CRIMINAL JUSTICE

CRIMINAL JUSTICE

SECOND EDITION

SUE TITUS REID, J.D., Ph.D.

Dean and Professor
School of Criminology
Florida State University

MACMILLAN PUBLISHING COMPANY

New York

Editor: Christine Cardone
Production Supervisor: Katherine Evancie
Production Manager: Ann Berlin
Text and Cover Designer: Natasha Sylvester
Illustrations: Vantage Art, Inc.

This book was set in Aster and Antique Olive by Waldman
Graphics, Inc. and printed and bound by Von Hoffmann Press.
The cover was printed by Von Hoffmann Press.

Macmillan Publishing Company
866 Third Avenue, New York, New York 10022

Collier Macmillan Canada, Inc.

Library of Congress Cataloging-in-Publication Data
Reid, Sue Titus.
  Criminal justice / Sue Titus Reid.—2nd ed.
  p. cm.
  Bibliography: p.
  Includes index.
  ISBN 0-02-399193-3
  1. Criminal justice, Administration of—United States.   I. Title.
HV9950.R45   1990
364′.973—dc19   89-2406
             CIP

Photo of Sue Titus Reid on p. vi © Glen Nelson.
Chapter Opening Photos: (1) The Bettmann Archive, Inc.; (2) Alan
Carey/The Image Works; (3) UPI/Bettmann Newsphotos;
(4) Carlin/The Picture Cube; (5) Robert W. Ginn/The Picture
Cube; (6) Sepp Seitz/Woodfin Camp & Associates; (7) Lionel J-M
Delevingne/Stock, Boston; (8) Bohdan Mrynewich/Stock, Boston;
(9) Dean Abramson/Stock, Boston; (10) Alan Carey/The Image
Works; (11) The Picture Cube; (12) AP/Wide World Photos;
(13) Jerry Berndt/Stock, Boston; (14) Stephen Ferry/Gamma
Liaison; (15) Danny Lyon/Magnum Photos; (16) Michael D.
Sullivan/TexaStock; and (17) Paul Conklin.

Color Insert Photos: Photo of Sue Titus Reid copyright © Glen
Nelson; Sue Carter Collins, Dr. George Kirkham, Debra Riley,
Howard Schleich, Melvin L. Tucker, JoAnn Van Meter, Mark
Wheeler and Brix, and James D. White by Doyle A. Woods, Jr.;
David Bachman, Kenneth L. Bergstrom, Bernard R. Cohen, Obie
Condry, Jr., John R. L. Isaacs, XV, J. D. Lamer, Eddie Laracuente,
Lieutenant Curt McKenzie, Charles E. Miner, Jr., Shirley D.
Minter, David E. Riddle, Jack C. Steele, F. Michelle Taylor, Pearl
Vann, Phil Welsh, Winnie Wentworth by Laura E. Nagy.

Printing: 1 2 3 4 5 6 7   Year: 0 1 2 3 4 5 6

To
Jack L. McNulty
and
John P. Scott
of the law firm of Savage, O'Donnell, Scott, McNulty, and Affeldt
with my appreciation for your excellent legal assistance
and your friendship over the years

BIOGRAPHY
Sue Titus Reid

Sue Titus Reid assumed the position of Dean and Professor of the School of Criminology, Florida State University in 1988 after serving 11 years as a Professor (and two as Associate Dean) at the University of Tulsa College of Law. She also served on the faculty of the University of Washington School of Law and was a visiting faculty member at the University of San Diego College of Law and the University of Nebraska Department of Sociology. Dr. Reid also served as Executive Associate of the American Sociological Association.

Dr. Reid's earlier teaching experiences were at Cornell and Coe Colleges in Iowa, where for 11 years she taught sociology and criminology courses, served as Acting Chair of the Sociology Department during part of her tenure at Cornell, and chaired the Sociology Department at Coe College. During those years, Dr. Reid was active in the Midwest Sociological Society, serving a term on the Board of Directors.

Dr. Reid graduated with honor from Texas Woman's University in 1960 and received graduate degrees in sociology from the University of Missouri-Columbia, with an M.A. in 1962 and a Ph.D. in 1965. She began her teaching career in 1963 while working on her Ph.D. In 1972 she graduated with distinction from the University of Iowa College of Law. She has been admitted to the Iowa Bar, the District of Columbia Court of Appeals, and the United States Supreme Court.

Dr. Reid's formal training in criminology began in graduate school, but her interest in the field dates back to her early childhood. She was strongly influenced in her career by her father who was born in jail where his father, the sheriff of a small East Texas County, lived with his family. As a child, she helped her father in his grocery store and was quite disturbed when, on three separate occasions, he was

victimized by criminals, one an armed robber. In each instance the offender took all the cash and checks; no one was ever apprehended.

Dr. Reid's interests in law and sociology and in teaching led her to her first major publication, *Crime and Criminology*, a basic text first published in 1976. This text, now in its fifth edition with a sixth edition in production, has been widely adopted throughout the United States and Europe. The text blends the philosophy of law, the causes of crime, and society's reaction to crime through the criminal justice system. Dr. Reid's interdisciplinary training qualifies her as one of the few academicians distinguished in both law and sociology.

In 1979 Dr. Reid was one of the youngest graduates ever selected to receive the Distinguished Alumna Award from Texas Woman's University. In 1980 she was one of four, and the only woman, selected from the field of law to be among those elected as Oklahoma Young Leaders of the '80s. In 1982 the American Society of Criminology elected her as a Fellow "for outstanding contributions to the field of Criminology." In 1985 she held the prestigious George Beto Chair in Criminal Justice at the Criminal Justice Center, Sam Houston State University, Huntsville, Texas.

Dr. Reid has traveled extensively in her pursuit of knowledge about criminal justice in the United States and in other countries. In 1982 she was a Member of the People-to-People Crime Prevention Delegation to the People's Republic of China. Several trips to Europe were highlighted by a three-month study and lecture tour of ten countries in 1985.

In addition to this text and her criminology text, Dr. Reid has published *The Correctional System: An Introduction, Criminal Law*, several book chapters, and scholarly articles on both law and sociology.

Preface

Many people consider crime the number one domestic problem in this country. In the 1988 presidential election, crime was a major issue. But the concern extends beyond the nature and frequency of crime to include official reaction to crime. The criminal justice system is seen as inadequate for preventing crime and as a questionable system for coping with crimes that do occur. Some people react with bitter criticism of the system, but with no meaningful suggestions for improvement. Others take the law into their own hands, fighting back, wounding, and, in some cases, killing those who attempt to make them crime victims. Still others take a close look at the system with the view of retaining the best parts and changing those elements that might be improved.

The latter view is taken in this book. The criminal justice system is explained and analyzed in terms of its procedures and the issues that arise in the execution of those procedures. This book also considers the interrelationships of the various parts of the system, for it is very important to understand that a change in one area of the system may, and usually does, have a significant impact on other areas of the system. Thus, longer sentences make it necessary to provide more space for incarceration, and recognition of the constitutional rights of inmates means that the increased populations cannot be confined in overcrowded conditions.

Although this second edition contains the same number of chapters as the first and the chapter titles are identical, many significant changes are incorporated within those chapters. New topics are added; others receive expanded coverage. Examples include drug and alcohol abuse and the recent emphasis on mandatory testing for substance abuse, AIDS, gangs, terrorism, and more extensive coverage of women and minorities in the criminal justice system.

All topics have been checked for the latest information available at the time of publication. All legal cases and citations have been checked to make sure those cases have not been overruled or changed. Older cases are used only where they represent classic statements of the law and are still in effect or where they represent the latest Supreme Court decision in an area.

Where possible, legal points are illustrated with recent cases, many from 1987 and 1988. Such recentness, however, presents problems in that some of these cases will be changed on appeal while this book is in production. All cases will be checked at the latest possible time before publication, but the careful reader will understand that the law is moving rapidly in criminal justice. What is correct today may be incorrect tomorrow.

This second edition also includes the latest relevant scholarly articles. Where possible, scholarly discussions are illustrated by recent media events to demonstrate the applicability of scholarly learning to what actually happens in the real world.

CHAPTER FORMAT

The chapter-opening format is slightly altered in this edition. The distinctions among procedures, issues, and system effect have been deleted to permit space for moving the key terms from the end to the beginning of chapters. This enables readers to focus early on the important concepts to be covered in each chapter. Key terms are also boldfaced the first time they appear within the chapter, and they are defined in the Glossary at the end of the text. The brief outline at the beginning of each chapter also contains a listing of the spotlights in that chapter.

The text of each chapter begins with a hypothetical scenario, Criminal Justice in Action (CJA). The CJA element raises some of the major topics of the chapter in the context of a real-life situation. It is intended to arouse your thinking about how the situation will be handled and how it should be handled. This element is not intended to address all the topics of the chapter, but only a few topics that are keys to an understanding of the focus of that chapter.

Hypothetical cases are also used within some chapters. In some situations you are asked to put yourself in the place of the criminal justice official and make a decision. In others you are asked to consider that you are the accused and must try to decide how you would respond to the situation.

The material within the chapters is illustrated and emphasized by tables, figures, maps, cartoons, and spotlights. Court cases are also used within the text. Experience has shown that students enjoy reading the actual court cases, but legal opinions are often long and difficult to understand. Thus, the cases have been carefully excerpted to illustrate only the topic under discussion.

Each chapter concludes with a detailed summary followed by essay questions designed to assist students in learning and analyzing the chapter's material.

ORGANIZATION OF THE TEXT

The text is divided into five parts. Part 1, "Introduction to the Criminal Justice System: The Criminal Event," begins with Chapter 1, an overview of the criminal justice system and criminal law. Chapter 2 follows, focusing on crime data. Chapter 3 explores the biological, psychological, and sociological explanations of criminal behavior. Chapter 4 focuses on crime victims.

Part 2, "Entry into the Criminal Justice System: Policing," focuses on one of the basic functions of the criminal justice system. The first of this part's three chapters contains a brief history of the emergence and structure of police systems in the United States. Chapter 6 focuses on what police actually do. Their three basic functions—law enforcement, order maintenance, and social services—are discussed. Chapter 7 is devoted to a close look at the major problems and issues of policing, such as role conflicts, stress, subcultures, women and minorities, and corruption among police officers and within police departments.

Part 3, "Processing a Criminal Case: The Criminal Court System," explores the procedures and issues that arise from arrest through sentencing and appeals. Chapter 8 sets the stage with a discussion of the court system. Chapter 9, "Prosecution and Defense," examines the role of the prosecutor both historically and currently, with an emphasis on prosecutorial discretion. After a look at the prosecutor, who represents the state (or federal government) in a criminal justice system, the focus shifts to defense attorneys, who represent defendants. The right to counsel, an important element of the American system of criminal justice, is examined in the context of the role of defense attorneys. The differences between public and private defense attorney systems are summarized, and the context in which defense attorneys work is examined.

Chapter 10, "Pretrial Procedures," and Chapter 11, "Trial and Appeals," describe basic procedures that occur throughout the pretrial and trial phases of a criminal case. Special attention is given to the process of sentencing, the focus of Chapter 12. This discussion includes an analysis of varying court reactions to the new federal sentencing guidelines.

Part 4, "Confinement and Corrections," focuses on corrections, with four chapters examining the methods of confining offenders in total institutions or of placing them in the community under supervision. The discussion begins in Chapter 13, "The History and Structure of Confinement," with a look at the history of prisons and jails, a distinction between those two types of confinement facilities, and a discussion of the federal and state prison systems. Attention is also given to the problems of local jails.

Chapter 14, "Life in Prison," focuses on inmates and guards and the interaction between these two types of people who spend so much time in confinement facilities. Particular attention is given to the methods of social control that involve both inmates and guards. How inmates cope with the pains of imprisonment, along with a distinction between the adjustment of male and female inmates, is also considered.

Many legal issues have been raised concerning the incarceration of offenders. Chapter 15, "Conditions of Incarceration: The Courts React," explores some of the major issues and explains how lawsuits may be filed by inmates or their attorneys. Part 4 closes with Chapter 16, "Probation, Parole, and Community Corrections," which examines the preparation of inmates for release, problems faced on release, and supervision of the offender in the community.

The final part of the text, Part 5, "Juvenile Justice: A Special Case," contains one chapter on the juvenile system, a special approach that was developed for the processing of juveniles who get into trouble with the law or who are in need of supervision or care because of neglectful parents or other guardians. This chapter explains the juvenile justice system, contrasts that system with the adult criminal court system, and considers the changes in the juvenile system that have resulted from recent decisions of the United States Supreme Court. The chapter also considers the processing of serious juvenile offenders in the criminal court, the use of capital punishment, and finally, the juvenile in corrections.

Two Appendices assist the reader with legal issues. Appendix A reprints selected amendments of the United States Constitution. These amendments are cited throughout the text. Appendix B explains the abbreviations and references that are used in legal case citations. Individual indexes assist the reader who desires quick access to names, subjects, and legal cases cited in the text.

ACKNOWLEDGMENTS

Many individuals contributed significantly to the writing and production of this text, and to all of them I am grateful. My former law student at the University of Tulsa, Chrisie Brightmire, began the research prior to my departure from Tulsa in the summer of 1988. Lenny Krzycki, Ph.D. candidate in the School of Criminology at Florida State University, completed the research and updated citations.

My sister, Jill Pickett, typed and helped edit the entire manuscript, compiled the indexes and the Glossary, and provided humor, support, and reinforcement throughout the writing and production of this text. Jill, her family, and our mother assisted us with their love and understanding when we were frantically trying to meet publication deadlines.

Shortly after I completed the first draft of this text I moved from Tulsa, Oklahoma to Tallahassee, Florida to assume the position of Dean and Professor of the Florida State University School of Criminology. Preparing my office and my home for the move was handled with efficiency, energy, and enthusiasm by Anne Montesano who, with my niece and nephew, Rhonda and Clint Pickett, took charge of all of the unpacking and arranging of my office and home. Their excellent help enabled me to concentrate on this manuscript and my new job.

The FSU School of Criminology staff took charge of many of the final details involved in publishing a book. To Mary Harris, Judy Waters, Edwina Ivory, Debbie Orth, and Kathleen Rose I give my special thanks. Diane Crompton joined our staff as Executive Secretary while the book was in production, and she handled the permissions and other jobs that are necessary in the early production stages. Most importantly, Diane kept the office running smoothly at all times.

My colleagues, staff, and graduate students provided encouragement and much needed humor during the writing and production of this book. To all of them I say thank you for your understanding and your support.

FSU Provost and Vice President for Academic Affairs, Augustus B. Turnbull III, clearly indicated in our early discussions concerning the FSU School of Criminology deanship that he would be supportive of my interest in continuing research and writing. Without his support it would not have been possible for me to complete this text. To him and our president Bernard F. Sliger I owe great appreciation for their encouragement and support of my total professional commitments.

My attorneys helped me through the problems of selling one home and buying another and, most importantly, adjusting to the difficulties created by three automobile accidents and the resulting injuries and law suits. To Jack L. McNulty and John P. Scott, this book is dedicated. The encouragement and medical expertise of my doctors was also invaluable. In particular I am grateful to Dr. Charles H. Wingo and Dr. Frederick A. Koehler, for their excellent medical care during the completion of this text.

A text revision may be greatly enhanced by careful reviews by colleagues in the field. To the following colleagues in the criminal justice field I owe a special thanks for the time and effort you devoted to my manuscript: Steven J. Cox, Illinois State University; Patricia A. Koski, The University of Arkansas; Vern Rich, Radford University; Donald Hugh Smith, Old Dominion University; Lawrence F. Travis III, University of Cincinnati; and Joseph B. Vaughn, Central Missouri State University.

The ancillary materials make this second edition of *Criminal Justice* a complete package. A *Student Study Guide* is available for the second edition that includes key terms, chapter summaries, chapter objectives, test questions and student exercises. An *Instructor's Manual and Test Bank* is available to professors and includes summaries, key terms, objectives, and supplementary material for class projects and demonstrations.

The seemingly endless hours that are required for writing and producing a book were greatly eased by the professional expertise of the publishing staff. The College Division of Macmillan Publishing Company provided me with excellent assistance. My Acquisitions Editor for this and *Criminal Law*, Christine Cardone, has become a friend as well as a professional colleague. Chris provides leadership and guidance without stifling creativity or questioning the author's professional expertise. She knows what to suggest, and she does it with a sense of perspective and of reality, while maintaining a high degree of professionalism. D. Anthony English, Editor in Chief, provided leadership and an incredible sense of humor just when all of us needed to laugh. Production Supervisor Katherine Evancie, Production Manager Ann Berlin, and Text Designer Natasha Sylvester guided the manuscript through production with a minimum of problems for the author.

Sue Titus Reid

Brief Contents

Detailed Contents

PART 2 ENTRY INTO THE CRIMINAL JUSTICE SYSTEM: POLICING

137

PART 3   PROCESSING A CRIMINAL CASE:
THE CRIMINAL COURT SYSTEM   263

PART 4 **CONFINEMENT AND
CORRECTIONS**   469

PART **5**   **JUVENILE JUSTICE: A SPECIAL CASE**   627

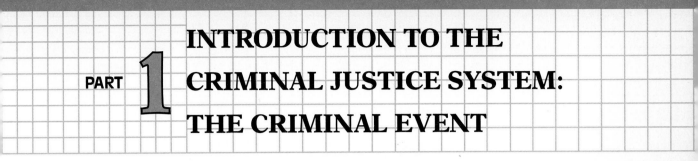

1

INTRODUCTION TO THE CRIMINAL JUSTICE SYSTEM: THE CRIMINAL EVENT

Criminal justice systems throughout the world vary considerably; even in the United States there are differences among the various state systems. The federal system also has unique features. But all criminal justice systems must deal with common problems. They must count the numbers of criminal acts committed. They must decide the philosophy on which their reactions to those crimes will be based. They must decide how to respond to victims of crime. And, they must attempt to explain criminal behavior, for policy decisions will be affected by those explanations.

Part 1 features the criminal justice systems in the United States, although many of the procedures and issues also are common to other systems. The first chapter presents an overview of common features of the criminal justice systems in the United States. The philosophy on which these systems is based is explained and contrasted to the approach used in some other countries. Chapter 1 also discusses the nature and purpose of the criminal law and contrasts criminal and civil law. Chapter 2 continues this introduction into the criminal event by discussing and analyzing the methods by which data on crime are secured. Chapter 3 focuses on the various explanations of criminal behavior. Chapter 4 focuses on victims of crime.

The chapters in Part 1 set the stage for the more intensive discussion of the basic parts of the criminal justice system—police, prosecution and defense, courts, and corrections—that constitute the remainder of the text.

Chapter 1. The System of Criminal Justice
Chapter 2. The Incidence of Crime
Chapter 3. Explanations of Criminal Behavior
Chapter 4. Victims of Crime

The System of Criminal Justice

Joe, a 19 year old with a criminal record; Susan, a 15 year old with no history of contact with the police; Peter, a 12 year old who often refuses to go to school; and Harry, a 20 year old with no prior record are all apprehended by the police after they steal an automobile. The police officer arrests Joe and Harry and radios for another officer to take them to the police station for further processing.

Susan, who is a juvenile, is taken to a juvenile detention center. The apprehending officer decides not to take official action against Peter, also a juvenile. The officer drives Peter home, talks to him and his parents, gives Peter a warning that the next time he is ap-

prehended he will be taken to the juvenile detention center, and advises the parents to seek professional counseling for Peter.

In Joe's case, after looking at the evidence and Joe's prior record, the prosecutor files charges and the case proceeds to trial. Joe is convicted and sentenced to five years in prison. After three years, however, he is released on parole. After reviewing Harry's case, the prosecutor decides not to press charges; Harry is released with a warning. Susan's case is processed through the juvenile court; she is sent to a correctional institution for juveniles where she will remain until she reaches her majority age, 16.

INTRODUCTION

The facts in the preceding scenario illustrate some of the procedures and issues of the **criminal justice system** and will be elaborated on throughout the chapter. This chapter provides a brief introduction to that system, which includes the entire system of criminal prevention, detection, apprehension, trial, sentencing, and punishment.

The chapter begins with an overview of the institutions within the criminal justice system; it then explains the stages of the system before proceeding to the important topic of the interrelationship of the various institutions and stages. This interrelationship is even more important when observed in the context of the wide range of decision-making discretion permitted in the criminal justice system.

An examination of the philosophy on which the American system of criminal justice is based is followed by a discussion of the purpose of the system as a method for controlling behavior. The use of a formal system must be understood in the context of other methods of social control; thus, law and the formal criminal justice system will be explained in the framework of less formal methods of social control.

Criminal law, the basis of the criminal justice system, is examined for its sources, its distinction from civil law, and its elements. The extent to which the criminal law should be used as a method of social control is also discussed.

OVERVIEW OF THE SYSTEM

The United States' system of criminal justice is really many systems, for states organize and operate their systems in different ways. The federal system also has some unique features. But American criminal justice systems also have many common features; those features are emphasized throughout this text.

Institutions and Stages

In the United States, the most common organization of criminal justice systems is one consisting of four institutions: police, prosecution, courts, and corrections. In Figure 1.1, these four institutions are noted, along with a diagram of the steps by which a case goes through the system. All of the stages in Figure 1.1 will be discussed in more detail where appropriate throughout the text; at this point, it is important to see the entire system at once to understand the interrelationship of its parts.

A case may enter the system when a **crime** is reported to the police or when police observe behavior that appears to be criminal. After a crime is reported, the police usually will conduct a preliminary investigation to determine whether there is sufficient evidence that a crime actually has been committed. In the case of the car thieves, this investigation was simple. The apprehending officer radioed the license number of the car to the police department, where a fast computer check indicated that the car had been stolen.

The officer must then decide what to do. This officer decided to arrest the adults, apprehend the older juvenile, and release the younger juvenile. These facts and Figure 1.1 illustrate that the criminal justice systems in this country usually consist of two separate systems: one for adults and one for juveniles. In many cases when juveniles are apprehended, police officers will take them home or send them home with a warning, and no further official action is taken. But juveniles also may be officially processed through the juvenile court system. As Figure 1.1 indicates, that system is not as extensive as the adult system; it is based on a different philosophy. Juvenile justice will be discussed in the last chapter of the text, along with the exceptional cases in which juveniles may be tried in criminal courts.

The case of the car thieves also illustrates that not all arrested suspects proceed to the end of the criminal justice system. In fact, most cases do not go that far. Police may decide that no crime has been committed or that a crime has been committed but there is not enough evidence on which to arrest a suspect. A suspect may be arrested but quickly released for lack of evidence. Persons who remain suspects through booking, the initial appearance, and the preliminary hearing (as indicated in Figure 1.1) may be dismissed; or the charges may be dropped at any of those stages. These decisions may be made for lack of evidence or other reasons, some of them highly controversial, such as political pressures. Even after formal charges have been made against the accused, those charges may be dropped or reduced.

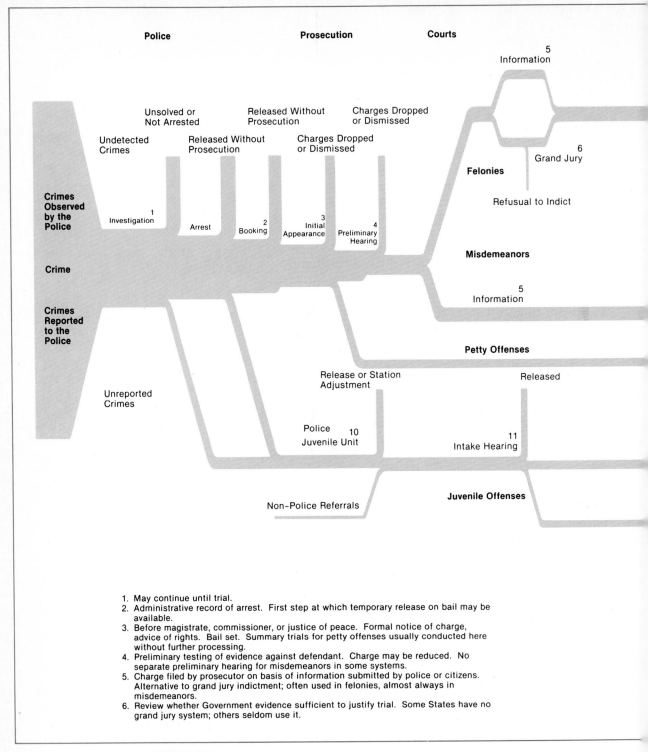

Police   **Prosecution**   **Courts**

1. May continue until trial.
2. Administrative record of arrest. First step at which temporary release on bail may be available.
3. Before magistrate, commissioner, or justice of peace. Formal notice of charge, advice of rights. Bail set. Summary trials for petty offenses usually conducted here without further processing.
4. Preliminary testing of evidence against defendant. Charge may be reduced. No separate preliminary hearing for misdemeanors in some systems.
5. Charge filed by prosecutor on basis of information submitted by police or citizens. Alternative to grand jury indictment; often used in felonies, almost always in misdemeanors.
6. Review whether Government evidence sufficient to justify trial. Some States have no grand jury system; others seldom use it.

FIGURE 1.1
Institutions and Stages in the American System of Criminal Justice. *Source:* President's Commission on Law Enforcement and Administration of Justice,

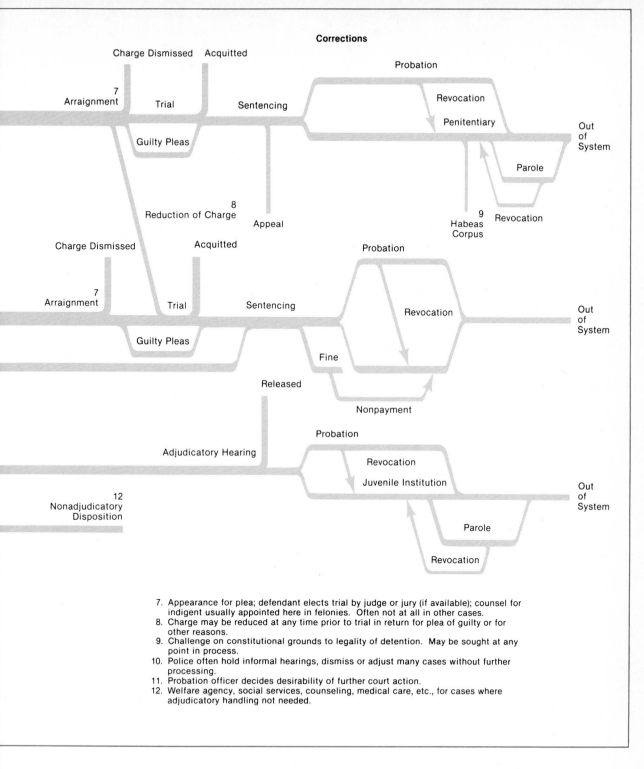

Corrections

Charge Dismissed   Acquitted

Probation

7
Arraignment   Trial   Sentencing   Revocation

Guilty Pleas   Penitentiary   Out of System

Parole

8
Reduction of Charge   Appeal   9   Revocation
                                              Habeas Corpus

Charge Dismissed   Acquitted   Probation

7
Arraignment   Trial   Sentencing   Revocation   Out of System

Guilty Pleas   Fine

Released   Nonpayment

Probation

Adjudicatory Hearing   Revocation
                             Juvenile Institution   Out of System

12
Nonadjudicatory Disposition   Parole

Revocation

7. Appearance for plea; defendant elects trial by judge or jury (if available); counsel for indigent usually appointed here in felonies. Often not at all in other cases.
8. Charge may be reduced at any time prior to trial in return for plea of guilty or for other reasons.
9. Challenge on constitutional grounds to legality of detention. May be sought at any point in process.
10. Police often hold informal hearings, dismiss or adjust many cases without further processing.
11. Probation officer decides desirability of further court action.
12. Welfare agency, social services, counseling, medical care, etc., for cases where adjudicatory handling not needed.

The Challenge of Crime in a Free Society (Washington, D.C.: U.S. Government Printing Office, 1967), pp. 8–9.

Suspects who proceed to trial may not be convicted. Despite strong evidence against them, suspects may receive a verdict of not guilty. Or, the suspect may be convicted but placed on probation, fined, or sentenced to work in the community in place of being sent to prison. Those sent to prison may not serve their full term. Joe's case illustrates that a parole board may have the authority to grant early release.

The criminal justice system thus is a process as well as a set of stages, and many factors may affect the processing of a suspect through the system or out of it. Throughout the text those factors will be considered, but two other very important factors are relevant to an overview of the system: the interrelationship of the system's parts and the considerable discretion within the system.

Interrelationship of the Parts of the System

Some of the most crucial problems in the criminal justice system have occurred as the result of a failure to recognize the effect that a change in one part of the system will have on the remaining parts. The components of the criminal justice system do not operate independently; the functions often overlap. A change in one area usually will have an impact on what happens in other parts of the system. In many instances the effects are not planned; they are often not even contemplated. The results may create more problems than they solve.

The facts of the car theft illustrate the system's effect. Joe was paroled after serving three years of a five-year sentence. If Joe and others were not paroled and must serve their full terms, prisons would be more crowded. On the other hand, if they were released early, they might commit more crimes, thus increasing the crime rate. The police arrested Harry but he was not prosecuted. If prosecutors often refuse to prosecute, the police may stop arresting in those types of cases. But if prosecutors insist on prosecuting most or all arrests, the increased caseload would put pressures on the court system. If the increased prosecutions resulted in more convictions, they also would put pressure on the correctional system.

Official processing of all juveniles apprehended by the police would put stress on the facilities and personnel of the juvenile justice system and might not be a positive move for the juveniles or for society. Refusal to deal with these problems, however, might result in an increase in juvenile crime or in other problems among juveniles.

The Role of Discretion

A second important characteristic of the criminal justice system is the wide discretion given authorities within it. **Discretion** means that individuals may use their own judgment to make important decisions. The case of the car thieves illustrates several types of discretion. The police officer decided to arrest the two adults and to take the older juvenile to the juvenile detention center. He chose not to process the younger juvenile officially. The prosecutor chose to file charges against Joe, who had a criminal record, but not against Harry, who had no prior record.

TABLE 1.1

Discretion in the Criminal Justice System

Who Exercises Discretion?

These crimnial justice officials . . .	. . . must often decide whether or not or how to—
Police	Enforce specific laws
	Investigate specific crimes
	Search people, vicinities, buildings
	Arrest or detain people
Prosecutors	File charges or petitions for adjudication
	Seek indictments
	Drop cases
	Reduce charges
Judges or magistrates	Set bail or conditions for release
	Accept pleas
	Determine delinquency
	Dismiss charges
	Impose sentence
	Revoke probation
Correctional officials	Assign to type of correctional facility
	Award privileges
	Punish for disciplinary infractions
Paroling authority	Determine date and conditions of parole
	Revoke parole

Source: Bureau of Justice Statistics, *Report to the Nation on Crime and Justice: The Data*, 2d ed., (Washington, D.C.: U.S. Government Printing Office, 1988), p. 59.

Discretion may be exercised by various persons within the criminal justice system. Table 1.1 indicates the positions that have the greatest discretion: police, prosecutors, judges or magistrates, correctional officials, and paroling authorities. The table also briefly describes the types of discretion exercised by personnel in each area.

Although discretion can be abused, it is not necessarily a negative aspect of the system. It can be a very positive factor. In the case of Peter, official processing through the juvenile system may be the most negative action that could be taken by the officer. On the other hand, it could be a positive action that would lead to solving some of Peter's problems. The problem is that we often do not know the answers to such complicated situations, and officers must use their best judgment. It is possible to establish guidelines for the exercise of discretion, but it is not possible to eliminate all need for discretion.

In addition, attempts to abolish discretion in one area of the system may increase discretion in other parts of the system. Thus, if longer sentences are instituted to control crime and these sentences are perceived as too harsh by juries, those juries might not convict persons they believe are guilty. In those cases, the system would have no alternative but to free the accused.

Philosophy of the System: The Adversarial Approach

The two philosophies underlying most criminal justice systems are the **inquisitory** and the **adversary** approaches. The systems in the United States are characterized by the adversary philosophy. The two approaches may be distinguished in several ways. The adversary approach assumes innocence. The accused do not have to prove their innocence; the prosecutor, representing the state, must prove their guilt. The inquisitory system assumes guilt, and the accused must prove that they are innocent. This difference between the two approaches is related to another basic contrast: the inquisitory approach places a greater emphasis on conviction than on the process by which that conviction is secured. The adversary approach, however, requires that proper procedures be followed, procedures designed to protect the rights of the accused.

Due Process and Equal Protection   In the United States the adversary system embodies the basic concepts of **equal protection** and **due process.** These concepts are considered necessary to create a system in which the accused has a fair chance against the tremendous powers of the prosecutor and the resources of the state. Theoretically, the protections will prevent the prosecutor from obtaining a guilty verdict for an innocent defendant. In reality, justice does not always prevail.

The impossibility of explaining exactly what is meant by the concept of due process is illustrated by this comment of a former U.S. Supreme Court justice:

> "Due Process". . . cannot be imprisoned within the treacherous limits of any formula. Representing a profound attitude of fairness between man and man, and more particularly between the individual and government, "due process" is compounded of history, reason, the past course of decisions, and stout confidence in the strength of the democratic faith we possess. "Due process" is not a mechanical instrument. It is not a yardstick. It is a process.[1]

The basis for the rights to due process and equal protection comes from the Fourteenth Amendment to the Constitution:

> nor shall any State deprive any person of life, liberty, or property, without due process of law; nor deny to any person within its jurisdiction the equal protection of the laws.

The Supreme Court has decided numerous cases in which it has been argued that the due process or equal protection rights of individuals have been violated. It would take an extensive course in constitutional law to explore these concepts adequately, but we can look at them briefly.

Essentially, the concept of due process means that those who are accused of crimes and who are processed through the criminal justice system must be given the basic rights guaranteed by the Constitution. For example, defendants may not be subjected to unreasonable searches and seizures by the police. When questioned about acts that upon conviction may involve a jail or prison term, they do not have to answer questions by the police until they have an attorney. If they do not wish to talk then, they may remain silent. If they cannot afford an attorney, the state must provide one for them. They do not have to testify against themselves at the trial. Certain rules of evidence at the trial must be observed.

Defendants may not be tried twice for the same offense; once a judge or jury has decided that the defendant is innocent, the state may not bring those same charges again in an effort to wear down the defendant. In short, the state must conduct the criminal trial and the processes preceding and following that trial by the rules embodied in the Constitution as interpreted by the Supreme Court of the United States and according to the established procedural statutes.

The equal protection clause of the Fourteenth Amendment is also the subject of frequent lawsuits. That clause declares that the state may not attempt to enforce statutes against persons solely because of specific characteristics such as race, age, or sex. The state or federal government, however, may draft statutes that, for example, distinguish between males and females if there are significant reasons for doing so.

This brief excerpt from *Liberta v. Kelly*, a case arising under New York statutes and decided by a federal court in 1988, indicates the reasons why the federal court upheld the state's exclusion of females as **defendants** from its rape and sodomy statutes. According to the federal court, the New York statute did not violate the Equal Protection clause of the federal constitution.[2]

Liberta v. *Kelly*

[Briefly, the facts are as follows. Mario Liberta and Denise Liberta were separated, and Denise had obtained two protective orders, which required Mario to live apart from Denise and their young son but which also granted him visiting privileges with the child. Mario had a history of physically abusing his wife. On the occasion in question, he persuaded her to let him see the child in her presence, indicating that he would bring a friend with him. The friend quickly left, however, and Mario forced Denise to perform oral sex on him while the child watched; he then raped Denise. After a long discussion of other issues in this case, the court focused on the defendant's argument that he had been denied equal protection of the law because the New York sodomy and rape statutes included only men as defendants.]

Women and men thus are not similarly situated with regard to rape. Rape is unquestionably a crime that requires male participation as a practical matter, and only male rape of a female can impose on the victim an unwanted pregnancy. These facts, in our view, provide an "exceedingly persuasive justification," for a statute that provides heightened sanctions for rapes committed by men. Moreover, it cannot be contended that a rape statute punishing only men "demean[s] the ability or social status" of either men or women, particularly in the context of a penal code that prohibits coercive sexual conduct by women. The exclusion of women from [the New York statute] therefore, does not deny men equal protection of the laws.

In recent years, several states have changed their rape and sodomy statutes to include females as perpetrators, but the point of this case is that it is not necessarily a violation of equal protection to define these crimes as crimes that may be committed only by males.

The Equal Protection clause, like the Due Process clause, must be examined in the context of the facts of a given case. This is why it is impossible to state "the law" on most issues. Such elasticity of United States' laws is important but at times frustrating to one who wants a definitive answer immediately. The issues in this text must be understood in the context of this flexibility.

Crime Control Versus Due Process Models   The adversary model of due process and equal protection frequently comes under attack. The system is seen as hindering law enforcement and, consequently, crime prevention and control. Reference is often made to the conflict between what the noted scholar Herbert L. Packer called the **crime control model** of criminal justice and the **due process model.**

The goal of the crime control model is the quick and efficient processing of people who violate the law. The due process model, in contrast, places priority on the dignity, autonomy, and individual rights of persons accused of crimes. The crime control model is similar to an assembly line, whereas the due process model is more of an obstacle course. Within the criminal justice system, support for the due process model comes mainly from the courts and defense attorneys, whereas the main support for the crime control model comes from the prosecution and the police.[3]

Although Packer made these observations two decades ago, his comments are relevant today. By the provisions of our federal and state constitutions, and court decisions interpreting those documents, we have a system that is basically a due process model. There is no question, however, that observation of the defendants' rights creates obstacles for law enforcement. If authorities could accuse anyone of a crime regardless of available evidence, could search and seize at will, could interrogate suspects for unlimited periods of time when those suspects did not have attorneys, could physically and psychologically coerce confessions, and could violate other recognized rights, there might be more convictions in the criminal courts. But that approach might also increase law violations, for more people would become angry at the system. Some people argue that our system has gone too far in recognizing the rights of the accused; others argue that it has not gone far enough.

PURPOSE OF THE CRIMINAL JUSTICE SYSTEM

The Need for Social Control

Every society has certain functions that must be performed in order for the society to continue existing. Some provision must be made for replacing members, providing food and other needed resources such as housing and clothing, creating a sense of belonging sufficient to maintain the group, and deciding how much deviation from the norms of the group will be permitted and what will be done to those who deviate. Societies must also transfer these norms to new members, a process sociologists call **socialization.**

Informal Social Control   The process of socialization involves teaching members the appropriate behavior within that society. Sociologists use the term **norms** to refer to behavior defined as appropriate. An early sociologist, William Graham Sumner, used the terms **folkways** and **mores** to refer to these informal methods of **social control**. Folkways are the customary or routine ways of performing activities, such as gathering wild fruits and vegetables and killing wild animals for food. Folkways also govern interpersonal relationships. In earlier societies, if a man raped your daughter, you might be permitted to kill the offender for revenge. Private revenge, in many cases, was not only acceptable, but expected; it was thought that the society's welfare depended on such actions.[4]

When these customary ways of solving problems become important to the welfare of society, they become mores and are then considered the right or wrong way to act. But not all folkways become mores. It may not be important to the society whether you kill wild animals for food or gather wild fruits, but it may be very important whether you take action against someone who steals your cow or rapes your daughter. Mores are not habits or customs that we may choose to avoid. They govern required behaviors. Mores tell people how to behave.

Among primitive societies, folkways and mores usually are sufficient for regulating the behavior of members. With limited or no technology, fewer types of jobs or functions exist than in more complex societies. Most people take care of their own needs. They grow or capture their own food and make their own clothing and housing; they have no need for exchanging goods and services. Historical evidence indicates that for the most part such societies live in internal peace more often than in war or conflict. They have some kind of a normative structure, but it is not formal law. Neither civil nor criminal law but submission to custom controls most of their behavior.[5] Because the society does not need many rules to regulate activities outside the group, informal methods of social control are very effective.

The family is the main agency of social control, but other members of the society also are influential in controlling members' behavior. Such societies are usually characterized by a minimum of conflicting and competing interests, and those who deviate from the norm are easily and quickly spotted. The community can react with informal sanctions. These informal sanctions, often more effective than laws, may be a disapproving glance, an embarrassed silence following an action, a smile, a nod, a frown, a social invitation, or social ostracism. The threat of being banished from a society could be a serious deterrent to deviant behavior among such groups. The key to the success of these informal methods of social control is that the groups are closely knit.

As societies become more complex, the informal methods of social control are less effective. Among earlier sociologists who studied the movement from informal to formal methods was Émile Durkheim, who believed that, as societies grew more complex, a division of labor developed.

They then moved from what Durkheim classified as mechanical (the less complex type of society in which members are highly integrated through their cultural and functional similarities) to organic solidarity (the more complex type of society in which members are integrated because they are functionally interdependent). With the increasing complexity of society comes the need for formal social controls.[6]

Emergence of Law as Social Control   Law has emerged as the most formal method of social control, but scholars do not agree on how that evolution occurred. Two major models have been used to analyze the evolution of law: **consensus approach** and **conflict approach**. The consensus approach views law as the formalization of the views and values of the people. Sumner, in his discussion of folkways and mores, viewed laws as evolving through social interaction, reflecting the values of society and eventually becoming formalized. The laws could not, however, change the folkways and mores. Underlying the laws must be a consensus of values held by the people in society. The contrasting position involves the use of a conflict model. This model sees conflict among various groups in society and postulates that the conflict is resolved when the groups in power achieve control. The powerful use the law to control the behavior of minority groups within society.[7]

Regardless of whether law is viewed as emerging through consensus or conflict, it does provide the basis for the criminal justice system; and it may be distinguished from other methods of social control. Law, at least in theory, is more specific. Criminal laws define the nature of offenses and the punishments to be administered for conviction of those offenses. Laws must be clear enough to give adequate notice to potential transgressors that they are in danger of violating those laws.

Law, a formal enactment made by a legislative body or by a court, is supposed to be applied to all who transgress its provisions unless there is some justification or defense for their behavior. Law specifies **sanctions,** and only those sanctions specified may be applied. Law also differs from other institutions of social control in that its sanctions are applied exclusively by organized political agencies. Law usually does not reward conforming behavior. It is concerned mainly with negative sanctions. Unlike other forms of social control, in most cases the legal system provides the right of appeal.

BASIS OF THE SYSTEM

Sources of Law

Although many people think of law as those provisions written in the statute books after passage by legislatures, laws actually come from three sources: constitutions, statutes, and court decisions. State legislatures pass statutes that apply to actions in their respective states. Congress passes statutes that apply to the federal government as well as to the District of Columbia. These statutes are called **statutory law**; they may apply to any type of activity, although they may not conflict with the constitutions of

Our modern laws were and still are heavily influenced by the English common law, created by English judges. (Culver Pictures)

the respective **jurisdictions**. These statutes apply only to the jurisdiction in which they are passed, with the exception that no state may enforce statutes conflicting with the rights guaranteed by the U.S. Constitution. That document, as well as state constitutions, also specifies some laws.

Statutory Law   Some statutes define the procedures that are appropriate for law enforcement. These are called *procedural laws*. Others define the elements that are necessary for an act to constitute a violation of the civil or criminal law. They are called **substantive laws**. For example, the crime of murder may be defined as the killing by one human being of another with malice aforethought. Convicting a person of murder requires proof of these statutorily provided elements: that a person has been killed, that the person was killed by the accused, and that the killing involved malice aforethought.

What does *malice aforethought* mean? It refers to the requirement of an intent to kill and the absence of any legal justification for that killing. But if the statute does not define that element, then court decisions, another source of law, may be used for a definition.

Case Law   Law that comes from court decisions is called **case law**, which often derives from the English **common law**. *Common law* refers to those customs, traditions, judicial decisions, and other materials that guide courts in decision making but that have not been enacted by legislatures into statutes or embodied in the Constitution. The common law developed in England after the Norman Conquest in 1066. Before that time there was no distinction among law, custom, religion, and morality. Decisions might be different in different communities.

The Normans, however, wanted to establish some unity, so the king employed representatives to travel to the various jurisdictions. These representatives kept the king informed about the different jurisdictions and also carried news to each jurisdiction of what was happening in the others. "The result of all this was that the legal principles being applied began to be similar, or common, in all parts of England. Thus, the terms 'Common Law of England,' and 'Common Law.' "[8] Case law is just as important as statutory law. The English common law has significantly influenced the development of law in the United States.

Administrative Law   Another source of law that may be important to an understanding of criminal law is **administrative law**. State legislatures and Congress may and do delegate rule-making power to some state and federal agencies. The Board of Parole is given the authority to make rules governing the release of inmates on parole; prison officials may be given the authority to make rules that regulate the daily operations of those institutions; the Federal Bureau of Investigation has the power to make rules governing the enforcement of laws under its jurisdiction. Such rules must be made according to specific procedures and guidelines. These rules are very important, but normally the violation of administrative rules is not viewed as criminal.

Violation of administrative rules, however, may become criminal under some circumstances. Suppose that an administrative agency with the power to enforce rules concerning pure food discovers that a restaurant is serving spoiled food. The agency may issue an order to the restaurant to stop the practice, though it is not a criminal action. But if the practice is not stopped, the administrative agency may get a court order for enforcement; if that order is violated, the restaurant officials may be cited for **contempt of court**, a criminal offense. But even in those cases, violators are not viewed in the same way as those who violate the criminal law, and data on violations of administrative rules and regulations are not a part of official crime data.

Criminal Law Compared to Civil Law

Criminal law is the basis for the actions that take place in the criminal justice system. But criminal and civil law are not always distinguishable; in some instances they overlap. Therefore, it is important to understand the theoretical difference between criminal and civil law.

The **civil law** permits legal actions for those who are harmed by others. It is used to uphold certain institutions such as the family. Civil laws regulate marriage and divorce or dissolution, the handling of dependent and neglected children, and the inheritance of property. They protect the legal and political systems, organize power relationships, and establish who is superordinate and who is subordinate in given situations.

Civil law governs many types of activities that will not be discussed in this book. One area of civil law that often is closely related to criminal law is **torts**. The word *tort* comes from a Latin word that means twisted. It refers to actions that are twisted, crooked, or not straight. A tort is sometimes referred to as a civil wrong.[9] In torts cases, the law permits the injured party to sue the person responsible for the death or injury (or damage to property) that results. If the suit is successful, the losing party will have to pay for those damages.

Torts include such varied actions as injury and death caused by the negligence of others and damage to one's reputation caused when people make false comments that are slanderous, such as accusing a person of being a criminal or of having a sexually transmitted disease. Also included are unsafely designed or constructed products that result in injuries to persons or damage to property. An example from an area of tort law that has recently gained more recognition in the courts will illustrate one type of tort, as well as the close relationship between torts and crimes. Some landlords have been required to pay damages to tenants who have been criminally attacked on the rented premises. The legal theory is that the landlord was negligent in not providing adequate locks, lights or, in some cases, guards.

Tenants do not always win these cases. The courts look at all of the circumstances before determining whether landlords are liable. Usually the courts require the landlord to have had some notice of criminal activity in the area and the cost of additional locks and security to have been a reasonable expenditure. Further, they may require the criminal activity to have taken place in central areas such as laundry rooms in which tenants should have a reasonable expectation of security and in which individual tenants would have no way of providing extra security for themselves.

When courts hold that landlords are liable in such cases, they are not saying that the individuals who committed the criminal acts are not responsible. The underlying assumption is that the criminal activities might have been prevented with adequate precautions by the landlords. Spotlight 1.1 contains another example of a case that may involve both a tort and a crime.

In cases constituting both a crime and a tort, how do the legal actions differ? In a torts case, the action is brought by the person who has been wronged. In a criminal case, the action is brought by the state or federal government because it is assumed that society's rights as well as those of the victim have been invaded. In a torts case, the losing party may be ordered to pay damages to the victim. In a criminal case, the person who is found guilty may be ordered to pay money to the victim as compensation for the crime; but the offender also may be ordered to pay a fine to the state, engage in some type of community work service, or serve time in prison.

Civil and criminal cases are governed by different procedural rules. They also differ in the evidence that may be presented and the extent of proof needed to win the case. Whether the action is civil or criminal also

SPOTLIGHT 1.1
AN ACT MAY BE A CRIME AND A TORT

The following facts illustrate one situation in which an act may constitute both a crime and a tort. About 8:15 A.M. on a weekday, Sallie, a secretary in a large office building in the downtown area of a medium-sized city, parked her car in a parking garage and left for work. As she entered the elevator to go to the third floor where she worked, a man she had never seen also entered the elevator. He stopped the elevator between floors and raped Sallie. He was later apprehended, charged with first-degree rape, convicted, and sentenced to prison for 15 years.

Since the defendant had no money, Sallie knew that it would be useless to sue him for the tort of assault and battery. Instead she brought an action in tort against the company that designed the elevator. At the subsequent trial, her attorney proved that the cost of installing an alarm button in the elevator would have been $100. The attorney successfully argued that if the elevator had had an alarm button, Sallie might have hit the button, sounded the alarm, and gotten help in time to prevent the attack. The court awarded Sallie $500,000 as compensation for the cost of medical care, for the pain and suffering she sustained from the attack, and for the wages she lost while she was unable to work.

The act of rape is a crime as well as a tort, but this case illustrates that even if the victim cannot get financial compensation in a civil case against her assailant, she might be successful in a tort action against a third person.

---

may determine the type of court in which the trial will take place. In some cases, the action may not be considered a crime the first time it occurs. A first offense of driving while intoxicated is considered a traffic violation and not a crime in some jurisdictions, but a second or third offense may be a crime.

The distinction between a civil and a criminal violation is extremely important because of the more serious repercussions encountered by one accused of violating a criminal as compared to a civil law. In addition to the possibility of a prison sentence for conviction of violating the criminal law, persons accused of a crime may expect social repercussions even if they are found not guilty. Some people lose their jobs as soon as they are formally charged with a crime, particularly when the crime involves sexual offenses. It is important that the criminal law not be taken lightly and that the term *criminal* be used only in referring to people who have been convicted of a criminal offense. A careful analysis of the meaning of crime is necessary.

The Concept of Crime

Crime may be defined as an "act or omission prohibited by law for the protection of the public, the violation of which is prosecuted by the state in its own name and punishable by incarceration."[10] Some states define certain acts as violations or infractions. Those acts may be subject to fines or other minor penalties in the criminal law or to civil penalties, but the commission of those acts is not considered criminal. When an act is neither defined nor processed as a crime, it should not be labeled a crime.

Classification of Crimes

Crimes usually are classified according to the seriousness of the offense; two main categories are used for this purpose. **Misdemeanors** are the less serious offenses, and **felonies** are the more serious offenses. Misdemeanors generally are punishable by a short jail term, fine, probation, or some other penalty that does not involve incarceration in a prison. Felonies usually are punishable by more than a year in jail, incarceration in a prison, or capital punishment.

Crimes are also classified as **mala in se** and **mala prohibita**. *Mala in se* refers to acts that are generally considered to be criminal in nature, acts such as murder and rape. *Mala prohibita* refers to acts that are not so generally regarded as criminal; they are criminal because the legislature has designated them as crimes. Examples of *mala prohibita* crimes today are laws regulating the consensual sexual conduct of adults, the use of drugs, and the use of alcohol by certain age groups.

Elements of a Crime

The elements that must be proved for conviction of a crime will vary from crime to crime and from jurisdiction to jurisdiction. There are some common elements that distinguish crime from noncrime, however.

An Act (*Actus Reus*)   In the American system of law, a person may not be punished for his or her thoughts; an act, or the omission of an act, must be committed. But some crimes do not require an act as we traditionally think of the term. In the crime of conspiracy, which involves an agreement between two or more people to commit an illegal act, the agreement constitutes the act. A crime may also be committed when a person is an accomplice to another who actually commits the criminal act.

In some cases, a crime also may be committed when a person has made an attempt to commit an act defined as a crime but has not actually committed that act. The person must have made a substantial attempt to commit the crime. A very early English case established the crime of attempt. The defendant was accused of putting a lighted candle and some combustible materials in the house he was renting. The house was not burned, but the defendant was convicted. The court said, "The intent may make an act, innocent in itself, criminal; nor is the completion of an act, criminal in itself, necessary to constitute criminality."[11]

Failure to act may constitute a crime but only when a person has a legal duty to act. If a child is drowning and two people watch without making any effort to rescue the child, the lack of action of one may be a crime whereas that of the other might not meet the requirements of a criminal act of omission. In the first instance, the observer is a parent with a legal duty to aid the drowning child. But if the other person is not a close relative, has no contractual obligation to the child, and has not in any way placed the child in that position of peril, he or she may not have a legal duty to come to the aid of the child. Failure to do so does not constitute a crime, no matter how reprehensible the lack of action may be from a moral point of view.

In order for an act to be criminal, it must be voluntary. A driver who has a sudden epileptic seizure while driving a car, during which he or she loses control of the car, strikes another car, and seriously injures or kills the driver of the other car, would not necessarily have committed a crime. But the driver who has had prior attacks of a similar nature might be found guilty of a crime for recklessly creating a situation of danger to others by driving a car with the knowledge that loss of control may occur.

An Unlawful Act   A crime is an act prohibited by the criminal law. Under the United States' concept of criminal law, a person cannot be punished for acts that may be considered to be socially harmful but are not prohibited by the criminal law. The law also must be reasonably clear about the conduct that is prohibited. A statute will be declared void when "men of common intelligence must necessarily guess at its meaning and differ as to its application."[12]

An Intent (*Mens Rea*)   For an act to be a crime, the law requires the element of intent or **mens rea**, "a guilty mind." This requirement is to distinguish those acts that may be harmful to others but for which the actor had no immoral or wrong purpose. Negligent actions may cause harm to others, who may recover damages in a civil tort suit. But the law requires a guilty or immoral mind for those acts to be considered criminal. Former Supreme Court justice Oliver Wendell Holmes, Jr., described the meaning of this distinction when he said, "Even a dog distinguishes between being stumbled over and being kicked."

The intent requirement is very complex. Neither court decisions nor scholarly legal writings provide an easily understood meaning. Furthermore, the intent requirement may vary from crime to crime. But it is clear that some kind of intent must be present in order for an act to constitute a crime. In simple terms, an intent to do something means that the actor means to bring about the consequences of his or her actions or at least is substantially certain those actions will follow. But the actor does not have to intend the specific result that occurs. A person who fires a gun into a crowd intending to kill a specific person, misses that person, and kills another could still be convicted of the crime of murder.

In this example, the intent comes from the evidence that the individual purposely and knowingly took the action that resulted in the death of another. This usually is the easiest kind of case in which to prove intent, but the required intent need not be that obvious. Criminal intent also may be found in cases in which the action is extremely reckless or negligent. The example in Spotlight 1.2 illustrates a scenario in which prosecutors argue that the *reckless* actions of parents provide the criminal intent necessary to constitute a crime.

Another example is that of the landlord held responsible in tort for a criminal attack on a tenant. Add to that case these facts: The tenant was raped in the laundry room that was located in an unlighted area on the premises of the apartment units. She was the fourth tenant raped in that room in two weeks, and she died as a result of the attack. Despite repeated

SPOTLIGHT 1.2
FAILURE TO USE SEAT BELT: A TRAFFIC VIOLATION OR A CRIME?

A statutory requirement that drivers and passengers in automobiles wear seat belts is becoming more common in this country. This statute generally states that adults who are transporting children of specified ages are responsible for adequately securing those children in seat belts. The statute is not generally considered criminal in nature, and the penalty for violation is usually a fine.

In some cases, however, parents who did not properly place small children in seat belts are being prosecuted for homicide, a crime, when an accident occurs and the child is killed. Prosecutors argue that the parent's failure to observe the law is the cause of the child's death and that such violations are so reckless and so negligent that they constitute the requisite intent for a criminal prosecution.

requests from tenants, nothing had been done by the landlord to increase security. A court might find that, in addition to negligence sufficient to establish a tort, the failure to act was so grossly negligent or reckless that it constituted the criminal intent necessary for conviction of a crime.

The definition of criminal intent in cases of reckless and negligent behavior is not easy. The Model Penal Code reproduced in Spotlight 1.3

SPOTLIGHT 1.3
THE MODEL PENAL CODE'S DEFINITION OF CRIMINAL INTENT

Sec. 2.03. . . .

(2) Kinds of Culpability Defined.

(a) Purposely.

A person acts purposely with respect to a material element of an offense when:

(i) if the element involves the nature of his conduct or a result thereof, it is his conscious object to engage in conduct of that nature or to cause such a result; and

(ii) if the element involves the attendant circumstances, he is aware of the existence of such circumstances or he believes or hopes that they exist.

(b) Knowingly.

A person acts knowingly with respect to a material element of an offense when:

(i) if the element involves the nature of his conduct or the attendant circumstances, he is aware that his conduct is of that nature or that such circumstances exist; and

(ii) if the element involves a result of his conduct, he is aware that it is practically certain that his conduct will cause such a result.

(c) Recklessly.

A person acts recklessly with respect to a material element of an offense when he consciously disregards a substantial and unjustifiable risk that the material element exists or will result from his conduct. The risk must be of such a nature and degree that, considering the nature and purpose of the actor's conduct and the circumstances known to him, its disregard involves a gross deviation from the standard of conduct that a law-abiding person would observe in the actor's situation.

(d) Negligently.

A person acts negligently with respect to a material element of an offense when he should be aware of a substantial and unjustifiable risk that the material element exists or will result from his conduct. The risk must be of such a nature and degree that the actor's failure to perceive it, considering the nature and purpose of his conduct and the circumstances known to him, involves a gross deviation from the standard of care that a reasonable person would observe in the actor's situation.

Source: The American Law Institute, Model Penal Code, Proposed Official Draft (Philadelphia, Pa.: The American Law Institute, May 4, 1962), Article 2, "General Principles of Liability." Copyright 1962 by The American Law Institute. Reprinted with the permission of The American Law Institute.

has been drafted as a guide to use in defining those kinds of culpability as well as the two more common kinds of intent: purposely and knowingly.

Intent may not be required in a few specific cases, such as those in which people are held responsible for the criminal acts of others. Suppose, for example, that you are the owner of a bar in a college town. You employ another person to serve the drinks while you are out of town. That person serves liquor to a minor who leaves the bar drunk, drives a car, wrecks the car, and kills another person. You and the driver may be charged with a crime.

A second exception to the intent requirement is the **felony-murder** rule. Suppose you have agreed with a friend that together you will rob a store. Your friend carries the gun, enters the store, and gets the cash while you watch at the front door and then drive the getaway car. Your friend gets scared and kills the store attendant. Under the felony-murder rule, you might be held criminally responsible for that murder. It occurred while you were engaged in a felony, robbery with a firearm, in which it is reasonable to assume that serious bodily injury or death might result. Likewise, if you purposely set fire to a building, thinking the building is empty, you may be held criminally responsible for the deaths of people inside that building.

The felony-murder doctrine does not exist in all states; where it is effective, it generally applies only to deaths that follow the commission of inherently dangerous felonies such as forcible rape, robbery, arson, and burglary, and the U.S. Supreme Court has limited its application.[13]

Attendant Circumstances   Acts may be criminal in some circumstances but not others. As previously stated, failure to act to save a drowning child constitutes a criminal omission only if the person has a legal duty to assist that child. It is also true that some acts that normally are criminal, such as forcible rape, may not be criminal unless certain circumstances exist. Under the common law and under most statutes in this country, until very recently, there was a marital exclusion for the crime of rape. That meant that a husband could not be convicted of raping his wife unless he forced her to have sexual intercourse with another man. He, however, had unlimited sexual access to her. Many states have changed their rape statutes to eliminate the marital exemption.

Concurrence of Act and Intent   For an act to be a crime, the act and the intent must occur together. *A* might intend to kill *B* today but not do so. One week later, after *A* and *B* have resolved their differences, they go hunting. *A* accidentally falls while preparing to shoot a deer, the gun fires, and *B* is killed. *A* should not be charged with murder since, at the time he fired, he did not have a criminal intent.

Causation   A final element of all crimes is that there must be proof that the result is caused by the act. If *A* shoots and hits *B*, wounding *B* slightly, *A* may be charged with attempted murder (if the elements of that crime can be proved). But *A* should not be charged with murder if *B* dies of causes totally unrelated to the act of shooting. **Causation** in criminal law is too intricate and complex to discuss in this text. It is important to know, however, that *legal cause* is a crucial element that must be proved before a person is convicted of a crime.

Defenses in Criminal Law

Some acts that normally would be considered crimes are not considered so if they are committed under circumstances that raise legal **defenses** or justifications. Killing another person is not a crime if that act is done by a police officer acting under a reasonable belief that the accused is committing a felony and that the only way to protect the officer and others is to shoot to kill. Likewise, a private citizen may wound or kill in self-defense or defense of others. The rules regarding defenses are, like most areas of law, very complex. But it is clear that one may not use excessive force, force that is greater than is necessary to protect oneself and others in these situations.

Another defense is infancy. Under the common law, as well as all of our state statutes, children under a specified age are considered legally incapable of having the guilty mind necessary for a crime. There are also situations in which the law will recognize the defense of insanity. The insanity defense, though widely known, is used infrequently. This highly controversial defense is familiar because of the developments since John W. Hinckley was found not guilty by reason of insanity in his trial for attempting to assassinate then President Ronald Reagan and others.

Entrapment also is a familiar defense. The defense is used by defendants who argue that they would not have engaged in the criminal conduct had a police officer (or other government agent) not induced them to commit the crime. The Supreme Court's general rule for determining whether government conduct constituted entrapment was stated in 1958. In *Sherman v. United States*, the Court said, "To determine whether entrapment has been established, a line must be drawn between the trap for the unwary innocent and the trap for the unwary criminal."[14] That line is often difficult to draw. Spotlight 1.4 details a recent but unsuccessful use of the entrapment defense in the highly publicized case of John Zaccaro, Jr.

PURPOSE OF THE CRIMINAL LAW

An analysis of the legal definition of crime may answer the question of the kinds of acts that are defined as criminal, but it does not answer the question of which acts should be included within the criminal law. Historically, the purpose of the criminal law has been the subject of considerable debate. Some argue that only those acts that are clearly criminal should be included and that the criminal law should not be used to try to control behavior that many people do not believe to be wrong. Others take the position that the law is the most effective method of social control and therefore should embrace even those acts that some may consider to be

SPOTLIGHT 1.4
THE ENTRAPMENT DEFENSE: ZACCARO'S UNSUCCESSFUL CASE

John A. Zaccaro, Jr., son of John Zaccaro and Geraldine A. Ferraro (unsuccessful Democratic vice-presidential candidate in 1984), was tried and convicted of illegally selling one-quarter gram of cocaine to Laura Manning, an undercover police officer. Zaccaro's attorney argued unsuccessfully that his client was entrapped by the attractive woman and that he therefore should be found not guilty.

The jury, however, believed the prosecutor, who argued that Zaccaro's sale to the undercover officer was just another illegal drug sale. Authorities began their investigation of Zaccaro after an anonymous tip alleged that the college student was selling drugs.

Geraldine Ferraro acknowledged that her son was in possession of the illegal drug but argued that the sale was a setup and that her son was targeted by authorities because of her political campaign.

Zaccaro was sentenced to house arrest, which means he could remain in his apartment rather than go to prison, but his activities were restricted. Many people criticized the sentencing judge for what they perceived as a lenient sentence.

---

mala prohibita rather than *mala in se*. Among the most controversial areas are the inclusion within the criminal law of some kinds of sexual behavior and the sale of alcohol and drugs.

Sexual Behavior

In a 1969 publication two scholars referred to the criminal law in the United States as the most moralistic in history, characterized by sex offense statutes designed "to provide an enormous legislative chastity belt

Despite arguments that sexual behavior between consenting adults in private should not be included within the reach of criminal law, prostitution is illegal in almost all U.S. jurisdictions. (Joel Gordon)

encompassing the whole population and proscribing everything but solitary and joyless masturbation and 'normal coitus' inside wedlock."[15] In recent years, many states have repealed criminal statutes that proscribe sexual behavior between consenting adults. They have limited those statutes to sexual behavior that is the result of force against any person, is committed consensually but with an underage person, or is committed in public. Many states still retain the common law approach, however, and provide criminal penalties for adult consensual sexual behavior thought to be deviant by some members of the population. In a controversial decision in 1986, *Bowers v. Hartwick*, the U.S. Supreme Court upheld the right of states to do so. This case involved consenting homosexual behavior between two men.[16]

It is argued that inclusion of homosexual behavior within the criminal law is necessary to control the spread of Acquired Immune Deficiency Syndrome (AIDS), a deadly disease that thus far has been found more frequently among homosexual than heterosexual individuals. But the concern with the spread of AIDS goes beyond these situations. In 1987, a federal court in Minnesota upheld a defendant's conviction for assault with a deadly or dangerous weapon. The charge was based on the biting of two correctional officers by an inmate who was infected with AIDS.[17] The fear of AIDS is cited by some as the reason for the increased acts of random violence against the 11 million homosexuals in this country. "According to gay-rights groups, hate-motivated assaults have nearly tripled in recent years."[18]

Alcohol and Drugs

Considerable debate is taking place throughout many countries in the world concerning the role of the law in attempting to regulate alcohol and drugs. In recent years, many countries have significantly increased the penalties for the illegal sale and possession of alcohol and drugs. This movement raises important questions regarding the purpose of the criminal law.

The critical question is not whether we should try to regulate some or all of these activities (although we do not even agree on that issue), but whether the criminal law is the best way to attempt control. How does the offense of driving under the influence of alcohol or driving while intoxicated compare with another related act, public drunkenness, that also is considered to be criminal in many jurisdictions? Should the criminal law be used to regulate both offenses? Clearly, driving while intoxicated is a serious problem. Many fatal automobile accidents are caused by drunk drivers. But what about the public drunk who is wandering around but not harming anyone? Should that person be processed through the criminal justice system? If so, what do we do with the person after conviction? What is an appropriate penalty?

What has been the result of arresting people for public drunkenness? In most cases, the arrestees have overcrowded the jails and received no counseling or other services that would assist them in coping with the problem. Some jurisdictions, realizing the impact of the problem on the

Although drinking may be considered by many to be a private matter that should not be included within the criminal law, most people would agree that driving while intoxicated is a public matter that should be considered criminal. (Spencer Grant/ Stock Boston)

rest of the criminal justice system, have removed public drunkenness from the jurisdiction of criminal law and provided alcohol treatment and other plans for handling the problem.[19]

Others have retained public drunkenness statutes. The California statute was unsuccessfully challenged, with a 1986 decision in *Sundance v. Municipal Court* in the Supreme Court of California upholding the practice of routinely arresting and jailing people for public drunkenness. The court, however, noted that arrests for public drunkenness, which constituted 32.1 percent of all misdemeanor arrests in 1975 when the complaint was originally filed, were second only to traffic arrests in Los Angeles County. The court also noted that although those arrested for public drunkenness may be diverted into treatment centers, this is not done in many cases.[20]

Several reasons are given for including alcohol- and drug-related acts within the criminal law. First is the symbolic value of the legislation: by criminalizing the acts, the society makes it clear that they are unacceptable.

Second, it is assumed that criminalization has a deterrent effect: if the act is a crime, most people will decline to commit it. This reason requires more careful consideration. There is no significant evidence indicating that the threat of criminal punishment is a deterrent to public drunkenness. In fact, the trial court in *Sundance* concluded that jailing public drunks might even be counterproductive. The California Supreme Court declared that that finding "applied only to chronic alcoholics, while the statute applies to all members of the public," and there therefore was no legal reason to declare the statute unconstitutional.[21]

Furthermore, most medical personnel take the position that chronic alcoholism is a disease, not a condition over which the alcoholic has free will. The United States Supreme Court, however, does not agree with this position. In 1988, *Traynor v. Turnage*, a case involving veterans' benefits, the Court classified alcoholism as "willful misconduct," not as a disease.[22]

Driving while under the influence of alcohol or drugs, however, is another issue. Deaths from such drivers reach the 50,000 figure in a two-year period, costing as much as $21–24 billion in economic losses for property damage alone.[23] Concern with deaths caused by persons driving under the influence (DUI) of a controlled substance, in recent years, has led to enhanced penalties for conviction of such offenses. At first the campaign to reduce violations of the DUI statutes appeared to be working, with deaths attributed to such offenses declining by 11 percent from 1982 to 1985. But in 1986 such deaths rose by 7 percent, leading some to conclude that the apparent deterrent effects of stiffer penalties for DUI are only temporary.[24]

It is also argued that because the use of alcohol (and drugs) is related to criminal behavior the criminal law must be employed. An earlier study of prisoners and their use of alcohol and drugs indicated that many inmates had been using drugs or alcohol at the time of their criminal acts. Even if some of the inmates exaggerated their reports of alcohol use, concluded the study, "It is clear that alcohol has played a major role in the lives of many prison inmates." Furthermore, almost half the inmates said they had been drinking just before the commission of the criminal act for which they were incarcerated at the time of the study. More than three-fifths reported that they had been drinking heavily.[25]

A later report of the Bureau of Justice Statistics indicated that more than half of all convicted jail inmates admitted that before committing the offenses for which they were currently serving time they were "pretty drunk" or "very drunk." Specifically, nearly 70 percent of those convicted of manslaughter had been drinking before the offense, and 49 percent of those convicted of murder or attempted murder were drinking before committing the criminal act.[26]

The use of drugs is also tied to crime rates. A 1988 study of 1,483 offenders in Texas found that the typical inmate is a "high school dropout with a drug or alcohol problem" and concluded that if more prisons are built "at the expense of education and social programs," the problem will only get worse.[27]

Studies of the effect of substance abuse on the crime rate must be analyzed carefully. Although it is unreasonable to ignore the possible effect of substance abuse present in so many instances when crimes are committed, the concurrence of alcohol or drug abuse and criminal activity does not necessarily mean that there is a direct cause-and-effect relationship. It is possible that the use of drugs and alcohol represents a life-style adopted by some criminals and has nothing to do with the commission of crimes. In those cases, attempts to enforce laws regulating the abuse of alcohol and drugs will not have a significant long-term effect on criminal activity.

Recent researchers have found that "race, poverty, population size, and age composition provide the 'best explanation' for variations in the level of criminal activity," and that although alcohol-related variables may aid our understanding of criminal behavior, "their impact is secondary and probably ancillary," once social disorganization, as measured by variables such as race, poverty, population size, and age composition, have been accounted for.[28] This is not to suggest that enforcement of the laws is an unreasonable means of indicating society's disapproval of substance abuse. Enforcement of these laws also may discourage some people from law violations.

Even if we decide that public drunkenness, driving while intoxicated, substance abuse, or all of these offenses should be included within the realm of the criminal law, we should consider carefully what penalties to assess. What is accomplished by jailing a public drunk other than to get him or her off the streets? In most cases, there is no long-term positive result. For that matter, what is accomplished by jailing a person for DUI? Would it be more effective to impose a heavy fine and restrict or prohibit driving for a long period of time? Or is a jail term necessary to convince drivers that drunk driving will not be tolerated? If so, is that jail term worth the cost to society when new facilities must be constructed to handle the large populations of incarcerated people?

Criminalization of Crimes Without Victims

This discussion of the purpose of the law raises the issue of whether the criminal law is used too extensively and therefore goes beyond the purpose of protecting the public's safety and welfare and interferes with the behavior of private persons. Those who take this position argue that the criminal law is being used to encompass victimless crimes, or crimes without victims. The results are said to be harmful in the long run. Police may invade personal rights of privacy in order to enforce the law; courts, jails, and prisons may be overcrowded as the result of processing these people through the criminal justice system; black markets may develop to supply the prohibited products such as drugs and alcohol; and attempts to enforce unpopular and unsupported criminal statutes may create disrespect for the law. Critical police resources may be diverted from more important functions.

Critics of the current war against drugs also argue that the Reagan administration approach denies to some sick people the drugs needed for treatment, noting that some drugs, such as marijuana and heroin, are helpful in the treatment of cancer pain, nausea due to radiation and chemotherapy, and glaucoma. Arnold S. Trebach, an internationally acclaimed drug policy expert, argues that, although victimizing millions, current drug policies bring little benefit to anyone. According to Trebach, "We do not now have, and never had, the capability to manage a successful war on any drug." We should be fighting on another front with goals such

SPOTLIGHT 1.5
THE DRUG PROBLEM: SUGGESTIONS FOR REFORM

- Make it legal for adults to grow and possess marijuana for personal use.
- Recognize that all drugs, legal and illegal, may be abused by some people but not by most users.
- Impose greater controls on the real killers, tobacco and alcohol, and less on such drugs as marijuana, heroin, and cocaine.
- Allow doctors to provide clean drugs and needles

to their addict-patients so as to improve their health, curb the spread of AIDS, and reduce crime.
- Provide a wide range of affordable treatment options to any person suffering from the disease of addiction to any drug, legal or illegal, as often as needed.

Arnold S. Trebach, *The Great Drug War* (New York: Macmillan Publishing Co., 1988).

as those suggested by Trebach in his most recent book, *The Great Drug War*, and listed in part in Spotlight 1.5.[29]

Supporters argue that the criminal law is a necessary symbol of morality and that removal of *mala prohibita* acts from the criminal law would place society's stamp of approval on the behaviors in question. Resolution of these two positions regarding the use of the criminal law to control morality involves religious, moral, and ethical considerations as well as legal and empirical issues. In the final analysis, the answer may be a very personal one. But it is clear that whatever position is taken, it will have important repercussions on the criminal justice system.

SUMMARY

This introductory chapter was designed to set the stage for our study of criminal justice. It began with an overview of the system, emphasizing that the criminal justice system in the United States is really many systems, but they do have common features. The elements of the systems are similar, including the four basic institutions of the police, prosecution, courts, and corrections, as well as the stages the accused goes through from the time of apprehension through incarceration and release. In later chapters, all of those institutions and stages will be discussed. This chapter, however, focused on an overview of the basic philosophy of the American criminal justice systems and emphasized the interrelationship of the parts of those systems. Too frequently, changes are made in the system without careful consideration of the impact of those changes on other aspects of the system.

Examples of changes that have had negative ef-

fects may be seen in the analysis of the criminalization of consensual sexual behavior and the use of alcohol and some drugs. These areas in particular, along with others, raise the question of what is the real purpose of criminal law. What are we trying to accomplish when we include these behaviors within the criminal law? Do we accomplish those goals? Is it possible that there are more negative than positive results? The purpose of this discussion is not to suggest that any or all of the activities discussed should not necessarily be targeted by the criminal law but, rather, to encourage serious analysis and thinking about the *total* effects of criminalizing certain acts.

Any discussion of the nature and purpose of criminal law must be understood within the context of the adversary system, with its important philosophies of due process and equal protection. Central to this discussion is a distinction between the crime control and the due process models. It is quite possible, perhaps even probable, that a more severe approach to crime, such as that exemplified by the crime control model, would be more successful in reducing crime rates. But at what cost?

In the U.S. system, individual rights are important. They are embodied in the Bill of Rights of the U.S. Constitution and in most state constitutions. Throughout this text it will be important to compare these rights with the often conflicting rights of victims, society, and the need to control crime. Drawing the lines in creating the boundaries of the criminal justice system is difficult at best. This text is designed to encourage the reader to *think* about where those lines should be drawn and *why*.

This chapter also introduced the concepts of crime and of criminal law. Although both are extremely complex and cannot be detailed in an introductory text, it is important to understand the basic elements of a crime and to be able to distinguish criminal law from civil law. Crime requires a criminal act (which also includes a failure to act where there is a legal duty to do so) and a criminal state of mind, which combine to cause the prohibited result. Some statutes also require attendant circumstances, and where those exist, they constitute an element of the crime.

Some acts that would otherwise be criminal may not be so if adequate defenses are proved. There are numerous defenses in criminal law; not all are recognized in all jurisdictions. The more commonly known ones, insanity and entrapment, were mentioned, with the latter illustrated by the unsuccessful attempt of John Zaccaro in his trial on illegal drug sales.

The topics discussed in this chapter will reappear throughout the text, and the reader may wish to return to this chapter for review from time to time. The remainder of the book will look more closely at the important procedures, issues, and the system effect of the components of the criminal justice system. To continue this introduction to the criminal event, the next chapter is devoted to data on crime.

STUDY QUESTIONS

1. What are the four basic institutions or components of a criminal justice system?

2. Why is it important to anticipate all of the results that might occur when one component of the criminal justice system is changed?

3. Why is discretion important in the criminal justice system? Who exercises discretion?

4. What is meant by the *adversary system*? How do the processes of equal protection and due process relate to that system? How does this system conflict with the crime control model?

5. What is meant by *social control*? How does law compare to other methods of social control?

6. What are the important sources of law? How do they differ?

7. What are some of the differences between *criminal* and *civil law*? Distinguish between *tort* and *crime*.

8. Name and explain the basic elements of a *crime*.

9. What kinds of behavior should be included in the criminal law? What are the positive and negative implications of inclusion in each case?

ENDNOTES

1. Joint Anti-Fascist Refugee Committee v. McGrath, 341 U.S. 123, 162–163 (1951), Justice Frankfurter concurring.
2. Liberta v. Kelly, 839 F.2d 77, 93 (2d Cir. 1988), *cert. den.*, 57 USLW 3231 (1988) citations omitted.
3. Herbert L. Packer, "The Courts, the Police and the Rest of Us," *Journal of Criminal Law, Criminology, and Police Science* 57 (September 1966): 238–43. See also Herbert L. Packer, *The Limits of the Criminal Sanction* (Palo Alto, Calif.: Stanford University Press, 1968). For a recent anal-

ysis, see Philip Jenkins, *Crime and Justice: Issues and Ideas* (Monterey, Calif.: Brooks/Cole Publishing Company, 1984), pp. 36–56; and Samuel Walker, *Sense and Nonsense about Crime: A Policy Guide* (Monterey, Calif.: Brooks/Cole Publishing Company, 1985).

4. William Graham Sumner, *Folkways* (New York: Dover Publications, 1906), pp. 1–79.

5. See William Seagle, *The Quest for Law* (New York: Alfred A. Knopf, 1941).

6. Émile Durkheim, *The Division of Labor in Society*, trans. G. George Simpson (New York: Free Press, 1947).

7. See William J. Chambliss, "Elites and the Creation of Criminal Law," in William J. Chambliss, ed., *Sociological Readings in the Conflict Perspective* (Reading, Mass.: Addison-Wesley, 1973). See also Jerome Hall, *Theft, Law and Society*, rev. ed. (Indianapolis: Bobbs-Merrill, 1952). For a brief but excellent overview of the conflict perspective, see Michael J. Lynch and W. Byron Groves, *A Primer in Radical Criminology* (New York: Harrow and Heston, 1986).

8. Hazel B. Kerper, *Introduction to the Criminal Justice System* (St. Paul, Minn.: West Publishing Co., 1972), p. 27.

9. W. Page Keeton, gen. ed., *Prosser and Keeton on the Law of Torts*, 5th ed. (St. Paul, Minn.: West Publishing Co., 1984), p. 2.

10. MODEL PENAL CODE, Section 1.1014(1).

11. Rex v. Scofield, Cald. 397, 400 (1784).

12. Connally v. General Construction Company, 269 U.S. 385, 391 (1926).

13. See Enmund v. Florida, 458 U.S. 782 (1982) and Tison v. Arizona, 107 S.Ct. 3201 (1987).

14. Sherman v. U.S., 356 U.S. 369 (1958). For a recent case in which the defense was not successful, see U.S. v. Toro, 840 F.2d 1221 (5th Cir. 1988).

15. Norval Morris and Gordon Hawkins, *The Honest Politician's Guide to Crime Control* (Chicago: University of Chicago Press, 1969), p. 15.

16. Bowers v. Hardwick, 478 U.S. 186 (1986).

17. U.S. v. Moore, 669 F.Supp. 289 (D.Minn. 1987), *aff'd.*, 846 F.2d 1163 (8th Cir. 1988).

18. "Open Season on Gays: AIDS Sparks an Epidemic of Violence against Homosexuals," *Time* (7 March 1988), p. 24.

19. See "Jailing Drunk Drivers: Impact on the Criminal Justice System," *National Institute of Justice Reports* (Washington, D.C.: U.S. Government Printing Office, July 1985), pp. 2–5.

20. Sundance v. Municipal Court, 232 Cal.Rptr. 814 (Cal. 1986).

21. Sundance v. Municipal Court, 232 Cal.Rptr. 814 (Cal. 1986).

22. Traynor v. Turnage, 480 U.S. 916 (1988).

23. National Institute of Justice, *Jailing Drunk Drivers: Impact on the Criminal Justice System* (Washington, D.C.: National Institute of Justice, November 1984), p. 1.

24. "Deaths from Drunken Driving Increase," *New York Times* (29 October 1987), p. 12, referring to a study by Dr. Ralph Hingson, chief of social and behavioral sciences at the Boston University School of Public Health. For an earlier study on the deterrent effect of laws against DUI, see H. Laurence Ross, *Deterring the Drinking Driver: Legal Police and Social Control* (Lexington, Mass.: Lexington Books, 1982).

25. "Prisoners and Alcohol," U.S. Department of Justice, Bureau of Justice Statistics Bulletin (Washington, D.C.: U.S. Government Printing Office, January 1983).

26. News Release, Bureau of Justice (National Institute of Justice, November 1985).

27. "Most Convicts Used Drugs, Study Shows," *Tulsa World* (7 April 1988), p. 14C, referring to an internal study conducted for the Texas Board of Pardons and Paroles.

28. R. Thomas Dull and David J. Giacopassi, "The Impact of Local Alcohol Ordinances on Official Crime Rates: The Case of Tennessee," *Justice Quarterly* 4 (June 1987): 311.

29. News release from Macmillan Publishers about the recent book by Arnold S. Trebach, *The Great Drug War* (New York: Macmillan Publishing Co., 1988). Trebach also is the author of *The Heroin Solution* (1982). See also James A. Inciardi, *The War on Drugs: Heroin, Cocaine, Crime, and Public Policy* (Palo Alto, Calif.: Mayfield Publishing Co., 1986).

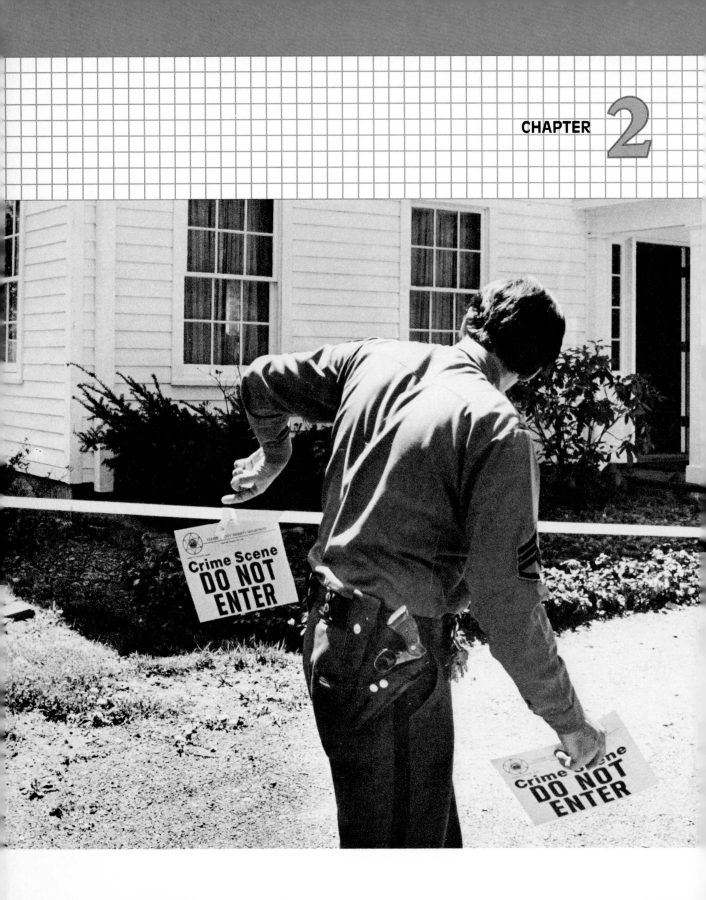

The Incidence of Crime

OUTLINE

KEY TERMS

The following actions occurred within a one-week period in a medium-sized city in the Northeast. Each illustrates a point that is pertinent to the collection of data on crime.

Jane, age 14, stole two leather purses from a department store. She was apprehended by the store manager, but because of Jane's age, the manager decided not to call police and proceed with formal charges.

Paul was murdered when he entered his home while two men were burglarizing the premises. One of the murderers was apprehended, arrested, convicted, and sentenced to life in prison. The other was never apprehended.

Auditors discovered that half a million dollars was missing from the largest bank in the city. After a thorough investigation, bank officials were shocked to find that Charles, one of the vice-presidents, had embezzled the money. Charles had deposited most of the money in a foreign bank. No official criminal charges were filed after Charles and the other bank officials agreed to a repayment plan and Charles agreed to resign.

Mary's car was stolen from the parking lot at her apartment. She reported the theft, but the car was never recovered. Mary was without a car for two weeks. During that time she rode the bus to work. Early one morning she was attacked just before she got to the bus stop. Mary's assailant forced her into his car, drove to a park, and raped her. He threatened to kill her if she reported the crime to the police. Mary did not report the rape.

INTRODUCTION

The actions of the criminals and victims in the CJA illustrate some of the problems encountered in measuring criminal activity. Not all crimes are reported to the police. Not all crimes that are reported are cleared by arrest; fewer still are cleared by conviction. This means, of course, that no source of data can be completely accurate in its measure of criminal activity. Despite the impossibility of detecting all criminal activity or successfully prosecuting and convicting all guilty parties who are detected, crime data serve a very important function. Crime data are utilized by official agencies in determining policies and budgets. They are utilized by police officials who must decide the best utilization of their officers and other resources.

Crime data may be used by official agencies and private citizens who are determined to make their communities safer for all who live there. Social scientists who study criminal behavior use crime data, both official and unofficial, in their analyses of why and under what circumstances people commit criminal acts. And as the 1988 presidential election illustrated, crime data may be used for political reasons, in an effort to convince voters of the success or failure of the opposition's crime prevention efforts.

The point then, is not to dismiss crime statistics because of problems of inaccuracy, but rather to analyze carefully the various sources of data and determine which sources are best for a particular purpose. This chapter examines and analyzes the most common methods for collecting data on crime: official reports of reported crimes; data secured from victims; and data from self-report studies. Following the description of the sources of data, the discussion compares those sources and analyzes the problems of collecting data by each method. The chapter then turns to an overview of the amount and types of crime as determined by official data.

SOURCES OF CRIME DATA

In this country there are two major sources of official data on crime: the *Uniform Crime Reports (UCR)* and the *National Crime Survey (NCS)*. Table 2.1 explains the purposes of these two sources and their differences. Basically, the UCR reports data on crimes that come to the attention of the police either through their own observations or through reports from others. As Table 2.1 indicates, the UCR includes two crimes not included by the NCS, murder and arson. Murder is not included in NCS data because those data are based on interviews with crime victims. Arson is not included because it is too difficult to measure with the techniques used in the NCS. Of the two sources, the UCR is the one most frequently used.

Uniform Crime Reports

The **Uniform Crime Reports** (UCR) include data on crime collected by the Federal Bureau of Investigation (FBI). The FBI publishes the official report once a year. Seven crimes were originally selected because of their seriousness and frequency to constitute the UCR Crime Index. Known as Part I, or **index offenses,** they include murder and nonnegligent manslaughter, forcible rape, robbery, aggravated assault, burglary, larceny–theft, and motor vehicle theft. Congress added arson to the index in 1978.

Each month law enforcement agencies report the number of **crimes known to the police;** that is, the number of Part I offenses verified by police investigation of the complaint. The number of actual crimes in the index category is reported whether or not any further action was taken in the case. A crime known to police is counted even if no suspect is arrested and no prosecution occurs. If a criminal activity involves several different crimes, only the most serious is reported as an index offense. If a victim is raped, robbed, and murdered, only the murder is counted in the UCR. Offenses known to police do not indicate how many persons were involved in a particular reported crime. The data are used to calculate a **crime rate.** The national crime rate is calculated by dividing the number of Part I reported crimes by the number of people in the country (data obtained from census reports). The result is expressed as a rate of crimes per 100,000 people.

The UCR also reports the number of Part I offenses that are cleared. Offenses are cleared in two ways: by arrest when a suspect is arrested, charged, and turned over to the judicial system for prosecution; and by circumstances beyond the control of the police. A suspect's death or the victim's refusal to press charges normally signal the end of police involvement. Crimes are considered cleared whether or not the suspect is convicted of the crime.

TABLE 2.1 _____

Comparison of the *Uniform Crime Reports*
and the *National Crime Survey*

	Uniform Crime Reports	**National Crime Survey**
Offenses measured:	Homicide Rape Robbery (personal and commercial) Assault (aggravated) Burglary (commercial and household) Larceny (commercial and household) Motor vehicle theft Arson	Rape Robbery (personal) Assault (aggravated and simple) Household burglary Larceny (personal and household) Motor vehicle theft
Scope:	Crimes reported to the police in most jurisdictions; considerable flexibility in developing small-area data	Crimes both reported and not reported to police; all data are available for a few large geographic areas
Collection method:	Police department reports to FBI or to centralized state agencies that then report to FBI	Survey interviews; periodically measures the total number of crimes committed by asking a national sample of 49,000 households encompassing 101,000 persons age 12 and over about their experiences as victims of crime during a specified period
Kinds of information:	In addition to offense counts, provides information on crime clearances, persons arrested, persons charged, law enforcement officers killed and assaulted, and characteristics of homicide victims	Provides details about victims (such as age, race, sex, education, income, and whether the victim and offender were related to each other) and about crimes (such as time and place of occurrence, whether or not reported to police, use of weapons, occurrence of injury, and economic consequences)
Sponsor:	Department of Justice Federal Bureau of Investigation	Department of Justice Bureau of Justice Statistics

Source: Bureau of Justice Statistics, *Report to the Nation on Crime and Justice: The Data*, 2d ed. (Washington, D.C.: U.S. Government Printing Office, 1988), p. 11.

One official source of crime data is the *Uniform Crime Reports* collected and published annually by the Federal Bureau of Investigation (FBI). (PhotoEdit)

Several persons may be arrested and one crime cleared, or one person may be arrested and many crimes cleared. The clearance rate is the number of crimes solved, expressed as a percentage of the total number of crimes reported to the police. The clearance rate is critical in policy decisions because it is one measure used to evaluate police departments. The higher the number of crimes solved by arrest, the better the police force looks in the eyes of the public. Figure 2.1 gives an indication of the percentage of crimes cleared by arrest on a national basis in 1987.

Figure 2.1 indicates that crimes of violence are much more likely to be cleared by arrest than are property crimes. Victims (or families in the case of murdered victims) are more likely to report violent crimes than property crimes to police and report them quickly. Victims of personal violence as compared to victims of property crimes also are more likely to be able to give police pertinent information that might lead to an arrest. Murder is the crime most likely to be cleared by arrest; burglary is least likely, but motor vehicle theft and larceny–theft also have very low clearance rates.

In addition to data on crimes reported and arrest information for Part I offenses, the UCR publishes the number of arrests for the less serious Part II offenses. Examples of these offenses are other assaults (simple), forgery and counterfeiting, fraud, embezzlement, stolen property, vandalism, prostitution and commercialized vice, other sex offenses, drug abuse violations, driving under the influence, drunkenness, and disorderly conduct.

Arrest information in the UCR is presented in two forms: (1) the total estimated numbers of arrests by crime for each of the recorded offenses and (2) the number of arrests made during one year for each of the serious offenses per 100,000 population. The UCR does not report the numbers of persons arrested each year because some individuals are arrested more

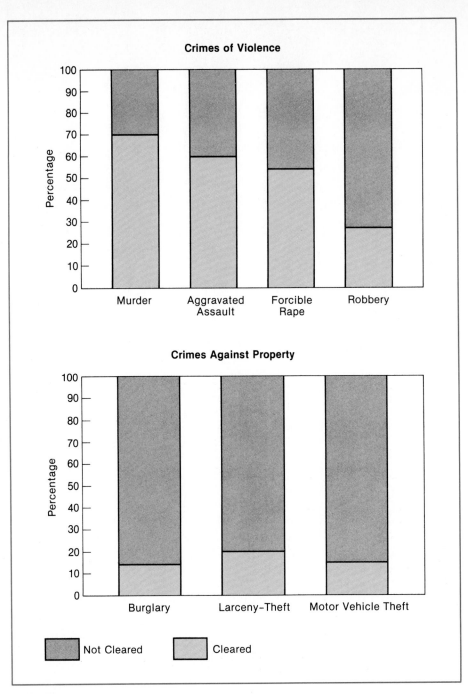

FIGURE 2.1
Crimes Cleared by Arrest, 1987. *Source:* Federal Bureau of Investigation, *Crime in the United States: Uniform Crime Reports, 1987* (Washington, D.C.: U.S. Government Printing Office, 1988), p. 154.

than once during the year. The actual number of arrested persons, therefore, is likely to be smaller than the total number of arrests.

Limitations of the UCR   The most serious limitation of the UCR is that it does not include all crimes that are committed. Some have argued that UCR data are significantly lower than the actual incidence of crime.[1] The UCR does not record all criminal activity for several reasons.

Refusal to Report Crimes   Police observe few crimes while they are occurring; most police work begins with a report of criminal activity. If victims and witnesses refuse to report crimes, police are seriously hindered in their ability to detect crime. The Bureau of Justice Statistics (BJS) reports that most crimes are not reported to the police. In general, victims report only 48 percent of the violent crimes of rape, robbery, and assault; 26 percent of personal thefts; and 37 percent of the crimes of burglary, larceny, and motor vehicle thefts. Victims are more likely to report completed crimes than attempted crimes and a crime that results in an injury, especially if that injury is serious.[2]

Economic loss also is important in analyzing crime reporting. The higher the value of stolen property or the cost of an injury, the more likely it is that the victim will report the crime. Victims who had some confrontation with the offender are more likely to report crimes than those who had no contact. Several reasons are given for not reporting crimes. Table 2.2 contains the BJS data on the most important reasons for reporting and for not reporting crimes. As the table indicates, of those who do not report crimes to the police, 35 percent indicated that they did not think the crime serious enough to warrant reporting.

The BJS statisticians also analyzed the data by type of crime, finding that for violent crimes, victims who did not report most frequently cited as their reason that the incident was not serious or that it was a personal or private matter. This was particularly the case with the crimes of aggravated and simple assaults.

Table 2.2 also indicates the reasons for reporting crimes, indicating that 40 percent of those who reported the crimes said that they did so for economic reasons: to collect insurance or to recover property. Data not included in Table 2.2 indicated that the most frequently mentioned reason victims of violent crimes gave for reporting their victimization was to keep the crime from happening again.

Mary, the rape victim in this chapter's CJA, illustrates a typical reaction: Victims of rape often do not report the crime to the police. Rape victims may think that nothing will be done about the crime and that they will be suspected of encouraging the crime particularly if the rape were committed by an acquaintance, as is often the case. Rape victims may not want to go through a trial in which they will have to face the alleged rapist and submit to intensive cross-examination. They may also be too embarrassed to relate the details of the crime to police or to their own families. In some cities, after police have been given special training to deal with rape victims and counseling services have been made available, there has been an increase in reported rapes.

TABLE 2.2

Most Important Reason Victims Give for Not Reporting
or for Reporting Crimes to Police

Reasons for Not Reporting		Reasons for Reporting	
Not serious		Economic	
Object recovered or offender		In order to collect insurance	8
unsuccessful	5	Desire to recover property	32
Did not think it important		Obligation	
enough	30	Because it was a crime	8
Nothing could be done		Because you felt it was your	
Didn't realize crime happened		duty	7
until later	7	To keep it from happening	
Property hard to recover due to		again	20
lack of identification number	4	To stop or prevent this incident	
Lack of proof, no way to find/		from happening	9
identify offender	16	To punish offender	7
Police wouldn't do anything		There was evidence or proof	1
Police wouldn't think it was		Need for help after incident due	
important enough—wouldn't		to injury	1
want to be bothered	7	Other	8
Police would be inefficient,			
insensitive	4		
Reported to someone else	11		
Private/personal matter or took			
care of it myself	9		
Did not want to take time, too			
inconvenient	2		
Afraid of reprisal by offender or			
his family or friends	1		
Other	7		

Source: Bureau of Justice Statistics, *Reporting Crimes to the Police* (Washington, D.C.: U. S. Department of Justice, December 1985), p. 8.

Delay in Reporting Crimes   Crime data from the UCR also are affected by the speed with which victims report crimes to the police. A study in Kansas City disclosed that probabilities of arrest decline quickly as delays in reporting crimes increase.[3] Other studies have confirmed these findings and indicated some of the reasons why citizens delay in reporting the crime.

Delay may be caused by inability to decide whether to report the crime. There are three reasons for this indecisiveness. Some citizens want to verify that a crime has been committed. Others take some actions to cope with the crime before calling the police. Still others experience conflict about calling the police; so they try to avoid making a quick decision. Once the decision to call the police has been made, there may be further delays. A phone may not be readily available. The caller may not know the police number. The caller may have trouble communicating with the police complaint taker.[4]

Police Discretion in Recording Crime   UCR data also are affected by police decisions. Crimes are included in the UCR only if the police decide there is sufficient evidence to believe that a crime has been committed. Police have wide discretion in making that decision. An earlier study by Donald J. Black, who studied police-citizen interaction to determine which variables were related to the probability that a citizen's complaint of a crime would become an official crime report, found that police were more likely to record the reported crime in these cases:

1. The crime was a felony rather than a misdemeanor.
2. The reporting citizen requested formal rather than informal disposition of the case.
3. The victim and the alleged offender were not related.
4. The complainant showed deference to the police.

Black found no relationship between the race of the complainant and the police decision to take official action, but he did find some evidence of a relationship between socioeconomic status and police reaction to complaints about crime.[5]

Other scholars have argued that police may individually, or as a department, want to downplay the amount of crime in their areas; consequently, they do not record all reported crimes even when there is sufficient evidence that a crime was committed. In an earlier study of police reporting of thefts, David Seidman and Michael Couzens concluded that official crime data are misleading. Because they are used as official data by people who are under pressure to have those data show certain things, they can be, and are, manipulated to show higher or lower crime rates.[6]

An earlier internal investigation disclosed that Chicago police were throwing out fourteen times more crime reports than comparable police departments but that in 40 percent of those cases there was sufficient evidence that a crime had been committed. Chicago police blamed the department for this situation, arguing that the policies on recording or discarding reported crimes were unclear. They also claimed that departmental officials wanted the crimes discarded. After department policies were changed, the department showed a 25 percent increase in crime. Police say this was a direct result of paperwork changes.[7]

Concern with the lack of accuracy of the FBI crime data led the U.S. Justice Department to pay over $1 million to consultants to analyze the reporting system and suggest improvements. Preliminary suggestions were to conduct audits of local crime-reporting agencies and require reporting jurisdictions to send separate reports of crimes to the FBI in place of the monthly summaries now requested. Such reports, it is argued, would provide a greater base for research on the nature of crime and victimization.

The preliminary report of the consultants also indicated that some jurisdictions seriously underreport their crimes and arrests whereas others overreport. In the case of underreporting, the auditors-consultants found that in one city the police believed that a reported low crime rate was essential to keeping the high level of tourism in the area. Other reasons for police underreporting were "political or fiscal considerations, police administrative procedures, dispatchers, omitting certain incidents from the system, individual officers' reporting decisions, and misclassifications." Police might exaggerate the number of crimes to justify hiring more police officers. Or they might exaggerate the number of arrests to achieve a better reputation for the department in the community.[8]

Crimes Not Included   Current and previous FBI reports of crime rates based on the index offenses do not include crimes that might involve far greater victimization in terms of cost but that are not classified as Part I offenses. This chapter's CJA gives an example. Even if Charles had been prosecuted and convicted, his crime of embezzling half a million dollars would not have been recorded as a Part I offense. Embezzlement is a Part II offense, and those offenses are not included in the FBI rates of serious crime. More important, **white-collar crimes** are frequently handled informally, as in this case; or they are handled by administrative agencies rather than criminal courts and thus are not officially counted as crimes. Other kinds of crime are not recorded as either Part I or Part II offenses; for example, computer crimes, organized crime, and corporate crimes. Yet, the economic impact of both of these areas of crime is widespread, resulting in far greater total financial damage to the society than the theft crimes included in the UCR.

NIBRS: The New Approach   The FBI recognizes that more data are needed. The director stated in a 1988 report, that "in this age of information, UCR has not kept pace with the increasing need for law enforcement and other criminal justice practitioners to identify the extent and dimensions of crime." In response to that need, the FBI in 1988 published details of its new approach: **National Incident-Based Reporting System,** or (NIBRS). NIBRS views crime, along with all its components, as an incident (see Spotlight 2.1) and recognizes that the data constituting those components should be collected and organized for purposes of analysis. The FBI refers to *elements* of crimes, among which are the following:

1. Alcohol and drug influence
2. Specified location of the crime
3. Type of criminal activity involved
4. Type of weapon used
5. Type of victim
6. Relationship of victim to offender
7. Residency of victim and arrestee
8. Description of property and their values.[9]

The FBI's new approach, NIBRS, will collect data on 22 crime categories, listed in Spotlight 2.2, rather than limiting collection to the current Part I 8 offenses. The new system is expected to improve our knowledge of crime, but it will take some time to implement completely. Data in this chapter are based on the traditional methods of collection since only they are available as of this publication.

In 1988, the FBI announced its new reporting plan, the National Incident-Based Report System (IBR or NIBRS), which will view crime as an incident containing several characteristics, as illustrated by this diagram.

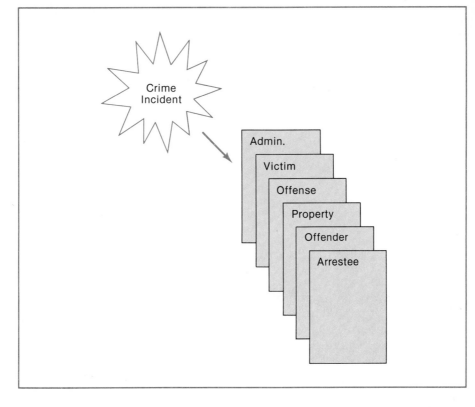

Source: National Incident Based Reporting System, a pamphlet published by the Federal Bureau of Investigation.

National Crime Survey Data

The existence of unreported crime, often called the *dark figure of crime,* that never becomes part of official crime data led to the establishment of another method of measuring crime. It was thought that if victims do not report crimes to the police, perhaps they will do so on questionnaires submitted to samples of the general population. Earlier victimization surveys indicated that many crimes were not reported to the police.[10]

Victimization surveys, currently conducted by the Bureau of Justice Statistics, are called the **National Crime Survey** (NCS). The NCS is based on the results of interviews with persons in about sixty thousand households each six months. Household members are questioned about whether

SPOTLIGHT 2.2
CRIME CATEGORIES IN THE NEW FBI APPROACH TO CATEGORIZATION

Following is a list of offenses that will be included in the new FBI reporting system utilizing the Incident-Based Reporting System. These categories will be used instead of the more limited list of eight offenses in the current index or Part I Offenses of the FBI's *Uniform Crime Reports.*

1. Arson
2. Assault
3. Bribery
4. Burglary
5. Counterfeiting
6. Destruction of property
7. Drug offenses
8. Embezzlement
9. Extortion
10. Fraud
11. Gambling
12. Homicide
13. Kidnapping
14. Larceny
15. Motor vehicle theft
16. Pornography
17. Prostitution
18. Robbery
19. Sex offenses forcible
20. Sex offenses nonforcible
21. Stolen property
22. Weapons violation

Source: National Incident Based Reporting System, a pamphlet published by the Federal Bureau of Investigation.

they have been the victims of rape, robbery, assault, household burglary, personal and household larceny, and motor vehicle theft. The NCS also involves research on large samples in twenty of the largest cities in the country, along with eight impact cities. These surveys include questions on business as well as personal victimizations.

The NCS is a valuable addition to the UCR. In addition to disclosing some crimes that are not reported to the police, the surveys indicate the reasons people give for not reporting crimes. However, the data are dependent on victim recall and perception, which may not always be accurate. Despite the possible inaccuracy of victim reports, victimization studies add to our knowledge of criminal activity. After reviewing the victimization studies, Gwynn Nettler summarized their findings. The findings that relate to specific characteristics of victims are discussed in a subsequent chapter on victims. The findings that relate to overall crimes are as follows:

1. Much more crime is committed than is reported to the police.
2. Reporting crimes to police is a function of the gravity of the crime and the victim's conception of the utility of reporting.
3. The rank order of the frequency of serious offenses reported by victims closely parallels that given by official statistics.
4. There are no huge surges in the amount of crime—so-called crime waves.[11]

James K. Stewart, director of the National Institute of Justice, and Steven R. Schlesinger, director of BJS, announced a jointly sponsored program in 1986. The purpose was to entice social scientists to submit proposals for revising and enhancing the data base of the NCS. The response was disappointing, but another request for proposals was issued in 1987. Perhaps some investigators will meet the challenge of the two government agencies in improving a system that these agency directors proclaim is

> now viewed as a storehouse of information on who is being victimized under what conditions. Its design principles have been adopted by numerous European nations and, most recently, by the United Nations. Few scholars about the world would argue that comparable information can be obtained by any less concerted an effort.[12]

Comparison of the NCS and the UCR Neither the UCR nor the NCS data give the complete picture of criminal activity. But it is hoped that using the two sources will provide a much better picture of the real crime figure. The sources may be used to supplement each other, but it is necessary to be careful in comparing them, for they are based on different time periods, use slightly different definitions of the crimes included, and employ different methods of counting crime.[13]

Some of the methodological problems in comparing these sources of crime data can be solved. Clearly, more research is needed to determine the precise relationship between reported crime and reported victimization. It may be that information from one crime data source can be used to test or predict the other, or further research may make it possible to ascertain criminal activity in areas not actually measured. Research is progressing rapidly in this area now that victimization surveys are conducted on a regular basis.[14]

One final point needs to be made in regard to both sources. Neither the UCR nor the NCS can estimate the extent to which a few offenders are responsible for large numbers of crimes. These reports only tell us how many crimes occurred, not how many of those crimes can be traced to the same offenders; and how many arrests were made, not how many times a particular person was arrested. More specialized studies indicate that a large percentage of those who enter prison to serve time have previously been convicted of other criminal offenses. Though these **recidivists** are relatively few in number, many suspect they account for an extremely large percentage of our crime.[15]

Self-Report Data

In addition to the UCR data and surveys of the population that indicate how many people have been victimized, self-report studies are used to gather data on the extent and nature of criminal activity. **Self-report data** (SRD) are acquired by two methods. One is the interview, in which the person is asked questions about illegal activities. The other is the questionnaire, usually anonymous. Variations of these two methods are listed in Table 2.3. Until recently, self-report studies were conducted mainly with juveniles, but the method increasingly is being used to study adult career criminals.[16]

TABLE 2.3

Methods for Measuring the Amount of Crime by Self-Reports

1. By asking people to complete anonymous questionnaires.
2. By asking people to complete anonymous questionnaires in a circuitous fashion and validated against later interviews or police records.
3. By asking people to confess to criminal acts on signed questionnaires validated against police records.
4. By having people complete anonymous questionnaires identified by number and validated against follow-up interviews and the threat of polygraph ("lie detector") tests.
5. By interviewing respondents.
6. By interviewing respondents and validating their responses against official records.

Source: Gwynn Nettler, *Explaining Crime*, 3d ed. (New York: McGraw-Hill, 1984), p. 81.

SRD have been criticized on several grounds. The first problem is that of accuracy. The danger exists that respondents, especially juveniles, will overreport their involvement in illegal activities. There also is the possibility that respondents will not remember their criminal activities. Other criticisms of SRD indicate that the surveys include too many non-serious, trivial offenses and sometimes omit serious crimes such as burglary, robbery, and sexual assault. Furthermore, self-report studies include too few blacks.

Taken together, these criticisms raise serious questions. White respondents tend to report greater involvement in less serious crimes that occur more frequently, and blacks tend to report illegal acts that are less frequent but more serious. One study found that black male offenders fail to report known offenses three times more often than white male offenders.[17]

Differences by sex have also been reported. Such findings do not invalidate the use of self-reports, but they do suggest that it may be necessary to compare these results with other measures and to develop more sophisticated methods for data analysis.[18]

Self-report studies may yield more useful data in the future. A new program, the **National Youth Survey** (NYS), is using interviews with adolescents over a five-year period to gather crime involvement data. The NYS has been structured to overcome many of the criticisms of other self-report studies.[19]

Crime Classification System

As an alternative to the UCR and NCS, the Police Executive Research Foundation is currently testing the **Crime Classification System** (CCS) under a grant from the United States Bureau of Justice Statistics. CCS is designed to measure and examine the harm inflicted on victims and the context in which crimes occur. In addition to providing a more useful data base for criminal justice agencies, it is believed that CCS will facilitate the understanding of crime by the general public and the news media.

One of the most significant differences between CCS and the UCR is the ability of CCS to measure the differences in the severity of crimes to different victims. For example, a woman who was beaten and robbed of $3,000 in a parking lot would appear under the same UCR classification as a 12 year old whose lunch money was taken after being beaten and knocked to the ground in the school playground by two other students. Both crimes, although vastly different in the harm inflicted on the victim and the context in which they occurred, would appear in the UCR data as a strong-arm robbery. CCS is currently being field tested in four sites, with additional testing to be conducted later in larger police departments.[20]

ANALYSIS OF CRIME DATA

All methods of counting and compiling the number of crimes have problems. How *crime* is defined and how crimes are counted will affect the results of all the methods. The refusal of people to report crimes may be a factor in all methods. The selection of samples in victimization and self-report studies will affect the data. Probably no method will ever accurately record all crime. But this does not mean that the methods may not be used for policy making and for studying criminal acts and criminal behavior. It just means that we need to be careful in interpreting crime data, particularly when those data are used to study why people commit crimes. A brief look at the variable of race indicates the problem.

Official data on crime indicate that higher rates of crime are committed by blacks than whites. Reports of crime data based on self-reports do not disclose such differences; data based on victimization surveys are closer to official data. Such discrepancies could lead to the conclusion that none of the measures are useful, but some researchers have looked more carefully and concluded that the differences may be in the selection of samples: "Most of the self-report studies published to date have had too few blacks to provide a meaningful test." The difference also may be explained by the type of offense contained in the self-report studies: "Most self-report scales have been dominated by items that are of low seriousness and high frequency, and whites tend to report greater involvement in these events while blacks tend to report involvement in less frequent, more serious offenses."[21] The solution therefore may be to reconceptualize the nature of the self-reports rather than to assume they are better (or worse) than official measures of crime.

It is also important not to place unreasonable demands on the data. Official data may not report all crime, but as one scholar has noted, they do indicate the extent of the "socially recognized volume of crime." They are useful as "indicators of the relative distribution of crime across cities. That is, although they do not specify the exact incidence of crime in a city, they tell us with some accuracy which cities have more crime than others."

The official UCR data have been collected for a longer period than any of the other methods and thus provide some measure of trends in crime.[22]

Official data also contain information about arrests and therefore contain data not available to the other methods. Persons accused of crime do not become part of the actual system of criminal justice unless they are apprehended by police. As noted in the first chapter, it is important that the designation *criminal* not be applied to people who have not been processed through the system. Mistakes may be made in that processing; politics may play a part in the outcome; but official labeling is significant and should be studied as such.

On the other hand, data on the extent of crime that is not reported and the reasons it is not reported are valuable for social scientists and policy makers. Information secured through self-reports is crucial to our understanding of the extent and nature of criminal activity, as well as of our knowledge of people who commit crimes. The self-report study approach also has provided valuable information on the career criminal, discussed in the next chapter.

It is important, too, when comparing crime data from these different sources, to consider whether the data refer to crime rates at a particular time or to trend data covering a period of years. In a recent article, Scott Menard examines short-term trends using the three main sources of data: *Uniform Crime Reports,* victimization data, and self-reports. Menard found that the UCR data, when compared to the other two sources, "produce very different short-term trends." When only UCR Part I, or index, offenses are considered, the UCR more often indicates upward trends, with victimization and self-report data showing more stability in crime rates. Menard says his study may suggest

> that rates of actual criminal behavior may generally be stable or may fluctuate randomly over time, but rates of discovery of crime by the police and rates of arrest are increasing, with few exceptions.[23]

Menard's findings may mean that police are becoming more efficient, and with that increased efficiency, discovery of crime and arrests increase. Certainly, these findings illustrate the need to analyze carefully each source of data before drawing conclusions.[24]

CRIME IN THE UNITED STATES: AN OVERVIEW

In the foreword to the 1982 *Uniform Crime Reports,* the director of the FBI announced with cautious optimism that the rate of serious crime was down 3 percent from 1981. The cautiousness of his optimism stemmed from the fact that in the 1970s the crime rates dropped twice, only to turn back upward shortly thereafter. In the 1984 *Uniform Crime Reports,* the director announced that crime had declined for the third straight year with fewer index offenses reported to law enforcement that year than in any year since 1978. He cautioned that the unprecedented three-year period of decline might be coming to an end because there had been a slight increase in crime during the last quarter of 1984.[25]

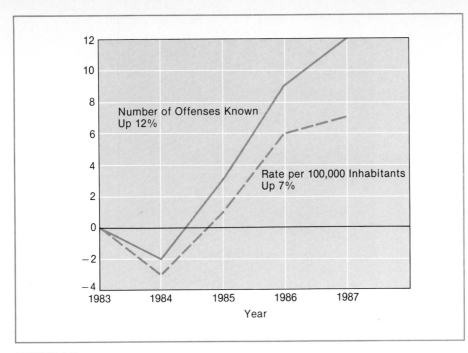

FIGURE 2.2

Crime Index Total. *Source:* Federal Bureau of Investigation, *Crime in the United States: Uniform Crime Reports, 1987* (Washington, D.C.: U.S. Government Printing Office, 1988), p. 43.

According to the UCR, the number of crimes reported to the police and the crime rate began climbing in 1984, leading the director of the FBI to say, "There are few social statements more tragic than these."[26] The increase continued through 1987, as indicated in Figure 2.2, which compares the number of offenses and the crime rate of index offenses from 1983 through 1987.

Until recently, NCS data indicated a downswing in crime victimization. The 1982 data, compared to 1981, with a general downturn of 1.7 million victimizations, represented "one of the most sweeping, single-direction changes to have taken place since the program's inceptions."[27] The decrease in reported crime victimizations continued through preliminary reports of 1987, as indicated in Figure 2.3, when crime victimizations were at their lowest level since the Bureau of Justice Statistics began publishing crime victimization data in 1975.[28]

Later reports of 1987 data, however, indicated a slight rise (1.8 percent) in the number of victimizations, although the victimization rate remained stable. "The increase in the number of victimizations was largely caused by an increase in household crimes, which rose 2.3 percent from the 1986 level. . . ."[29]

The steady crime rates in 1980 and 1981, followed by the decline in the number of offenses and the crime rates between 1982 and 1984, as measured by the UCR, along with the decreasing rates of victimization as measured by the NCS, led many (particularly in the Reagan administra-

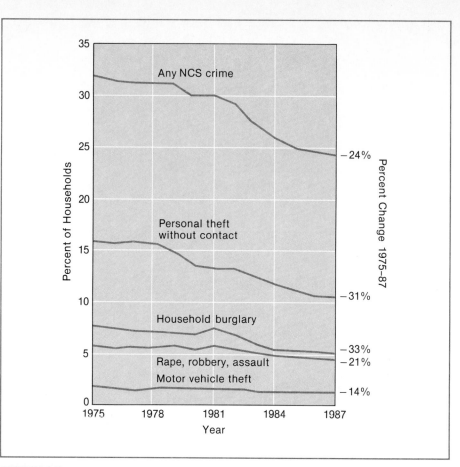

FIGURE 2.3
Households Touched by Selected Crimes of Violence, 1975–1987. *Source:* Bureau of
Justice Statistics, *Households Touched by Crime, 1987* (Washington, D.C.: U.S.
Department of Justice, June 1988), p. 1.

tion) to argue that a get-tough policy on crime was responsible for decreasing crime. Others were more cautious, taking the position that crime
must be viewed over a period of time before accurate conclusions may be
drawn. With the increase in recent years, in the number of crimes and the
crime rate, as measured by the UCR, and the 1987 increase in NCS data,
the more cautious approach may be the preferred one, although the proponents of a get-tough policy may still point to the decreases in reported
victimizations.

It is also useful to analyze crime data by individual crimes. The FBI
has historically divided the data into two major categories, Part I and Part
II offenses. Part I offenses contain the more serious and frequently committed crimes, and they are subdivided into two categories: *violent crimes*
(murder and nonnegligent manslaughter, robbery, aggravated assault, and
forcible rape) and *property crimes* (burglary, larceny–theft, motor vehicle
theft, and arson).

PART 1 Introduction to the Criminal Justice System: The Criminal Event

Property Crimes

Most of the serious crimes committed in this country are not violent personal crimes; they are crimes against property. Officially, data show that **property crimes** dropped 2 percent between 1983 and 1984, but rose 5 percent between 1984 and 1985, rose 6 percent between 1985 and 1986, and 3 percent between 1986 and 1987.[30] The most frequently committed property offense is larceny–theft.

Larceny–Theft **Larceny-theft** is the unlawful taking, carrying, leading, or riding away of property from the possession or constructive possession of another. It includes crimes such as shoplifting, pocket picking, purse snatching, thefts from motor vehicles, thefts of motor vehicle parts and accessories, and bicycle thefts in which no use of force, violence, or fraud occurs. In the UCR, this crime category does not include embezzlement, con games, forgery, and cashing worthless checks. Motor vehicle theft is also excluded from this category since it is a separate crime index offense. In 1987 larceny–thefts constituted 56 percent of the Crime Index, and 62 percent of all property crimes. Only 20 percent of these crimes were cleared by arrest. The estimated loss nationally from this crime was $3 billion.[31]

Modern Types of Theft The UCR category of larceny–theft does not include some thefts in which we are experiencing tremendous losses. Credit card thefts, our fastest growing crime according to some experts, are not included. These thefts indicate the interrelationship between individual criminal activity and organized crime. Muggers, prostitutes, and burglars often steal credit cards and then sell them to credit card rings for $15 to $50 per card. Losses per year as a result of credit card thefts and fraud

Political extremist Lyndon H. LaRouche, Jr., wearing cap, arrives at his sentencing hearing in which he was sentenced to 15 years in prison for scheming to defraud federal tax collectors and failing to repay more than $30 million in loans from political supporters. (Bary Thumma/AP Wide World)

Shoplifting has become a major type of theft. (John Coletti/ Stock Boston)

are high. One credit card ring in the East made $2 million in fraudulent charges per week in 14 different states.[32]

Theft by computer also is not included in UCR data. As early as 1982, a *Chicago Tribune* editorial described computer crime as follows:

> Computer crime is already an international problem of formidable dimensions and is expected to increase with the growth of electronic data processing. . . .
> As the paperless, totally wired society of the future moves from science fiction toward reality, high-tech crooks are bound to proliferate. And they won't be easy to outwit.[33]

Earlier reports estimated that every year in this country computer thieves steal more than $100 million, but experts think that is only the tip of the iceberg and losses may run as high as $40 billion a year.[34] In recent years legislators have struggled to enact statutes to cover computer crimes, as computer hackers have gained access to banks and even to the Department of Defense computer network. The main problem, however, is that many computer hackers are never caught.[35]

Computer crimes also illustrate what may be a growing acceptance of some kinds of crime. Cracking computers has become a rite of passage to some teenagers and college students. Rather than stealing and hot-wiring cars, they steal information from computers. Encouraged by the popular movie *War Games*, in which illegal access to computer data leads to the brink of World War III, they turn their intellectual talents to their home computers and an attempt to see what information they can obtain. According to the 414s, the Milwaukee youths who named themselves after their area code, they are not trying to steal; they are just having fun. The 414s said their project was easy. Once they found a likely target, they tried various passwords until they broke into more than 60 business and government computer systems in Canada and the United States. Said one of the youths, "It was like climbing a mountain; you have the goal of reaching the top or accessing a computer, and once you reach the peak, you make a map of the way and give it to everybody else."[36]

The actions of the 414s illustrate more than the possibility of using computers to steal information from other systems; the reaction of the young people also illustrates the common attitude that such actions are all right if you do not mean to be committing a crime. The blame is also placed on those who have unsecured computers, as the following comment from one of the 414s illustrates. "It got out of hand . . . but it's not all our fault either. There is no security in it or nothing."[37]

Burglary   The second major type of property crime, according to the UCR, is **burglary,** defined as "the unlawful entry of a structure to commit a felony or theft. The use of force to gain entry is not required to classify an offense as burglary." Burglary in the UCR is "categorized into three sub-classifications: forcible entry, unlawful entry where no force is used, and attempted forcible entry." In 1987, 3.2 million burglaries were estimated to have occurred, representing a 1 percent decrease after a 5.5 percent increase. The 1987 burglaries accounted for an estimated property loss of $3.2 billion, with an average of $960 per burglary. Most of the burglaries (70 percent) involved a forcible entry, with two of every three burglaries taking place in residences. Only 14 percent of these crimes were cleared by arrest.[38]

Motor Vehicle Theft   The greatest increase in property crimes between 1985 and 1986 occurred in **motor vehicle theft,** with the volume up 11 percent and the rate up 4.9 percent. Between 1986 and 1987, the number of offenses rose 5.3 percent, whereas the rate rose 4.3 percent. Motor vehicle theft includes vehicles other than automobiles and also includes attempted thefts. The category, however, does not include thefts of items from within a motor vehicle; those are included in larceny–theft.[39] In 1987 an estimated 1,288,674 motor vehicle thefts occurred, representing 11 percent of all property crimes. The estimated annual loss was over $6 billion, with an average of $4,964 per stolen vehicle.[40]

Arson   **Arson** did not become a Part I index offense until 1979; thus, trend data are not available for this crime as for other Part I offenses. Data are not available for all reporting agencies, and the FBI warns that as a result caution must be used in interpreting arson data. The most frequent targets of arson were structures (in contrast to mobile property such as motor vehicles), comprising 55 percent of all arsons. Of the structures, 61 percent were residential properties.[41]

Violent Crimes

We have already noted that most of the reported crimes in this country are property crimes, not **violent crimes** against the person, and that some rates of violent personal crime have declined while others have risen.

Many fires are deliberately caused, but arson is often difficult to prove. (David Kennedy/TexaStock)

Crimes included by the FBI in the index offenses of violent personal crime are robbery, aggravated assault, murder and nonnegligent manslaughter, and forcible rape.

Robbery   The term **robbery** is frequently used to refer to what is actually theft rather than robbery. Since property is taken in both crimes, what is the difference? Theft involves many different methods of taking of the property of another and may even be called by different names: larceny by trick or false pretensions, embezzlement, and burglary. Robbery is different from these kinds of theft in that it involves an element of force or the threat of force to the person. Robbery involves the same elements as larceny but adds two elements that make it a violent crime: taking the property from the person or the presence of the person and using force or threatening to use force.

In some cases the line between larceny and robbery is a very fine one, and not all scholars agree on how or where to draw that line. Thus, a crime such as purse snatching, which occurs so quickly that the victim

Four armed bandits who arrived in a limousine took over the exclusive New York City Hotel Pierre for nearly 2½ hours during which they handcuffed 19 persons and singled out about 50 safe deposit boxes, shown at right. (UPI/Bettmann)

does not have time to offer resistance or to be scared, is often classified as larceny rather than robbery. But even in that case, the fear that the victim suffers *after* the incident may be greater than the concern a victim has after a burglary or larceny. It is this fear of violence, as well as the possibility of violence, that entitles robbery to be classified as a violent personal crime.

Between 1985 and 1986, the number of robberies in this country increased by 9 percent, constituting 36 percent of all violent crimes. But between 1986 and 1987 the number of offenses decreased by 4.6 percent, constituting 4 percent of all index crimes and 35 percent of all violent crimes. The average loss per robbery was $631. The total estimated loss from the crime of robbery was $327 million.[42]

Aggravated Assault   Aggravated **assault** is a violent personal crime that involves an illegal attack on a person, which is done for the purpose of causing death or serious bodily harm. Although some aggravated assaults are conducted without a weapon, many involve the use of a deadly weapon. Aggravated assaults are considered to be serious, violent crimes because they frequently result in bodily harm and, at times, death. Aggravated assault was the only index crime to reflect a rise between 1981 and 1982, with a 1 percent increase in volume. Although 1983 data showed a decrease of 2 percent, the number of aggravated assaults rose in 1984 by 5 percent and between 1984 and 1985 increased 5.5 percent. Between 1985 and 1986 the number of aggravated assaults increased by 15.4 percent, but between 1986 and 1987 the increase was only 2.5 percent.[43] In 1987, 21 percent of the reported assaults were committed with firearms, 32 percent with blunt objects or other kinds of dangerous weapons other than knives, 21 percent with knives or other cutting instruments, and the remainder with hands, fists, and feet.[44]

In January, 1989, coroners carry the body of a dead man in the schoolyard of the Cleveland Elementary School in Stockton, California after he allegedly shot and killed six children and wounded many others before killing himself. (Walt Zeboski/AP Wide World)

Murder and Nonnegligent Manslaughter   The UCR defines **murder** and nonnegligent **manslaughter** as the "willful (nonnegligent) killing of one human being by another." In 1986 the volume of this crime, representing a rate of 8.9 deaths per 100,000 population, increased by 8.6 percent over 1985, but between 1986 and 1987 the volume decreased by 2.5 percent and the rate decreased by 3.5 percent.[45]

Americans must face the fact that they live in one of the most violent of all societies. Although random, violent murder is apparently reaching into areas once considered very safe, such as luxury resorts and quiet upper-class neighborhoods, most people who are victims of murder are acquainted with their assailants and are often relatives. In 1987, 57 percent of the murders committed in this country were perpetrated by persons who knew their victims before the crime, leading the UCR to conclude that "murder is primarily a societal problem over which law enforcement has little or no control." In 1987, 17 percent of all killings involved relatives.[46]

Forcible Rape   The UCR defines forcible **rape** as "the carnal knowledge of a female forcibly and against her will. Assaults or attempts to commit rape by force or threat of force are also included; however, statutory rape (without force) and other sex offenses are not included in this category."[47] **Statutory rape** refers to consensual sexual intercourse that involves a female who is under the legal age of consent.

In 1986 reports of forcible rape were up 3.2 percent from 1985, but the number of offenders declined 4 percent between 1986 and 1987. The five- and ten-year trends show that the number of offenses in 1987 rose 11 percent over the 1983 level and 21 percent above the 1978 level. In 1987 of the offenses reported, 81 percent were rapes by force and the remainder

A San Diego police officer and the body of a child killed in the 1984 rampage that resulted in the deaths of 20 people at a McDonald's restaurant. (Paul Richards/UPI Bettmann)

were attempts or assaults to commit forcible rape. The number of arrests for forcible rape decreased 2 percent from 1986, and the national clearance rate was 53 percent.[48]

SUMMARY

This chapter has provided an overview of the data on crime and how those data are secured. The three basic methods for collecting crime data were described and analyzed. The official data of the *Uniform Crime Reports* indicate the amount of crime as recorded by police departments and reported to the FBI. This source underrepresents the actual amount of crime as measured by surveys of households in which samples of the population are asked to indicate whether they have been victims of crime.

In recent years, the FBI has recognized the limitations of its method of collecting and recording crime data. Its most dramatic change, to begin soon, will be NIBRS, the National Incident-Based Reporting System. NIBRS views crime as an *element*, which involves many attributes, including alcohol and drug abuse; types of victims, weapons, and criminal activity; victim's and arrestee's residency; relationship between victim and offender; and a description of property and their values. Collection of these additional elements of criminal acts will greatly enhance our ability to analyze crime more extensively.

The second source of crime data, the *National Crime Survey* conducted by the Bureau of Justice Statistics, is also an official source of data on crime. It is valuable because it indicates that many victims do not report their victimizations to the police. The NCS also reports data on why people do not report victimizations. It does not, however, give any information on arrests, and it is dependent on the accuracy of perception and reporting of crime victims.

The third major source of crime data, self-reports, contains data that are not secured by either of the official methods. Through this method we can get information on characteristics of people who say they have committed crimes. SRD thus provides valuable information for social scientists who study why crimes are committed, as well as for officials who must make decisions concerning the use of resources aimed at crime control and prevention. SRD also allow us to study repeat offenders. The major problem with this approach is that respondents may underreport or overreport crimes.

All the sources of data may be used to analyze the nature and extent of crime, but it is important to analyze carefully the time periods and the definitions of crimes being measured before comparing data from the various sources. Data in this chapter focused primarily on the UCR; a subsequent chapter on victims will look more closely at victimization data. The UCR indicates that despite a downswing in both the volume and rate of crime during the early 1980s, recent years have seen that trend reversed, although there are still some decreases in particular crimes.

This chapter has emphasized that crime data may be affected by a number of factors, including police reporting, police efficiency, willingness of victims and witnesses to report crime and their accuracy in doing so, and even changes in methods of reporting. It is also important, however, to analyze factors that might cause persons to engage in criminal rather than law-abiding behavior; thus, the next chapter will focus on causes of crime.

STUDY QUESTIONS

1. Describe and contrast the major sources of data on crime.
2. Explain the FBI's new system of data reporting.
3. What are the advantages and disadvantages of self-report studies?
4. What have been the major changes in the amount of crime in this country since 1982?
5. What are the major differences between *violent crimes* and *property crimes*?

ENDNOTES

1. See, for example, Michael J. Hindelang, "Variations in Sex-Race-Age-Specific Incidence Rates of Offending," *American Sociological Review* 46 (August 1981): 461–74.
2. These data from the BJS come from one source: Bureau of Justice Statistics, *Reporting Crimes to the Police* (Washington, D.C.: U.S. Department of Justice, December 1985), pp. 1–3.
3. Kansas City Police Department, *Response Time Analysis*, Vol. 1. *Methodology*; Vol. 2. *Part I Crime Analysis* (Kansas City, Mo., Author, 1977).
4. William Spelman and Dale K. Brown, *Calling the Police: Citizen Reporting of Serious Crime* (Washington, D.C.: National Institute of Justice, October 1984); pp. xxiv–vii.
5. Donald J. Black, "Production of Crime Rates," *American Sociological Review* 35 (August 1970): 733–48.
6. David Seidman and Michael Couzens, "Getting the Crime Rate Down: Political Pressure and Crime Reporting," *Law and Society Review* 8 (Spring 1974): 457–93.
7. See, for example, Hindelang, "Variations in Sex-Race-Age-Specific Incidence Rates of Offending." For additional information on the relationship between police policies and crime rates, see J. Q. Wilson and B. Boland, "The Effect of the Police on Crime," *Law and Society Review* 12 (1978): 367–90; and J. Q. Wilson, "The Dilemmas of Police Reform," in A. L. Guenther, ed.,

Criminal Behavior and Social Systems, 2d ed. (Chicago: Rand McNally, 1976), pp. 392–404.
8. David Burnham, "Changes in F.B.I. Crime Report Weighed," *New York Times*, (19 November 1984), p. 13.
9. See Federal Bureau of Investigation, *Uniform Crime Reporting: National Incident-Based Reporting System*, Vol. 1. *Data Collection Guidelines* (Washington, D.C.: U.S. Department of Justice, July 1, 1988).
10. For a discussion of early victimization surveys, see Michael Hindelang, *Criminal Victimization in Eight American Cities: A Descriptive Analysis of Common Theft and Assault* (Cambridge, Mass.: Ballinger Publishing Co., 1976.) For later analyses of crime victimization studies, see R. M. O'Brien, *Crime and Victimization Data* (Beverly Hills, Calif.: Sage Publications, 1985); and W. G. Skogan, *Issues in the Measurement of Victimization* (Washington, D.C.: U.S. Government Printing Office, 1981).
11. Gwynn Nettler, *Explaining Crime*, 3d ed. (New York: McGraw-Hill, 1984), pp. 71–73 (italics omitted).
12. National Institute of Justice and Bureau of Justice Statistics, *Supplementing the National Crime Survey: Research Solicitation* (Washington, D.C.: U.S. Department of Justice, 1987), no page number.
13. See Larry J. Cohen and Mark J. Lichback, "Al-

ternative Measures of Crime: A Statistical Evaluation," *Sociological Quarterly* 23 (Spring 1982): 253–66.

14. See Edwin W. Zedlewski, "Deterrence Findings and Data Sources: A Comparison of the Uniform Crime Reports and The National Crime Surveys," *Journal of Research on Crime and Delinquency* 20 (July 1983): 262–76.

15. "Examining Recidivism," Bureau of Justice Statistics, *Special Report*, U.S. Department of Justice (Washington, D.C.: U.S. Department Printing Office, 1985).

16. See "Career Criminals and Criminal Careers," *Criminal Justice Research at Rand* (Santa Monica, Calif.: Rand Corporation, 1985), pp. 3–7. See also John D. Hewitt, Eric D. Poole, and Robert M. Regoli, "Self-Reported and Observed Rule-Breaking in Prison: A Look at Disciplinary Response," *Justice Quarterly* 1, no. 3, (1983): 437–47.

17. Michael J. Hindelang, Travis Hirschi, and Joseph G. Weis, "Correlates of Delinquency: The Illusion of Discrepancy between Self-Report and Official Measures," *American Sociological Review* 44 (December 1979): 995–1014. See also a book by the same authors, *Measuring Delinquency* (Beverly Hills, Calif.: Sage Publications, 1981). For a review of these and other criticisms of self-report studies, see Delbert S. Elliott and Suzanne S. Ageton, "Reconciling Race and Class Differences in Self-Reported and Official Estimates of Delinquency," *American Sociological Review* 45 (February 1980): 95–110.

18. See Douglas A. Smith and Laura A. Davidson, "Interfacing Indicators and Constructs in Criminological Research: A Note on the Comparability of Self-Report Violence Data for Race and Sex Groups," *Criminology* 24 (August 1986): 473–88.

19. For an extensive discussion of the new structure of the NYS, see Elliott and Ageton, "Reconciling Race," pp. 95–110.

20. David H. Konstantin, "CCS: The Crime-Data Frontier," *Law Enforcement News*, 11 (February 1985), pp. 1, 5.

21. Hindelang, "Variations in Sex-Race-Age-Specific Incidence Rates of Offending," p. 462. See also Hindelang, "Race and Involvement in Common Law Personal Crimes," *American Sociological Review* 43 (February 1978): 93–109.

22. Wesley G. Skogan, "The Validity of Official Crime Statistics: An Empirical Investigation," *Social Science Quarterly* 55 (June 1974): 25–26.

23. Scott Menard, "Short-Term Trends in Crime and Delinquency: A Comparison on UCR, NCS, and Self-Report Data," *Justice Quarterly* 4 (September 1987): 468, 470.

24. See H. C. Covery and Scott Menard, "Response to Rapid Social Change: The Case of Boomtown Law Enforcement," *Journal of Police Science and Administration* 12 (1984): 164–69; and W. R. Gove, M. Hughes, and M. Geerken, "Are Uniform Crime Reports a Valid Indicator of the Index Crimes: An Affirmative Answer with Minor Qualifications," *Criminology* 23 (1985): 451–501.

25. William H. Webster, *Crime in the United States, Uniform Crime Reports, 1984* (Washington, D.C.: U.S. Government Printing Office, 1985), p. iii.

26. William H. Webster, *Crime in the United States: Uniform Crime Reports, 1985* (Washington, D.C.: U.S. Government Printing Office, 1986), p. iii.

27. *Criminal Victimization in the United States: 1973–1982 Trends*, Bureau of Justice Statistics, *Special Report*, (Washington, D.C.: U.S. Department of Justice, 1983).

28. Bureau of Justice Statistics, *Households Touched by Crime, 1987* (Washington, D.C.: U. S. Department of Justice, May, 1988), p. 1.

29. Bureau of Justice Statistics, *Criminal Victimization 1987* (Washington, D.C.: U.S. Department of Justice, October 1988).

30. *Uniform Crime Reports, 1985*, p. 41; *1986*, p. 41; and *1987*, p. 41.

31. *Uniform Crime Reports, 1987*, pp. 29, 32.

32. "ABC News" (13 December 1982), special assignment.

33. Published in *Justice Assistance News* 3 (October 1982): 7.

34. August Bequai, *Computer Crime* (Lexington, Mass.: D.C. Heath and Co., 1978), p. xiii. See also Bequai, *How to Prevent Computer Crime: A Guide for Managers* (Somerset, N.J.: John Wiley and Sons, Inc., 1983).

35. For a recent discussion of computer crime and computer security, see Dorothy B. Francis, *Computer Crime* (Bergenfield, N.J.: E. P. Dutton and Company, 1987).

36. "Beware. Hackers at Play: Computer Capers Raise Disturbing New Questions About Security and Privacy," *Newsweek*, (5 September 1983), p. 42.

37. "F.B.I. Is Studying Computer 'Raids'," *New York Times* (12 August 1983), p. 9. For a discussion of computer crimes, see Sue Titus Reid, *Crime and Criminology*, 5th ed. (New York: Holt, Rinehart and Winston, 1988), pp. 313–19.

38. *Uniform Crime Reports, 1986*, pp. 24, 25; *1987* pp. 24, 25.

39. Ibid., *1986*, p. 31; *1987*, p. 34.

40. *Uniform Crime Reports, 1987*, p. 34.

41. Ibid., pp. 37, 38.

42. Ibid., *1986*, p. 17, 18; *1987*, pp. 17, 18.

43. *Uniform Crime Reports, 1982*, p. 21; *1983*, p. 16; *1984*, p. 22; *1985*, p. 22; *1986*, p. 22; and *1987*, p. 22.

44. *Uniform Crime Reports, 1987*, p. 22.

45. *Uniform Crime Reports, 1986, 1987*, p. 7.

46. Ibid., *1987*, p. 11.

47. Ibid., p. 13.

48. Ibid., pp. 14, 15.

CHAPTER **3**

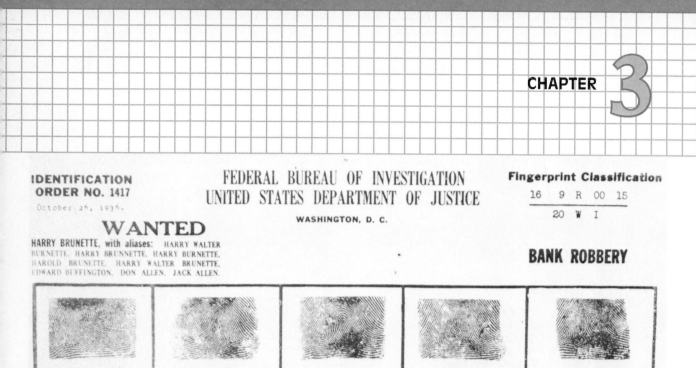

IDENTIFICATION ORDER NO. 1417
October 26, 1936.

FEDERAL BUREAU OF INVESTIGATION
UNITED STATES DEPARTMENT OF JUSTICE
WASHINGTON, D. C.

Fingerprint Classification

16 9 R 00 15
20 W I

WANTED

HARRY BRUNETTE, with aliases: HARRY WALTER
BURNETTE, HARRY BRUNNETTE, HARRY BURNETTE,
HAROLD BRUNETTE, HARRY WALTER BRUNETTE,
EDWARD BUFFINGTON, DON ALLEN, JACK ALLEN.

BANK ROBBERY

Photograph taken June 4, 1931.

DESCRIPTION

Age, 25 years (born Green Bay, Wisconsin, August 9, 1911); Height, 5'9 3/8"; Weight, 158 pounds; Build, medium and muscular; Hair, medium chestnut; Eyes, yellow orange azure; Complexion, fair; Occupation, librarian; Nationality, French-American; Marks and scars: oblique scar first joint left ring finger; oblique scar base of neck.

RELATIVES

Mrs. Theresa Brunette, mother,
John Brunette, brother,
  907 Jackson Street, Green Bay, Wisconsin.
Mrs. May Huempfner, sister,
  841 West James Street, Green Bay, Wisconsin.
Frank Brunette, brother, Muskegon, Michigan.
George Brunette, brother,
  1732 Eleventh Avenue, Green Bay, Wisconsin.
Walter Brunette, brother,
  3118 North 25th Street, Milwaukee, Wisconsin.

ARREST NUMBERS

#22793 PD Toledo, Ohio.
#9397   Boys Industrial School, Waukesha, Wisconsin.
#6605   State Reformatory, Green Bay, Wisconsin.
#1052   PD Green Bay, Wisconsin.
#63878 State Penitentiary, Columbus, Ohio.

Harry Brunette

A complaint was filed before United States Commissioner Floyd E. Jenkins, Milwaukee, Wisconsin, August 27, 1936, charging Harry Brunette and another with robbing the Seymour State Bank, Seymour, Wisconsin, on August 19, 1936, in violation of the Federal Bank Robbery Act.

Law enforcement agencies kindly transmit any additional information or criminal record to the nearest office of the Federal Bureau of Investigation, United States Department of Justice.

If apprehended please notify the Director, Federal Bureau of Investigation, United States Department of Justice, Washington, D. C., or the Special Agent in Charge of the office of the Federal Bureau of Investigation listed on the back hereof which is nearest your city.

(OVER)   Issued by: JOHN EDGAR HOOVER, DIRECTOR.

Explanations of Criminal Behavior

OUTLINE

KEY TERMS

The Kelley family had four children: Jacqueline, Harold, Sherry, and Joshua. Jacqueline was an excellent student and a very good athlete. On Saturdays she worked for a neighbor—cleaning house, baby sitting, and doing yard work. Jacqueline had never been in trouble with juvenile authorities or the police; neither had she been disciplined at school. She graduated from high school at the top of her class and went to college.

Harold was a very poor student who frequently refused to go to school. Harold and his close friends started smoking and drinking while they were in grade school. At age 13, they were apprehended for shoplifting in a neighborhood store. The store manager gave them a warning. Two weeks later they were apprehended by police while they were breaking into a liquor store late at night. All the youths were turned over to the juvenile authorities.

Harold and his best friend Joe spent two years in a training school for juveniles. Joe, a very bright, upper-class boy, was frequently visited by his family. Because of his excellent behavior at the school, Joe was occasionally permitted weekend visits to his home. Harold's parents never visited him although Jacqueline wrote to him frequently and visited when possible.

Sherry, the Kelley's third child, had always had trouble in school; she tried hard, but her IQ was significantly below normal. By the time she was twelve, she was discouraged with school. But she was very attractive and discovered that she could get a lot of attention by flirting. She met an older man who proclaimed an interest in her and led her into prostitution.

Joshua, the youngest Kelley, was born with slight brain damage and a large scar on his face, but he was a charming little boy and very well behaved. Mr. Kelley, however, could not cope with Joshua's physical and mental problems. Mr. Kelley had been drinking heavily for years, a habit that contributed to his problems of supporting his family. The day he was fired from his job, Kelley came home drunk. When Joshua tried to hug his father, Kelley attacked him. When Mrs. Kelley tried to intervene, she was beaten badly.

This scene was repeated often in the next two years, and Mrs. Kelley finally filed for a divorce. She got a part-time job and went to night school. Within two years she finished her bachelor's degree and was employed as a teacher. She was able to support herself and her four children. She began taking an interest in Harold, who had been released from the training school and was on his own. Harold started back to school, finished high school, and was never again in trouble with the law.

Joshua was not able to cope with his father's leaving. Despite his father's rejection, Joshua loved his father and wanted very much to be close to him. Joshua resented his mother's diligent attempts to be both a mother and a father; when he was ten, he ran away from home and became involved in juvenile activities. He was in and out of correctional institutions and prisons until he reached 40, at which time he became a law-abiding citizen.

INTRODUCTION

The cases of Harold, Sherry, Joe, and Joshua illustrate some of the typical patterns of juvenile and criminal behavior that have captured the attention of scientists who have attempted to explain criminal behavior. The problem is even more difficult when a person like Jacqueline, who came from a similar environment and the same parents as three of the law violators, never manifested serious behavioral problems and did not get into difficulties with juvenile authorities or the police.

The cases of these young people involve the variables of age, sex, and socioeconomic status, three variables frequently associated with juvenile and criminal behavior—at least as those behaviors are measured by *official* data. Below-normal intelligence, problems with education, physical deformities, and family disturbances also are variables often associated with criminal behavior. But how important are they in explaining *why* these young people engaged in illegal activities?

To say that most crimes are committed by young males who live in urban areas, are poorly educated and usually unemployed, and come from turbulent family backgrounds is not to explain *why* these people commit criminal acts. Many people with one or more of these characteristics are not apprehended by the police and subsequently processed through the criminal justice system. Some people who are highly educated, beyond youth in age, from stable families, and have held good jobs for a long period become involved in crime. It is important, therefore, to study theories that might explain criminal behavior.

The purpose of this chapter is to examine briefly the main approaches used to explain criminal behavior. The chapter begins with an introduction to the scientific study of criminal behavior. Attention then is given to the reasons why it is important to understand criminal behavior. Public policy decisions concerning the ways in which society should react to crime and criminal behavior ideally would be made on the basis of scientific information. Too often, however, such decisions are made using assumptions that may not be supported by evidence. The primary focus in public policy today appears to be a belief that sufficient punishment will keep people from committing crimes. It is therefore necessary to examine this presumption.

Scientists in many disciplines have become involved in explaining criminal behavior. Although the chapter concentrates on the sociological approach, brief attention is first given to psychological and biological approaches. The major sociological approaches then are discussed, followed by a brief look at two special categories of offenders: females and career criminals. In the final section, the interrelationship of the psychological, biological, and sociological approaches is examined in the context of substance abuse and criminality.

CRIMINAL BEHAVIOR: THE SEARCH FOR CAUSES

Although it is not possible to say which event or characteristic, or combination of events or characteristics, caused criminal behavior in a given situation, scientists have tried to look for critical and recurrent factors related to criminal behavior. But even those factors must be analyzed within a total theoretical framework. We look for "an invariant relationship of certain *key* factors to a given set of conditions which, in the majority of instances in which these conditions occur, is always apt to be present."[1] If criminologists can identify characteristics of individuals or of society that are highly associated with criminal behavior, they will then have a basis for establishing programs designed to prevent crime.

Criminologists are professionals who study, among other issues, why people become criminals. They are not the only ones who engage in this endeavor, but their focus differs from that of other scientists. All who study criminal behavior to understand what causes that behavior are faced with some difficult problems. The most important is the meaning and measurement of **causation.**

It is important to understand the difference between cause and relationship. In this chapter's CJA there may be a relationship between family problems, low intelligence, physical deformity, or socioeconomic status and delinquency, but that does not mean that the delinquency is *caused* by any or all of those variables. This is true even though some of these variables frequently are present in delinquent or criminal behavior. The frequency of association of some of these variables and illegal acts does, however, permit researchers to draw the reasonable conclusion that they do not occur together by chance. Thus, low intelligence or family violence may indeed be factors that should be considered in an analysis of criminal behavior. Certainly, the combination of several of the variables present in the CJA should be given careful attention.

A wide range of variables has been considered by some to be important in explaining criminal behavior. They include characteristics of the environment, such as climate, temperature, and density of cities; characteristics of the person, such as intelligence, physical deformity, color of hair, body type and size, age, sex, socioeconomic status, and race. Some variables that have dominated the literature on crime causation are not so easily measured; they include interactions among people and processes of learning as well as reactions to early life experiences, self-concept, and pressure of friends.

Volumes have been written on these and other variables thought to effectively explain criminal behavior. Only a sampling of approaches and theories can be presented in this chapter. The main purpose here is to present an overview that will provide the background necessary for an understanding of subsequent discussions in the text. Of particular importance is the need to recognize that the explanations accepted by public officials may significantly affect how those officials determine law and public policies regarding crime and how they allocate resources for the criminal justice system.

PUBLIC POLICY DECISIONS AND EXPLANATIONS OF CRIME

Members of legislatures, courts, administrative agencies, and many other institutions within society, as well as individual citizens, must make decisions on how to react to crime and to criminals. These decisions may be made for reasons having nothing to do with reality; on the other hand, they may be influenced by the results of scientific analyses of human behavior, particularly criminal behavior.

In recent years social scientists have had some influence on these decisions; it is important that this influence continue. Judges, lawyers, legislators, and other public officials need to understand the meaning and purpose of the criminal law. For the student of criminal justice, it is important to develop an analytical approach toward the evidence and decision making in the field, but it is also important to understand that this kind of approach will not be shared by all.

How crime is defined and explained will affect reactions to criminals. Sterilization of mentally defective persons was once rather common; it was believed that mental defects caused criminal behavior. Belief that the environment was a prime factor led to programs to clean up the poor areas of the city and to provide jobs and better housing for people who lived in those areas.

Belief that juvenile delinquents can be salvaged from a life of crime led to the emergence of the juvenile court as a separate institution from the adult criminal court. The philosophy of **rehabilitation** characterized the juvenile court, as well as all of corrections, until recently. Another concept that has influenced public policy in criminal justice is deterrence.

The Philosophical Basis: Deterrence Theory

The belief that criminal behavior is rational behavior that people will engage in if they think they will derive more benefit than pain from that behavior leads to a punishment philosophy. It is assumed that if punishments are severe enough, people will not engage in criminal behavior. This philosophy of **deterrence** currently is one of the main justifications for the punishment and sentencing that characterize the criminal justice systems in this country. Deterrence may be relevent to any of the approaches to explaining criminal behavior and therefore deserves further attention before the chapter focuses on specific explanations of criminal behavior. A belief in the philosophy of deterrence is also important to an understanding of many of the public policy decisions that are made.

Deterrence is generally considered to be of two types: individual (or specific) and general. **Individual deterrence** refers to the effect of punishment in preventing a particular individual from committing additional crimes. In the past this form of deterrence often involved **incapacitation,** or taking actions to make it impossible for a particular offender to repeat the crime for which he or she had been convicted. The hands of the thief would be amputated; rapists would be castrated; prostitutes would be disfigured in ways that would repel potential customers. Today, incapacitation takes the form of incarceration. Most people can be restrained from criminal acts if they are incarcerated and closely guarded. Clearly, they are prevented from committing criminal acts if a sentence of capital punishment is carried out.

Some very important questions, however, remain unanswered about specific deterrence. How many convicted persons would be repeat offenders, or **recidivists,** if they were not incarcerated or were punished in other ways? If Harold and his friends, featured in this chapter's CJA, had been punished for shoplifting, would they have refrained from engaging in subsequent illegal acts? How many people, especially those who are imprisoned, become more criminal because of the punishment they receive? Are most punishment efforts concentrated on those least likely to be deterred by punishment; for example, the alcoholic, the drug addict, and the sex offender? Some research indicates that, in fact, punishment is either not effective in deterring these offenders or effective for only a brief period.[2]

The second type, **general deterrence,** is based on the assumption that punishing individuals convicted of crimes will set an example for potential violators who, being rational people and wishing to avoid such pain, will not violate the law. Pro and con reactions to whether this is the case usually are based on conjecture, faith, or emotion, with little significant empirical data. This approach leads to dogmatic statements that cloud the issues.

Deterrence is questioned by scholars. One reason that the research is questionable is that many researchers do not ask some of the critical questions and measure some of the variables that may be influential in deterrence. Punishment may have a deterrent effect for some types of people or crimes but not for others. Perhaps punishment is effective in deterring a woman from shoplifting, but it will not necessarily stop her from poisoning her husband. Perhaps certain types of people are deterred by laws whereas others are not.[3]

In murder and other violent crimes, offenders are often under the influence of drugs or alcohol or are consumed by passion, as in domestic situations. Most of these people are probably not thinking very rationally at the time of the crime, and the threat of punishment might not be effective. Consider, for example, the murder cases discussed briefly in Spotlight 3.1. Although you would probably need more facts for a careful analysis, given what you do know, what do you think would have been an effective deterrent in each case? Do any of the crimes appear to have been the result of careful calculation in which case the behavior might have been deterred by the fear of severe punishment? How should each be handled in terms of general deterrence?

It is also possible that punishment is a deterrent but only one variable in a complex interplay of variables that keep many of us from committing crimes. The reason we do not commit crimes is not because we fear legal punishment, but because we fear social disapproval from our peers and we possess a moral commitment to the legal norms.[4] In determining whether the existence of legal punishment deters most people from committing crime, we need to consider the severity of the punishment and the degree of certainty that the punishment actually will be imposed. It is said that the *actual* certainty of punishment influences people's *perceived* certainty; and that if they believe certainty of punishment is high, they will be deterred from violating the law. The conclusions of some studies question the validity of this assumption.[5]

It may also be necessary to consider the type of punishment for a specific type of crime. Recent research has provided "tentative evidence

SPOTLIGHT 3.1
VIOLENT CRIMES: CASES FOR DETERRENCE?

What, if anything, might have constituted an effective specific deterrent in each of the following actual cases of criminal or alleged criminal activity? What punishments might constitute a general deterrence for each type of crime?

1. In March 1987 Russell W. Bledsoe, known to most of his California friends, neighbors, and legal colleagues as a bright, effective, and respected attorney, was shot to death by a federal agent who attempted to serve a federal search warrant in Bledsoe's home. The agent fired only after Bledsoe attempted to kill him.

A search of Bledsoe's home uncovered 61 pistols and shotguns, money, and files, clearly linking him with an international drug ring. Bledsoe, 71, who had been under police surveillance for a year, was known locally as a quiet man who was active in his parish and strongly opposed to drugs. There was nothing in his daily behavior to suggest his criminal connections.

2. In February 1988 authorities in Rochester, Minnesota, arrested David Brom, a 16-year-old accused of the ax murders of four members of his family. Most knew Brom as a quiet, gentle young man who wrote poetry; some described him as a person who would not hurt anyone. A few knew that he liked rock music and one of his favorite groups was Suicidal Tendencies.

On the day of the murders, Brom adopted a punk appearance, by dying his hair black, spiking it on the back of his head, and shaving the sides of his head. Previously, he had told some friends that he wanted to hurt his family. They thought of that conversation as one of a typical teenager frustrated by adults in his life.

3. In November 1987 Tom Knighten, a Dallas, Texas, police officer, personally faced the issue of crime causation as he pondered the death of a fellow officer, allegedly shot and killed by Knighten's 16-year-old son, two other teenagers, and a 23-year-old woman.

Knighten and his wife reared their children in what they considered to be a good home. Although the son now accused of murder had recently manifested some personal problems, it was not until

Knighten discovered that his son's friends were in possession of illegal drugs that he became concerned. He sent his son for drug testing four times in one year; all tests were negative. The teenager was sent to a psychiatrist, who concluded that his problems were not serious and warned the parents that the son needed some space and freedom.

Knighten and his wife were pleased with their son's new friend. He said he was a 17-year-old transfer student but turned out to be a 21-year-old undercover drug agent who said he had twice bought drugs from the son. The agent was later killed, allegedly by the four youths; police think Knighten's son fired the shots.

Police believe there were two motives for the killing: (1) the "friend" was finally suspected of being an agent, and (2) the alleged killers were involved in a satanic cult the nature of which Knighten would not discuss since the information is relevant to his son's defense.

4. A man arrested for stealing radios from Toyota Cressidas said he did so because someone driving that model had once referred to him by a racial slur. Raymond Herrera admitted stealing more than 400 radios from cars at Chicago's O'Hare airport. Most of the cars were Cressidas. Police believe Herrera stole to support his drug habit.

5. In May 1988 a 17-year-old Oklahoma teenager allegedly shot and killed her 16-year-old brother because, she said, he took her glass of orange juice.

6. In March 1988 Robert E. Chambers, Jr., after a long and bitter trial, but before the jury verdict, accepted a plea bargain and entered a guilty plea in the death of Jennifer Levin. Chambers had testified that he did not intend to hurt Levin but that they got into an argument and that he accidentally killed her after she "squeezed his testicles so painfully" that he reacted in a frenzy.

Chambers is from an affluent family and grew up with all the advantages that money can buy. The prosecution offered a plea bargain to avoid another trial which seemed inevitable when the jury, after nine days of deliberation, still could not reach a verdict. Under the terms of the plea bargain, Chambers is to serve from 5 to 15 years in prison.

that increasing jail populations has a moderate negative impact on property crimes, especially burglary and larceny, and a weaker impact on aggravated assault as a violent crime."[6] It is thus necessary to consider the issue of deterrence very carefully before concluding that a particular approach explains *why* crime does or does not occur.

THE HISTORICAL BEGINNINGS OF CAUSATION THEORIES

Free Will: The Classical Approach

Deterrence theory is based on the assumption that behavior is purposeful. Humans choose to behave in certain ways. But *why* do they make these choices? This question has been of great importance to philosophers throughout history, but we turn to the eighteenth-century writers for the development of the doctrine of free will that underlies deterrence theory. During that century, the **classical school** of criminology dominated thinking about criminal behavior. The leader of the school was Cesare Beccaria, whose major treatise, *An Essay on Crime and Punishments*, was first published in 1764.[7]

Beccaria and his followers argued that human behavior is purposive and based on **hedonism,** the pleasure–pain principle: people choose those actions that give pleasure and avoid those that give pain. Therefore, pun-

Cesare Beccaria advocated that punishment should fit the crime. (Culver Pictures)

A California neurosurgeon who refused to improve his rental units after a court order found him guilty of violating the health, fire, and building codes of the city of Los Angeles was found in contempt of court and ordered to serve a 30-day jail term. The day he completes that term he will be escorted from jail to one of his rental units where, under court order, he must live for 30 days. In pronouncing the sentence, the judge said that she hopes it will bring the doctor in "contact with some sense of human decency."

The doctor's case was brought to court by tenants who complained that he refused to maintain the rental units in compliance with city codes. The apartments have rats, leaky roofs, broken windows, and an unreliable hot water supply. One tenant reported that her children had been bitten by insects and rats. The doctor was given 36 months to bring the rental units up to code standards. When he did not do so, the court ordered the jail and apartment-living sentence.

ishment should be assigned to each crime in a degree that would result in more pain than pleasure for those who committed the forbidden act. The punishment also should be appropriate for the act committed. It was assumed that such punishment would deter most people from engaging in criminal acts. But those who persisted in acting in criminal ways would be getting the punishment they deserved for the particular acts they committed. Punishments were to be set by the legislature. No defenses were allowed. The law was rigid, structured, and theoretically impartial. The view of the classical school that punishment should fit the crime is often seen today in sentences designed to fit the particular crime committed, as illustrated in Spotlight 3.2.

The classical approach was seen as too rigid by some thinkers. The **neoclassical school** tempered the law by adding defenses. Children were not considered capable of free will and would not be under the jurisdiction of the criminal law even if they engaged in criminal activities. Likewise, the mentally ill were not considered criminally responsible for their acts; so the insanity defense became a part of the criminal law.

Determinism: The Positive School

The classical and neoclassical philosophies of letting the punishment fit the crime soon gave way to the philosophy of the **positivists:** that the punishment would fit the criminal. The positivists rejected the harsh legalism of the classical and neoclassical schools and substituted the doctrine of determinism for that of free will. They focused on the **constitutional causes of crime,** individual aspects of the criminal instead of the legal aspects of the crime. They emphasized a philosophy of individualized, scientific study and treatment of criminals. This study was to be based on the findings of the physical and social sciences that were emerg-

Lombroso advocated that punishment should fit the criminal. (Historical Picture Service, Inc.)

ing at the time the positivists wrote. "Their emergence (in the late eighteenth century) symbolized clearly that the era of faith was over and the scientific age had begun."[8]

Led by the Italian Cesare Lombroso (1835–1909), the positivists emphasized the importance of empirical research in the study of criminals. They disagreed on the cause of crime: some saying that it was the constitution of the body; others emphasized the social and psychic component, thus introducing the concept of environment into the study of crime. The importance of these factors, however, lies in the underlying assumptions that we can study the criminal and we can change the criminal; thus, they set the foundation for the philosophy of rehabilitation that dominated the criminal justice system until recently.[9] Taken together, the classical and positivist schools of thought were forerunners of the developments in the three main areas that today are used to explain criminal behavior: psychological, biological, and sociological.

PSYCHOLOGICAL AND BIOLOGICAL EXPLANATIONS

Many of the psychological and biological explanations of behavior are closely related, and a wide range of explanations may be categorized as psychological or biological. Some of the earliest claimed that criminal behavior resulted when persons were possessed of devils. In recent years, this explanation of criminal behavior has reemerged, as police and others have confronted cult members engaged in criminal activity. Spotlight 3.3 focuses on some recent cases.

Thirteen victims were found buried in Mexico near the Texas border. The suspects in custody say they killed at the demand of Adolfo de Jesus Constanzo, who believed that human sacrifices would protect the cult members from harm. (Brad Doherty/Brownsville Herald/AP Wide World)

Earlier explanations of criminal behavior also centered on personality traits of individuals, with some traits found more frequently in criminals than in noncriminals. It was also argued that all people have criminalistic tendencies, but that in most, those tendencies are curbed by inner controls developed through the process of **socialization** during early childhood. When those controls are not properly developed, the criminal tendencies are acted out or projected inward, producing reactions that cause mental conflict, which may lead to criminal behavior. In the extreme, these individuals lose touch with reality.

Earlier biological explanations were illustrated by the work of Lombroso, mentioned earlier. His approach focused in part on biological differences between criminals and noncriminals. Although Lombroso wrote about other types, he was best known for his category of the born criminal. Criminals were seen as biologically different from noncriminals, and those biological differences, according to Lombroso, could be measured. His work was questioned by others, but the biological approach is back in vogue in some circles today.

The biological approach to explaining criminal behavior has recently received widespread attention in the popular media. The *New York Times* has referred to current research links between defective genes and manic-depressive illness.[10] *Newsweek* reports that twins "share traits and emo-

He was disillusioned with his family's religion, rebellious against what he termed "stupid Christian morals" and anxious to find like minds willing to act on their views.

So the 20-year-old Dallas man ran a classified ad in a local newspaper earlier this year seeking anyone interested in "Crowleyanity"—his term for the philosophy of Aleister Crowley, an English occultist considered the father of modern satanism and black witchcraft. He said the ad brought about 30 replies. "If I want something, I believe I should be able to do anything, and I mean anything, to get it. Even if it hurts somebody else," said the man, who refused to be identified.

"Crowley says, 'Do what you will, shall be the whole of the law.' That fits me, and I wanted to find other people to start a group that believed that and wanted to practice Crowley's magic."

Law enforcement authorities believe the man's reasons for embracing a black religion mirror those of a small but disturbing number of teenagers and adults here [in Dallas, Texas] and across the country.

Sandi Gallant, a San Francisco Police Department officer recognized as the country's first ritual-crime expert, terms satanism and other deviant occult beliefs "the fad of the '80s."

Police, educators and mental health workers believe it is a fad that has spawned a small but significant nationwide wave of violence and crime.

Among the most publicized recent incidents are: a January murder-suicide in Newark, N.J., in which a 14-year-old killed himself and his mother after becoming obsessed with satanism; a December 1987 baseball-bat bludgeoning death of a 19-year-old in Carl Junction, Mo., in which three teen-age, self-styled devil worshipers have been charged; and the January shoestring strangulation of a 14-year-old Atlanta-area girl in which a Georgia police investigator said the three teenagers charged "performed a satanic ritual, and in it, the murder victim was their sacrifice." . . .

Experts say there is no completely accurate profile of likely participants because leaders usually collect a hodgepodge of beliefs salable as what one officer described as "something that can fulfill any need or desire, so it attracts a variety of people."

But in general, many say, the resulting belief systems attract intelligent and bored young, middle-

---

tional bonds, communicate with each other in mysterious ways and provide tantalizing insights into human nature."[11] *Newsweek* has also given its readers a brief "guide to hormones" explanation, noting that scientists are discovering more and more hormones and the role they play in human behavior. "Behavior has glandular links, whether it be anxiety, aggression, eating disorders or suicide."[12] *Time*, referring to studies by researchers at the Minnesota Center for Twin and Adoption Research, reports that "key characteristics may be inherited."[13]

The scholarly literature also is carrying an increasing number of research articles linking behavior with biological, chemical, and neurological elements of the human body.[14] Scientists are telling us that our moods and behavior may be determined by what we eat or what we inherit; but the emerging sociobiology, which has given us more insights into animal behavior, is highly controversial in its application to human behavior.[15] The application of these findings and conclusions also presents problems for trial courts, as judges determine whether the "evidence" should be permitted in a trial on the issue of whether the defendant was legally responsible for his or her conduct.[16]

The renewed emphasis on the use of the physical sciences to explain behavior, particularly criminal behavior, has recently focused on a very

class adults and troubled teenagers by celebrating self-indulgence and providing an outlet for those angry at conventional religion and social mores.

Experts say young followers are often loners or misfits seeking companionship, much like a 15-year-old boy from north Dallas County who claimed he had joined in blood-drinking rituals, animal sacrifices and other satanic rites to find friends.

His parents and probation officer said his involvement in the adult-led group was a factor in his rapid transformation from a normal youth into a delinquent and runaway.

Police say that the nature of such religion—and the power it can give a leader over others—makes it attractive to other extremists. . . .

A University of California–Berkeley sociologist and expert on cults said current interest in deviant occult religion may be rooted in the same social currents responsible for the New Age movement.

"A weakening of traditional religion coupled with the reach of television and other mass communication has created a virtual supermarket of ideas in which seekers are free to pick elements of belief systems as obscure as shamanism, paganism and Egyptian magic," said the expert, Richard Ofshe.

"And something that catches on in California can spread instantaneously, fueling institutions and organizations in the business of promoting what has become a New Age market," he said. "On the dark side of this, the opposite side of New Age, you have an identical ability to spread ideas instantaneously.

"For teenagers, you also have a highly competitive music industry that appears to be fashioning and selling much of what is termed heavy-music by promoting a satanic theme.

Such music, occult films and television shows can lead teenagers to experiment with occult concepts drawn from the same available array of belief systems," he said.

An FBI behavioral sciences expert believes some of the rising interest stems from a simple itch to ride the edge of social convention.

"People want to see forbidden things. They're kind of like moths flying around a damn flame just to see how close they can get without getting burned.

"And you must consider how little is forbidden today," said the agent, assigned to the FBI training academy at Quantico, Va. "We accept things now that would've been unheard of 20 years ago. That's one reason why what's attractive is so much more extreme."

Source: Lee Hancock, "Crimes in the Name of Satan. Occultism: The Fad of the '80s?" *Dallas Morning News* (20 April 1988), p. 1C. Reprinted with permission of The Dallas Morning News.

controversial work. *Crime and Human Nature* was published in 1985 and written by James Q. Wilson, a Harvard professor who has written widely on many areas of criminal justice, and Richard J. Herrnstein, a Harvard psychologist. Wilson and Herrnstein argue that the evidence shows that criminals are more likely than noncriminals to be fat and athletic. However, the authors quickly point out that it probably is not body build that causes the criminal behavior but rather the aggressive temperament that goes with the body type. Wilson and Herrnstein also emphasize the relationship between low intelligence and certain hormones and criminal behavior. Again, they emphasize that "these biological tendencies interact in complicated ways" with methods of child rearing, but their point is that sociological explanations of criminal behavior are not sufficient and that too little attention has been paid to biological factors.[17]

The Wilson and Herrnstein book has been praised by many and severely criticized by others. In evaluating this book and any other attempts to explain criminal behavior, we must analyze the conclusions critically. Unfortunately, Joseph Gusfield is probably correct when he concludes:

> Pushed into the public arena, its findings are likely to be distorted. Agreement and disagreement will doubtless depend less on the analysis of materials than on whether the reader's pet ox has been gored or massaged.[18]

It is important to understand that by far the greatest majority of people who have the biological, psychological, or physiological traits linked by such investigators with criminal behavior do not engage in criminal behavior. The Wilson and Herrnstein approach should not be allowed to eradicate the importance of sociological explanations of criminal behavior.

SOCIOLOGICAL EXPLANATIONS

Sociological explanations of criminal behavior have dominated the formal discipline of criminology. The theoretical approaches are numerous, and the research in many areas is vast. Only a sample of the sociological contributions can be made here.

The Ecological Approach

Sociologists who study the **ecology** of crime are interested in examining the way in which criminal behavior is related to the distribution of elements of the social structure and changes within that structure. Such studies were conducted extensively in the 1920s and 1930s in Chicago and other large cities as sociologists studied the growth patterns of the cities. They noted that delinquent and criminal behavior appeared to be related to those changes. Rates of illegal behavior were high in certain areas of the city and low in others. The areas with high rates of crime were characterized by physical deterioration and declining populations. In many cases, these areas of high crime rates previously had been characterized

High crime rates are frequently found in low-income areas, but that does not necessarily mean that poverty is the cause of crime. (Joel Gordon)

as nice residential areas with little or no crime, located near the center of the city. But as the city grew and businesses moved into the area, the people who could afford to do so moved out. The areas deteriorated and became characterized by high rates of crime, delinquency, truancy, and other social problems.[19]

Ecological studies, along with crime data indicating that many people who are convicted of crimes are from low-income areas, have led some to conclude that poverty *causes* criminal behavior. The early ecologists did not draw that conclusion; they were looking for reasons why poverty often is a characteristic of criminals. But ecologists also recognized that other factors might be involved in explaining the cause of the criminal behavior. Differential law enforcement is an example; people living in poor areas of the city might be more likely to be arrested for illegal behavior than people living in more affluent areas.

More recent analyses of the relationship between poverty or unemployment and crime note that the

> connection between crime and unemployment [or economic conditions generally] is likely to be quite complex. . . . The inconsistent . . . results of so many studies of the crime-economy link arise in large measure . . . from relying on an overly simple model of choice, one in which a person chooses between crime and work on the basis of stable preferences and without regard to the preferences of others.[20]

Such simple models look mainly to the monetary aspect of poverty without analyzing the social values, other variables that might (or might not) be associated with poverty.

For example, it commonly is argued that higher unemployment will result in higher crime rates. Although there is little recent empirical support for this belief,[21] there is some evidence that unemployment is related to *some* but not to other types of crime[22] and that unemployment has some relationship to rates of imprisonment.[23] But, when other variables are controlled, the relationship between crime and unemployment or imprisonment is not so clear.[24] It therefore is important to look not only at economics and crime but to consider other variables. For example, race and ethnic heterogeneity have been found to be related to crime along with income inequality, with some evidence that the impact of income inequality on crime increases as ethnic heterogeneity increases.[25]

It also may be important to look at the type and extent of poverty, the size and type of neighborhood, and even the extent of marital discord in studying the relationship between economics and crime. A study of neighborhoods in Manhattan, New York, found that the rates of homicide were highest in the neighborhoods characterized by *extreme* poverty and *pervasive* marital discord.[26]

Many researchers who study the relationship of economics, race, and crime do so in the context of violent crimes. The California Commission on Crime Control and Violence Prevention is an example. That commission, although recognizing that official crime rates are higher among minority and low socioeconomic groups, also emphasized the need to analyze more carefully all variables that might be involved, as indicated in Spotlight 3.4. Other recent research has indicated that the extent of the rela-

SPOTLIGHT 3.4
ECONOMIC FACTORS AND INSTITUTIONAL RACISM: CAUSES OF CRIME?

Findings of the California Commission on Crime Control and Violence Prevention

- Although most minorities are law-abiding and non-violent, arrest rates are highest for minorities of low-socioeconomic status. The accuracy with which arrest data reflect actual rates of minority criminal activity has long been debated. Federal Uniform Crime Report data, however, are consistent with locally reported arrest data, thereby suggesting their accuracy.
- Racial minorities receive differential treatment by the criminal justice system after arrest. Blacks and Hispanics are more likely to be institutionalized for their crimes than are Whites.
- It is impossible to separate the effects of race and ethnic status from the effects of socioeconomic status because a large number of minority people fall within the low-socioeconomic status category. While there has been improvement in the economic condition of some minorities, the fact remains that a large proportion are jobless or under-employed, and receiving at- or below-subsistence level income. The interaction of institutional racism and economic factors contributes substantially to high crime and violence rates within some minority groups.
- High crime rates among some minority groups, particularly Black and Hispanic, may be due to the relegation of a substantial number of their members to a permanent underclass. Members of the underclass are denied participation in mainstream American life—economically and politically. This condition fosters alienation, deprivation and powerlessness, which, in turn, may lead to a negative form of adaptation whereby members of these groups react with violence; additionally, crime may be perceived as the only means available for achieving an affluent life style.

Source: An Ounce of Prevention: Toward an Understanding of the Causes of Violence (Sacramento, Calif.: Commission on Crime Control and Violence Prevention, 1982), p. 5.

---

tionship between, for example, social class and violent crime, varies depending on the way in which researchers define the concept of social class.[27]

The key to analyzing the influence of the ecological distribution of people or poverty on crime is to recognize that we are not explaining *the* cause of crime. Nor are we trying to say that aspects of the social structure, rather than characteristics of the individual criminal, cause crime. Rather, we are attempting to explain why the crime *rates*, even with changes in the population, are consistently higher in depressed areas than in more affluent areas of the city.[28] The need to look more carefully at several variables associated with criminal behavior is also illustrated by an analysis of social disorganization, or anomie, and crime.

Anomie and Crime

Official data indicate that many offenders come from families characterized by instability and violence. Many offenders have relatives who have been in prison. Most offenders are poorly educated and below normal in verbal skills. Others have neurological abnormalities associated with aggressive behavior. Some would interpret this information as proof that any or all of these variables cause criminal behavior. Sociologists, on the other hand, look carefully at these variables to try to discover what they have in common. The variables of education, verbal skills, family problems and violence, and neurological abnormalities represent biological, psychological, and sociological variables, but some sociologists have argued that all indicate a condition of **anomie.**

Durkheim's Concept of Anomie   *Anomie* literally means lawlessness. It has been used by sociologists to describe the lack of cohesion in some groups or societies. A noted sociologist, Émile Durkheim, discussed his understanding of the concept in 1893 when he offered an explanation for the understanding of criminal behavior in relation to anomie. According to Durkheim, as societies grow, they become more complex and less cohesive. The result is a state of normlessness that is more conducive to deviant behavior. That deviancy may result in criminal activity. The deviancy also may be positive. Durkheim believed that if a society is flexible enough to allow people to deviate positively from the norm, it must also expect negative deviation and criminal acts.[29]

Merton's Concept of Anomie   The abstract nature of Durkheim's contribution to our understanding of the relationship between anomie and crime has been refined by the contributions of sociologist Robert K. Merton. According to Merton, all societies have goals for their members. The goals are the things worth striving for, and pressure exists to attain these goals. The society also designates appropriate means for attaining these goals.

Some societies place greater emphasis on the goals than on how they are attained, whereas in other societies the means of attaining goals may become goals in themselves. Americans tend to emphasize success and goals. One manifestation of this emphasis is seen in the use of money as a measure of success. Americans generally want "just a bit more" no matter what they have, and in many cases, attaining the money becomes more important than how the money is attained.[30]

From the description of a cultural emphasis on goals and how to achieve those goals, Merton goes to the methods of individual reaction or adaptation to these goals and means. His position is diagrammed in Table 3.1, which features five types of adaptation, each defined in terms of ac-

TABLE 3.1

Merton's Anomie: A Typology of Modes of Individual Adaptation

Modes of Adaptation	Culture Goals	Institutionalized Means
Conformity	+	+
Innovation	+	−
Ritualism	−	+
Retreatism	−	−
Rebellion	±	±

Note: (+) signifies "acceptance"; (−) signifies "rejection"; (±) signifies "rejection of prevailing values and substitution of new values."

Source: Robert K. Merton, *Social Theory and Social Structure,* enlarged ed. (New York: Macmillan Publishing Co., Inc., 1968), p. 194. Copyright © 1957 by The Free Press, renewed 1985 by Robert K. Merton.

ceptance or rejection of the goals and means of society. In a stable society, the most common type of adaptation is conformity, which involves accepting both the goals and the socially approved means of attaining them. The next type of adaptation, innovation, involves accepting the goals but adopting different ways of achieving them. Pointing to studies disclosing that most people admit that at some time they have engaged in criminal behavior, Merton quotes one that illustrates the adaptation of innovation. When a minister was asked why he made false statements about a commodity he sold, he replied, "I tried truth first, but it's not always successful." According to Merton, the pressures that might lead to this adaptation are greatest in the lower class, where legitimate opportunities for achieving goals by acceptable means often are not available.

A third method of adaptation, ritualism, involves a scaling down of society's goals to a level one can attain; but it still allows one to engage almost compulsively in the appropriate methods for attaining the goals. This adaptation may be illustrated by the reaction, "Don't aim high and you won't be disappointed." This type of adaptation most often will be found among the lower middle class, which is characterized by severe training in the proper way of doing things.

Merton's fourth type of adaptation, retreatism, is probably the least common type. In this mode, the individual retreats from the goals and the means. This adaptation is frequently used by people who have often failed in their attempts to achieve the goals by proper means. These people, according to Merton, are *in* the society but not *of* it. Examples are chronic drunkards, drug addicts, vagrants, psychotics, and outcasts. A final type of adaptation, rebellion, involves rejecting the goals and means and attempting to substitute new values for both.

Merton's theory of anomie has been criticized because it does not explain why we choose one type of adaptation over another, a criticism that Merton acknowledged. Others have criticized the approach because it does not explain the apparent nonutilitarian reasons why many youngsters engage in delinquent behavior. They may see crime as fun, and the goals of society may have no effect on their decisions to engage in delinquent or criminal activities. The approach does not explain the destructive nature of some delinquent activity. Nor does Merton take into account the possibility that we do not all agree on the goals and that our society is characterized by conflict not agreement or consensus.[31]

Some recent research suggests that the relationship between anomie or normlessness and crime must be analyzed more closely than Merton does. For example, among those who live in a state of normlessness, some engage in criminal activity and others do not. What distinguishes them? One study found that the individual's perception of power or the lack of power is important.

> Normlessness does not lead to trouble with the law among persons who also believe they are powerless to achieve their ends. It is only among persons who do not believe they are powerless—who see themselves as active and effective forces in their own lives—that normlessness is related to trouble with the law.[32]

It also may be true that anomie or normlessness is indicative of other characteristics of the social setting related to criminal (or delinquent) behavior. One approach is the study of subcultures.

Subcultural Explanations

Merton's concept of anomie has been influential in the development of another explanation of delinquent behavior: the subcultural approach. This approach is characterized by several theories and numerous empirical studies. The theorists do not agree on the nature of the subculture, but they do agree that delinquency is related to the emergence of a **subculture,** which is really a culture within a culture. The subculture has its own rules and regulations as well as methods of control over its members. The values of the subculture often are contrary to those of the larger society.

Lower-Class Boys and Middle-Class Values Albert K. Cohen has described the subculture by discussing the reactions of lower-class boys to middle-class values. Middle-class values are emphasized at school and other social institutions as well as through the media. Lower-class boys accept those values, but they cannot achieve them through the means established as acceptable by the middle class. After repeated attempts, they develop a subculture that will enable them to achieve the goals of status and success that they find unobtainable by middle-class values.[33] The middle-class values that they have found unobtainable are listed in Spotlight 3.5.

Cohen described the nature of the subcultural adaptation of the lower-class boy. The adolescent culture is characterized by the following:

Nonutilitarian. The boys steal "for the hell of it" rather than take items they really need or desire.

Malicious. The boys appear to delight in activities that make others uncomfortable.

Negativistic. The values of the subculture usually are just the opposite of middle-class values.

Versatility. The boys steal a variety of objects.

Short-run hedonism. Members of the gang subculture often gather for no specific purpose; their activities are oriented toward immediate pleasure, with no thought or plans for the future.

Group autonomy. The boys resist outside social controls; their controls are from within the group only.

According to Cohen, a subculture with these six characteristics enables its lower-class members to achieve status and success within their group and thus provides one method of adjustment to the frustrations they encounter when they try to achieve middle-class values by middle-class methods.

Techniques of Neutralization Gresham Sykes and David Matza disagree with Cohen's thesis that lower-class boys develop a subculture whose values

SPOTLIGHT 3.5
SUMMARY OF MIDDLE-CLASS STANDARDS FACED BY THE
LOWER-CLASS BOY: COHEN'S APPROACH TO SUBCULTURE

1. Ambition is a virtue; its absence is a defect and a sign of maladjustment. Ambition means a high level of aspiration, aspiration for goals difficult of achievement. It means also an orientation to long-run goals and long-deferred rewards . . . an early determination to "get ahead." . . .
2. The middle-class ethic is an ethic of individual responsibility. It applauds resourcefulness and self-reliance, a reluctance to turn to others for help. . . .
3. Middle-class norms place a high evaluation on the cultivation and possession of skills and on the tangible achievements which are presumed to witness to the possession of skills and the application of effort. Outstanding performance of almost any kind is applauded . . .
4. Middle-class norms place great value on "worldly asceticism," a readiness and an ability to postpone and to subordinate the temptations of immediate satisfactions and self-indulgence in the interest of the achievement of long-run goals. . . .
5. Rationality is highly valued . . .
6. The middle-class value system rewards and en-

courages the rational cultivation of manners, courtesy and personality. . . .
7. The middle-class emphasizes the control of physical aggression and violence . . .
8. Recreation should be "wholesome." That is, one should not "waste" time but spend his leisure "constructively." . . .
9. . . . Middle-class values emphasize "respect for property." This . . . means a particular cluster of attitudes regarding the nature of property rights and the significance of property . . .

What the Delinquent Subculture Has to Offer

. . . Certain children are denied status in the respectable society because they cannot meet the criteria of the respectable status system. The delinquent subculture deals with these problems by providing criteria of status which these children *can* meet.

Source: Albert K. Cohen, *Delinquent Boys: The Culture of the Gang* (New York: Free Press, 1955), pp. 88–91; 121. Copyright © 1955 by The Free Press, renewed 1983 by Albert K. Cohen.

---

are at odds with those of middle-class society. In developing their theory of techniques of neutralization, Sykes and Matza argue that the shame and guilt exhibited by delinquents when they violate society's norms indicate that they are not rejecting those norms. Further evidence of their support of society's values is that they believe only certain people are appropriate targets for delinquent and criminal activity. The delinquent shows admiration for some law-abiding citizens and in other ways indicates that he has at least accepted some of society's norms. Sykes and Matza take the position that the delinquent who cannot achieve those norms rationalizes or neutralizes the norms. The delinquent's behavior does not indicate a rejection of society's norms, as Cohen suggests, but is an "apologetic failure. . . . We call these justifications of deviant behavior techniques of neutralization."[34]

Differential Opportunity Theory   Another subculture theory, **differential opportunity,** developed by Richard Cloward and Lloyd Ohlin, sees the individual in relation to both the legitimate and the illegitimate opportunity structures of society. Merton emphasized that not all people have equal access to legitimate ways of doing things; other theories emphasize that not all people have access to illegitimate ways of doing things. Cloward and Ohlin analyze behavior by the individual's access to both types of opportunities. They analyze the differential access to legitimate or illegitimate opportunities for three types of subcultures.

In the *criminal subculture*, found mainly in lower-class neighborhoods, the successful criminal is visible and willing to associate with juveniles. These juveniles have limited access to adults who could serve as role models who have attained success through legitimate means. The juveniles thus live in a structure that permits and facilitates illegitimate instead of legitimate activities.

The *conflict subculture* emerges in areas characterized by a lack of organization and stability. The community is disorganized and cannot provide young people with access to legitimate ways to achieve success; this leads to frustration and discontent among the youths. But access to criminal opportunity systems is also limited by this disorganization. Combined with weak social controls, this lack of organization leads to the emergence of conflict subcultures, often characterized by violence.

The third type of subculture, *retreatist*, is composed of youths who failed in the other two types; they tend to retreat, often into drugs. "When both systems of means are simultaneously restricted, it is not strange that some persons become detached from the social structure, abandoning cultural goals and efforts to achieve them by any means."[35]

Miller's Lower-Class Theory In his analysis of the subculture of delinquent boys, Walter Miller argued that these boys are responding to a distinct lower-class subculture. This subculture is dominated by women who are the heads of most of the households. Men are not usually present in the homes; when they are present it is generally not in a stable form of marriage. There may even be a series of men in the home; Miller called this situation *serial monogamy*. These men do not participate as much in the family situation as is characteristic of other classes. For most of the males growing up in these families, the one-sex peer unit, or gang, is the most significant factor in their lives instead of the family unit.

This lower-class culture in which young males are reared may be distinguished from middle and upper classes by six focal concerns: trouble, toughness, smartness, excitement, fate, and autonomy, which are defined in Spotlight 3.6. After explaining these focal concerns, Miller concludes that the result is a cultural system quite distinct from other cultural systems within the society, that this system is growing even more distinct from other classes, and that it is growing in size.[36]

Critique of Subculture Theories All these subculture theories have been the subject of empirical research and criticism. The critiques vary but the general approach may be criticized in that it does not explain why some boys who are exposed to the elements of the subculture become delinquent whereas others are law-abiding citizens. The approach also has been criticized as being circular in its explanation. "It is said to explain one kind of behavior by reference to attitudes and other behaviors that are of the substance of what is to be accounted for. It is as though one were to say,

Some subcultural explanations of criminal activity focus on youth groups and distinguish them from adult groups. (Mary Ellen Mark)

SPOTLIGHT 3.6
FOCAL CONCERNS THAT DISTINGUISH THE LOWER CLASS FROM OTHER CLASSES: MILLER'S APPROACH TO SUBCULTURE THEORIES

1. *Trouble* means to get into difficult situations with official authorities or agencies of the middle class.
2. *Toughness* involves several characteristics, such as physical prowess as demonstrated by outstanding skill and athletic ability; masculinity, which can be symbolized by tattooing; a lack of concern with art, viewing women as objects to be conquered; and bravery when threatened physically.
3. *Smartness* refers to the ability to outsmart or outfox, dupe, or con others and avoid having others successfully treat you in the same manner.
4. *Excitement* refers to the attempts of the lower-class youths to avoid the routine and monotony in their lives. This is done through the use of alcohol, drugs, gambling, and so on.
5. *Fate* refers to the belief by lower-class youths that they are not in control of much of what happens to them. Life is determined by luck or fortune, or the opposite.

6. *Autonomy* refers to the stated desire to go it alone. "I don't need no help from anyone." The irony of the situation, however, is that despite this stated rejection of authority, many of the youths seek highly structured and authoritarian environments.

Miller also spoke of two additional concerns of importance to adolescents: belonging and status. *Belonging* means that one has demonstrated knowledge of the group norms, as well as a desire to conform to those norms. The opposite of belonging is exclusion. *Status* is demonstrated by the possession of the qualities described above as focal concerns.

Source: Paraphrased from Walter B. Miller, "Lower Class Culture as a Generating Milieu of Gang Delinquency," in Marvin E. Wolfgang et al., eds., *The Sociology of Crime and Delinquency*, 2d ed. (New York: John Wiley & Sons, 1970), pp. 352–61. Reprinted by permission.

'People are murderous because they live violently' or 'People like to fight because they are hostile,' " without ever explaining why people live violently or why they are hostile.[37]

The Gang

Much emphasis has been placed recently on the influence of youth gangs on criminal behavior; however, this is not a new approach. The subculture theories were preceded by the classic study of Frederic M. Thrasher, who saw the juvenile gang developing from the social disorganization in the transitional zones of cities. In his study of 1,313 gangs in Chicago, Thrasher saw the gang developing as a result of innocent play groups that eventually came into conflict over space in the crowded and physically deteriorated areas of the inner city.[38]

Modern gangs do not fit Thrasher's descriptions. News publications today frequently report on the latest gang violence. In a 1985 article, *Newsweek* described some Chicago murders attributed to local gangs, concluding that

> Chicago is in the throes of some of its worst gang violence since the 1930s. Youth gangs that once battled over turf have evolved into small criminal empires fighting for control of thriving narcotics, auto-theft, gun-running and extortion operations.[39]

Youth gangs are frequently involved in delinquent and criminal activity. (J. P. Laffont/Sygma)

In 1988, *Newsweek's* presentation on gangs was even stronger, noting their differences from the earlier gangs that fought over turf. The popular news magazine described the gangs, which now operate in dozens of cities across the country:

> Gang conflicts have become a form of urban-guerrilla warfare over drug trafficking. Informers, welchers and competitors are ruthlessly punished; many have been assassinated.[40]

Although the popular news media focus mainly on the drug and violence aspect of gangs, social scientists have studied the total culture of the gang. Ruth Horowitz, who spent many hours personally observing gangs and talking with members in Chicago over a three-year period, writes about the interaction of gang members, nongang youths, and adult members of the community in which the gangs operate. She explains how the latter two groups come to understand and tolerate (if not accept) gang violence.

Gang violence is seen as an element of honor, she points out. Young men are taught to be independent and to defend themselves. In their cultural setting, this often requires violence. For a parent to supervise the gang member's behavior too closely would compromise his honor and development as a man. It also might alienate him from the approved family and community activities in which he takes part. Furthermore, it would be unacceptable to call in the police to control the violence, for that would constitute public questioning of the son's behavior. In short, although parents and other adults in the community see the gang's activities as violent, they do not view the members themselves as dangerous people. "The cultural and existential solution is to work with gang members to maintain a relationship of mutual toleration and to engage in negotiations which allow community life to proceed in an orderly, if tenuous, fashion."[41]

Recent sociological studies of female gangs, conducted by sociologists such as Horowitz, Campbell, and others, find that girls join gangs for the same reason as boys: to find a sense of belonging that they have not otherwise found. They accept some of the values of mainstream society but reject others. They do not view themselves as criminals even though some of their activities are against the law. They rationalize their behavior by saying it is necessary in their society or by denying responsibility for what they do. Female gang members are aggressive against other women but not against men.[42]

The Conflict Approach

The social structure theories discussed earlier generally can be described as theories that represent consensus in society's definitions of what constitutes criminal or abnormal and noncriminal or normal behavior. The **conflict approach** is based on the assumption that the norms, values, and laws of society are characterized by conflict, dissension, and clash. The conflict approach is difficult to define and explain because the theorists do not agree on the elements of conflict theory—or for that matter, on what this approach should be called. The conflict approach is often referred to as *radical criminology, the new criminology,* or most frequently as *critical criminology.*

Some conflict theorists talk about conflict arising between primary and secondary cultures or societies. Thus, one who moves to the United States from another society may experience conflict between his or her former and current societal norms.[43] Others talk about conflict between interest groups *within* the same society. An example would be conflicts between races within the United States. Conflict may also exist between weak and powerful groups, with the powerful groups exerting pressures over the weaker ones. Political organizations may be analyzed as examples of this kind of conflict.[44]

Critical Criminology   Critical criminology is concerned with the ways in which people, especially lower-class people, are oppressed, manipulated, and misunderstood. Critical criminology can be explained as utilizing a subordinate ideology in its analysis of crime. It gained prominence in the 1960s, a period of social change and social turmoil, during which some began to reexamine the issues of social fairness, equality, and justice. Scholars began to take renewed interest in a Marxist perspective for proposing solutions to what they viewed as economic and radical injustice. Questions were asked in reference to why certain behaviors came to be defined as crimes; why certain persons were more likely to engage in criminal behavior; and the extent to which the criminal justice system was biased in the way it processed and treated criminals. This approach was based on the philosophies of Karl Marx, who came to be viewed as a humanistic scholar.

Critical criminology is a critique of capitalism. It encompasses a historical account of how crime, law, and social control develop within a wider social, economic, and political perspective. This is a departure from traditional criminology and suggests that traditional criminology fails to recognize how material conditions and crime evolve together.[45]

Critical criminologists argue that common crimes, those listed in the FBI's *Uniform Crime Reports*, are not the ones most costly to society, either economically or socially. They also suggest that the crimes that cost society the most—such as corporate crimes, environmental crimes, fraud, violation of human rights, racism, sexism, dangerous working conditions that lead to serious bodily injury or death, and the manufacture and sale of hazardous products—generally escape being officially labeled criminal. Critical criminologists believe that crime and criminology cannot be understood apart from understanding the processes by which people come to be defined as criminal, which in turn cannot be understood apart from considerations of power and privilege, which are tied in with the society's economic system.

For purposes of analysis, Marx used the term *mode of production.* A person's role in the mode of production (that is, his or her relation to the production of capital) designates the social class to which that individual belongs. Categories include those who own the means of production and those who work for the owners, or wage workers. The critical position also states that capitalist societies produce a group of people whose relationship to production is marginal or nonexistent, the unemployed or underemployed. How people relate to the mode of production will determine their class status, and their class status will determine how they relate to society politically and economically.

Critical criminologists also emphasize the causal connection between political and economic status and inequality and crime. The approach argues that class stratification and inequality in large part are due to political and economic factors as these relate to antagonism between owners and wage workers in the capitalistic system.

They explain crime by stating that the criminal justice system serves as an instrument of those who own and control the means of production. These people are the ones with power: they control the laws and therefore define as illegal those behaviors they find bothersome and exclude those behaviors they do not find to be a problem. The powerful also control the enforcement of laws; thus, they dominate the less powerful, or subordinate, in society in the entire criminal justice system, ranging from arrest to incarceration or capital punishment.

Critical criminology has been criticized for not defining its terms clearly enough to permit empirical measurement of its concepts. It is labeled a perspective rather than a theory, a perspective whose conclusions rest on conjecture. But the approach has forced some to reexamine the criminal justice system and consider carefully whether the law is applied fairly or whether income and race determine how it will be applied. "If a 'critical criminology' can help us solve that issue, while still confronting the need to control crime, it will contribute a great deal."[46]

The Labeling Perspective

An explanation of criminal behavior that is in some ways similar to the conflict approach is the **labeling perspective.** Both approaches are concerned primarily with *why* some people are designated criminal, whereas others who engaged in the same behavior are not. The behavior per se is not at issue, but the reaction of official agencies to that behavior. Some people who drive while intoxicated are not arrested and charged even when observed by police and other people; others are arrested and formally charged.

The point of the labeling approach is that the difference between those who are arrested and those who are not is not intrinsic to the behavior in question. The difference is in the way people react to and label that behavior. Sociologist Howard Becker describes the situation in these terms:

> Deviance is *not* a quality of the act a person commits, but rather a consequence of the application by others of rules and sanctions to an 'offender.' The deviant is one to whom that label has successfully been applied; deviant behavior is behavior that people so label."[47]

The point then, according to labeling perspective, is to explain *why* the label is applied to some and not to others. Some groups may be more likely than others to be labeled criminal. For example, low-status groups, which do not have power to press public officials, may be more likely to be so labeled. Further, people with status and power are more likely to afford private attorneys and know their legal rights. They thus may be more likely to negotiate a better plea bargain. Groups with power are more likely to have the symbols and strong institutions associated with success and law-abiding behavior, such as continuous success, strong family ties, and friends who can successfully intervene on their behalf. If they are convicted, they are more likely to be placed on probation rather than sentenced to prison and less likely to become involved in future crimes.[48]

Criticism of labeling theory has included the allegation that it is a perspective and not a theory. Some have argued that not only has the labeling approach not been systematically developed into a theory and tested empirically, but that empirical tests in this area are "both impossible and ridiculous."[49] Testing is not possible until the terms have been defined precisely, in such a way that they can be measured. It is also argued that the labeling approach avoids the important issue of causation, while erroneously suggesting that the actor is too passive. Insufficient attention is given to the interaction between the person labeled and those who do the labeling. The approach fails to recognize that some labeling can have positive effects, whereas it overemphasizes the effect of labeling on the individual.[50]

Differential Association

The approaches or theories discussed thus far are concerned mainly with the structure of society and how that structure might relate to criminal activity. But these approaches do not tell us *why* people become criminals. They can only tell us that turbulent family backgrounds, unemployment, social class, subcultures, or other social structural variables are often characteristic of those who are formally labeled criminal. Some people who are exposed to these variables do not become criminals. What is the difference?

One social process approach to explaining crime and delinquency is **differential association** theory, introduced and developed by Edwin H. Sutherland. Sutherland believed that criminal behavior develops in the same way as noncriminal behavior and that both may be explained by a learning process. Through the process of communication within small groups, people learn definitions that are either favorable or unfavorable to violating the law. The definitions accepted by a particular person will be influenced by the intensity, frequency, length, and kind of contact that occurs during the learning process.[51]

In developing his theory of differential association, Sutherland was reacting against theories based on biological inheritance. He also argued that impersonal agencies of communication such as newspapers and movies had little effect. It is the interaction that occurs within small intimate groups over a period of time that Sutherland thought important in explaining human behavior. Learning, not imitation, is important.

Sutherland also emphasized that criminal behavior cannot be explained by basic needs and values since many people satisfy those same needs and values through noncriminal behavior. "Thieves generally steal in order to secure money, but likewise honest laborers work in order to secure money." Explaining criminal behavior as a response to the need for money, says Sutherland, is like explaining it in terms of perspiration, "Which is necessary for any behavior, but which does not differentiate criminal from noncriminal behavior."[52]

Differential association has been criticized as unclear, consisting of terms that cannot be defined easily for purposes of research. It also has been argued that the theory does not cover all types of criminal behavior; nor does it explain why some people who have the opportunity to learn criminal behavior choose instead to be law-abiding citizens.[53] Despite these and other criticisms, differential association theory has produced a vast literature of theoretical development as well as empirical testing. It has influenced other theorists to develop similar explanations of criminal behavior.

Control Theory

A final sociological approach to the understanding of criminal behavior, like learning theory, involves psychological as well as sociological principles. Control theory is based on the assumption that human beings have to be taught how to behave properly. This learning occurs through the process of socialization. Through the family, peers, and other associates, the young learn how to behave. There are various approaches within control theory, but they all agree on the central assumption that social behavior requires social training. "Disagreement arises only in describing *how* human beings become socialized, in ascertaining *how much* difference the process makes to conduct, and in *assigning weights* to the various influences that mold us."[54]

Through the process of socialization, we develop inner controls, sometimes called *conscience*. When these inner controls are weak, criminal behavior may result. A strong inner commitment to society's values may result in the development of a favorable self-concept, thought by some to be positively associated with law-abiding behavior. In contrast, alienation from society and a weak self-concept may be highly associated with criminal behavior.

One form of control theory discussed frequently today is Travis Hirschi's social bond theory. According to Hirschi, what we must explain is not why some people commit crimes but why others do not do so. He believes that the degree of the individual's bonding to society is the key to the explanation. Social bond consists of four components: attachment, commitment, involvement, and belief.[55]

Attachment refers to our affective ties to people whose opinions are important to us and therefore have an impact on our behavior. *Commitment* is the "rational component of conformity" and refers to the energy and time that we are willing to put into the way we live. If we expend that commitment on activities like smoking and drinking rather than on conventional activities, we will be more prone to deviant behavior.

Involvement refers to our concern with and immersion in conventional values and is a consequence of commitment. If we are involved in conventional activities, we will have less time for involvement in nonconventional ones. The fourth component, *belief*, means that we attribute moral validity to conventional values. We see them as right. Delinquent and criminal behavior become more likely with the weakening in these four elements of the social bond.[56]

In an empirical study of young people in California, Hirschi found that youths who have positive attitudes toward teachers and school, positive attitudes toward their own accomplishments, and close ties to their parents were less likely to be involved in delinquent behavior than young people who did not have such attachments and commitments.[57]

Social control theory and Hirschi's approach in particular have been criticized as placing too much emphasis on commitment to conventional values and too little emphasis on the effect of self-concept and peer pressure on the behavior of young people. Hirschi recognizes some of these criticisms but has stated his belief that future research "will supplement rather than seriously modify the control theory."[58]

SPECIAL CATEGORIES OF OFFENDERS

Some of the problems of explaining crime may be examined in the context of particular categories of offenders. Offenders have been categorized in many ways. In this discussion two types will be examined: female offenders and career criminals.

Female Offenders

Most of the study and analysis of criminal behavior historically has focused on the juvenile or adult male offender, perhaps because women and girls have constituted a much smaller percentage of apprehended delinquents and criminals, also, most people who studied criminal behavior were men. Whatever the reason, during the past two decades women have received more attention in the analysis of criminal behavior as well as in the study of victimization.

Official arrest data indicate that women are responsible for only a small percentage of crime but that in recent years their rate of increase has been almost twice as fast as that of men. The increase in arrest rates of women has occurred mainly in arrests for property crimes. Total arrests of women remain considerably below those of men.

Official arrest rates are the subject of debate. Scholars do not agree on whether they represent increased criminal activity among women, an increased willingness on the part of officials to arrest women, or changes in policies regarding women. There is also disagreement over the nature of female criminality.

Scholars place more attention on female crime today than in the past, but they disagree on the reasons that distinguish crimes committed by women from those committed by men. (Stuart Rosner/Stock Boston)

In 1975, Freda Adler wrote *Sisters in Crime*, in which she argued that female criminality was increasing and that women were becoming more involved in crimes generally thought to be male crimes.[59] Some scholars agreed with Adler in taking the position that female criminality is increasing and also becoming more violent.[60] But the official data on arrests show that rates of arrests for males and females for violent crimes have increased at about the same rate and that most female arrests are for larceny–theft, representing 80 percent of females arrested for index crimes and 20 percent of all females arrested in 1987.[61]

It has been suggested by some researchers that these arrests for larceny–theft represent primarily an attempt of the females to support their drug habits. According to one study, the "data strongly imply a causal relationship between addiction to narcotics and property crime levels" although women also have found other criminal ways, such as prostitution and drug dealing, to support drug habits.[62]

The high rates of arrests of females for larceny–theft (many of which are for shoplifting) compared to other crimes, along with his other research, has led sociologist Darrell J. Steffensmeier, who has written extensively on female criminality, to conclude that although "women may be a little more active in the kinds of crime they have always committed," they are "still typically nonviolent, petty property offenders." Their crimes still reflect the traditional roles women have played in this society.[63]

Overall arrest rates continue to be much higher for men than women. In 1987, 82 percent of all arrests were of men. Men accounted for 78 percent of index crime arrests, constituting 89 percent of arrests for violent crime and 76 percent of arrests for property crimes.[64]

More research is needed to explain fully the differences between male and female criminality, but that research must be narrowed to consider other variables that also might be influential in explaining these differences. For example, type and seriousness of crime should be considered.[65]

Differences between the criminal activity of black and white females should be compared.[66] Differential treatment in the entire criminal justice system should also be analyzed. There is some evidence that women are treated more leniently than men during the initial stages of the process (arrest, pretrial, and trial) but more severely at sentencing.[67] The debate on whether female criminals are significantly different from male criminals continues, with scholars warning against premature conclusions and assumptions based on simplistic explanations for the nature of behavior.

Career Criminals

Recent research has focused on career or habitual criminals, those criminals who have engaged in serious criminal activity over a sustained period of time. It is argued that we may be attempting the impossible in trying to find a theory that explains all criminality and that it would be profitable from an explanatory point of view to concentrate on the sociological, psychological, and biological characteristics of career criminals. The recent research on career criminals is illustrated by the research of the Rand Corporation.

The intensive analyses that Rand researchers have conducted on the subject have been done with data secured from self-reports of criminals, rather than on official data. They found these reports to be highly reliable and informative. The Rand research reports that most crimes are committed by a few criminals, that they are young when they begin their careers, that they are men with poor employment records, that they think of themselves as criminals, and that they intend to resume criminal activity upon release from prison.

Such findings have implications for policy making in criminal justice. "Based on these findings, the Rand researchers concluded that, if these high-rate offenders could be identified for selective prosecution and sentencing, the criminal justice system would operate much more effectively and efficiently." Unfortunately, these studies are not yet generalizable to the entire population because of the limited sample.[68]

INTERRELATIONSHIP OF THE APPROACHES

Detailed criticism could be given of all the attempts to explain criminal behavior, but there are some common problems in the research of psychological, biological, and sociological explanations. The basic problem is one of isolating the factors being analyzed. Is it possible to say "this is environment" and "this is heredity"? This problem has led many researchers to take the position that we can no longer think in either-or terms. The approach to explaining criminal behavior must be an interdisciplinary one. We cannot ignore the biological or psychological factors when we are

SPOTLIGHT 3.7
RESEARCHERS DISCOVERING WHY SOME TEENS ARE MORE DANGEROUS

Researchers are finally beginning to understand why some teen-agers sail through the turmoil of adolescence and others stumble from one dangerous episode to the next, endangering themselves and others in the process.

Recent studies have found, for instance, that the teen-agers most likely to get into trouble have a type of risk-taking personality that may be present almost from birth. The research indicates that this type of personality, known as Type T (T for thrills) may be inherited and that Type T children may actually be physiologically different from children who are less prone to taking risks.

Type T teen-agers are the ones who get into fights at the drop of a hat, race cars at enormous speeds and indulge in unrestrained sexual activity. They are the kids who abuse alcohol and drugs at earlier ages, and they may also be the ones who are most likely to kill themselves—a phenomenon that is increasing among teen-age boys at an alarming rate.

If there is an inborn personality trait that leads some children to be risk takers, psychologists stress that it may be an asset to children who learn to channel it in constructive ways. A series of studies at the University of Wisconsin involving hundreds of children have shown that Type T teen-agers are more creative than other children, possibly because they take the mental risks necessary for creative success.

"There are these two powerful forces—destructive risk-taking and creative risk-taking—that arise from the same group of kids," said Frank Farley, a professor of educational psychology at the University of Wisconsin who coined the term Type T. "Which way they channel their energies depends a lot on how they are raised and educated."

Farley and other researchers who dissected teen-age risk-taking at a conference recently in Bethesda, Md., say no one really knows for sure the biological basis for this type of risk-taking personality. Farley hypothesizes that Type T children have physiological systems—heart rates, skin temperatures, sweat glands—that are slower to respond to external stimulation. As a result, these people spend their lives seeking the extra thrills they need to feel stimulated. Below a certain level, Farley speculates, their senses are understimulated.

Farley sees Type T personalities as one extreme in a continuum of human behavior. The flip side is something he calls the "little t" personality—the shy, inhibited child who will do anything to avoid taking risks. A growing body of evidence suggests that the personalities of these shy children—like their "big T" counterparts—may be molded at birth. Physiologically, they require comparatively low levels of stimulation and, in fact, may try to avoid risks in an effort to calm their hyperactive nervous system.

Not all teen-agers who take crazy risks are Type T personalities. Some get into trouble because of bad parenting or because they are emulating their parents. One recent study at the University of California at Berkeley, for instance, found that the drinking habits of fathers closely correlated with their sons' later involvement in drugs and alcohol. This correlation did not hold for girls; instead, the Berkeley study found that girls were more likely to misbehave in adolescence—for instance, engaging in sexual promiscuity and taking drugs—if their mothers were experiencing psychological problems.

Teen-agers, of course, have always engaged in reckless and seemingly irrational behavior. Adolescence, which marks a difficult transition from dependency on parents to independence as adults, is a stressful time for almost every child. Research shows that risk-taking behavior is magnified by the dramatic hormonal and developmental changes that take place with puberty.

One recent study of 1,000 Type T people, interviewed at various ages, showed that risk-taking behavior, particularly involving physical activities, is highest during late adolescence. It begins to climb at age 10, peaks between the ages of 14 and 19, and then starts declining in the early 20s.

Understanding why teen-agers take risks has become an increasingly urgent topic because the consequences are more dangerous than ever before, the researchers say. Unprotected sex, which teen-agers have always experimented with, now raises the specter of AIDS in addition to unwanted pregnancies. Addictive drugs are cheaper and more available to the teen-age population than ever before, and despite the increase in the drinking age, alcohol remains readily available to most teens.

With both parents working, or divorced, teens in many families get less of the support and guidance they need.

Statistics bear out this concern. Adolescents are the only age group in which mortality has risen since 1960. Three-quarters of teen-age deaths are caused by accidents, homicides, and suicides, and accidents alone account for 60 percent.

"Young people are dying of their own reckless behavior," said Lewis Lipsitt, a developmental psychologist at Brown University who organized the conference on risk-taking at the National Institute of Mental Health.

Suicides among young white males have risen sharply over the last decade (this is not the case with white females or with blacks), and some researchers believe alcohol and drug abuse is a major factor. A 15-year British study found that suicides increased only among teen-agers whose blood contained traces of alcohol or drugs. Among those whose blood contained no such traces, there was no increase.

"This suggests the increased suicide rate among young white males is being brought about by the increased availability of drugs and alcohol," said David Shaffer, a psychiatrist and authority on suicide at New York State Psychiatric Institute. "In a certain vulnerable type of personality, the substance abuse leads to impaired judgment and suicidal behavior."

As some studies show, many of these vulnerable teen-agers are Type T risk-takers. Farley, for instance, said he has found that Type T adolescents are twice as likely to get into automobile accidents than their shy, "little t" counterparts. They are also more likely to drink and to drive fast, and they experiment with sex a year earlier, on the average, than "small t" teens.

In 20 years of research, Farley said, he has identified certain psychological characteristics that seem to define the Type T individual. "They look for uncertainty, high risk, novelty, variety, complexity, high intensity and conflict," he said. "They do best in unstructured situations—open classrooms, for instance, where there's a lot of activity going on and a lot of interaction."

People with "little t" personalities prefer certainty and familiar situations and avoid variety and risk. They do best in a structured environment, where the teacher is completely in control and teaches at a fixed pace in a traditional classroom mode.

Farley and other researchers believe that this type of personality may be genetically based, because it is present from early childhood. Two long-term studies in Chicago and Baltimore found that students who showed the greatest readiness to learn and explore in kindergarten also were more ready to explore in adolescence, including experimentation with drugs and alcohol.

Conversely, children who did poorly on the readiness test for first grade had a higher likelihood of being depressed 10 years later, said Dr. Sheppard Killam, a psychiatrist who conducted these studies and is now chairman of the Department of Mental Hygiene at John Hopkins University. "Those who explore drug use are not depressed," Killam said. "These seem to be two separate developmental pathways for children."

Some researchers have found evidence that the risk-taking teen-agers differ markedly physiologically from their shyer, more inhibited peers. In one study of 50 junior high students, Farley found that those who matched the Type T profile sweat less when exposed to various stimuli.

Farley speculates that because the physiological systems of Type T teen-agers are slow to respond to stimulation, they need an extra boost of excitement to feel stimulated. Conversely, "little t" children may get all the excitement they need from low levels of stimulation. Thus, they crave familiar situations and security.

A newly published report on extremely shy children seems to support this hypothesis. In two five-year studies, Harvard psychologist Jerome Kagan and colleagues found that extremely inhibited children were more likely than their outgoing peers to experience increased heartbeats, dilations of the pupils and muscle tension when confronted by strangers or unfamiliar situations. These phenomena were noted when the subjects were two years old and were still present at age 7.

"It appears that a small percentage of children are born with a biological disposition that would tend to make them shy," said J. Stephen Reznick, a Yale University psychologist who was one of the researchers.

Although the precise biological components of risk-taking remain unknown, most researchers agree that enough is known about its behavioral signs to identify at an early age those children who may grow up to be troublemakers.

"If parents, teachers and counselors identified these kids early on, they could rechannel these kids' energies into exciting, positive and diverse experiences.

Source: Alison Bass, *Boston Globe*, reprinted in *Tulsa World* (5 May 1988), p. Z-A-S (Special Features Section). Reprinted courtesy of The Boston Globe.

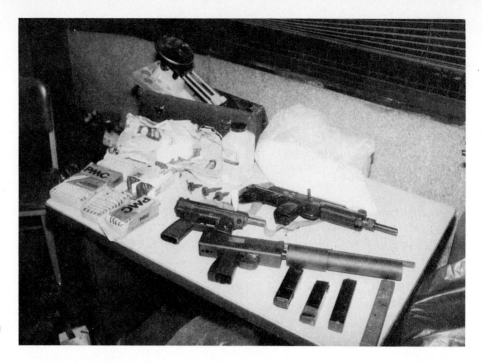

Close-up of an illegal drug and arms cache seized in a raid on a Harlem apartment. (Jeffrey Smith/Woodfin Camp)

analyzing criminal behavior from a sociological point of view. "Both social and biological variables and their interactions are important for our complete understanding of the origins of antisocial behavior."[69]

Substance Abuse and Criminal Behavior

The three basic areas of explanations of criminal behavior—psychological, biological, and sociological—may be used in attempts to explain the relationship between substance abuse and criminal behavior. The excessive use of alcohol and drugs may be related to biological or psychological dependency. Substance abuse may be related to one or more sociological variables. It may also be associated with a combination of psychological, biological, and sociological factors. Spotlight 3.7, which focuses on violent behavior in young people, illustrates that some researchers are looking not only at the possible link between heredity and behavior but also at the relationship between sociological variables, such as family problems, and violent behavior.

Scientists do not have all the explanations for the relationship between substance abuse and behavior, but data indicate that the problem of substance abuse often occurs before or during criminal activity. Beginning with Marvin Wolfgang's studies in the early 1950s, evidence has indicated that a very high percentage of those involved in violent criminal acts had been drinking at the time the act occurred. Wolfgang's study of homicide disclosed that either the victim or the offender had been drinking in 64 percent of the homicides.[70]

Studies of violent criminal acts in other countries have disclosed similar patterns of drinking during or right before the violent act. After an extensive study of the literature on alcohol and crime, investigators for the National Institute of Justice concluded that, "It is our judgment that alcohol use is an important factor in the occurrence of some crime. If we begin to understand *how* alcohol use exerts its causal influence, the relative importance of alcohol use to the occurrence of criminal behavior can be estimated."[71]

A study of 12,000 inmates in state prisons indicated that one-third had been drinking heavily just before they committed the offense for which they were then incarcerated. Twenty percent said that they drank heavily every day of the year before they entered prison for the current offense. Almost 16 percent had been in an alcohol treatment program at least once. Habitual offenders and those convicted of the violent personal crimes of rape and assault, as well as those convicted of burglary, were heavier drinkers than other types of offenders. Rates of drinking were also high among whites, American Indians, and inmates in the age group 18 to 25.[72]

Studies have also disclosed a very high rate of drug use among some offenders. Although the precise nature of the relationship is not clear, there is evidence that changes in drug use are associated with changes in the extent of criminal activity.[73] The relationship between substance abuse and criminal behavior continues to be a major focus of government and private research. Some of the research mentioned earlier in this chapter is aimed at discovering what kinds of penalties might deter deviant behavior such as driving under the influence. Other research focuses on the issue of causation.[74]

SUMMARY

Attempts to explain why people engage in criminal behavior are not new; the process has existed for centuries. What is new is a more systematic approach to the study. Beginning with the eighteenth-century efforts of Beccaria, Lombroso, and others, scientists have attempted to refine their techniques for studying human behavior. Volumes have been written on the approaches to a study of criminal behavior, and scholars continue to argue about which approaches best explain criminal behavior. An introductory course can cover only a very small sampling of those approaches.

This chapter began with a brief look at the subject of causation and continued with a discussion of deterrence theory. Deterrence theory is very important because of its effect on public policy. Most public officials look at crime with the goal of explaining the behavior in order to institute policies that will deter that kind of behavior. Unfortunately, the pressure to prevent and deter crime may lead some officials to conclusions that are not based on empirical data, such as the assumption that by increasing the length and severity of sentences, criminal behavior will be deterred. That approach was taken during the classical period when it was assumed that criminal behavior is rational. This eighteenth-century approach is quite in vogue today despite the lack of empirical evidence to support its assumptions.

Criminal behavior has also been studied in relation to the environment. Sociological studies of the nature and structure of the city and its relationship to delinquent and criminal behavior were quite popular in the earlier part of this century. The policy implications of that approach may be seen in attempts to improve living and working conditions in slum areas, as well as to provide meaningful recreational opportunities for those who live in high-crime areas.

Later emphasis on the social process by which criminal behavior is acquired led to the emergence of theories of anomie, in which social disorganization was a primary focus. Studies of the group involvement of juveniles led to the development of subculture theories of criminality. Still others have taken the position that crime is the result of conflicts within society or of the process of labeling. Others have focused on crime as a reaction to legitimate or illegitimate opportunities within the social structure.

The belief that all behavior, including criminal behavior, is learned led Edwin Sutherland to develop the theory of differential association, one of the most recognized of all sociological theories. According to Sutherland, criminal behavior is learned through socialization in small groups and involves all the processes involved in the learning of any kind of behavior. Social control theorists, who have commanded significant attention in the study of criminal behavior, also look at the socialization process, but they focus on the lack of a sufficient development of inner controls as an explanation of delinquent and criminal behavior.

The final section focused on attempts to explain female criminality and the careers of habitual criminals. In a sense these two categories represent the extremes in criminal behavior. Official data indicate that women constitute a very small percentage of arrests for serious crimes. The combination of official data and self-reports indicates that habitual criminals account for a very large percentage of serious crimes. Scholars disagree on the causes of female criminality and career criminality.

The problems in explanation do not mean that research is meaningless, but they indicate that we must be careful in drawing conclusions about research on the causes of criminal behavior. Continued efforts to develop systematic theories and to test those theories empirically should be given high priority in the criminal justice system.[75] Explaining criminal behavior by any or all of these theories may require that, in addition to analyzing the behavior of the criminal, researchers must consider the situation in which the behavior occurs and the behavior of victims or potential victims. The next chapter focuses on victims of crime.

STUDY QUESTIONS

1. What is meant by *deterrence*? What did the classical theorists contribute to our understanding of the concept?

2. How was the classical approach altered by the neoclassical thinkers? The positivists?

3. What is ecology? How has it been related to crime?

4. What is meant by *anomie*? How does the concept relate to crime?

5. Compare the contributions of the various subculture theorists.

6. What is the difference between pluralist conflict theory and critical criminology? How do those approaches compare to labeling theory?

7. What is social control theory?

8. What is differential association theory?

9. How would you compare female criminality to male criminality?

10. What is the relevance of studying career criminals?

11. What is the relationship between drug abuse and crime?

12. What are the problems with assuming that criminal behavior can be explained by any of the approaches discussed in this chapter?

ENDNOTES

1. Albert K. Cohen, cited in Herbert A. Block and Frank T. Flynn, *Delinquency: The Juvenile Offender in Society Today* (New York: Random House, 1956), p. 60.

2. See David J. Pittman and C. Wayne Gordon, *Revolving Door* (New York: Free Press, 1968); and H. Laurence Ross, *Deterring the Drinking Driver:* *Legal Policy and Social Control* (Lexington, Mass.: Lexington Books, 1982).

3. See Jack P. Gibbs, *Crime, Punishment and Deterrence* (New York: Elsevier Science Publishing Co., 1975); and Franklin E. Zimring and Gordon J. Hawkins, *Deterrence: The Legal Threat in Crime Control* (Chicago: University of Chicago Press,

1973). For a discussion of methodological problems of research in this area, see John Hagan, ed., *Deterrence Reconsidered: Methodological Innovations* (Berkeley, Calif.: Sage Publications, 1982).

4. Harold G. Grasmick and Donald E. Green, "Legal Punishment, Social Disapproval and Internalization as Inhibitors of Illegal Behavior," *Journal of Criminal Law and Criminology* 71 (Fall 1980): 325–35.

5. For a review of the literature, see Jerry Parker and Harold G. Grasmick, "Linking Actual and Perceived Certainty of Punishment," *Criminology* 17 (November 1979): 366–79. See also H. Frances Pestello, "Deterrence: A Reconceptualization," *Crime and Delinquency* 30 (October 1984): 593–609.

6. Gary W. Sykes, Gennaro F. Vito, and Karen McElrath, "Jail Populations and Crime Rates: An Exploratory Analysis," *Journal of Police Science and Administration* 15 (March 1987): 13. See also Peter Greenwood, *Selective Incapacitation: A Method of Using our Prisons More Effectively*, National Institute of Justice Reports (Washington, D.C.: U.S. Government Printing Office, 1984), pp. 4, 6–7.

7. Cesare Beccaria, *An Essay On Crime and Punishments* [1764], trans. Henry Paolucci (Indianapolis: Bobbs-Merrill, 1963). For a scathing critique, see Graeme Newman, *Just and Painful: A Case for the Corporal Punishment of Criminals* (New York: Macmillan Publishing Co., 1983), pp. 71–72 (2d ed., 1987).

8. Stephen Schafer, *Theories in Criminology* (New York: Random House, 1969), p. 123.

9. Cesare Lombroso, *Crime, Its Causes and Remedies*, trans. H.P. Horton (Boston: Little, Brown, 1911). For a discussion of modern positivism, see Michael Gottfredson and Travis Hirschi, eds., *Positive Criminology* (Beverly Hills, Calif.: Sage Publishers, 1987).

10. "Defective Gene Tied to Form of Manic-Depressive Illness," *New York Times* (26 February 1987), p. 1, referring to the works of scientists at the Miami School of Medicine in Florida, the Massachusetts Institute of Technology, and the Yale University School of Medicine.

11. "All About Twins," *Newsweek* (23 November 1987), p. 58.

12. "A User's Guide to Hormones," *Newsweek* (12 January 1987), p. 52.

13. "Exploring the Traits of Twins," *Time* (12 January 1987), p. 63. For earlier criminological explanations utilizing the body-type approach, see W. H. Sheldon, *The Varieties of Human Physique: An Introduction to Constitutional Psychology* (New York: Harper and Row, 1942); and Sheldon Glueck and Eleanor Glueck, *Physique and Delinquency* (New York: Harper and Row, 1956). For more recent developments, see Juan B. Cortes with Florence M. Gatti, *Delinquency and Crime: A Biopsychosocial Approach* (New York: Seminar Press, 1972).

14. See Sarnoff A. Mednick and Jan Volavka, "Biology and Crime," in Norval Morris and Michael Tonry, eds., *Crime and Justice: An Annual Review of Research*, vol. 2 (Chicago: University of Chicago Press, 1980), pp. 103–4. See also David C. Rowe, "Sibling Interaction and Self-Reported Delinquent Behavior: A Study of 265 Twin Pairs," *Criminology* 23 (May 1985): 223–40; Rowe, "Genetic and Environmental Components of Antisocial Behavior: A Study of 265 Twin Pairs," *Criminology* 24 (August 1986): 513–32.

15. See "Sociobiology Yields Fresh Insights into the Behavior of Animals: Application of Theories to Humans Is Contested," *New York Times* (15 October 1985), p. 18; and F. H. Marsh and Janet Katz, *Biology, Crime, and Ethics—A Study of Biological Explanations for Criminal Behavior* (Cincinnati, Ohio: Anderson Publishing Co., 1986).

16. See John H. Beckstrom, *Sociobiology and the Law: The Biology of Altruism in the Courtroom of the Future* (Champaign: University of Illinois Press, 1985).

17. James Q. Wilson and Richard J. Herrnstein, *Crime & Human Nature* (New York: Simon and Schuster, 1985).

18. Joseph Gusfield, review of *Crime and Human Nature* in *Science* 231 (January 1986): 414.

19. See, for example, Clifford R. Shaw and Henry D. McKay, *Juvenile Delinquency and Urban Areas*, rev. ed. (Chicago: University of Chicago Press, 1972); Roland J. Chilton, "Continuity in Delinquency Area Research: A Comparison of Studies for Baltimore, Detroit, and Indianapolis," *American Sociological Review* 29 (February 1946): 71–83; and Bernard Lander, *Towards an Understanding of Juvenile Delinquency* (New York: Columbia University Press, 1954). For a discussion of the conclusions of the Chicago ecological school, see Clifford R. Shaw et al., *Delinquency Areas* (Chicago: University of Chicago Press, 1929), pp. 198–204.

20. Wilson and Herrnstein, *Crime and Human Nature*, pp. 335, 336.

21. See, for example, Allan V. Horwitz, "The Economy and Social Pathology," *Annual Review of Sociology* 10 (1984): 95–119.

22. See David Cantor and Kenneth C. Land, "Employment and Crime Rates in the Post-World War II United States: A Theoretical and Empirical Analysis," *American Sociological Review* 50 (1985): 317–32.

23. See George A. Galster and Laure A. Scaturo, "The U.S. Criminal Justice System: Unemployment and the Severity of Punishment," *Journal of Research in Crime and Delinquency* 22 (1985): 163–89.

24. Robert Nash Parker and Allan V. Horwitz, "Unemployment, Crime, and Imprisonment: A Panel Approach," *Criminology* 24 (November 1986): 751–73. See also Theodore G. Chiricos, "Rates of Crime and Unemployment: An Analysis of Aggregate Research Evidence," *Social Problems* 34 (1987): 187–212; and Theodore G. Chiricos and Edmond J. True, "Unemployment and Property Crime: Aggregate Effects in the 1970's," paper presented at the 37th Annual Meeting of the Society for the Study of Social Problems, August 1987, Chicago.

25. See William R. Avison and Pamela L. Loring, "Population Diversity and Cross-National Homicide: The Effects of Inequality and Heterogeneity," *Criminology* 24 (November 1986): 733–49. See also Peter M. Blau, *Inequality and Heterogeneity* (New York: Free Press, 1977); and Harvey Krahn et al., "Income Equality and Homicide Rates: Cross-National Data and Criminological Theories," *Criminology* 24 (1986): 269–295.

26. Steven F. Messner and Kenneth Tardiff, "Economic Inequality and Levels of Homicide: An Analysis of Urban Neighborhoods," *Criminology* 24 (May 1986): 297–317.

27. David Brownfield, "Social Class and Violent Behavior," *Criminology* 24 (1986): 421–38.

28. See Rodney Stark, "Deviant Places: A Theory of the Ecology of Crime," *Criminology* 25 (November 1987): 893–909.

29. For a discussion of Durkheim's theory of anomie, see Émile Durkheim, *The Division of Labour in Society*, paperback ed. (New York: Free Press, 1964), pp. 374–88; and Durkheim, *The Rules of Sociological Method* [1938] (New York: Free Press, 1964), p. 66.

30. Robert K. Merton, *Social Theory and Social Structure*, enlarged ed. (New York: Free Press, 1968).

31. Edward Sagarin, *Deviants and Deviance: An Introduction to the Study of Disvalued People and Behavior* (New York: Holt, Rinehart and Winston, 1975), pp. 108–9.

32. Catherine E. Ross and John Mirowsky, "Normlessness, Powerlessness, and Trouble with the Law," *Criminology* 24 (May 1987): 272.

33. Albert K. Cohen, *Delinquent Boys: The Culture of the Gang* (New York: Free Press, 1955).

34. Gresham M. Sykes and David Matza, "Techniques of Neutralization: A Theory of Delinquency," in Marvin E. Wolfgang et al., eds., *The Sociology of Crime and Delinquency*, 2d ed. (New York: John Wiley and Sons, 1970), pp. 292–99, quotation on pp. 295 (emphasis omitted) and 298. For the results of a more recent test of this theory, see Robert S. Agnew, "Neutralizing the Impact of Crime," *Criminal Justice and Behavior* 12 (June 1985): 221–39. For a recent analysis of neutralization theory, see John E. Hamlin, "The Misplaced Role of Rational Choice in Neutralization Theory," *Criminology* 26 (August 1988): 425–38.

35. Richard A. Cloward and Lloyd E. Ohlin, *Delinquency and Opportunity: A Theory of Delinquent Gangs* (New York: Free Press, 1960), pp. 161–71, 175, 186.

36. Walter B. Miller, "Lower-Class Culture as a Generating Milieu of Gang Delinquency," in Wolfgang et al., eds., *Sociology of Crime and Delinquency*, pp. 351–63.

37. Gwynn Nettler, *Explaining Crime*, 3d ed., (New York: McGraw-Hill Book Co., 1984), p. 246.

38. Frederic M. Thrasher, *The Gang* [1963], abridged ed. (Chicago: University of Chicago Press, 1972).

39. "Chicago's Gang Warfare," *Newsweek* (28 January 1985).

40. "The Drug Gangs," *Newsweek* (28 March 1988), p. 23.

41. Ruth Horowitz, "Community Tolerance of Gang Violence," *Social Problems* 34 (December 1987): 449. See also Horowitz, *Honor and the American Dream* (New Brunswick, N.J.: Rutgers University Press, 1983). For a more recent study of Chicago gangs, see G. David Curry and Irving A. Spergel, "Gang Homicide, Delinquency, and Community," *Criminology* 26 (August 1988): 381–405.

42. Anne Campbell, "Self Definitions by Rejection: The Case of Gang Girls," *Social Problems* 34 (December 1987): 451–66; Campbell, *The Girls in the Gang* (New York: Basil Blackwell, 1984)

43. See Thorsten Sellin, *Culture, Conflict, and Crime* (New York: Social Science Research Council, Bulletin No. 41, 1938). For a brief but excellent recent article on Sellin, see Peter P. Lejins, "Thorsten Sellin: A Life Dedicated to Criminology," *Criminology* 25 (November 1987): 975–88.

44. See Austin T. Turk, *Criminality and the Legal Order* (Chicago: Rand McNally and Co., 1971); and Turk, *Political Criminality: The Defiance and Defense of Authority* (Beverly Hills, Calif.: Sage Publications, 1982).

45. See Michael Lynch and W. Byron Groves, *A Primer in Radical Criminology* (New York: Harrow and Heston, 1986).

46. Gresham M. Sykes, "The Rise of Critical Criminology," *Journal of Criminal Law and Criminology* 65 (June 1974): 212–13.

47. Howard S. Becker, *Outsiders: Studies in the Sociology of Deviance* (New York: Free Press, 1963), p. 9.

48. Stuart L. Hills, *Crime, Power and Morality* (Scranton, Pa.: Chandler, 1971), pp. 19–21. See also Joan Petersilia, "Racial Disparities in the Criminal Justice System: A Summary," *Crime and Delinquency* 31 (1985): 15–34; and Roland Chilton and Jim Galvin, "Race, Crime and Criminal Justice," *Crime and Delinquency* 31 (1985): 3–14.

49. Charles T. Tittle, "Labelling and Crime: An Empirical Evaluation," Chapter 6 in Walter R. Gove, ed., *The Labelling of Deviance* (New York: Holsted Press, 1975), p. 158.

50. For a recent study, see Gordon Basemore, "Delinquent Reform and the Labeling Perspective," *Criminal Justice and Behavior* 12 (June 1985): 131–69.

51. Edwin H. Sutherland and Donald R. Cressey, *Principles of Criminology*, 10th ed. (Philadelphia: Lippincott, 1978), pp. 80–82.

52. Ibid., p. 82. For recent analyses of differential association, see the special issue of *Crime and Delinquency* (July 1988), published after the 1987 death of Donald Cressey.

53. See Donald R. Cressey, "The Theory of Differential Association: An Introduction," *Social Problems* 8 (Summer 1960): 3.

54. Nettler, *Explaining Crime*, p. 289, emphasis in the original.

55. Travis Hirschi, *Causes of Delinquency* (Berkeley and Los Angeles: University of California Press, 1969), p. 10.

56. Ibid., pp. 230–31.

57. Ibid., pp. 54, 66.

58. Ibid., pp. 230–31. For other analyses of social control theory, see Robert Agnew, "Social Control Theory and Delinquency: A Longitudinal Test," *Criminology* 23 (February 1985): 47–62; Randy L. LaGrange and Helene Raskin White, "Age Differences in Delinquency: A Test of Theory," *Criminology* 23 (February 1985): 19–46; and Donald Black, ed., *Toward a General Theory of Social Control* (New York: Academic Press, 1983).

59. Freda Adler, *Sisters in Crime: The Rise of the New Female Criminal* (New York: McGraw-Hill Book Co., 1975), pp. 19–20.

60. See, for example, Richard Deming, *Women: The New Criminals* (Nashville: Thomas Nelson, 1977).

61. Federal Bureau of Investigation, *Crime in the United States: Uniform Crime Reports, 1987* (Washington, D.C.: U.S. Government Printing Office, 1988), p. 164.

62. M. Douglas Anglin and Yin-ing Hser, "Addicted Women and Crime," *Criminology* 25 (May 1987): 393.

63. Darrell J. Steffensmeier, "Crime and the Contemporary Woman: An Analysis of Changing Levels of Female Property Crime, 1960–75," *Social Forces* 57 (December 1978): 566–84.

64. *Uniform Crime Reports, 1986*, p. 164.

65. See, for example, Merry Morash, "Gender, Peer Group Experiences, and Seriousness of Delinquency," *Journal of Research in Crime and Delinquency* 23 (February 1986): 43–67.

66. See the works of Vernetta D. Young, "Gender Expectations and Their Impact on Black Female Offenders and Victims," *Justice Quarterly* 3 (September 1986): 305–27; and John H. Laub and M. Joan McDermott, "An Analysis of Serious Crime by Young Black Women," *Criminology* 23 (February 1985): 81–98.

67. See Ronald Barri Flowers, *Women and Criminality: The Woman as Victim, Offender, and Practitioner* (Westport, Conn.: Greenwood Press, 1987); Clarice Feinman, *Women in the Criminal Justice System*, 2d ed. (New York: Praeger Publishers, 1985); and William Wilbanks, "Are Female Felons Treated More Leniently by the Criminal Justice System?" *Justice Quarterly* 3 (December 1986): 517–29.

68. *Criminal Justice Research at Rand* (Santa Monica, Calif.: Rand Corporation, January 1985), p. 4. See also Joan Petersilia, *Criminal Career Research: A Review of Recent Evidence*, in Norval Morris and Michael Tonry, eds., *Crime and Justice*, vol. 2 (Chicago: University of Chicago Press, 1980); Petersilia et al., *Criminal Careers of Habitual Felons* (Santa Monica, Calif.: Rand Corporation, 1977); Petersilia, *Who Commits Crime: A Survey of Prison Inmates* (Cambridge, Mass.: Odelgeschlager, Gunn, and Hain, 1981); and Donna Hamparian et al., *The Young Criminal Years of the Violent Few*, U.S. Department of Justice (Washington, D.C.: U.S. Government Printing Office, 1985). See also Michael Gottfredson and Travis Hirschi, "Career Criminals and Selective Incapacitation," in Joseph E. Scott and Travis Hirschi, eds., *Controversial Issues in Crime and Justice* (Beverly Hills, Calif.: Sage Publications, 1988), pp. 199–209.

69. Mednick and Volavka, "Biology and Crime," pp. 143–44, emphasis in the original.

70. Marvin E. Wolfgang, *Patterns in Criminal Homicide* (Philadelphia: University of Pennsylvania Press, 1958).

71. James J. Collins, *Alcohol Use and Criminal Behavior: An Executive Summary*, National Institute of Justice (Washington, D.C.: U.S. Government Printing Office, November 1981), p. 32.

72. Bureau of Justice Statistics Bulletin, *Prisoners and Alcohol* (Washington, D.C.: U.S. Government Printing Office, Jaunary 1983), p. 1.

73. Summarized in Bernard A. Gropper, *Probing the Links between Drugs and Crime*, National Institute of Justice (Washington, D.C.: U.S. Government Printing Office, February 1985).

74. See, for example, Richard E. Johnson et al., "The Role of Peers in the Complex Etiology of Adolescent Drug Use," *Criminology* 25 (May 1987): 323–40; and James D. Orcutt, "Differential Association and Marijuana Use: A Closer Look at Sutherland (with a Little Help from Becker)," *Criminology* 25 (May 1987): 341–58.

75. Recent developments in sociological theory are covered in more detail in a recent journal that focuses its entire issue on theories; see volume 25 of *Criminology* (November 1987).

Victims of Crime

OUTLINE

KEY TERMS

On April 5, 1988, Kuwait Airways Flight 422, while in route from Bangkok to Kuwait, was seized by armed gunmen who held the plane and 31 hostages for 15 days. Other hostages were released earlier; two men were killed. The hijackers were demanding the release of 17 Shi'ite Moslems who were imprisoned in Kuwait after being convicted of the 1983 bomb attacks on the French and American embassies in Kuwait. They threatened to kill all their hostages. After an undisclosed agreement, the hostages were freed.

In May 1982, six gunmen burst into the Sea Crest Diner in Old Westbury, New York. The diner was crowded with people ranging in age from 16 to the early 60s. Approximately 80 people were robbed of their jewelry and cash, forced to undress, and then told to engage in sexual acts. Women who did not have male companions were told to engage in sex with other women; couples were singled out and commanded to perform specific sexual acts; one woman was raped; two people were shot. One victim said, "The degradation and humiliation seemed to transcend the robbery." Victims reacted with disbelief, hysteria, reality,

and then anger. Men as well as women responded like victims of rape. According to one counselor, "They are afraid to be out alone; they experience a loss of independence and . . . guilt feelings. They feel like there was something they could do." Five men pleaded guilty to terrorizing victims at the Sea Crest, at one other diner, and at a private home. They were sentenced to 15 to 30 years in prison.[1]

Around the same time that those crimes were committed, the following crimes also occurred. Henry, a 21-year-old black man, was seriously wounded by Chris, a black acquaintance, after the two got into a fight at a bar. Police were called; Chris was arrested, but he was never charged with a crime. Cathy, who lived in a high-crime area, returned home to find her front door open, her house in disarray, and her television and video recorder missing. She called the police, who investigated the crime, but no suspects were arrested. Eric, a 50-year-old middle-class professional, was apprehended for sexually molesting his 5-year-old granddaughter.

INTRODUCTION

The crimes in the CJA represent many of the points that will be made in this chapter. The crimes that occurred on Flight 422 and in New York received extensive media attention. When the judge sentenced the five defendants in the Sea Crest Diner case, he said, "These men are guilty of the most gross, base, horrendous crimes conceived by man. . . . They should serve every single last possible day that is consistent with the law." The District Attorney argued that we are all victims "of these rampaging thugs. Of course, the most obvious victims of these five spineless parasites . . . are the unfortunate individuals who fell prey to their self-indulgent, immoral, inhumane and antisocial crime spree."[2]

We may all be victims of the Sea Crest crimes or of the hijacking of Flight 422. It may be that such random violence is the type of crime people most fear, but these crimes do not represent the ones we are most likely to experience. The crimes committed against Cathy (property crime) and Henry (violent crimes more often involve a black male assailant and a black male victim) are more typical of victimization in this country, but those crimes were not even reported by the media. Eric's alleged sexual molestation of his granddaughter was reported widely and represents what some think is an increasing crime, sexual abuse of children. But it is also a crime that often is not reported to authorities.

This chapter discusses these and other types of victimization. After a brief historical overview, the chapter focuses on victimization data to identify the victims of crime. An analysis of the relationships between victims and offenders is an important part of that discussion. The discussion then looks briefly at how people react to victimization and the threat of victimization.

The second major part of the chapter focuses on three categories of victims: the elderly, children, and women. These categories were not chosen because they represent most victims but because in recent years the popular media, as well as social scientists and government commissions, have focused considerable attention on them. Legislatures and courts also have made changes to encourage the cooperation of these victims in the criminal justice system and to provide compensation for these and other victims of crime.

THE STUDY OF VICTIMS

Victims of crime historically have been ignored by scholars and researchers in criminology and by institutions that could assist them. In the past decade attention has been given to the study of victims and providing services for them. Professional societies such as the National Organization for Victim Assistance (NOVA) have been instrumental in passing federal and state legislation concerning victims. NOVA has provided assistance to thousands of victims in this country and works directly with local organizations to improve services at that level. Workshops on **victimology** have increased knowledge and understanding of the problems. Scholarly researchers writing on victimology have also found a forum for their writings in professional journals focusing on this important topic.[3]

The Reagan administration approached the problems of victims by appointing a Task Force on Victims of Crime. That task force submitted its final report to the president in December 1982. In the introduction to that report, the task force chairman referred to the president's reasons for emphasizing the needs of victims:

> [President Reagan] recognized that in the past these victims have pleaded for justice and their pleas have gone unheeded. They have needed help and their needs have gone unattended. The neglect of crime victims is a national disgrace. The President is committed to ending that neglect and to restoring balance to the administration of justice.[4]

Concern with the needs of victims has led to national legislation on their behalf. In response to the Victim and Witness Protection Act of 1982, a national statute, the United States Attorney General's office has issued detailed guidelines concerning the treatment of crime victims and witnesses by the prosecutors and investigators of the Department of Justice. These guidelines will lead to the protection of the privacy of victims and witnesses and to the provision of medical and social services as well as counseling. Notification of court proceedings, restitution, and other programs available for the assistance of victims and witnesses are also provided. Many states have passed legislation to aid victims. But like many other reforms in the criminal justice system, legislation aimed at assisting victims has also created legal problems. Some of those problems will be discussed in this chapter.

DATA ON VICTIMS

Concern for victims of crime must begin with the collection of data on victims. Chapter 2 noted that one method of gathering data on crime is to ask samples of the population whether they have been victims of crime during a specified period. This is the procedure taken by the Bureau of Justice Statistics (BJS), which publishes the **National Crime Survey** (NCS) data.

National Crime Survey: Overview of the Data

In September 1983, the BJS issued a special report containing a brief analysis of the 1982 NCS data. The 1982 data, compared to 1981, with a general downturn of 1.7 million victimizations, represented "one of the most sweeping, single-direction changes to have taken place since the program's inception. Virtually all categories of crime contributed to the reduction, and there were no statistically significant increases."[5]

In October 1987, the NCS data indicated that reported victimizations had continued to decline and had reached the "lowest level in the 13-year history of the NCS, about 18% below the . . . victimizations recorded in the peak year of 1981." The October 1988 report, however, indicated an increase in the most recent data, 1987, which rose 1.8 percent over 1986. Figure 4.1 shows the victimization trends between 1973 and 1987. The overall increase in victimizations was due mainly to an increase in household crimes, which rose 2.3 percent from the 1986 level.[6]

Characteristics of Victims

The NCS data include information on characteristics such as the age, sex, and race of crime victims.[7] Analyses of data on victimization for years have indicated differences in the rates of victimization of specific groups within the population. Young people, males, blacks, Hispanics, divorced or separated, unemployed, and those with an income of less than $3,000 are the most frequent victims of violent crime.

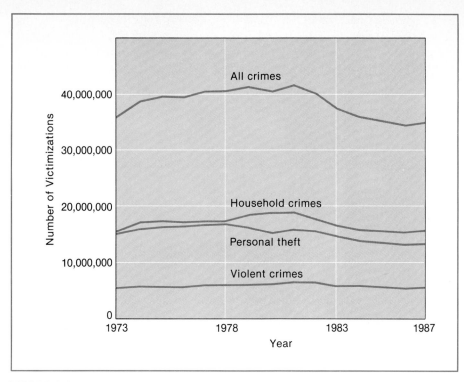

FIGURE 4.1
Victimization Trends: 1973–1987. *Source:* Bureau of Justice Statistics, *Criminal Victimization, 1987* (Washington, D.C.: U.S. Department of Justice, October 1988), p. 1.

Trend data on victimization indicate that men were much more likely than women to be victims of violent crime, with the rates of robbery and assault twice as high for them. Rates of personal larceny without contact also were higher for men. For crimes of violence or theft, the elderly were least frequently the victims, and those persons in the age group from 12 to 24 were most frequently crime victims. The rates of victimization decrease with each age group after the age of 24; this pattern holds when sex is also considered a variable. Males in the age group from 12 to 24 were particularly vulnerable to the crimes of assault, robbery, or personal larceny.

Blacks were far more often the victims of crime than whites but had only slightly higher rates than members of other minority races. When the variables of race and sex are compared, the highest rates of victimization for violent crimes are among black males, followed by white males, black females, and white females.

Table 4.1 contains a listing of characteristics of crime victims as indicated by the literature on victimization. But for most people, data on victimization have little meaning unless they are interpreted to show the *probabilities* of becoming a crime victim.

Friends and relatives may also be viewed as victims of the crimes committed on their loved ones. Here friends of Nicholas Corwin, an elementary school child killed during a shooting rampage at his school, attend his funeral. (Mark Elias/AP Wide World)

PROBABILITIES OF BECOMING A VICTIM OF CRIME

A careful reading of Table 4.1 indicates some factors that are important in determining the probability that you will become a crime victim. Several of those findings indicate that the amount of crime is associated with the area of the city in which you live. No area is immune to crime, but living within the areas of high mobility and disorganization—areas often located near the center of the city—will increase the probability that you will become a crime victim. Spending time in public places, appearing vulnerable and desirable, and living alone or as a female single parent are other factors that increase your chances. But what does all this mean? The data are more meaningful if analyzed using sociological theories, some of which were discussed in the last chapter.

The ecological approach looks at the relationship between people and their environment. This approach has been refined by Oscar Newman, who developed the concept of defensible space. According to Newman, crimes could be reduced by an alteration in the physical environment in which people live. Residential environments inhibit crime when they are a "physical expression of a social fabric that defends itself." This may be done by increasing physical security to the point that the area appears to be an "environment under the control of its residents." It might also be done by creating the illusion that neighbors are watching the area carefully for signs of potential criminals. Lighting is also important. Lighting makes detection of criminal activity easier; well-lighted areas are less likely to become targets of criminal activities than areas with little or no lighting.[8]

TABLE 4.1

Who Are the Victims of Crime?

1. In general, people are less likely to be victims of crime the farther they live from America's central cities. . . .
2. Men are more frequently robbed by strangers than women are.
3. Men who live alone, and unrelated people living in households, suffer disproportionately from robbery. . . .
4. Households headed by women suffer above-average victimization by burglary and larceny, and children in such households experience the highest rates of aggravated assault of all demographic categories. . . .
5. At all levels of income, blacks suffer more violent attacks than whites or members of other ethnic groups. . . .
6. Whites suffer less from burglary as their income rises, but blacks suffer more from burglary at higher income levels. . . .
7. For whites of both sexes, victimization by violence decreases from the city outward; for blacks of both sexes, rates of violent victimization remain constant by distance from cities. . . .
8. According to victims' reports, blacks are overrepresented as offenders in rape, robbery, assault, and personal larceny. . . .
9. The amount of interracial crime varies among American cities as a function of the amount of black criminality. . . .
10. The more time a person spends in public places, the more likely he or she is to suffer personal victimization. . . .
11. Victimization is not distributed randomly; some people experience "more than their share." . . .
12. The chance of being a victim of crime increases among people who share the demographic characteristics of more likely offenders. . . .
13. Predators choose their victims from among persons who appear vulnerable and desirable, and who are convenient. . . .

Source: Gwynn Nettler, *Explaining Crime,* 3d ed. (New York: McGraw-Hill Book Co., 1984), pp. 73–74, italics omitted.

Social integration might also explain vulnerability to criminal activity. The concept of anomie, as developed by Durkheim and Merton and discussed in Chapter 3, may be useful in explaining victimization. Neighbors who do not interact frequently with each other may be less inclined to watch for criminal activity in the area, and criminal activity is less likely to be detected quickly.

A sociological theory not discussed earlier is the routine activity theory of Lawrence Cohen and Marcus Felson. Cohen and Felson explain crime as the convergence of three elements: people who are motivated to commit crimes, suitable targets for criminal activity, and an absence of people to prevent the criminal activity. For example, a person who is inclined to commit crime may do so upon seeing an unlocked, partially open door disclosing a television set that could be carried away easily. The crime is even more likely if the potential offender knows that no one is home or likely to come home. This approach may explain the higher rates of victimization for property crimes among women who are heads of households, men who live alone, and unrelated people living together. These people frequently are gone from home, thus leaving the home without what Cohen and Felson call *capable guardians*.[9]

These and other theories related to the opportunity to commit crime should not be interpreted to mean that victims cause the crime. A woman who is raped while hitchhiking does not cause the rape, nor should she be blamed for that crime. What the theories suggest is the potential for victims and potential offenders to converge in certain circumstances with the result of a greater probability that crime will occur. But it is also important to look beyond the circumstances under which the potential victim and potential offender may come together and consider the relationship between the victim and the offender.

Relationship Between Victims and Offenders

The relationship between offender and victim is an important variable in some crimes. Violence in the form of assault or murder is usually preceded by social interaction, and physical violence is more likely if both the offender and the victim define the situation as one calling for violence. If only one is prone to physical violence, the altercation probably will not become a physical one. In this sense, the victim may contribute to his or her own injury or death.

Often the social interactions have been preceded by numerous other interactions, some of these recent. In an earlier study of homicide victims, Marvin Wolfgang found that one-fourth of the victims precipitated the event that led to their deaths. These victims were the first to strike a blow, show force with a deadly weapon, or use that weapon.[10] Many rape victims have also had prior contact with their assailants.[11] Chapter 2 noted that evidence of substance abuse is often found in both victims and offenders.

The 1985 NCS data indicate that 61 percent of violent crimes were perpetrated by strangers. BJS cautions, however, that there is good reason to suspect that domestic violence is underreported because victims do not wish to have their family members arrested. If that is true, it is possible that most violent crimes are committed by friends, family members, or acquaintances.

Men are much more likely than women (69 versus 48 percent) and whites are more likely than blacks to be attacked by strangers. Robberies usually are committed by strangers (three out of four), as are 57 percent of all forcible rapes. Violent crimes against persons in lower-income groups are more likely to be committed by nonstrangers than violent crimes against higher-income groups.[12]

Risk of Violent Crime

The chances that you will become a victim of violent crime cannot be determined from the victimization data collected and analyzed by the BJS, because not all violent crimes are covered by the NCS data. The BJS recently developed a new measure of the risk of becoming a victim of violent crime. The Crime Risk Index discloses the percentage of the population that was victimized by violent crime in a given year.

Using this new index in an analysis of data from the five-year period of 1978–1982, BJS reported in 1985 that Americans have a 3 percent chance each year of becoming victims of the violent crimes of murder, manslaughter by drunk drivers, kidnapping, child abuse, or other violent crimes not measured by the National Crime Survey. The 3 percent figure applies only to a given year. Over a lifetime, the chances of becoming a victim of rape, robbery, or assault would be much higher.[13]

In its most recent publication at the time of this writing, the BJS submitted the following report based on 1975–1984 annual victimization data:

1. Four out of six people will be victims of the violent crimes of rape, robbery, and assault (or of attempts to commit these crimes) at some time during their lives.
2. Approximately one-half of the population will be victimized by violent crimes more than once.
3. When two or more violent crimes are considered, black men are almost twice as likely as black women and more than three times as likely as white females to be victimized.
4. Nearly one of every twelve females will be the victim of forcible rape or attempted rape. One out of every nine black females will fall into this category.
5. Blacks are almost twice as likely as whites and men are 70 percent more likely than women to be victimized by robbery.
6. Nearly all of the American population will be victimized by personal theft at least once; approximately seven of every eight will be victimized three or more times.
7. Attempted assaults will victimize about three of every four people, with men far more likely than women to be crime victims.[14]

THE COST OF CRIME

Economic Loss

The cost of crime is usually measured by economic loss to crime victims, but until recently such data were not available. BJS data indicate that the total economic loss for one year was $10.9 billion. That figure includes the cost of property taken, property damaged, and medical expenses. Of the $10.9 billion, 75 percent resulted from property crimes against the household. Household burglary accounted for more than one-third of the total economic loss. More than 93 percent of the $10.9 billion occurred without contact between victims and offenders. Only 2 percent of the total loss involved medical expenses.[15]

These BJS figures on the economic cost of crime to direct victims do not cover the cost of crime to society. The increase in costs for other elements of the criminal justice system is significant but not easily measured.

Neither do these data reflect the cost to society nor to individual crime victims not covered by the BJS survey. For example, the President's Commission on Organized Crime issued its final report in April 1986. According to that report, organized crime will take profits as high as $75 billion in 1986. On the average, each American will suffer a $77 loss through lost jobs and taxes, as well as face increased competition in the economy. Though the commission's report has generated controversy (the commission itself was characterized by internal disagreement), the report indicates some of the effects on this country of indirect victimization by criminal activity.[16]

BJS data do not include the effect on society or individuals of crimes committed by business organizations, computer crimes, or white-collar crimes. These types of crimes may involve far greater dollar losses than the crimes reported by the BJS and the UCR, but their effects are not very obvious to individual citizens. One final cost of crime is crucial, although it cannot be measured economically. The psychological and physical injuries sustained by crime victims may have a far greater effect on their lives than do their economic losses. The changes that crime victims and potential victims make in their life-styles are also important in analyzing the cost of crime.

THE FEAR OF CRIME AND CITIZENS' REACTIONS

In recent years, media attention to random, violent personal crime in this country has indicated that Americans have a great fear of crime. *Newsweek* described the year 1981 as "the year that mainstream America rediscovered violent crime . . . confirmation that random mayhem has spilled out of bounds and that a sanctuary can become a killing ground almost at whim."[17] The fear of violent crime by strangers who often pick their victims randomly led former Supreme Court Chief Justice Warren F. Burger to refer to the "reign of terror in American cities." One privately funded study of crime concluded that "the fear of crime is slowly paralyzing American society."[18]

Other reports disagree with these statements. Data reported by Wesley G. Skogan and Michael G. Maxfield, based on their intensive study of how people cope with crime, do not disclose widespread fear.[19] A BJS report of data gathered from 20,000 persons indicated that 32 percent felt their neighborhoods were very safe from crime, whereas 59 percent said they were fairly safe, and only 10 percent said they were unsafe. Ninety percent felt very or fairly safe at their places of work.[20]

The study by Skogan and Maxfield indicates that the fear of crime is not always correlated with the probability of crime. The greatest fear is exhibited by the elderly, but rates of victimization are much higher for the young than for the old. Likewise, rates are higher for men than for women, but more women than men indicate a fear of crime. The greater indication of fear expressed by women and the elderly may be a reaction to media presentations of violent personal crimes. It also may be true that personal crimes are not higher for these two groups of citizens precisely because they alter their life-styles to avoid situations that might be conducive to victimization.[21]

Life-Style Changes Spotlight 4.1 relates the facts of a violent personal crime against an elderly woman. The probability that an elderly person will be victimized in this way is not great, but for many elderly people, it is not the *probability* of becoming a victim that is crucial, but the *possibility*. For the elderly, a purse snatching may have a far more serious effect than it would have on younger victims. The elderly are more likely to be seriously injured in any altercation between the assailant and the victim. Such direct contact also may be much more frightening to an elderly person. The loss of money may be more serious to a person living on a fixed income. For the elderly, fear of crime often leads to severe changes in life-style, to the point that they refuse to leave their apartment or house.

Women may adjust their life-styles to decrease their chances of becoming crime victims. They often are advised by police and others to do so. In various cities police have reported that a high percentage of rapes are committed against victims who have been careless. They were walking alone at night, hitchhiking, sleeping in apartments with unlocked doors or windows, or going out with someone they met at a bar. Other women, because of their fear of crime, may avoid going places they would like to go and thereby reduce the probability that they will be victimized. But they also deprive themselves of a life-style they prefer. For them, one cost of crime is decreased personal freedom.

Women and the elderly are not the only ones who make changes in life-style because of a concern with crime. In early March 1986, the BJS released the results of a study of the measures taken by the 20,000 people in their survey the previous year. About 38 percent of the respondents indicated that they participate in neighborhood watch programs when

Although females, compared to males, are less frequently the victims of violent crime, they indicate more fear of becoming victims. (Sylvia Plachy)

SPOTLIGHT 4.1
AN ELDERLY VICTIM

She was on her way to mass on a sunny June day in 1981, happy that although she was ill, she was alive. She had lived long enough to see her children grow up and to enjoy her grandchildren. She was able to walk, despite her 78 years, and to enjoy the beautiful sunny day. She was traveling to Old Town in Chicago from her home on the South Side, where she had lived since she came to this country from Ireland in the 1920s. On that day she was saying her rosary as she held her beads, and did not hear the man approach her from behind. She feared no one, for it was 10:40 A.M. and a lot of people were around,

including the children playing at a nearby school. Those factors, however, made no difference to her assailant, for he obviously knew the odds were against getting caught when he attacked an older person. As he professionally kneed her in the back, she fell to the ground, stunned, while he grabbed her by the throat, turned her around and smashed her eyes, temporarily blinding her. He then threw her down, grabbed her purse, and escaped in his Cadillac. The robber got only $9 in cash and a Social Security check that was unsigned. The victim stopped payment before he could cash the check.

they are available. Seven percent of the households had burglar alarms. About one-third of the respondents either have a burglar alarm, participate in a neighborhood watch program, or engrave their valuables with an identification number. All these measures involve either money or time, both significant costs of crime.[22]

Following terrorist incidents during 1985–1988 in several foreign countries where Americans were visiting, many Americans changed their plans to travel abroad. The fear of crime may not have been the only reason for such changes, but it certainly was one factor along with the falling value of the American dollar. Although the dollar continued to fall in 1987, Americans in increasing numbers traveled abroad, and the figures rose again in 1988. The recent terrorist incidents perhaps produced only short-term fears.

The apparent increase in fear of crime, with resulting changes in lifestyle, has led some scholars to conclude that fear of crime is a serious problem. "Left unchecked, it can destroy the fabric of civilized society, causing us to become suspicious of each other, locking ourselves in our homes and offices, and relinquishing our streets to predators."[23]

The unrealistic fear of crime—that is, fear that exceeds the probability of crime—has now become a focus of research. The Police Foundation received a grant from the National Institute of Justice to study the problem and implement ways of reducing unrealistic fear of crime. Early reports indicate some success in this endeavor.[24] Before conclusions are drawn, more research is needed on the effect of crime on potential as well as actual crime victims. Some information is available on the reaction of particular types of victims. Because of the research attention given recently to the elderly, children, and women as victims of crime, attention will be given here to those categories of victims.

FOCUS ON TYPES OF VICTIMS

Although the elderly, children, and women constitute only a small percentage of the total victims of crime as measured by official data, special attention has been given to these three categories of victims. The lack of attention until recently may have been because these categories of people have not been involved in conducting studies of crime, but it may also be due to the hesitancy of these victims to report victimization. All the crimes discussed here are sensitive and difficult for some people to discuss; in some cases, such as incest, people react with total disbelief. This lack of comfort in discussing the types of criminal victimization may be a factor in the previous lack of attention given to these crimes.

Many of the crimes discussed in this section occur within the family and constitute a type of **domestic violence**. They may be interrelated, but crimes against the elderly, children, and women are not limited to the domestic scene.

The Elderly as Victims

The increasing percentage of the population classified as elderly may account for some of the current attention focused upon crimes against this group. It also may be that crimes against the elderly are actually increasing and the data on these crimes do not represent just an increased reporting of the crimes. The elderly are not frequently the victims of violent crimes, which constitute only 6 percent of crimes against the elderly. Robbery constitutes approximately 45 percent of those violent crimes. The two graphs in Figure 4.2 indicate that the most frequent crime against the elderly is personal larceny without contact and that the crimes against the elderly have been on the decline, at least according to BJS data.[25]

It is important to keep in mind during this discussion that official data show that most elderly are not victimized, and, according to a recent study, most elderly do not fear becoming the victims of crimes.[26] This does not mean that crimes against the elderly are not a critical problem. The official data do not include many of the crimes committed against the elderly by members of their own family. This type of crime has become the focus of recent research on the elderly and crime.[27]

We do not know the extent of family abuse of the elderly, but estimates run from between 500,000 and 1 million annually.[28] According to the chairman of a subcommittee to the House Select Committee on Aging, "domestic violence against the elderly is a burgeoning national scandal." Witnesses before that committee testified that abuse includes not only violent attacks upon the person of the elderly, but also such acts as withholding food, stealing their savings and social security checks, verbal abuse, and threats of sending the elderly family member to a nursing home.[29]

Violence against elderly parents has been referred to as the King Lear syndrome (after the aging character in Shakespeare's play who was mistreated by his two daughters), **granny bashing**, granslamming, parental abuse, and elder abuse. Unlike other forms of violence, this type cuts across socioeconomic and racial lines. "Professional families did it, working-class families did it, black families did it, and white families did it," says a geriatrics specialist who studied the problem.[30]

We do not know much about what causes abuse of elderly parents. It has been suggested that the roots of the problem may lie in child abuse, "for there is considerable evidence of intergenerational transmission of family violence. . . . Children reared in an environment of violence batter their children and spouses and in turn may find themselves exposed to violence in their latter years from their own children, who in turn were brought up by violent parents."[31] Therefore, it is important to look at the much more studied problem of child abuse.

Children as Victims

Children are frequently the victims of crime in our society. Some are abused by their parents or other relatives. The abuse may be physical,

Both personal and property crimes are especially feared by the elderly, many of whom change their lifestyles significantly in an attempt to avoid victimization. (F. Carter Smith/NYT)

nonsexual, sexual, or psychological. Children are also victimized by non-family members. This type of abuse frequently involves **sexual abuse**, both for the sake of personal gratification and for financial exploitation, as in the use of children in pornography.

Several cases of child abuse that recently have been reported are summarized in Spotlight 4.2. These cases are probably not typical of all

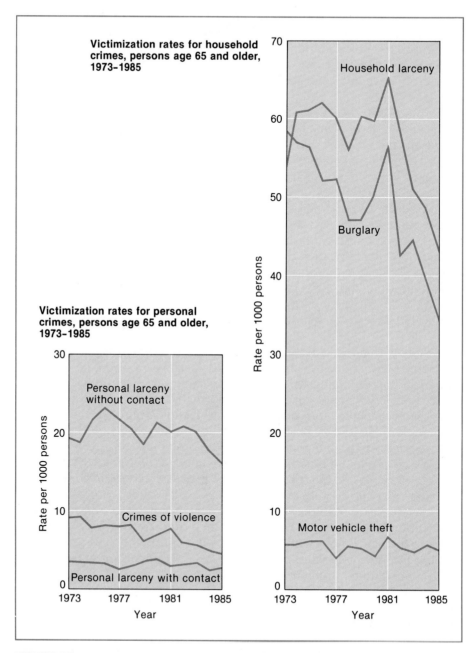

FIGURE 4.2
Characteristics of Crimes Against the Elderly. *Source:* Bureau of Justice Statistics, *Elderly Victims* (Washington, D.C.: U.S. Department of Justice, November 1987), p. 2.

1. Cheryl Pierson, 16, a high school cheerleader who claimed that her father sexually abused her for years, pleaded guilty to manslaughter after the death of her father. Pierson, who claimed she saw no other way out of her problems, was sentenced to six months in jail and five years probation. Her boyfriend, Sean Pica, whom she hired to kill her father, was sentenced to 8 to 24 years in prison.

2. Darlwin Carlisle, 9, had to have both legs amputated because of frost bite, suffered while she was locked in an unheated attic. Authorities, who charged Carlisle's mother with felony neglect, believe the child had been in the attic for several days.

3. Lisa Steinberg, 6, whose death was attributed to severe beatings by her adoptive parents, showed signs of physical abuse, but reports indicate that her teachers and social workers were not properly trained to detect child abuse. Lisa's 17-month-old brother, who was also in the custody of the couple charged with murdering Lisa, was found tied to a chair, drinking spoiled milk. Authorities now question the legality of the adoption of these children, and the boy's biological mother has been granted per-

manent custody of the child. Joel Steinberg was convicted of manslaughter in the beating death of Lisa.

4. Lou Ann Powell, a pregnant Chicago drug addict, allegedly traded one of her babies for $50 worth of cocaine. Authorities have charged Ms. Powell with the felony of child abandonment and are seeking to sever her legal ties to her two children.

5. In Tulsa, Oklahoma, in the summer of 1987, authorities found a 16-year-old boy chained to a bed that was soaked with urine and guarded by a German shephard. The boy is partially mentally retarded, diabetic, and autistic.

6. In Houston, Texas, a 7-year-old emaciated boy was found locked in a bathroom with two dogs. Authorities believe the boy had been there for at least four years. The child escaped through a bath-room window and went to a service station to report the situation. Houston police, indicating this was one of the worst cases of child abuse they had ever seen, arrested the parents who were charged with injury to a child.

---

that occur, but they illustrate that extreme abuse of children may not be detected until the child is killed, or in the case of Pierson, participates in killing a parent.

Parental Abuse of Children   The term **child abuse** usually refers to the abuse of children by their own parents or guardians. Such abuse has been called "the ultimate crime, the ultimate betrayal."[32] Although the term is diffi-cult to define, it generally refers to actions by parents who deliberately or inadvertently inflict physical harm on their children in contrast to cases of neglect, where the parent is passive.

Data on parental abuse of children are difficult to obtain because the behavior usually is not reported, but the incidents of such abuse are thought to be on the rise. In 1982 the reported incidence of child abuse in the United States increased by 10 percent, according to a survey of the 50 states conducted by the National Committee for Prevention of Child Abuse. The survey also disclosed that deaths attributed to child abuse increased by over 40 percent in many states.[33]

The National Committee for Prevention of Child Abuse reported in 1986 that during the first half of 1985 child abuse reports had increased by 9 percent but that the category of sexual abuse showed a 24 percent increase, compared to a 35 percent increase the previous year. The data for this survey came from 50 state Child Protective Service agencies.[34]

One study disclosed that boys are abused as frequently as girls and that, in approximately 60 percent of the cases of child abuse by parents, the mother is the perpetrator of the crime. High-income families are not immune to the problem, but reports of cases of child abuse are more extensive among low-income families, perhaps because those families are more frequently in contact with social welfare agencies whose personnel might report the crimes. Children of all ages are affected, but half of the reported cases in one study were of children under 6, a particularly important finding "because the younger the child the more serious the physical consequences of abuse and neglect." Of those who die from child abuse, 60 percent are under 2.[35]

Mothers are the most frequent child abusers in all kinds of abuse except sexual. Studies have not identified a particular type of mother who will most likely abuse a child, but she most often is a socially isolated person who probably came from a background of inadequate nurturing. She is a person who is not able to sublimate or redirect her anger. She has a low threshold for the typical activities of children and a poor concept of herself.[36]

These same characteristics also may be true of fathers, but their abuse of children more often is sexual than nonsexual. The crime of **incest,** sexual relations with a member of the immediate family, is often referred to as the crime no one talks about, but today it is gaining more attention, with approximately 50,000 cases of father–daughter incest reported each year. But the data are thought to be quite inaccurate because of the silence surrounding the crime.

In incest cases, children usually cooperate in the warning not to tell anyone about the sexual behavior. "Daddy's little girl is locked into a

Joel Steinberg, left, disbarred lawyer, was convicted of first-degree manslaughter in the battering death of Lisa Steinberg, his illegally adopted 6-year-old daughter. (Richard Drew/UPI Bettmann)

conspiracy of silence, torn between shame and a need to keep the family together, nurturing her father's adult needs while shrouding the behavior in secrecy." Retrospective studies of adult women indicate that one out of ten women were sexually abused by a member of their family.[37]

Abuse of Children by Friends and Strangers   Today more attention is being focused on the various kinds of abuse of children, along with an emphasis that the trusted family friend, or even a family member other than the parent, may become the abuser. The focus usually is on sexual abuse, specifically **statutory rape,** which involves sexual intercourse with the consent of a person considered by law to be too young to give consent.

A survey of 521 parents in Boston contained interesting information on the problem of sexual abuse. Most parents think the perpetrators of such crimes are strangers, a myth that may indicate why most parents do not warn their children about the possibility of sexual abuse by friends, siblings, parents, or other relatives. Nearly one parent in ten indicated that his or her own child had been the victim of sexual abuse or attempted abuse, whereas nearly half of the parents indicated that they knew a child who had been victimized sexually. Of those children, 37 percent were 6 or younger. Fifteen percent of the mothers and 6 percent of the fathers reported that they had been sexually abused as children, and in one-third of those cases, the abuse occurred before the child was 9 years old. Children of both sexes were abused, but the abuser was most often a man.[38]

Children also are exploited for sexual and financial reasons through pornography. In 1982 an affluent, divorced mother of five was arrested and charged with 13 felony counts of distributing child pornography and 2 misdemeanor counts of distributing obscene material. When police searched her home, they found stockpiles of files and magazines depicting sex involving children, adults, and animals. Although she was on public welfare, she had an estimated $500,000 annual net income from the sale of these materials. She controlled 80 percent of the child pornography market.[39] In 1984 the "Kiddie Porn Queen" pleaded guilty on two counts of mailing obscene material. She was sentenced to two 10-year prison terms and fined $20,000.

Prosecutions for "kiddie porn" may be very difficult, however. In 1988 the Supreme Judicial Court of Massachusetts ruled that a statute making it a crime knowingly to permit a child younger than 18 "to pose or be exhibited in a state of nudity . . . for the purpose of visual representation or reproduction in any book, magazine, motion picture film, photograph, or picture" was too broad and therefore unconstitutional.

In *Commonwealth v. Oakes*, defendant Douglas Oakes was successful in appealing his conviction under this statute. The pictures were described as nonpornographic, nonobscene, and not taken with the intent of commercial distribution. The photos pictured the stepdaughter nude from the waist up. The statute was found to be too broad since it would cover a parent who, for example, took a picture of a naked 1-year-old child "running on the beach or romping in a wading pool."[40]

Consequences of Violence Against Children   Many children who are the victims of violence exhibit violent behavior against other children and adults during their childhood. That some will turn on their own families is indicated by the Pierson case in Spotlight 4.2. Studies of juvenile offenders indicate that many were victims of child abuse or witnessed the abuse of other children. "Once violence begins in the home, it spreads like a cancer throughout society," with many of the victimized children becoming adults who abuse their own children.[41]

Not all researchers agree that abused children frequently become abusive parents. After reviewing 40 articles in professional journals, Yale child development psychologist Edward Zigler concluded that many of the studies were questionable because of the research methods utilized. According to Zigler, only 25 to 35 percent of abused children become abusers, and those who do not become abusers had at least one loving and caring parent.[42]

Abused and neglected children also suffer physical reactions. Many have significant impairment of neurological functions, retardation, or impairment of intelligence; many have personality disorders. Child victims often go through the **rape trauma syndrome,** beginning with the acute phase in which the child's life is extremely disrupted, followed by a long-term phase in which the child tries to reconstruct his or her life. In the acute phase, he or she may have dreams and nightmares, often with the offender as victim of a violent act. They may manifest fears of going out alone or fears of being alone with an adult. Even when the child does not manifest problems, sexual abuse may be considered a time bomb that will go off later in the victim's adult sexual experiences.

Women as Victims

Men are much more likely than women to become the victims of criminal activity in this country. Yet surveys indicate that women are much more frightened than men of the possibility of becoming a crime victim. Is the fear because women are becoming more conscious of crimes and more willing to talk about victimization or is it because of the violent crimes often aimed at women, such as purse snatching, rape, and other sexual assaults?

Forcible Rape   The FBI defines forcible **rape** as "the carnal knowledge of a female forcibly and against her will." The FBI crime index includes attempted forcible rape but not statutory rape, which involves consensual sexual intercourse but with a person who is under the legal age of consent. The number of rapes in 1986 increased by 3.2 percent over 1985, but between 1986 and 1987, the number of rapes decreased by .4 percent. Eighty-one percent of the 91,111 rapes reported in 1987 were forcible rapes.[43]

Forcible rape by strangers is probably the crime most feared by women of all ages,[44] but a close look at the reported offenses indicates that young women (16 to 24) are two to three times more likely to be rape victims than are women as a whole. Thus, most rape victims are young and white, but those data must be understood in terms of the population distribution. There are more white than black women in the total population. The likelihood that a black woman will be a rape victim is significantly higher than that of a white woman.[45]

BJS victimization data indicate that women are twice as likely to be raped by a stranger as by an acquaintance, friend, or family member, but the reason may be because women are less likely to report rape in the latter category. Most victims are raped by only one offender.[46] Thus, the reported gang rape discussed in Spotlight 4.3 is not typical of forcible rapes, but again, it may represent a situation many women fear.

Significant social science research on rape, rape offenders, and rape victims has been conducted only recently. Several theories have been ad-

Spotlight 4.3
WHO ARE RAPE VICTIMS?

Rape victims often complain that they are victimized two or three times: once by the rapist, then by people who do not believe they are really victims, and finally by the criminal justice system. These are discussed in the text, but the first two are further illustrated by the alleged facts of a 1988 gang-rape in Texas and by a recent study of attitudes toward date rape.

In early 1988, a 19-year-old mother of two left a family barbeque that she attended with her husband and other family members. She had planned to walk the two blocks to their home to check on the children, who had been left with her grandmother. One of the children was ill. The victim reported that she was abducted and taken to a ranch where 20 to 30 men were watching an illegal cockfight. According to the woman, she was raped by 15 to 20 men during a four hour ordeal, part of which was watched by some of the men at the cockfight.

The victim and her husband, who live in San Diego, a small Texas town, have been laughed at, scorned, and ridiculed by neighbors and other residents of the community. The couple, with their two children, have been hidden by authorities to protect them from being harmed by relatives of the ten defendants indicted on charges of rape and aggravated kidnapping. At the time of publication, two men had been convicted of rape and aggravated kidnapping.[1] Although this case is not a "typical" case of forcible rape, it does illustrate how, in a case in which it would be difficult to argue that the woman "asked for it," the victim still suffers from the reaction of others to the alleged crime. This type of reaction might be more typical in cases of date rape.

A 1988 survey of 1,700 sixth, seventh, eighth, and ninth grade students, conducted by the Rhode Island Rape Crisis Center, revealed that some of the young people condoned some types of date rape. Twenty-four percent of the boys and 16 percent of the girls responded that it is acceptable for a man to have forced sexual intercourse with a female if he has spent money on her. Forced kissing was acceptable by 51 percent of the boys and 41 percent of the girls when the boy had spent a "lot of money," defined as $10 to $15 dollars, on the woman.[2]

One-half of the respondents indicated that if a woman walks alone at night or dresses seductively, she is asking to be raped. If a couple has been dating for six months, it is acceptable for him to force her to have sexual intercourse according to 65 percent of the boys and 47 percent of the girls. If the couple is married, those responses jump to 87 percent of the boys and 79 percent of the girls.

Although this study is too small to permit generalizations to the total population or, for that matter, to other age groups, it may indicate some reasons for date rape. Forced sexual intercourse is not viewed as rape by some people. These responses were given prior to the students' participation in a rape crisis seminar. After that seminar, "less than 25 percent of the participants thought rape or forced kissing was appropriate in any situation."

[1]Summarized by the author from media sources.

[2]These results were reported in the *Dallas Morning News*, (3 May 1988), p. 6A.

vanced to explain the crime. Social scientists do not agree on these explanations, but some variables are associated with high rates of rape. Examples are high rates of divorced or separated women, poverty, and the social inequality of women in relation to men.[47]

Recently increased attention has been given to a form of forcible rape not previously recognized: **date rape.** Date rape is forcible rape in which the victim has consented to the company of the offender but has not agreed to have sexual intercourse. Women are less likely to report these rapes. It thus is possible that most rapes are not committed by strangers, as the official crime data indicate.

Studies of college students report that 12 to 25 percent of women report that they have been victims of rape or attempted rape, while from 7 to 35 percent of men report that they have committed forcible or attempted forcible rape.[48] Some college men also report that they have been victims of date rape in that they were psychologically coerced to have sexual intercourse with their dates. Some reported that women threatened to blackmail them by reporting damaging information or threatened that the relationship would end if the men did not engage in sexual intercourse.[49]

Victims of rape and other forms of sexual assault often complain that they are blamed for the rape. This chapter's CJA indicated that women and men experienced humiliation and degradation as a result of the robbery and sexual assaults at the Sea Crest Diner. Spotlight 4.3, mentioned earlier in relationship to gang rape, also indicates that some young people condone date rape, thus reacting to alleged victims not as real victims but as people who "get what they deserve."[50]

There is empirical evidence that rape may have long-term effects. A study comparing 20 rape victims with 20 nonvictims disclosed that even after a year the rape victims were more anxious, suspicious, fearful, and confused than their nonvictim counterparts.[51] Another study found that rape victims had problems with eating habits: some exhibiting nervous overeating; others not eating. Over half suffered prolonged problems that may indicate lack of a feeling of self-worth. Almost half had sleeping problems. Victims also feared being alone on the street as well as at home. Half had problems with social activities, reporting that their normal social activities altered after the rape. Many had problems with their general feelings toward men they knew.[52]

Domestic Battering   A second type of crime in which women are the most frequent victims is domestic battering. The term *domestic battering*, rather than wife battering, is used for two reasons. First, husbands may be battered; and, second, many instances of domestic battering occur between people who are not married. Either they have been married and are divorced (perhaps only separated); or they have never been married to each other but have lived together; or, even in the absence of cohabitation, they have established an intimate relationship.

Data on domestic battering probably are less accurate than data on any other crime, including forcible rape. Many women, 48 percent according to National Crime Survey Data reported in Spotlight 4.4, will not report the crime. The NCS reports an estimated 2.1 million women an-

SPOTLIGHT 4.4
DOMESTIC VIOLENCE AGAINST WOMEN

The Bureau of Justice Statistics has reported the following findings relevant to the issue of what actions might be taken to prevent domestic violence against women:

- From 1978 to 1982 the National Crime Survey showed that once a woman was victimized by domestic violence, her risk of being victimized again was high. During a six-month time period following an incident of domestic violence, approximately 32 percent of the women were victimized again.
- Close to half of all incidents of domestic violence against women discovered in the National Crime Survey (48 percent) were not reported to police.
- The most common reason given by women for not reporting domestic violence to police was that the woman considered the crime a private or personal matter (49 percent). Fear of reprisal from the assailant was the reason in 12 percent of unreported crimes.
- For the estimated 52 percent of incidents of domestic violence that were brought to police attention, one of the most common reasons given by women for reporting the crime to the police was to prevent future recurrences (37 percent).
- Evidence from the National Crime Survey for 1978

to 1982 indicated that calling the police did seem to help prevent recurrences. An estimated 41 percent of married women assaulted by their husband who did *not* call the police were subsequently assaulted by him within an average six-month time period; for women who *did* call the police, 15 percent were reassaulted. Calling the police was thus associated with 62 percent fewer subsequent assaults.

- About a third of the incidents of domestic violence against women in the National Crime Survey would be classified by police as "rape," "robbery" or "aggravated assault." These are felonies in most states. The remaining two-thirds would likely be classified by police as "simple assault," a misdemeanor in most jurisdictions. Yet, based upon evidence collected in the National Crime Survey, as many as half of the domestic "simple assaults" actually involved bodily injury as serious as or more serious than 90 percent of all rapes, robberies, and aggravated assaults.

Source: Bureau of Justice Statistics, *Preventing Domestic Violence Against Women* (Washington, D.C.: U. S. Department of Justice, August 1986), p. 1.

---

nually are victimized by domestic violence and that seven out of ten of these acts are committed by the woman's spouse, ex-spouse, boyfriend, or ex-boyfriend. The NCS thus does not confine the term *domestic battering* to spouse abuse.[53]

Social scientists Murray Straus and Richard Gelles, two highly regarded researchers in this area, think domestic violence to be much higher than the NCS figure, estimating the figure to be as high as 6 million annually. Straus and Gelles also found that one out of every six couples in this country engage in at least one incidence of violence each year and that during the years of their marriage the chances are greater than one in four (28 percent) that a couple will engage in physical violence.[54]

Domestic violence also includes violence of wives against their husbands. For centuries women have been murdering their husbands. "It was inevitable that battered husbands would be discovered."[55] One of the problems with getting accurate data on domestic violence is that some define it as including marital rape, while others include marital rape within the definition of forcible rape.

Marital Rape Historically, a husband had unlimited sexual access to his wife; she was expected, and in most cases expected herself, to comply with his sexual desires. Legally he could be charged with rape only if he forced her to have sexual intercourse with a third person. No amount of force on his part would classify his sexual intercourse with his wife as rape, and this was true even if the couple had legally separated. This common-law provision became a part of most state rape statutes. The Texas statute is an example, defining rape as follows: "A person commits an offense if he has sexual intercourse with a female not his wife without the female's consent."[56]

In 1977 Oregon became the first state to repeal the marital rape exemption.[57] Oregon, upon a complaint by Greta Rideout, filed criminal charges against her husband, John, and and he was tried under this statute. This was the first marital rape trial in the United States, but on December 27, 1979, John Rideout was acquitted. Shortly thereafter, the Rideouts reconciled, although the reconciliation did not last very long. In 1979 James K. Chretien, convicted of raping his estranged wife, was believed to be the first person in the United States to be convicted of marital rape. He was sentenced to from 3 to 5 years in prison.

Over one-third of the states now permit prosecution of husbands for the crime of marital rape. In some states in which the marital rape exemption has not been specifically eliminated by statute, courts have refused to rule that the exemption is implicit within the rape statutes. According to the Georgia Supreme Court, "When a woman says I do," she does not "give up her right to say I won't." The Georgia court held that neither the rape nor the aggravated sodomy statutes implied a marital exemption.[58]

Although we do not have accurate data on the extent of marital rape, some reports indicate that marital rape is a "common form of family violence" and that "the effect on these women is profound." The forms of abuse are serious, with many women reporting repeated rapes by their husbands over a period of years. In one study women reported being raped by their husbands twice as often as they reported rape by strangers. Of a sample of 644 married women over 18, 12 percent reported being raped by their husbands.[59] A later study by noted scholars in this field, David Finkelhor and Kersti Yllo, indicated that approximately one in ten wives is victimized by marital rape. Despite this frequency, many people still think of marital rape as a domestic problem, not a violent crime.[60]

THE CRIMINAL JUSTICE SYSTEM AND CRIME VICTIMS

Recent changes in the criminal justice system's reaction to victims has led one authority to conclude that the decade of the 1980s might well be viewed historically as the decade in which crime victims were finally recognized as "central characters in the criminal event, worthy of concern, respect, and compassion."[61]

Research in the 1980s has provided some information on how victims react to crime. Some of the findings are summarized in Spotlight 4.5. These and other findings have led to significant changes in the criminal

SPOTLIGHT 4.5
CRIME TAKES PSYCHOLOGICAL TOLL: A BRIEF OVERVIEW
OF RESEARCH ON VICTIMS' REACTIONS TO CRIME

Only recently have people come to realize that victims of crime experience crisis reactions similar to those experienced by victims of war, natural disasters, and catastrophic illness.

Research in 1975 focused on victim experiences both with crime and with the criminal justice system. The findings had a significant impact on the thinking of criminal justice planners and the development of programs for victims and witnesses. Researchers at Marquette University interviewed 3,000 victims and witnesses from cases active in Milwaukee County's court system and 1,600 persons identified as victims of serious personal crimes by a previous National Crime Survey.

They found mental or emotional suffering to be the most frequent problem expressed by victims in general, while time and income loss posed the greatest difficulties for victims involved in the court process. The fear and emotional distress experienced by victims often extended as well to the victims' families and friends.

The study produced a wealth of policy recommendations to improve the treatment of victims and witnesses in the courts. Many have since been widely adopted.

The Milwaukee study introduced the term "secondary victimization" to characterize the distress experienced by the family and friends of crime victims. In 1982, a research team from the New York Victim Services Agency, pursuing this theme, questioned 240 New York City victims of robbery, nonsexual assault, and burglary. They asked about problems and needs stemming from the crime and about organizations and individuals to whom victims turned for assistance.

While few victims had sought assistance from organizations, virtually all had received help from friends, neighbors, or relatives. The help ranged from listening while victims "ventilated," to aiding in apprehending the criminal, to lending money, to helping with replacement of doors, windows, and locks.

The New York researchers then contacted supporters named by the victims and interviewed them about the costs (and benefits) incurred in helping

the victims. Most supporters reported being glad to help, but many said that their own fears about crime had been heightened because of the victim's experience. Such reactions were most prevalent among family members and neighbors of victims.

The study showed that the effects of crime hit hardest among the poor. Psychological distress and crime-related problems were more common among the less affluent and less educated, and these differences persisted at least up to four months after the crime. Similarly, poorer, less educated supporters were more likely than affluent supporters to report that providing assistance had placed a burden on them.

In a surprising finding, an earlier study revealed that nearly as many burglary as robbery victims underwent a "crisis reaction" during the weeks following victimization. In fact, according to researchers at the American Institutes for Research, the impact of crime on victims' emotions and everyday behaviors was actually greater for burglary than for robbery victims.

Psychological reactions of victims were examined in depth under a 1984 NIJ study funded in response to a Victims Task Force recommendation. Researchers at the Medical University of South Carolina interviewed female victims of sexual assault, robbery, aggravated assault, and home burglary, identified through a random victimization study.

Psychological adjustment of victims was measured against that of a sample of nonvictims. Details were gathered about current psychological status, previous mental health history, treatment history, and about the crime itself. This research provides the first reliable information about the proportions of victims in various crime categories who experience serious adjustment problems. Results indicate that victims of sexual assault suffer more adverse psychological reactions and adjustment problems than victims of robbery and burglary.

Source: Robert C. Davis, "Crime Victims: Learning How to Help Them," *NIJ Reports* No. 203 (May–June 1987): 2–3, footnotes omitted.

justice system. But it has not been an easy journey for crime victims; nor have they yet seen all of their problems solved. Victim reaction, however, has been a key factor in these changes.

Victims Respond to the System

In 1982, Ronald Reagan established the President's Task Force on Victims, which was followed in 1984 by the Attorney General's Task Force on Family Violence. Both commissions interviewed crime victims and others. Most of the victims spoke negatively about their treatment in the criminal justice system. Here are the comments of three victims:

1. To be a victim at the hands of the criminal is an unforgettable nightmare. But to then become a victim at the hands of the criminal justice system is an unforgivable travesty. It makes the criminal and the criminal justice system partners in crime.
2. I will never forget being raped, kidnapped, and robbed at gunpoint. However, my sense of disillusionment of the judicial system is many times more painful. I could not in good faith urge anyone to participate in this hellish process.
3. How can the system have gotten this far away from what it is supposed to be?[62]

The criminal justice system's reaction to some victims of crime means that they are twice victimized: once by the criminal and once by the system in a variety of ways. First, the victim may be blamed for the crime. Particularly in the case of sexual assault, the response of the system may be that the victim asked for it by being in a questionable place such as a bar, or by hitchhiking on the highway, or by having a questionable reputation. This is referred to as **victim-precipitation.** Second, victims may find that police and others are not sympathetic to domestic violence problems, that they view those actions as domestic problems, not violence. Some rape victims have complained about the reactions of police and prosecutors, alleging that these professionals have not tried to understand the problems suffered by the victims.

Studies have shown, however, that many victims are satisfied with the handling of their cases by professionals. Table 4.2 contains data from a study of victims in six cities. These results disclose that although victims indicated greater satisfaction with police than with prosecutors and judges, over 50 percent responded that they were satisfied or very satisfied with all of these practitioners in the criminal justice system. But when asked their opinions about courts, the victims responded less favorably. As Table 4.3 indicates, only 30 percent of the victims believed the court system cares about victim's needs, and only 32 percent believed that courts do as good a job as can be expected.

When asked how the system could be improved, 36 percent of the victims responded, "Treat offender more harshly," while 30 percent wanted practitioners to keep victims better informed of the court proceedings. Victims were better informed in systems that had developed

TABLE 4.2

Victim Satisfaction with Practitioners, Six Sites

	Victims Satisfied With			
	Police	Prosecutor	Judge	Victim Assistance Staff
Percent satisfied or very satisfied	80	67	54	67
Number of victim respondents	338	290	208	153

Note: There were two other categories: "dissatisfied" and "very dissatisfied."

Source: Brian E. Forst and Jolene C. Hernon, Bureau of Justice Statistics, *The Criminal Justice Response to Victim Harm* (Washington, D.C.: U.S. Department of Justice, June 1985), p. 4.

special programs for victims and witnesses than in systems that did not have such programs.[63]

In 1988, citizens of Florida, by an overwhelming majority, passed a constitutional amendment that provides for granting victims of crime, and the next of kin of homicide victims, the qualified right to be informed, to be present, and to be heard at all crucial stages of criminal proceedings in their cases. Florida law already provided some aspects of victim compensation and, in most cases, the right of victims to appear or to submit a written statement to the sentencing court.

The System Responds to Victims

Several significant changes have been made recently in the criminal justice system in response to a growing concern about the needs and rights of crime victims.

Training of Police and Prosecutors   Many jurisdictions have started training police and prosecutors to be sensitive to the needs of particular types of victims such as victims of rape and domestic violence, as well as very

TABLE 4.3

Victim Attitudes About the Court System

(W = 301) Percent who agreed that:

Guilty offenders are not punished enough	86
In general, judges make fair decisions	63
Courts do about as good a job as we can expect	32
The court system cares about victims' needs	30

Source: Brian E. Forst and Jolene C. Hernon, Bureau of Justice Statistics, *The Criminal Justice Response to Victim Harm* (Washington, D.C.: U.S. Department of Justice, June 1985), p. 5.

Information from victims is essential; here, an officer interviews a victim in her home. (Phyllis Graber Jensen/Stock Boston)

young victims. Some departments have special units of officers designated to handle rape cases or incidents of domestic violence.

Revised Arrest Policies   Victims of domestic violence have frequently complained that police view their problem as a domestic problem, not as an act of violence, and that police do not arrest the offender. If police do arrest, prosecutors will not file charges. Police response to that complaint has been that without the cooperation of victims prosecution of domestic violence cases usually will not be successful and that most victims will not cooperate. Victims respond that they are afraid that if they cooperate their spouses will later retaliate.

Some departments have responded to this situation by emphasizing that domestic violence is violence that threatens society like any other violent crime. Such violence is not to be considered "just a domestic dispute." In an attempt to remove the responsibility (and thus increased chances of retaliation by the offender) from the victim, some police departments have instituted a policy of mandatory arrests in domestic battery cases. Mandatory arrests remove from police the discretion to avoid the situation, mediate, or recommend civil action only. If called to the scene of a domestic battering, police must arrest if they have probable cause to believe that battering has occurred.

One of the earlier studies of the effects of mandatory arrest of domestic batterers occurred in Minnesota, where it was reported that the conviction rate of batterers went up significantly after the institution of the policy. There were also fewer repeat offenders among the arrestees.[64] Studies in other cities have found similar results.[65]

Changes have also been made in arrests of alleged child abusers. Although many are still reluctant to do so, an increasing number of public welfare professionals, teachers, and doctors will report suspected child abuse, and all states now have legislation requiring them to do so. Despite this, underreporting still is a problem.[66]

Changes in Judicial and Court Procedures Legislative and administrative changes in the roles of prosecutors and judges also have been made. Training programs for prosecutors have given them greater understanding of the unique problems suffered by victims of child and domestic abuse. Provision of counseling services for victims, court-ordered counseling for those found guilty of child abuse or domestic violence, greater restrictions on pretrial release of suspects, and many other changes have been made.[67]

Some changes have been made in court procedures to make it more comfortable and less embarrassing for victims to testify. Testifying in court is a difficult experience for most people, but that experience may be traumatic for a crime victim, particularly a victim of a sensitive personal crime such as rape. In the past, rape victims could be asked questions about their prior sexual experiences. Today, some jurisdictions prohibit such questions on the grounds that the information is not relevant to the case on trial, will prejudice the jury, and will discourage rape victims from agreeing to testify. Exceptions may be made, as in the case of the victim's prior sexual experience with the defendant.

Court rules have been relaxed on some cases when children are the victims of sexual abuse. Children often do not understand the sexual experience and find it very difficult to explain what happened. Prosecutors may use anatomically correct dolls and ask the children to demonstrate what happened. Rules regarding direct testimony of complaining witnesses have also been relaxed in some courts when the victims are children. Some courts now permit the testimony of a child victim to be presented to the court by videotape.[68] Others permit doctors or nurses to testify concerning what the child said to them and thus eliminate the child's direct testimony in court. There are, however, legal problems with such changes. State and federal courts are not in agreement over whether the defendant's right to confront his or her witnesses and cross-examine

Testifying in court may be particularly traumatic for a child. (Steve Skloot/Photo Researchers)

them in court is violated when the state permits doctors, nurses, parents, or others to testify regarding what the child said rather than having the child testify in court.[69]

Laws governing parental rights to children are also being changed. Experts predicted in early 1988 that one of the top priorities in state legislation during the immediate future would be revision of laws that make it almost impossible to remove a child from his or her biological parents.[70]

One of the problems with changing trial procedures to accommodate the needs of victims of sexual abuse is illustrated by a United States Supreme Court case involving the right of the press to report the details of a trial. Although the Supreme Court has ruled that it would be an infringement of the First Amendment right of public access to a criminal trial to have a statute that automatically excluded the public and the press from the trial of a defendant accused of sexually assaulting a child, there might be some cases in which the exclusion would be permitted. The Court gave its reasons in *Globe Newspaper Co. v. Superior Court, Etc.*[71]

Globe Newspaper Co. v. Superior Court, Etc.

The state interests . . . are reducible to two: the protection of minor victims of sex crimes from further trauma and embarrassment, and the encouragement of such victims to come forward and testify in a truthful and credible manner. We consider these interests in turn.

We agree with respondent that the first interest—safeguarding the physical and psychological well-being of a minor—is a compelling one. But as compelling as that interest is, it does not justify a mandatory closure rule, for it is clear that the circumstances of the particular case may affect the significance of the interest. A trial court can determine on a case-by-case basis whether closure is necessary to protect the welfare of a minor victim. Among the factors to be weighed are the minor victim's age, psychological maturity, and understanding, the nature of the crime, the desires of the victim, and the interests of parents and relatives.

[Regarding the second interest] . . . Surely it cannot be suggested that minor victims of sex crimes are the only crime victims who, because of publicity attendant to criminal trials, are reluctant to come forward and testify. The State's argument based on this interest therefore proves too much, and runs contrary to the very foundation of the right of access: . . . namely, "that a presumption of openness inheres in the very nature of a criminal trial under our system of justice."

Victim Participation in Criminal Proceedings   Victims also have been permitted to become involved in some criminal proceedings. For example, California permits some involvement at sentencing; Minnesota permits involvement during **plea bargaining.**[72] The Supreme Court has ruled, however, that at death sentence hearings the constitutional rights of defendants are not consistent with evidence of a Victim Impact Statement (VIS) to the extent that that statement contains information on the severe emotional impact of the crime on the family, the personal characteristics of the victim, and the family members' opinions and characterizations of the crime and of the offender. The Court explains its decision in this brief excerpt from *Booth v. Maryland*.[73]

Booth v. Maryland

One can understand the grief and anger of the family caused by the brutal murders in this case, and there is no doubt that jurors generally are aware of these feelings. But the formal presentation of this information by the State can serve no other purpose than to inflame the jury and divert it from deciding the case on the relevant evidence concerning the crime and the defendant. As we have noted, any decision to impose the death sentence must "be, and appear to be, based on reason rather than caprice or emotion." The admission of these emotionally-charged opinions as to what conclusions the jury should draw from the evidence clearly is inconsistent with the reasoned decisionmaking we require in capital cases.

The use of VIS in other sentencing contexts may be questioned legally as new cases arise, but the policy has already been characterized as "a mere genuflection to ritualistic legalism." The policy may serve as a placebo, however, "in that it creates the impression that something is being done." Perhaps, the use of a VIS is important for that reason, and it makes little difference that the victim does not realize that the sentencing agreement "is *almost entirely* mediated by legally relevant variables."[74]

Victim Compensation Legislation   Another area in which the criminal justice system has attempted to respond to the needs of victims is the provision of **victim compensation programs.** Beginning in 1965 with California, the first state to adopt a victim compensation program in this country, the trend toward adoption of these programs moved quickly. Unfortunately, many states have not provided adequate funding for the programs, leaving victims with only an illusion that they will receive financial aid, medical care, and counseling assistance for the injuries and losses they have suffered as the result of crime.

The provisions of state victim compensation programs vary considerably. The state plans also differ in methods of application, eligibility requirements, and minimum and maximum awards available. Because of the wide range of provisions of the various state plans, it has been suggested that a model plan be drafted and adopted by all states. It is also important to evaluate the victim-witness programs carefully, although this is not always done.[75]

Despite their popularity, state victim compensation programs have been severely criticized. The passage of legislation in this area gives the impression that something is being done for the victim. But, for the following reasons, many crime victims are not adequately compensated, if at all:

1. Restrictions concerning residency and financial eligibility.

2. Minimum payments (for example, no payments for a claim of under $100).
3. Maximum payments that do not reach the extent of the loss suffered.
4. Lack of compensation for all property loss or for pain and suffering.
5. The exclusion in many plans of compensation to those who have been victimized by members of their own families.

Also, it is not clear that the programs meet other goals, such as increased crime reporting. One researcher found that the reluctance of victims to report crimes has not been significantly altered by the presence of victim compensation programs. Nor is the attitude of compensated victims toward the criminal justice system significantly improved.[76]

Congress passed a victim compensation bill that applies to victims and witnesses involved in federal crimes, the Victim and Witness Protection Act of 1982. The act contains various provisions designed to prevent harassment of victims and witnesses. It establishes guidelines for fair treatment of crime victims and witnesses in the criminal justice system. It requires victim impact statements at sentencing, contains more stringent bail requirements, and provides that the sentencing judge must order defendants to pay **restitution** to victims or state reasons for not so ordering.[77]

The restitution provisions of the 1982 law have been challenged in the courts. Those decisions will be discussed in more detail in Chapter 12, "Sentencing." Here it is relevant to note that the basic problem is one of conflict between the rights of defendants and the rights of victims, once again illustrating the system effect of a reform measure.[78]

Congress also passed the Comprehensive Crime Control Act and the Victims of Crime Act of 1984, which authorizes federal funds be distributed by the Office of Justice Programs through its Office for Victims of Crime and Bureau of Justice for state victim compensation and assistance programs. That law, which is often called VOCA (Victims of Crime), provided that federal funds stopped after September 30, 1988, but Congress reauthorized the program to continue through 1994.[79]

Civil Rights of Crime Victims   Chapter 1 discussed the relationship between torts and crime and noted that some acts may constitute both. But until recently, there was little litigation on tort liability arising out of crimes, perhaps because, even in cases in which the offender was convicted, there was no reason to sue since he or she had no financial assets.

In recent years, however, courts have recognized the rights of crime victims, under certain circumstances, to recover civil damages from other than the offender. These third party liability actions have mushroomed since the California case of *Tarasoff v. Regents of the University of California*, in which the California Supreme Court held that psychotherapists who have knowledge that their patients might harm reasonably foreseeable persons have a duty to warn those persons.[80]

In *Tarasoff*, the psychotherapist's patient threatened to kill a specific person and later did so. Since this case, courts have focused on situations in which it is reasonable to hold a third party liable for a duty to warn. Later cases have held hospitals, landlords, business owners, and others liable for criminal acts that occur on their premises in situations in which the third party might have prevented those criminal acts by taking precautions such as providing more lighting and security.[81]

A number of factors must be considered in these cases; not all victims will win all cases. But this growing area of tort law provides additional avenues for crime victims who, despite their legal right to sue the offender for civil damages, have in effect had no recourse because of the offender's lack of resources.

SUMMARY

This chapter explored the recently developed and rapidly expanding study of victimology. The chapter's CJA opened the discussion with a series of scenarios designed to show the broad range of crimes and victims. Widely publicized but infrequently occurring crimes, such as the terrorism aboard Kuwait Airways Flight 422, command far more attention by the media and the public than larceny or even violent crimes committed by friends or acquaintances.

The CJA's fact patterns do not tell the whole story, however; for in a real sense, we are all victims of crime. The physical injuries and economic losses from crime are much easier to assess than some of the other losses, but emotional and psychological reactions also deserve attention. Another cost of crime is the fear that exists, not only among people who have already been victimized but also among other citizens. The extent and nature of that fear are debatable. Women and older people show greater fear than other citizens, but they are less likely than men and young adults to become victims of criminal activity. Women, the elderly, and children, however, are the focus of national attention today, particularly when they are victims of violence or sexual abuse.

Women, the elderly, and children are not the people most victimized. The chapter examined data on crime, noting that most violent crimes are committed against black men and that although official data indicate that most violent crimes against the population in general are committed by offenders not known by the victims, it is possible that the data would be quite different if more crimes were reported. Date and marital rape, sexual offenses committed by family members against children, and family abuse of the elderly are crimes that frequently go unreported.

Despite the lack of complete knowledge of actual offenses committed, it is possible, using data from the FBI's *Uniform Crime Reports* and the Bureau of Justice Statistics' data on victimization, to construct probabilities of our becoming crime victims. Both of these government sources, along with private and government-sponsored research, continue to improve the means of measuring actual crimes committed.

The effects of victimization is another area in which victimology is being expanded. Particular focus has been on the effects of sexual crimes. Authorities are debating whether sexual abuse of children leads to violence of those victims against their own children: the evidence points both ways, and more research is needed. Now that the society is more receptive to the problems, many adult women who were sexually victimized during their childhood are speaking publicly about their problems, indicating that the effects of such victimization are indeed long-term.

A final focus of this chapter was on the criminal justice system and its treatment of criminals. Despite some research indicating that many victims were pleased with the system; and although many changes have been made, the system still in many cases creates a "second victimization." Efforts to recognize the rights of victims have taken such measures as victim compensation, revised court procedures, and victim participation in the criminal justice process.

Like most changes in the system, however, recognizing the rights of victims creates other needs, such as training programs for professionals within the system and financial backing for those programs as well as for victim compensation plans. The recognition of victim rights also might compromise the rights of defendants, as indicated by the refusal of the Supreme Court to permit the emotional Victim Rights Statements introduced at the sentencing phase of a recent capital punishment case. Changes within the system that were designed to make it easier for children to be witnesses in sexual abuse cases also demonstrate the problem of denying defendants their rights when recognizing victims' needs. Relaxing the rules of evidence to allow doctors, nurses, or parents to testify in court regarding what a child said about his or her alleged sexual abuse may deny the defendant the right to confront and cross-examine the witness. Excluding the press from the trial of a defendant accused of sexually abusing a child may protect the child from media publicity, but it denies the public its right to know about the court proceedings.

The rights of victims and the rights of defendants may come into conflict. Nevertheless, changes made in the system to help victims may produce positive results such as increased reporting of crime and more arrests and convictions. But what appear to be positive results may create problems for the system and society because of the increased need for jails and prisons. A study of crime victims thus provides another example of the need to assess the effect that changes in one aspect of the system will have on the rest of the system and of society.

STUDY QUESTIONS

1. What progress has been made recently in the study of victims?

2. Discuss the characteristics of crime victims and of their offenders.

3. What are your chances of becoming a crime victim?

4. What life-style changes might you consider because of the risk of crime?

5. Is the fear of crime realistic?

6. Discuss the extent and effect of *child abuse.*

7. Compare women and men as victims and as abusers of spouses.

8. What changes have been made in the criminal justice system to improve the plight of crime victims?

ENDNOTES

1. *New York Times* (4 June 1983), p. 10.
2. "Five Get 30-Year Terms for Crime Spree on L.I.," *New York Times* (8 December 1982), p. 18. For an interesting analysis of victimization as affecting all members of society and suggestions of how to deal with victimization, see Robert Elias, *The Politics of Victimization: Victims, Victimology, and Human Rights* (New York: Oxford University Press, 1986).
3. For a brief account of the history of victimology, along with a discussion of most of the important areas of the subject, see Andrew Karmen, *Crime Victims: An Introduction to Victimology* (Monterey, Calif.: Brooks/Cole Publishing Co., 1984).
4. President's Task Force on Victims of Crime, *Final Report* (Washington, D.C.: U.S. Government Printing Office, 1982).
5. Bureau of Justice Statistics, *Criminal Victimization in the United States: 1973–82 Trends* (Washington, D.C.: U.S. Department of Justice, September 1983).
6. Bureau of Justice Statistics, *Criminal Victimization 1986* (Washington, D.C.: U.S. Department of Justice, October 1987), p. 1; *1987* (October 1988), p. 1.
7. These data are taken from Bureau of Justice Statistics, *Criminal Victimization 1985,* (Washington, D.C.: U.S. Department of Justice, 1986).
8. Oscar Newman, *Defensible Space* (London: Architectural Press, 1972).
9. Lawrence E. Cohen and Marcus Felson, "Social Change and Crime Rate Trends: A Routine Activity Approach," *American Sociological Review* 44 (August 1979): 588–608. See also Marcus Felson, "Routine Activities, Social Controls, Rational Decisions and Criminal Outcomes," in Dereck Cornish and Ronald V. Clarke, eds., *The Reasoning Criminal* (New York: Springer-Verlag,

1986); and Marcus Felson, "Routine Activities and Crime Prevention in the Developing Metropolis," *Criminology* 25 (November 1987): 911–32.

10. Marvin Wolfgang, *Patterns in Criminal Homicide* (Philadelphia: University of Pennsylvania Press, 1958), p. 252.
11. See A. Nicholas Groth with H. Jean Birnbaum, *Men Who Rape: The Psychology of the Offender* (New York: Plenum Press, 1981).
12. *Criminal Victimization 1985*, p. 5.
13. Bureau of Justice Statistics, *Special Report, The Risk of Violent Crime* (Washington, D.C.: U.S. Department of Justice, May 1985).
14. Bureau of Justice Statistics, *Lifetime Likelihood of Victimization* (Washington, D.C.: U.S. Department of Justice, March 1987), p. 3.
15. Bureau of Justice Statistics, *Special Report, The Economic Cost of Crime to Victims* (April 1984).
16. "Crime Panel Issues Its Final Report," *New York Times* (2 April 1986), p. 1.
17. "The Plague of Violent Crime," *Newsweek* (23 March 1981), p. 46.
18. "The Curse of Violent Crime: A Pervasive Fear of Robbery and Mayhem Threatens the Way America Lives," *Time* (23 March 1981), p. 16.
19. Wesley G. Skogan and Michael G. Maxfield, *Coping with Crime: Individual and Neighborhood Reactions* (Beverly Hills, Calif.: Sage Publications, 1981), p. 75.
20. News release, Bureau of Justice Statistics (10 March 1986).
21. For an analysis of the interaction of race, gender, and age on the fear of crime, see Suzanne T. Ortega and Jessie L. Myles, "Race and Gender Effects on Fear of Crime: An Interactive Model with Age," *Criminology* 25 (February 1987): 133–152.
22. News release, Bureau of Justice Statistics (10 March 1986).
23. Hubert Williams and Antony M. Pate, "Returning to First Principles: Reducing the Fear of Crime in Newark," *Crime and Delinquency* 35 (January 1987): 53.
24. Ibid., 53–89. See also Wesley G. Skogan, "The Impact of Victimization on Fear," *Crime and Delinquency* (January 1987): 135–54.
25. Bureau of Justice Statistics, *Elderly Victims* (Washington, D.C.: U.S. Department of Justice, November 1987), p. 2.
26. See Ronald L. Akers, et al., "Fear of Crime and Victimization among the Elderly in Different Types of Communities," *Criminology* 25 (August 1987): 487–505.
27. See M. J. Quinn and S. K. Tomita, *Elder Abuse and Neglect—Causes, Diagnosis, and Intervention Strategies* (New York: Springer Publishing Co., 1986); Peter Yin, *Victimization and the Aged*, (Springfield, Ill.: Charles C Thomas, 1985); and K. A. Pillemer and R. S. Wolf, eds., *Elder Abuse—*

Conflict in the Family (Boston: Auburn House Publishing Co., 1986).
28. "Unveiling a Family Secret," *Newsweek* (18 February 1980), p. 104.
29. "Congress Panel Hears of Physical Abuse of the Elderly," *New York Times (22 April 1980), p. B1.*
30. Ibid., p. 106.
31. Michael D. A. Freeman, *Violence in the Home: A Socio-Legal Study* (Westmead, Farnborough, Hampshire, England: Gover Publishing Co., 1980), p. 239 [first published in 1979 by Saxon House]. See also Susan K. Steinmetz, *The Cycle of Violence: Assertive, Aggressive, and Abusive Family Interaction* (New York: Praeger Publishers, 1977).
32. Officer Dick Ramon, head of the sex-crimes unit of the Seattle Police Department, quoted in "Child Abuse: The Ultimate Betrayal," *Time* (5 September 1983), p. 22.
33. "Reports of Child Abuse on Rise," *Justice Assistance News* (4 May 1983), p. 4. See also Diana E. H. Russell, *Sexual Exploitation: Rape, Child Sexual Abuse, and Workplace Harassment,* (Beverly Hills, Calif.: Sage Publications, 1984). For an extensive discussion of the male victim of sexual assault, see E. Porter, *Treating the Young Male Victim of Sexual Assault—Issues and Intervention Strategies* (Syracuse, N.Y.: Safer Society Press, 1986).
34. "Child Abuse Rises," *American Bar Association Journal* 72 (February 1986): 34.
35. Judith Miller and Mark Miller, "Protecting the Rights of Abused and Neglected Children," *Trial* 19 (June 1983): 69. See also Richard Gelles, "Violence towards Children in the United States," *American Journal of Orthopsychiatry* 48 (October 1978): 580–92; and Gelles, *Family Violence*, 2d ed. (Beverly Hills, Calif.: Sage Publications, 1987), pp. 23–26.
36. Study by psychiatrists Brant Steele and Carl Pollock, cited in Ruth Inglis, *Sins of the Fathers: A Study of the Physical and Emotional Abuse of Children* (New York: St. Martin's Press, 1978), p. 69.
37. Laura Meyers, "Incest: No One Wants to Know," *Student Lawyer* 9 (November 1980): 30. For a study that found cases of incest to be highest among siblings, see David Finkelhor, *Sexually Victimized Children* (New York: Free Press, 1979). See also Robert L. Geiser, *Hidden Victims: The Sexual Abuse of Children* (Boston: Beacon Press, 1979); Joseph Shephen, *Incest: A Biosocial View* (New York: Academic Press, 1983); David Finkelhor, *Child Sexual Abuse: New Theory and Research* (New York: The Free Press, 1984); Deborah Daro, *Confronting Child Abuse* (New York: The Free Press, 1987); and David Finkelhor and Associates, *A Sourcebook on Child Sexual Abuse* (Beverly Hills, Calif.: Sage Publishers, 1986).
38. David Finkelhor, "Sexual Abuse: A Sociological

Perspective," *Child Abuse and Neglect* 6 (1982): 95–102.

39. "Woman Charged with Dealing in Child Pornography," *New York Times* (22 August 1982), p. 18.

40. Commonwealth v. Oakes, 401 Mass. 602 (1988), *vacated and remanded*, Massachusetts v. Oakes, 57 U.S. Law Week 4787 (June 21, 1989). Procedural and substantive issues beyond the scope of this text are involved in the appeal of this case. Simply stated, subsequent to the time the case was heard by the U.S. Supreme Court, the statute in question was amended to add a "lascivious intent" requirement to the "nudity" portion of the statute and to eliminate exemptions contained in the prior version. This change made the case moot before the Supreme Court, since the amendment cured the overbroad issue, which was the only issue decided by the Massachusetts court and on appeal before the Supreme Court. Since the Massachusetts court did not decide whether the original statute was applicable to the case of Oakes, the Supreme Court sent the case back for that determination.

41. Miller and Miller, "Protecting the Rights of Abused and Neglected Children," p. 70. For a recent analysis of the effects of child abuse on children, see Gail Elizabeth Wyatt and Gloria Johnson Powell, eds., *Lasting Effects of Child Sexual Abuse* (Beverly Hills, Calif.: Sage Publications, 1988).

42. "Study Says Abused Children Not Destined to Be Abusers," *Dallas Morning News* (18 September 1987), p. 10A, referring to an article in the *American Journal of Orthopsychiatry*. For a review of the literature and an analysis of the relationship between child victimization and later criminality, see Ronald Barri Flowers, *Children and Criminality: The Child as Victim and Perpetrator* (Westport, Conn.: Greenwood Press, 1986). For a collection of scholarly articles on child abuse, see Richard J. Gelles and Jane B. Lancaster, eds., *Child Abuse and Neglect: Biosocial Dimensions* (Hawthorne, N.Y.: Aldine de Gruyter, 1987).

43. Federal Bureau of Investigation, *Uniform Crime Reports: Crime in the United States 1986* (Washington, D.C.: U.S. Government Printing Office, 1987), pp. 13, 14; and *Uniform Crime Reports: Crime in the United States: 1987* (Washington, D.C.: U.S. Government Printing Office, 1988), pp. 13, 14.

44. See Mark Warr, "Fear of Rape among Urban Women," *Social Problems* 32 (February 1985): 238–50.

45. Bureau of Justice Statistics, *The Crime of Rape* (Washington, D.C.: U.S. Department of Justice, 1985), pp. 1, 2.

46. Ibid., p. 2

47. See, for example, M. Dwayne Smith and Nathan Bennett, "Poverty, Inequality, and Theories of Forcible Rape," *Crime and Delinquency* 31 (April 1985): 295–305; this is a special issue on rape and contains several other pertinent research articles. See also Larry Baron and Murray A. Straus, "Four Theories of Rape: A Macrosociological Analysis," *Social Problems* 34 (December 1987): 467–89.

48. For a review of the literature on these findings, see R. Lance Shotland and Lynne Goodstein, "Just Because She Doesn't Want to Doesn't Mean It's Rape: An Experimentally Based Causal Model of the Perception of Rape in a Dating Situation," *Social Psychology Quarterly* 46 (September 1983): 220–32. See also Neil M. Malamuth, "Rape Proclivity among Males," *Journal of Social Issues* 37 (1981): 138–57; and Mary P. Koss et al., "The Scope of Rape: Incidence and Prevalence of Sexual Aggression and Victimization in a National Sample of Higher Education Students," *Journal of Consulting and Clinical Psychology* 55 (April 1987): 162–70. See also S. Estrich, *Real Rape* (Cambridge, Mass.: Harvard University Press, 1987).

49. "As Victims of Date Rape, Men Should Just Say No," *Tulsa World* (5 June 1987), p. A11, reporting on a study by Cindy Struckman-Johnson, a psychologist at the University of South Dakota.

50. See Joyce E. Williams and Karen A. Holmes, *The Second Assault: Rape and Public Attitudes* (Westport, Conn.: Greenwood Press, 1981).

51. Dane G. Kilpatrick, Patricia A. Resick, and Lois J. Veronen, "Effects of a Rape Experience: A Longitudinal Study," *Journal of Social Issues* 37 (1981): 105–22.

52. Thomas W. McCahill et al., *The Aftermath of Rape* (Lexington, Mass.: D.C. Heath and Co., 1979).

53. Bureau of Justice Statistics, *Preventing Domestic Violence against Women* (Washington, D.C.: U.S. Department of Justice, August 1986), p. 3.

54. See Gelles, *Family Violence*, p. 92. See also Murray Straus, Richard Gelles, and Susanne Steinmetz, *Behind Closed Doors: Violence in the American Family* (New York: Doubleday/Anchor Books, 1979). For a recent analysis of domestic violence from a feminist point of view, see Kersti Yllo and Michelle Bograd, eds., *Feminist Perspectives on Wife Abuse* (Beverly Hills, Calif.: Sage Publications, 1988).

55. Gelles, *Family Violence*, pp. 137, 142.

56. TEX. PENAL CODE ANN, tit. 21, Section 21.02(a).

57. OR. REV. STAT, Section 163.375 (repealed 1977).

58. Warren v. State, 336 S.E. 2d 221 (Ga. 1985).

59. Report of Dr. Diana Russell, presented to the American Sociological Association, quoted in *New York Times* (29 November 1982), p. B20.

60. David Finkelhor and Kersti Yllo, *License to Rape: Sexual Abuse of Wives* (New York: Free Press, 1987).

61. Robert C. Davis, "Crime Victims: Learning How

to Help Them," *NIJ Reports* no. 203 (May–June 1987): 2.

62. *President's Task Force on Victims of Crime, Final Report*, pp. 5, 9, 13.

63. Brian E. Forst and Jolene C. Hernon, Bureau of Justice Statistics, *The Criminal Justice Response to Victim Harm* (Washington, D.C.: U.S. Department of Justice, June 1985), p. 6.

64. For detailed information on the analysis of the effect of these arrests in Minnesota, obtain a copy of the report, "Police Responses to Domestic Assault: Preliminary Findings," from the Police Foundation, 1919 K St., N.W., Suite 400, Washington, D.C. 20006, telephone (202) 833–1460. For other information on the deterrent effect of arresting domestic violence offenders, see Lawrence W. Sherman and Richard A. Berk, "Deterrent Effects of Arrest for Domestic Assault," *American Sociological Review* 49 (April 1984): 261–71.

65. See Richard A. Berk and Phyllis J. Newton, "Does Arrest Really Deter Wife Battery? An Effort to Replicate the Findings of the Minneapolis Spouse Abuse Experiment," *American Sociological Review* 50 (1985): 253–262. These and other studies are discussed in "Protecting Battered Women: A Proposal for Comprehensive Domestic Violence Legislation in New York," *Fordham Urban Law Journal* 15, no. 4 (1986–1987): 999–1048.

66. "Child Abuse Prompts New Look at Law," *New York Times* (1 January 1988), p. 5.

67. For a discussion of these and other changes, see Gail A. Goolkasian, *Confronting Domestic Violence: The Role of Criminal Court Judges* (Washington, D.C.: U. S. Department of Justice, 1986).

68. See State v. Warford, 389 N.W. 2d 575 (Neb. 1986). For a discussion and analysis of the legal issues, see "Face–to Television Screen—to Face: Testimony by Closed-Circuit Television in Cases of Alleged Child Abuse and the Confrontation Right," *Kentucky Law Journal* 76, no. 1 (1987–1988): 273–99.

69. See Cassidy v. Maryland, 536 A.2d 666 (Md. Ct. Spec. App. 1988), *cert. den.* State v. Cassidy, 212 Md. 602 (1988), holding inadmissible the testimony of a doctor who testified that the alleged victim said that her "daddy" abused her.

70. "Child Abuse Prompts New Look at Laws."

71. Globe Newspaper Co. v. Superior Court, Etc.,

457 U.S. 596, 607–10 (1982), footnotes omitted. For a discussion, see "Protecting the Rape Victim Through Mandatory Closure Statutes: Is It Constitutional?" *New York Law School Law Review* 32, no. 1 (1987): 111–136.

72. CAL. CONST. Art. 1, Section 28; MINN. STAT. ANN., Section 611A.03(1). For a discussion see Sarah N. Welling, "Victims in the Criminal Process: A Utilitarian Analysis of Victim Participation in the Charging Decision," *Arizona Law Review* 30, no. 1 (1988): 85–117.

73. Booth v. Maryland, 482 U.S. 496, *reh. den.*, 483 U.S. 1056 (1987), cases and citations omitted. For a discussion see "Constitutional Law: Victim Impact Statements and the Eighth Amendment," *Harvard Journal of Law and Public Policy* 2 (Spring 1988): 583–93.

74. Anthony Walsh, "Placebo Justice: Victim Recommendations and Offender Sentences in Sexual Assault Cases," *Journal of Criminal Law and Criminology* 77 (Winter 1986): 1139, emphasis in the original.

75. For a detailed description of the evaluation of a proposed program, see Thomas Blomberg, Gordon Waldo, and Carol Bullock, *A Study of Jacksonville's Proposed Crime Victim Intake Center*, available from the authors, School of Criminology, Tallahassee, Florida, 32312.

76. See William E. Hoelzel, "A Survey of 27 Victim Compensation Programs, *Judicature* 10 (May 1980): 485–96. For a recent account of victim-witness programs, see Peter Finn and Beverly N. W. Lee, *Establishing and Expanding Victim-Witness Assistance Programs*, National Institute of Justice (Washington, D.C.: U. S. Dept. of Justice, August 1988).

77. U.S.C., tit. 18, Section 3579, as amended by P.L. 100-690, Section 7121 (1989).

78. For a discussion of this problem, see Deborah P. Kelly, "How Can We Help the Victim without Hurting the Defendant?" *Criminal Justice* (Summer 1987): 14–17; 38–40.

79. U.S.C., tit. 42, Section 10601.

80. Tarasoff v. Regents of the University of California, 131 Cal. Rptr. 45 (Cal. 1976).

81. A brief discussion of these cases may be found in the short article by Frank Carrington, "Crime Victims' Rights: Courts Are More Willing to Grant Remedies, *Trial* 24 (January 1988): 79–83.

PART 2

ENTRY INTO THE CRIMINAL JUSTICE SYSTEM: POLICING

The President's Commission on Law Enforcement and Administration of Justice emphasized in its 1967 report that police occupy the front line in this country. In a real sense, claimed the commission, our ability to do what we want, free from the fear of crime, depends on the police. But despite the responsibilities and powers granted to the police, they cannot deal effectively with crime without the cooperation of victims and witnesses. We already noted that such cooperation is not always given. Yet, police are blamed if crime rates increase and if reported crimes are not solved.

Part 2 explores the nature, organization, function, and problems of policing in an attempt to place this important aspect of the criminal justice system in proper perspective. Chapter 5 discusses the history of policing and explains how a formal police system emerged. It explains the different levels of public police systems in this country and then looks at private police. The administration and organization of police systems is also considered.

Chapter 6 describes what police actually do, ranging from performing many services within the community to the dangerous job of apprehending violent criminals. Police functions are discussed in the context of legal requirements and empirical social science research. Part 2 closes with a focus on some of the many problems and issues in policing.

The Emergence and Structure of Police Systems

CRIMINAL JUSTICE IN ACTION

Peter, who has just reached his thirteenth birthday, lives in a quiet rural area in which everyone knows everyone. Peter is caught stealing his neighbor's automobile. The neighbor talks to Peter and his parents and agrees that, if Peter will work 50 hours on the neighbor's farm, he will not report the theft to the police. The agreement is accepted, and Peter never has a criminal or juvenile record.

Abe, who is almost 14, lives in a suburban area. He also steals a car from his neighbor, who catches him in the criminal act. The neighbor screams angrily at Abe and calls the police, who arrive quickly and initiate formal proceedings against Abe. Abe is taken before the juvenile court, adjudicated delinquent, and sent to a training school for juveniles.

Harry, a young adult, steals a car in a large metropolitan area, but he is not apprehended. The police investigate the reported theft but are never able to link the theft with Harry.

INTRODUCTION

The brief hypothetical scenarios described in this chapter's CJA illustrate a common crime, auto theft, occurring in different settings. In a small and simple society, effective law enforcement by informal methods is often possible, but in larger, more complex societies that kind of control is usually ineffective. The scenarios are not meant to suggest that no formal action is ever taken in rural areas or that formal action is always taken in urban areas. Rather, the point is that informal methods of control are much more likely to be taken and to be effective in rural than in urban areas. The focus of this chapter is the emergence and development of *formal* **police** systems.

Policing is one of the most important functions in the entire criminal justice system. "The strength of a democracy and the quality of life enjoyed by its citizens are determined in large measure by the ability of the police to discharge their duties."[1] Almost one-half of the total expenditures for civil and criminal justice go for police protection, and although those expenditures have been increased significantly in recent years, the increase has not been sufficient. Total government spending for justice represents only 2.9 percent of the total government budgets, compared to, among other categories, 20.8 percent for social insurance payments, 18.3 percent for national defense and international relations, and 13.0 percent for education.[2]

This chapter and the following two chapters discuss policing: its past, present, and future. The discussion begins with a history of policing to explain the reason for the formal systems of public policing today. The history is traced from its informal beginnings in other countries to today's formal systems in the United States. The decentralized system of policing that exists in this country is examined by its major categories: local, state, and federal policing systems. Private policing also is examined.

The chapter then focuses on the administration and organization of police departments, looking at these subjects in historical perspective as well as at the issues they raise today. The recruitment, training, and education of police is considered as these topics pertain to the need for professionalism in policing.

HISTORY OF POLICING

Although formal policing is a relatively modern development, some form of policing has existed for centuries. When societies were small and cohesive, with most members sharing common goals and activities, it was usually possible to keep order without a formal police structure. The rules and regulations of the society were taught to new members as they were socialized, and most people observed the rules. Others could be coerced into observing those rules by informal techniques of social control. If that did not work and if rules were violated, crime victims might handle the situation informally, as in the case of Peter in this chapter's CJA. The victim might also be permitted to take private revenge against the offender.

In some countries informal policing was organized beyond the immediate family or individual concerned. England had the **frankpledge system,** in which families were organized into **tithings** (ten families) and **hundreds** (ten tithings) for purposes of protecting each other as well as for enforcing the laws. The frankpledge was a system of mutual pledge or mutual help, with all adult members responsible for their own conduct and that of others in the system. If the group failed to apprehend a lawbreaker, the English Crown fined all members of the group.

Individual private policing had its limits, however, and as societies grew in size and complexity, public policing was needed. The appointment of **constables** in England in the twelfth century signaled the beginning of public policing in that country. The constable, who was not paid, was apparently responsible for taking care of the weapons and the equipment of the hundred.

A second kind of police officer emerged when hundreds were combined to form shires, which were analogous to counties. The king appointed a shire-reeve to supervise each shire. The shire-reeve was the forerunner of the **sheriff.** Originally the shire-reeve was responsible only for making sure that citizens adequately performed their law enforcement functions, but later the sheriff's duties were expanded to include apprehending law violators. The sheriff was assisted in his duties by his constables, but the sheriff was the only paid official.

During the reign of Edward I (1272–1307), the **watch system,** the immediate forerunner to modern police systems, emerged in England. The watch system was developed as a means of protecting property against fire and for guarding the walls and gates of the cities. But the watchmen were also responsible for maintaining order and monitoring public behavior and manners. The London watchmen carried clubs and swords. They did not wear uniforms and could be distinguished from other citizens only by the lanterns and staffs they carried. Originally they were to patrol the streets at specified intervals during the night, announcing that all was well. As the city grew, a day shift was added.

Police officers today have more sophisticated equipment for performing their duties, but their jobs are also more complex and dangerous than in the past. (Rhoda Sidney/Stock Boston)

In 1326, Edward II supplemented the shire-reeve–supervised mutual pledge system by creating an office of justice of the peace. The justices were appointed by the king, and their original function was to assist the sheriff with the policing of the counties. Later the justices assumed judicial functions. As the central government took on greater responsibility for law enforcement in England, the constables lost their independence as officials of the pledge system and were under the authority of the justices.

Constables performed functions such as supervising night watchmen, taking charge of prisoners, serving summonses, and executing warrants, and the justices performed judicial functions, thus beginning the separation of the functions of the police and the judiciary. This distinction between the police functions of the constable and the judicial functions of the justices, with the constables reporting to the justices, remained the pattern in England for the next 500 years.

The mutual pledge system began to decline, however, as many citizens failed to perform their law enforcement functions within the system. The early police officials were not popular with citizens; nor were they effective. Citizens were also dissatisfied with the watch system and its inability to maintain order and prevent crime. English life was characterized by rising levels of crime, a perceived increase and greater severity of public riots, and an increase in public intoxication resulting from a rise in drinking among the lower classes.

Public drunkenness became a serious problem. Not used to drinking, people were unpredictable and often violent in their behavior on the streets. The result was a great rise in violent crimes and theft. The government responded by improving city lighting, increasing the number of watchmen, and increasing the punishment for all crimes. But the watchmen were not able to control the frequent riots that occurred; neither could they protect citizens and their possessions. The public responded by refraining from entering the streets at night without a private guard and by arming themselves. The rich moved to safer areas, leaving behind them the residential segregation characteristic of contemporary society.[3]

The rise of industrialization in England also contributed to the need for a formal police force. As more people moved to cities and life became more complex, maintaining law and order also became more difficult, and the less formal system of policing was not sufficient.

Modern Policing: The London Beginning

Although scholars still debate how and why formal police systems emerged, the beginning is usually traced to England, where Londoners protested the ineffectiveness of the watch system and agitated for a formal police force. Some believed that a police force constantly patrolling the town would reduce and eventually eliminate crime in the streets. Others feared that the concentration of power necessary for a formal police force would lead to abuses, especially if the force were a national one. Eventually the tension between these two positions was resolved by the establishment of local police systems.[4]

Dissatisfaction with the constable system led the English to experiment with other systems. In the mid-eighteenth century John Fielding and Henry Fielding, London magistrates, instituted a system called the **Bow Street Runners.** The Fieldings selected constables with a year of experience and gave them the police powers of investigation and arrest. The constables were given some training and were paid a portion of the fines in the cases they prosecuted successfully.

Increased concern about safety and security in London led to pressures from citizens to improve police protection. Between 1770 and 1828, a total of six commissions appointed by the English Parliament investigated policing and made suggestions, but an attempt in 1785 to establish a metropolitan police force was defeated by the opposition of powerful commercial interests. None of the English efforts were successful in establishing a satisfactory police force until 1829.[5]

That year the first modern police force, the Metropolitan Police of London, was founded in London by Sir Robert Peel. The men employed by the force were sometimes called *Peelers* and sometimes *Bobbies* after the founder. Working full-time and wearing special uniforms, the officers' primary function was to prevent crime. They were organized by territories and they reported to a central government. Candidates had to meet high standards to qualify for a job as a police officer in London. The system has been described as follows:

> Peel divided London into divisions, then into "beats." The headquarters for the police commissioners looked out upon a courtyard that had been the site of a residence used by the Kings of Scotland and was, therefore, called "Scotland Yard." . . . [I]n 1856 Parliament required every borough and county to have a police force similar to London's.[6]

London set the example; the rest of England was slow to follow, but other countries quickly began establishing modern, formal police systems. Some countries developed a centralized police system, but a decentralized system developed in the United States.[7]

EMERGENCE OF POLICING IN THE UNITED STATES

People in the United States saw a variety of policing systems in the early days. The English immigrants brought many aspects of their system to this country. The constable was in charge of towns, and the sheriff had jurisdiction over policing counties. Before the American Revolution, these positions were filled by the governors appointed by the Crown, but afterward, most constables and sheriffs obtained their positions by popular elections.

The English watch system was adopted by many of the colonies. As early as 1631, Boston had a watch system; New Amsterdam (later New York) developed a watch system in 1643. The New York City system was said to be typical of that system of policing in this country. Bellmen regularly walked throughout the city, ringing bells and providing police services. Later they were replaced by a permanent watch of citizens and still later by paid constables. Professional, full-time police were not appointed in New York City until 1845.

One of the most familiar kinds of policing, still in use in rural areas today, was the **posse.** Under the posse system, a sheriff could call into action any number of citizens over a certain age if they were needed to assist in law enforcement.

In some early systems in this country, law enforcement officials were paid by local government. Others were paid by private individuals.

> By the early nineteenth century, American law enforcement was a hodgepodge of small jurisdictions staffed by various officials with different power, responsibilities, and legal standing. There was no system, although there were ample precedents for public policing.[8]

It did not take long, however, for Americans to realize that these methods of policing did not produce the efficiency and expertise necessary to control the urban riots and increasing rates of crime and violence that accompanied the industrialization, increased complexity, and growth of American cities. A professional police system was needed; the movement toward that goal began in Boston in 1837. By the late 1880s, most American cities had established municipal police forces, although the county sheriff system continued to provide policing services in rural areas. State police systems were gradually added, followed by the federal system. The state and federal systems were not, however, to supersede the local systems.[9]

DECENTRALIZED POLICING: THE U.S. SYSTEM

The United States system of policing is a decentralized one, operating on several levels. This decentralized approach is advantageous because the policing needs of areas vary with the size and nature of the population. Therefore, it is important to examine the different levels of police systems regarding their unique needs as well as the general problems police encounter regardless of the area. This section discusses the major levels of police systems: rural, county, municipal, state, and federal. Even within those levels there are significant differences. After a brief look at the data on police officers, the general characteristics and problems of policing at each level will be discussed.

On October 31, 1987, the 12,149 city, county, and state police agencies employed a total of 480,383 officers and 160,785 civilians for a rate of 2.6 per 1,000 inhabitants.[10] Most of the employees are employed in cities, with the highest number in the largest cities, as would be expected because of the larger population.

Local Policing

Local policing includes police agencies at the rural, county, and municipal levels. Most studies of police focus on municipal policing. Few criminal justice texts even discuss rural policing, and usually only slight attention is given to county police systems, leaving the impression that these levels of policing are not important. This conclusion is erroneous because local and county levels of policing cover significant geographical areas of the country. In fact, the majority of police agencies in this country are located in small towns, villages, or boroughs.

Rural Policing   Throughout the United States, but particularly in southern and western regions, many towns and villages are too small to support a police department. Some of these areas depend on the county police system for protection. But others have their own systems, usually consisting of an elected official. This official is sometimes called a *constable,* who has policing duties similar to those of the county sheriff. Constables may not be trained in law or policing; yet they have the power to enforce laws, to arrest, to maintain order, and to execute processes from the **magistrate's** courts, which are courts of limited **jurisdiction,** often called *justice of the peace courts.*

Rural policing is very important but often plagued with financial and personnel problems. One officer cannot adequately police even a small area for 24 hours a day. Citizens are frequently without police protection; local police officers are overworked; and in many jurisdictions funds are not available for the support services necessary to adequate policing. Some of the problems of rural justice, including the entire criminal justice system, are illustrated by Spotlight 5.1.

Rural officers usually do not have sufficient resources for investigating criminal activity. They are more isolated from other officers. Quick backup services from other officers may be a scarce luxury rather than a daily reality. Working conditions of rural police may be less desirable than those of police officers at other levels. Salaries usually are significantly lower and not necessarily compensated for by a lower cost of living. Initial training is more limited and usually not geared to the unique problems of rural policing. Officers must often train in urban settings, because in many areas there are not enough rural police to justify separate training centers. As a result, those officers may have unrealistic expectations of rural policing. Many rural officers do not have the opportunity for continued education and training.

Budget planning and other activities concerning policing in rural areas might be town projects, with police officers involved in heated discussions from which their urban counterpart might be shielded by police administrators. This high visibility and total immersion in local problems and politics also might affect the social life of the officer, who finds it impossible to go anywhere in the area without being viewed as a police officer. For rural officers, long periods of inactivity may lead to boredom and lowered self-concept. In comparison to urban police, rural police may face even greater citizen expectations for a variety of services not connected with law enforcement.

On the positive side, some rural officers enjoy the greater involvement in community activities with local citizens. The lower crime rates, particularly the lower rates of violence, may increase police security. The lack of complexity in the police system might be seen as a positive rather than negative factor. Problems associated with a lack of security, when only one officer is assigned to an area, might be eliminated or greatly reduced by cooperation from the next level, county policing. In many areas, the rural police are limited to traffic functions and some ministerial

```
┌─┬─┬─┬─┐
├─┼─┼─┼─┤
├─┼─┼─┼─┤
├─┼─┼─┼─┤
└─┴─┴─┴─┘
```

SPOTLIGHT 5.1
A RECENT LOOK AT RURAL JUSTICE

When the Rural Justice Center looked for a place exemplifying some of the most vexing problems of rural justice in the United States, it came here to Robeson County which has a volatile population mix of whites, blacks and Indians, and a district attorney who has put more people on death row than any prosecutor in the United States.

So when two Tuscarora Indians took 19 hostages at the local newspaper recently, they did more than dramatize longstanding grievances about the criminal justice system in an insular county some people refer to as the Great State of Robeson (pronounced ROB-uh-son).

The situation also was a reminder that many of the most troubling issues of criminal justice are played out in areas far removed from the legal mainstream. The Rural Justice Center, a non-profit research and consulting organization based in North Conway, N.H., says 79 percent of the courts of general jurisdiction in the country—those other than specialty courts, like probate courts—are in rural areas, serving 55 million citizens.

"They are neglected by the judicial administration community in the same way rural communities are neglected by an urban-based society," said Kathryn Fahnstock co-director of the Rural Justice Center.

The two men arrested, Eddie Hatcher, 30, and Timothy Jacobs, 19, face possible life imprisonment on federal charges. They surrendered after state officials agreed to investigate allegations of discrimination and corruption in Robeson County. The American Indian Movement also said it would investigate and aid in their defense.

In some ways, Robeson is as distinctive a county as can be found in the United States. Its population of more than 100,000 spread out over 944 square miles in southeastern North Carolina is divided fairly equally between whites, blacks and Indians. Whites are the largest group, about 40 percent of the population, followed by Indians, with 35 percent. . . .

Robeson is one of the poorest counties in North Carolina. Because of its situation on Interstate 95 midway between New York and Florida, it has become a major drug distribution center, officials say. The sheriff's office made 400 drug arrests last year.

And few justice systems are dominated by one man the way Robeson County's is by District Attorney Joe Freeman Britt, a tall, flamboyant prosecutor who has been listed in the Guinness Book of World Records as the "deadliest prosecutor." By July 1987, he had won 44 death verdicts.

"He's the best prosecutor in the world," said John Wishart Campbell, a local defense attorney. "He's a fair man who treats everyone the same. He's mean to everyone."

To his admirers, Britt, who has run unopposed each election since he was first appointed to the post in 1973, is the spirit of law and order incarnate.

"The people who are in trouble are the ones who make the noise, but most people sit back and say, 'Attaboy, Joe,'" said Buddy Parker, a local businessman. "Most people think he's a super man."

To Britt's detractors, the system he runs is a caricature of the worst problems of rural justice, with the law being administered capriciously for the benefit of those in power. . . .

"Robeson County is not an isolated case," said Dr. Robert Schneider, a professor of political science at nearby Pembroke State University. "It's an extreme case of what has been a national tragedy, the systematic denial of due process for people in our legal system."

In various reports, the Rural Justice Center has said that isolation, excessive interdependence among those in the justice system and the intimacy of small-town life often mitigate an adversary system meant to protect the rights of defendants.

duties, with the major law enforcement handled by the county sheriff and county police officers. The county may contract with the rural community to provide these services.

And the group says rural areas often lack social services and aggressive defense attorneys to balance a vigorous law-enforcement system.

Critics and admirers agree that Britt runs a highly effective prosecutorial system.

Of 1,192 felony cases disposed of during the 1986–87 fiscal year in Britt's district, the largest portion of which is Robeson County, 933 were decided by guilty pleas to the original charges, six by guilty pleas to lesser charges, 67 by a finding of guilty by a jury, and 36 by findings of not guilty, according to the North Carolina Administrative Office of the Courts. The rest were dismissed or disposed of in other ways.

Of all 21,844 criminal cases filed by law enforcement officials, including traffic cases, less than 7 percent were dismissed, an extremely low figure, the Rural Justice Center says.

In a 1983 study, the center reported numerous abuses in the system. It said bail often was set too high and used as punishment rather than to ensure the appearance of defendants at trials. Court calendars are set so that people can spend days or even weeks in court waiting for their cases to be called.

It said that defendants are discouraged from seeking counsel and that, in 65 percent of the felony cases with counsel that were studied, the defense attorney did not file any motions. In every case but one, the defendant said his attorney spent less than 30 minutes discussing the case with him.

Neither Britt nor his assistants would respond to the criticisms, but local defense lawyers defended the system and their own performance. They said that, while problems existed, in general the system worked well, especially considering the county's poverty and high crime rate.

Franklin Freeman, director of the state's Administrative Office of the Courts, said some of the report's charges were still accurate, but others had been rectified. He said some of the most serious complaints such as accusations that innocent people often pleaded guilty, were unsubstantiated. . . .

Robeson County Citizens for Better Government has formed . . . to try to address community problems. Joy J. Johnson, a black minister and a leader of the group, said the hostage incident and other protests reflect a new level of activism in the minority communities.

"We have a new generation now," he said. "They're not going to take what my generation put up with."

As a result of such attitudes, proposals for changes in the judicial system are being considered by state officials. For example, Freeman said a study was planned for this spring on whether a full-time public defender's office should be established to replace the current practice of judges' appointing local lawyers to represent indigent defendants.

Local officials deny the ferment reflects broad-based problems. Sheriff Stone said he hears general criticisms but is met with silence when asked for specific complaints.

"You will always find some people, I call them radicals, but I think they're a small minority," he said. "For the most part, we have three races that live together as peacefully as you'll find anywhere."

And even most critics say the problems have less to do with race than with class and a history of poor education that has left the county with crime, poverty and illiteracy problems.

"These problems don't go back 10 years—they go back 100 years," said Harbert Moore, a leader in the Indian community. "It's sort of like the national debt. It just gets bigger and bigger."

Source: Peter Applebome, "How Rural Justice Differs," *New York Times News Service*, reprinted in *Dallas Morning News* (11 February 1988), p. 42A. Copyright © 1988 by The New York Times Company. Reprinted by permission.

County Policing   Some county police agencies are also rural, but the county system is larger and usually employs as the primary law enforcement officer a sheriff whose main law enforcement functions are described in Spotlight 5.2. The county sheriff may also have numerous other functions unrelated to law enforcement, such as acting as the county coroner, collecting county taxes, or supervising any number of county government activities. If the department is large enough, the county police department may have a deputy sheriff and law enforcement officers assigned to patrol the county and enforce order.

The sheriff is considered the most important law enforcement officer in the county, but in practice, the functions of the sheriff's officer are usually limited to the unincorporated areas of the county, with law enforcement in the incorporated areas handled by the municipal police in the larger cities.

As Spotlight 5.2 indicates, the sheriff is an elected official. Previously sheriffs often served for very long periods. But a 1988 study in Texas indicates that with changing times, it is becoming difficult if not impossible for long sheriff tenures to continue. Political activists have been successful in unseating several sheriffs who have served for years, leading some authorities to refer to the office of incumbent sheriff as "an endangered species."[11]

One study in 15 southern and southwestern states divided sheriffs into small rural, medium rural, and urban counties. Table 5.1 contains data on the comparisons of sheriffs in these categories. Of particular interest is the significantly lower tenure of small rural as compared to medium rural and urban sheriffs. Sheriffs in rural areas remain in the position only about half as long as their counterparts in larger areas, suggesting that the traditional view of the elected sheriff in rural areas having a stronghold on local politics and remaining in office for a long time is a dated stereotype. Urban sheriffs were also more educated, had been in police work longer, and were older than the sheriffs in less populated areas.

SPOTLIGHT 5.2
THE COUNTY SHERIFF

At the county level of government, the sheriff is the primary law enforcement officer. He is an elected official whose term usually spans from two to four years and whose jurisdictional responsibility primarily covers unincorporated portions of each county. His functions include keeping the peace, executing civil and criminal process, patrolling the area, maintaining the county jail, preserving order in county courts, and enforcing court orders. The sheriff as a rule performs only restricted law enforcement functions in incorporated areas within a county and then usually only when the city requests his participation in such activities as patrol or investigation.

Source: The President's Commission on Law Enforcement and Administration of Justice, *Task Force Report: The Police* (Washington, D.C.: U.S. Government Printing Office, 1967), p. 8.

TABLE 5.1

Personal Characteristics of Rural Sheriffs Compared
with Urban Sheriffs in 15 Southern Counties

	Small Rural	**Medium Rural**	**Urban**
Median Age	45.5 yrs.	46.7 yrs.	48.9 yrs.
Median Education	12.2 yrs.	12.1 yrs.	12.4 yrs.
Median Years—Police Work	8.6 yrs.	9.0 yrs.	11.8 yrs.
Median Years—Sheriff	2.8 yrs.	5.0 yrs.	4.9 yrs.
Sought Other Political Office	21%	19%	17%
In-Service Training	87%	76%	87%
(n)	(179)	(207)	(256)

Note: Small Rural—Counties with a population density less than or equal to 20 persons per square mile.
Medium Rural—Counties with a population density greater than 20 persons per square mile and less than or equal to 44 persons per square mile.
Urban—Counties with a population density of 45 persons or more per square mile.
Source: Adapted from Roger Handberg and Charles M. Unkovic, "Changing Patterns in Rural Law Enforcement: The County Sheriff as a Case Study," in Shanlor Cronket et al., eds., *Criminal Justice In America*, National Institute of Justice (Washington, D.C.: U.S. Government Printing Office, June 1982), p. 72.

The study of southern sheriffs also indicated that none were women, and the few blacks were in areas with a predominantly black voting population. Rural sheriffs were more likely to have been born in the areas they served. Urban sheriff departments were generally three or four times larger than rural departments, and rural sheriffs were more frequently in charge of jails, a responsibility that drained their resources and personnel.[12]

The lack of law enforcement attention to routine investigations probably accounts for at least some of the differential in urban and rural official crime data, thus providing another example of the effect an action in one area of the criminal justice system may have on other elements in the system.

Larger county police departments may contract their services to smaller county or rural departments. The county department may also employ county **marshals,** sworn officers who perform mainly civil duties of the courts, such as delivering papers to initiate civil proceedings. Marshals also may serve papers for the arrest of criminal suspects.

Larger county police departments have investigative units that service the district attorneys who bring the prosecutions in the county. These departments will be staffed by sworn officers and by support personnel. Departments too small for investigative units may contract for such services from the municipal or urban police departments in the area or the Federal Bureau of Investigation (FBI).

Municipal Policing Most studies of policing focus on municipal departments; most of the issues and problems also center around policing at this level. Consequently, the discussions in the following two chapters apply

Most police work in municipal areas. Here police are investigating drunk and disorderly conduct in a large city. (Sepp Seitz/Woodfin Camp)

mainly to municipal policing. Here some comments will be made about the differences between municipal, or urban, policing and the other local levels.

Municipal police departments differ from other local police agencies mainly in their size, organization, complexity, and services. Although they may service smaller geographic areas than rural or county systems, most municipal police systems will have more employees and provide more extended services. The complexity of the departments leads to greater problems in staffing, organization, and meeting the needs of the public. Municipal departments, however, usually will have more resources both within the department and within the community, and in some cases, these resources will be shared with rural and county systems on a contract basis. On the other hand, the expectations of citizens for services from municipal police departments are often greater than at the rural or county levels, whereas the mandate of the department is often less defined and more open ended.[13]

Municipal departments, in contrast to departments at other levels, may encounter more difficult political problems with their governing bodies. The police department will be competing with more agencies for funding. The costs of policing are highest in urban areas. Population changes also may present more problems. Many large cities have experienced significant changes in the numbers of people who actually live in the city compared to the number who come in daily to work. The residential tax base goes down as the need for services, order maintenance, and law enforcement increases.

Crime rates generally are much higher in urban than rural or county areas. The composition of the population also may present greater policing problems. Urban areas have a more heterogeneous population as well as a greater number of the unemployed, the transient, and those who have already been in trouble with the law.

State Policing

State police patrol highways and regulate traffic. They have the primary responsibility for enforcing some state laws and provide services, such as a system of criminal identification, police training programs, or a communications system for local law officials. The organization and the services provided by state police vary from state to state. No national or central control exists except for some standards of the United States Department of Justice and the United States Department of Transportation. This lack of centralization stems from the historic distrust of national police systems, as well as from the different law enforcement needs of different states. For example, in 1835 the Texas Rangers, a group of uneducated and untrained men, were recruited and given authority to protect the Texas border from the Mexicans. After Texas was admitted to the union, the Rangers were retained, still with the primary duty of patrolling the southern border of Texas.

The Texas Rangers became the first state-supported organization of police in this country. As police functions expanded, the role of the Texas Rangers also expanded, as did their training. Spotlight 5.3 describes the evolution of the Texas Rangers and explains how state police may assist rural or county police in performing various police functions.

The industrialization and expansion of the country led to many problems that could not be handled adequately at the local level, and although Texas had the first state police agency, Pennsylvania's system became the

A Texas state trooper poses with 567 pounds of cocaine he found while searching a vehicle during a traffic stop in central Texas. (Lynne Dobson/ TexaStock)

early model for state police in the United States. In the late 1870s, a powerful secret organization, the **Molly Maguires,** responded to anti-Irish riots in Pennsylvania by forming Irish labor unions that used violence to terrorize the state's coal-producing regions. The Molly Maguires controlled all hiring and firing. Employers who ignored their mandates were often killed. The terrorists threatened the growing Pennsylvania economy, which was heavily dependent on mineral wealth. The state was sparsely settled, and local police authorities could not control the Molly Maguires. "The Pinkerton Detective Agency, a private national organization, was eventually brought in to infiltrate the Molly Maguires, and twenty of its members were successfully prosecuted for murder and other crimes."[14]

In 1905 the governor of Pennsylvania succeeded in convincing the state legislature to appropriate funds for a constabulary to help in preventing future disasters such as those caused by the Molly Maguires. The movement toward state policing did not occur quickly, however, for many still feared that the next step would be national police and political repres-

SPOTLIGHT 5.3
TEXAS RANGERS LIVE THE LEGEND

An image of the state of Texas is inlaid in silver on his ivory-handled, .45-caliber pistol, and a small ruby marks the northern territory he's charged to roam.

A hand-tooled, leather holster hangs on his hip, and clipped to a rack in his car is the standard-issue, good-guy, white cowboy hat.

Weldon Lucas will tell you not to mistake his pistol, which is always cocked, for a *pearl-handled* one—"those are for showboats"—and he's sad to say that the cowboy hat seldom comes down from its rack.

"I don't wear the hat much," says the 45-year-old Lucas. "In fact, that's a summer hat, and I've been meaning to get a winter one up there."

For more than six years, Lucas, a modern-day Texas Ranger, has patrolled the high plains of Denton and Cooke counties. Like all Rangers, he takes a fierce pride in the force's rich lore—the storied "shoot first, ask questions later" myth.

But times have changed, and the demands on a Ranger differ dramatically from those their predecessors faced. No longer the high sheriffs in the state's counties, Texas Rangers are a cross between backwoods diplomats and dogged investigators.

Tradition and legend aside, Lucas says, the swath the Rangers still cut through Texas commands respect, most notably in the small towns and communities where they serve.

And Lucas, a robust man with a razor-edge haircut, rarely eases up on the bravado. With his slow swagger and western attire, Lucas could have walked off the Hollywood stage set where *The Comancheros* was filmed. . . .

A Ranger must function as a smooth-talking liaison between local, county and federal law enforcement agencies, he says, as well as providing a backup for the difficult cases the smaller forces don't have the manpower or resources to see through.

"It is expected that we solve a case. That's what Rangers did in the past, and that's what we must live up to," Lucas says emphatically. "We are an assisting and investigative arm. We try to stay behind the scenes, and we've got to get along with everybody.

"We can't shoot criminals or make up laws to bring them in like they did in the 1800s and early 1900s. But we have the ability to get things in the courthouse, and that's what we do."

The force traces its origin to 1823 when Stephen F. Austin hired 10 men to serve as "Rangers." But it wasn't until the Texas Revolution began in 1835 that the force was officially recognized and given legal status to operate across the state.

Early on, they were frontier defenders charged with fighting Indian and Mexican raiding parties and later battling outlaws, feudists, rustlers and oil-field rioters.

sion. But the use of automobiles and increased problems with traffic on state roads and highways in the twentieth century created an obvious need for state police.

State police are similar to the state patrol. Both have uniformed, sworn officers who carry weapons, and "when the activities of the state patrol are added to the services provided by the county sheriffs and a state bureau of investigation, the services rendered are very close to those offered by a state police system."[15] The state patrol and the state police differ primarily in their law enforcement powers. State patrol officers in most jurisdictions are primarily traffic control officers, although they may also be empowered to enforce criminal laws violated in their presence, on the highway, or within sight of or adjacent to the highway. But they do not have general powers of law enforcement for all state laws as state police have. State police, in contrast to the state patrol, may have their own investigation units as well as a forensic science laboratory.

State police also differ from the state patrol in that the state police

Most of the 94 Rangers in Texas today still operate independently. In rural areas, a sole Ranger might cover several counties that stretch over hundreds of miles. But bullets and bullheadedness have been traded for subpoenas and sophisticated investigative disciplines—like blood-splatter and voter-fraud analyses.

As part of the Texas Department of Public Safety, the Rangers have forensic labs, helicopters, airplanes and state-of-the-art surveillance systems at their fingertips.

Still, all the sophisticated equipment in the world can't replace the dreary, and often dangerous, police work that has to be done. . . .

The bulk of Lucas' day is spent driving his territory, which ranges from the neon and fast-food strips in Denton and Lewisville to the back roads of Cooke County, where towns like Prairie Point and Lois alternate with lush horse ranches and scraggly woods. . . .

"I have the luxury of dropping everything and spending a lot of time on an investigation. Up here the county and local investigators get snowed under with the everyday stuff," the Ranger says. "And we don't get the easy ones."

Lucas, whose 24 years of DPS duty includes stints as an undercover agent and supervisor of a narcotics division, says he's cleared about 80 percent of his murder cases.

"He is an excellent investigator," says Phil Adams, Cooke County's district attorney. "We use him because he's very good, but we also try not to tie up his time on the routine stuff."

Some of the Rangers' investigative methods have been anything but routine. Again, Lucas attributes it to frontier bravado.

Rangers have been known, he says, to send Christmas and birthday cards and other surprises to those they suspect might have commited a crime—just to let them know they're still on the trail.

He says that sometimes the best thing a Ranger can do is just show up.

When the Denton County town of Hackberry was in the midst of a coup a year ago, Lucas' sullen appearance wasn't lost on the town's 260 residents. A political feud had come to a head when two aldermen took control of town records, moved City Hall and appointed new town officials.

Lucas was not too happy about being dragged into the middle of such a political fiasco.

"You go into these town squabbles, and half of the town loves you and the other half hates you," Lucas says. "But hey, that's all right. In fact it's good for the mystique of the Ranger because they all respect you."

Source: Joe Drape, "Texas Rangers Live the Legend, *Dallas Morning News* (6 March 1988), p. 29A. Reprinted with permission of The Dallas Morning News.

system often includes specialized forms of policing, such as control over fishing and gaming laws, regulation of gambling and horse racing, and regulation of alcohol sales. The Alcohol Board of Control is a state agency responsible for investigating requests for liquor licenses and may also have the power to establish rules concerning the conditions under which liquor may be sold. This same board may also be in charge of enforcing state laws concerning the sale of dangerous drugs.

Federal Policing

Enforcement of criminal laws in the United States historically has been viewed as the function of states, although states may and do delegate some of their powers to local police agencies. The Constitution does not provide for a central police agency. It gave the federal government specific power to enforce only a limited number of crimes. The Constitution also provides that all powers not delegated to the federal government are reserved to the states. But the Constitution also gives Congress the power to pass laws that are "necessary and proper" for the exercise of Congressional powers. Over the years Congress has passed statutes on federal crimes. The United States Supreme Court has upheld the power of Congress to do so in many cases.

Today the number of crimes included in the *United States Criminal Code* has grown to the point that when Congress, after years of attempts, passed a new criminal code in 1984, almost 800 pages were required to print the code. Despite the number of crimes that can be enforced at the federal level, the relative number of criminal cases processed at that level is small compared to the number at the state and local levels. Less than 50,000 police are employed at the federal level, compared to approxi-

William Sessions, center, Director of the Federal Bureau of Investigation, pictured as he arrived at a Senate Judiciary Committee hearing on his nomination. (John Duricka/AP Wide World)

mately one-half million sworn officers at the state and local levels. Federal law enforcement includes federal prosecutors and federal police agencies. The federal level of policing is quite complex and encompasses more than 50 enforcement agencies.

The first federal police agency was established in 1789 to deal with smuggling. In the following years, federal policing was narrowly focused on federal activities such as the mails, but in 1868 Congress authorized a federal detective force, followed in 1879 by the establishment of the Department of Justice. This department was established for crime detection and prosecution. Congress passed a statute that regulated mail fraud, the first criminal statute giving the federal government jurisdiction over crimes that usually had been prosecuted at the state level.

Other statutes expanding federal criminal jurisdiction followed. In about 1919 a criminal division was established within the Department of Justice. Five years later, J. Edgar Hoover was appointed director of the Justice Department's Bureau of Investigation, which later became the Federal Bureau of Investigation (FBI). Hoover headed that organization until his death in May 1972.[16]

The foundation for the modern era of federal criminal control began in the 1930s and continued until the end of World War II. During that period many crimes were added to the federal criminal code. The modern era followed. Beginning in the 1950s, it was characterized by a new perception of the federal government's role in crime prevention and control. Crime was seen as a national problem, with the federal government having a special responsibility to assist states and local governments in enforcing laws, investigating criminal activity, and preventing crime. The modern era brought another expansion of federal criminal statutes and an increase in federal law enforcement personnel.

The Federal Bureau of Investigation   The largest federal criminal law enforcement agency (with the exception of the military) is the Federal Bureau of Investigation in the Department of Justice. The department, with about 8,000 agents, is the primary agency charged with enforcing all federal laws not assigned to other special agencies. The FBI headquarters are located in Washington, D.C. Field officers are located in major cities throughout the United States and in San Juan, Puerto Rico. The director of the FBI is appointed by the president of the United States, by and with the consent of the Senate.

The investigative work of the FBI is performed by special agents. All agents are trained at the FBI Academy, located on the United States Marine Corps Base at Quantico, Virginia. In addition to special agents, the FBI employs approximately 11,000 persons, who perform such functions as fingerprint examinations, clerical and receptionist duties, computer programming, and laboratory work.

The FBI is not a national police force. It is primarily an investigative agency. FBI agents may investigate crimes over which the federal government has jurisdiction by statute; they may also investigate state and local crimes when requested by those agencies. The FBI crime laboratory provides investigative and analysis services for other law enforcement agencies. Perhaps best known are the fingerprinting services. The FBI maintains fingerprint cards on more than 65 million persons. The FBI's National Crime Information Center maintains a file on missing persons.

The National Crime Information Center of the FBI stores information on serialized stolen property, persons for whom an arrest is outstanding, and criminal histories on some persons. This information, which can be quickly retrieved, is available to other law enforcement agencies. The facilities and scientific expertise of the FBI laboratory are available to other law enforcement agencies upon request. There is no charge for these services.

The training facilities of the FBI Academy are used by other agencies for training law enforcement officers; some foreign officers are accepted into the program. The academy provides continued education and training for officers. Another important function of the FBI is the collection of national data on crimes known to the police and on arrests.

Over its history, particularly during the long years it was headed by J. Edgar Hoover, the FBI has been criticized severely as well as praised highly. During most of its existence, the FBI has had only loose directives from Congress. A strong leader like Hoover was able to take advantage of that situation and build a powerful, extremely influential organization that allegedly held great power even over the presidents under whom Hoover served. Yet, "given the history of informal direction and loose supervision, and in spite of excesses and Hooverian eccentricities, the Bureau has achieved a generally high level of professionalism."[17]

The FBI provides outstanding career opportunities for young people who want to be involved in law enforcement. This agency, like other federal law enforcement agencies, should be viewed as a supplement to, not a replacement of, state and local agencies.

Other Federal Law Enforcement Agencies   In addition to the FBI, the Department of Justice contains two major law enforcement agencies: the Drug Enforcement Administration (DEA) and the Immigration and Naturalization Service (INS). The DEA previously was part of the Treasury Department and called the *Bureau of Narcotics*. It was shifted to the Justice Department in 1973. The FBI also has some drug enforcement powers, so the DEA and the FBI engage in some cooperative work. The INS polices the borders of the United States, trying to prevent the entrance of illegal aliens. The INS also is in charge of admitting foreigners who qualify for United States citizenship.

Some federal law enforcement agencies are part of the Treasury Department. The Customs Service handles inspections at points of entry into the United States. The Internal Revenue Service (IRS) is in charge of laws regulating federal income tax and its collection. The Bureau of Alcohol, Tobacco and Firearms (ATF) has jurisdiction over laws and licensing requirements regarding the sale of alcohol and drugs and over federal gun control laws and the collection of taxes connected with these areas. The Secret Service is responsible for protecting the president, vice-president, and other specific officials, as well as for investigating forged government checks, other securities, and counterfeiting activities.

Other federal agencies also are concerned with law enforcement, li-

Many federal law enforcement officers receive their formal training at the FBI Academy in Quantico, Virginia. (Sue Titus Reid)

censing, or both. The Food and Drug Administration (FDA) oversees the enforcement of the vast number of laws regulating the sale and distribution of pure food and drugs. The Department of Agriculture has an Office of Investigation that investigates fraud in the area of food stamps as well as in aid to disaster victims, subsidies to farmers and rural home buyers, and in other activities of the department. Criminal law enforcement divisions are also found in the Securities and Exchange Commission (SEC), the Department of Labor, the U.S. Postal Service, and other federal organizations.

United States Marshals   The president of the United States, with the consent of the Senate, appoints nearly 100 persons, one for each federal judicial district, as United States marshals. These marshals are assisted by deputy marshals. Their major function is to transport federal prisoners between prison and court and to escort them to home or jobs when they have temporary leaves. Witnesses at federal trials who need protection will receive that protection from federal marshals. The marshals are in charge of seizing and auctioning federal property, taken by others but that federal courts have authorized must be returned. As sworn police officers, U.S. marshals make arrests for federal offenses and perform other police functions such as controlling riots.

The International Level

The function that federal agencies can provide for local and state police is illustrated by the participation of the federal government in **INTERPOL,** a world police organization established for cooperation among nations involved in common police problems. INTERPOL was founded in 1923 but did not function actively until after its reorganization in 1946. The United States became a member in 1938. INTERPOL is to "track and apprehend criminal fugitives, thwart criminal schemes, exchange experience and technology, and analyze major trends of international criminal

SPOTLIGHT 5.4
POLICING AT THE INTERNATIONAL LEVEL: INTERPOL

As law enforcement agencies battle new breeds of crime spawned by advances in modern technology, INTERPOL is becoming an ever more important tool for criminal investigation. Its world association of national police forces places a global network of services at the disposal of police officers whose cases extend to foreign jurisdictions. Established for mutual assistance in detecting and deterring international crimes and criminals, INTERPOL provides the only practical means by which most local enforcement authorities can pursue a criminal matter outside the country.

INTERPOL gives U.S. law enforcement agencies access to the police resources of 136 nations around the world. The service is free to the local agency,

and it has become increasingly important in the investigation of such crimes as traffic in drugs, guns, and stolen works of art, laundering of money, electronic funds transfer fraud, counterfeit currency, and acts of international terrorism.

In recent years, the United States has increased its participation in INTERPOL to help strengthen the organization's capabilities to fight international criminal activities that threaten the security and the economies of many countries.

Source: Michael Fooner, "INTERPOL: Global Help in Fight Against Drugs, Terrorists, and Counterfeiters," *NIJ Reports,* National Institute of Justice (September 1985), p. 3.

activity. Any police official of any member country may initiate a request for assistance on a case that extends beyond his country's territory."[18] The importance of INTERPOL is illustrated in Spotlight 5.4.

Analysis of Decentralized Policing

Decentralized policing has the main advantage of giving recognition to the rights of local and state authorities to organize and manage their own affairs. Some aspects of policing are unique to particular areas; state and local autonomy give the people in those areas the power to solve their problems in ways they think are best under the circumstances.

Decentralization also preserves the strong belief in state's rights that has permeated all areas of government in the United States. It allows states to be creative and innovative in solving their internal problems of overlap, duplicity of services, or even hostility among the various police agencies. Agencies at the local, state, and even federal levels may cooperate while maintaining their own independence.

The disadvantages of decentralization are that, in addition to overlap and a duplicity of services, some needs may fall through the gaps between agencies. Competition between agencies also may create problems. The jurisdiction of police officers within each level of government is limited to the area in which that person is a sworn officer of the law. With only a few exceptions, such as an officer in hot pursuit of a suspected criminal, officers may not cross those jurisdictional boundaries for the purpose of law enforcement without being invited to do so by the officers in charge of the next jurisdiction. Even when officers desire help from officers in another jurisdiction, obtaining such help may be difficult because of bureaucratic policies.

PRIVATE POLICE AND SECURITY FORCES

In addition to public policing, an important development all over the world is the growth of private policing. Businesses employ security guards to protect their premises from shoplifting and to secure the personal safety of employees and shoppers. Security guards are frequently employed to escort women employees from their places of work to their automobiles at night, particularly in high-crime areas. Apartment owners also have increased their use of private security forces, as have neighborhood associations. Increasingly common are guard gates at which drivers entering the association area are required to stop and present adequate identification before being granted permission to enter the premises.

On college campuses **private security forces** are often hired for night work in addition to the regular security of the institution. Some serve as escorts for women students who attend night classes. The need for private security and private police has risen as citizens have felt a lack of sufficient security provided by public police.

Types of Systems

Whereas some businesses have their own private investigators and security personnel, others contract for those services from professional firms. The oldest and largest of the firms providing investigative and security services is Pinkerton's, founded in 1850 by Allan Pinkerton. Pinkerton was the first detective of the Chicago Police Department. Local, state, and federal agencies, as well as private companies and individuals, employed the services of Pinkerton's. "The term 'private eye' had its source in the unblinking eye that was Pinkerton's trademark for many years." Pinkerton's, headquartered in New York City, has over 100 offices and over 12,000 clients in the United States and Canada. The primary business of Pinkerton's today is to supply private security guards, but the firm also provides private consultants, electronic surveillance devices, and some investigation service.[19]

Private security is also provided by alarm companies. The most frequently used security program today is alarm systems; increasing numbers of systems are being installed in private residences and in businesses. Fire and burglar alarm systems are most common, but alarm companies also install access control systems, fixed security equipment, and perimeter security systems. Most alarm systems are installed by relatively small companies, although some companies have services available nationally. The most sophisticated systems are constantly monitored for increased protection and may involve extensive, and very expensive, systems.

Private security also is provided by armored vehicles with armed guards for transporting precious jewels, money, and other valuables. Cour-

Many private residential areas employ private security guards. (David Hall)

ier services provide fast delivery for valuables and papers that must be transported quickly and safely. Private security services also may be employed for emptying cash machines, delivering money from businesses to bank drops after hours, and many other activities in which business persons or private citizens feel a need for added security. Other services include security training courses, screening of personnel for businesses, technical countersurveillance to determine whether bugging devices have been installed, security consultation, and drug detection. Private security vaults are used frequently by people who want access to their valuables after regular banking hours.[20]

Growth of Private Security and Characteristics of Personnel

An estimated 1 million people are employed in private security, and by 1990 an additional 215,000 persons will be employed. Expenditures for private security protection now exceed expenditures for public security, as indicated in Figures 5.1 and 5.2. The most rapid growth for private security occurred in the late 1970s and early 1980s at a time when public police agencies were experiencing reductions in personnel, hiring freezes, and a general stabilization of allocated resources.[21]

The quality of private security guards has improved with this growth. The average guard today is a well-trained young white man with a high school education (and an increasing number with some college education). This description compares to the 1969 study that found the average guard to be an "aging white male, poorly educated, usually untrained and very poorly paid . . . [with] little education beyond the ninth grade."[22]

Relationships Between Public and Private Policing

Some attempts have been made to study the relationships between public law enforcement and private security systems. A 30-month national study sponsored by the National Institute of Justice (NIJ) of the Department of Justice highlighted some of the problems between the two systems as well

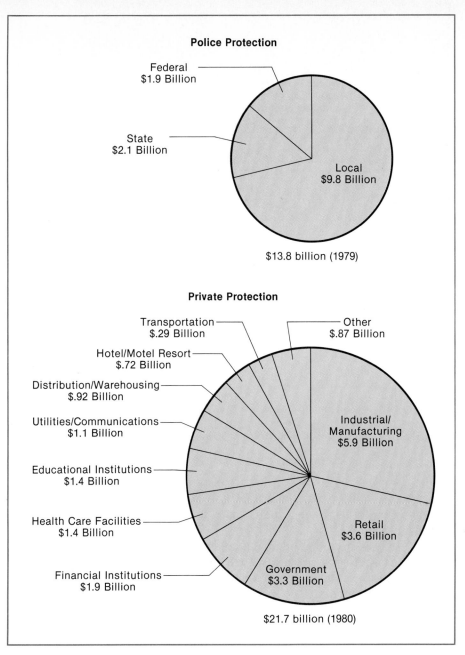

Police Protection

Federal
$1.9 Billion

State
$2.1 Billion

Local
$9.8 Billion

$13.8 billion (1979)

Private Protection

Transportation
$.29 Billion

Other
$.87 Billion

Hotel/Motel Resort
$.72 Billion

Distribution/Warehousing
$.92 Billion

Utilities/Communications
$1.1 Billion

Industrial/
Manufacturing
$5.9 Billion

Educational Institutions
$1.4 Billion

Health Care Facilities
$1.4 Billion

Retail
$3.6 Billion

Financial Institutions
$1.9 Billion

Government
$3.3 Billion

$21.7 billion (1980)

FIGURE 5.1

Gross Expenditures for Protection in the United States. *Source:* William C.
Cunningham and Todd H. Taylor, *The Growing Role of Private Security,* National
Institute of Justice, Research in Brief (Washington, D.C.: U.S. Department of Justice,
October 1984), p. 17, footnotes omitted.

as some of the progress in solving those problems. It was found that the
two systems share many common goals, such as recovering stolen property, protecting life and property, and deterring and discovering criminal
activity. But the study also indicated that public law enforcement officials

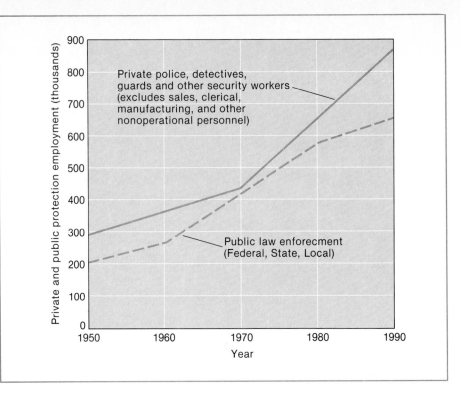

FIGURE 5.2
Trends in Private and Public Protection Employment. *Source:* Bureau of the Census and Bureau of Labor Statistics publication. Reprinted in William C. Cunningham and Todd H. Taylor, *The Growing Role of Private Security*, National Institute of Justice, Research in Brief (Washington, D.C.: U.S. Department of Justice, October 1984), p. 18.

rate private security personnel poorly in almost every area of their work and that they do not have a high regard for the ability of private security to prevent crime.

The NIJ study concluded that there is still a "climate of suspicion and distrust between private security and law enforcement," although some progress toward cooperative efforts has been made. There was evidence of a willingness to cooperate and to transfer some responsibilities from public law enforcement to private security. Some efforts have been made to integrate the activities and increase the understanding between private security personnel and public law enforcement officers.[23]

Other issues have arisen concerning private police protection. Despite recent legislation in many states, some still do not have licensing requirements for private security. In those jurisdictions, there are few if any checks on the quality of security services or on the training of security personnel. Many states have enacted statutes providing for regulation of private security, but even in those cases, many issues remain. There has been opposition to these measures. Some question licensing fees, required psychological tests, and statutes that are not broad enough to include all types of private security.[24] Increased reliance on private security forces also raises the moral and ethical question of whether our society can afford to have a system in which necessary police protection is available only to those in the upper income brackets.

ADMINISTRATION OF POLICE SYSTEMS

Administration and management of any large department presents numerous challenges and problems, but these may be particularly acute in publicly supported police departments. The police department frequently is the largest and most complex agency in the criminal justice system, with officers at the lower levels exercising tremendous authority over the lives of citizens. The functions performed by these people are varied and complex, although the training for the job usually focuses on only one of those functions—law enforcement.[25]

Despite the importance of police administration, until recently little attention was given to the issues and problems of administration. Indeed, in contrast to the well-planned development of the English police system, the American police system's development was preceded by little planning because of a basic mistrust of a professional police force. Early systems were characterized by corruption and inefficiency. The result was that, at the turn of this century, police forces in our metropolitan areas "were caught in a vicious circle of political manipulation, low prestige, small public expectations, and neither the will nor the pressure to improve."[26]

Early Reform Efforts

Widespread corruption, inefficiency, and a realization of the often negative impact of partisan politics on police systems gave rise in the early 1900s to a study of the role of police administration in improving the quality of policing and to the increased use of private security guards.

These early efforts were assisted by the work of the major reformer August Vollmer, often referred to as the father of modern police management systems or (as Spotlight 5.5 indicates), the dean of American chiefs of police. As chief of the Berkeley, California, Police Department, Vollmer instituted a summer program in criminology at the University of California at Berkeley and began an emphasis on the importance of formally educating police.

In 1931 the School of Criminology was founded at Berkeley. In 1933 it granted the first police degree, an A.B. degree with a minor in criminology. In 1930 the first two-year college police program was begun at San Jose Junior College, but the first grants to such programs did not begin until 1966. These programs were to offer courses in liberal arts, behavioral sciences, public administration, law, and government.

Others who were influential were Bruce Smith, who contributed to police professionalism through his writings and as a professional police consultant, and O. W. Wilson. Wilson was influential as a police chief emphasizing advanced training for officers in Wichita, Kansas, in the late 1920s. He was dean of the School of Criminology at Berkeley and a coauthor of a widely acclaimed text on police administration.[27] He perhaps

SPOTLIGHT 5.5
AUGUST VOLLMER: DEAN OF AMERICAN CHIEFS OF POLICE

He never went any further than the seventh grade in school, but held the rank of full professor at the University of Chicago and the University of California.

Architect of some of the major contributions of the present century to crime control, the man—August Vollmer, Dean of American Chiefs of Police and for 32 brilliant years, the chief of police of Berkeley, California—became known the world over as a social scientist who pioneered the application of scientific method in police service. The scores of innovations that he introduced have since become standard practice in the American police field and in civilized countries throughout the world. Even a partial inventory of these contributions provides a factual account of the march toward professionali-zation in this branch of the public service.

The Vollmer system of police administration attracted national and international attention, illumi-nating the way for an emerging profession and launching the American police services into a period of transition, the full implications of which are not yet generally understood. The author has traveled the length and breath of Europe, the Mediterranean,

the Holy Land, the Orient, and Southeast Asia and found it to be true everywhere—the mere mention of his name in police circles caused eyes to light up. The connotation was always the same—a scientific police service.

He gave to the people of Berkeley the lowest crime and delinquency rates of any city in Berkeley's population class. The odds under which he achieved this unusual record can best be understood on pointing out that Berkeley is located in a dense metropolitan area around San Francisco Bay in a state posting some of the highest crime rates in the nation. In addition, he developed a police system costing less per capita than in any other city in Berkeley's class and, yet, paid his officers higher salaries than could be found anywhere in the police services.

Source: V. A. Leonard, "August Vollmer: Dean of American Chiefs of Police," *The Police Chief* 48 (February 1981): 65, footnote deleted. Copyright held by The International Association of Chiefs of Police, Inc., P.O. Box 6010, 13 Firstfield Road, Gaithersburg, MD 20878, USA. Further reproduction without express written permission from IACP is strictly prohibited.

---

was best known for his contributions in the 1960s as superintendent of police in Chicago.

Vollmer, Smith, and Wilson strongly influenced the emergence of a professional model for policing, including not only the use of management skills at the administrative levels of policing, but also the application of modern technology in improving police work. The result was a model characterized by "a tight quasi-military organization; rigorous discipline; a streamlined chain of command; higher recruitment standards; a lengthy period of preservice training; the allocation of available personnel ac-cording to demonstrated need; and extensive use of vehicles, communi-cations, and computer technology."[28]

A Professional Model of Policing

What was needed was a professional model of policing. As sociologist Jerome Skolnick often has emphasized in his analyses of policing, profes-sionalism involves more than technological advancement. The needed phi-losophy of professionalism must rest on a set of values conveying the idea that the police are as much an institution dedicated to achieving legality in society as they are an official social organization designed to control illegal conduct through arrests. The problem of policing in a democratic society is not merely a matter of obtaining newer police cars and a higher order of technical equipment nor of recruiting people who have to their credit more years of education. What must occur is a significant alteration in the ideology of police so that police professionalism rests on the values of a democratic legal order rather than on technological proficiency.[29]

The professional model of policing gained momentum with the reports of the President's Commission on Law Enforcement and Administration of Justice in 1967 and the National Advisory Commission on Criminal Justice Standards and Goals in 1973. According to the 1981 report of the United States Commission on Civil Rights, "These two commissions, in particular, gave added impetus to some specific suggestions, such as the more effective use of police personnel and, most emphatically, the requirement that police officers have some college education."[30]

The need for professional police systems became obvious in the 1960s. With television bringing into the American home the violent clashes between police and minorities, including the young as well as racial and ethnic groups, the urban riots of the 1960s indicated the need to train police in handling orderly protests as well as violence and law enforcement.

During the 1960s, police and other elements of the criminal justice system became the focus of the federal government. In 1965 President Lyndon Johnson appointed the President's Commission on Law Enforcement and Administration of Justice. This commission issued several reports in 1967. In 1965 Congress established the Office of Law Enforcement Assistance, and in 1968 the **Law Enforcement Assistance Administration** (LEAA). Until its demise in 1982, LEAA provided over $7 billion for research, development, and evaluation of various programs in criminal justice, some of which went for hardware in police departments (a source of criticism of the LEAA). Money also was provided for police education through the **Law Enforcement Education Program** (LEEP). The result was the development of criminal justice departments throughout the country. Most of them focused on the education of police.

Recruitment   Recruitment and training of police personnel are critical processes in the establishment of an efficient and effective police force; yet the Commission on Civil Rights found that standards for selecting police recruits do not accurately reflect and measure the qualities needed for adequate job performance. In addition, the standards contribute to discrimination against women and minorities. The commission recommended the review of current selection standards "to ensure that they are job-related. Those standards that tend to disqualify minorities and women disproportionately should be subjected to a high degree of scrutiny." The commission also emphasized the importance of psychological testing.[31]

The difficulty, however, is that desirable qualities and characteristics are never defined in acceptable and measurable terms. Perhaps the problem is that in the past the focus has been on the people and their qualities, the assumption being that if different types of people were attracted to policing, the profession would be improved. Some have assumed that cer-

Affirmative action has resulted in active recruiting of women and minority police officers. (Karen Griggs/Sygma)

tain types of people, for example, authoritarian and cynical people, are attracted to policing. Others argue that the system of policing creates these personalities.[32]

In an analysis of the literature on police personalities, two researchers concluded that it is not possible to draw conclusions about whether police possess a distinct personality, and if so, when and how it is acquired. Nor is it possible to eliminate all undesirable candidates by use of psychological testing as part of the recruitment and selection process. However, psychological tests are useful in conjunction with other recruitment and selection methods such as personal interviews. The personal interview is the device most widely used for selecting job applicants, but the limited studies of its use among police indicate that "there is no strong evidence of the reliability with which it predicts future performance."[33]

Despite the lack of conclusive data on the predictability of psychological and other tests or job interviews, all should be used in recruiting and selecting police recruits. It is also important to give the recruits an indication of the context in which policing occurs as well as the nature of the job. This information might alleviate the stress caused by unrealistic expectations by recruits.

Successful recruitment of police officers requires more research into the characteristics most highly associated with effective policing. We do know that good policing requires many qualities, including intelligence and the abilities to think independently, to switch roles, to understand other cultures and subcultures, to switch functions, and to understand the importance of freedom and the dangers of abusing authority. Minimum qualifications for officers in one large police department in the midwest are listed in Spotlight 5.6, which reprints in part the recruitment poster used to advertise in that department. The minimum education require-

SPOTLIGHT 5.6
NOTICE OF OPENINGS FOR POLICE OFFICERS

Minorities and Women Are Encouraged to Apply

1987 Salary Schedule
  Probationary Patrolman $16,500
  2nd Year Patrolman $21,259
  3rd Year Patrolman $25,022

Requirements

1. Be a resident citizen of the United States
*2. Must be 21 to apply and not over 35 years of age

*You cannot have reached your 36th birthday prior to swearing-in date.

3. Have a High School diploma or GED Certificate
4. Not have been convicted of a felony
5. Have weight in proportion to height
6. Have vision no less than 20/100 uncorrected, correctable to 20/30 – Normal Color Vision
7. Have blood pressure of no higher than 150/90
8. Not have been dishonorably discharged from the military
9. Be a resident of Marion County (thirty days after appointment)
10. Possess a valid driver's license from the State of Residence

---

ment is only a high school diploma or its equivalent. An increasing number of departments are requiring at least some college education.

Higher Education   College education for police first received significant attention from August Vollmer in 1917, when he recruited part-time police officers from students at the University of California. Despite his emphasis on the importance of higher education and his reputation as an outstanding police administrator, Vollmer did not succeed in getting many police departments to follow his lead. During the Depression when jobs were scarce, college-educated men were recruited by police departments, but that practice ceased with the end of the Depression. California slowly added college-educated men to the police forces, but elsewhere the phrase *college cop* was often heard.

In 1967 the President's Commission on Law Enforcement and the Administration of Justice recommended that the "ultimate aim of all police departments should be that personnel with general enforcement powers have baccalaureate degrees."[34] The government provided financial incentives and support for the development of programs for higher education of police. By early 1980 it was estimated that approximately half of the police officers in this country had received some college training under the federally funded programs. But in the early 1980s the federal funding was cut; many programs were reduced or abolished; local budgets were cut; and some departments that had established policies requiring police officers to have a college degree were either changing those requirements or extending the date for their enforcement.

The emphasis on higher education of police also has been criticized. In the first place, many of the criminal justice programs that provide police education have come under severe attack. Critics argue that there is too much emphasis on technical skills at the expense of a broad educational background. The National Advisory Commission on Higher Education for Police Officers criticized higher-education programs for police for "servicing the status quo" rather than offering police a broadening experience that would enable them to expand the ability to tackle their professional problems.[35]

The commission also recommended recruiting college-educated young people rather than sending recruits to college. Persons entering law enforcement should be educated in programs in which no more than one-fourth of the courses are law enforcement courses. Ideally, recommended the commission, police would be recruited from those who are broadly trained in the liberal arts and therefore qualified to enter other professions.

In 1985 the New York Police Department announced the establishment of the Police Cadet Corps, a program designed to improve the educational level of police by attracting college-educated people into policing. Only one-fourth of the new police in New York City have college degrees. The Police Cadet Corps will provide scholarships and training to interested sophomores who, after 80 hours of training, will be issued uniforms and paid $5 an hour to work as apprentices with police officers. The students will not carry weapons. Students will receive up to $1,500 in interest-free loans during their junior and senior years. The loans will be cancelled if after graduation the recipients are accepted into the police department and serve for two years.[36]

Training   In emphasizing the need to attract educated people into policing, the importance of training in skills should not be overlooked. In its 1967 report, the Task Force on Police of the President's Commission on Law Enforcement and Administration of Justice emphasized the importance of adequate police training, noting that the problem was particularly acute in small police departments. Many larger departments had expanded police training, but the task force concluded that "current training programs, for the most part, prepare an officer to perform police work mechanically but do not prepare him to understand his community, the police role, or the imperfections of the criminal justice system." Few of the programs reviewed by the commission provided training on the use of discretion in policing.[37]

The commission's final recommendations on the training of police included providing instruction on "subjects that prepare recruits to exercise discretion properly and to understand the community, the role of the police, and what the criminal justice system can and cannot do." The commission recommended "an absolute minimum of 400 hours of classroom work spread over a four-to-six-month period so that it can be combined with carefully selected and supervised field training." In-service training at least once a year, along with incentives for officers to continue their education, should also be provided.[38] In 1973 the National Advisory Commission on Criminal Justice Standards and Goals put police training into perspective with some harsh comments: "Perhaps no other profession has such lax standards or is allowed to operate without firm controls and without licensing."[39]

In 1981 the Commission on Civil Rights, in emphasizing the need for formal training of police, concluded that most of the programs examined "do not give sufficient priority to on-the-job field training, programs in human relations, and preparation for the social service function of police officers, including intervening in family-related disturbances." The commission also found that even firearms training was usually inadequate and, in addition, "subject to the ambiguities found in statutes and departmental policies." Because of this ambiguity, said the commission, it is imperative that police be exposed during training to situations in which the use of firearms might or might not be appropriate and that they also be trained in the use of alternatives to deadly force. The commission also recommended that police receive training in the social services they are expected to perform.[40]

As in any profession, it is important that police training change as the demands of the job changes. In 1987 and 1988 the *New York Times* ran a series of articles discussing the efforts of the city's police department to do just that. The training program even emphasized such problems as dating among officers or between officers and academy instructors or administrators. The New York recruits were trained more thoroughly in the social sciences than in the past. They were taught how to deal with prejudices and how to respond without force to potentially disruptive behavior. Police commissioner Benjamin Ward emphasized that New York City's recruits need "more training in subduing violent people without using guns and in 'overcoming a mindset' that makes them reluctant to retreat," since retreat is the best way to handle some situations.[41]

The Federal Law Enforcement Training Center   A brief look at the training of federal officers will indicate some types of courses and program involved in police training. The Federal Law Enforcement Training Center (FLETC) was established by Congress in 1970 to provide training for officers in the various federal agencies other than the FBI, which has its own training center. A central training center was thought to be the most effective and efficient way to provide the necessary training for the recruits in the numerous federal agencies employing law enforcement personnel.

Training operations began in 1970 in temporary facilities in the Washington, D.C., area. The permanent facility was to have been built in Maryland; but when it became necessary to find another location, the Glynco Naval Air Station near Brunswick, Georgia, was selected. Today that facility provides training for officers in 59 federal agencies as indicated in Table 5.2, which is included here to demonstrate the wide range of federal agencies involved in some form of law enforcement. In 1984, at the request of the Bureau of Indian Affairs (BIA), FLETC assumed responsibility for operating an FLETC Indian Police Academy near Tucson, Arizona. This facility is now a satellite operation of FLETC and provides training for BIA and tribal police personnel. The facility also is used by FLETC for some short-term training programs for federal officers in the western part of the United States.

The Attorney General's Task Force on Violent Crime recommended that consideration be given to using FLETC for advanced and specialized programs for training state and local law enforcement officers. After par-

TABLE 5.2 _____

Federal Law Enforcement Training Center
Member Agencies and Participating Organizations

Executive Branch

Agriculture	▪ Forest Service
Commerce	▪ National Bureau of Standards
	National Marine Fisheries Services
	Office of Security
Defense	▪ Naval Investigative Service
Health and Human Services	▪ Saint Elizabeths Hospital
	National Institutes of Health
	Social Security Administration
Interior	▪ Bureau of Indian Affairs
	Bureau of Land Management
	National Park Service
	U.S. Fish and Wildlife Service
	Bureau of Reclamation
	Office of Surface Mining, Reclamation and Enforcement
Justice	▪ Immigration and Naturalization Service
	U.S. Marshals Service
	Drug Enforcement Administration
	Bureau of Prisons
State	▪ Office of Security
Transportation	▪ Federal Aviation Administration
	U.S. Coast Guard
Treasury	▪ Bureau of Alcohol, Tobacco and Firearms
	Bureau of Engraving and Printing
	Internal Revenue Service
	U.S. Customs Service
	U.S. Mint
	U.S. Secret Service

President's Council on Integrity and Efficiency

Statutory Inspector's General Offices: Agriculture
Commerce
Defense
Education
Energy
Health and Human Services
Housing and Urban Development
Interior
Labor
State
Transportation
Agency for International Development
Environmental Protection Agency
General Services Administration
National Aeronautics and Space Administration
Small Business Administration
Veterans Administration

Legislative Branch

Congress
- Government Printing Office
  Library of Congress Police
  U.S. Capitol Police

Judicial Branch

Supreme Court
- Supreme Court Police
  Federal Judicial Center

Independent

Amtrak
- Northeast Corridor Police

Central Intelligence Agency
- Office of Security

Environmental Protection Agency
- Criminal Enforcement Division

Federal Emergency Management
  Agency
- Office of the Inspector General
  Security Division

General Services Administration
- Federal Protection and Safety

Smithsonian
- National Zoological Park
  Office of Protection Services

Tennessee Valley Authority
- Land Between the Lakes Patrol
  Public Safety Service

Totals: 19 Member Agencies/59 Participating Organizations

Source: Pamphlet, *Summary of Operations and Programs,* Federal Law Enforcement Training Center, Glynco, Ga.

---

ticipating in a pilot program FLETC established a national center for state and local training. This center provides training generally not available in state and local law enforcement departments, including such areas as fraud and financial operations, cargo theft, advanced arson for profit, undercover investigative techniques, child abuse and exploitation investigation techniques, and specialized juvenile justice law enforcement matters.

Training of federal officers varies according to the type of officer and the agency in which the officer will be employed. Most recruits, however, participate in basic training that includes eight major areas of study, which are briefly described in Table 5.3. In 1984, FLETC graduated 14,255 students; between 1970 and 1984 the center graduated 88,251 students.

ORGANIZATION OF POLICE DEPARTMENTS

The organization and management of police departments received considerable attention from the President's Commission on Law Enforcement and Administration of Justice. Some of the commission's conclusions, stated in its 1967 report on police, were the lack of qualified leadership; resistance to change; lack of trained personnel in research and planning, law, business administration, and computer analysis; inefficient use of

TABLE 5.3

Topics of Study, Basic Training: Federal Law Enforcement Training Center

Legal

The legal study covers rules and principles of law, especially those related to investigation, detention, arrest, and search and seizure.

Enforcement Techniques

Enforcement techniques include fingerprinting, description and identification, law enforcement photography, collecting and preserving evidence, and identifying narcotics.

Behavioral Science

Behavioral science includes courses on the awareness of individual, group, social, and cultural motivators and their effect on human behavior; sources of potential human relations problems and alternative means of preventing and resolving conflicts; recognition of various sources of stress and how to deal with stress; participation in defusing crisis and noncrisis situations in a safe and humane manner. Hired role-players as well as video equipment are used.

Enforcement Operations

Enforcement operations cover the basic knowledge of the various operational procedures specific to job functions as criminal investigators or uniformed police officers. The former receive instruction in using techniques such as working with informants, conducting a surveillance, executing search warrants, and working undercover operations. The latter receive instruction in radio communications, note taking, report writing, and various operational skills and patrol procedures. Specialized training is also provided in computers, firearms, physical techniques, and driver specialties for officers and investigators in the basic and advanced programs.

Computer/Economic Crime

Computer/Economic crime includes courses that teach computer skills to investigators of the various law enforcement organizations employed to work in the area of economic crimes. Provides instruction in the investigation of white-collar crime and the understanding and employment of computers as investigative tools. Also includes courses in white-collar crime, computer fraud and data processing investigation, and procurement and contract fraud.

Firearms

Firearms covers fundamental training in the safe and accurate operation of a weapon.

Physical Techniques

Physical techniques include training in the physical activities in law enforcement, motivation to proper physical conditioning, arrest techniques, and self-defense as well as emergency medical procedures and water survival.

Driver and Marine

This category covers vehicle limitations, skills in recognition of traffic hazards; instruction in the improvement of reflexes and decision-making ability; defensive driving; skid control; highway response driving; instruction in four-wheel-drive vehicles for officers in such agencies as the National Park Service and the Border Patrol. Courses for advanced training in this area include handling of small boats in the law enforcement environment; navigation; the rules of the road, mechanical troubleshooting; pursuit, board and search; and firing from aboard a boat.

Source: Adapted from *Summary of Operations and Programs,* Pamphlet of the Federal Law Enforcement Training Center, Glynco, Ga.

---

personnel; and departmental organization that does not incorporate "well-established principles of modern business management."[42]

The commission graphed one model of departmental organization, the traditional model, characterized by a hierarchical structure with the police chief as the central authority in the organization. Heads of departments, such as internal investigation, community relations, administration bureau, operations bureau, and services bureau, report directly to the chief. Each of these heads have subordinate administrators reporting directly to them. Under this model, the police department is organized around specialized functions such as patrol, traffic, personnel and training, and data processing, all of which are subunits of the major divisions of administration, operations, and services. This particular model has major units concerned with internal investigations and community relations. Some departments also will have a unit specializing in crime prevention.

The chain of command in this traditional model is clear. Subordinates in each unit report directly to their division heads, who report directly to the chief. This authoritarian model involves many rules and regulations, with little input from subordinates in developing those rules and regulations. It may be a very efficient model for making some kinds of quick decisions, for prescribing safety measures, and for internal control of subordinates, and it often results in high production output.

This model has been criticized for being too authoritarian and for establishing policing units that are too specialized. For example, if a police officer assigned to the patrol division encounters a problem with a juvenile, under the traditional model that juvenile should be turned over to the juvenile division, even though the patrol officer in that district may have more knowledge of the individual juvenile and his or her background. Controlling traffic and issuing traffic citations is the specialty of the officers in the traffic division; so they should be called for handling these problems in the patrol officer's district. The officer may arrest a suspect for violating a crime, but the investigation of that crime will be conducted by a detective in another division. There may be overlap in the record keeping of these various divisions in addition to the obvious fragmentation of functions.

Criticism of the traditional method of organizing police departments has led to adoption of other models of organizations. The knowledge-problem type of organization focuses on a less extensive division of labor, fewer rules and regulations, and few levels of authority. The emphasis is on solving problems, and power comes from the ability of employees to succeed in that goal, not from the title of their positions. Its emphasis is on gaining knowledge and using that knowledge to adapt to new situations. It thus provides greater flexibility, which may be necessary for some types of decisions and problem solving, while permitting greater involvement of subordinates in the police force. Since much of police work requires officers to make on-the-spot decisions, this model may be more effective than the traditional model in developing the ability to make such decisions effectively.[43]

Team Policing

The president's commission, in its analysis of organizations of police departments, emphasized the problems that may be created by too much specialization and fragmentation. The commission recommended a concept called **team policing**, in which patrol and criminal investigation in a specified area would be under unified command. Each team unit would be headed by a field supervisor and consist of a team of agents, law enforcement officers, and community service officers. At the beginning of each shift of duty, the team would meet with the supervisor and be briefed on the problems in that area at that time. The supervisor would then assign team members to duties for that shift, but those assignments could be changed as situations changed. If a major crime were reported or a riot started, reassignments might be necessary, and the supervisor would have the authority to make those changes.

The police department would still have specialists. On occasion those specialists might be brought into the team's district. The emphasis in team policing, however, is on improving community relations and increasing crime detection and prevention by using the same team members in one area. A team field supervisor and the team members are responsible and accountable for all police activities in their area, not just for some specialized functions. It is also assumed that this arrangement will increase the flow of information from citizens to the police department. Team policing may be oriented toward the community or toward neighborhoods within the community. Police teams could also be organized around time periods of shifts, but most have focused on geographic areas.

The most successful efforts at team policing are those characterized by an increased involvement of subordinates in decision making, an assumption by the team of total responsibility for police services in their area (24 hours a day, seven days a week), and a combination of patrol and investigative functions within the team.[44]

SUMMARY

The first chapter introduced the subject of social control and explored the differences between informal and formal methods of control. This chapter illustrates those differences with reference to the need for a formal police system. The history of informal and formal policing methods in England and the United States was examined. Many factors contributed to the need for formal policing, but in both countries the increasing complexity that resulted when society became industrialized was a crucial factor. The rising levels of criminal activity, public unrest, and riots that accompanied industrialization also demonstrated the inability of informal methods of policing to provide adequate protection.

The formal system of policing that evolved in the United States, a decentralized system with local, state, and federal levels, results in overlap and gaps between levels; but it also permits states and localities to experiment with methods that might be effective in light of the problems that distinguish their policing needs from those of the federal government. The various levels of policing cooperate in some functions, such as investigation and training. The federal training center, in response to specialized needs of states and localities, has developed programs for training state and local law enforcement officers. This training is particularly important to police departments that cannot afford to provide the specialized training needed by a relatively small number of officers.

Formal, public policing systems long have been the object of great criticism; some citizens have reacted by employing private police or by having security devices installed in their homes or businesses. Conflict between public and private policing developed and continues, although there also is some evidence of cooperation between the two. Many states recently have taken measures to establish minimum requirements for licensing private security firms.

Dissatisfaction with policing also led to an emphasis on professionalism, on developing attitudes and values among police officers that would enable them to deal more effectively with the human problems they encounter in their work. Higher education and more extensive training were emphasized in the 1970s, but not everyone agrees that these changes are necessary or even desirable. With budget cuts in the 1980s, many departments have not implemented the more stringent education and training requirements. Other departments are making efforts to adapt their recruiting and training programs to the changing roles of police.

The nature and quality of policing may also be affected by the manner in which the police department is organized. It has been argued that the traditional, authoritarian model of organization is not as effective as the team policing model in which officers are less specialized, assigned to one area, and responsible for all police services in that area. Experimentation with team policing has produced some positive results, but changes in tradition do not come easily for any group of people, and the police have not been an exception. Some continue to prefer the more traditional approach to policing.

The type of police organization and administration, the types of people who are attracted to policing through the recruitment efforts of police agencies, and the type of education and training of those recruits will significantly affect the way those persons perform their police functions. Thus this chapter provides a framework in which to examine police functions and services.

STUDY QUESTIONS

1. Why do we have a formal system of policing?

2. Explain the meaning in the development of modern policing of the following: Bow Street Runner, Peeler, posse, and Molly Maguire.

3. Compare local, state, and federal police systems. What are the advantages and disadvantages of decentralized policing?

4. What are some of the unique problems of rural law enforcement?

5. What are *U. S. marshals*?

6. What is the role of private police agencies?

7. How would you describe the administration of early police systems in this country?

8. Trace the development of the professional model of policing.

9. What factors should be emphasized when recruiting young people into the police profession?

10. What are the pros and cons of requiring a college education for police recruits?

11. Discuss some of the problems and changes in society today that might alter the way police should be trained.

12. Evaluate the traditional, authoritarian model of organizational structure of police departments.

ENDNOTES

1. Herman Goldstein, *Policing in a Free Society* (Cambridge, Mass.: Ballinger Publishing Co., 1977), p. 1.
2. Bureau of Justice Statistics, *Justice Expenditure and Employment, 1985* (Washington, D.C.: U.S. Department of Justice, March 1987), p. 1.
3. Jonathan Rubinstein, *City Police* (New York: Ballantine Books, 1973), p. 5.
4. For a summary of the work in this area, see Alexander W. Pisciotta, "Police, Society, and Social Control in America: A Metahistorical Review of the Literature," *Criminal Justice Abstracts* 14 (December 1982): 514–39.
5. David H. Bayley, "Police: History," in Sanford H. Kadish, ed., *Encyclopedia of Crime and Justice*, vol. 3 (New York: Free Press, 1983), pp. 1122–23.
6. Louis B. Schwartz and Stephen R. Goldstein, *Law Enforcement Handbook for Police* (St. Paul, Minn.: West Publishing Co., 1970), p. 34.
7. For recent analyses of the British police system, see Avrom Sheer, *Public Order and the Law* (New York: Basil Blackwell, 1988), which explores the role of the police in British society; and Simon Holdaway, *Inside the British Police: A Force at Work* (New York: Basil Blackwell, 1983). Written by a sociologist who was previously employed as a police sergeant, this book examines the modern British police system based on his observations of everyday policing in Great Britain.
8. Bayley, "Police: History," p. 1124.
9. Ibid.
10. Federal Bureau of Investigation, *Uniform Crime Reports: Crime in the United States, 1987* (Washington, D.C.: U.S. Government Printing Office, 1988), p. 227.
11. "Sheriffs Losing Posts in Southeast Texas: Political Activist Cites Changing Times," *Dallas Morning News* (18 April 1988), p. 13A.
12. Roger Handberg and Charles M. Unkovie, "Changing Patterns in Rural Law Enforcement: The County Sheriff as a Case Study," in Shanlor Cronk et al., ed., *Criminal Justice in America*, National Institute of Justice (Washington, D.C.: U.S. Government Printing Office, June 1982), pp. 71–74.
13. Egon Bittner, "Police: Urban Police," in Kadish, ed., *Encyclopedia of Crime and Justice*, vol. 3, p. 1133.
14. Robert Borkenstein, "Police: State Police," in ibid., p. 1133.
15. Ibid., p. 1134.
16. This history of law enforcement is summarized from Norman Abrams, "Federal Criminal Law Enforcement," in ibid., vol. 2, pp. 779–85.
17. Richard E. Morgan, "Federal Bureau of Investigation: History," in ibid., p. 774.
18. Michael Fooner, "INTERPOL," in ibid., vol. 3, p. 912.
19. James S. Kakalik and Sorrel Wildhorn, *The Private Police: Security and Danger* (New York: Crane Russak and Co., 1977, copyright Rand Corporation), p. 68.
20. William C. Cunningham and Todd H. Taylor, *Crime and Protection in America: A Study of Private Security and Law Enforcement Resources and Relationships: Executive Summary* (Washington, D.C.: U.S. Government Printing Office, May 1985), pp. 19–22.
21. William C. Cunningham and Todd H. Taylor, *The Growing Role of Private Security*, National Institute of Justice, Research in Brief (Washington, D.C.: U.S. Department of Justice, October 1984), pp. 17–18.
22. William C. Cunningham and Todd H. Taylor, "Ten Years of Growth in Law Enforcement and Private Security Relationships," *The Police Chief* 1 (June 1983): 30–31. For a more recent analysis of the rapid growth of private policing and the effect it has had on public policing, see Clifford D. Shearing and Philip C. Stenning, *Private Policing* (Beverly Hills, Calif.: Sage Publications, 1987).
23. Cunningham and Taylor, ibid., p. 32. See also the study describing the efforts of the police department and private security companies in Oakland, California, to collaborate on crime prevention as well as the problem of residents' fear

of crime. A. J. Reiss, Jr., *Policing a City's Central District—The Oakland Story*, U.S. Department of Justice, National Institute of Justice (Washington, D.C.: U.S. Government Printing Office, 1985).

24. See for example, the Oklahoma Security Guard and Private Investigator Act, ch. 42A, title 59, Sections 1750.1–1750.12 of the OKLA. CODE.

25. The basis for this discussion comes from the article by Herman Goldstein, "Police Administration," in Kadish, ed., *Encyclopedia of Crime and Justice*, vol. 3, pp. 1125–31.

26. Bruce Smith, *Police Systems in the United States* (New York: Harper Bros., 1960), pp. 104–5, quoted in George D. Eastman and James A. McCain, "Education, Professionalism, and Law Enforcement in Historical Perspective," *Journal of Police Science and Administration* 9 (June 1981): 122.

27. See O. W. Wilson and Roy Clinton McLaren, *Police Administration*, 4th ed. (New York: McGraw-Hill Book Co., 1977).

28. Goldstein, "Police Administration," p. 1126.

29. Jerome H. Skolnick, *Justice without Trial* (New York: John Wiley and Sons, 1966), pp. 238–39. The second edition was published in 1975.

30. *Who Is Guarding the Guardians? A Report on Police Practices*, a Report of the United States Commission on Civil Rights (Washington, D.C.: U.S. Government Printing Office, 1981), p. 6.

31. Ibid., pp. 154–55.

32. See Arthur Neiderhoffer, *Behind the Shield: The Police in Urban Society* (Garden City, N.Y.: Doubleday Publishing Co., 1969).

33. Elizabeth Burbeck and Adrian Furnham, "Police Officer Selection: A Critical Review of the Literature," *Journal of Police Science and Administration* 13 (March 1983): 68.

34. President's Commission on Law Enforcement and Administration of Justice, *The Challenge of Crime in A Free Society* (Washington, D.C.: U.S. Government Printing Office, 1967), p. 109.

35. Quoted in *New York Times* (30 November 1978), p. A10. For a recent analysis of police education, see David L. Carter et al., *The State of Police Education: Policy Direction for the 21st Century* (Washington, D.C.: Police Executive Research Forum, 1989).

36. "New York City Starting a Police Cadet Corps," *New York Times* (4 September 1985), p. 1.

37. President's Commission on Law Enforcement and Administration of Justice, *Task Force Report: The Police* (Washington, D.C.: U.S. Government Printing Office, 1967), p. 138.

38. *The Challenge of Crime in a Free Society*, pp. 112–13.

39. National Advisory Commission on Criminal Justice Standards and Goals, *A National Strategy to Reduce Crime* (Washington, D.C.: U.S. Government Printing Office, 1973), p. 83.

40. *Who Is Guarding the Guardians?*, p. 155.

41. "New York Police to Get Training to Cut Slayings," *New York Times* (8 January 1988), p. 14. See also "At Police Academy, Recruits are Trained to Keep Prejudices in the Lockers," *New York Times* (24 March 1987), p. 16; and "Police Academy Adapts to Changing New York," *New York Times* (6 February 1987), p. 10.

42. President's Commission, *Task Force Report: The Police*, p. 44.

43. Thomas J. Sweeney, "Police Organization," in Bernard L. Garmire, ed., *Local Government Police Management* (Washington, D.C.: International City Management Association, 1977), pp. 111–114. For results on a recent study of police organizations, see Robert H. Langworthy, *The Structure of Police Organizations* (Westport, Conn.: Greenwood Press, 1986). For a brief but thorough overview of police organizational structure, see Charles R. Swanson, Leonard Territo, and Robert W. Taylor, *Police Administration: Structures, Processes, and Behavior*, 2d ed. (New York: Macmillan Publishing Co., 1988), pp. 101–26.

44. See Lawrence W. Sherman et al., *Team Policing: Seven Case Studies* (Washington, D.C.: Police Foundation, 1973).

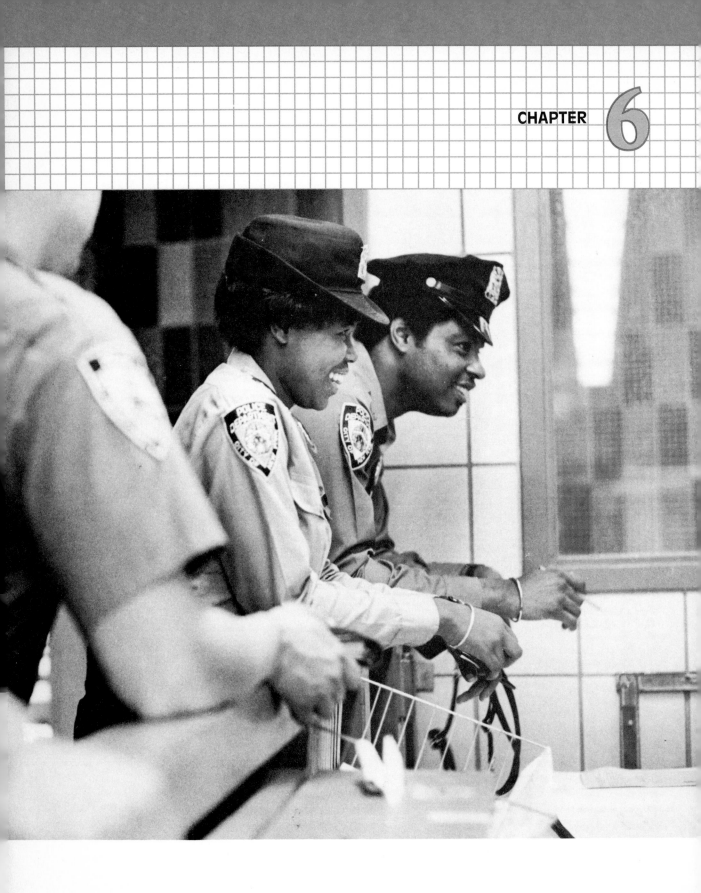

Policing in a Modern Society

KEY TERMS

adversary system
arrest
booking
contraband
curtilage
discretion
due process
exclusionary rule
felony
frisk
informant
magistrate
Miranda warning
misdemeanor
probable cause
search and seizure
search warrant
warrant

A police officer, while out on routine patrol at midnight on a Friday night, observed a car weaving down the highway, going five miles over the speed limit. The officer turned on his siren and lights and directed the car to stop. After checking the operator's driver's license, the officer inquired where the person was going and why he was speeding. The driver replied that the did not realize he was speeding but that he was in a hurry to get home because his contact lens was causing pain. Something apparently flew into his eye and temporarily blurred his vision. He considered it unsafe to stop by the side of a busy highway. He was trying to get to his home only a mile away.

When asked where he had been, the driver replied that he was an A student in a criminal justice program and had been at a friend's house studying since the library closed at 11 P.M. When asked whether he had been drinking, the driver replied that he had had only one beer. The driver answered all questions politely and nondefensively.

What would you do if you were the police officer? Would you ticket the driver for driving over the speed limit? Would you believe his response about the contact lens? Would you believe what he told you about drinking only one beer? Would it make any difference in your decision if you had stopped him at 3 A.M. rather than at midnight?

INTRODUCTION

The hypothetical scenario in this chapter's CJA illustrates one of the most important aspects of policing, the wide range of discretion that police have in deciding when and how the law will be enforced. This chapter focuses on what police do in a modern society, but those functions can be understood only in the context of the wide range of discretion given to police in performing their jobs. The chapter will begin with an examination of the importance of discretion and how it might be controlled.

The major focus of the chapter is the wide range of police functions. Police in the United States are expected to prevent crime, apprehend and arrest criminals, enforce traffic ordinances and other laws, maintain order in domestic and other kinds of personal disputes, control riots and other disturbances, and perform numerous miscellaneous services. Police must perform these functions in the context of political, legal, and popular expectations that often are unrealistic and conflicting.

Some of the functions assigned to police are shared by other persons or agencies, which often results in conflict concerning the role of police. But police are given greater discretion and greater power in performing their tasks than are other agencies. Why? We have already talked about the need for formal social control. The functions of police may be viewed in that perspective. "Broadly, then, we may define the role of the police as the coercive regulation of social behavior among the members of a community in the interests of the protection of life and the preservation of order."[1]

The *possibility* that disorder, or even violence, may occur convinces us that the force of the police should handle the situation. Therefore, we are willing to grant police the *power* to intervene when such intervention is necessary. "This lends homogeneity to such diverse procedures as catching a criminal, driving the mayor to the airport, evicting a drunken person from a bar, directing traffic, crowd control, taking care of lost children, administering medical first aid, and separating fighting relatives.[2]"

The functions of policing are varied. After a brief overview of the three major areas of functions, we will discuss each area, beginning with order maintenance and the performance of various services before concentrating on law enforcement. The section on law enforcement includes a brief overview of the legal context in which law enforcement occurs. The discussion then focuses on traffic control and enforcement of traffic laws before discussing the procedures and issues surrounding stopping, arresting, searching and seizing, and interrogating persons suspected of criminal activity. In the final sections, attention is given to police patrol and the investigative functions of policing.

DISCRETION IN POLICING

Chapter 1 included a discussion of **discretion** and indicated that wide discretion exists in the criminal justice system. Perhaps, that discretion is greatest in policing. Police have wide discretion in determining whether to begin the formal processing of the criminal justice system. When they see a person who appears to be violating the law, police may refuse to acknowledge that action. Or, they may investigate the situation and decide that they do not have sufficient reason to think a crime has been committed. They also might decide that a crime has been committed but not by the suspect, or that the suspect may have committed the crime but for some reason should not be arrested.

How the officer exercises discretion may be determined by a number of factors. Let's return to the facts in the hypothetical scenario in this chapter's CJA, in which you were asked to decide what you would do if you were the police officer in that situation. You could, of course, give the driver a verbal warning and let him go. You could give him a speeding ticket. If you had sufficient reason to think that he had been drinking to the point that he was legally drunk, you could ask him to get out of the car and perform some simple tests. Or, you might just arrest him and take him to the police station to begin the official processing in the criminal justice system.

Now, think about the results of your decision. If the driver is telling the truth and you decide to arrest him, what have you accomplished by your action? Is it not possible that the negative effect of the arrest and subsequent experiences he will have in the criminal justice system will outweigh any benefit that society would get from this arrest? On the other hand, if he has been drinking too much, even if he is not legally drunk, is it not possible that an arrest will cause him to think before he gets in a car again after drinking? Or, will it not affect his behavior at all? What about the behavior of his friends who will certainly hear about your actions?

Perhaps, by now you have decided what action you would take. Let's add some factors to the scenario. Suppose that, when you begin to talk to the driver, he curses you and tells you to mind your own business. Would this affect your decision whether to write a speeding ticket or perhaps make an arrest for driving while intoxicated?

Police must make such decisions as these daily. Selective enforcement of laws is necessary because our system could not process all cases of law violations even if we chose to do so. The discretion of policing is very important because the police most often are the ones responsible for the initial entry of a person into the criminal justice system. The necessity to exercise discretion without adequate guidelines puts tremendous pressure on police.

> The police really suffer the worst of all worlds: they must exercise broad discretion behind a facade of performing in a ministerial fashion; and they are expected to realize a high level of equality and justice in their discretionary determinations though they have not been provided with the means most commonly relied upon in government to achieve these ends.[3]

In recent years, however, more attention has been given to the need to prepare police for the appropriate use of discretion.[4] Police must make decisions about the most appropriate way to handle problems. The exercise of discretion is not the problem but the abuse of discretion, whether it involves the police or anyone else in the criminal justice system. The possibility for abuse might be minimized with the establishment of guidelines, but guidelines can never specify all of the facts that might occur in situations in which the police must make decisions. Flexibility is needed in many situations, and police officers must have the authority and the self-confidence to make individual decisions that may not be covered by the guidelines.

THE ROLE OF THE POLICE: AN OVERVIEW

Although the popular image of police sees them as primarily apprehending and arresting criminals, this function actually constitutes a very small part of the daily life of a police officer. In reality, police perform a variety of functions not directly related to law enforcement. A second major function of policing is order maintenance. Although order maintenance is sometimes used synonymously with the third major function, providing various services, the two are distinct. James Q. Wilson says the key to order maintenance is the management of conflict situations to bring about consensual resolution. Wilson believes that order maintenance is the *main* function of the police and that it is important because police encounter more problems in this area than in social service or law enforcement (with the exception of traffic violations). Also, they often face danger in performing the order maintenance function.[5] A third function of policing is the provision of services, ranging from helping people with directions when they are lost to driving them to the service station for gas when they are stranded on the highway.

There appears to be agreement that law enforcement, order maintenance, and community services are the three basic areas of police functions in this country; but there is no agreement over whether they should be the basic functions. Nor is there agreement on how police time and resources should be allocated among the three areas. It is clear, however, that the areas are not discrete; there is considerable overlap. Attention to an order maintenance problem or provision of a particular service may prevent the situation from escalating into criminal behavior. Order maintenance and service provision also may alert the police to violations of the criminal law.

ORDER MAINTENANCE

Police are charged with maintaining order, particularly in areas in which crime might erupt. James Q. Wilson defined *order* as the absence of disorder, by which he means behavior that tends to disrupt the peace and tranquility of the public or that involves serious face-to-face conflict between two or more persons. According to Wilson the maintenance of order, "more than the problem of law enforcement, is central to the patrolman's role for several reasons."[6]

First, many police departments receive more calls for help in maintaining order than in enforcing the law. Some of these complaints may result in arrests, but most do not. Police may be called to quiet down noisy neighbors; they may be asked to intervene in disputes between friends and associates who cannot solve their differences and who appear to be on the brink of fighting. Public drunks wandering around the city alarm some people, who call the police to handle the situation. Some of these activities may violate local ordinances, but most of the situations involve activities that are not criminal, although they may be obnoxious to those who call the police.

Order maintenance is a very important function of police for a second reason. Maintaining order may subject the police and others to physical danger. A large protest group may turn into a riot. Domestic disputes frequently lead to violence between the spouses or against the police. Domestic problems often occur late at night; other resources are not available to the complainant.

A third reason listed by Wilson as underscoring the importance of the order maintenance function of police is that in this area police exercise

> substantial discretion over matters of the greatest importance (public and private morality, honor and dishonor, life and death) in a situation that is, by definition, one of conflict and in an environment that is apprehensive and perhaps hostile.[7]

Emphasis on Order Maintenance: The Controversy

Not all scholars and practitioners agree on the emphasis that should be placed on the order maintenance function of policing. George L. Kelling analyzes order maintenance in the context of the reforms of policing popular in this century. As professionalism in policing was emphasized, evaluation of individual police and of police departments focused on tangibles such as arrests and quick response time of police to citizen calls.

> Police behavior that did not lead to arrests . . . was neither organizationally recognized nor rewarded. Police actions were rarely seen as ends in themselves but instead were viewed as means to "process persons" into the justice system.

Police concentrated on crime prevention, arrests, and apprehension of criminals, thus emphasizing law enforcement over the maintenance of order or provision of services. This approach, says Kelling, decreased police corruption and improved the internal management of policing, but it also resulted in less emphasis on order maintenance.[8]

Kelling argues that the focus on law enforcement has not significantly lowered crime rates but that a decreased involvement of police in order maintenance has had negative effects. His position is that increased police attention to order maintenance improves relationships between the police and the community, which results in greater cooperation of citizens with the police. Citizen fear of crime is reduced; community support of the police is improved; police feel less isolated from the community; and crime detection and prevention increase.[9] Kelling, along with James Q. Wilson, advocates a significant enlargement of the order maintenance function of policing. Neither believes this approach would endanger law enforcement.[10]

The Kelling and Wilson position has been challenged by Carl B. Klockars, who argues that American police, historically and today, maintain "an extraordinarily strong crime-fighting mandate," seen by them and others as the primary mission of policing. To reduce that emphasis by increasing resources for order maintenance is undesirable. It would not significantly reduce crime because the police do not have control over many of the factors that produce crime. The financial cost would be much greater and would be at the sacrifice of a reduction in the number of calls for service to which police could respond quickly.

Klockars suggests one solution might be to use foot patrols in high-density areas, particularly business areas. The increased costs might be financed partially by voluntary, tax-deductible contributions by the business people, who stand to gain the most from the increased presence of police in the area. The problem with that suggestion, warns Klockars, is that a study of a foot patrol experiment in Newark revealed that commercial residents perceived "a deterioration in their neighborhoods: more activity on the street, more crime-related problems, reduced safety, more victimization, poorer police service, and greater use of protective devices." Klockars is not arguing against order maintenance, but only against an extended and more systematic and costly approach that would require significant changes in the administrative structure of police departments.[11]

In his support of the order maintenance function of policing, which he calls *street justice*, Gary W. Sykes emphasizes that at the local level order maintenance is the main function of police. It can be justified "on moral grounds as part of the community building and maintaining functions." Sykes warns that "to deny to citizens this police role has profound moral consequences and abandons those less capable of protecting themselves to the unchecked forces of private power."[12]

COMMUNITY SERVICE FUNCTION

Police perform a variety of services unrelated to law enforcement. James Q. Wilson maintains that such services are performed by police only because of historical accident and community convenience, that there is no good reason for police to perform such services, and that the services should "be priced and sold on the market."[13]

The President's Crime Commission was concerned about the amount of time police spend in community services. The commission looked at the arguments pro and con. Performing community services takes away police time that might otherwise be spent in law enforcement. But the performance of certain community services by police might deter criminal activity as well as improve the public's image of the police. The commission concluded that

> in the absence of conclusive proof to the contrary . . . the performance of
> many of the nonenforcement duties by the police helps them to control
> crime and that radically changing the traditional police role would create
> more problems than it would solve. . . . [But,] the community should
> take a hard look at such police assignments as running the dog pound, tax
> collection, licensing, jail duty or chauffeur duty, which are related neither
> to law enforcement nor to performing essential community services on the
> streets.[14]

The report of the President's Crime Commission should be considered seriously. Removal of unnecessary community service functions does not mean that the police should not continue to be involved in community services that are either directly or indirectly related to crime prevention or order maintenance. Police in many cities have instituted plans to increase their involvement in community activities.

Police officer helps teach retarded youngster to fish. (Mike Douglas/Image Works)

Operation Identification is a service that relates directly to crime prevention. Police departments provide the equipment and officers to visit in community groups and individual homes to assist residents in marking their possessions so that in case of theft the goods may be identified more quickly and easily. Officers also give talks on crime prevention, emphasizing to residents what they can do to make it less likely that they will become the victims of property or personal crimes. Educating women on the prevention of rape is a frequent topic of these sessions. Visiting with school children to educate them in crime prevention is another type of police social work.

Police may also perform a very important community service function that indirectly relates to crime prevention. Police are dependent on the cooperation of citizens for effective crime prevention, but many citizens do not have a good image of the police and do not wish to cooperate with them. Any kind of community involvement of police may have a positive effect on their images. Spotlight 6.1 illustrates New York City's

SPOTLIGHT 6.1
POLICE GAINING A COMMUNITY ROLE

One day a few weeks ago, a large garbage container appeared on Columbus Avenue near 62nd Street in Manhattan. The bin, provided for a nearby construction project, blocked the fire hydrant in front of a restaurant. Police Officer Edward Acevedo, who walks past the restaurant nearly every day as part of his duties as a member of the Community Patrol Officer Program in the 20th Precinct, called the Sanitation Department. The container was moved the next morning.

It was a small job but an important one, the sort of thing that for years New Yorkers have complained their police were too busy or uncaring to do. But since the department began its first "C-POP" project in Brooklyn nearly three years ago, officers in precincts around the city have increasingly been helping with just such little problems.

"It's rewarding," said Officer Acevedo. "It's nice to have people wave at you for a change."

The program, one of Police Commissioner Benjamin Ward's pet projects and now operating in 44 of the city's 75 precincts, was designed for the city by the Vera Institute of Justice. Other cities, including Houston, have adopted community patrols. Boston is considering establishing a program and officers from Philadelphia and Rio de Janeiro recently visited New York because their departments are considering starting similar units.

Mark H. Moore, Guggenheim Professor of Criminal Justice Policy and Management at Harvard University's John F. Kennedy School of Government, says that beyond helping calm community fears, foot patrols are "extremely important adjustments in the basic strategy of policing American cities."

"It has become increasingly apparent," he said, "that to be effective in dealing with violent crime, one needs enormous amounts of assistance from the community, to give evidence, to give testimony. If the police fail to build confidence and personal relationships with the people in the community, they've lost then some capacity for fighting violent crimes."

In Brooklyn, foot-patrol officers have organized Halloween parties for children and settled disputes between churchgoers and residents annoyed by the worshipers' parked cars. In the Bronx, they have shooed peddlers from the sidewalks in front of stores and persuaded a resident to remove a pile of junked cars from his yard. And, of course, they have arrested criminals too.

In the beginning, residents and merchants were so shocked to find men and women in blue introducing themselves as the neighborhood's new

response to the community service function of policing. It is important that police not spend so much time in community service functions that the law enforcement and order maintenance functions are neglected.

Community Service Officers

One way to solve the time commitment problem is to train and assign special officers to community service functions, one of the suggestions made by the President's Crime Commission. In 1983 in Tulsa, Oklahoma, the police department began a Community Service Officer program. Officers in this program go through 12 weeks of training, compared to the 16 required of officers in the other police departments. A high-school education is the maximum required for these officers, compared to 108 hours of college for other police officers. The salary also is lower. The community service program, however, provides career opportunities for qualified

community patrol officers, they called local precincts and community boards to complain about police impersonators. Officers found it hard to win the people's confidence.

"Now, if I'm on vacation for two weeks or so, they start calling to ask where I am," said Officer Joe Martinez, who walks a beat on Westchester Avenue in the 43rd Precinct in the Bronx.

The officers keep detailed notebooks, listing the stores and public places on their beats and noting such trouble spots at the school where toughs gather or the tavern that is often rowdy on Friday nights. Each month they plot the location of crimes and nuisance conditions and submit plans to their sergeants for dealing with the problems.

"It did make a very visible difference in the community from the very outset," said Frank Marchiano, the district manager of Community Board 7 in the Sunset Park section of Brooklyn, in the 72d Precinct. The precinct was the first to receive a community patrol program, in the summer of 1984. There are at least two in each borough now, and Commissioner Ward hopes to expand the program citywide. Police officials said Mayor Koch's plan to hire nearly 2,000 more officers will make it easier to achieve that goal.

The police acknowledge that the effectiveness of an officer on foot is limited, and the foot patrols are not replacing radio cars. Experienced officers assigned to foot patrols are replaced by new recruits.

"It's more helpful in quality-of-life things than in actual crimes, I think," said Sgt. Tom Poidevin, who supervises the program in the 43d Precinct. But Sergeant Poidevin and others say the informal intelligence gathered by the foot officers, and their familiarity with their communities, do help to solve crimes.

"One of our guys was getting a lot of burglaries on his post, and he kind of thought he knew who was doing them," the sergeant recalled. "He got a radio car out there and waited with them and saw the guy and got him."

Other officers speak of the personal satisfaction and sense of independence they have gained in the program. Officer Martinez said he takes less sick leave than he used to. "I'm not as agitated as I used to be," he said. "Now if I talk about work, instead of talking about the negative, I can talk about the positive things."

Source: Todd S. Purdum, "Police Gaining a Community Role," *New York Times* (10 May 1987), p. E7. Copyright © 1987 by The New York Times Company. Reprinted by permission.

young people who either cannot or prefer not to attend college. Community service officers are certified law enforcement officers; they carry guns, and they may arrest law violators.

Community service officers have provided excellent services to the community. The system was designed to relieve some of the pressures on the time of other officers and to save the community money. The program supervisor said the program was designed "to relieve police officers of routine chores and place them back on field duty and to provide security at municipal facilities at a price less than what it would cost to use regular officers." The use of community service officers at the Tulsa airport alone saved $60,875 in one year.[15]

LAW ENFORCEMENT

The third major area of police functions is law enforcement. In the United States we not only empower the police to enforce the law, but we expect that they will do so. We also expect police to prevent crime, in many cases without our help. But the ability of police to handle crime is limited, and they are dependent on citizens for assistance, although they do not always get that assistance.[16]

The law enforcement function of policing cannot be understood adequately except in the context of the legal requirements that must be observed by police officers performing this aspect of policing. Thus, before discussing particular law enforcement activities, it is necessary to understand the legal context of law enforcement.

Constitutional Provisions, the Courts, and Law Enforcement

The power to use coercive force to intervene in the daily lives of people is a tremendous power. It is a power necessary for police to perform their functions properly and efficiently. Earlier we discussed the difference between the crime control and the due process models of law enforcement. If police followed only the crime control model, their jobs might be performed more efficiently and more quickly. But the **adversary system** recognizes basic fundamental rights that fall under the concept of **due process**. Observation of those rights is viewed by some as creating unreasonable obstacles for police; by others it is seen as important to the philosophy on which our Constitution is based.

The Bill of Rights of the United States Constitution contains many provisions critical to an understanding of the criminal justice system in this country. The first eight amendments to the Constitution specify 23 separate rights, 12 of which concern criminal procedures. These provisions of the Bill of Rights of the Constitution require interpretation. Over the years the Supreme Court has heard and decided many cases involving these basic rights. Legislative branches of government have passed numerous statutes for enforcing the basic rights. It is not possible for us to consider all of those statutes or decisions, for criminal procedure is a very complex area of law. But it is possible to consider the overall picture of the conflict between the due process and the crime control models of law enforcement in the context of the criminal justice system.

Subsequent chapters, where appropriate, will discuss amendments to the Constitution. This chapter is concerned primarily with the Fourth Amendment and a portion of the Fifth Amendment as set out in Spotlight 6.2 Those amendments also apply to certain pretrial procedures that involve police, and those issues will be discussed in a subsequent chapter. This chapter considers the application of constitutional rights to the police functions of stopping and questioning suspects; arresting and conducting immediate searches of the person, home, or automobile of suspects; and the practices of custodial interrogation and initial investigation. The discussion begins with a brief look at traffic control, an area of law enforcement in which many police officers engage and one that may lead to the detection of serious crimes.

Traffic Control and Enforcement of Traffic Laws

Traffic control is a very important aspect of law enforcement. The flow of traffic usually is controlled by stop signs and lights, but during high peak times police may direct traffic. Police also enforce state and local ordinances governing the operation of motor vehicles. This function includes enforcing requirements that vehicles be licensed and inspected, as well as ticketing motorists who commit moving violations. Violations of this type normally involve a simple procedure in which the police officer signs a statement indicating the violation and gives a copy to the motorist, explaining that the ticket, if unchallenged, may be handled by mail or in person at the police station. Court appearances are not required unless the ticket is challenged. Most people do not challenge these tickets. The officer may decide not to issue a ticket; a verbal or written warning may be given instead.

It has been suggested that traffic control functions of policing could be performed by persons specially trained in that area and not by police

SPOTLIGHT 6.2
FOURTH AND FIFTH AMENDMENTS, UNITED STATES CONSTITUTION

Fourth Amendment

The right of the people to be secure in their persons, houses, papers, and effects, against unreasonable searches and seizures, shall not be violated, and no Warrants shall issue, but upon probable cause, supported by Oath or affirmation, and particularly describing the place to be searched, and the persons or things to be seized.

Fifth Amendment

No person . . . shall be compelled in any criminal case to be a witness against himself. . . .

Police often use motorcycles for transportation when they are patrolling traffic. (William Edward Smith/The Picture Cube)

officers who are trained in law enforcement techniques. It is a waste of police time. The contrary position emphasizes that in performing the function of traffic control, police may keep situations from escalating into criminal activity.

Enforcement of statutes and ordinances designed to regulate the flow of traffic and to create safe conditions for drivers and pedestrians also is an important police function. Excessive speed on any street or highway, speeding in school zones or failing to stop for school buses, and driving under the influence of drugs or alcohol are dangerous. Apprehension of people who violate traffic ordinances may lead to disorder and violence. Therefore, it is important that trained police officers be in charge of such apprehensions, which also may lead police to evidence of criminal activity such as stolen automobiles, violations of drug laws, escaped felons, wanted persons, burglaries, and other crimes. Apprehension of traffic violators as well as of persons suspected of having committed crimes begins with the investigatory stop, which may or may not lead to arrest.

The Investigatory Stop Leading to Arrest

The police may be notified or they may observe a situation that gives them a reasonable basis for stopping and questioning a person. Because of the importance of this initial stop and the serious effect that it may have on the individual, we will return to the hypothetical case that was the subject of this chapter's CJA. Put yourself in the place of the suspect rather than the police officer. The case will be traced from your apprehension by the police through arrest and booking at the police station. The discussion will indicate proper police procedures, but it will be followed by an example of improper procedures for the purpose of illustrating how easily the initial police stop may go too far. This will be a brief introduction to the procedures and issues at the initial stage of police-suspect contact. Some of these subjects will be discussed in more detail in subsequent chapters on pretrial procedures and the right to counsel and later in this chapter, when the topics of interrogation and investigation are discussed.

The officer observes your car weaving as well as speeding and signals you to stop. When asked whether you have been drinking, you reply that you have had one beer. The officer does not believe you, particularly since he can smell liquor on your breath. You are then told to get out of your car and walk a straight line. You do not perform this task very well. The officer now believes that you are under the influence of alcohol, places you under **arrest**, and indicates that you will be taken to the police station. You are understandably quite concerned about what might happen to you, and you begin to wonder about the practical and legal aspects of your case. What can the police do?

The police at this stage should inform you that you are under arrest, that you have a right to remain silent, that anything you say might be used against you in subsequent proceedings, that you have a right to an attorney, and that if you cannot provide one, the state will provide counsel for you. You have all of these rights because you have been arrested for an offense that could involve jail confinement. In some areas a first offense

Police have the power to make investigatory stops under certain circumstances; such stops often lead to arrests. (Tom Zimberoff/Sygma)

for driving while intoxicated (DWI) is a less serious offense and does not carry a possible jail term. In that case, the police do not have to give these warnings.

The police should also tell you that you will be permitted to make a phone call from the police station. Usually you are limited to one call. You will be asked to take a blood or breath test to determine the extent of alcohol in your body. You have a right to refuse to take this test, in which case the officer must tell you the consequences of that refusal, as indicated in Spotlight 6.3, an example of a form that must be completed by the arresting officer and given to the arrestee who refuses to take the alcohol test. The nature of the form will differ from jurisdiction to jurisdiction.

The nature of the procedures following arrest will also differ. In some police departments, it is departmental policy to permit the person arrested for DWI to be released to the custody of an adult relative, friend, or attorney. Others will require that the person remain at the police station for a period of hours until sober.

You are taken to the police station for **booking,** a process that involves entering into the police log your name and when, where, and for what purpose you were arrested. You also may be fingerprinted and photographed. If it is local policy not to release persons arrested for DWI for a specified number of hours, you will be retained at the police station for that time period. You will be placed in a jail cell or a drunk tank until you are sober.

At the initial stop, the police have considerable discretion. They could have decided not to make the stop. They could have stopped your car but not arrested you. They could have released you with a verbal or a written warning. The police must make important judgment calls at the stage of stopping and questioning suspects, for it would be an inefficient use of police time to arrest people who were not violating the law. It would also be a violation of your rights for the police to arrest you without good reason to think that you had committed a crime. Consider the following case.

SPOTLIGHT 6.3
POLICE OFFICER DWI STATUTORY WARNING

Date _____

Time _____

Place _____

_____ , _____ , _____
Full Name of Suspect (print or type)   Drivers License/I.D. No. or None   Date of Birth

You are under arrest for the offense of Driving While Intoxicated. I request that you submit to the taking of a specimen of your **Breath/Blood** (strike one) for the purpose of analysis to determine the alcohol concentration or the presence of a controlled substance or drug in your body.

If you refuse to give the specimen, that refusal may be admissible in a subsequent prosecution. Your drivers license, permit, or privilege to operate a motor vehicle will be automatically suspended for 90 days after notice and a hearing, if requested, whether or not you are subsequently prosecuted as a result of this arrest. If you do not possess a license or permit to operate a motor vehicle, you may not be issued a license or permit to operate a motor vehicle for a period of ninety (90) days after notice and a hearing, if requested. Further you have the right within twenty (20) days after receiving written notice of a suspension or a denial of a license or permit to request in writing a hearing on the suspension or the denial.

I certify that I have orally informed you of the consequences of a refusal and have provided you with a complete and true copy of this statutory warning.

Signed _____
(Officer)

I have requested that you give a specimen of your Breath/Blood (strike one). I have informed you of the consequences of not giving a specimen. You have refused to give a specimen. I request that you sign this statement indicating your refusal.

Signed _____
(Suspect)

I certify that the above named individual was duly admonished as to the consequences of his/her refusal to give a specimen of Breath/Blood (strike one). He/She refused to give a specimen and he/she further signed/refused to sign (strike one) the statement set out above when requested to do so by this officer.

Signed _____
(Officer)   Badge No. or ID. _____

Department _____

Address _____
Street (P.O. Box)   City   State   Zip Code

Going Beyond the Bounds of the Law   Thirty-six-year-old Edward Lawson—tall, black, muscular, and long-haired—walked almost everywhere he went. Lawson was stopped by police approximately 15 times between March 1975 and January 1977. Police in California were relying on a California statute that prohibited a person from loitering or wandering

> upon the streets or from place to place without apparent reason or business and who refuses to identify himself and to account for his presence when requested by any peace officer to do so, if the surrounding circumstances are such as to indicate to a reasonable man that the public safety demands such identification.[17]

Each time he was stopped, Lawson refused to identify himself. He was arrested five of the times he was stopped, convicted once, and spent several weeks in jail. The Lawson case illustrates the tension between the claim of police that, in order to combat crime, they must be able to stop and question people who look suspicious, and the right of citizens to be free of intrusions into their privacy.

Lawson appealed his convictions to the United States Supreme Court, which reversed them on the grounds that the statute under which Lawson was convicted was vague. The problem with the California statute was not that the police initially stopped a person. According to the Court, "Although the initial detention is justified, the State fails to establish standards by which the officers may determine whether the suspect has complied with the subsequent identification requirement." The Court indicated that giving a police officer such discretion "confers on police a virtually unrestrained power to arrest and charge persons with a violation," and therefore "furnishes a convenient tool for 'harsh and discriminatory enforcement by local prosecuting officials against particular groups deemed to merit their displeasure.' "[18]

The Lawson case makes it clear that police may not use a vague statute for purposes of stopping, questioning, and otherwise harassing individuals. But the case also makes it clear that the police may stop and question individuals. How can the police tell when they can go beyond initial questioning and make an arrest? Some basic legal principles must be explained.

Arrest, Search, and Seizure

The process of stopping and questioning people may lead to arrest, which is a crucial step in the criminal justice proceedings because most cases are initiated by arrest, as Spotlight 6.4 indicates. The process of **search and seizure** is closely tied to the process of arrest, but a clear understanding of these processes is impossible without a brief introduction to the Fourth Amendment of the Constitution. That amendment prohibits unreasonable searches and seizures, as Spotlight 6.2 indicates. This provision of the Constitution is pertinent to our discussion here since stopping and arresting a person may, under some circumstances, constitute a seizure of

SPOTLIGHT 6.4
THE IMPORTANCE OF ARREST: MOST CRIMINAL CASES ARE INITIATED BY ARREST

When a crime has been committed, a suspect must be identified and apprehended for the case to proceed through the system

Sometimes a suspect is apprehended at the scene; however, extensive investigations may be required to identify a suspect, and, in many cases, no one is identified or apprehended. Law enforcement agencies have wide discretion in determining when to make an arrest, but to arrest a suspect properly they must obtain an arrest warrant from the court prior to arrest or they must be able to show that at the time of arrest they had probable cause to believe that the suspect committed the crime. A suspect who is arrested (taken into physical custody) must then be booked (official recording of the offenses alleged and the identity of the suspect). In some States law enforcement agencies must fingerprint suspects at the time of arrest and booking.

Most persons enter the criminal justice system through arrest, but some enter in other ways.

A person may be issued a citation by a police officer requiring a court appearance to answer a criminal charge. Generally, a citation creates an obligation to appear in court. However, in some jurisdictions, a payment of money can be made in lieu of a court appearance; the common example of such a provision is the case of a minor traffic violation. Alternatively, a person may be issued a summons (a written order by a judicial officer requiring an appearance in court to answer specific charges). A third way of entering the criminal justice system is through indictment by a grand jury. Such indictments usually follow the referral of allegations and evidence by the prosecutor. Occasionally, a grand jury will issue an indictment pursuant to a criminal investigation initiated by the prosecutor. Such an indictment is commonly known as a "grand jury original."

Source: Bureau of Justice Statistics, *Report to the Nation on Crime and Justice: The Data*, 2d ed. (Washington, D.C.: U.S. Government Printing Office, 1988), p. 67.

---

the person and must therefore follow proper procedures or be ruled an unreasonable seizure by the courts.

Arrest and Search Warrants   With some exceptions, the Supreme Court requires that arrests and searches may not be made until the police secure a **warrant**. A 1948 decision indicated the purpose of the **search warrant**, but the principle also applies to arrests. The Court, in *Johnson v. United States*, interpreted the meaning of the Fourth Amendment that protects against unreasonable searches and seizures and requires that search warrants may be issued only upon probable cause.[19]

Johnson v. *United States*

The point of the Fourth Amendment, which often is not grasped by zealous officers, is not that it denies law enforcement the support of the usual inferences which reasonable men draw from evidence. Its protection consists in requiring that those inferences be drawn by a neutral and detached magistrate instead of being judged by the officer engaged in the often competitive enterprise of ferreting out crime. . . . When the right of privacy must reasonably yield to the

The canine patrol is often used for searching suspects, weapons, and drugs. (Michael Hanulak/ Photo Researchers)

right of search is, as a rule, to be decided by a judicial officer, not by a policeman or government enforcement agent.

The Meaning of Probable Cause　The Fourth Amendment requires that a warrant shall not be issued except upon a finding of **probable cause**. Probable cause is also required in those exceptions, to be discussed, in which arrest, search, and seizure are permitted without a warrant. It is necessary to understand the meaning of that term. The term *probable cause* really means reasonable cause. What is reasonable must be decided in light of the facts of any situation. To constitute probable cause, the facts of the

Police radios permit officers to call for information that may give them probable cause to make an arrest. (Picture Cube)

situation must be such that a reasonable person would, upon hearing those facts, conclude that a crime probably had been committed.

The Establishment of Probable Cause   How is probable cause established? Facts sufficient to lead a reasonable person to conclude that a crime has been committed by a particular person or that a particular kind of **contraband** may be found at a specified location may be secured in various ways. One of the most controversial ways occurs when the facts come from an **informant**, who may have a history of criminal activity, or from an anonymous source. The Supreme Court considered the latter in a 1983 case. In *Illinois v. Gates*, the police received an anonymous letter indicating that two specified people, a husband and wife, were engaging in illegal drug sales and that on May 3 the wife would drive their car, loaded with drugs, to Florida. The letter indicated that the husband would fly to Florida to drive the car back to Illinois with the trunk loaded with drugs. The letter further stated that the couple currently had about $100,000 worth of drugs in their basement in Illinois.

After receiving this information, a police officer secured the address of the couple. He also found out that the husband had made a May 5 reservation to fly to Florida. The flight was put under surveillance, which revealed that the suspect took the flight, spent the night in a motel room registered to his wife, and the next morning left in a car with a woman. The license plate of the car was registered to the husband suspect. The couple were driving north on an interstate highway frequently used for traffic to Illinois.

With these facts, the police secured a warrant to search the house and automobile of the couple. The police were waiting for the couple when they returned to their home in Illinois. Upon searching the house and car, the police found drugs that the state attempted to use against the couple at trial. The Gates's motion to have the evidence suppressed at trial was successful, and the Illinois Supreme Court upheld the lower court on this issue. The U.S. Supreme Court, however, disagreed, established a new test, the "totality of circumstances," and held that in this case, independent police verification of the allegations from the anonymous source provided sufficient information on which a **magistrate** could have probable cause to issue the warrants.[20]

The Court's totality of circumstances test in the *Gates* case is very important. Police often receive anonymous tips about a crime that is being committed or about to be committed. Such information does not in and of itself constitute probable cause. The police must verify the anonymous tips.

Sometimes police secure information from known informants. Their information may be used to establish probable cause, but the Supreme Court has established rules that must be followed in such cases. There must be underlying circumstances that would lead a reasonable person to conclude that the informant is reliable and credible in what he or she is saying, and there must be underlying circumstances that indicate a basis for the conclusions drawn by the informant.[21] If the informant is a police officer, credibility might not be questioned although it would still be necessary to show why that person has reason to have such information. But when the informant is a known or suspected criminal, as is frequently the case, establishing credibility is more difficult.[22]

Exceptions to the Search Warrant Requirement   When police arrest or search without a warrant, they make the initial determination of probable cause. When they first secure a warrant, the judge or magistrate makes that determination. The principles are the same in both cases, but the Court allows only a few exceptions to arrest and search without a warrant.[23]

One exception to the warrant requirement is a search that occurs when an officer makes a lawful arrest. This type was first mentioned by the Supreme Court in 1914; but in a 1948 decision, the Court emphasized that the right to search the person, even when the arrest is proper, is a limited privilege.[24] After arrest, some warrantless searches, such as searches of possessions or of the person when the suspect is booked into jail, may be proper; warrantless searches made for the protection of the officer or others also are permitted and will be discussed under the stop and frisk rules.

Inspections and regulatory searches are permitted, too. These would involve searching the possessions of individuals who wish to board airplanes or cross borders. Because both are considered unique areas by the laws of search and seizure, they do not require probable cause. Although such searches are required, individuals have the option of refusing, in which case it is legal to refuse to permit them to cross the border or board the aircraft.

Warrantless searches also may be conducted legally when a person consents to the search. This consent may be given to a search prior to arrest, at the time of arrest, or later at the police station. It may involve searching possessions, automobiles, homes, or persons. The critical factor is whether the consent was made knowingly and voluntarily. In some cases, consent to a search may also be given by a third party.

Search of the Home   The United States Supreme Court has said that the "physical entry of the home is the chief evil against which the wording of the Fourth Amendment is directed."[25] The Court recognizes a difference between searches and seizures within a home or office and the search of a person's property in other places.

> It is accepted, at least as a matter of principle, that a search or seizure carried out on a suspect's premises without a warrant is *per se* unreasonable, unless the police can show that it falls within one of a carefully defined set of exceptions based on the presence of "exigent" circumstances.[26]

An example of an unreasonable entry into and search inside of a home occurred in *Mapp v. Ohio*. When police arrived at the home of Ms. Mapp without a search warrant, she, after calling her attorney, denied them entrance. The police advised their headquarters of that response and put the house under surveillance. About three hours later, with more officers on the scene, police again attempted entry. When Ms. Mapp did not quickly come to the door, the officers forced their way in through one of the doors to the house. In the meantime Mapp's attorney arrived, but the police would not let him enter the house or see Mapp. The following excerpt explains subsequent events.[27]

Mapp v. *Ohio*

It appears that Miss Mapp was halfway down the stairs from the upper floor to the front door when the officers, in this high-handed manner, broke into the hall. She demanded to see the search warrant. A paper claimed to be a warrant, was held up by one of the officers. She grabbed the "warrant" and placed it in her bosom. A struggle ensued in which the officers recovered the piece of paper and as a result of which they handcuffed appellant because she had been "belligerent" in resisting their official rescue of the "warrant" from her person. Running roughshod over appellant, a policeman "grabbed" her, "twisted [her] hand," and she "yelled [and] pleaded with him" because "it was hurting." Appellant, in handcuffs, was then forcibly taken upstairs to her bedroom where the officers searched a dresser, a chest of drawers, a closet and some suitcases. They also looked into a photo album and through personal papers belonging to the appellant. The search spread into the rest of the second floor, including the child's bedroom, the living room, the kitchen, and a dinette. The basement of the building and a trunk found therein were also searched. The obscene materials, for possession of which she was ultimately convicted, were discovered in the course of that widespread search.

At the trial no search warrant was produced by the prosecution, nor was the failure to produce one explained or accounted for. At best, "There is, in the record, considerable doubt as to whether there ever was any warrant for the search of the defendant's home."

The seized evidence was used against Mapp at trial, and she was convicted of "knowingly having had in her possession and under her control certain lewd and lascivious books, pictures, and photographs." The U.S. Supreme Court reversed the conviction.

Scope of the Search What happens if the police, in connection with a lawful arrest, search the entire house of the suspect? In *Chimel v. California*, the Court considered that question. In *Chimel*, police officers, with a warrant authorizing the arrest of the suspect, proceeded to search the house thoroughly. They had no search warrant. The Court, in reversing the conviction, limited the areas that may be searched for weapons, if necessary, to protect the life of the officer and others. The person may also be searched to the extent necessary to prevent destruction of evidence. The officer may search the area "within the immediate control" of the arrestee, such as a gun lying on a table near the suspect.[28]

In later cases the Supreme Court has elaborated on the scope of the lawful search of a home and its **curtilages**. In *United States. v. Dunn*, decided in 1987, the Court said that curtilage questions should be resolved with particular reference to four factors: the proximity of the area claimed to be curtilage to the home, whether the area is included within an enclosure surrounding the home, the nature of the uses to which the area is put, and the steps taken by the resident to protect the area from observation by people passing by.

The Court then held that a barn 60 yards from the house and outside the area surrounding the house enclosed by a fence was not part of the curtilage.[29]

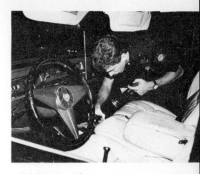
Vehicles may be searched without search warrants under some circumstances. (Bob Daemmrich/ Image Works)

Automobile Searches   In *Carroll v. United States* the Court held that, when police stop an automobile and have probable cause to believe it contains contraband, it is not unreasonable to search that vehicle. However, the Court in *Carroll* did not deal with the scope of that permissible search. In *Chambers v. Maroney*, the Court held that a search warrant is not necessary "where there is probable cause to search an automobile stopped on the highway; the car is moveable, the occupants are alerted, and the car's contents may never be found again if a warrant must be obtained." Each case must be judged on its facts, for the Court has made it clear that not all warrantless searches of cars are lawful.[30]

Subsequent decisions in this area indicate the difficulty the Court has had in articulating rules. In 1981 in *Robbins v. California*, the Court held that, when police stopped a car for proceeding erratically, smelled marijuana smoke as the door was opened, searched the car and found two packages wrapped in opaque plastic, they went beyond the scope of a legitimate search without a warrant when they opened the packages.[31] One year later in *United States v. Ross*, the Court reconsidered its position by examining the extent to which police officers, who have legitimately stopped an automobile and who have probable cause to believe that contraband is concealed somewhere within it, may conduct a probing search of compartments and containers within the vehicle whose contents are not in plain view. "We hold that they may conduct a search of the vehicle that is as thorough as a magistrate could authorize in a warrant particularly describing the place to be searched." The Court emphasized, however, that such searches must be based on probable cause.[32]

In 1985 in *United States v. Johns*, the Court held that a warrantless search of packages held for three days after seizure by customs officials was not unreasonable. Customs officials had been observing what appeared to be a drug-smuggling operation. They saw several packages removed from two small airplanes that had landed in a remote section of the airport. The packages were then loaded onto two pickup trucks. The customs officers approached the trucks, smelled marijuana, and saw packages that were wrapped in plastic bags and sealed with tape. Some of the individuals were arrested, and the packages were seized and placed in a Drug Enforcement Agency warehouse. Three days later, without a search warrant, officers opened the packages and found marijuana. In ruling that the search was proper even without a warrant, the Supreme Court indicated that the warrantless search of a vehicle need not occur contemporaneously with the lawful seizure of the items searched. The Court emphasized, however, that officers may not hold vehicles and their contents indefinitely before they complete a search.[33]

The Court has also held that warrantless inventory searches of automobiles (and persons) are permissible in some cases. In 1987, in *Colorado v. Bertine*, the Court reviewed several prior decisions and upheld the inventory search described in the first part of this excerpt. The excerpt also gives the Court's reasons for holding that the search in *Bertine* did not violate the defendant's Fourth Amendment rights.[34]

Colorado v. *Bertine*

On February 10, 1984, a police officer in Boulder, Colorado arrested respondent Steven Lee Bertine for driving under the influence of alcohol. After Bertine was taken into custody and before the arrival of a tow truck to take Bertine's van to an impoundment lot, a backup officer inventoried the contents of the van. The officer opened a closed backpack in which he found controlled substances, cocaine paraphernalia, and a large amount of cash. . . .

[A]n inventory search may be "reasonable" under the Fourth Amendment even though it is not conducted pursuant to warrant based upon probable cause. In *Opperman*, this Court assessed the reasonableness of an inventory search of the glove compartment in an abandoned automobile impounded by the police. We found that inventory procedures serve to protect an owner's property while it is in the custody of the police, to insure against claims of lost, stolen, or vandalized property, and to guard the police from danger. . . .

In our more recent decision, *Lafayette*, a police officer conducted an inventory search of the contents of a shoulder bag in the possession of an individual being taken into custody. In deciding whether this search was reasonable, we recognized that the search served legitimate governmental interests similar to those identified in *Opperman*. We determined that those interests outweighed the individual's Fourth Amendment interests and upheld the search.

In the present case, as in *Opperman* and *Lafayette*, there was no showing that the police, who were following standardized procedures, acted in bad faith or for the sole purpose of investigation. In addition, the governmental interests justifying the inventory searches in *Opperman* and *Lafayette* are nearly the same as those which obtain here. In each case, the police were potentially responsible for the property taken into their custody. By securing the property, the police protected the property from unauthorized interference. Knowledge of the precise nature of the property helped guard against claims of theft, vandalism, or negligence. Such knowledge also helped to avert any danger to police or others that may have been posed by the property.

These cases illustrate some of the facts under which the Court has held that warrantless searches of automobiles are permissible. Each case, however, must be analyzed in light of its peculiar facts, and not all will agree on whether the search is constitutional. The Supreme Court continues to decide difficult cases involving the search of vehicles, and the controversy in this area may be expected to continue.

Body Searches   The search of bodily cavities by police perhaps is the most controversial search and seizure issue. Some searches are permitted, but there are limitations on the type, time, place, and method of search. The classic case involving body searches was decided in 1949 when three deputy sheriffs of the County of Los Angeles, relying on some information that a man named Rochin was selling narcotics, went to Rochin's home and entered the home through an open door. They then forced open the door of the second-floor bedroom, where they found Rochin, partially clothed, sitting on the bed where his wife was lying. The officers saw two capsules beside the bed and asked, "Whose stuff is this?" Rochin grabbed the capsules and swallowed them. The officers, applying force, tried to remove the capsules, and when they were unsuccessful, handcuffed Rochin and took him to the hospital. They ordered his stomach pumped and the drugs were used as evidence in the subsequent trial, at which Rochin was convicted. In the brief excerpt, the United States Supreme Court gives the reasons why the search and seizure were illegal.[35]

Rochin v. *California* _____

[T]he proceedings by which this conviction was obtained do more than offend some fastidious squeamishness or private sentimentalism about combating crime too energetically. This is conduct that shocks the conscience, illegally breaking into the privacy of the petitioner, the struggle to open his mouth and remove what was there, the forcible extraction of his stomach's contents— this course of proceeding by agents of government to obtain evidence is bound to offend even hardened sensibilities. They are methods too close to the rack and the screw to permit of constitutional differentiation.

Searches of bodily cavities are permitted under some circumstances. Safety and security within jails and prisons is sufficient for strip searches of inmates. Body cavity searches also may be conducted at the borders into the country when customs officials have reason to believe a person is smuggling contraband into the country by carrying the contraband, usually illegal drugs, in bodily cavities. This crime is referred to as *alimentary canal smuggling*. Probable cause is not required for the search of bodily cavities in these cases; customs officials need only have a reasonable suspicion that a traveler is commiting the crime of alimentary canal smuggling to conduct the search.

The Supreme Court recently decided a case on this issue. The case involved a woman who arrived in Los Angeles from Bogota, Columbia. Customs officials became suspicious when, in examining her passport, they noted that she had made numerous recent trips to Miami and Los Angeles. She was carrying $5,000 in cash and told officers that she planned to purchase goods for her husband's store, but she had made no hotel reservations nor any appointments with merchandise vendors. Customs officials suspected that she was smuggling drugs within her body. A pat-down search by a female officer revealed that the suspect's abdomen was firm and that she was wearing elastic underpants lined with a paper towel.

Officials asked the suspect to consent to an x-ray, which at first she agreed to do, but she then withdrew her consent. At that point she was given three choices. She could return to Columbia on the next available flight, submit to an x-ray, or remain in detention until she produced a bowel movement that would be monitored. She chose to return to Columbia but no flight was available, so she was detained for 16 hours. During that time she refused to use the toilet facilities provided for her (a wastebasket placed in a restroom). She refused to eat or drink. Officials finally obtained a court order for an x-ray and bodily search of her rectum. They found a cocaine-filled balloon. During the next four days of detention, the suspect excreted numerous balloons filled with cocaine, totaling more than half a kilogram of the drug.

In upholding the bodily search as legal, the Supreme Court indicated that the right to privacy is diminished at the border. The rights of suspects are important, but the government has a great interest in preventing drug smuggling. The test used by the Court for such searches at the border is whether customs officials, "considering all the facts surrounding the traveler and her trip, reasonably suspect that the traveler is smuggling contraband in her alimentary canal."[36]

In contrast is a case involving proposed surgery to remove a bullet from a suspect who refused to consent to the surgery. The Court held that that search and seizure would be unreasonable. The prosecution claimed that the bullet would link the suspect to the crime. Initial investigation had shown that the surgery would involve only a minor incision that could be conducted with a local anesthetic; on the basis of that evidence, the lower court granted the request to conduct the surgery. Further evidence, however, indicated that the bullet was deeply imbedded and that removal would require a general anesthetic.

The court noted that the interest of individuals in their right to privacy as well as health and life must be considered against the government's interest in combating crime. A surgical procedure to remove evidence may be unreasonable and therefore illegal if it "endangers the life or health of the suspect . . . and [intrudes] upon the individual's dignitary interest in personal privacy and bodily integrity." In this case, said the Court, there was considerable medical uncertainty regarding the safety of the procedure.[37]

Arrest Without a Warrant   Historically, under the English common law, police were permitted to make lawful arrests without an arrest warrant if they had probable cause to believe that a **felony** had been committed and that it was committed by the person to be arrested. Today, either by court decisions or by statutes, this rule exists in most jurisdictions. On the other hand, under the common law in case of a less serious offense, a **misdemeanor**, police were permitted to arrest without a warrant only if the act constituted a breach of peace that occurred within the presence of the officer.

Today, either by court decisions or by statute, most jurisdictions permit police to make a warrantless arrest for any misdemeanor committed in their presence. If the offense is not committed in the officer's presence, however, a warrant is usually required for an arrest of a suspected misdemeanant, even if the officer has overwhelming evidence that the suspect committed the offense. "Committed in the presence of the officer" does not usually mean that the officer must have actually seen the crime committed; rather, it usually is interpreted to mean that the officer has probable cause to believe that the misdemeanor was committed in his or her presence.

In the case of warrantless arrests of suspected felons in which the felony was committed in the presence of the officer, the arrest has been upheld when it appeared that the officer had time to get an arrest warrant before effecting the arrest. This has been true even in cases in which the Court refused to recognize the search and seizure as legal.

A 1984 case illustrates the refusal of the Court, under some circumstances, to sanction a warrantless arrest for a minor offense. *Welsh v. Wisconsin* involved a driver whose car was observed moving erratically down the road, eventually leaving the road. No damage was caused, but the witness suggested to the driver that he should wait for assistance in moving his car. The suspect refused and left the scene. When the police arrived, the witness reported that the driver of the abandoned car was either very sick or intoxicated. The police traced the car registration and went to the home of the suspect.

The suspect's daughter admitted them to the home where, without an arrest warrant, they arrested the suspect for driving while intoxicated. The suspect was taken to the police station where he refused to take a breath-analysis test. Under Wisconsin law, a person who unreasonably refused to take the test faces revocation of his or her driver's license. But the law also provides that it is reasonable to refuse to take the test if the arrest is not lawful.

The Supreme Court held that the refusal to take the breath analysis test was reasonable because the arrest without a warrant was unlawful. The Court emphasized the particular facts of the case. The suspect was arrested for a *civil*, not a criminal offense. Under Wisconsin law, the first offense of driving while intoxicated is a civil offense. The penalty for this offense does not involve a jail or prison term. The suspect was no longer a threat to public safety because he was not continuing to drive his car. He was in his own home, where, as the Court has often emphasized, an arrest (or search) without a warrant generally is not permissible. The Court held that, under the facts of this case, the arrest without a warrant was not lawful.[38]

This case, considered with the hypothetical one posed earlier in the chapter, in which you were arrested for driving while intoxicated, points out the difficulty that officers may have in deciding whether they have probable cause to arrest without a warrant. The facts of these two cases are similar, and it could be argued that in both there is probable cause to believe that the driver was intoxicated. But the differences in the factual situations are critical. You are in the car stopped by the officers; they personally observed your erratic driving as well as your apparent intoxication, an inference made stronger by your inability to perform a test designed to provide a simple measure of intoxication. In the Wisconsin case, the suspect is no longer in the car but in his own home when arrested. The police did not observe his erratic driving. Another critical difference is that, in the jurisdiction in which you were arrested in our hypothetical case, driving while intoxicated is a criminal offense carrying a maximum five-day jail term even for first offenders. In the Wisconsin case, a first offense is a civil, not a criminal matter.

Stop and Frisk   Most of the previous discussion has been concerned with situations in which police have probable cause to arrest. But what happens if the police do not have a search warrant, stop a person, think the person may be armed, and conduct a warrantless search. Some discretion must be allowed the police officer who, based on experience, perceives that a crime might be committed and that the suspect may be armed, thus constituting a threat to the life or health of the officer and others who may be present. It is permissible for the police to conduct pat-down searches, or **frisk**, in some cases.

In *Terry v. Ohio*, Detective Martin McFadden of the Cleveland Police Department noticed two men standing on a street corner in front of several stores. The men made many trips up and down the street, peering into store windows. They also talked to a third man, whom they followed up the street after his departure. McFadden, who had 39 years of experience as a police officer, suspected that the men were casing the stores for purposes of a robbery. He approached the men, identified himself as a police officer, and asked their names. The men only mumbled responses, at which point the detective spun Terry around and patted his breast pocket. Officer McFadden removed the pistol that he felt and then frisked the second man, also finding a pistol. The third man was frisked but did not have a weapon.[39]

How does this case compare to your hypothetical arrest? Should the officers have had the legal right to search your person and your automobile at the time you were arrested? Do you think Officer McFadden should have had the legal right to search the three men for weapons, although he did not have probable cause to think they were committing a crime and therefore could not lawfully arrest them?

In *Terry*, the Supreme Court emphasized that even such brief detention of a person without an arrest is a seizure of that person, and such intrusions are not just petty indignities but, rather, constitute "a serious intrusion upon the sanctity of the person, which may inflict great indignity and arouse strong resentment." On the other hand, the Supreme Court recognized that police officers are injured and killed in the line of duty. They cannot be expected to take unreasonable risks. Consequently, the Court concluded that "when an officer is justified in believing that the individual whose suspicious behavior he is investigating at close range is armed and presently dangerous to the officer or to others," a brief search is permissible. The case clearly limits the range of a warrantless search to a pat-down for weapons. In the case of the hypothetical arrest, the officers did not have reason to think you were armed; so even a pat-down search would have been an unjustified intrusion and illegal.

Interrogation

Another important law enforcement function of policing is that of interrogation. Police must be able to question the suspects they stop, but that need to question must be balanced with the right of suspects not to have to testify against themselves, as guaranteed by the Fifth Amendment (Spotlight 6.2). The interrogation function of the police and the limits on it raise some of the most controversial issues in criminal law and criminal procedure.

It is clear now that police may not use physical force to extract confessions, but what about the use of psychological pressure to encourage suspects to give incriminating statements to the police? Consider the *Miranda* decision, decided by the Supreme Court in 1966. Miranda was arrested, taken into custody, and identified by the complaining witness. He was held and interrogated for two hours by police who admitted that they did not tell him he had a right to have an attorney present. The police obtained from Miranda a written confession that said his confession was voluntary, made with full knowledge that it could be used against him, and that he fully understood his legal rights. That confession was admitted into evidence at the trial, and Miranda was convicted. The Supreme Court of Arizona upheld the conviction, emphasizing that Miranda did not ask for an attorney. The U.S. Supreme Court reversed the conviction in a lengthy decision, discussing the dangers of establishing psychological environments in which the accused, even if innocent, would confess. To protect suspects from impermissible psychological interrogation, the Court handed down the **Miranda warning**, outlined in this brief excerpt from the case.[40]

Miranda v. Arizona ⎯⎯⎯⎯⎯⎯⎯⎯⎯⎯⎯⎯⎯⎯⎯⎯⎯⎯⎯⎯⎯⎯⎯⎯⎯

[U]nless other fully effective means are devised to inform accused persons of their right of silence and to assure a continuous opportunity to exercise it, the following measures are required. Prior to any questioning, the person must be warned that he has a right to remain silent, that any statement he does make may be used as evidence against him, and that he has a right to the presence of an attorney, either retained or appointed. The defendant may waive effectuation of these rights, provided the waiver is made voluntarily, knowingly and intelligently. If, however, he indicates in any manner and at any stage of the process that he wishes to consult with an attorney before speaking there can be no questioning. Likewise, if the individual is alone and indicates in any manner that he does not wish to be interrogated, the police may not question him. The mere fact that he may have answered some questions or volunteered some statements on his own does not deprive him of the right to refrain from answering any further inquiries until he has consulted with an attorney and thereafter consents to be questioned.

The Interpretation of *Miranda*   The *Miranda* decision has been the subject of frequent litigation, and a number of cases have reached the U.S. Supreme Court. These cases indicate the problems with which the Court has been concerned. One of the most important questions raised by *Miranda* is at what point the warning must be given. *Miranda* refers to the point of "custodial interrogation." In *Miranda* the Court makes a footnote reference to an earlier case, *Escobedo v. Illinois,* in which the Court referred to an investigation as beginning when the police had gone beyond a general inquiry into alleged criminal acts and actually focused their investigation on the accused.[41]

Numerous articles were written shortly after the Court decided *Escobedo* and *Miranda,* and numerous cases were litigated on the issues raised by these cases. The mid-1980s also witnessed considerable scholarly and unscholarly reactions to the meaning of police interrogation. In addition to numerous articles in major law review publications, the leading police interrogation manual was revised.[42] The U.S. Department of Justice, headed by Attorney General Edwin Meese, issued a report on *Miranda*.[43] And the Supreme Court narrowly interpreted the *Miranda* holding in two of its 1986–1987 cases.[44]

The Court had previously established some exceptions to the *Miranda* rule, one of which was *New York v. Quarles,* in which the Court established a public safety exception. *Quarles* involved a woman who stopped a police car shortly after midnight and told the officers that she had just been raped by a man who subsequently fled into a nearby supermarket. The police entered the store, saw a man who fit the description given by the woman, chased, caught, and handcuffed him. Without giving the *Miranda* warning, the police, upon noticing an *empty* brown shoulder holster, inquired, "Where is the gun?" The suspect answered, the police found the gun, and it was used as evidence at trial. In upholding the use of that evidence, the Court gave its reasons in the brief excerpt that follows.[45]

New York v. *Quarles*

We hold that on these facts there is a "public safety" exception to the requirement that Miranda warnings be given before a suspect's answers may be admitted into evidence. . . .

We conclude that the need for answers to questions in a situation posing a threat to the public safety outweighs the need for the prophylactic rule protecting the Fifth Amendment's privilege against self-incrimination. We decline to place officers such as Officer Kraft in the untenable position of having to consider, often in a matter of seconds, whether it best serves society for them to ask the necessary questions without the *Miranda* warnings and render whatever probative evidence they uncover inadmissible, or for them to give the warnings in order to preserve the admissibility of evidence they might uncover but possibly damage or destroy their ability to obtain that evidence and neutralize the volatile situation confronting them.

The intellectual problem of the 1980s and 90s is essentially the same as that of the 1960s: how to protect the privilege against self-incrimination while permitting police to secure confessions essential for conviction in many cases.[46] The Supreme Court continues to face many questions on the issues surrounding confessions, with the justices disagreeing among themselves on the resolution of the issues. In this area of criminal procedure we must analyze carefully the facts of each case and how the Court applied its decision to those facts.

In the next chapter we will look at other recent cases dealing with the ultimate effect of a violation of the *Miranda* rule—the **exclusionary rule**, requiring that evidence illegally seized or confessions obtained in violation of the rule must be excluded from the subsequent trial. Concern with cases in which the suspect was freed because excluding illegally seized evidence meant that the prosecution could not prove guilt beyond a reasonable doubt has led to severe criticism of the *Miranda* warning and the exclusionary rule. Strong support for abolition came from President Ronald Reagan and his administration.

In analyzing the *Miranda* rule and the subsequent interpretations of that rule, we must recall the purpose of the adversary system: the search for truth, coupled with the belief that truth is not to be obtained by unreliable confessions from bewildered, beaten, or terrified suspects. The purpose of the *Miranda* requirement is not to suppress the truth but, rather, to avoid violating the rights of citizens during police interrogations.

POLICE ON PATROL

The President's Crime Commission declared in 1967 that the "heart of the police law enforcement effort is patrol, the movement around an assigned area, on foot or by vehicle, of uniformed policemen." Yet, although all police experts would agree that patrol is important, there is little agreement over how much and what kind of patrol is most effective.[47]

Purposes of Patrol

Patrol has several purposes. In the first place, the presence of an officer on patrol may eliminate the opportunity for someone to commit a crime, even if that presence does not decrease the desire to engage in the unlawful action. The presence of a police officer where the crime would be committed increases the chances of apprehension and arrest. The potential criminal may think that the officer's presence would eliminate the opportunity to commit the crime successfully.[48]

A second purpose of police patrol is to give the officers an opportunity to assess the possibilities for crime violations and thereby prevent them from occurring. This may be done by getting to know the people in the area, stimulating high ethical standards, and working to eliminate forces found to produce crime. Favorable interactions with citizens may prevent their desire to commit crime and may enhance the positive interactions between citizens and the police. Police officers who give assistance to persons having personal problems, in effect, may be preventing criminal activities, for such problems often precede criminal involvement.

Police patrol has a third purpose, that of providing officers with a quick opportunity to investigate crimes that have occurred. Further, the existence of 24-hour-a-day patrol means that police are available, in contrast to most other professionals, for assistance in various services. Police may report violations of building codes or safety standards, lack of trash pickup, and many other activities of importance to other agencies. These activities illustrate how patrol, a form of law enforcement, overlaps services to citizens and to other agencies.

Types of Patrol

Police may patrol on foot, on horseback, on bicycles, on motorcycles, in cars, in helicopters, or in airplanes. They may patrol alone or in groups of two or more. Today in large cities it is common for some officers to be accompanied on patrol by dogs, referred to as the canine patrol. Dogs may be trained to sniff for drugs, for weapons thought to be associated with the crime, or for people and their possessions. These types of patrol all have their advantages and disadvantages, but one common source of disagreement in policing is the controversy over which is the best type of patrol.

A Traditional Model of Patrol

Traditionally, police patrol has been viewed as providing services to citizens as well as preventing crime, detecting crime and apprehending criminals, recovering stolen property, and providing a sense of community and safety for citizens. The presence of a uniformed officer is seen as the most effective way to accomplish these goals, although plainclothes detectives also are used in some situations. Analyses of what police do while on patrol vary, but generally patrol officers are involved in four kinds of functions: calls for service, preventive patrol, administrative tasks, and officer-initiated activities.

Calls for Service   Police perform a variety of services for citizens. Calls to the police department for service often will take priority over other activities of the patrol officer. If the officer is engaged in preventive patrol when a call comes from the dispatcher, the call normally will take precedence; for police departments frequently emphasize the importance of rapid response to calls. Some officers complain that they cannot engage in effective preventive patrol because of the demand for services and the pressure from other patrol officers in their districts if they are not available to assist with those calls.

In an extensive analysis of all kinds of police patrol, investigators concluded that

> not all calls merit a response by a mobile unit and that not all calls require an immediate response. Departments that have developed alternative response methods and realistic response time goals have been more successful in providing patrol services than departments that have indiscriminately attempted to deal with every citizen request as an emergency.[49]

The National Institute of Justice (NIJ), in the 1980s, sponsored research into the question of the effectiveness of differential response systems. In a study of police in Wilmington, Delaware, and Birmingham, Alabama, researchers found that only about 15 percent of citizen calls to police were "critical," meaning that they required immediate police response. Of the calls, 55 percent did not require immediate response, and 30 percent could be handled by an alternative method.[50]

NIJ also sponsored research on a police system called *management-of-demand* (MOD), by which police establish policies for handling by an alternative method calls which do not demand immediate police attention. For example, a telephone report might be taken by police personnel, thus eliminating the need for a uniformed officer to go to the scene of the alleged crime. Research indicated that citizens did not become dissatisfied with police under this system and that crime rates did not increase.[51]

Joan Petersilia, a researcher at the Rand Corporation, which conducts extensive research on criminal justice issues, summarized the research as follows:

- In the areas studied, less than 5 percent of arrests made for serious crimes could be attributed to fast police response.
- The time it takes for a citizen to report a crime is the major factor in determining whether or not an on-scene arrest takes place and whether witnesses are available. When victims and witnesses delay in calling the police after a crime, variation in the speed of police response accounts for so small a proportion of total elapsed time that it has almost no effect on arrest probabilities.
- Most service calls are not critical in nature and do not require fast response by patrol units. Many can potentially be handled by other means, some of them by civilian police personnel or other agencies.
- Citizens do not become dissatisfied with different types of police response, provided they are told in advance how their calls will be handled.[52]

It thus would appear reasonable for police to devise an alternative response system for some calls.

Preventive Patrol   When officers are not dispatched by the police department to respond to calls for services, order maintenance, or law enforcement, they may walk, ride, or drive through their districts without specific assignments. It is assumed that they are on preventive patrol; their presence will deter people from engaging in criminal activity. They may have total discretion on how they use this noncommitted time, and there probably will be few checks on their activities, illustrating again the discretion given police officers. Some studies indicate that police spend more time on preventive patrol than in other activities. (See Figure 6.1). But how effective is preventive patrol?

In 1972 the Police Foundation sponsored an extensive study of the effects of police patrol in Kansas City, with the investigators concluding the following: the overwhelming evidence is that decreasing or increasing routine preventive patrol within the range tested in this experiment had no effect on crime, citizen fear of crime, community attitudes toward the police on the delivery of police service, police response time, or traffic accidents.[53] James Q. Wilson, in an evaluation of the Kansas City experiment, cautions that the results should not be misinterpreted.

> The experiment does not show that the police make no difference and it does not show that adding more police is useless in controlling crime. All it shows is that changes in the amount of random preventive patrol in marked cars does not, by itself, seem to affect, over one year's time in Kansas City, how much crime occurs or how safe citizens feel.

Wilson points out that very different results might have occurred if changes had been made in *how* the police were used and not merely in the number of marked patrol cars placed in one area.[54]

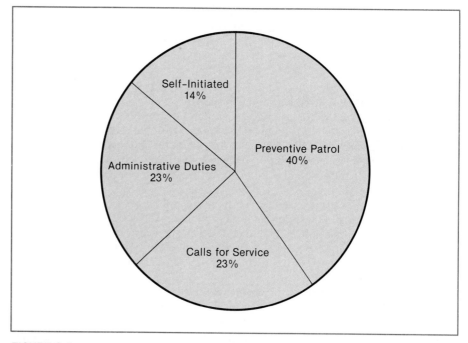

FIGURE 6.1
Analysis of Patrol Workload in Kansas City. *Source:* William G. Gay, Theodore H. Schell, and Stephen Schack, *Improving Patrol Productivity*, vol. 1, *Routine Patrol* (Washington, D.C.: U.S. Government Printing Office, July 1977), p. 3.

Foot patrol of police officers, used frequently in the past, has recently come back into practice in some areas. (Sylvia Plachy)

The major proponent of the effectiveness of patrol, O. W. Wilson, argues that despite that conclusion, "the fact remains that in the few situations in recent history in which police response was obviously not immediately available . . . wholesale looting and lawlessness have been the result."[55]

More recent analyses of the relationship between amount of time police spend on patrol and the incidence of crime indicate that the relationship is more complex than previously recognized.

For example, in some instances, the rates of robbery have actually *increased* when police patrol has increased. This may be because citizens are more likely to report robberies when they know that police are concentrating more time and effort on detecting that crime.[56] It also may be the result of police who patrol aggressively. Clearly, more research is needed on the precise interrelationship between police patrol and crime rates.

Police patrol may have a positive effect on the relationships between the community and the police, too. Interviews over a four-year-period disclosed that the Neighborhood Foot Patrol program in Flint, Michigan, improved relationships between the police and the community; it also reduced the disparity between blacks and whites in their perceptions of police effectiveness. Residents of the community indicated their belief that the police on foot patrol were more responsive to their needs than had been the case before the experimental program.[57]

Administrative Tasks Patrol officers also spend time in administrative duties, such as preparing reports, transporting papers and prisoners, preparing the patrol vehicle, running departmental errands, and appearing in court. Some of these functions (such as preparing the vehicle) can be handled by others; streamlining bureaucratic work also can reduce the amount of time patrol officers must spend in administrative tasks. Reports must be filed, but officers legitimately complain about the time consumed in writing reports simply because the police department has inadequate support personnel.

Officer-Initiated Activities   Patrol officers in the Kansas City study spent only 14 percent of their time in activities they initiated: services, crime prevention, law enforcement, or order maintenance. Officers may be concerned about getting too far away from their radios. The pressure to be available for calls is severe in many departments, and some officers have reported that their colleagues are quite critical of officers who are frequently unavailable to answer dispatch calls in their districts.

Some researchers have suggested that the noncommitted time of patrol officers should be more directed and structured, resulting in a more productive and efficient use of patrol time.[58] Others have suggested that rather than viewing patrol mainly in terms of responding to citizen calls, police departments should focus all patrol efforts on particular problems underlying criminal activity.

Problem-Oriented Policing

Although police patrol has always been concerned with problems, the emphasis today is on *problem-oriented policing*. This approach, based on research findings of the past 20 years, is based on the belief that police effectiveness can be increased if the expertise and creativity of line officers are utilized to develop innovative methods for solving the underlying problems that cause or influence criminal behavior. Spotlight 6.5 diagrams and explains the problem-oriented approach.

Problem-oriented policing may focus on underlying problems in any or all of the three traditional areas of policing: order maintenance, law enforcement, and community service. It is not designed to eliminate police reaction to citizen calls but rather to enhance the effectiveness of policing by identifying underlying problems and attempting to solve those problems.

Problem-oriented policing is in effect in some police departments.

INVESTIGATION

The success or failure of the prosecution of a suspect for a particular crime may—and often does—depend on the investigative abilities of the police before, during, or after the suspect's arrest. Evidence may be quickly destroyed or never found. Without physical evidence, it may be impossible to link the alleged criminal activity with the suspect.

In larger departments, criminal investigation may be the responsibility of specialists, and police officers may not be closely involved in the process. In many cases, however, the police officer who makes the arrest will be a critical element in the investigative process. In large police de-

The Problem-Solving Process

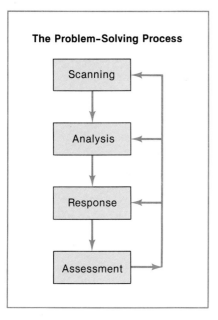

The Problem-Solving Process

Scanning → Analysis → Response → Assessment

Explanation

1. *Scanning.* Instead of relying upon broad, law-related concepts—robbery, burglary, for example—

officers are encouraged to group individual related incidents that come to their attention as "problems" and define these problems in more precise and therefore useful terms. For example, an incident that typically would be classified simply as a "robbery" might be seen as part of a pattern of prostitution-related robberies committed by transvestites in center-city hotels.

2. *Analysis.* Officers working on a well-defined "problem" then collect information from a variety of public and private sources—not just police data. They use the information to illuminate the underlying nature of the problem, suggesting its causes and a variety of options for its resolution.

3. *Response.* Working with citizens, businesses, and public and private agencies, officers tailor a program of action suitable to the characteristics of the problem. Solutions may go beyond traditional criminal justice system remedies to include other community agencies or organizations.

4. *Assessment.* Finally, the officers evaluate the impact of these efforts to see if the problems were actually solved or alleviated.

Source: William Speiman and John E. Eck, "Newport News Tests Problem-Oriented Policing," *National Institute of Justice Reports* (January–February 1987): 2–3, 4.

---

partments, the investigative function of the patrol officer is limited. Most of the investigation, at least in serious cases, is conducted by specialized officers in the Criminal Investigation Unit of the department. These investigators conduct various kinds of activities, as indicated in Spotlight 6.6.

Research on the Investigatory Process

In 1975, Peter Greenwood of the Rand Corporation began an extensive study of the investigatory process in the United States. Bernard Greenberg at the Stanford Research Institute also conducted a study. Both wrote extensive reports and suggested reforms. The National Institute of Justice funded research projects to implement some of those reforms.[59] The results have been summarized as follows:

SPOTLIGHT 6.6
MAJOR FUNCTIONS PERFORMED BY UNIFORMED CRIME INVESTIGATORS IN THE OCEANSIDE, CALIFORNIA, POLICE DEPARTMENT

1. Total crime scene management
2. Crime scene photography
3. Develop latent prints using powders and chemicals
4. Conduct interviews/interrogations
5. Obtain search/arrest warrants
6. Collect, preserve, and catalog physical evidence
7. Crime scene sketch
8. Collect body fluids
9. Make impressions
10. Make composites using the "Identi-Kit" process
11. Conduct neutron activation tests
12. Attend autopsies
13. Operate artificial lighting systems
14. Maintain field activity records
15. Conduct followup investigations

Source: Lt. Gene N. Berry, "The Uniformed Crime Investigator: A Unique Strategy to Protect and Serve," *FBI Law Enforcement Bulletin* 53 (March 1984): 3.

- Many serious crimes are not—and often cannot be—solved.
- Patrol officers are responsible, directly or indirectly, for most arrests. Either they arrest the suspect at the scene or they obtain identifications (or useful descriptions) of the criminal from victims or witnesses when the crime is initially reported.
- Only a small percentage of all index arrests result from detective investigations that require special organization, training, or skill. Special investigations bring very few *unknown* criminals to justice.
- Investigators play a critical role in the postarrest process, particularly in collecting evidence that will enable the prosecutor to file formal criminal charges.[60]

It may be concluded that, although we should not reduce the total police resources, we could probably be more efficient by reallocating some of the resources to different functions within the investigative process. Most of the initial investigations could be assigned to patrol units that would be directed by local commanders. The quality of these initial investigations would be improved if the patrol force had the services of more generalist-investigators. Cases also should be screened before investigations begin. Screening would indicate that some complaints should not be investigated. These changes would permit detectives to concentrate their investigative efforts on more serious crimes.

Investigative Techniques

Police spend considerable time looking for witnesses to testify and recovering evidence that a crime has been committed and committed by a particular person. Much of their efforts are futile, for sufficient evidence cannot be found.

Fingerprinting is one of the most effective types of evidence. This technique has been available in the United States since it was first used

Investigation is an important function of policing. Here, detectives inspect some items that were handled by bandits in the famed Cartier jewelers in the Waldorf Astoria hotel in New York City. (UPI Bettmann Newsphotos)

around 1900 by Scotland Yard in London. Recently, however, investigators have been able to use computers to assist with fingerprint identification.

One prosecutor has emphasized the potential impact of this development, which "could revolutionize law enforcement in a way that no other technology has since radios were put in patrol cars." This is because the computer can pick out the identifying qualities much faster than a human conducting the process by hand.[61]

Another new technique is the use of DNA, or deoxyribonucleic acid, "which carries the genetic information that determines individual characteristics such as eye color and body size." This technique is close to 100 percent accurate, compared to traditional blood and semen tests, which are only 90 to 95 percent accurate.[62]

These new techniques have been very successful in assisting police and prosecutors to identify evidence sufficient for conviction in recent cases. As this science of forensic evidence expands, more effective evidence will be used in criminal trials.

SUMMARY

This chapter has focused on the major functions of policing, emphasizing that all of those functions are carried out in settings that involve considerable police discretion. We have already seen that discretion is a crucial element in many areas of criminal justice, but perhaps it is most evident in policing. Despite the checks on what police can and cannot do in apprehending, arresting, interrogating, and searching and seizing, there are virtually no checks on their decisions not to intervene.

Police functions include maintaining order, providing a variety of services, and enforcing the law. For each of these areas, we discussed the ways that the functions are carried out, as well as some of the controversies concerning them. There is little agreement on the relative merit of using police for functions other than law enforcement, but clearly many situations that at first do not involve criminal activity may escalate into illegal action without adequate intervention.

The law enforcement function of policing can be understood only in view of the legal constraints on that function. The conflict between the crime control and the due process models comes into play dramatically in law enforcement. Police could make more arrests and conduct more thorough investigations if they did not have to observe the due process rights of defendants, but our society places great emphasis on the right of individuals to be free from unreasonable intrusion by the government. This does not mean that police cannot arrest, search and seize, interrogate, and investigate, but only that these functions must be performed within the limits of due process.

The legal rules regarding what police may and may not do, however, are not always clear. Once again, discretion becomes important. With the discretion to decide what to do in a particular situation and without a definite legal mandate, police often face the need to make a quick decision at the risk of violating the civil rights of suspects. This is not an easy task, and it presents serious role conflicts for police.

The Fourth Amendment's prohibition against unreasonable search and seizure and the Fifth Amendment's provision that a person may not be forced to incriminate himself or herself are the key constitutional bases of what police can and cannot do in law enforcement. The investigatory stop, the brief detention, the arrest, and searching and seizing are important police activities regulated by constitutional requirements, court interpretations of those requirements, and departmental policies.

A look at a few key cases on the law of arrest, search, and seizure should make it obvious that it is impossible to state what "the law" is in this area. The facts of a particular case must be analyzed carefully in light of previous court decisions. Reasonable minds often will differ as to the conclusion in any given case. It is important to analyze case law very carefully, looking not only at the actual holding of a case but the reasons given by the judges (or justices) for making that decision.

In some cases police are permitted to arrest, search and seize without a warrant, although the Su-

preme Court prefers warrants. Again, it is impossible for police to know in every case whether they face exceptions to the warrant requirement. Law enforcement is frequently ambiguous, leaving considerable discretion to the individual officer, who later may be second-guessed by the courts.

Interrogation is another important law enforcement function of policing. The Supreme Court also has issued decisions in this area. The Court requires that the *Miranda* warning be given in cases in which a person might be deprived of his or her liberty, but it is not always clear when interrogation has begun and the warning must be given. Failure to comply with *Miranda* requirements may result in the exclusion of evidence from the trial, an issue that will be discussed in the next chapter. In recent years, in the words of some, the Court has "watered down" the *Miranda* decision. The "public safety" exception of the *New York v. Quarles* case is an example. Other examples will also be discussed in Chapter 7.

Police patrol, an important function, is controversial, too. The traditional patrol model—in which police respond to calls for service, engage in preventive patrol and administrative tasks, and initiate some actions to deter or apprehend criminals—has been carefully researched. As a result, some police departments have instituted differential response systems and management-of-demand policies to reduce the number of occasions in which a patrol officer responds directly to the scene of a call for help. Problem-oriented policing, in which police focus on the problems underlying criminal activity, is gaining more attention today, too, with some departments reporting a significant reduction in crime by use of this method.

Investigation is the final police function discussed in this chapter. Traditionally, the police have spent considerable time investigating crimes at the scene of their occurrence without significant effectiveness. Recently, investigative techniques have been improved by the use of forensic science, especially DNA.

Policing has changed in many ways in recent years. This chapter touched on only a few areas in which changes have been tried. Some police activities, such as the handling of domestic violence, are discussed elsewhere. Some will be discussed in the next chapter, in which we focus on problems of policing.

STUDY QUESTIONS

1. Why is discretion important in policing? Will guidelines help curb abuses?

2. Should order maintenance remain a police function? Why, or why not?

3. Should police officers be expected to perform services for individuals if those services are not directly related to law enforcement or order maintenance? Why, or why not?

4. What functions do police have in traffic control and in enforcing traffic laws and ordinances? Should nonuniformed personnel be used instead of uniformed police for any of these functions?

5. Under what circumstances may police stop, question, and arrest a suspect?

6. Why are warrants usually required for arrest and search?

7. What is the meaning of *probable cause*?

8. How may police establish probable cause?

9. Under what circumstances may police search without a *warrant*? Arrest without a warrant?

10. When may police search a home? How much of the home may be searched?

11. Under what circumstances may an automobile be searched?

12. When may bodily searches be conducted?

13. What is meant by *stop and frisk*? What are the general rules for this type of police action?

14. What is the *Miranda* warning? Why is it important?

15. What exceptions has the Court made to the *Miranda* warning?

16. What is the importance of police patrol? How might it be improved?

17. What is meant by *problem-solving policing*? Evaluate this approach.

18. What improvements might be made in police investigation?

ENDNOTES

1. Michael K. Brown, *Working the Street: Police Discretion and the Dilemmas of Reform* (New York: Russell Sage Foundation, 1981), p. 5.

2. Egdon Bittner, "The Police Charge," *The Functions of the Police in Modern Society* (Bethesda, Md.: National Institute of Mental Health, 1970); quoted in Richard J. Lundman, *Police Behavior: A Sociological Perspective* (New York: Oxford University Press, 1980), p. 38.

3. Michael R. Gottfredson and Don M. Gottfredson, *Decision Making in Criminal Justice: Toward the Rational Exercise of Discretion*, (Cambridge, Mass.: Ballinger Publishing Co., 1980), Chapter 3, "The Decision to Arrest," p. 87.

4. For an often cited discussion of police discretion in general, see Kenneth Culp Davis, *Police Discretion* (St. Paul, Minn.: West Publishing Co., 1975).

5. James Q. Wilson, *Varieties of Police Behavior: The Management of Law and Order in Eight Communities* (Cambridge, Mass.: Harvard University Press, 1968), p. 21.

6. Ibid., pp. 16, 17.

7. Ibid., p. 21.

8. George L. Kelling, "Order Maintenance, the Quality of Urban Life, and Police: A Line of Argument," in William A. Geller, ed., *Police Leadership in America: Crisis and Opportunity* (Chicago: American Bar Foundation, 1985), p. 297.

9. Ibid., p. 308.

10. See James Q. Wilson and George L. Kelling, "Police and Neighborhood Safety: Broken Windows," *Atlantic Monthly* 249 (March 1982); pp. 29–38.

11. Carl B. Klockars, "Order Maintenance, the Quality of Urban Life, and Police: A Different Line of Argument," in Geller, ed. *Police Leadership*, p. 316, quoting *The Newark Foot Patrol Experiment* (Washington, D.C.: Police Foundation, 1981), p. 88.

12. Gary W. Sykes, "Street Justice: A Moral Defense of Order Maintenance Policing," *Justice Quarterly* 3 (December 1986): 510.
13. Wilson, *Varieties of Police Behavior*, p. 5.
14. President's Commission on Law Enforcement and Administration of Justice, *The Challenge of Crime in a Free Society* (Washington, D.C.: U.S. Government Printing Office, 1967), pp. 97–98.
15. "Tulsa Police Officials Praise Community Service Program," *Tulsa World*, (15 September 1985), p. 4B, col. 1.
16. See The President's Commission on Law Enforcement and Administration of Justice, *Task Force Report: The Police* (Washington, D.C.: U.S. Government Printing Office, 1967).
17. CAL. PENAL CODE, Section 647(e).
18. Kolender et al. v. Lawson, 461 U.S. 352, 360, 361 (1983).
19. Johnson v. U. S. 333 U.S. 10, 13–14 (1948).
20. Illinois v. Gates, 462 U.S. 213 (1983).
21. Aguilar v. Texas, 378 U.S. 108 (1964).
22. See U.S. v. Simpson, 813 F.2d 1462 (9th Cir. 1987), *cert. den.*, 108 S. Ct. 233 (1987), upholding the use of a prostitute to obtain information on a drug dealer.
23. Katz v. United States, 389 U.S. 347, 357 (1967).
24. Weeks v. United States, 232 U.S. 383 (1914); Trupiano v. U.S. 334 U.S. 699 (1948).
25. U.S. v. U.S. District Court, 407 U.S. 297, 313 (1972).
26. Coolidge v. New Hampshire, 403 U.S. 443, 474–475, (1971).
27. Mapp v. Ohio, 367 U.S. 643, 644 (1961).
28. Chimel v. California, 395 U.S. 752 (1969).
29. United States v. Dunn, 480 U.S. 294 (1987), *reh. den.*, 481 U.S. 1024, *on remand*, 817 F.2d 18 (1987).
30. Carroll v. U.S., 267 U.S. 132 (1925); Chambers v. Maroney, 399 U.S. 42, 51 (1970).
31. Robbins v. California, 453 U.S. 420, 428 (1981).
32. U.S. v. Ross, 456 U.S. 798, 800 (1982).
33. U.S. v. Johns, 469 U.S. 478 (1985).
34. Colorado v. Bertine, 107 S. Ct. 738 (1987), footnotes and citations omitted. Citations for the mentioned cases are South Dakota v. Opperman, 428 U.S. 364 (1976) and Illinois v. Lafayette, 462 U. S. 604 (1983).
35. Rochin v. California, 342 U.S. 165 (1952).
36. U.S. v. Montoya de Hernandez, 473 U.S. 531 (1985).
37. Winston v. Lee, 470 U.S. 753 (1985).
38. Welsh v. Wisconsin, 466 U.S. 740 (1984).
39. Terry v. Ohio, 392 U.S. 1 (1968). See also U.S. v. Hensley, 469 U.S. 221 (1985).
40. Miranda v. Arizona, 384 U.S. 436, 444, 445 (1966).
41. Escobedo v. Illinois, 378 U.S. 478 (1964).
42. Fred E. Inbau et al., *Criminal Interrogation and Confessions*, 3d ed. (Baltimore: Williams & Wilkins, 1986).
43. U.S. Department of Justice, Office of Legal Policy, *Report to the Attorney General on the Law of Pre-Trial Interrogation* (Washington, D.C.: U.S. Government Printing Office, 1986).
44. See Colorado v. Connelly, 479 U.S. 157 (1986), and Colorado v. Spring, 479 U.S. 564, (1987). For a discussion of the latter, see "Fifth Amendment—Validity of Waiver: A Suspect Need Not Know the Subjects of Interrogation," *Journal of Criminal Law & Criminology* 78 (Winter 1988): 828–852.
45. New York v. Quarles, 467 U.S. 649 (1984).
46. For a discussion of these recent developments, see Donald A. Dripps, "FOREWORD: Against Police Interrogation—And the Privilege Against Self-Incrimination," *Journal of Criminal Law & Criminology* 78 (Winter 1988): 699–734.
47. *The Challenge of Crime in a Free Society*, p. 95.
48. For more information on the functions of patrol, see the source from which this summary is taken: O.W. Wilson and Roy Clinton McLaren, *Police Administration*, 4th ed. (New York: McGraw-Hill Book Co., 1977 pp. 320–21.
49. William G. Gay et al., *Improving Patrol Productivity*, Vol. 1. *Routine Patrol* (Washington, D.C.: U.S. Government Printing Office, July 1977), p. 60.
50. For a brief summary and analysis of the research on police response to calls for service, see Joan Petersilia, *The Influence of Criminal Justice Research* (Santa Monica, Calif.: Rand Corporation, 1987), pp. 10–13.
51. See Michael F. Cahn and James Tien, *An Alternative Approach in Police Response: Wilington Management of Demand Program* (Washington, D.C.: U.S. Department of Justice, National Institute of Justice, 1981), reviewed in Petersilia, ibid., p. 12.
52. Petersilia, ibid., pp. 12–13.
53. George L. Kelling et al., "The Kansas City Preventive Patrol Experiment," in Carl B. Klockars, ed., *Thinking About Police: Contemporary Reading* (New York: McGraw-Hill Book Co., 1983), p. 160. For the full report, see *The Kansas City Preventive Patrol Experiment: A Summary Report* (Washington D.C.: The Police Foundation, 1974).
54. James Q. Wilson, *Thinking about Crime* (New York: Vintage Books, 1975), p. 99.
55. Wilson and McLaren, *Police Administration*, p. 323.
56. See Herbert Jacob and Michael J. Rich, "The Effects of the Police on Crime: A Second Look," *Law and Society Review* 15 (1980–1981): 109–22, refuting the findings of an earlier study by James Q. Wilson and Barbara Boland.
57. See R. C. Trojanowicz and D. W. Banas, *Impact*

of Foot Patrol on Black and White Perceptions of Policing, National Neighborhood Foot Patrol Center, Michigan State University, 560 Baker Hall, East Lansing, MI 48824. Document free.
58. Gay et al., *Routine Patrol*, p. 6.
59. See Bernard Greenberg et al., *Felony Investigation Decision Model—An Analysis of Investigative Elements of Information* (Menlo Park, Calif.: Stanford Research Institute, 1975); and Peter Greenwood et al., *The Criminal Investigation Process* (Lexington, Mass.: D. C. Heath and Co., 1977).
60. Petersilia, *The Influence of Criminal Justice Research*, p. 16.
61. "Taking a Byte out of Crime," *Time* (14 October 1985), p. 96.
62. Debra Cassens Moss, "DNA—The New Fingerprints," *American Bar Association Journal* (1 May 1988): 66.

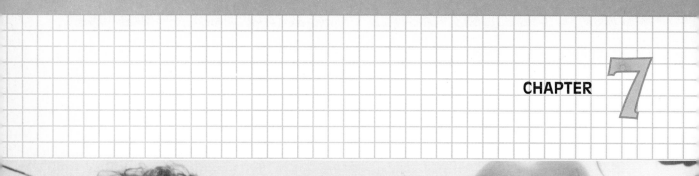

Problems and Issues in Policing

Sharon and Jerry, white police officers on patrol in a predominantly black area of a large city, responded to a call to investigate a reported burglary in progress. As they arrived on the scene, two men ran out of an apartment and down the alley. Sharon and Jerry yelled, "Police, Freeze. Drop your weapons." One of the men followed the orders; the other reached for what the officers thought was a gun. Jerry fired a shot at that suspect, wounding him seriously. The suspect, a 15-year-old black, died a week later. He had been carrying a toy pistol.

After the incident, Jerry was suspended pending an investigation. The investigatory committee, consisting of police officers and administrators, found no improper behavior, but Jerry was unable to return to work. He could not sleep well; he had nightmares about the shooting. He lost confidence in himself; he questioned his actions and often remarked

that if he had not fired, the young man would still be alive. Jerry's problems affected his family life; soon his wife filed for divorce; his children began to avoid him.

Prior to this incident, Sharon and her husband had been very active socially with a group of police officers and their spouses. She found these colleagues and their families to be a great source of support in helping her adjust to the emotional reaction she had to the wounding and subsequent death. Although she had not fired the shot, Sharon felt partly responsible for Jerry's actions. Jerry had been her patrol partner for several months. She knew that Jerry was involved in the illegal sale and abuse of drugs, but she had not reported his behavior to the department. On the night in question, Jerry had appeared to her to be under great stress, although he was not under the influence of drugs at that time.

INTRODUCTION

This chapter's hypothetical scenario illustrates some of the problems and issues that policing creates for officers, for police departments, and for the community. The use of deadly force is always controversial, even when that force is legally appropriate. But when deadly force is used by a police officer of one race against a citizen of another, particularly a juvenile, the action may become even more controversial. In some cities, this kind of incident has been followed by serious rioting.

The scenario also illustrates the stress that policing may create for officers who are not prepared to cope with the results of their use of deadly force. It indicates the problems some officers have in resisting the opportunities for corruption and other illegal activities. Their colleagues often do not know what to do when they discover the illegal activities. A common reaction is to do nothing.

Police officers may or may not experience more stress than other professionals, but stress clearly is a part of policing. Some officers handle that stress successfully with the aid and support of other officers and their families; some, however, become involved in the police subculture to the exclusion of other social contacts. This may lead to negative rather than positive reinforcement.

The facts surrounding the response of Sharon and Jerry to a call for police service illustrate only a few of the problems and issues that might occur as police officers go about their daily activities. In considering problems and issues in policing, we must realize that no problem is pervasive. Our purpose is to discuss problems and issues that arise in policing, not to suggest that all police, or even most police, encounter the problems and do not resolve them successfully. Policing, like all other professions, has some bad apples, but many police officers work very hard to serve the public.

Policing, however, presents officers and administrators with some serious role conflicts. Conflicts over allocation of the officer's time; investigations that may compromise the officer's integrity or lead the public to question the officer's investigative techniques, and processing domestic violence calls are only a few of the problem areas that may cause role conflict in policing.

Role conflicts, the threat of danger, methods of evaluating job performance and the degree of job satisfaction, and other problems may create stressful situations that in turn lead to professional and personal problems. Some police react by becoming involved in a police subculture, where they feel comfortable and accepted while off duty. Others may become involved in corruption or in overzealous enforcement of the law. A few turn to brutality against crime suspects. The line between appropriate police use of deadly force and brutality often is not easy to draw, but court decisions give us some guidelines. Recruiting and training women and racial minority officers, along with problems that arise within the department once these individuals are hired, present another critical area of concern in modern policing.

How to handle the problems of policing also is debatable. Several methods have been suggested and will be discussed in this chapter. This chapter is not meant to exhaust all the problems and issues associated with policing. The focus here is on the problems associated primarily with police functions and how those problems affect the police officer and the community.

ROLE CONFLICTS IN POLICING

In any profession it is necessary for people to adjust to conflicting role demands, but those conflicts may be greater in policing than in most other professions. We expect the police not only to solve crimes but also to prevent crimes. We also expect police to respond cheerfully, quickly, and efficiently to a host of public services. At the same time, police are expected to be polite, even when being verbally attacked, and to be effective in securing evidence of crimes without violating the constitutional rights of citizens.

Police are expected to enforce laws that are widely violated; but if they arrest a prominent, influential citizen, they may find that strict enforcement is not expected. In short, police are expected to perform impossible tasks with limited resources and conflicting demands. It may not be possible to have perfect police under our system, as Spotlight 7.1 indicates.

SPOTLIGHT 7.1
IN SEARCH OF A PERFECT POLICEMAN

The perfect policeman?

He'd know law like a lawyer and have a judge's ability to tell right from wrong.

He'd have a doctor's knowledge of medicine, and the tenderness and compassion of a nurse.

The perfect cop would have the speed and strength of an Olympic athlete, the manners of a Japanese diplomat and the intelligence of a college professor.

On any occasion the officer would risk his life to protect the worldly goods of the rich while at the same time being content with a salary that precluded his having many worldly goods of his own.

The perfect policeman could be man or woman.

If a human being had all the attributes he needed to be the perfect cop, he'd probably be something else. So would she. It might be easier to be president.

This summer at the political conventions, I watched with interest the behavior of the police in San Francisco and Dallas. The character of the police force in any city is as different from that of another city as its skyline. You'd think that, like the city itself, the San Francisco police force would be more liberal, more relaxed than the police in Dallas, but that didn't seem to be so.

Unfortunately for its national image, several television news cameramen were in attendance when a handful of demonstrators were administered a brutal beating by a special forces unit of the San Francisco Police. A demonstrator was seen not only being beaten with nightsticks but being speared in the stomach and kidneys by one cop while his arms were pinned by three others.

It was the sort of action that must make the good cops everywhere cringe.

On the second day in San Francisco, I walked up to one of three officers standing on a barricaded corner and asked where Folsom Street was. I had a car parked in a lot there and had lost my bearings. The officer shrugged indifferently and said he didn't know. I could see he didn't care, either.

Fifteen minutes later, after a lot of wandering and some better advice, I ended up on the same corner with the three cops.

"If anyone else asks you where Folsom Street is," I said. "you're standing on it."

He shrugged again in a why-don't-you-go-back-where-you-came-from manner. The people trying to enhance San Francisco's image as a friendly convention city, which it generally is, would have cringed.

Later that same week, I asked another cop for directions. He thought for a minute, then took out a pencil and, placing an envelope on the hood of a nearby car, proceeded to give me detailed, accurate and friendly directions. The secretary of the Chamber of Commerce himself couldn't have been nicer. It was hard to believe the two cops belonged to the same police force.

In Dallas, the police were on their best behavior, but you had the nervous feeling it didn't come easily to them. Wednesday of that week, I pulled up near the Convention Center in a car with a camera crew. The cameraman started to get out when a nearby policeman yelled, "Hey, you. Get back in that car."

I don't know what the security problem was but his tone of voice alone constituted unnecessary force.

"Just going to take some pictures of the demonstrators, Officer," the cameraman said in a conciliatory voice.

"You get out of that car, you're going to jail," the Dallas cop said quite finally.

In New York, where I spend a lot of time, the police have been so consistently put down that they've lost interest in law and order. They've given up.

If a New York policeman had to choose between interrupting a murder in progress in a nearby apartment or ticketing a car parked four minutes overtime at a meter, he'd probably give the ticket and ignore the murder. They've had too many bitter experiences.

I can't decide which style of police work I like best.

Source: Reprinted by permission: Tribune Media Services, Inc. Andy Rooney is a columnist syndicated nationally through the Tribune Media Services, Inc.

Police also experience conflicts created by administrators.

[P]atrolmen lead something of a schizophrenic existence: they must cope not only with the terror of an often hostile and unpredictable citizenry, but also with a hostile—even tyrannical—and unpredictable bureaucracy. [P]olice discretion is to be understood in terms of an enduring conflict between the uncertain requirements of police work and the demand of administrators for control.[1]

Allocation of Police Time

Part of the conflict in police roles is created because there is little agreement on how police should allocate their time among law enforcement, order maintenance, and social services. Part of this conflict might be solved if recruits were better informed about the time pressures of police departments. Studies of why people call police departments illustrate this time pressure. Earlier studies of police allocation of time gained considerable attention. James Q. Wilson sampled calls to the Syracuse (New York) Police Department in 1966 and found that only 10.3 percent of those calls related to law enforcement, compared to 30.1 percent for order maintenance. Requests for services dealing with accidents, illnesses, and lost or found persons or property constituted 37.5 percent (the largest category of calls), whereas 22.1 percent called for information.[2]

In another study Albert J. Reiss, Jr., analyzed the calls to the Chicago Police Department. His findings were similar to those of Wilson in one respect: 30 percent of the calls were on noncriminal matters. But Reiss found that 58 percent of the calls were related to law enforcement matters.[3] Richard J. Lundman, in studying police activities in five jurisdictions, also found law enforcement to be the most frequent category of activities in which police engaged, constituting slightly less than one-third of all police activities.[4]

The different findings of these studies may be attributed to the different methodology used for assessing time allocation of police. Wilson and Reiss analyzed calls made to police departments; Lundman observed officers on patrol. Perhaps a more important variable in explaining the difference lies in the failure to specify carefully which activities would be included in each category.

In a study by Gordon P. Whitaker and others, telephone calls to police were categorized as crime, 36 percent; order maintenance, 22 percent; service, 30 percent; or traffic, 12 percent, with each category carefully defined. The investigators admitted, however, that four categories "are clearly too broad to be of much benefit in designing operational policies and procedures, but they do permit some useful generalizations about requests for service."[5]

Carefully defined, narrow categories may produce a more accurate picture of police allocation of time. Eric J. Scott categorized over 26,000 calls to police departments, and the results are reproduced in Table 7.1. Each of the categories in Table 7.1 was subdivided into more specific categories. For example, the category "assistance" included animal prob-

Police render services in a variety of circumstances. Here an office administers aid to an individual who survived a suicide attempt. (Jim Anderson/Woodfin Camp)

Order maintenance is an important but time consuming and potentially dangerous function of policing. (Alon Reininger/ Woodfin Camp)

lems, property check, escorts and transports, utility problems, property discovery, assistance to motorists, fires, alarms, crank calls, unspecified requests, and other.[6]

According to Scott, the failure of other investigators to define each category carefully is a serious problem since "the addition or subtraction of a particular call from some categories can cause a large change in the percentage of calls attributable to that category.[7] The various studies thus are not comparable because we cannot be sure how specific types of calls in the various studies were coded. Scott also was concerned with the problem of coding calls as crime or noncrime. Many police activities involve a little of each and thus cannot be accurately coded into two discrete categories.

These studies of the allocation of police time have important implications for recruitment of police, as well as for understanding the role conflict of those already in policing. If people are attracted to policing because they think most of the officer's time will be spent in exciting chases of dangerous criminals and have no concept of the often dull, routine periods of waiting for action, they might be quite unhappy as police officers. If they have no concept of the service functions of policing and are not trained to perform those functions, life on the beat might come as an unpleasant surprise.

Police officers also may encounter the problem of having supervisors who do not give equal credit to successful performance of the three functions of policing. Catching dangerous criminals might result in a faster

TABLE 7.1

Frequency and Percentage of Citizen Calls to Police, by Type of Problem

Type of Problem	Number of Calls	Percent of Calls	Range by Department
Violent Crimes	642	2%	0–3%
Nonviolent Crimes	4,489	17%	8–20%
Interpersonal Conflict	1,763	7%	1–10%
Medical Assistance	810	3%	1–7%
Traffic Problems	2,467	9%	5–15%
Dependent Persons	774	3%	1–4%
Public Nuisances	3,002	11%	4–15%
	1,248	5%	3–9%
Suspicious Circumstances			
Assistance	3,039	12%	8–30%
Citizen Wants Information	5,558	21%	14–43%
Citizen Gives Information	1,993	8%	5–15%
Internal Operations	663	2%	0–10%
Total	26,418		

Source: Eric J. Scott, *Calls for Service: Citizen Demand and Initial Police Response*, National Institute of Justice (Washington, D.C.: U.S. Government Printing Office, July 1981), p. 26.

promotion than successfully performing routine order maintenance or social service functions. Police officers may experience a similar response from other police officers and from the community.

Proactive Versus Reactive Policing

Regardless of how police activities are categorized, it is clear that police do not spend most of their time engaging in the stereotype held by many: catching dangerous criminals. In fact, many police officers spend very little time in actual crime detection. Police work is mainly **reactive** not **proactive;** that is, police depend on the assistance of victims, witnesses, and other citizens to report crimes.

There have been some changes in recent years. In the previous chapter we examined problem-oriented policing, whereby police identify problems that may be creating the criminal situation and try to eliminate those problems. Police also have become proactive in other areas, particularly in identifying career criminals and processing domestic violence.

Identification of Career Criminals In the past two decades there has been an increasing emphasis on career criminals, or those individuals who are repeat offenders over a long period of time. Research indicates that a few people commit most of the crimes; thus, it is assumed that concentrating on these career or habitual offenders would be a sound approach to crime reduction and prevention. Concentration on these offenders also is seen as a way to reduce prison overcrowding.[8]

Prosecutors began more vigorous prosecutions of career criminals, and police departments began developing targeting programs whereby they would watch or track individuals known to be frequently involved in criminal activity. Police use various tactics, some of which are highly controversial. For example, the use of police decoys (such as policewomen posing as prostitutes, police officers infiltrating the drug scene and "buying" drugs and then arresting the sellers) and informants who are involved in crime have led to criticisms that police are compromising themselves through such endeavors. Police and other supporters of these techniques argue that such proactive work is the only effective way to apprehend many criminals.[9]

Evaluations of one such program, the Repeat Offender Project (ROP) in Washington, D.C., brought interesting results:

- The work of the Repeat Offender Project substantially increased the likelihood of arrest of the persons it targeted.
- Those arrested by ROP officers had longer and more serious arrest histories than a comparison sample.
- Persons arrested by the ROP unit were more likely to be prosecuted and convicted on felony charges and more likely to be incarcerated than comparison arrestees.[10]

The related success of ROP led to widespread dissemination of the results. A survey conducted in 1985 disclosed that 33 police departments had established units to handle proactive work in apprehending career criminals. Several other states have since added programs.[11]

Processing Domestic Violence Cases   Our earlier discussion of domestic violence indicated that some jurisdictions have instituted a policy of mandatory arrests. In the past, it was uncommon for police, when called to the scene of domestic violence, to arrest the alleged offender. Victims of domestic violence would frequently ask police to "stop the violence" but would not agree to cooperate if an arrest were made.

Under a policy of mandatory arrest, the police officer must arrest the alleged perpetrator of domestic violence if there is sufficient evidence that such violence has occurred. This approach has resulted in more arrests in cases of domestic violence, with police acting on their own without waiting for victims to insist on pressing charges.

Evaluations of greater arrest rates in domestic violence cases indicate that this approach is more successful in preventing further domestic violence than when police did not arrest. Such results led the Attorney General's Task Force on Family Violence (appointed in 1984) to recommend that

> To provide the most effective response, operational procedures should require the officer to presume that arrest, consistent with state law, is the appropriate response in cases of family violence.[12]

Despite the apparent success of the mandatory arrest practices, police still encounter conflicts in domestic violence situations. Many spouses do not want the offender arrested; if police insist and make the arrest, the "victim" may become hostile, belligerent, even violent. Thus, what appears to be a positive change in policing may actually result in greater role conflict for police officers.

Stress in Policing

In recent years increasing attention has been given to stress and the effects it has on people in various professions. A variety of harmful physical results may occur when individuals do not handle stress successfully. Whereas all people may be affected in some way by stress on their jobs,

In recent years, more attention has been placed on training police for effective intervention in domestic violence situations. (Donna Ferrato/Black Star)

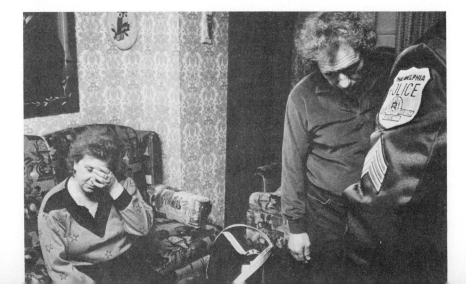

Stress may result from frequent exposure to human problems. Here police administer mouth-to-mouth resuscitation to a heart attack victim before the ambulance arrives. (Ellis Herwig/Stock Boston)

studies have found evidence of particularly high rates of stress in some professions; policing has been called the most stressful. And the effect goes beyond the individual officer. "Police work ... affects, shapes, and at times, scars the individuals and families involved."[13]

Some studies indicate that police have higher rates of divorce, suicide, and other manifestations of stress than are found among people in other professions;[14] but most of the research contains serious methodological problems, and we therefore should be cautious about accepting the conclusions. On the other hand, if the differences are real, several factors might explain the higher rates of stress among police officers.

1. Police work is a male-dominated profession, and men have a higher suicide rate.
2. The use, availability, and familiarity with firearms by police in their work make for a high lethality factor with little chance for resuscitation.
3. There are psychological repercussions to constantly being exposed to potential death.
4. Long and irregular working hours do not promote strong friendships and do strain family ties.
5. There is constant exposure to public criticism and dislike for "cops."
6. Judicial contradictions, irregularities, and inconsistent decisions tend to negate the value of police work.[15]

Higher rates of suicide and divorce among police officers, if indeed the rates are higher than those of other professionals, may not be *caused* by stress unique to policing. For example, what explains the fact that, although suicides are very high among American police officers, such is not true with British police?[16] Is the difference explained by the cultures of the two countries? In analyzing suicide rates among police in this country, one researcher emphasized the need to use caution in concluding that the stress of policing *causes* any particular problem. For example, police have high rates of digestive disorders. But, if that physical problem is caused by improper eating habits rather than stress unique to policing, the latter cannot be the cause of a higher incidence of digestive disorder among police than among other professions or occupations. In fact, there are reports that police officers may be among the poorest eaters in America, with a very high rate of consumption of fast food and junk food!

Other variables that might explain the high rates of physical, emotional, and domestic problems among police are as follows:

1. Social class background;
2. The subculture of violence in which police work;
3. Social isolation, role conflicts, and role ambiguities that are not unique to policing;
4. Organizational problems;
5. Other working conditions, any one of which may also be characteristic of other occupations and professions.

The difference in policing may be the *combination* of these alleged causal factors. We need to conduct research on police stress, controlling for variables that might be relevant to explaining differences in reaction to stress, if such exist.

Stressors Unique to Policing   This discussion suggests that stress in policing may be no different from stress in other occupations and professions. But there is one major difference; police are trained to injure or kill, and if the situation requires, they are expected to use that ability. Indeed, they may be sanctioned for not using their weapons. It is this requirement, say some officers, that is clearly unique in creating stress in policing.

A psychologist notes that in a war, military officers may cope by defining the opposition as bad—all of them. "The role is so well accepted and shared." But that is not true of our police officers who, indeed, may be highly criticized, even sanctioned, for a killing. Officers who kill also may be socially isolated from their colleagues. Routine procedure is to suspend officers pending investigation of a shooting. Said one officer, "I felt as alone as I ever had in my whole life. They take you out of a group and make you stand alone." Another officer spoke of the nightmares, the flashbacks, and the social isolation that he felt after he killed a person in the line of duty. "I consider myself part of a class of people other people don't understand."[17]

Professors at Michigan State University have found that officers who kill in the line of duty suffer postshooting trauma that may lead to severe problems, including ruining their careers. Studies indicate that 70 percent of these officers leave the police force within seven years after the shooting.[18] The case of Jerry in this chapter's CJA illustrates this reaction. Recently some police departments have recognized the need for psychological counseling as part of the professional assistance provided for police.

Stress Reduction Programs   The Commission on Civil Rights emphasized the need to provide stress management programs and services for police. Citing Los Angeles as a city with this type of comprehensive program, the commission nevertheless noted that most police departments lack such programs, despite the recent emphasis on stress as "an important underlying factor in police misconduct incidents." The commission recommended that

> Police officials should institute comprehensive stress management programs that include identification of officers with stress problems, counseling, periodic screening and training on stress management.[19]

The Los Angeles police psychology program, designed to provide therapy for police officers and their families, was started in 1968 when a pioneer in police psychology, Martin Reiser (sometimes called the father of police psychology), was employed by the department and given the title of department psychologist.[20]

Theodore H. Blau, a clinical psychologist in private practice in Tampa, Florida, offered his counseling services as a volunteer with the Manatee County Sheriff's Office in Bradenton, Florida. Blau later completed police academy training and is now a police inspector. He insists that all police departments should have psychologists available for counseling officers and administrators, and he emphasizes techniques that alert police to stress-related problems before the problems become too severe.[21]

Other cities have also started stress reduction programs for police, but the critical and as yet unanswered question is whether they are effective. Some officers say that they have been helped by such programs, but the empirical evidence raises some questions. After studying stress prevention programs, one group of researchers concluded that when such programs are applied to all personnel "across the board, without reference to individual need or desire to change," they are not successful in preventing stress-related problems. "It is suspected that stress prevention programs will have no effect on job performance at all."[22] On the other hand, counseling made available on a voluntary basis to officers who wish help may be successful in reducing the impact of stress-related problems.

THE POLICE SUBCULTURE

One way of handling role conflicts and stress is to withdraw from the sources of those conflicts and stress into a more comfortable situation. If sufficient numbers of a group do so, a subgroup or **subculture** will be formed. The subculture will have values and expectations that distinguish it from the dominant culture but that solidify its members.[23]

An earlier analysis of the life-styles and self-concepts of police compared them to minority groups.

> Both suffer from a "lack of respect," both see the larger community as an enemy which does not understand them, both are aggressive in their response to those not in their community, both stay within their own group and both see the other as a threat and strike out at the other.[24]

But police isolation may not be limited to their relations to minorities in the community. Police also may become isolated from people who might otherwise be their friends, if it were not for the police officer's authority and responsibility to regulate the daily lives of citizens. Traffic

Police often develop a subculture, socializing with other officers. Here a police officer gives an emotional salute at the funeral of her fiancee, a fellow officer who was shot to death. (AP Wide World)

violations are an example. Police are also supposed to enforce other frequently violated laws, such as laws regulating the use of drugs and alcohol. "The nature of the policeman's role tends to overflow the norms of friendship and to violate the integrity of trust on which friendships must rest." It would be difficult to form an intimate relationship with someone who is expected "to arrest you for common and petty violations which intimates would ordinarily know about."[25]

Earlier studies suggested that police are a homogeneous group involved in a police subculture and manifesting a distinct personality type. They were said to be authoritarian, cynical, punitive, rigid, physically aggressive, assertive, and impulsive risk takers.[26] Police were viewed as people who look for negatives and who stereotype situations, making quick judgments when they think crime is involved. Such attitudes may even lead to violence.

It was assumed that the best way to alleviate police cynicism was to increase professionalism. Eric D. Poole and Robert M. Regoli tested the relationship between these two variables and concluded that although "commitment to a professional ideology reduces cynicism among police," the relationship between these two variables is more complex than was thought by earlier researchers.[27] In a later study, Regoli and his colleagues emphasized the need to look more carefully at dimensions of each of the variables: cynicism and professionalism.[28]

Research also indicates a relationship between professionalism and cynicism among police chiefs, although there are some differences when comparing chiefs to other police officers. There are also differences over time. For example, cynicism "is highest for police chiefs during their early years and gradually declines with experience." Cynicism also varies according to the size of the chief's police agency, with those in larger agencies showing lower cynicism.[29]

There is also some evidence that police officers, like police chiefs, become less cynical as their length of service on the police force increases.[30] Taken as a whole, the research on police cynicism indicates the importance of looking carefully at all variables that might account for cynicism and analyzing those variables in their full complexity. It simply is not sufficient to find cynicism and professionalism (or any other trait) among police officers or chiefs and draw the conclusion that the relationship is a simple one.

WOMEN AND RACIAL MINORITY OFFICERS

Women have been involved in policing for a long time, but as Spotlight 7.2 indicates, they have usually held subordinate roles. Despite an emphasis in recent years on recruiting more women, their total numbers in policing are still small compared to men. In 1987 only 8 percent of sworn officers were women.[31]

Recruitment

The recruitment of more women and racial minorities was emphasized by the Commission on Civil Rights, which found the following to be true:

SPOTLIGHT 7.2
THE HISTORY OF WOMEN IN POLICING IN THE UNITED STATES

The participation of women in policing in this country has been traced back to 1854, when six females were appointed as matrons in New York City. Their duty was to search and guard female prisoners at the city jail and at Blackwell's Island. These women had no enforcement powers; they were considered to be civilian employees.

The appointment of the matrons provided encouragement for other groups that then became involved in appointing women in police departments or prisons. In the 1870s, members of the Women's Temperance Union attended courts and visited prisons and jails in Portland, Maine. They hired a person whose function was to visit the institutions and see that women were not mistreated. By 1877 the city was paying the salary of this steady visitor, who was then hired full-time as a matron. The successful hiring of women as matrons in New York and Maine led to similar hirings in other states, but their sole function was to guard and search women inmates.

In 1893, at the death of a police officer in the city of Chicago, the officer's widow was appointed as patrolman. She worked in that capacity for 30 years until she retired on pension.

By 1900, several prominent organizations were providing strong impetus to the hiring of women police officers; in 1905, Lola Baldwin of Portland, Maine, was given temporary police powers for the sole purpose of dealing with women and girls at the Lewis and Clark Exposition.

It was not, however, until 1910 that a woman received regular appointment as a police officer. Mrs. Alice Stebbins Wells, a graduate theological student and social worker, was influential in convincing the Los Angeles Police Commission and the city council that they should create a position of policewoman. They agreed, and Wells was appointed. "Her chief duties would comprise the subversion

and enforcement of laws concerning juveniles and women at dancehalls, skating rinks, movie theaters, and other places of recreation for young people and women." Wells lectured throughout the United States and in many other countries as police departments expressed interest in hiring women to perform functions that male officers "might be inadequate to deal with." Because of her efforts, by 1916 women police officers were employed in 25 cities in 20 states. Some occupied executive positions.

During World War I women served as quasi-police, patroling around military training camps to keep prostitutes away from the servicemen, and assisting with runaway women and girls. Their work was sufficient to convince many police departments that they should hire more women after the war and that the functions of policewomen should be extended beyond the historical ones of matrons and clerks. New responsibilities consisted of working with women and children offenders. The work of the women was excellent, leading the International Association of Chiefs of Police in 1922 to pass a resolution concerning the value of women in police departments.

The progress of women in policing suffered a setback during the depression, for jobs were scarce and many departments thought it more important to hire men than women. During World War II women again entered policing, this time to serve as supplements to men who were going off to war. After the war, many of the positions held by women were again terminated. "And, so it went. From their inception to the late 1960s, policewomen were met by discrimination, silent contempt, and double standards."

Source: Paraphrased by the author from Barry D. Mishkin, "Female Police in the United States," *The Police Journal* 54 (January 1981): 22–25.

Serious underutilization of minorities and women in local law enforcement agencies continues to hamper the ability of police departments to function effectively in and earn the respect of predominantly minority neighborhoods, thereby increasing the probability of tension and violence.

While there has been some entry of minority and women into police service in recent years, police departments remain largely white and male, particularly in the upper-level command positions. Utilization figures for

women hardly approach tokenism, although studies have indicated that as a rule women perform at least as well as men on the force.

In light of that finding, the commission recommended that "[p]olice department officials should develop and implement affirmative action plans so that ultimately the force reflects the composition of the community it serves."[32]

Other researchers have also emphasized the critical role of recruiting women and minorities to police work. Lack of women in the police force creates a doubt among women that police will be sensitive to their particular needs, for example, as rape victims. Lack of sufficient racial minority representation may lead minorities to doubt the reasonableness of police use of deadly force against minorities.[33]

The Commission on Civil Rights found that efforts by police departments to recruit women and racial minorities may be hindered by the community's perceptions that the department really is not seriously committed to such recruitment. Such perceptions, said the commission, are created in different ways; for example, newspaper reports of the way police handle cases involving women and racial minorities, complaints of former members of the police force, and the treatment received by women and minorities who applied but were turned down as recruits by the police department. Perceptions of racism also are created by the lack of advancement opportunities for women and racial minorities within the department, as well as by the high rates of attrition during the training process of those who are recruited. The commission concluded that in addition to an emphasis on recruitment, "Minorities and women, through the implementation of equal opportunity programs, should hold positions that lead to upward mobility in the ranks, allowing them to compete for command positions."[34]

The progress made in recruiting women and racial minorities is difficult to assess. Ellen Hochstedler, in her study of affirmative action programs in police systems, emphasized that the lack of data in police systems makes it impossible for us to have a correct historical data base against which to measure the current situation. In addition, she says, it is

Recruitment of police officers may begin at an early age. Here, a three-year-old boy shows off a uniform tailored from those worn by Tallahassee, Florida police officers. (Mark Foley/AP Wide World)

Court orders and active recruitment of women and minorities has increased their representation among police. (Sepp Seitz/ Woodfin Camp)

very difficult to assess the effects of measures adopted pursuant to affirmative action plans. Typically, there is no baseline data of adequate specificity to allow direct measurement of the effects of a change in policy or standards.

Evaluation of the effects of attempts to recruit and hire women and racial minorities, therefore, is difficult if not impossible. But, according to Hochstedler, the data reveal that the attitudes of police administrators are crucial in determining whether affirmative action programs are perceived with resentment or pride by employees in the system. Furthermore, there is evidence that affirmative action programs pertaining to minorities have been more successful than our efforts to involve women in policing. Hochstedler concludes that a quota system is necessary in order to remedy the situation.[35]

Recruitment of women and minority officers has had some help from the courts, with both groups having successfully filed affirmative action cases under federal statutes. Women, for example, have successfully argued that they were discriminated against in hiring, assignments while on the job, and promotions. One female officer, Penny E. Harrington, successfully filed numerous affirmative action suits during her 22-year career

TABLE 7.2

Ranks of Minorities in the New York City Police Department, 1987

Officers	1974		1980		1987	
White	20,391	(89.1%)	15,985	(85.4%)	19,280	(77.3%)
Black	1,859	(8.1%)	1,792	(9.5%)	2,730	(10.9%)
Hispanic	643	(2.8%)	947	(5.1%)	2,790	(11.2%)
Asian/Pacific Islander	0		n.a.		135	(0.5%)
Sergeants						
White	2,500	(95.6%)	2,130	(94.4%)	2,358	(81.2%)
Black	89	(3.4%)	85	(3.8%)	330	(11.4%)
Hispanic	26	(1.0%)	40	(1.8%)	206	(7.1%)
Lieutenants						
White	967	(97.2%)	758	(96.9%)	957	(94.5%)
Black	24	(2.4%)	16	(2.1%)	34	(3.4%)
Hispanic	4	(0.4%)	8	(1.0%)	21	(2.1%)
Captains and above						
White	357	(99.4%)	385	(98.0%)	449	(97.2%)
Black	1	(0.3%)	6	(1.5%)	9	(1.9%)
Hispanic	1	(0.3%)	2	(0.5%)	4	(0.9%)

Source: "New York's Police Feel the Chill of Racial Tension," *New York Times* (1 November 1987), p. 6E. Copyright © 1987 by The New York Times Company. Reprinted by permission.

with the Portland, Oregon, Police Department. In 1985 she was appointed police chief, the first woman in that capacity in a major city. After a 17-month tenure, Harrington resigned. She had been criticized for numerous alleged management failures in her administration. Harrington's response was that no other chief had ever been subject to such close scrutiny and second-guessing by the media, the community, and the police union.

After a decade of decisions on affirmative action policies concerning minorities and women, the Supreme Court in 1987 held that it is permissible for employers to give preferential treatment in jobs on the basis of sex and race. *Johnson v. Transportation Agency, Santa Clara, Co., California* involved a white man who argued that he was unfairly discriminated against when his employer promoted a white woman to a position for which he, too, was qualified.[36]

In *Johnson*, the Court upheld the voluntary affirmative action plan of the Transportation Agency. Under this plan, in making promotions to positions in which women and minorities traditionally have been excluded or underrepresented, the agency was authorized to consider sex or race as a reason for a promotion. No quota was mentioned, but the policy did call for short-range goals of actively promoting women and minorities.

SPOTLIGHT 7.3
FEMALE OFFICER SAVORS EXCITEMENT, VARIETY OF URBAN POLICE WORK

Her gun came out of the holster so fast, even she seemed surprised.

Officer Gayle Kansier was the first to arrive at the Ross Avenue business to answer a call that gave every appearance of being a routine break-in.

Routine, until an arm reached out from the battered front door.

"He's coming out," she yelled, pulling her gun as a bystander ducked behind the police car and traffic began to slow on Ross, drivers craning to catch a flicker of the nighttime drama. Unflinching, Ms. Kansier let her training take over.

Only later, after the helicopter gave up its search for the suspect who had fled from the rear of the business and the K-9 unit departed after flushing another suspect, would Ms. Kansier suggest that this had been a routine incident.

"This looks like a big deal to someone who's not trained in police work," she said, driving her patrol car to the Lew Sterrett Justice Center with a surly, handcuffed suspect. "But it's just what we're trained to do."

It was a night of "routine" patrol for Ms. Kansier, starting with a flurry of shoplifting reports at con-venience stores in Oak Lawn and ending 10 hours later with the burglary suspect in jail.

Sandwiched between were the slices of urban police work that attracted Officer Kansier, 31, to Dallas in 1981 from a rural Michigan police force, where she had had her fill of barking dog complaints and traffic citations.

It was the challenge of working on a larger police force and the fact that Dallas was hiring in the early 1980s when northern cities were cutting back, that brought her south. But the rhythm and excitement of the work have kept her here, she said.

"I want to work with all types of people," she said. "And in the central sector, you get so much diversity—the worker, the rich folks, minorities, Mexicans, blacks, whites, Vietnamese, the gay community. You don't have time to develop stereotypes."

Likewise, Ms. Kansier has never felt bound by stereotypes frequently applied to women. "I'm not a tiny, petite woman," she said. "I didn't figure I'd have any problems in this line of work because I work out, run and lift weights. I can handle my end of it."

In 1987, in *U.S. v. Paradise*, the Court also upheld the Alabama affirmative action plan that established a one-for-one racial quota for promotions. The Court said this action is permissible because of the long history of excluding blacks from employment as state troopers.[37]

Despite affirmative action policies, blacks and women are still underrepresented in major police departments, particularly in the higher ranks. Table 7.2 indicates that minorities occupy a very small percentage of the higher ranks in the New York Police Department.

The small number of minority and female officers may create problems for those officers, although some officers report that they are satisfied. Spotlight 7.3 illustrates the job satisfaction of one female officer. Ironically, that officer is with the Dallas Police Department, which in recent years has had serious racial problems within the department as well as between police and the community. Much of the tension has centered on the use of deadly force by police. Blacks claim that too often force is used against blacks. The city's racial tension has been cited as the main factor leading to the resignation in 1988 of Police Chief Billy Prince. Prince, who claimed he was not forced out of office, said the job he held for six years was at times "like being on a runaway roller coaster."[38]

The only problems occur during an occasional arrest, she said. "Either the suspect will be nice to you or they'll be threatened by you being a woman. . . . They're going to pick at anything that looks like a weakness. You just learn to take the verbal abuse."

In the ritual of patrol work, Officer Kansier turned her squad car toward East Dallas side streets as the prostitution activity started up that late afternoon, about the time commuter traffic began to wind itself through neighborhood streets.

"Where you going, Muffin?" Officer Kansier called out to the young woman strolling down Annex Street in a recycled wedding dress.

"To the store," said the woman not bothering to glance in the direction of the patrol car.

"We're not going to have to play the game tonight, are we?" the officer asked. "We have an understanding, don't we? Because if we don't, you can get in the car and we'll talk it over."

Prostitution is a frustrating game, Officer Kansier conceded. "You get rid of the whores and you still have the pimps, the dope and all the junk that goes with it. It's cat and mouse."

Two hours later, she was dispatched to an apartment on Ross Avenue, where a woman had complained that her husband tore the telephone out of the wall and roughed up their 2-year-old son.

"I'm not a referee in a family match," Officer Kansier told the wife, who protested when her husband was being handcuffed and taken to the jail. "Lady, maybe you better look at your definition of love and decide whether it means you let someone hit your kids."

Later, Officer Kansier took an extra 10 minutes to scour the state penal code, certain there was a new state law relating to the abuse of children. She was right.

"I'm good at this," she said when she returned to her patrol car in search of other flaws in the night.

"You have to be able to read people, be able to talk to people. You have to have the ability to go from a hot situation, cool yourself off and go on to the next. You have to be quick."

Minutes later, back on Ross Avenue, Ms. Kansier showed how quick when the burglar attempted his getaway straight into her path—as quick as she could draw her gun.

Source: "Officer Savors Excitement, Variety of Urban Police Work," *Dallas Morning News* (30 November 1986), p. 15A. Reprinted with permission of The Dallas Morning News.

Job Performance Evaluation and Job Satisfaction

Some studies have been conducted of the job satisfaction and job performance of women compared to men and of black compared to white police officers. In one study in which blacks, compared to whites, were found to be slightly happier with police work, the investigator emphasized that variables other than minority status may be more important in influencing job satisfaction and job performance. "Affirmative action programs, racial composition of the police department, the type of city administration, and the attitudes of the service community may have more impact upon work attitude than generalizations about the effect of minority status within a work organization reflect."[39] The same caution should be applied to studies of job performance and job satisfaction of women in policing.

Other variables might also be important in analyzing job performance and job satisfaction. There is evidence that men and women choose police work for different reasons, with men more likely to enter the profession for reasons of security and women more frequently indicating that they chose this profession because they wanted to help others. This difference is consistent with the image of women as superior to men in conflict resolution and mediation, but this advantage of women also may be viewed as a disadvantage.

The image of women as sympathetic, understanding, warm, and non-aggressive is inconsistent with the stereotype of police officers as tough, aggressive, masculine, and authoritarian. These images may have influenced police administrators, who view their female officers as less effective than male officers on patrol. But the evidence indicates that male and female officers obtain about the same results in handling angry or violent citizens and in working with other police officers. Women are as effective as men on patrol. Injuries on the job also are about evenly distributed between the sexes.[40]

What about the physical differences between men and women and the effect those differences might have on policing? One researcher has indicated that whereas men "potentially have a higher plateau of fitness and strength than do women, this does not necessarily indicate that the physical jobs of policing are beyond the physical abilities of all women." Improved training could prepare the physically unfit of both sexes. Furthermore, studies indicate than when police officers get into difficulties resulting in serious injury or death, the reasons usually are not the lack of physical fitness or strength but circumstances beyond the control of the officer or a mistake in judgment.[41]

POLICE CORRUPTION

Police officers have many opportunities for engaging in corruption, defined by sociologist Lawrence W. Sherman as follows:

> A public official is corrupt if he accepts money or money's worth for doing something that he is under a duty to do anyway, that he is under a duty not to do, or to exercise a legitimate discretion for improper reasons.[42]

Opportunity for corruption varies with greater opportunities available in larger cities, but corruption may be found in all types of police departments.

James Q. Wilson, who has written extensively about policing, analyzed police corruption according to the type of organization in the police department. He defined three types of law enforcement styles and found those styles to be related to the degree of police corruption.[43] According to Wilson, the greatest degree of police corruption is found in departments characterized by the *watchman style*, in which police are expected to maintain order, not to regulate conduct. Low salaries and the expectation that police will have other jobs increase the probabilities that police will be involved in corruption.

Corruption is found to a lesser degree in departments characterized by the *legalistic style*, with its emphasis on formal police training, recruiting from the middle class, offering greater promotional opportunities, and viewing law as a means to an end rather than an end in itself. Formal sanctions are used more frequently than informal ones, with police giving less attention to community service and order maintenance than to law enforcement.

Corruption is not a serious problem in the third type of style, the *service style*. In this management style, law enforcement and order maintenance are combined, with an emphasis on good relationships between the police and the community. Command of the police is decentralized, with police on patrol working out of specialized units. Higher education and promotional opportunities are emphasized, and police are expected to lead exemplary private lives.

Sherman also analyzed police corruption according to ideal types. His first type, the *rotten apples*, is a department characterized by a few police officers who accept bribes and engage in other forms of corruption. Those people generally are uniformed patrol officers, but they are loners who will accept bribes for overlooking traffic violations. Some work in groups, termed *rotten pockets*, accepting bribes for nonenforcement of the law. Members of the vice squad are often found in this type.[44]

A second type of corruption Sherman called *pervasive organized corruption*, describing the highly organized hierarchical organization of the political processes of the community, going beyond the police force. Many police departments are characterized by widespread but unorganized corruption, labeled by Sherman as *pervasive unorganized corruption*. In addition to identifying these types, Sherman also analyzed the external opportunities that might be conducive to police corruption.[45]

Examples of Police Corruption

In 1970 John V. Lindsay, mayor of New York City, in response to allegations of corruption in that city's police department, issued an executive order establishing the Knapp Commission. The commission's report, published in 1972, reported widespread police corruption. Rookies were quickly initiated into the system; many became corrupt; others just became cynical. The commission found that police were involved with organized crime (the most lucrative form of corruption), payoffs from citizens, especially for traffic citations, and accepting money for overlooking violations of licensing ordinances.[46]

The Knapp Commission also found widespread involvement of police in drugs. Although most of the corruption in this area involved accepting bribes for overlooking drug violations, some police were also selling drugs.

In 1981 five New York City police officers were indicted on charges that they hired themselves out to protect people from arrest. Two years later, an undercover investigation into police conduct led to indictments against 19 present and former police officers. Four of the officers pled guilty to lesser charges. One of those who became an informant testified that within two months after he joined the New York City Police Department, he became a thief and continued his illegal activities for the 15 years he was with the department. He said he committed numerous larcenies, mainly to pay his gambling debts.[47]

SPOTLIGHT 7.4
THIRTY YEARS OF POLICE OFFICERS RULING AS A COURT ARE EXPOSED IN RHODE ISLAND

For at least 30 years the Police Department [in Central Falls, Rhode Island] held its own legal proceedings at police headquarters, with detectives and police officers issuing summonses and presiding over traffic and misdemeanor cases, in violation of state law and the United States Constitution.

The practice, which was exposed last month by The Providence Journal and halted on the advice of the state Attorney General, is clearly illegal, according to judges and other authorities. While no criminal charges have been filed, lawyers and judges who may have participated could be subject to professional discipline, officials said.

Local officials here now acknowledge that their traffic and misdemeanor courts were illegal, but add that they were well-intentioned attempts to streamline the course of justice and unburden the state courts of minor cases.

Practice Was Unquestioned

Police Chief Robert Choquette of Central Falls said the informal hearings also helped keep residents from becoming entangled in the criminal justice system.

"It would scare the hell out of a person who hadn't dealt with the police, quiet them down and keep them out of the criminal system," the Chief said.

Officials here said that the practice went unquestioned simply because it had existed for so long. Residents, meanwhile, seemed divided over the propriety of the police handling cases that should have been referred to a state court in Pawtucket, a mile away.

The police summoned people who were slow to pay traffic tickets to appear at "Traffic Court" at the Central Falls police station or face arrest. No court of any kind has legally existed here for about 30 years, said City Solicitor Raymond Cooney.

Authority Was Exceeded

The police also ordered people who complained of or were suspected of misdemeanors to report to the police chief to "show cause" why a warrant should not be issued for their arrest, Mr. Cooney said. When people came to the station, police officers would hold informal hearings, often without lawyers and always without oaths and recordkeeping.

Mr. Cooney acknowledged that the police acted beyond their authority.

New York Police Department officials contend that only a very small percentage of police officers in that city are involved in corruption. Undercover tests of integrity, whereby some officers are assigned to make secret reports on the behavior of other officers, they say, have virtually eliminated organized corruption. Others contend that corruption has not been eliminated in the New York City Police Department or any other; they hold that it is inevitable.

> Corruption is endemic to policing. The very nature of the police function is bound to subject officers to tempting offers. . . . Solutions, so far, seem inadequate and certainly are not likely to produce permanent results.[48]

Even New York City police commanders expressed concern about the use of drugs by their police officers. The serious implication of the drug use of officers was underscored by a report that concluded, "Nar-

---

"Police have no authority to summon a person to the station or arrest them for not showing up," he said. Police officers may arrest a person caught in a criminal act, question him and bring them into state court for arraignment. Police officers may also serve a summons that has been issued by a judge and may ask a judge to authorize an arrest.

Mr. Cooney said officials of several successive city administrations never thought about the legality of the long-established police courts until they read critical comments in the Providence newspaper on Aug. 26.

But state judges and legal officials said they were appalled.

"It's shocking and unbelievable that in 1987, there is a completely illegal court like the one in Central Falls that is routinely violating people's constitutional rights," said Robert K. Pirraglia, a state district court judge. "It may have been well meaning but is a recipe for dictatorship."

Judge Pirraglia said that lawyers or judges who attended or knew of the illegal proceedings without reporting them could face charges of unethical conduct.

"Most bewildering, is how it could have gone on all these years," he added. "I've been to Central Falls hundreds of times and never heard of this so-called traffic court."

Mayor Carlos A. Silva Jr. did not return several telephone calls seeking comment.

Municipal Court Sought

Daniel J. Issa, a state senator and former city council member, said he and other city officials knew of the procedures but did not know they violated any laws.

"I was as shocked as the rest of the city to learn that what the police were doing was illegal," he said. He said he will file legislation in January to set up a municipal court here.

Mr. Cooney said the police began dispensing justice after a district court above the old police station was closed 30 years ago. Since then, all traffic violations and criminal misdemeanors were to be referred to state court in Pawtucket.

Instead, the police routinely summoned people who failed to pay $5 to $15 traffic fines to appear before a police officer at headquarters. At this hearing, the person summoned could pay the fine, ask to have it dismissed or go to district court if no agreement could be reached, Mr. Cooney said.

About $40,000 a year in fines and numbered receipts went to the city treasury, said Daniel J. Vassett, the treasurer. "For 20 years, annual audits haven't shown any missing funds," he said.

Source: New York Times (7 September 1987), p. 9. Copyright © 1987 by The New York Times Company. Reprinted by permission.

cotics is perceived as the department's number one corruption hazard.''[49] That statement was made in 1983. In 1988, experts warned that the integrity of the New York City Police Department was being threatened by rampant drug trafficking and efforts to control that problem. Criminologists studying the New York City system agreed that some types of corruption (such as systematic payoffs from gambling operators) had been significantly decreased in the 16 years since the Knapp Commission found pervasive corruption. But the researchers, along with police commanders, warned that the recent recruitment of more than 17,000 police from a society in which drug use is fairly common, has led to drug-related corruption.[50]

In September 1988, seven present and former Boston police officers were found guilty of extorting thousands of dollars in bribes from nightclub and restaurant owners in the neighborhoods patroled by those officers. Some of the officers had served more than 30 years in the Boston Police Department.[51] Police corruption also occurs in smaller towns. Spotlight 7.4 explains some of the long-term illegal acts of police in Central Falls, Rhode Island.

VIOLENCE AND THE POLICE

Historically, the police have been viewed as necessary in establishing law and order, often by applying justice on the spot. Although violence between police and citizens was reported earlier, the violence and unrest that occurred in the 1960s led to demands for larger and better trained police forces. During that decade predominantly white police and minority citizens often clashed in hot, crowded cities. Student protesters frequently found themselves in conflict with the police, and the police were experiencing disillusionment with a system that they did not believe protected their interests. They, too, became more active. Police unions were established. They were viewed by many as representing hostility by the police.

In short, the decade of the 1960s brought open violence between police and citizens, and the 1970s brought more cases of police violence and corruption. Meanwhile, crime rates began to rise and citizens demanded greater police protection. Demands for a more professionalized police force were also heard, but the allegations of police misconduct were predominant. In analyzing police misconduct, we begin with violence against the police, a phenomenon that police may use for justifying their own violent acts.

Violence Against the Police

A 1980 magazine article entitled "The War on the Cops" referred to a new breed of pathological killers in New York City. These killers were described as madmen who engaged in random killings with no apparent motive. "The police have fallen victim not to the incorrigible, but to the uncontrollable." In a 33-day period in 1980, the four police killed were

242

more than the number killed in the previous year. In addition, during that period six police were badly injured. The new breed of killers was described as

> a small but virulent strain of violent, conscience-free, "Clockwork Orange" street criminals and mentally deranged men and women who have managed—admittedly, with little effort—to defeat the programs designed to constrain and heal them.

This new type of murderer is seen as a person who has nothing to lose and who views prison time as a natural part of life. They are people for whom the juvenile justice system has been a failure, young people who have spent much of their lives in institutions and who have no future orientation. For them, incarceration is no threat. It is a realistic way of life.[52]

Despite this new form of violence against police in New York City, a systematic study of the killings of police officers in that city led to the conclusion that killing a police officer, in most cases, is a functional act done to avoid arrest.[53] Not all police officers are convinced, and some place the cause in the structure of society. "It's a more violent society, and police are its victims as much as everyone else."[54] In 1987, 72 law enforcement officers were killed in the line of duty. That figure represents six more deaths than in 1986, which was the lowest year since 1968 when four officers were killed.[55]

In January 1988, John Glenn Chase, a Dallas police officer, was killed in a downtown parking lot while some bystanders urged the black, mentally ill, homeless man to kill the officer who was pleading for his life. Hundreds of Dallas police officers flew to Des Moines, Iowa, for the slain officer's funeral, also attended by numerous police and citizens in that city.

Chase's death and the circumstances under which it occurred became a "major issue in this city—one of race." White police Chief Billy Prince accused black city council members of spreading malicious rumors about the police department and referred to these critics as "little more than freeze-dried experts." Blacks called for Prince's resignation, which was later tendered, although Prince and others claimed he was not forced to resign.[56]

The reactions of citizens in Dallas, many of whom demonstrated strong support for the police department, is not unusual. Killings of police officers in the line of duty elicit strong public reaction. It is common after each of these crimes to hear demands for more police, banning of hand guns, reinstituting capital punishment (where it does not exist, for example, in New York state), incarcerating violent offenders in special prisons, imposing stiffer sentences, and abolishing parole for violent offenders.

The number of police officers killed by citizens does not tell the complete story. Police have also encountered a growing hostility from the public that, in many cases, has resulted in verbal abuse and physical attacks short of murder. Several cities in Texas, for example, have experienced increases in physical assaults against police, as indicated in Figure 7.1. That figure also indicates an increase in killings of police in Dallas over a 12-year period.

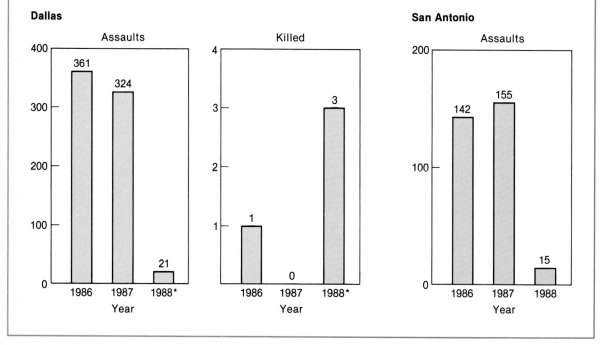

Assaults on Police

Texas			United States		
Year	Killed	Assaulted	Year	Killed	Assaulted
1986*	5	4,380	1986*	66	64,259
1985	7	3,617	1985	78	61,724
1980	10	3,163	1980	104	57,847

*Latest complete data available

Violent Assaults on Police by City

Dallas

Assaults
400 —
361
324
300 —
200 —
100 —
21
0 —
1986 1987 1988*
Year

Killed
4 —
3
3 —
2 —
1
1 —
0
0 —
1986 1987 1988*
Year

San Antonio

Assaults
200 —
155
142
100 —
15
0 —
1986 1987 1988
Year

FIGURE 7.1
Violence Against the Police in Texas. *Source:* "Rise in Assaults on Law Officers Causing Alarm," *Dallas Morning News* (20 March 1988), p. 42A. Reprinted with permission of The Dallas Morning News.

Although it is debatable which comes first and which causes which, there are indications that violence against police officers is accompanied by violence by police officers. The Police Foundation, in its study published in 1977, focused only on police use of deadly force, but the authors indicated that they were "acutely aware of the interrelationship between acts committed *by* the police and acts committed *against* them."[57]

Police Violence

In a classic and frequently cited article on police brutality published in 1968, Albert J. Reiss, Jr., began his discussion with a 1903 quotation by a former police commissioner of New York City:

> For 3 years, there has been through the courts and the streets a dreary procession of citizens with broken heads and bruised bodies against few of whom was violence needed to affect an arrest. Many of them had done nothing to deserve an arrest. In a majority of such cases, no complaint was made. If the victim complains, his charge is generally dismissed. The police are practically above the law.[58]

Until recently, however, little research had been conducted on police brutality. During the summer of 1966, Reiss conducted a study of the interactions of police with citizens in Boston, Chicago, and Washington, D.C. In discussing the results of that study, Reiss pointed out the difficulty of defining police brutality, but he listed six of the most common complaints of citizens.

1. The use of profane and abusive language;
2. Commands to move on or get home;
3. Stopping and questioning people on the street or searching them and their cars;
4. Threats to use force if not obeyed;
5. Prodding with a nightstick or approaching with a pistol;
6. The actual use of physical force or violence itself.[59]

This list covers a wide range of behavior, not all of which would be considered brutality by everyone. Reiss emphasizes the importance to the citizen of the status degradation aspect of police behavior, "the judgment that they have not been treated with the full rights and dignity among citizens in a democratic society."[60] Police brutality may lead to death, as alleged in Spotlight 7.5, but the use of deadly force by the police is the root of most controversy surrounding police behavior.

Police Use of Deadly Force: The Fleeing Felon Rule

The use of **deadly force** by police has been defined as "such force as under normal circumstances poses a high risk of death or serious injury to its human target, regardless of whether or not death, serious injury or any harm actually result."[61] Police officers may legally use deadly force under some circumstances. If they use deadly force improperly, the officers (and the police department) may be liable to the injured person (or, in the event of death, to the family of the deceased) in a civil suit. Most rules for the use of deadly force come from federal statutes. Most of the suits are concerned with police use of deadly force to arrest fleeing suspects who were apparently engaging in nonviolent felonies. Violent felonies are felonies, such as armed robbery, that create a risk of bodily harm or death. Un-

SPOTLIGHT 7.5
ALLEGED POLICE BRUTALITY: THE HEMPHILL, TEXAS, CASE

In February 1988, a grand jury composed of two black women, two white women, and two white men concluded that the death of Loyal Garner, Jr., was a homicide. Garner and two of his friends were apprehended by police as they crossed the Louisiana–Texas border and entered the small East Texas town of Hemphill. On Christmas Day 1987, the three were arrested.

Garner, who was arrested for driving while intoxicated, was allegedly beaten by three white police officers. Garner died on December 27, 1987. The officers were charged with first-degree murder and violating Garner's civil rights. The officers were released on $25,000 bond each pending trial. In July

1988, the officers were acquitted on the civil rights charges, but they await trial on the murder charges.

Calling the killing "senseless and tragic," one state legislator is planning to introduce legislation calling for the death penalty for peace officers who kill a person in their custody unless the homicide is necessary for self-defense or for protecting another's life. Garner's widow and his parents have filed a civil action against the town of Hemphill, alleging wrongful death. Garner's two friends have also filed civil suits for damages for the physical injuries and emotional distress they suffered as a result of the incident.

---

armed burglars, however, do not generally represent a substantial risk of serious bodily harm or death to a police officer if they are not immediately apprehended.

Shooting any fleeing felon was permitted historically. Because all felonies were punishable by death, it was assumed that any felon would resist arrest by all possible means. The rule permitting officers to shoot **fleeing felons** developed during a time when apprehending criminals was more difficult. Police did not have weapons that could be used for shooting at a long distance, nor did they have communication techniques that would enable them to quickly notify other jurisdictions that a suspect had escaped arrest. It therefore was possible for fleeing felons to escape if not immediately apprehended and begin a new life in another community without fear of detection by the local police.[62]

As more efficient weapons were developed, it became easier for police to apprehend felons, and many did so by use of deadly force even though the fleeing felons were not dangerous. Such actions were not necessary to protect the officer and others, nor were they necessary to apprehend the felon. Despite these developments, however, many states codified the common-law rule that permitted police officers to use deadly force in apprehending fleeing felons. This practice was condemned by many commentators and scholars, but the practice was not generally prohibited by the courts before 1985.

On 27 March 1985, the U.S. Supreme Court ruled that Tennessee's fleeing felon statute was unconstitutional under the facts of the case. *Tennessee v. Garner* involved an unarmed boy who was killed by a police officer as the youth fled from an unoccupied house. The officer could see that the fleeing felon was a youth and apparently unarmed. But the officer argued that he knew that if the youth got over the fence, he could escape;

so he fired at him. The Tennessee statute allowed an officer to shoot a suspect if it appeared to be necessary to prevent the escape of a felon.[63]

In *Garner*, the Court emphasized that the use of deadly force by police officers must be reasonable to be lawful. Such use is reasonable in the following circumstances:

1. To prevent an escape when the suspect has threatened the officer with a weapon.
2. When there is a threat of death or serious physical injury to the officer or others.
3. If there is probable cause to believe that the person has committed a crime involving the infliction or threatened infliction of serious physical harm and, where practical, some warning has been given by the officer.

The Tennessee statute that permitted an officer to shoot a fleeing felon therefore may be constitutional in some instances. But used against a young, slight, and unarmed youth who had apparently been involved in a burglary, such force was unreasonable and therefore unlawful.

The CJA in this chapter gives an example of a situation in which it is difficult to know whether an officer may legally shoot a fleeing felon. *Garner* allows the use of deadly force if necessary to prevent an escape when the suspect has threatened the officer with a weapon, or when there is a serious threat to the officer or others. Do those conditions exist in the CJA? The answer will be determined by whether a reasonable officer in that situation would have thought the fleeing felon had a gun, was reaching for the gun, and would have threatened the life of the officer or others. The knowledge that the felon was fleeing an alleged burglary and that there was no evidence of violence makes the case more difficult.

Effects of Unreasonable Force by Police and Citizens

The effects of unreasonable force, especially that which causes death, go beyond the immediate victims and their families. One reaction to police use of excessive force is the feeling by minorities in the community that the police are out to get them. Approximately 50 percent of the victims killed by police officers are black. Studies indicate, however, that this high percentage for blacks might not necessarily represent a policy of discrimination against minorities, although some investigators believe there is evidence that "police have one trigger finger for blacks and another for whites."[64]

Presidential commissions studying urban riots have uniformly noted the effect of police brutality on such incidents. When the public perceives an act by a police officer to be unfair, unreasonable, unnecessary, or harassing, especially when minorities are the victims, that perception may provide the impetus for urban riots.[65] This is not to suggest that police actions *cause* the riots. Police have no control over the root causes of civil disturbances, such as unemployment, lack of educational opportunities, poor housing, and inadequate health care facilities; but police can reduce violent confrontations by the policies they adopt. The United States Commission on Civil Rights, in its report issued after field investigations and public hearings in Philadelphia and Houston in 1979, along with the results of a national conference of police experts and community officials, emphasized the importance of hiring more racial minorities and upgrading their positions on police forces. The commission cited the recent study of the National Minority Advisory Council on Criminal Justice:

> Central to the problem of brutality is the underrepresentation of minorities as police officers. . . . It has been shown that the presence of minority police officers has a positive effect on police-community relations.[66]

This report of the Commission on Civil Rights emphasized the far-reaching effect of police brutality. In Miami, for example, after a white police officer was acquitted in the killing of a black citizen he had pursued in a high-speed chase for a traffic violation, rioting began in the black community, resulting in destruction, violence, and the death of 18 people. Earlier commissions also underscored police violence as a catalyst in urban rioting in the 1960s.[67]

Violence against police also has serious repercussions. Officers who survive may have physical injuries or psychological problems that preclude further work as police officers. Families and friends of those who are killed are also victims of such violence. One study indicated the following reactions of survivors of police who are killed in the line of duty:[68]

- Having difficulty concentrating and making decisions, feeling confused, having one's mind go blank;
- Feeling hostile;
- Feeling different from others, feeling alone, being uncomfortable in social situations;
- Fearing people, places, and things, and being anxious of one's ability to survive;
- Reexperiencing the traumatic incident through flashbacks, dreams, or thoughts;
- Feeling emotionally numb, having less interest in previously enjoyed activities, or being unable to return to prior employment;
- Having less ability to express positive and negative emotions;
- Having difficulty falling asleep or remaining asleep;
- Feeling guilty about the way one acted toward the deceased or as if one could have prevented the death.

THE CONTROL OF POLICING

Although only a minority of police officers may be guilty of misconduct, any misconduct should be subject to discipline; more important, policies and programs should be developed to avoid as much misconduct as possible. Police misconduct may be controlled from within the department or by outside agencies.[69]

Regulation by Police Departments

The efficient operation of any department requires internal discipline of employees; in the case of police departments, it also is important that the public's image of internal operations be positive. It therefore is essential, said the Commission on Civil Rights, that police departments have an effective system of internal discipline that will "include clear definition of proper conduct, a reliable mechanism for detecting misconduct, and appropriate sanctions, consistently imposed, when misconduct has been proven." Policies must be clearly articulated.[70]

Police departments should actively and fairly enforce their written policies. If the police believe that they will never be reprimanded for violating the policy, the policy may be ineffective in curbing abuse of discretion. The Commission on Civil Rights recommended that "every police department should have a clearly defined system for the receipt, processing, and investigation of civilian complaints." Once a violation of policy is found, "discipline imposed should be fair, swift, and consistent with departmental practices and procedures."[71] Police departments should take measures to identify violence prone officers in an attempt to avert problems.

Regulation by Courts: The Exclusionary Rule

Courts have also attempted to regulate police behavior. If police illegally seize evidence or improperly secure confessions, that evidence may be excluded from trial. This procedure is the result of the U.S. Supreme

"Which one of you did that bang-up job of getting evidence against the East Side mob by going through their garbage?" (Wayne Stayskal/Tampa Tribune)

Court's **exclusionary rule.** In 1914 the Supreme Court held that the Fourth Amendment (which prohibits unreasonable searches and seizures) would have no meaning unless the courts prohibited the use of illegally seized evidence. Consequently, when the police violated that provision, the evidence they seized could not be used in *federal* cases. In 1961 the Court ruled that the exclusionary rule also applied to the states.[72]

The exclusionary rule is highly controversial, mainly because it applies after the fact. When the illegally seized evidence is excluded from the trial, we already know who the suspect is and, in many cases, believe that the guilt is obvious. Thus, when the judge rules that the gun allegedly used in the murder cannot be used against that person in court because the evidence was obtained illegally by the police and the suspect goes free because we do not have enough legal evidence for a conviction, there is strong public reaction of disbelief and outrage.

Arguments in Favor of the Exclusionary Rule The exclusionary rule serves a symbolic purpose. If police violate the rights of individuals to obtain evidence to convict alleged criminals, the government, in a sense, is supporting crime. When this occurs, the government becomes a lawbreaker, and "it breeds contempt for law; it invites . . . anarchy."[73]

The symbolic purpose is important, but the second reason for the exclusionary rule is a practical one: it is assumed that the rule will prevent police from engaging in illegal searches and seizures. According to the Supreme Court, the exclusionary rule "compels respect for the constitutional guaranty in the only effectively available way—by removing the incentive to disregard it."[74]

Of course, it is difficult to know whether that statement is true because illegal searches that may be conducted to harass or punish generally take place in secret and thus may not be reported. Research on the issue reports inconclusive evidence. There is evidence, however, that the existence of the rule has led some police departments to increase the quantity and quality of police training, thus educating officers in what they may and may not do in the areas of search and seizure.[75]

Arguments for Abolishing the Exclusionary Rule In recent years the exclusionary rule has come under severe attack, with many people calling for its abolition or at least its modification. Their arguments generally are the reverse of the arguments in favor. First is the argument of the symbolism of abolition, based on the view that, when people see guilty persons going free because of a technicality, they lose respect for law and order, and the entire criminal justice system is weakened. The public's *perception* of letting guilty people go free is crucial.

Second, the abolitionists contend that the exclusionary rule should be eliminated because it results in the release of guilty people. It makes no difference how many: one is too many, argue the abolitionists. Third, the possibility of having evidence excluded from trial because it was not properly seized leads defendants to file numerous motions to suppress evidence, which takes up a lot of court time and contributes to their congestion. In criminal cases, objections to search and seizure are the most frequently raised issues.[76]

Police must be careful in searching and seizing evidence. If they do not follow proper guidelines, the evidence may be excluded from the trial. (Bob Daemmrich/Image Works)

Exceptions to the Exclusionary Rule   Several exceptions to the exclusionary rule have been suggested. Under the **good faith exception,** illegally obtained evidence would not be excluded from trial if it could be shown that the police secured the evidence in good faith; that is, they reasonably believed that they were acting in accordance with the law. The good faith exception has been rejected by some state legislatures and adopted by others. It is opposed by the American Bar Association and the American Civil Liberties Union. In the 1983–1984 term, in *Massachusetts v. Sheppard*, the Supreme Court adopted the good faith exception, holding that when police conduct a search in good faith, even though the technical search warrant is defective, the seized evidence will not be excluded from the trial.[77]

It is considered likely that the Supreme Court also will extend the good faith exception to warrantless searches that are objectively reasonable. The Court has permitted, for example, the use of evidence seized by officers who had a warrant to search one apartment but searched the wrong apartment and found illegal drugs. In *Maryland v. Garrison*, the Court reasoned that because the search was in good faith and excluding its use in such cases would not deter police, who thought they were searching an apartment included in the warrant, nothing positive would be gained by applying the exclusionary rule.[78]

During its 1987–1988 term, the Court ruled that evidence secured by police who conducted a warrantless search through garbage left for collection outside an individual's home need not be suppressed under the exclusionary rule. According to the Court, the individuals who left the garbage outside their dwelling did not have a reasonable expectation that such garbage would not be viewed by others.

> It is common knowledge that plastic garbage bags left on or at the side of a public street are readily accessible to animals, children, scavangers, snoops, and other members of the public.[79]

A variation of the good faith exception to the exclusionary rule occurred in November 1988, when the Court ruled that a defendant's constitutional rights are not violated when police officers lose or destroy evidence that might have been used to establish the defendant's innocence provided the officers' actions were made in good faith. The case, *Arizona*

SPOTLIGHT 7.6
THE RETURN OF THE CHRISTIAN BURIAL CASE: THE SUPREME COURT ADOPTS THE INEVITABLE DISCOVERY RULE

The Christian burial case is back, 15 years after young Pamela Powers was assaulted sexually and murdered and an escaped mental patient led Iowa police to her frozen body in a snow-covered ditch. . . .

It was Christmas Eve 1968 when 10-year-old Pamela Powers disappeared while visiting a YMCA in Des Moines.

A short time later Williams left the YMCA, where he had rented a room and asked a 14-year-old boy to help him load a large bundle into his car. Williams drove off before police could be alerted. The bundle, the boy would later say, had "two legs in it and they were skinny and white."

Williams disappeared until Dec. 26, when he telephoned a Des Moines attorney from Illinois. On the attorney's advice, Williams turned himself in to police in Davenport, Iowa, where he was arrested and arraigned.

Two officers were dispatched from Des Moines, 160 miles away, to retrieve him. The officers had agreed with Williams's Des Moines attorney and another defense lawyer in Davenport not to question the prisoner on the drive home. Williams already had received five separate Miranda warnings and had been told by his lawyers to remain silent.

But before too long, one of the officers in the car, Detective Cletus Leaming, began talking to Williams. The detective knew that Williams was a former mental patient and that he was deeply religious.

"I want to give you something to think about while we're traveling down the road," the detective said. "They are predicting several inches of snow for tonight, and I feel that you yourself are the only person that knows where this little girl's body is, that you yourself have only been there once, and if you get a snow on top of it you yourself may be unable to find it. . . . I feel that we could stop and locate the body, that the parents of this little girl should be entitled to a Christian burial for the little girl who was snatched away from them on Christmas Eve and murdered."

Leaming's "Christian burial speech" proved persuasive and Williams directed the officers to the body. The speech ended a widespread search for the victim of a horrible crime, but it also started a debate that would span three decades over the rights of a twice-convicted murderer.

In his opinion for the 5–4 majority in *Brewer v. Williams,* now-retired Justice Potter Stewart held that the speech amounted to interrogation and that Williams had a right to legal counsel during the interrogation. Although he had led police to the little girl's body, Williams had not made "an intentional relinquishment or abandonment of a known right or privilege," the Court said.

The Fateful Footnote

Justice Stewart upheld the reversal of Williams's 1969 murder conviction, noting in a footnote that the state courts should have ruled inadmissible incriminating statements that Williams made to the

v. Youngblood involved an Arizona case in which Larry Youngblood was convicted of the kidnapping, molestation, and sexual assault of a 10-year-old boy.[80]

The police in *Youngblood* had failed to refrigerate the victim's semen-stained clothing or to make tests capable of showing whether the semen came from Youngblood. Results of such tests might have shown that Youngblood was not the offender in the case. Justice Rehnquist, writing for the majority, argued that the omission can "at worst be described as negligent."

Since the Supreme Court adopted the good faith exception to the exclusionary rule, some state courts have held that it does not apply under

detective as well as "any testimony describing his having led the police to the victim's body."

But the footnote didn't take away all of the evidence against Williams. "Evidence of where the body was found and of its condition," Justice Stewart wrote, "might well be admissible on the theory that the body would have been discovered in any event, even had incriminating statements not been elicited from Williams. . . . In the event that a retrial is instituted, it will be for the state courts in the first instance to determine whether particular items of evidence may be admitted."

Before the year ended, Williams was convicted a second time for the girl's murder and sentenced to life in prison without possibility of parole.

The Iowa trial judge obeyed the U.S. Supreme Court's mandate and kept from the jury any evidence relating to Williams's statements to Leaming and the circumstances under which the body was found. But the trial court also took the rest of Justice Stewart's footnote to heart and refused to suppress evidence gleaned from the body itself.

As it had done before, the Iowa Supreme Court affirmed the conviction (285 N.W. 2d 248).

. . .

[In its 1983–1984 term, the U.S. Supreme Court again considered the case.]

Inevitable Discovery Exception Added to Exclusionary Rule

Earlier in the term, on June 11, the Court created an "inevitable discovery" exception to the exclusionary rule.

. . .

[In *Nix v. Williams*] the Court rejected the court of appeals' requirement of a showing of good faith on the part of the police, saying that this would place courts in the position of withholding from juries relevant and undoubted truth that would have been available absent any unlawful police conduct. This would place the police in a worse position than they would have been if there had been no unlawful conduct, the Court said, and it fails to take into account the "enormous societal cost of excluding truth in the search for truth in the administration of justice."

Justice Stevens concurred in the judgment, calling attention to the protracted litigation, which he blamed on the officer who made the "Christian burial" plea. Justice White wrote a short opinion taking exception to Justice Stevens's characterization of the police officer.

Justice Brennan, joined by Justice Marshall, dissented. They were willing to accept the inevitable discovery exception but argued that the inevitability should be proved by clear and convincing evidence rather than by a mere preponderance of the evidence.

Source: Barry Adler, "The Return of the Christian Burial Case," *American Bar Association Journal* 70 (January 1984): 100–2, referring to the case, *Brewer v. Williams,* 430 U.S. 387 (1977). The discussion of the 1984 adoption of the inevitable discovery rule comes from Rowland L. Young, "Supreme Court Report," *American Bar Association Journal* 70 (September 1984): 126.

their state constitutions. Since this involves enlarging, not reducing a Supreme Court interpretation of the federal constitution, such interpretations are permissible.[81]

In its 1983–1984 term, the Supreme Court adopted the **inevitable discovery** exception to the exclusionary rule. According to this rule, evidence that police seize illegally will be admitted at trial if it can be shown that the evidence would eventually have been discovered by use of legal methods. The details of the case are contained in Spotlight 7.6. Writing for the Court in *Nix v. Williams*, Chief Justice Warren E. Burger said, "Exclusion of physical evidence that would inevitably have been discovered adds nothing to either the integrity or fairness of a criminal trial."[82]

Community Relations

A final method of controlling police activities is through community involvement and improved police-community relationships. It is vital that relationships between police and the community be improved. We already have seen that police are not in a position to apprehend most criminals without the support of citizens. The United States Commission on Civil Rights emphasized that the men and women who are authorized to make arrests in this country depend to a great extent today on the cooperation of the public. "Perhaps the most valuable asset these officers can possess is credibility with the communities they serve."[83]

Good police-community relationships take on an even greater importance as budgetary restraints force reductions in police forces, making police even more dependent on citizen assistance in crime control. The importance of these contacts is emphasized by studies indicating that citi-

Police services may include visits to schools. Here officers conduct a workshop on the dangers of drugs. (David Grossman/Photo Researchers)

Police-community relations are very important. (Mark and Evelyn Bernheim/ Woodfin Camp)

zens who have positive images of the police are more likely to report crimes than those who have negative images. Those most likely to have negative images of the police are members of the lower class, blacks, and other nonwhites—persons who feel a general alienation from the political process and those who perceive an increase in crime in their neighborhoods.[84]

One problem with these studies, however, is that they tend to be descriptive and based on socioeconomic, racial, or ethnic factors. It has also been argued that, in studying police-community relationships, attention should be given to such factors as "the frequency and nature of past contacts with police officers, residential history, and arrest records." After conducting that type of study, investigators found evidence to refute the argument that certain segments of the population will have negative images of police no matter how the police behave.

> Socioeconomic factors such as race, age, and income appear to have little
> direct effect on attitudes toward police. The primary factor determining
> general satisfaction with police and police service seems to be actual
> personal contact with specific police officers in a positive context.[85]

The findings of this study also minimized the effect of efforts by the police to educate the community, finding instead that what really counts is contact with the police in an *official* capacity.

On the whole, however, police do not receive extremely high marks for their work. But contrary to what might be expected, negative reactions to the police are not necessarily related to police performance of their jobs. For example, *not* giving a ticket when one should have been given may be seen as negative, not positive. In one study, negative reactions to the police resulted mainly from the way police behaved when they took action. Regulatory actions of police were seen as positive when they

> resulted from a prompt response, being informative about the reasons for the police actions, and for being nice, polite, and helpful (e.g., calling an ambulance or aiding the citizen to cope with consequences of the situation). . . . In no case did the policeman have to engage in dangerous or extraordinary feats to be positively evaluated; he simply had to respond in a sincere and personal way to the individual.[86]

A recent emphasis on community-oriented policing (COP) has received the research efforts of several investigators, such as Jerome Skolnick and David Bayley, who closely observed police work in Newark, Detroit, Denver, Houston, Oakland, and Santa Ana. They report that COP has been effective in reducing crime, as illustrated by the 25 percent reduction in Newark, New Jersey.[87] Similar results were found by Albert J. Reiss, Jr., in his study of policing in Oakland, California.[88]

COP may take many forms. Some were noted in the previous chapter, such as foot, motorcycle, or horse patrol, in which the officers have a chance to learn first-hand the problems of the community and community citizens have an opportunity to know their police.[89] Crime prevention programs also are important. Police educate the community about various approaches to crime prevention. Community organization work in which police and the community work together to identify community problems also is helpful.[90]

Herman Goldstein, who has written extensively on numerous criminal justice issues, concludes that full development of the overall concept of community policing, including a "concern with the substance of policing as well as its form," could "provide the integrated strategy for improving the quality of policing."[91]

Civilian Review Boards

Members of the community may be involved in improving police-community relationships by means of civilian review boards, which review citizen complaints against police officers. These boards became popular after the civil disturbances of the 1960s and 1970s, primarily in areas in which minorities believed that police were discriminating against them. They were bitterly opposed by some police, and most either lasted only a short time or were not very powerful.[92]

The Civil Rights Commission emphasized that the civilian review boards created to hear complaints against police have not always been successful. "Their basic flaws were that they were advisory only, having no power to decide cases or impose punishment, and that they lacked sufficient staffs and resources." The commission recommended that, although the primary responsibility for disciplining police rests with police departments, it is imperative that the disciplinary process "be subject to some outside review to ensure . . . that a citizen not agreeing with the police department's disposition of a complaint has an avenue of redress to pursue."[93]

Some civilian groups are not merely advisory, however, and have proven quite effective. In 1984 an out-of-court settlement was reached in Los Angeles, giving the Los Angeles Police Commission (composed of civilians) full authority to authorize future undercover investigations by the police (an authority that was previously held by the chief of police). Under the terms of the settlement, the city was required to pay $900,000 to 143 plaintiffs who claimed that their civil rights were violated by the police, who spied on legal, political, and civil activities. The city also had to pay the fees of the American Civil Liberties Union attorneys who represented the plaintiffs. Guidelines were created and accepted; the attorneys reported that they had numerous requests from other police departments and civil liberties groups for copies of those guidelines.[94]

Tort Actions Against Police

Earlier, the text discussed the meaning of **torts,** noting that civil suits may be brought even in some cases that also involve crimes. The use of civil suits to bring actions against police (or other authorities) who violate civil rights of citizens is thought to be an effective deterrent for such illegal actions. Even if they do not deter other violations, tort actions, if successful, at least permit victims of abuse (or their families when the victims die) to recover monetary damages for their physical injuries (or death) and also for emotional and psychological damages.

Tort actions are brought under the Civil Rights Act and commonly called *1983 actions*, after the section of the U.S. Code in which the provision is codified.[95] Section 1983 actions also may be brought by persons injured as a result of police negligence, as for example, in high-speed chases that result in injuries (or death) to bystanders.[96] Damage awards may be quite high.

SUMMARY

This chapter has focused on some of the problems and issues connected with policing in a complex society. Many of the problems may be related to the role conflicts of policing. Most officers receive more training in law enforcement than in order maintenance and performing services. Many of them view policing primarily as law enforcement; and superiors often evaluate them by their work in that area. Yet, studies indicate that officers spend less time in law enforcement than in other police functions.

Police also face a lot of stress due to the nature of the job and the varying expectations of citizens. Some resent this situation, and many citizens have no hesitation in complaining if all police functions are not performed quickly, efficiently, and adequately. The real problem may lie in our unrealistic expectations of policing. At least in theory, we expect the police to enforce all laws; but in reality, we will not tolerate full enforcement—police will not and cannot do that anyway. We expect them to prevent crime. They have the same expectation, but that is not always possible either. We expect them to be authoritarian in enforcement situations, yet maintain a supportive and friendly approach in others. We expect them to handle all kinds of emergencies, yet we do not provide them the resources or authority for some. No matter what they do, for police the system has conflicts. There is conflict between aggressive crime prevention (the crime control model) and the rights of citizens to be free from unreasonable interference by the police (the due process model).

Most important, we cannot separate policing and its context from the rest of our society. The actions of the police "mirror the social relations of American society. Until those relations change we will continue to have a police problem."[97]

Problems and issues also have surrounded affirmative action programs aimed at employing more women and racial minorities in policing. These groups argue that police cannot understand their problems and gain the support of their members unless they are adequately represented among police officers. Others argue that recruitment efforts have lowered standards or that court decisions upholding affirmative action programs for increasing the number of women and racial minorities on a police force are unfair and create internal problems for police.

Corruption among police has been widely studied. Reports vary as to the pervasiveness and nature of corruption, but it is clear that at least some police are involved in drug transactions and other illegal acts. Departmental efforts to eradicate such illegal behavior are not always successful.

Violence and policing has also gained considerable attention. Violence against police and police violence against citizens both lead to serious repercussions. Police are permitted to use some violence, but the abuse of that violence is the focus of concern. Court decisions have required changes in the use of deadly force, for example, and some police departments have responded with a greater emphasis on proper training in the use of deadly force. Some have also established more detailed departmental policies on the use of such force.

Efforts to control improper policing have come from department regulations, court decisions, improvement of community-police relations, civilian review boards, and tort actions against police. The most controversial of these efforts has been the Supreme Court's exclusionary rule, whereby evidence obtained by police in violation of a suspect's constitutional rights may be excluded from use in that individual's subsequent trial. Recently, though, the Court has created some exceptions to the exclusionary rule, such as the good faith exception and the inevitable discovery rule.

Civil actions against police may serve as a deterrent to improper police behavior, and an increasing number of these suits are being filed under the Federal Code.

The problems of improving policing in the United States have been addressed recently by a prestigious panel of criminal justice professionals, who studied the problems on a national scale. Among the recommendations of the panel of experts are

> the creation of a national institution to develop and utilize top-quality police leadership, broader-based procedures for selecting police chiefs, and programs that would heighten public awareness of the changing role of law enforcement groups.

Also emphasized was the need to recruit "quality personnel from wider segments of society," in particular, women and racial minorities. The panel emphasized the need for widespread discussions of policing and the problems police face in today's complex society.[98]

Despite problems in policing, many officers are very satisfied with their professions. Problems exist in any profession; and, perhaps, it is good that we are never free of problems. Policing is not for everyone; but for those who enjoy a challenging, exciting job in which there is opportunity for service as well as hard work, policing is a viable choice.

Joseph Wambaugh, a police officer who later became a writer of best-selling novels, assessed his life in both professions. He does not miss the tedium and the bureaucracy of policing, but he does miss the loyalty and camaraderie of his police colleagues. "I find a lot of disloyalty in show business. In police work, it's totally different . . . for the period of time that you're working together [in policing] you are absolutely loyal to each other." In the final analysis, Wambaugh emphasized that driving a Mercedes rather than a VW is nice, but that he does not consider himself a success now and a failure when he was a police officer. "Being a cop was a good life."[99]

STUDY QUESTIONS

1. Discuss the reasons for role conflicts in policing. What is the relationship of time allocation to role conflicts?

2. What is meant by *proactive* and *reactive policing* and what changes are being made in the former type?

3. What is meant by *subculture*? How does that concept apply to policing?

4. What has been the result of efforts to recruit women and racial minorities into policing? What would you recommend for the future?

5. Are police cynical? Discuss in light of research summarized in this chapter.

6. Discuss the extent and effect of police corruption.

7. What is the relationship between violence against the police and violence by the police?

8. What is meant by the *fleeing felon rule*? Contrast its historical meaning with the Supreme Court's ruling in effect today.

9. What do you think would be the most effective way to control policing?

10. What is meant by the *exclusionary rule*? What are the pros and cons of this rule and what exceptions has the Supreme Court permitted?

11. What is *community-oriented policing*?

12. What is the purpose of permitting civil actions against police who abuse their power?

ENDNOTES

1. Mortan Bard and Joseph Zacker, "The Prevention of Family Violence: Dilemmas of Community Intervention," *Journal of Marriage and the Family* 33 (November 1971): 678.

2. James Q. Wilson, *Varieties of Police Behavior: The Management of Law and Order in Eight Communities* (Cambridge, Mass.: Harvard University Press, 1968), p. 19.

3. Albert J. Reiss, Jr., *The Police and the Public* (New Haven, Conn.: Yale University Press, 1971), pp. 63, 64, 71.

4. Richard J. Lundman, "Police Patrol Work: A Comparative Perspective," in Richard J. Lundman, ed., *Police Behavior: A Sociological Perspective* (New York: Oxford University Press, 1980), p. 55.

5. Gordon P. Whitaker et al., *Basic Issues in Police Performance*, National Institute of Justice (Washington, D.C.: U.S. Government Printing Office, July 1982), p. 40.

6. Eric J. Scott, *Calls for Service: Citizen Demand and Initial Police Performance*, National Institute of Justice (Washington, D.C.: U.S. Government Printing Office, July 1981), pp. 24–30.

7. Ibid., p. 27.

8. See Peter Greenwood with Alan Abrahamse, *Selective Incapacitation* (Santa Monica, Calif.: Rand Corporation, 1982); and Joan Petersilia, Peter Greenwood, and Marvin Lavin, *Criminal Careers of Habitual Felons* (Santa Monica, Calif.: Rand Corporation, 1978).

9. See George I. Miller, "Observations on Police Undercover Work," *Criminology* 25 (February 1987): 27–46.

10. Susan E. Martin and Lawrence W. Sherman, *Catching Career Criminals: The Washington, D.C.*
Repeat Offender Project (Washington, D.C.: U.S. Department of Justice, 1980), quoted in Joan Petersilia, *The Influence of Criminal Justice Research* (Santa Monica, Calif.: Rand Corporation, June 1987), p. 24. See also Martin and Sherman, "Selective Apprehension: A Police Strategy for Repeat Offenders," *Criminology* 24 (February 1986): 155–73.

11. William Gay and William Bowers, *Targeting Law Enforcement Resources: The Career Criminal Focus* (Washington, D.C.: U.S. Department of Justice, 1985).

12. *Attorney General's Task Force on Family Violence*, Final Report (Washington, D.C.: U.S. Department of Justice, 1984), p. 20. For analyses of the research in this area, see Lawrence Sherman, *Police Change Policy on Domestic Violence* (Washington, D.C.: Crime Control Institute, 1986).

13. Jerry Dash and Martin Reiser, "Suicide among Police in Urban Law Enforcement Agencies," *Journal of Police Science and Administration* 6 (March 1978): 18. For a recent analysis of some of the coping techniques police officers use to adjust to stress, see M. T. Charles, *Policing the Streets* (Springfield, Ill.: Charles C Thomas, 1986).

14. For a bibliography and discussion of these studies, see W. Clinton Terry, III, "Police Stress: The Empirical Evidence," *Journal of Police Science and Administration* 9 (March 1981): 67–68, 70.

15. Leonard Territo and Harold J. Vetter, "Stress and Police Personnel," *Journal of Police and Administration* 9 (June 1981): 200, referring to the work of Nelson and Smith, "The Law Enforcement Profession: An Incidence of Suicide."

16 David Lester, "Stress in Police Officers: An American Perspective," *The Police Journal* 56 (April 1983): 189. For a report on a study of stress among British police officers, see Gisli H. Gudjonsson, "Life Events Stressors and Physical Reactions in Senior British Police Officers," *The Police Journal* 56 (January 1983): 60–67.

17. Quoted in Anne Choen, "I've Killed That Man Ten Thousand Times," *Police Magazine* (July 1980): 17–23.

18. *Justice Assistance News* 4 (April 1983): 5.

19. *Who Is Guarding the Guardians? A Report on Police Practices*, Report of the United States Commission on Civil Rights (Washington, D.C.: U.S. Government Printing Office, October 1981), p. 156.

20. Reiser, who holds an Ed.D. degree, has written extensively about police psychology. His latest book is a collection of papers in the field, *Police Psychology: Collected Papers* (Los Angeles: Lehi Publishing Co., 1982).

21. Robert J. Trotter, "Psychologist with A Badge," *Psychology Today* (November 1987): 26–30.

22. Michael W. O'Neil et al., "Stress Inoculation Training and Job Performance," *Journal of Police Science and Administration* 10 (December 1982): 396.

23. See William A. Westley, *Violence and the Police: A Sociological Study of Law, Custom, and Morality* (Cambridge, Mass.: MIT Press, 1970).

24. Bill Sommerville, "Double Standards in Law Enforcement with Regard to Minority Status," *Issues in Criminology* 4 (Fall 1968): 39.

25. Rodney Stark, *Police Riots: Collective Violence and Law Enforcement* (Belmont, Calif.: Focus Books, 1972), p. 93.

26. See Arthur Niederhoffer, *Behind the Shield: The Police in Urban Society* (Garden City, N.Y.: Doubleday Publishing Co., 1969).

27. Eric D. Poole and Robert M. Regoli, "An Examination of the Effects of Professionalism on Cynicism among Police," *The Social Science Journal* (October 1979): 64.

28. Robert M. Regoli et al., "Police Professionalism and Cynicism Reconsidered: An Assessment of Measurement Issues," *Justice Quarterly* 4 (June 1987): 269. See also the following articles in that journal: Robert H. Langworthy, "Comment—Have We Measured the Concept(s) of Police Cynicism Using Niederhoffer's Cynicism Index?" (pp. 278–80); and Robert M. Regoli et al., "Rejoinder—Police Cynicism: Theory Development and Reconstruction," (pp. 281–86).

29. John P. Crank et al., "Cynicism among Police Chiefs," *Justice Quarterly* 3 (September 1986): 343–52. See also John P. Crank et al., "The Measurement of Cynicism Among Police Chiefs," *Journal of Criminal Justice* 15 (1987): 37–48.

30. Dennis Jay Wiechman, "Police Cynicism Toward the Judicial Process," *Journal of Police Science and Administration* 7 (September 1979): 340–45.

31. FBI, *Crime in the United States: Uniform Crime Reports, 1987* (Washington, D.C.: U. S. Government Printing Office, 1988), p. 228.

32. See *Who Is Guarding the Guardians?*, p. 2.

33. See Barbara Raffel Price and Robert Price, "Police Community Relations: Sex-Conscious Hiring and Professionalism," *Journal of Crime and Justice* 4 (1981).

34. *Who Is Guarding the Guardians?*, p. 154.

35. Ellen Hochstedler, "Impediments to Hiring Minorities in Public Police Agencies," *Journal of Police Science and Administration* 12 (June 1984): 227–40.

36. Johnson v. Transportation Agency, 480 U.S. 616 (1987). For an analysis of this decision, see "Johnson v. Transportation Agency: Are We All Equal?" *Creighton Law Review* 21 (No. 1, 1987–88): 333–58.

37. U.S. v. Paradise, 480 U.S. 149 (1987). For an analysis of this case, see "United States v. Paradise: Another Look at Alabama's Hiring Quota," *Creighton Law Review* 21, no. 1 (1987–1988): 303–31. For a study of women in state police positions, see Ralph A. Weisheit, "Woman in the State Police: Concerns of Male and Female Officers," *Journal of Police Science and Administration* 15 (June 1987): 137–44. The Supreme Court's affirmative action decisions became more conservative in its 1988–89 term, and many fear that the civil rights of minorities and women will continue to be eroded. See, for example, Martin v. Wilks, No. 87-1614, U.S. Law Week 57 (June 13, 1989), p. 4616.

38. "Prince Quits as Chief of Police," *Dallas Morning News* (13 April 1988), p. 1.

39. Eva S. Buzawa, "The Role of Race in Predicting Job Attitudes of Patrol Officers," *Journal of Criminal Justice* 9 (1981): 74–75.

40. B. Peter Block et al., *Policewomen on Patrol* (Washington, D.C.: Police Foundation, 1973). See also Bruce N. Carpenter and Susan M. Raza, "Personality Characteristics of Police Applicants: Comparisons Across Subgroups and with Other Populations," *Journal of Police Science and Administration* 15 (March 1987): 10–17.

41. Michael T. Charles, "Women in Policing: The Physical Aspect," *Journal of Police Science and Administration* 10 (June 1982): 198. See also Sean A. Grennan, "Findings on the Role of Officer Gender in Violent Encounters with Citizens," *Journal of Police Science and Administration* 15 (March 1987): 78–85.

42. Lawrence W. Sherman, ed., *Police Corruption: A Sociological Perspective* (Garden City, N.Y.: Doubleday Publishing Co., 1974), p. 6.

43. Wilson, *Varieties of Police Behavior.*

44. Sherman, ed., *Police Corruption*, pp. 7–8. For a discussion of corruption in four police depart-

ments, see Lawrence W. Sherman, *Controlling Police Corruption: The Effects of Reform Policies: Summary Report* (Washington, D.C.: U.S. Government Printing Office, 1978). See also Sue Titue Reid, "The Police," in Abraham S. Blumberg, ed., *Current Perspectives on Criminal Behavior*, 2d ed. (New York: Alfred A. Knopf, 1981), pp. 124–29.

45. See Sherman, *Police Corruption*, pp. 1–39.

46. *The Knapp Commission Report on Police Corruption* (New York: Braziller, 1972).

47. "Officer Says He Was Thief Soon After He Joined Force," *New York Times* (3 June 1983), p. 11.

48. Herman Goldstein, *Policing a Free Society* (Cambridge, Mass.: Ballinger Publishing Co., 1977), p. 218.

49. "Drug Abuse by Police Called New York Force's Key Worry," *New York Times* (26 June 1983), p. 15.

50. Todd S. Purdum, "Drugs Threatening Integrity of New York Police," *New York Times* (12 November 1988), p. 1D.

51. "Boston Jurors Convict Seven in Police Corruption Inquiry," *New York Times* (14 September 1988), p. 15.

52. Nicholas Pileggi, "The War on the Cops," *New York Times* (17 March 1980), pp. 31, 32.

53. Mona Margarita, "Killing the Police: Myths and Motives," *The Annals of the American Academy of Political and Social Science* 452 (November 1980): 63.

54. "When Police Officers Use Deadly Force," *U.S. News & World Report* (10 January 1983), p. 58.

55. *Crime in the United States, Uniform Crime Reports, 1987* (Washington, D.C.: U.S. Government Printing Office, 1988), p. 228. For a recent analysis of the killing of police, see S. G. Chapman, *Cops, Killers and Staying Alive—The Murder of Police Officers in America* (Springfield, Ill.: Charles C Thomas, 1986).

56. "Police Death Divides Dallas," *Tulsa World* (28 January 1988), p. A9.

57. Catherine H. Milton et al., *Police Use of Deadly Force* (Washington, D.C.: Police Foundation, 1977), p. 3.

58. Albert J. Reiss, Jr., "Police Brutality," *Transaction Magazine* 5 (1968); reprinted in Richard J. Lundman, ed., *Police Behavior: A Sociological Perspective* (New York: Oxford University Press, 1980), pp. 274–75.

59. Ibid., p. 276. See also Albert J. Reiss, Jr., *The Police and the Public* (New York: Ballantine Books, 1973).

60. Reiss, "Police Brutality," p. 276.

61. Milton et al., *Police Use of Deadly Force*, p. 41.

62. Lawrence W. Sherman, "Execution without Trial: Police Homicide and the Constitution," *Vanderbilt Law Review* 33 (January 1980): 74–75.

63. Tennessee v. Garner, 471 U.S. 1 (1985).

64. Arnold Binder and Peter Scharf, "Deadly Force in Law Enforcement," *Crime and Delinquency* 28 (January 1982): 1, 23. See also Frank Horvath, "The Police Use of Deadly Force: A Description of Selected Characteristics of Intrastate Incidents," *Journal of Police Science and Administration* 15 (September 1987): 226–38. For a recent study of police shootings in Philadelphia and New York, see James J. Fyfe, "Police Shooting: Environment and License," in Joseph E. Scott and Travis Hirschi, eds., *Controversial Issues in Crime and Justice* (Beverly Hills, Calif.: Sage Publishing Co., 1988), pp. 79–94.

65. See Milton et al., *Police Use of Deadly Force*, pp. 3–4, for a discussion of such findings.

66. National Minority Advisory Council on Criminal Justice, *The Inequality of Justice: A Report on Crime and the Administration of Justice in the Minority Community* (October 1980), pp. 15–16, as quoted in *Who Is Guarding the Guardians?* p. 2.

67. *Who Is Guarding the Guardians?* p. vi.

68. Frances A. Stillman, *Line-of-Duty Deaths: Survivor and Departmental Responses* (Washington, D.C.: U.S. Department of Justice, National Institute of Justice, January 1987), pp. 2, 3.

69. For a history and analysis of controlling policing, see Samuel Walker, "Controlling the Cops: A Legislative Approach to Police Rulemaking," *University of Detroit Law Review* 63 (Spring 1986): 361–91.

70. Ibid., p. 35.

71. Ibid., pp. 157, 159; see also pp. 58–79.

72. Weeks v. United States, 232 U.S. 383 (1914). Mapp v. Ohio, 367 U.S. 643 (1961).

73. Olmstead v. United States, 277 U.S. 438, 485 (1928), Justice Brandeis, dissenting.

74. Elkins v. United States, 364 U.S. 206, 217 (1960).

75. See Stephen H. Sachs, "The Exclusionary Rule: A Prosecutor's Defense," *Criminal Justice Ethics* 1 (Summer–Fall 1982). This journal contains a symposium on the pros and cons of the exclusionary rule and is an excellent source on the topic.

76. See Comptroller General of the United States, *Impact of the Exclusionary Rule on Federal Criminal Prosecutions* (Washington, D.C.: United States Government Printing Office, 19 April 1979), p. 1.

77. Massachusetts v. Sheppard, 468 U.S. 981 (1984). See also United States v. Leon, decided the same day, 468 U.S. 897 (1984).

78. Maryland v. Garrison, 480 U.S. 79 (1987). For a discussion, see "Maryland v. Garrison: Extending the Good Faith Exception to Warrantless Searches," *Baylor Law Review* 40 (Winter 1988): 151–66. For a recent analysis of the inevitable discovery rule, see "Criminal Law—The Inevitable Discovery Exception to the Exclusionary Rule—The Search for Its Principled Application

to Prewarrant Evidence," *Western New England Law Review* 10, no. 1 (1988): 59–98.

79. California v. Greenwood, 486 U.S. 35 (1988).
80. Arizona v. Youngblood, 109 S.Ct. 333 (1988), *reh. den.*, 109 S.Ct. 885 (1989).
81. See State v. Sundling, 395 N.W. 2d 308 (Mich. App.1986), *Appeal denied* (Apr. 7, 1987).
82. Nix v. Williams, 467 U.S. 431 (1984), *remanded*, 751 F. 2d 956 (1985), *cert. denied*, 471 U.S. 1138 (1985).
83. *Who Is Guarding the Guardians?* p. 2.
84. For a discussion of these findings, see Paul S. Benson, "Political Alienation and Public Satisfaction with Police Services," *Pacific Sociological Review* 24 (January 1981): 45–64.
85. Richard Seaglion and Richard G. Condon, "Determinants of Attitudes toward City Police," *Criminology* 17 (February 1980): 493.
86. Theodore Groves et al., "An Approach to Problems in Police-Community Relations," *Journal of Community Psychology* (October 1980): 359, 360.
87. See Jerome H. Skolnick and David H. Bayley, *The New Blue Line: Police Innovation in Six American Cities* (New York: Free Press, 1986).
88. Albert J. Reiss, Jr., *Policing a City's Central District: The Oakland Story* (Washington, D.C.: National Institute of Justice, 1985).
89. See M. J. Farrell, *The Community Patrol Officer Program: Interim Progress Report*, no. 2 (New York: Vera Institute of Justice, 1986).
90. See S. W. Greenberg et al., *Informal Citizen Action and Crime Prevention at the Neighborhood Level: Executive Summary* (Washington, D.C.: National Institute of Justice 1985).
91. Herman Goldstein, "Toward Community-Oriented Policing: Potential, Basic Requirements, and Threshold Questions," *Crime and Delinquency* 33 (January 1987): 28.
92. Gerald W. Lynch and Edward Diamond, "Police: Misconduct," in Sanford H. Kadish, ed., *Encyclopedia of Crime and Justice* (New York: Free Press, 1983), vol. 3, p. 1160.
93. See *Who Is Guarding the Guardians?* p. 163.
94. "Civilian Group is Given Power to Veto Spying by L. A. Police," *Criminal Justice Newsletter* 51 (March 15, 1984): 3.
95. U.S. Code, Chapter 42, Section 1983.
96. See Geoffrey P. Alpert and Patrick R. Anderson, "The Most Deadly Force: Police Pursuits," *Justice Quarterly* 3 (March 1986): 1–14.
97. Michael K. Brown, *Working the Street: Police Discretion and the Dilemmas of Reform* (New York: Russell Sage, 1981).
98. "Study of Future of Policing Recommends Several Reforms," *Criminal Justice Newsletter* 17 (15 February 1984): 4–6.
99. Quoted in Claudia Dreifus, "A Conversation with Joseph Wambaugh," *Police Magazine* (May 1980): 37, 38.

3 PROCESSING A CRIMINAL CASE: THE CRIMINAL COURT SYSTEM

The processing of a criminal case involves a complex series of stages that center around the criminal courts. The chapters in Part III will examine the pretrial, trial, and appellate procedures of the criminal court system. Chapter 8 begins with an examination of the structure of courts, how they are administered, what role judges play in the court system, and what might be done about the current crisis in courts created by the increase in cases at the trial and the appellate levels.

Attorneys play important roles in the trial of criminal cases. Prosecutors and defense attorneys are popularly seen as fighting their battles in the drama of a criminal courtroom. Their roles, however, are far more complex than the media portrays. Chapter 9 looks at the differences between the prosecution and the defense and analyzes their roles in the criminal justice system. Particular attention is given to the wide discretion of prosecutors.

The prosecution and defense of a criminal case begins long before the actual trial; in fact, most cases do not go to trial. Chapter 10 examines pretrial procedures including the frequently used and highly controversial process of plea bargaining. Chapter 11 focuses on the trial of a criminal case, examining each step of the trial and explaining the roles of defense, prosecution, and judge in the criminal trial. The appeal of a criminal case is also discussed.

Perhaps the most controversial process in the criminal justice system is the sentencing of persons who are found guilty of a criminal offense. This process warrants a separate chapter, and in Chapter 12 the recent trends in sentencing are examined, along with a description of the sentencing process and an analysis of the issues raised by sentencing.

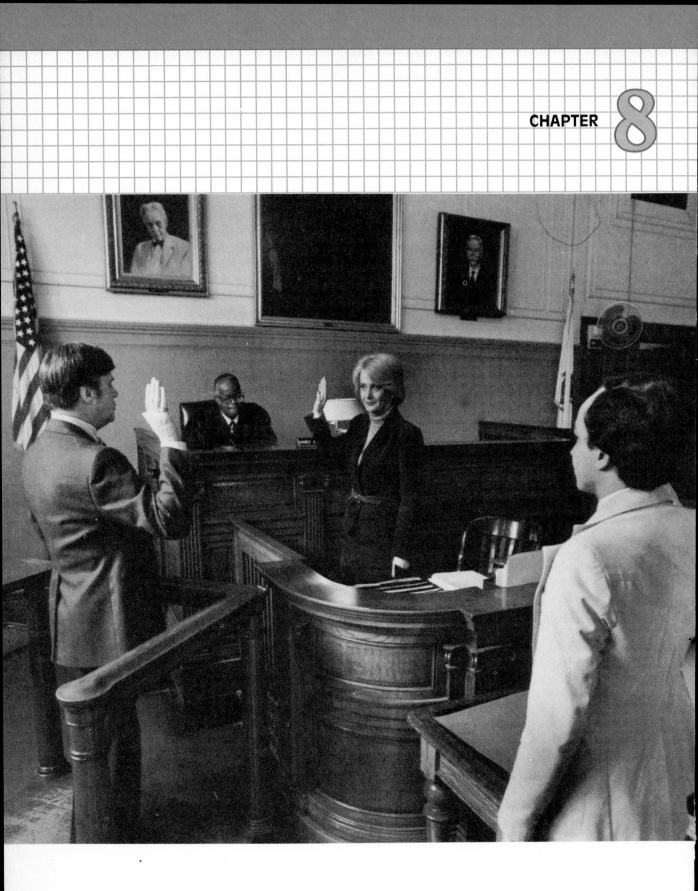

CHAPTER 8

Structure and Purpose of Courts

OUTLINE

KEY TERMS

Joseph, a 25-year-old man, spent too much money during the Christmas season and is unable to pay his January bills. He decides to rob a bank. Because bank robbery is risky, he asks an acquaintance, Stan, to help. Stan is very experienced but not very successful at robbing banks; he has just completed his second term in prison for armed robbery.

Stan provides the plan and the guns. Stan and Joseph enter the small bank in a nearby town, commit the armed robbery, and drive back to their home town. Local police see the car speeding and flash Stan to stop. He refuses to do so; a high-speed chase ends when Stan's car crashes into another car, killing the occupants. The police arrest Stan. He is charged with speeding (a traffic offense), reckless driving (a misdemeanor), and manslaughter (a

felony). Later investigations lead to probable cause to connect him with the armed robbery. After he is charged with that offense, he implicates Joseph, who is apprehended and arrested.

Both men plead not guilty and go to trial, but the courts are so crowded that they have to wait 2 months before they are tried. Both are found guilty of armed robbery, and Stan is found guilty of all other charges against him. The judge who sentences them on the armed robbery charge decides on penalties of 15 years for Stan, a third-time offender, and 2 years for Joseph, who has no prior convictions. Stan receives a fine for speeding, 2 weeks in jail for reckless driving, and 2 years in prison on the manslaughter charge.

INTRODUCTION

The activities of Stan and Joseph raise some of the crucial issues and procedures of the court system. The type of court that has the legal power to hear and decide each of the three major types of offenses—traffic, misdemeanor, and felony—is explained in this chapter, along with the differences between state and federal courts. The cases also raise the problem of overcrowding in the courts, a problem that results in delays in trials. This major problem in the criminal justice system will be addressed in this chapter. Other topics such as bail, sentencing, and sentencing disparity are discussed in greater detail in subsequent chapters, but a discussion of courts sets the stage for those discussions.

In the past decade increasing attention has been focused on the role of American courts in the criminal justice system. The first national survey of public attitudes toward courts was completed in 1978. The study showed that the general public ranked courts lower in prestige than many other social institutions. A majority of the public expressed dissatisfaction with the courts, indicating their belief that courts should be responsible for protecting society but that they have failed in this duty. Courts were seen as unfair and unequal in their treatment of individuals, and court personnel were not considered highly competent. The public indicated a desire for better-managed courts and greater public access to them. On the positive side, the study indicated that people were willing to pay more taxes to improve the court system. The most discouraging finding was that although the public generally lacks knowledge of courts, the more people know about courts, the greater is their dissatisfaction.[1]

The importance of courts cannot be overemphasized. Courts supervise many elements of the criminal justice system. The preliminary hearing and the arraignment take place in courts. Judges determine whether there is sufficient reason to hold a suspect brought in by the police. Judges supervise the actions of the prosecution and defense in the controversial procedure of plea bargaining. Judges decide whether to accept or deny a guilty plea. They supervise the grand jury in cases in which a grand jury indictment is required before a suspect can be tried.

Trials are supervised by courts. The process of sentencing occurs within courts. All motions after conviction, such as motions for a new trial, and all appeals take place within courts. Therefore, courts are critical in the system of criminal justice, and the actions that occur within them may significantly affect all other aspects of the criminal justice system.

This chapter begins with an introduction to some legal concepts that must be understood for an adequate examination of courts. It then examines court structure, pointing out the distinctions between the federal and the state systems. Both systems have trial and appellate courts, and those types will be explained. The highest court in the United States, the Supreme Court, is examined in more detail because of its importance in criminal justice. The second major section of the chapter examines the judge's role. The final section focuses on court congestion and discusses solutions to this major problem.

THE JUDICIAL BRANCH OF GOVERNMENT

The framers of the U.S. Constitution established three branches of government at the national level—legislative, executive, and judicial—and provided for the establishment of one supreme court. They envisioned a separation of the powers of these three branches, although there is some overlap. Federal judges and justices of the U.S. Supreme Court are appointed by the president, representing the executive branch, and confirmed by the Senate, representing the legislative branch. Because courts have limited enforcement powers, they usually rely on the executive branch for enforcement of their decisions. The court system must depend on the legislative branch of government for financial appropriations.

In the U.S. system of criminal justice the separate judicial branch is viewed as necessary for assuring that the constitutional and statutory rights of citizens are not controlled by political pressures. In practice, however, political pressures may enter into the selection of judges as well as into the organization and administration of courts and the judicial decision-making process.

DEFINITIONS OF LEGAL TERMS

It is necessary to understand some legal terms and concepts before the discussion proceeds. **Jurisdiction** refers to a court's power to hear and decide a case. Such power is given by the constitution or statute that created the court. A court's jurisdiction may be limited to a certain age group (for example the juvenile courts, with jurisdiction over juveniles, child custody, and adoption proceedings) or to a particular type of law. Some courts have jurisdiction only over minor offenses or misdemeanors. Others may hear only the more serious kinds of offenses, called *felonies*. Some courts may hear only civil cases, others only criminal cases. This chapter is concerned mainly with courts that have jurisdiction over criminal cases.

It also is important to understand the difference between original and appellate jurisdiction. **Original jurisdiction** refers to the jurisdiction of the courts that can first hear a case; that is, the court that may try the facts. **Appellate jurisdiction** refers to the jurisdiction of the court that can hear the case on appeal. When more than one court can hear a case, the courts have **concurrent jurisdiction.** When only one can hear a case, that court has **exclusive jurisdiction.**

Another limitation on courts is that they hear only cases and controversies. Courts will not decide hypothetical issues, and they will not give advisory opinions except in rare cases. Only when a dispute involves a legal right between two or more parties will a court hear the case. If the controversy ends before the end of the trial or the appeal, the court will not decide the case because the issue is now **moot,** meaning it is no longer a real case because no legal right between the parties needs to be resolved. Just as courts will not hear hypothetical cases, neither will they hear cases from uninvolved persons. A person must have **standing** to sue. In other words, the individual must have some private, substantive, legally protected interest that is being harmed or threatened.

Because it is important for the law to have stability, courts generally follow a rule of ***stare decisis*** ("to abide by, or adhere to, decided cases"), whereby previous decisions become precedents for current and future decisions. The law, however, also is flexible, and courts may overrule (specifically or by implication) their previous decisions. It is always important to distinguish between the rule of the court and the **dicta** of the judges or justices. At times when justices or judges write opinions, they expound on issues that are not part of the actual ruling of the court. These comments (called *dicta*), even if they represent the opinion of a majority of the court, must be recognized as such and not confused with the holding or rule of law of the court. For this reason it is necessary to read cases carefully and apply them only in terms of the *facts* of each case.

Appellate courts usually issue written opinions that are recorded in official reports. Decisions of the Supreme Court are officially recorded in the *United States Reports*, but this official printing takes a couple of years after a case has been decided. Thus, when new Supreme Court cases are cited, endnotes will reference those cases as printed in the *Supreme Court Reporter* or the *U.S. Law Week*.

Decisions of the Supreme Court are binding on all federal courts and on state courts where applicable; that is, where federal statutory or constitutional rights are involved.

Trial and Appellate Courts

It is important to distinguish trial and appellate courts. Both exist at the state and federal levels. Both are involved in making and interpreting the law, but it is generally said that trial courts try the facts of the case and appellate courts are concerned only with law, not facts. However, there are exceptions. Trial courts are the major fact finders in a case. The trial jury (or judge if the case is not tried to a jury) answers the basic question of fact: Was the accused guilty of the crime for which he or she is being tried? In making that finding, the jury will consider evidence presented by both the defense and the prosecution. Because the trial judge and jury hear and see the witnesses, it is assumed that they are in a better position than the appellate court to decide whether those witnesses are credible. Thus, it is argued, the appellate court should be confined to issues of law.

After the judge or jury has made a decision at the trial level, the defendant, if found guilty, may **appeal** that decision. In a criminal case, the defendant has a right of appeal, both in the state and in the federal court system, although he or she does not (except in a few specific cases) have the right to appeal to the highest court.

At the appellate level, the **appellant,** the defendant at trial, alleges errors in the trial court proceeding (for example, illegal confession admitted or minority groups excluded from the jury) and asks for a new trial. The **appellee,** the prosecution at trial, argues that errors either did not exist, or if they did exist, they did not prejudice the appellant, and therefore a new trial should not be granted.

On appeal, cases are heard by judges but not by juries. The appellate court looks at the trial court record, considers written briefs submitted by attorneys who use these briefs to establish and support their legal arguments, and hears oral arguments from counsel for the defense and the prosecution. It then determines whether there were any errors of law during the trial. The appellate court makes a ruling on those issues and either affirms the trial court ruling or sends the case back to the trial court for retrial. When the case is sent back for retrial, the appellate court is reversing and remanding the trial court on those issues. The appellate court also may affirm the trial court, in which case the finding of the trial court is upheld. It may reverse the case with prejudice, meaning that the case cannot be retried.

Appellate courts, in effect, are trying trial courts. This system allows the appellate courts to exercise some administrative control over trial courts, thus achieving more uniformity among courts than would otherwise exist. But trial court judges and juries exercise considerable power in the criminal justice system. Many cases are not appealed; in cases that are appealed and retried, the lower court often reaches the same decision as in the first trial.[2]

Prosecutors may also appeal on points of law, but the defendant may not be retried because of the constitutional provision against being tried twice for the same offense. However, the prosecutor who wins on appeal has a decision that may be of benefit in future trials.

Appellate courts also have the power of **judicial review** over acts of the legislative and executive branches of government, if those acts infringe on freedoms and liberties guaranteed by the state constitutions and by the Constitution of the United States. This power of judicial review represents the great authority of the courts. The Supreme Court has the power to declare acts of the president or of Congress unconstitutional.

The highest court of each state determines the constitutionality of that state's statutes in relation to its constitution. The Supreme Court is the final decision maker in the process of judicial review of the U.S. Constitution.

THE DUAL COURT SYSTEM

The United States has a dual court system consisting of state and federal courts, as indicated in Figure 8.1. State crimes are prosecuted in state courts. Federal crimes are tried in federal courts. State crimes are defined by state statutes. Federal crimes are defined by Congress.

Some acts violate both federal and state statutes, in which case the defendant may be tried in both courts. In this chapter's CJA, the armed robbery charges will probably be tried in a federal court since armed robbery of a bank is a federal offense if the bank is federally insured. It may also be a state offense. The other charges will be tried in local and state courts.

Lower federal courts and state courts constitute separate systems. Cases may not be appealed from a state court to a federal court except to

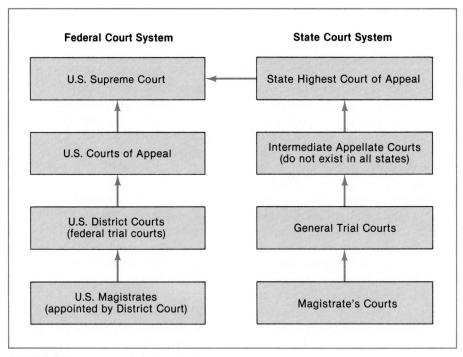

FIGURE 8.1
The United States Has a Dual Court System.

the U.S. Supreme Court and then only when a federal statutory or constitutional right is involved. Federal and state courts may hear only cases over which they have jurisdiction. Many of the cases brought in federal courts by state prisoners are appropriate to those courts because the inmates are alleging that federal rights have been violated.

A close look at the structure and organization of state and federal court systems will facilitate understanding of the subsequent discussions in this chapter, as well as the later discussions of pretrial and trial processes. The discussion begins with the state court systems since most criminal cases are tried in state and local courts.

State Courts

Considerable variation exists in the organization of state court systems. Diversity also exists within states, leading to problems that have prompted some states to move toward a unified court system. Despite the variety in systems, it is possible to make some general observations that will provide an overview of state court systems. This discussion focuses on courts that process criminal cases. The main aspects of the structure, function, and jurisdiction of state courts are summarized in Spotlight 8.1.

Courts of Limited Jurisdiction   In discussions about courts, frequent references are made to the lower courts. These are the courts of limited jurisdiction, so called because they are legally entitled to hear (that is, have jurisdiction over) only specific types of cases. Usually jurisdiction is limited to minor civil cases and criminal misdemeanors. But the jurisdiction over criminal cases also may be limited to certain kinds of misdemeanors, such as those that carry a jail or short prison term or some other less serious sanction. In this chapter's CJA, Stan might be tried for reckless driving in the same court that assesses his fine for speeding. Or the court that assesses the fine may not have jurisdiction over any of the other offenses.

Jurisdiction also may be limited to certain activities of the courts. The judges, often referred to as **magistrates,** presiding over these courts may conduct only certain pretrial procedures such as issuing warrants for searches or arrest, deciding bail, appointing counsel for defendants who are indigent, or presiding over the initial appearance or preliminary hearing.

Lower courts, which are called by various names, as indicated in Spotlight 8.1, should not be considered unimportant because of their limited jurisdiction. Subsequent chapters will indicate the importance of the pretrial procedures occurring in these lower courts. Certainly the power to grant or deny bail or some other method of pretrial release, rather than requiring the defendant to remain in jail, is a tremendous power.

Despite the importance of lower courts, these are the courts so frequently cited in criticisms. They are often underfinanced and staffed by part-time judges, who may be political appointees or elected officials in small towns where politics and courts are closely interrelated. In some cases, although the situation has improved in recent years, they are presided over by judges who are not legally qualified to render decisions.

SPOTLIGHT 8.1
STRUCTURE AND JURISDICTION OF STATE COURT SYSTEMS

COURT	STRUCTURE	JURISDICTION
Highest State Appellate Court (usually called the state supreme court)	Consists of five, seven, or nine justices who may be appointed or elected; cases decided by this court may not be appealed to the U.S. Supreme Court unless they involve a federal question, and then there is no right of appeal except in limited cases.	If there is no intermediate appellate court, defendants convicted in a general trial court will have a right of appeal to this court; if there is an intermediate appellate court, this court will have discretion to limit appeals with few exceptions such as in capital cases.
Intermediate Appellate Court (also called court of appeals; exists in approximately half of the states)	May have one court that hears appeals from all general trial courts; or may have more than one court, each with appellate jurisdiction over a particular area of the state. Usually has a panel of three judges.	Defendants convicted in general trial court have right of appeal to this level.
General Trial Courts (also called superior courts, circuit courts, district courts, court of common pleas)	Usually state is divided into judicial districts with one general trial court in each district, often one per county. Courts may be divided by function, such as civil, criminal, probate, domestic.	Jurisdiction to try cases usually begins where jurisdiction of lower court ends, so this court tries more serious cases. May also have appellate jurisdiction over cases decided in lower courts.
Courts of Limited Jurisdiction (also called magistrate's courts, police courts, justice of peace courts, municipal courts)	Differs from state to state; some states divide state into districts, with each having the same type of lower court. In other states, courts may be located in political subdivisions such as cities or townships, in which case the structure may differ from court to court. May not be a court of record, in which case the system will permit trial *de novo* in general trial court. Particularly in rural areas, magistrates may not be lawyers and may work only part-time.	May be limited to specific proceedings such as initial appearance, preliminary hearing, issuing search and arrest warrants, setting bail, appointing counsel for indigent defendants. Jurisdiction of cases is limited to certain types, usually the lesser criminal and civil cases. Some jurisdictions may hear all misdemeanors; others are limited to misdemeanors with minor penalties.

General Trial Courts General trial courts are also called by other names, as indicated in Spotlight 8.1. These courts usually have a wider geographic base than lower courts. In large areas, the general trial court may be divided by functions: traffic cases, domestic cases, civil cases excluding domestic and traffic cases, probate, estates and wills, and criminal. In the

CJA, for example, Stan might face speeding and reckless driving charges in traffic court and be tried in criminal court on the manslaughter charge. Smaller jurisdictions may have fewer divisions. A civil and a criminal division is one model frequently used.

The jurisdiction of general trial courts usually begins where the jurisdiction of the lower courts ends and includes the more serious cases. If the lower court is not a court of record, meaning that the court does not make provision for a transcript of the proceedings, a case appealed from the lower court to the general trial court may be tried *de novo*, which means that the case will be tried again. In that instance, the evidence will again be presented. Over time, however, evidence may be destroyed, and witnesses may die or forget. So the probability of being convicted when a case is tried *de novo* at this level may be less than the probability of conviction in the lower court.

Administrative Personnel in Trial Courts   Both of the court levels discussed thus far are at the trial level. Before considering state appellate courts, we must look briefly at the day-to-day operations of these trial courts. These procedures will also vary among jurisdictions.

The court clerk is the court officer charged by statute or court rules with the responsibility of maintaining all court records. The court clerk files the pleadings and motions and records any decisions made by the court. These are very important functions because judgments are not enforceable if they have not been properly filed. The court clerk will be assisted by a staff that in large jurisdictions may include a deputy for each of the court's divisions (such as traffic, probate, civil, and criminal). Various personnel also may be employed to handle the paperwork of the court.

The bailiff, perhaps best known for pronouncing "Hear ye, hear ye, this court of the Honorable Judge Smith is in session, all rise" prior to the judge's entry into the courtroom, has a variety of functions associated with keeping order. The bailiff may eject or otherwise discipline people who do not observe proper courtroom decorum. The bailiff may also transport defendants to and from the court, pass papers and exhibits to and from attorneys and the judge, run errands for the judge, and guard the jury room when deliberations are taking place. In some courts a deputy sheriff performs the functions of the bailiff. In the federal courts a deputy marshal may serve as bailiff.

In courts of record, a verbatim transcript of all proceedings will be kept by a court reporter. The transcript will not be transcribed unless parties request, in which case there will be a fee. If a criminal defendant is indigent, the state will pay for the transcript when it is required for an appeal. Court reporters may transcribe proceedings outside of court when attorneys are securing evidence for trial by questioning witnesses.

The minute clerk is an employee of the court who records an outline of what happens during the proceedings but does not maintain a verbatim transcript. The minute clerk might record the charges against the defendant, summarize the process of selecting the jury, perhaps note the time spent in that process, list the names of the jurors and alternates, summarize the evidence presented, and record the court's decision.

Intermediate Appellate Court   All states provide for at least one appeal from an adverse decision in a criminal trial, but only about half of the states have an intermediate appellate court, sometimes called a *court of appeals*. In states that have an intermediate appellate court, only one court may hear all appeals or courts in various districts may hear appeals from their respective geographical areas. Defendants who have been convicted in general trial courts have a right to appeal to this court where it exists. If it does not exist, they have a right of appeal to the highest court; but if the state has an intermediate appellate court, the defendant (except in capital cases) may not have a right to appeal to more than one appellate court. Thus, the defendant who loses an appeal in this court may have no other appeal unless he or she has other legal issues that might be raised, for example, in a federal court.

Highest State Appellate Court   If the state does not have an intermediate appellate court, cases may be appealed from the general trial courts to the highest court, which in most states is called the state supreme court. Justices of this court may be elected or appointed, and the court may have five, seven, or nine justices. In states with intermediate appellate courts, except in a few types of cases, the highest appellate court will have the power to limit the cases it will hear and decide. This court has the final decision on cases that involve legal issues pertaining to the constitution or statutes of the state in which the case is brought. If, however, the case involves any federal issues, the defendant may appeal to the U.S. Supreme Court, although that court hears only a limited number of the cases that petition it for review.

One final model of state appellate courts should be noted. Some states have two final appellate courts: one court makes the final decisions in criminal cases; the other makes final appellate decisions in civil cases.

The United States court system consists of both federal and state courts. (Barbara Rios/Photo Researchers)

Federal Courts

In the federal court system, U.S. magistrates, judicial officers appointed by the district court (as indicated in Figure 8.1), may have full jurisdiction over minor offenses along with jurisdiction over some of the pretrial steps of more serious offenses. The basic trial courts in the federal system are the United States district courts. These courts try cases in which individuals have been accused of violating federal criminal laws. They also try civil cases that meet specified criteria. Each state has at least one federal district court, and some states have several. In the federal district courts, cases are prosecuted by United States attorneys who are appointed by the president of the United States. The courts are presided over by appointed federal trial judges.

Cases appealed from federal district courts go to the appropriate intermediate federal appellate courts. These courts, referred to as *circuit courts*, are called the United States Court of Appeals for the First (Second, and so on) Judicial District. Figure 8.2 divides the country into the appropriate judicial circuits. For example, a case from a federal district court in Texas will be appealed to the United States Court of Appeals for the Fifth Circuit.

Decisions of the federal courts of appeals are not binding on state

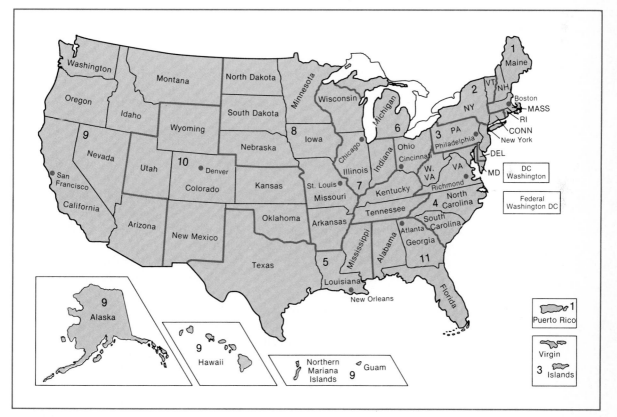

FIGURE 8.2
Federal Judicial Circuits. *Source:* West Publishing Company.

courts unless they involve federally created procedural rights that have been held to apply to the states or federally protected constitutional rights such as the right to counsel. The decision of one federal court of appeals is not binding on another court of appeals. The circuit courts may decide similar cases differently. The conflict may be resolved only by the U.S. Supreme Court, the final court of appeals in the federal system. The importance of that Court warrants a closer look.

THE UNITED STATES SUPREME COURT

The United States Supreme Court, traditionally held in high esteem, began its 1982 term with some of the most widespread criticism of its history. Three law professors, all former law clerks to Supreme Court justices, described the Court's opinions as mediocre, gobbledygook, and murky. One of the professors concluded that the biggest problem is that the Court just does not have many talented lawyers.[3] Six of the nine justices had already spoken out publicly about the problems of the Court, although they disagreed on the reasons as well as the solutions. Some blamed the delays in the court on the litigation explosion. Others argued that Congress had passed too many sloppy laws requiring Supreme Court interpretation. Others blamed the Court for mismanaging its own case docket.

In commenting on court delays, a *New York Times* editorial stated,

> More troubling than delay is the diminishing quality of the Court's final product. Wordy opinions ghost-written by law clerks get less and less editing by the harried jurists who sign their names to the prose. . . . [Yet, the *Times* concluded,] The High Court, despite generations of attack and controversy, remains one of the world's most trusted institutions.[4]

History and Purpose of the Court

The Supreme Court is the only court specifically established by the Constitution, which also gives Congress the power to establish "such inferior Courts as the Congress may from time to time ordain and establish." The Constitution further specifies a few cases in which the Supreme Court has original jurisdiction. The Court has appellate jurisdiction under such exceptions and regulations as determined by Congress. During the debates of the Constitutional Convention, it was recognized that the Supreme Court would have the power to review state court decisions when such decisions affected federal rights.

The basic function of the Supreme Court is to interpret federal laws and the U. S. Constitution. In fulfilling this function of judicial review, the Court is often accused of making law or of reshaping or changing the Constitution. In response to this allegation, constitutional law expert Paul A. Freund said, "Like a work of artistic creation, the constitution endures because it is capable of responding to the concerns, the needs, the aspirations of successive generations."[5]

If the Court is to interpret the Constitution according to the concerns, needs, and aspirations of the day, it will be subjected to criticism because these are issues on which reasonable minds differ. Technically, then, the Court does not make, but rather interprets, law. A former member of the Court said that the justices "breathe life, feeble or strong, into the inert pages of the Constitution and of statute books." One constitutional lawyer pointed out, however, that "it matters who does the breathing."[6]

Composition of the Court

Nine justices sit on the Supreme Court. Today the Court has eight male justices and one female, Sandra Day O'Connor, the first and only woman appointed to the Court. The Chief Justice presides over the Court. In the summer of 1986, Chief Justice Warren Burger announced his retirement. President Reagan nominated Associate Justice William H. Rehnquist as chief justice and Anthony Scalia as the new associate justice. Both were confirmed although there was active opposition to the promotion of Rehnquist.

In the summer of 1987 Associate Justice William A. Powell, 80, who was frequently the swing vote in the Court's 5–4 decisions, announced his retirement after 15½ years on the United States Supreme Court. Powell's departure gave President Ronald Reagan an opportunity to appoint a conservative to the Court, an act that many feared would swing the Court's decisions to a more conservative stance.

Reagan quickly nominated Judge Robert H. Bork, a strong conservative who was on the United States Court of Appeals for the District of Columbia. After one of the most bitterly fought (and expensive) confirmation battles, the Senate refused by a 58–42 vote to confirm Bork's nomination. In 1988 Judge Bork resigned his federal judgeship to devote his time to answering his critics, maintaining that much of the confirmation debate was based on false accusations.

President Reagan's earlier response to suggestions that the Senate might reject a conservative nominee was "And if I have to appoint another one, I'll try hard to find one that they'll object to just as much as they did to this one." He nominated Douglas H. Ginsburg, another conservative. Liberals promised another fight, but Ginsburg withdrew his nomination after admitting that on a few occasions in the 1960s (while he was a college student) and 1970s (while he was a Harvard law professor), he had smoked marijuana.

President Reagan's third appointment to fill the seat vacated by Justice Powell's retirement was Judge Anthony McLeod Kennedy, a federal appellate judge from California. Judge Kennedy's appointment was confirmed by a Senate vote of 97–0, and in February 1988 he took his seat on the U.S. Supreme Court, becoming the 104th justice on that Court. His confirmation brought the Court to full strength, but the Court had already conducted over one-half of its 1987–1988 term without a ninth justice.

Unlike Judge Bork, who had written numerous opinions on controversial subjects, Judge Kennedy's views on many sensitive issues were not known, leaving Supreme Court watchers to speculate as to whether Kennedy would provide the strong conservative vote President Reagan would like. But history shows that justices change over time, and efforts by the president to "pack the Court" are not always successful. Perhaps it was best said by Judge Bork's best friend, the late Professor Alexander M. Bickel of the Yale Law School:

> You shoot an arrow into the far-distant future when you appoint a Justice, and not the man himself can tell you what he will think about some of the problems that he will face.[7]

Operation of the Court

A case gets to the Supreme Court if the Court grants a **writ of certiorari** on an appealed case. A writ is an order from a court authorizing or ordering that an action be done. *Certiorari* literally means "to be informed of." When the Supreme Court grants a *writ of certiorari*, it is in effect agreeing to hear the case appealed from a lower court and ordering that court to produce the necessary documents for that appeal. If the Court denies *certiorari*, it is refusing to review the case. In those instances, the decision of the lower court stands.

Four of the justices must vote in favor of a writ in order for it to be granted. In an average term, the Court hears less than 4 percent of the cases filed. One of the obvious reasons for limiting the number of cases is

The nine U.S. Supreme Court Justices maintain offices, hear oral arguments, and conduct their conferences in the Supreme Court Building in Washington, D.C. (UPI Bettmann Newsphotos)

time. The justices hear oral arguments on many cases they accept for decisions, and they schedule approximately 1 hour per case for oral argument. They schedule oral arguments for 4 hours a day and 40 days during each term for a total of 160 hours.

The second reason the Court hears only a percentage of the cases filed was emphasized by a former chief justice of the Court:

> To remain effective, the Supreme Court must continue to decide only those cases which present questions whose resolution will have immediate importance far beyond the particular facts and parties involved.[8]

The Court often will hear cases when lower-court decisions on the issues in question have differed. The Court's decision becomes the final resolution of the issue, unless or until it is overruled by a subsequent Court decision, by a constitutional amendment, or in some cases, by Congressional legislation.

Cases that are accepted for review by the Supreme Court must be filed within a specified time before oral argument. The attorneys who argue before the Court are under a lot of pressure. They may be interrupted at any time by a justice's question. Attorneys are expected to argue their cases without reading from the prepared briefs. Each is limited to 30 minutes (sometimes an hour) for oral arguments, and the time limits are usually strictly enforced.

When it is in session, the Court hears arguments Monday through Thursday for two weeks of the month. On Friday, conference day, the justices discuss cases argued before them and decide which additional cases they will hear. A majority vote of the Court is needed for a decision in a case heard by the Court. If an even number of justices is sitting and there is a tie vote, the decision being appealed is affirmed.

The decision usually is announced in a written opinion, which often represents a majority opinion. **Concurring opinions** may be written by justices who voted with the majority but disagree with the reasons, agree with the decisions but for reasons other than those in the court's opinion, or agree with the Court's reasons but wish to emphasize or clarify one or more points. Thus, in some cases, the opinion of the Court may represent the views of only a plurality of the justices. Opinions concurring in part, dissenting in part, and dissenting entirely may also be written.

Judicial opinions are a very important part of the U. S. legal system. They are read carefully by lawyers, who use the arguments in future cases. The justices circulate among themselves drafts of their opinions, which are printed in secret and remain secret until the Court announces its decision in the case. In this way the entire Court participates in formulating an opinion; a written opinion is rarely the sole product of the justice whose name appears as writer. It is important to recognize that all justices are involved to some extent in all stages of all cases. The U.S. Supreme Court functions neither by committee nor by individual assignment.

Decisions of the Court are handed down on opinion days, which are usually three Mondays of each month of the term. The decisions then are public, and newspapers will pick up portions of the decisions thought to be of greatest interest.[9]

Suggestions for Improving the Efficiency of the Court

Various suggestions have been made for solving the problem of the over-load of cases heard by the Court. One recommendation is that the Court use summary procedures more frequently. In an increasing number of cases, the Supreme Court is responding with summary procedures, which means the Court acts on the case without hearing oral arguments or reading the briefs required for submission in cases heard before the Court. All the Court has before it in a summary procedure is the petition for hearing.

A second suggestion is the proposal for a National Court of Appeals that would have the function of choosing which cases would be heard by the Supreme Court. Justice John Paul Stevens has publicly supported this proposal, arguing that, by removing from the Court the time-consuming function of selecting which cases it should hear, the justices would be left more time for the important function of hearing and deciding cases.

Justice William J. Brennan, Jr., the senior member of the Court, who for years refused to acknowledge that the Court has too much work, responded that this proposal would "destroy the role of the Supreme Court as the framers envisaged it. . . . The screening function is second to none in importance." (Justice) Brennan concluded that if that role "were to be farmed out to another court, some enormous values of the Supreme Court decisional process would be lost."

Justice Brennan, however, supported the proposal of his colleague Justice Byron R. White that the Supreme Court reduce the frequency with which it hears conflicting cases from lower federal appeals courts. Brennan argues that the Court should not be expected to write more than the 150 opinions a year that is its current output: "There is a limit to human endurance." Justice White's suggestion is that a new appeals court be created. Unlike the current federal appellate courts, which have limited geographic jurisdiction, this one would have national jurisdiction and would hear cases in which the lower federal appeals courts have rendered conflicting decisions. The decisions of that new court could be appealed to the Supreme Court.[10]

Justice White also proposed that the Supreme Court limit appeals from federal appellate courts to those decisions that are decided by the lower court *en banc*, which means the case was decided by all of the judges on the court. Most of the cases in federal appellate courts are decided by a panel of three judges of the Court. Only a few are decided by all the judges on the court.[11]

A final suggestion relates to the Court's secrecy. When the justices have their conferences on Fridays, they begin by shaking hands. They then sit down and argue the cases, often voting more than once on a given case. No one else is permitted to hear these discussions. Many have argued for eliminating this secrecy on the U.S. Supreme Court. The popular book *The Brethren*[12] (published in 1979) was seen by some as an attempt to force the Court to become more open in its proceedings. Justice Lewis F. Powell, Jr., responded to the secrecy issue by emphasizing that the preparation of a final opinion may involve hours of discussion, drafting, more discussion, more drafts, and additional efforts to resolve differences among justices to the extent that is feasible. It is this unstructured and informal process . . . that simply cannot take place in public.

Powell further explained that

the integrity of judicial decision making would be impaired seriously if we had to reach our judgments in the atmosphere of an ongoing town meeting. There must be candid discussion, a willingness to consider arguments advanced by other justices, and a continuing examination and re-examination of one's own views. The confidentiality of this process assures that we will review carefully the soundness of our judgments. It also improves the quality of our written opinions.[13]

Despite criticisms of the Court, according to former Supreme Court Justice Robert Jackson,

The Supreme Court, whatever its defects, is still the most detached, dispassionate, and trustworthy custodian that our system affords for the translation of abstract into concrete constitutional commands.[14]

JUDGES IN THE CRIMINAL COURT SYSTEM

Judges historically have been held in high esteem by the U.S. public. Even when people have become disillusioned with the courts, their dissatisfaction usually has focused on the court as an institution, not on judges, who have continued to score high on occupational prestige scales.[15]

Recently, however, judges have come under severe criticism. In their decisions on pretrial release, they have been accused of releasing dangerous persons, who prey on the public, commit more crimes, and terrorize citizens. In their sentencing decisions, they have been accused of coddling criminals. Judges are easy scapegoats, and some critics are taking the opportunity to accuse judges of causing most of the critical problems in the handling of criminals in this country. Although some of the criticism is justified, much of it is not.

The Role of Judges in a Criminal Case

Judges begin their participation in the criminal justice system long before the trial occurs. After arrest, a suspect must be taken before a neutral magistrate who will determine whether there is probable cause to hold the suspect. Judges also determine when there is probable cause to issue a search warrant or an arrest warrant. They determine whether the accused will be released on bail or some other pretrial procedure or will be detained in jail awaiting trial.

Judges hear and rule on motions made by the defense and the prosecution before trial. They are the final decision makers for any plea bargain between the prosecution and the defense. Judges play a critical role

Judges preside over trials. Among other responsibilities, judges must make sure that attorneys observe the rules of evidence, the rights of defendants and victims, and that order is maintained in the courtroom. (Jerry Berndt/Stock Boston)

in the criminal trial. They also hear and rule on motions made after the trial and sentencing. Judges at the appellate level determine whether cases should be reversed or affirmed.

The Judge at Trial   At the trial, judges are referees. Theoretically they are neither for nor against a particular position or issue, but rather are committed to the fair implementation of the rules of evidence and law. They are charged with the responsibility of making sure that attorneys play by the rules of the game.

In the role of referee, the judge has tremendous power. For example, if the defense makes a motion to have some important evidence suppressed on the grounds that it was obtained illegally, the judge's decision whether to grant that motion might very well be the deciding factor in the case. Without the evidence, the prosecution may not be able to prove its case.

Although trial judges' decisions may be appealed, many are not. Many decisions that are appealed are not reversed, and even if the defense wins on appeal, considerable time has been lost—time that might have been spent by the accused in jail. Furthermore, the U.S. Supreme Court has emphasized that it is important to *prevent* problems at trial when possible and that responsibility of prevention lies with the trial judge.[16]

Another very important responsibility of the trial judge is to rule on whether expert testimony may be admitted. Many issues in criminal cases are beyond the common knowledge of judges; so it is necessary to submit expert testimony. There may be no problem in admitting the testimony of a physician who is to give information concerning the cause of death in a murder case.

It is more complicated, however, when attorneys wish to admit expert testimony on such defenses as the **battered woman's syndrome,** a new and highly controversial defense that presumes that prior beatings by her spouse (or another) produce violent reactions that lead the woman to murder the offending spouse. The trial judge must first decide whether there is sufficient scientific evidence on the defense to submit that to the jury. Some judges have allowed the defense; others refuse to allow experts to testify concerning the battered woman's syndrome. The judge who decides sufficient evidence exists to permit the defense must then determine whether the particular individual called by the defense or prosecution is qualified to testify regarding the defense.

A recent case illustrates the power of the trial judge in this regard. Defendant, convicted of second-degree murder, alleged on appeal that the trial court made a mistake in refusing to grant her request to be examined

Florida woman is arrested and handcuffed in a parking lot after she allegedly shot and killed her husband. After hearing evidence of the husband's previous physical abuse of his wife, the grand jury refused to indict her for his murder. Had the indictment been returned, her attorney planned to use the battered woman syndrome to argue that the wife killed in self defense. (Phil Coate/Tallahassee Democrat)

by a neurologist who could then testify at trial concerning whether defendant had postconcussion syndrome, which she argued, would mean she was not competent to stand trial. The appellate court upheld the trial court's ruling, as illustrated by this brief excerpt.[17]

State v. Hansen

The decision whether to appoint an expert is a matter within the discretion of the trial court and will not be reversed absent an abuse of discretion.

Dr. David's testimony [trial court granted defendant's request for an examination to determine whether she was competent to stand trial, by appointing two doctors to examine her] indicated that the presence of postconcussion syndrome was not highly probable. Moreover, the doctor indicated that even if the syndrome were present, Hansen would likely still be competent to stand trial. We refuse to adopt a rule that defendants are entitled to every psychiatric test imaginable regardless of possible result, and we find, following a review of the record, that the trial court did not abuse its discretion in denying Hansen's request for the appointment of a neurologist.

Another responsibility of the trial judge is to decide whether there is sufficient evidence to send the case to the jury for a decision on the facts being argued or whether the case should be dismissed for lack of evidence. Even if the judge sends the case to the jury and the jury finds the defendant guilty, the trial judge may reverse that decision if he or she believes the evidence is not sufficient to determine guilt beyond a reasonable doubt. This power is given to judges so they may serve as a check on jurors who might be too influenced by passion or prejudice despite the evidence in the case.

A judge may, after hearing the evidence in a case, also direct the jury to return a verdict of **acquittal.** This may be done even before the judge hears all the evidence. Once the verdict of acquittal has been entered, the defendant may not be retried on the same issue. To do so would violate the defendant's constitutional right not to be tried twice for the same offense.

In all of these and other activities at trial, not only the decision but also the demeanor and the attitude of the judge are important. The judge's behavior may not only influence the attitudes and decisions of jurors, witnesses, and victims at trial, but also the general public's image of the entire criminal justice system. The judge also has a tremendous influence over the flow of cases through the criminal courts. Poor management of the caseload will contribute to court congestion and risk impairing the rights of defendants to a fair and speedy trial.

The Judge at Sentencing   The role of the judge at sentencing and the effect of that decision has been stated concisely in a brief article on judicial sentencing:

The sentencing decision is probably the most important one made by a judge in a criminal case. By uttering a few words he determines whether a person will be free or imprisoned, and if the latter, for how long.[18]

Despite the tremendous importance of sentencing, until recently little attention was paid to preparing judges for this decision or to the importance of thorough presentence reports by probation or other officers of the court to assist judges in making the decision. Likewise, little attention was given to appellate review of judicial sentencing. The result has been alleged **sentence disparity** and considerable criticism from defendants, professionals in law and criminal justice, and the public.

Senator Edward M. Kennedy has called judicial sentencing a "national scandal,"[19] and investigators from Yale Law School, testifying before a congressional committee on their study on sentencing, said that "sentencing in the Federal courts is a judicial lottery marked by gross and shocking disparities."[20] A federal judge who is a frequent contributor to the literature on sentencing said that

A critical function of the judge occurs at the sentencing stage. (Wayne Miller/ Magnum)

> the almost wholly unchecked and sweeping powers we give to judges in the fashioning of sentences are terrifying and intolerable for a society that professes devotion to the rule of law.[21]

Empirical studies of judicial sentencing indicate that analyzing judicial sentencing differences is a complicated procedure.[22] Clearly, some of those differences result from a consideration of legally acceptable factors, such as prior record and nature of the current offense. Some of the differences may also be the result of unacceptable factors, such as sex, age, and race of defendants, as well as of the personality, background, and prejudices of the sentencing judges. It therefore is important, before concluding that judicial sentencing differences are unfair, unreasonable, or unconstitutional, to consider all the variables involved in the process of decision making.

To say that sentencing differences occur because judges have different socioeconomic backgrounds, different political beliefs, or even because some are men and some are women is not sufficient; for those variables may not be influential in determining sentencing differentials. The major problem in analyzing sentencing disparity, however, is the lack of an adequate measure of disparity. This chapter's CJA provides a typical example, with a 15-year sentence for Stan and a 2-year sentence for Joseph. Do you think the circumstances warrant the differential sentencing, or is this a case of sentencing disparity?

Differential sentencing is not necessarily explained by differences in judicial background, personality, sex, or any other characteristic of judges. There is empirical evidence that judicial sentencing decisions are significantly related to the recommendations made by probation officers. An analysis of the sentencing of adult felons in San Diego County, California, disclosed that the recommendations of probation officers are based on the severity of the offense charged, the extent of the prior record of the defendant, and the status of the defendant. Those recommendations almost always are accepted by judges with some slight modification on the basis of the defendant's status. The researchers concluded,

> If disparity across judges does exist, it seems likely that it does so because probation officers vary their recommendations across judges and not because different judges are influenced by different factors in their decisions.[23]

If this is true, we again see the interrelationship of the various elements and actors in the criminal justice system, a system that is complex and must be analyzed carefully before conclusions are drawn concerning solutions to its problems.

The sentencing decision is a difficult one; it may be impossible to achieve justice at this stage. As one judge concluded, "I am sure that I speak for my many colleagues when I state that the imposition of a criminal sentence is the most delicate, difficult, distasteful task for the trial judge."[24]

The Appellate Judge. Judges on appellate courts also have a tremendous responsibility. In those courts with the power to decide which cases they will hear, the judges (or justices, the term often used to refer to judges on the highest court of appeal in the state, as well as the Supreme Court of the United States) must decide whether to hear a case. If the judges refuse to hear a case that a defendant appeals, the lower-court decision will be upheld.

With the increasing number of cases on appeal, these decisions regarding which cases to hear are becoming even more critical. A refusal by the highest court of the state (or the Supreme Court) to hear and decide conflicting cases that come from various lower courts in their jurisdiction leaves the system with unanswered questions. Courts may continue to interpret the law differently, thus creating allegations that the law is not applied uniformly throughout the jurisdiction. On the other hand, appellate courts are facing more requests for appeals than they can adequately handle.

We already have noted that the decisions of trial judges may be reversed on appeal. But, as the excerpt from *State v. Hansen* indicates, appellate courts will not reverse trial courts unless they find "an abuse of discretion." Appellate courts usually defer to trial courts on issues in which the trial judge has an advantage because of his or her direct observation of the events that occurred at trial. This brief excerpt from a 1988 Colorado case illustrates this principle.[25]

People v. *McGuire*

Finally, we reject defendant's contention that the trial court abused its discretion in failing to grant a mistrial. During defense's closing argument, the complaining witness, in apparent responses to certain statements being made by defense counsel, audibly stated, "You're a liar." After arguments were concluded, defendant moved for a mistrial.

The right to a fair trial includes the right to a trial free from audience demonstrations which may contaminate or prejudicially affect the jury. However, a mistrial need be granted only in extraordinary circumstances to prevent any injustice. The decision to grant a mistrial should be left to the discretion of the trial court, which is best able to judge the effect of the claimed impropriety upon the jury.

We are in no position to second-guess the trial court upon the prejudice, if any, that occurred from this statement.

The fact that appellate judges infrequently overturn trial court decisions should not be implied to mean that the role of the appellate judge is not complicated and very important. Although appellate judges defer to trial judges on many issues, the most complicated and highly controversial issues often are decided at the appellate level. Nor is the role of an appellate judge devoid of problems, as indicated by Spotlight 8.2.

Appellate judges and justices frequently are faced with interpreting the laws and constitutions of their jurisdictions in ways that will have an effect on more than the parties before the court. In that respect, their decisions have a much wider effect than the decisions of trial courts. Their decisions, in contrast to those of trial court, usually are accompanied by written opinions, thus placing an even greater responsibility on judges to articulate why they decided a particular case in a particular way.

Selection, Training, and Retention of Judges

The first problem in deciding how to select, train, and retain judges is to decide what general qualities are wanted for judges. Oliver Wendell Holmes, former justice of the United States Supreme Court, said that judges should be a combination of Justinian, Jesus Christ, and John Marshall (a distinguished chief justice of the Supreme Court). Even Holmes recognized, however, that it would be extremely difficult, if not impossible, to find such persons.

SPOTLIGHT 8.2
THE APPELLATE JUDGE: A BRIEF VIEW FROM INSIDE

Patricia M. Wald, chief judge of the United States Court of Appeals for the District of Columbia, gives her view of the appellate judge's role, in this comment.

Appeals court judges are a bit like monks or conjugal partners locked into a compulsory and often uneasy collegiality, destined to spend their working lives dissecting each other's logic and syntax, constrained from many of the social and political diversions that make life tolerable for the rest of society, with only one chance to explain ourselves on paper and no defense after that, required in good conscience to decide hard questions we would just as soon not . . .

Source: Quoted in *American Bar Association Journal* (1 June 1988), p. 34.

Historically, judges have been white, male, and Protestant, with conservative backgrounds. Only recently have more women and minorities joined the judiciary, and many would agree, as Spotlight 8.3 indicates, that women and minorities represent values and viewpoints important to the judiciary.

Judges should be impartial and fair. They should be able to approach a case with an objective and open mind concerning the facts. Such objectivity will enable the judge to be fair, to insist that attorneys play by the rules of the game, and to see that due process is not violated. Judges should be well educated in the substantive law and in procedural rules and evidence. Judges should be able to think and write clearly. Their opinions are of great importance to attorneys and other judges, who use them to analyze how future cases might be argued and decided. Judges should have high moral standards, enabling them to withstand political and economic pressures that might influence decisions. They should be in good physical, mental, and emotional health. They should be good managers, since judges have considerable power over the management of the court system. They should be able to assume power sensibly, without abuse, and to exercise leadership in social reform where necessary and desirable.[26]

Irving R. Kaufman, a federal judge on the second circuit, wrote an

SPOTLIGHT 8.3
FEMALE AND MINORITY JUDGES

Historically, women were considered neither suitable nor capable to hold judgeships. As a justice of the Wisconsin Supreme Court said in 1875,

Our profession has essentially and habitually to do with all that is selfish and extortionate, knavish and criminal, coarse and brutal, repulsive and obscene. Nature has tempered women as little for the judicial conflicts of the courtroom as for the physical conflicts of the battlefield.[1]

Recently the demographic composition of the judiciary has changed. In 1981 Sandra Day O'Connor became the first woman to be nominated and confirmed as a member of the United States Supreme Court. In 1979 female judges organized the National Association of Women Judges.

Despite the appointment of Justice O'Connor and other women to the bench, women still represent only a small percentage of judges. They hold only 5 percent of the federal judgeships, and over one-third of the states have not yet named a woman to their appellate benches. Furthermore, female judges

have faced problems. At the fourth annual convention of the National Association of Women Judges, women indicated that they are often lonely in their positions and that they are still excluded from some all-male clubs where judges and attorneys meet for social occasions. Some believe that they have little influence in court administration and policy making, and limited influence and power in their bar associations. Some expressed dissatisfaction with what they call tokenism at both the state and federal levels, and strongly criticized the Reagan administration for appointing so few women judges when there are over 50,000 women practicing law in this country.[2] The women also complained that they receive less glamorous assignments than their male colleagues, "and are subjected to standards that are both stricter and sillier than those applied to men."[3]

Does it make a difference whether there are female judges? How are they treated? Some female judges and attorneys claim that women judges have

[1]Quoted in "Women Find Bar to Bench a Far Journey," *New York Times* (17 October 1982), p. EY15. The historical information on women as judges also comes from this article.

[2]"Some Problems Shared by Women on the Bench," *New York Times* (11 October 1982), p. 16.
[3]"Women Find Bar to Bench a Far Journey."

open letter to President Reagan shortly after Reagan's election. Kaufman addressed the issue of the qualities and characteristics that should be considered in the selection of federal judges, but his suggestions also are applicable to state and local judges. Regarding judicial temperament, Judge Kaufman noted that the word *temperament* is most often applied to judges and pedigreed dogs! But in seeking a definition of what it means for dogs, he offers us some understanding of what it means for judges: "The ideal canine temperament is a mixture of quiet dignity and an obedience that is not blind but exhibits character when the situation requires."

According to Kaufman, a

> judge's comportment must at all times square with the ideals of justice and impartiality that the public projects on us in our symbolic role. A judge must be reflective, perhaps even a bit grave, but must always demonstrate an openness consistent with our tradition of giving each side its say before a decision is rendered.

It is also important, says Kaufman, that a judge be able to "separate the dignity of the office from a sense of self-importance."[27]

greater sensitivity to the women who practice before the bar, as well as to female witnesses and victims. Women lawyers often complain that they are put down in various ways by men attorneys and judges, who make comments about their clothing or appearance in an attempt to distract the jury, referring to the women by their first names or as "sweetie" or "honey," all of which are unprofessional and unacceptable in the courtroom. This kind of conduct may not seem important to some, especially to those who have never been treated in this manner. But the differential treatment does send a message to the jury; the female witness is discredited in her testimony, and the professional competency of the female attorney is questioned.

It is argued that female judges have greater sensitivity to certain issues such as child support payments to mothers who are alone caring for their children, and to the problems of victims of rape and domestic abuse.

A strong argument may also be made for the necessity of having minority judges, although until recently little attention was paid to this need or, for that matter, the need for minority attorneys. Minority enrollments in law schools, however, are increasing, and minorities are becoming visible in the judiciary, although at a very slow pace.

In addition to the problem of the small number of minority attorneys and judges, problems are associated with the quality of legal education and legal experience available to minorities. Minorities generally have not been graduates of the best law schools; they do not practice with the big firms. In the past, they have been excluded from various state and local bar associations, and from memberships in country and business clubs where they could make important contacts. Minority lawyers and judges have encountered other problems. They have been criticized for becoming too preoccupied with their own status to provide adequate representation for the everyday needs of minorities.

Does it make a difference whether there are minorities on the bench? Some studies have shown that comparisons of decision making of minority judges with the decisions of nonminority judges do not reveal significant differences. But that is not the only point. Minorities should be recruited to the judiciary because they, too, deserve an opportunity to enter that profession. Likewise, minorities on the bench may serve a very important symbolic function to the people who appear before those judges, as well as to the general public.

Minorities are still underrepresented among judges, but some progress has been made. (Susan Lapides/Design Conceptions)

Selecting Judges Several methods have been used historically for selecting judges in the United States. During the colonial period, judges were appointed by the king, but after the Revolution, this practice ceased. In a majority of the colonies, judges were appointed by the legislators; in some, the appointment was made by the governor, with or without the required approval of his council, depending on the colony.[28]

As the colonies became states, they gradually began to select judges by popular election, but that method also quickly came under criticism, with frequent allegations of political control of judges leading in many cases to the selection of incompetent judges and corruption.

The merit plan for selecting judges is traced to Albert M. Kales, one of the founders of the American Judicature Society. The first state to adopt the merit plan was Missouri in 1940. This method is frequently referred to as the *Missouri Plan*, or, less commonly, the *Kales plan*, or the *commission plan*.

Merit selection plans vary extensively from state to state, but most plans include a nonpartisan commission that actively solicits, investigates, and screens candidates when judicial openings occur. A select number of names (usually three to five) will then be sent to the executive and an appointment made by that branch. The judge may then serve a probationary period (usually a year) and then may be required to run unopposed on a general election retention ballot. Voters are polled with a yes or no vote to decide whether this judge should be retained in office. A judge who receives a majority of votes (which is usually the case) will be retained. A merit selection plan does not assure that politics will not enter into the selection process, but the prescreening by a nonpartisan commission arguably places only qualified candidates in a position for election. However, criticisms remain, and politics plays an important role.

Earlier in the chapter the opposition to Supreme Court nominee Bork was mentioned. Allegedly politics was the main reason Chief Justice Rose Bird of the California Supreme Court was defeated in 1986. Bird was publicly denounced by the governor; she and two of her colleagues on the California Supreme Court were the first California appellate judges to lose a retention election. Although theirs was the most publicized election, two other state chief justices lost their positions in highly publicized elections in 1986: Chief Justice Rhoda Billings of North Carolina and Chief Justice Frank Celebrezze of Ohio.

The defeat of these justices raises the question of what role public opinion should be permitted to play in the selection or retention of judges. The California justices were ousted mainly for their opposition to capital punishment. But, if judges and justices must be responsive to public opinion, they lose their objectivity. On the other hand, when the legislature has enacted a capital punishment statute, it is arguable that the justices should support the enforcement of that statute unless they find it to be unconstitutional.

In an effort to avoid public pressures on judicial decision making, federal judges are appointed and essentially hold their jobs for life. Technically they are appointed by the president of the United States and confirmed by the Senate, but in reality the recommendations to the president often are made by the attorney general or the deputy attorney general, and the president accepts those recommendations. Members of the House and Senate often are very influential in nominating these judges, although the Justice Department also consults bar associations such as the American Bar Association. The constitutional provision for the appointment of federal judges and justices has been interpreted to mean that these judges and justices hold their appointments for life. They may be removed only for bad behavior, but that is seldom done.

Training of Judges   The United States does not have required formal training for most judges, although training is required in other countries such as England, France, and Japan. Many of our judges have not had formal training, have had limited experience as attorneys when they become judges, and have had no experience in the practice of criminal law. In some states local judges are not even required to be attorneys, although federal judges must be.

Despite the lack of a requirement for judicial training in order to be eligible to become a judge, we are making progress in providing training programs for newly appointed or elected judges. Most states now provide some kind of training program, and many are offering continuing education courses for judges in order to provide them with up-to-date training.[29]

Retention of Judges   Recruiting the right kind of attorneys and then giving them proper training in the judiciary is important, but retention of our best judges is becoming a serious problem. In the past a judicial appointment, especially to the federal bench, was the ultimate aim of many lawyers. But the increasing number of resignations of federal judges has led some to refer to the "revolving door" of the federal judiciary, with good candidates accepting appointment, staying a few years, and then leaving. For those who do stay, morale is affected as they realize the substantial cut they take in income by leaving private practice to accept an appointment to the bench.

Judicial salaries vary significantly from state to state. Although they are generally higher at the federal level, the level of compensation of federal judges was described by Judge Irving R. Kaufman in his open letter to President Reagan: "And as you know, we receive for our services little more than those fresh-faced lads a few years out of Harvard at the larger New York firms."[30] Salaries of federal judges were increased in 1987, although the increase was considerably lower than that recommended by the commission studying the issue, with the result that "U.S. judges [are] leaving the bench in record numbers to return to more lucrative private practices."[31] A congressional attempt to raise salaries in 1988 was unsuccessful.

Added to the problems of low pay and heavy workloads is the stress that judges may expect to experience. Judges deal with issues that are very important and highly controversial but issues that must be decided. As Judge Kaufman said, "Much tension accompanies the job of deciding the questions that all the rest of the social matrix has found too hard to answer."[32]

A clinical psychologist who studied stress extensively reports that judges are less likely than other professionals to express fatigue, uncertainty, temporary depression, and other signs of stress, for to do so might diminish their images in the eyes of others. Consequently, when judges face severe stress, they do not pick up the warning signs as quickly as other people. In addition, judges face several stressors not common to other professions. There is a lonely transition from the practice of law to a profession about which they may know very little except as outside observers. Usually at the peak of their legal careers when they become judges, they must give up many of their positions and even their friendships.

Judicial stress also may be caused by the code of judicial conduct requirement that judges divest themselves of contacts that might compromise their judicial decisions. Positions on the board of directors of corporations must usually be resigned. Their associations with practicing attorneys must be restricted, for they cannot discuss cases with attorneys outside of judicial proceedings, and even there, discussions are limited.[33]

Despite the stress and the relatively low salaries, many judges still say they enjoy their work, find it challenging, and wish to remain. Before his death in 1982, Justice Matthew Tobriner of the California Supreme Court, described by the governor of that state as "one of the most distinguished state court judges in the nation," called his 19 years of experience on the court "the greatest experience of my life."[34]

Control of Judges   At the opposite extreme of the problem of how to retain good judges is the delicate problem of how to get rid of bad ones. Like all professions, the judiciary is characterized by some who fall below the line in their professional and personal lives. Their shortcomings may significantly affect their abilities to function effectively as judges. Although the sexual behavior of adults may be considered their private business, the public considers it their business when judges engage in questionable sexual behavior. Excessive drinking may be tolerated in some circles, but excessive drinking by a judge, particularly if charged with driving while intoxicated, is another matter.

Language that may be acceptable in some circumstances might constitute cause for removal of a judge. A California judge was censured by the state judicial commission because of his use of racial slurs and his habit of beginning the court session with such comments as "Well, bring in the criminals." Such conduct, said the commission, is "prejudicial to the administration of justice and brings the judicial office into disrepute."[35]

Perhaps the most publicized comments of judges are those made by male judges who comment unfavorably on victims of alleged sexual abuse. A Wisconsin judge called a 5-year-old girl sexually promiscuous after she was allegedly molested by the man who lived with her mother. Angered citizens tried unsuccessfully to unseat him in a recall election. One of his colleagues, however, was unseated by citizens who were irate at his comment when a 15-year-old was accused of raping an 11-year-old coed in a high school stairwell. The judge said that whether women like it or not, they are sex objects. He admonished women to quit dressing in provocative clothing, suggesting that they are asking for what they get.

But how do we control such activities of judges? It is not easy to unseat judges, even after they have been convicted of a crime. They usually are asked to resign, but if they do not do so, it may take a lot of time to go through disciplinary channels to unseat them. Elected judges may be unseated by a recall vote. When judges are appointed, however, the process is more difficult.

California provides one example of a system for overseeing the behavior of the judiciary. The California Commission on Judicial Performance investigates complaints of misconduct and makes recommendations to the supreme court of the state. Various forms of discipline may be recommended, including removal of the judge from office. The commission declared an 82-year-old justice senile and unable to perform his judicial duties. The justice had engaged in behavior that indicated his inability to continue effectively in his position as a justice of the state supreme court. He would sit in court with an impassive glazed look, leave the bench to make personal phone calls or to check on the weather, fall asleep during oral arguments, and forget what action the court had recently taken. He was an example of a man who had performed in an exemplary manner for most of his career, but his mental and physical abilities had deteriorated because of age.[36] This justice was forced to retire, a procedure that, in contrast to removal, allowed him to retain his retirement pension.

At the federal level, where judges serve for life and can only be removed by impeachment, legislation provides some avenues for disciplining judges. The Judicial Councils and the Judicial Conduct and Disability Act of 1980 provide for several sanctions: certify disability, request the judge to retire, strip the judge of caseload "on a temporary basis," and censure or reprimand privately or publicly.[37]

CRISIS IN THE COURTS

Numerous problems exist in our criminal courts, some of which have been mentioned in the discussions in this chapter. But by far the most serious problem is the pressure placed on courts, on defendants, and on society by the increased numbers of cases tried and appealed. This increase has led to a crisis in our courts and the crisis continues despite the addition of more judges to the system.

Court Congestion

The number of federal judges has increased by 43 percent since 1970. But, despite this 43 percent increase, courts are still overcrowded. Between 1970 and 1986 the number of civil cases increased by 192 percent and between 1980 and 1986 by 51 percent. Since federal courts hear civil and criminal cases, this tremendous increase in civil cases also affects criminal cases.[38] The increase in cases filed has created a large backlog of cases in federal courts. Figure 8.3 indicates the number of cases, both civil and criminal, pending for specific time periods.

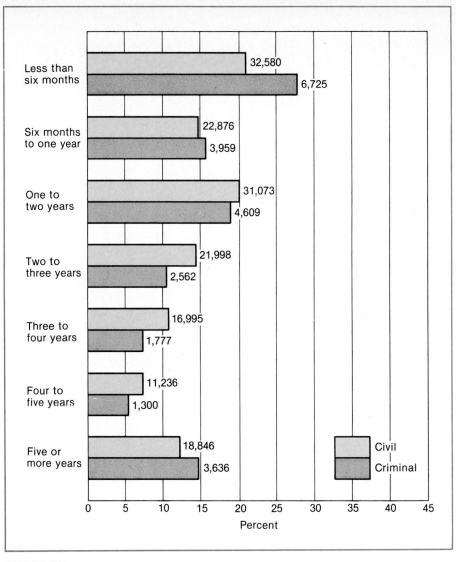

FIGURE 8.3
Age of Criminal and Civil Cases Pending in United States Attorneys' Offices. *Source: Statistical Report, United States Attorney's Office, Fiscal Year 1987* (Washington, D.C.: U.S. Department of Justice, 1988).
Note: Data as of September 30, 1987
       Total Cases: Criminal 24,586
                        Civil   155,584
       The figures do not include appeals.

Court congestion also exists at the appellate levels, both state and federal. Appellate filings in state courts have increased even faster than trial court filings, as Figure 8.4 indicates. The state court appellate workload increase in the past decade has surpassed the workload growth in most other components of the criminal justice system.

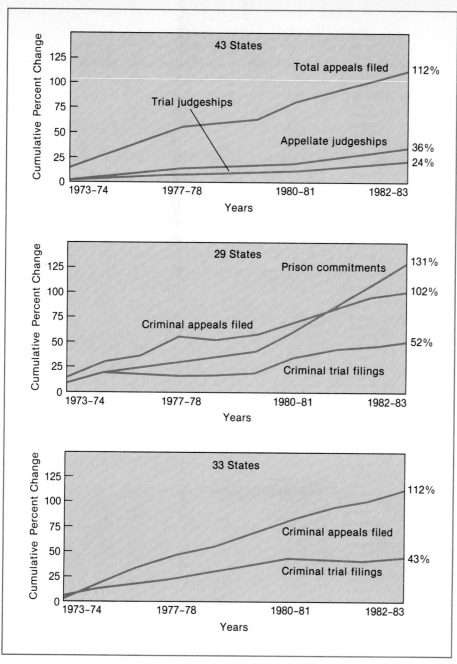

FIGURE 8.4
Cumulative Growth in Appeals Filed Compared to Other Factors, 1973–1983. *Source:*
Bureau of Justice Statistics, *The Growth of Appeals* (Washington, D.C.: U.S.
Department of Justice, February 1985), p. 3.

The rapid increase in court caseloads has raised serious questions as to
whether public safety is jeopardized when the outcome of criminal cases
can be delayed for many months and whether justice is being served when
it can take years to resolve a civil court case.[39]

Court congestion results in delayed trials. It has been argued that justice delayed is justice denied. That concept is based on the belief that when a trial is delayed, there is a greater chance for error. Witnesses may die or forget. Crowded court dockets also have created pressures that encourage plea bargaining and mass handling of some cases. Delayed trials also may deny defendants their constitutional right to a speedy trial.

For the accused who are not released before trial, court congestion may mean a long jail term in already overcrowded facilities. Because their court-appointed attorneys are so busy with other trial cases, defendants may not see them during that period. The accused are left with many questions, no answers, and a long wait, often under inhumane conditions in local jails. Those who are incarcerated before trial face more obstacles in preparation for trial.

Obvious injustices are created by an overworked court that must quickly decide cases presented by overworked prosecutors and defense attorneys. The image of inefficiency and injustice that the crowded court dockets and delayed trials project to the public colors their image of the entire legal system.[40]

There are many causes of court delays. One is the use of **continuances,** or postponements. The purpose of granting continuances is to guarantee a fair hearing. The defense or the prosecution may need more time to prepare; additional evidence may have come to light and need evaluating; additional witnesses may need to be located. But too often continuances are used by defense attorneys to collect their fees. They know that fees are difficult to collect after the trial. Defense attorneys therefore may tell clients that they will not go to trial until attorney fees are paid and then ask the court for a continuance.[41]

A second reason for congestion in criminal courts is that courts must

Court congestion today threatens the quality of court services. (Bill Bachman/ Photo Researchers)

handle some cases that, as was discussed in Chapter 1 of this text, perhaps should be processed in some other way. The criminal law is used in an effort to control behaviors, such as some types of alcohol and drug abuse, consenting sexual behavior between adults, prostitution, and gambling. This is not to suggest that we should not be concerned with these activities but only to question the reasonableness of using the criminal court for their regulation. Removal of some or all of these actions from the criminal court system would greatly reduce the number of cases in those courts.

Many suggestions have been made for solving the congestion of courts. First, as just mentioned, is to reduce the number of offenses covered by the criminal law. Building new court facilities and expanding the number of judges, prosecutors, defense attorneys, and support staff is another possible solution. Better management of court proceedings and court dockets is another. Some courts are using computers to speed up the paperwork. Other courts have been reorganized for greater efficiency.[42]

Alternatives to courts is another suggestion, based on the assumption that in many cases courts could be avoided. Although most of the alternatives, such as arbitration and mediation, apply primarily to civil cases, some can be used in criminal cases.[43] The expanded use of plea bargaining, whereby defense and prosecution reach an agreement out of court, is an example. This practice is used frequently and will be discussed in a subsequent chapter, along with the controversy that surrounds its use.

The director of the National Center for State Courts, however, has concluded that congestion and delays in court will not be solved by computerizing court calendars or by adding judges or courts, but only by changing the culture of lawyers: "Lawyers and judges will set the pace that suits them. Computerized docket controls may expedite some proceedings, but leisurely judges will not be hurried."[44]

The costs of these proposals must also be evaluated. We are not talking only about the cost of increasing the judiciary, estimated to take less than 2 percent of the average state budget. Expanding courts and increasing the number of judges involves both the direct cost of the expansions along with support staff and an increase in the number of prosecutors, defense attorneys, courtrooms, other facilities, and police and correctional personnel and facilities.

SUMMARY

An understanding of the nature and structure of the criminal court system is necessary for a study of the activities taking place within that system. Terminology also is important. If a court does not have jurisdiction, it cannot hear and decide the case. Cases must be brought before the proper court. Which court is proper may be determined by the seriousness of the offense, the type of offense, or both. Some courts may hear only criminal cases. Some may hear only petty offenses or misdemeanors whereas others hear only felony cases.

Trial courts base their decisions on *facts* that will or will not establish whether the defendant committed the alleged crime act or acts. Appellate courts usually are concerned only with questions of law. They ask, "During the trial, did the trial court commit any serious errors in law, such as the admission of evidence that should have been excluded?" If so, the case will be reversed and sent back for retrial. The appellate court might find less serious errors in law and not reverse the case.

Criminal cases may be appealed but not necessarily to the highest court. Cases in the state system may not be appealed to the lower federal appellate courts. If a federal constitutional right is involved in a state case, the Supreme Court of the United States may hear that case. Cases decided in state courts must be followed in the states in which they are decided. Thus, a California Supreme Court case is not binding on courts in Texas. Likewise, the decisions of a federal appellate court in California are not binding on other federal courts; nor are they binding on state courts in California.

Decisions on one level or jurisdiction may be used by other courts as reasons for their decisions if the judges choose to do so. Decisions of the U.S. Supreme Court are binding on state and lower federal courts. But, because the Supreme Court hears only a few of the cases it is asked to hear, many issues remain unsettled, for courts in different jurisdictions decide similar cases differently.

The primary figure in court efficiency and administration is the judge. Despite the importance of judges in the U.S. system, many who become judges are not specifically trained in judicial decision making or trial and appellate procedures. Some have had limited experience as trial lawyers. Yet, they are given vast powers in the criminal justice system. Most perform admirably; some need to be disciplined or removed, but the system is not very well equipped for that process.

Today courts often are criticized as being in a state of crisis because of the large backlog of cases, criminal and civil, at both the trial and the appellate levels. Some steps must be taken to reduce this backlog of cases; lawyers and judges have a great responsibility to solve this problem. But the role of the public also is important.

Significant changes cannot be made in the court system without the support, especially financial, of the public. It is imperative for us to realize that changes must be made in all areas of the criminal justice system. Significant changes in the courts will have an effect on the other elements of the system. If we create more courts so we can try, convict, and sentence more people to prisons and do not build sufficient and adequate facilities to accommodate that increase, we merely push the problems from one area of the system to another. Courts must be analyzed and altered in the total social context in which they operate.

STUDY QUESTIONS

1. What is meant by *jurisdiction*? How does it apply to the dual court system?

2. What is the difference between trial and appellate courts?

3. What is the relationship between state and federal courts?

4. What are the levels of courts in each of the two main court systems, state and federal?

5. How does a case get to the U.S. Supreme Court? What happens to a case that is appealed to that Court but not accepted by it? What changes would you suggest in the operation of the Supreme Court in order to handle the increasing workload it faces?

6. What do you think about the activities that surrounded President Reagan's last three nominations to the U.S. Supreme Court: Judges Bork, Ginsburg, and Kennedy?

7. What are the main roles of judges in trial courts? In appellate courts?

8. How are judges and justices selected? What are the advantages and disadvantages of each method?

9. Should an effort be made to recruit more female and minority judges? Why or why not? What methods would you suggest if you think more should be recruited?

10. What actions do you think should be sufficient to disqualify a person for a state judgeship? A federal judgeship? Appointment to the U.S. Supreme Court?

11. Would your answers to Question 10 differ if the issue were retention rather than appointment?

12. To what extent, if any, should public opinion be permitted to influence judicial appointment? Judicial retention?

13. How would you suggest that the current caseload crisis in trial courts be resolved?

ENDNOTES

1. This study was commissioned by the National Center for State Courts, and the results are summarized by Edward B. McConnell, director of that organization, in "Why People Today Distrust the Courts," *The Judges' Journal* 17 (Summer 1978): 12–16.

2. For a discussion of the purposes of appeal, as well as a comparison of our appellate system with other types, see Martin Shapiro, *Courts: A Comparative and Political Analysis* (Chicago: University of Chicago Press, 1981), pp. 49–64.

3. "Supreme Court Dissension," *Tulsa World* (3 October 1982), Sec. 1, p. 1, quoting William Van Alystyne of Duke University, Thomas Krattenmaker of Georgetown University, and A. E. Dick Howard of the University of Virginia.

4. "Supreme Court Blues," *New York Times* (4 October 1982), p. 18.

5. Paul A. Freund, *On Law and Justice* (Cambridge, Mass.: Harvard University Press, 1986), p. 54.

6. "Court at the Crossroads," *Time* (8 October 1984), p. 28, referring to a remark by Floyd Abrams in response to the earlier remark by former U.S. Supreme Court Justice Felix Frankfurter.

7. Quoted by Stuart Taylor, Jr., "Which Way Will Kennedy Tilt the Bench?" *New York Times* (7 February 1988), p. 4.

8. Chief Justice Fred M. Vinson, quoted in Ronald L. Carlson, *Criminal Justice Procedure*, 2d ed. (Cincinnati: W. H. Anderson, 1978), p. 243.

9. For more information on how the Supreme Court operates, see the recently published account by the chief justice, William Rehnquist, *The Supreme Court: How It Is. How It Was* (New York: William Morrow and Co., 1987), reviewed by noted constitutional law professor Laurence H. Tribe, in the 1 October 1987 issue of the *American Bar Association Journal*, pp. 142–43.

10. "Brennan Faults Stevens Bid on New Court to Cut Work," *New York Times* (10 September 1982), p. 11; "The Supreme Court: Justices Speaking Out on Reducing Their Caseload," *New York Times* (14 September 1982), editorial page.

11. See Richard A. Posner, *The Federal Courts: Crisis and Reform* (Cambridge, Mass.: Harvard University Press, 1985).

12. Bob Woodward and Scott Armstrong, *The Brethren: Inside the Supreme Court* (New York: Simon and Schuster, 1979).

13. Lewis F. Powell, Jr., "What Really Goes on at the Supreme Court?" *American Bar Association Journal* 66 (June 1980): 722.

14. Robert H. Jackson, "The Supreme Court as a Unit of Government," in Alan F. Westin, ed., *The Supreme Court: Views from Inside* (New York: W. W. Norton and Co., 1961), p. 80.

15. See James Willard Hurst, "The Functions of Courts in the United States, 1950–1980," *Law and Society Review* 15 (1980–81): 401–71.

16. See, for example, Sheppard v. Maxwell, 384 U.S. 333 (1966).

17. State v. Hansen, 751 P. 2d 951, 956 (Ariz. 1988), case citations omitted.

18. Marvin E. Aspen, "Sentencing: Judicial Function," in Sanford H. Kadish, ed., *Encyclopedia of Crime and Justice* (New York: Free Press, 1983), vol. 4, p. 1464.

19. Edward M. Kennedy, "Justice in Sentencing," *New York Times* (29 July 1977), p. A21.

20. "U.S. Court Sentencing Called Judicial Lottery," *New York Times* (10 June 1977), p. A28.

21. Marvin E. Frankel, *Criminal Sentences: Law without Order* (New York: Hill and Wang, 1973), p. 5.

22. For a review of the earlier studies, see Glendon Schubert, ed., *Judicial Decision-Making* (New York: Free Press, 1963) and A. Keith Bottomley, *Decisions in the Penal Process* (Toronto: University of Toronto Press, in association with the Centre of Criminology, University of Toronto, 1971). For more recent evidence, see Peter J. Van Koopen and Jan Ten Kate, "Individual Differences in Judicial Behavior: Personal Characteristics and Private Law Decision-Making," *Law and Society Review* 18, no. 2 (1984): 225–47.

23. Ebbe B. Ebbesen and Vladimir J. Koneeni, "The Process of Sentencing Adult Felons: A Causal

Analysis of Judicial Decisions," Chapter 12 in Bruce Dennis Sales, ed., *The Trial Process* (New York: Plenum Press, 1981): 446–47. See also Charles E. Frazier and E. Wilbur Bock, "Effects of Court Officials on Sentence Severity: Do Judges Make a Difference?" *Criminology* 20 (August 1982): 267–70.

24. United States v. Wiley, 184 F. Supp. 679 (D. Ill. 1960).

25. People v. McGuire, 751 P. 2d 1011, 1013 (Colo. App. 1987), case citations omitted.

26. For a more detailed discussion of these qualities, see Sheldon Goldman, "Judicial Selection and the Qualities that Make a 'Good' Judge," *The Annals of the American Academy of Political and Social Sciences* 462 (July 1982): 113–14.

27. Irving R. Kaufman, "An Open Letter to President Reagan on Judge Picking," *American Bar Association Journal* 67 (April 1981): 443.

28. For a brief history of the process of judicial selection, see Larry C. Berkson, "Judicial Selection in the United States: A Special Report," *Judicature* 64 (October 1980): 176–93.

29. For a recent analysis of the extent and nature of judges who are not legally trained, see Doris Marie Provine, *Judging Credentials: Nonlawyer Judges and the Politics of Professionalism* (Chicago: University of Chicago Press, 1986), reviewed by John H. Culver in *Justice Quarterly* 4 (March 1987): 159–62.

30. Irving R. Kaufman, "An Open Letter to President Reagan on Judge Picking," p. 444.

31. Gary A. Hengstler, "U.S. Judges Get Pay Increases," *American Bar Association Journal* (1 April 1987): 30.

32. "By and Large We Succeed," *Time* (5 May 1980), p. 70.

33. Isaiah M. Zimmerman, "Stress: What It Does to Judges and How It Can Be Lessened," *The Judges' Journal* 20 (Summer 1981): 4–9, 48–49.

34. *New York Times* (9 April 1982).

35. "Judge Faces Censure for Ethnic, Racial Remarks," *Los Angeles Times* (5 March 1982), p. 3.

36. William Wood, "Benching Incompetent Judges," *Student Lawyer* 5 (5 March 1977): 18–21, 53.

37. Judicial Councils Reform and Judicial Conduct and Disability Act of 1980, Pub. L. No. 96–458, 94 Stat. 12035.

38. *The Federal Civil Justice System*, Bureau of Justice Statistics (Washington, D.C.: U.S. Department of Justice, July 1987), p. 4.

39. Bureau of Justice Statistics, *Bulletin*, "The Growth of Appeals" (Washington, D.C.: U.S. Government Printing Office, February 1985), p. 1.

40. For an analysis of the lower courts, see Malcolm M. Feeley, *The Process Is the Punishment: Handling Cases in a Lower Criminal Court* (New York: Russell Sage, 1980).

41. See Laura Banfield and C. David Anderson, "Continuance in the Cook County Criminal Court," *University of Chicago Law Review* 35 (Winter 1968): 279–80. See also Maureen Mileski, "Courtroom Encounters: An Observation Study of a Lower Criminal Court," *Law and Society Review* 5 (May 1971): 473–538. For a report on similar findings in Cleveland, see Lewis Katz, Lawrence Litwin, and Richard Bamberger, *Justice Is the Crime* (Cleveland: Press of Case Western Reserve University, 1972).

42. For a discussion of changes in the New Jersey Supreme Court, see Randall Guynes and Neal Miller, "Improving Court Productivity: Two New Jersey Experiences," *NIJ Reports* 208 (March–April 1988): 2–6.

43. See, for example, Erdwin Pfuhl, Jr., and David L. Altheide, "TV Mediation of Disputes and Injustice," *Justice Quarterly* 4 (March 1987): 99–116; and Tony F. Marshall, *Alternatives to Criminal Courts* (Brookfield, Vt.: Gower Publishing Co., 1985).

44. James J. Kilpatrick, "Help for Our State Courts," *San Antonio Express* (19 February 1982), p. A20.

Prosecution and Defense

KEY TERMS

adversary system
assigned counsel
beyond a reasonable
  doubt
charge
continuance
crime control model
defense attorney
discretion
due process
due process model
grand jury
indictment
information
jurisdiction
paralegals
pro se
prosecuting attorney
prosecution
public defender
right to counsel
waiver

Fred and Harry, friends for several years, got into a fight at a bar one night. The situation escalated and resulted in injury to both men. The bartender called the police. The police arrived, called an ambulance to take both men to the hospital, and placed Fred and Harry under arrest. Another friend, Steve, was so enraged at the arrests that he verbally abused and hit the officer. He was placed under arrest and taken to the police station for booking.

You are the **prosecuting attorney** in the jurisdiction where these crimes occurred. You believe that you have sufficient evidence to charge Fred and Harry with attempted murder, but before you do that, Harry dies. You also have sufficient evidence to charge Steve with simple assault on a police officer, a misdemeanor that carries a penalty of 6 months to

1 year in jail. You know that Steve is a college student who has never been in trouble with the police. You also know that he has a part-time job, has worked steadily at that job while attending college, and that he has lived in the community with his family for 5 years.

After Harry dies, you can **charge** Fred with murder. You believe you have sufficient evidence to charge him with first-degree murder. Conviction on that charge would result in a sentence of life or death; there is no provision for a term of years. You could also charge him with second-degree murder, which carries a penalty of 10 years to life. You know that Fred has had only minor contact with the law; he was arrested for simple assault but not charged with that offense. He was convicted of burglary and served a 1-year prison term.

First-year law students preparing to become attorneys.

INTRODUCTION

The cases of Fred, Harry, and Steve present some of the problems that confront prosecutors. If you were the prosecutor in the jurisdiction in which these cases were reported, what decisions would you make? Would you prosecute all of the offenses? What are the reasons for your choices? How would your role as a prosecutor in the criminal justice system differ from that of the defense attorneys representing Fred, Harry, and Steve?

The adversary philosophy that characterizes the system of criminal justice in the United States perhaps is best illustrated by an analysis of the **prosecution** and defense of a criminal case. We have already seen that underlying the adversary philosophy is the belief that the best way to obtain the facts of a criminal case is to have an advocate for each side who will be subjected to examination by the opposing side. The primary figures in this process are the prosecuting attorney and the **defense attorney.** It is important to understand their functions before looking at the specific procedures in which they engage before, during, and after the criminal trial.

The previous chapter on courts set the stage for this discussion of prosecution and defense. Although the prosecutor and the defense attorney perform important functions outside the court, the court must accept or reject any negotiations that have been made between them concerning a guilty plea. The judge will preside over the formal pretrial, trial, and posttrial procedures engaged in by these two important positions in the criminal justice system. The prosecutor and the defense attorney are important figures at various stages in the criminal justice system. This chapter will provide an overview of their respective roles in the adversary system.

PROSECUTION AND DEFENSE IN THE ADVERSARY SYSTEM: AN OVERVIEW

As Chapter 1 pointed out, advocates of the **adversary system** believe it is the best method for getting the facts while recognizing important rights of the accused. It is assumed that each advocate, the prosecution and the defense, will be diligent in investigating witnesses and securing physical evidence to present on behalf of his or her case. The evidence then will be presented to a neutral body (the judge or a jury) for resolution. The process will be presided over by a judge whose function is to see that the prosecution and the defense observe all the rules of the system and do not violate a defendant's **due process** rights.

Critics of the adversary system argue that it is not an effective way of obtaining facts because advocates do not emphasize the search for truth, but the importance of winning the case. Critics claim that the adversary system is based on the incorrect assumption that defense and prosecution will be equal, both in ability and in their desire to find the truth. The result, say the critics, is a battle of wit and guile, having little to do with finding the truth. To the contrary, there may be efforts to suppress the truth.

The U.S. criminal justice system is an adversarial one, with attorneys representing each side. (Comstock)

In reflecting on this controversy over the most appropriate and accurate method of ascertaining the facts in a criminal case, we must keep in mind the **due process model** as compared to the **crime control model** of criminal justice systems. If the only goal of the system is to prove that a crime was committed and that a particular person committed that crime, the due process requirements observed in this country do not make sense. They create obstacles for the police and the prosecution in their investigations of criminal activities. They make it more difficult for the prosecution to prove its case at trial. But, if the due process model is important, as it is in our system, certain procedures must be recognized.

The purposes and functions of prosecution and defense must be analyzed in the context of the due process model. The duty of the prosecutor is to seek justice but not at any price. The duty to uphold the criminal law does not give prosecutors the license to violate individual rights in the process. On the other hand, the right to counsel, so important in our system of justice, does not give defense attorneys the right to defend at any cost. Both the prosecution and the defense are bound by constitutional limitations and the ethics of the legal profession.

PROSECUTION

The prosecution of a criminal case refers to the process by which formal criminal charges are brought against a person accused of committing a crime. There are various kinds of prosecution systems, some of which are described in Spotlight 9.1, but this chapter focuses on the public system of prosecution in the United States.

Emergence of Public Prosecution

Simple societies often are characterized by a system of private prosecution in which crime victims are permitted to take action against those who have allegedly committed crimes against them. As societies become more complex, some continue to permit private prosecutions, with the victim bringing the charges although the state actually carries out the formal prosecution. In some systems, however, the public prosecutor may have the authority to dismiss the case after a private party has initiated prosecution.

In the U.S. colonies, each colony had an attorney general or prosecutor with the authority to initiate prosecutions, but these attorney generals usually left the prosecution of criminal cases to victims. There was considerable abuse of the system, however, with some victims initiating criminal prosecutions in order to pressure defendants to make financial settlements with them. Because the penalties for many criminal offenses were quite severe, it was not uncommon for the accused to settle financially, thus in effect buying freedom from criminal prosecution.

Such abuses finally led to the exercise of the power of public prosecution by the colonial attorney general. It soon became evident, however, that one attorney general and one colonial court could not handle all the

SPOTLIGHT 9.1
PROSECUTION SYSTEMS IN SELECTED COUNTRIES

England

According to English law, any person may initiate a prosecution unless a statute prohibits the right. When a statute states such a prohibition, it requires the Director of Public Prosecutions to handle the case. . . . The number of statutes requiring the Director's office to act is fairly small. Thus, most cases may be prosecuted by any person.

The public's general authority to prosecute is based on the common-law belief that a true system of public prosecution should be available to members of the public, rather than limited to an agent of the central government. In reality, however, this obligation has been exercised primarily by the police. Since the advent of modern police forces in the nineteenth century, the English citizenry have adopted the view that the initiation of prosecutions is a task that rightly falls within the duties of the police.

Sweden

At the top of the administrative hierarchy is the Chief State Prosecutor who is responsible for the Swedish prosecutorial system. Appointed by the Cabinet, the Chief State Prosecutor has the specific duty to prosecute cases before the Supreme Court. The Chief is also responsible for initiating actions in the lower courts when the accused is a civil servant, judge, or military commander who has allegedly violated a law that violates the public trust, such as bribery. State prosecutors are responsible for public prosecutions within their county or region. There are 24 state prosecutors who are appointed by the Cabinet. . . . Finally, there are 86 district prosecutors who work at the local level, and they handle most of the cases in the district courts.

Swedish prosecutors tend to be actively involved in the preliminary investigation of a case, especially if it is considered serious in nature. They decide whether or not to charge the accused and would subsequently conduct the prosecution before the court. Thus, the prosecutor is afforded a good deal of power in the administration of justice. Although most prosecutions are instituted by the prosecutor's office, the Code of Judicial Procedure permits injured parties to initiate prosecutions by applying to the court for a summons against the accused.

Japan

[In Japan, criminal cases are prosecuted by procurators.] At the top of the procuratorial bureaucracy is the Supreme Public Procurator's Office. . . . It supervises all of the other procurator offices. There is one procurator office located in each of the courts. The Procurator General administers the entire system, and this official, along with the other members of the upper echelons of the procurator service, are appointed by the Cabinet. The other procurators are selected by the Procurator General.

The purpose of the procurator is to prosecute criminal cases and to determine how a case will be disposed. Although the police usually conduct most of the criminal investigations, the procurator has the authority to investigate, arrest and detain suspects. . . . Although the procurator's office is afforded a good deal of independence and is perceived as a part of the judiciary, nonetheless, it is part of the executive branch of government. The Minister of Justice has a certain amount of control over procurators but does not control the actual investigation and disposition of cases. There is one exception to this rule: the Minister can control the procurator's investigation into delicate political inquiries. Although this authority is rarely utilized, it has become a controversial political issue when this power is actually employed by the Minister.

Procurators are expected to be impartial in determining how a case will be disposed, and to promote this they are protected from arbitrary dismissal. Procurators can be removed from office if they are either physically or mentally disabled, or as a form of disciplinary action. . . . Procurators must retire at age 63 with the exception of the Procurator General who retires at age 65.

Source: Richard J. Terrill, *World Criminal Justice Systems: A Survey* (Cincinnati: Anderson Publishing Co., 1984), pp. 48, 196–97; 265–66.

prosecutions in a colony. Gradually a system developed by which prosecutors in each county would bring local prosecutions in the emerging county courts. These county prosecutors were viewed as local and autonomous, not as arms of the colonial government.[1]

The system of public prosecution differed from colony to colony. Some counties distinguished between the violation of state and local ordinances and had a separate prosecution system for each. Today all states have local and state prosecution systems. Local jurisdictions may have local ordinances applicable only to those jurisdictions, and local prosecutors will be responsible for prosecuting violations of those ordinances. Serious offenses, however, will be designated by state statutes, although they generally will be prosecuted in local courts by local prosecutors. A federal system of prosecution also exists; it is discussed later.

SPOTLIGHT 9.2
DALLAS PROSECUTOR: THIRTY-SIX YEARS A LAW-AND-ORDER ICON

"On a death penalty case you usually don't want a juror over 60 who might die tomorrow, but you never know," Henry Wade said, sitting back in his chair and meditating on his own private calculus of punishments.

"I had two jurors who were 85, and one of them jumped up and threatened to whip the defense lawyer," said Mr. Wade, the Dallas County District Attorney. "He gave the defendant the death penalty and showed up the next day to ask if I'd killed him yet. He wanted to save his soul for the Lord. The man was some kind of off-brand church, and he was kind of nutty on religion, but he was a good juror for us."

There are few certainties in the legal system, but for the last 36 years the one overwhelming constant here has been the dominating presence of Henry Wade, who has served as something of a law-and-order icon since he became District Attorney in 1950.

Mr. Wade's career has had some conspicuous moments in the national eye. There was the prosecution in 1964 of Jack Ruby, who killed Lee Harvey Oswald. In 1970, his office was sued by a woman who sought an abortion, and thus his name is part of Roe v. Wade, the landmark Supreme Court decision. And there was the Lenell Geter case, ending

in 1984, in which a young black engineer with no criminal background was finally freed after being given a life sentence for a robbery prosecutors later said he did not commit.

But as Mr. Wade prepares to step down at the end of the year, the national recognition of his office as one of the most relentless prosecutorial machines in the country pales before Mr. Wade's status locally.

Few people have defined Dallas's conservative instincts as decisively as the 71-year-old Mr. Wade. It is as hard for people here to think of the District Attorney's office without Henry Wade as it is to think of the Dallas Cowboys without Tom Landry.

His former chief lieutenant, Doug Mulder, said, "It was the most efficient and effective prosecuting machine in the country."

Some critics say it was too efficient and effective, seeking Draconian sentences and concentrating more on convictions than justice. Others, especially citing the Geter case, say it has slipped in recent years.

But Mr. Mulder recently summed up the prevailing mood when he told Mr. Wade at a roast in his honor, "Thanks for being the only legend most of us will ever know."

Mr. Wade's incessant cigar chewing, folksy drawl

Organization and Structure of State and Local Prosecution Systems

Most prosecutors are elected officials. That means they are subject to the pressures of local and state politics, but it is argued that the election of this important official will make the person more accountable to the people. Some prosecutors have been in office for long periods of time and even attained national recognition, as Spotlight 9.2 indicates. Note, however, that this spotlight also indicates some of the criticisms of the prosecutor.

More than 8,000 state, county, and local prosecution systems exist in the United States. There is no uniformity in the title of the office; it may be called the *solicitor, district attorney, county attorney, attorney general, prosecuting attorney, commonwealth's attorney, district attorney general,* or

and fondness for dominoes and mucking about on his 140-acre farm have given him an artfully deceiving image. Melvin Belli, who unsuccessfully defended Mr. Ruby, called Mr. Wade "a country bumpkin."

But the folksy manner masked a keen legal mind and a fierce competitive streak. Mr. Wade's career has been marked, at times to a point bordering on caricature, by a belief in the efficacy of punishment.

As a prosecutor, he asked for the death penalty 30 times and got it 29 times. In his last court appearance in 1973, before he restricted himself to administrative duties, he won 5,005-year prison terms for two kidnappers.

Even his critics say one of Mr. Wade's achievements has been to keep the office independent locally. His first crusade in the early 1950's was against drunken drivers, and victims came from all parts of town.

He says one of his proudest achievements has been keeping organized crime activity to a minimum in Dallas.

But tough prosecution has not had much impact on Dallas's crime rate, where property crime has been among the highest in the nation.

"It has been a model for Texas, a solid office, an honest office, but its glory days are long gone," said Peter Lesser, a local defense attorney who has twice run for district attorney himself, unsuccessfully, once against Mr. Wade and once to succeed him. "Henry Wade built a great house, but if you leave

the roof alone for 36 years, it's going to leak."

If the Geter case was Mr. Wade's most recent and least pleasant foray into the national spotlight, the Ruby prosecution is still his best known.

After a gap of 23 years, the passions of the case have mellowed, and when Mr. Wade reminisces on it, he does so with a vague half-smile, as if evoking a distant, bizarre spectacle.

"There must have been 300 reporters crowding around," he recalled of the scene the night of the assassination of President Kennedy here Nov. 22, 1963. "And suddenly there's Ruby," he said, "yelling, 'Henry, you're wanted on the telephone.' It turned out to be a disk jockey called the Weird Beard. Ruby had called him and said he could get an exclusive interview." The next day, Mr. Ruby shot and killed Oswald, a crime for which Mr. Wade won a conviction and death penalty.

He mused for awhile on Mr. Belli's courtroom strategy and Mr. Ruby's unlikely plans to make a fortune on a restaurant in Chicago at the end of the trial. "No question he had some loose cells in his brain," he said of Mr. Ruby, but when asked if he ever felt any sympathy for him, Mr. Wade's rueful smile immediately flicked off.

"I'm not inclined to feel sorry for any defendants in a trial," Henry Wade said.

Source: Peter Applebome, "Dallas Prosecutor: 36 Years a Law-and-Order Icon," Special to the *New York Times* (22 July 1986), p. 8. Copyright © 1986 by The New York Times Company. Reprinted by permission.

assistant solicitor general. Normally, the local office has **jurisdiction** over a limited geographical area, although some have statewide jurisdiction.

Prosecutors may work alone or with many assistant attorneys. Many prosecutors work in rural areas or small towns. Three-fourths of the approximately 3,000 local prosecutors operate from small offices with less than four assistants, and many work alone. They may be assisted in their work by law students who serve as interns.

Prosecution in Rural Areas   The advantages of rural prosecution are numerous. Small towns and rural areas usually have lower crime rates, and the processing of cases may be more informal. Caseloads are usually lighter, so rural district attorneys may have more time to prepare cases. Most prosecutors are acquainted with the other lawyers, judges, and court personnel on a professional as well as a social level. Most cases are handled individually; and all personnel, from the judge to the probation officer, usually give each case considerable attention.

In rural areas most cases are settled by guilty pleas. Since rural judges and juries tend to give harsher sentences, defense attorneys are less likely to advise taking cases to trial, and more defendants are willing to plead guilty without a trial.

Rural prosecutors handle a different type of population and different types of cases than urban prosecutors. Violent crimes such as armed robbery are rare; the usual case is driving under the influence of alcohol. Typical activities of a rural prosecutor involve prosecuting livestock thieves, handling schoolyard fights or vandalism, or investigating thefts of farm equipment. Rural prosecutors also give legal advice to local government agencies.[2]

One disadvantage of rural prosecution is that salaries are very low; many prosecutors maintain a private law practice in order to survive financially. Another disadvantage is that rural prosecutors manage without a full-time staff, adequate office equipment, or resources to investigate crimes. The criminal justice system also can be affected; when the sole prosecutor has an unexpected illness or emergency, the court cannot process cases. A single prosecutor may have difficulty handling complicated crimes, exceptional cases, or lengthy investigations alone.[3]

Prosecution in Suburban Areas   The suburban prosecutor may be in the most enviable position of all. The homogeneous nature of the population means the prosecutor's role is easier to define. Suburban prosecutors respond to fixed crime patterns and are accurate barometers of community values and standards. In an affluent community, residents will expect a defendant-oriented, treatment approach in the criminal justice system. Thus, prosecutors can easily establish an office policy for handling cases. Defendants in the suburbs are less likely to be the anonymous poor, the uneducated, and the unemployed of the urban area. The major type of crime is against property, and the processing of criminal cases is more standardized and orderly.

The suburban prosecutor has more funds and resources than the rural office. The land development, population increases, and growth in the tax base in suburban areas provide greater resources for its criminal justice system. Suburban prosecutors are in the best position to experiment and evaluate within a relatively controlled environment and to offer a rare opportunity for testing and analyzing the effect of changes in the criminal justice system.[4]

Prosecution in Urban Areas   Prosecution in urban areas is often more complex than prosecution in rural and suburban areas because of the differences in the type and extent of the crime rates. Crime rates generally are higher in large urban areas and include the more serious personal crimes of violence, such as armed robbery and murder. Caseloads are also higher. Some urban prosecutors are so busy that they may not see the files of cases involving less serious offenses until a few minutes before they arrive in court to prosecute the cases.

Salaries of urban prosecutors often are not competitive with those of attorneys in private practice, and for that reason it is difficult to attract the most qualified attorneys. Many who do become prosecutors may not stay long because of low salaries or job burnout, or because they view the job as only a training ground. For whatever reason, staff turnover is often high. On the positive side, salaries for urban prosecutors are usually higher than for those in suburban and rural areas; offices are better equipped and better staffed; and some attorneys find the variety in the types of crime prosecuted in large cities to be a challenge not found in other areas of legal work.

Urban prosecution offices also may involve programs not available in smaller offices. In recent years, many urban prosecution offices have added programs for crime victims and witnesses. Special prosecutors may be trained to work with rape victims and with children who are victims of sexual and other forms of abuse.

State Prosecution Systems   Prosecutions at the state level differ from state to state, but these systems are headed by a state attorney general, usually an elected official, who is the chief prosecutor for the state. The attorney general will have jurisdiction throughout the state for prosecuting violations of state crimes, although some of that responsibility may be delegated to local levels. The attorney general may also issue opinions on the constitutionality of state statutes.

The attorney general of the state will appoint assistant attorney generals. These assistants may be assigned to specific areas of responsibility, such as supervising legal services at state correctional facilities or providing legal services for state institutions such as colleges and universities.

Many young attorneys view the office of the state attorney general as an excellent place to begin a legal career. If the attorney general moves on to a higher elected office, such as governor of the state or United States congressman or senator, the assistant attorney general may be offered a position in the new administration. The legal experience to be gained in the state attorney general's office is excellent preparation for other kinds of law practice. It provides the young lawyer with valuable contacts in the legal profession.

Prosecution at the Federal Level The Judiciary Act of 1789 provided for prosecutors at the federal level. Today these prosecutors are called United States attorneys. One U.S. attorney heads each of the 95 federal judicial districts in the United States. U.S. attorneys are appointed by the president, who often accepts the recommendations of the members of the Senate and House of Representatives from the area in which the U.S. attorney will work. These officials and their nearly 2,000 assistant U.S. attorneys, along with nearly 400 lawyers in the U.S. Department of Justice, have jurisdiction for prosecuting violations of federal laws such as those diagrammed in Figure 9.1. The U.S. Department of Justice is headed by the attorney general, an attorney who is appointed by the president and confirmed by the Senate.

The U.S. attorneys act under the general supervision of the U.S. attorney general, but in reality they are rather free to develop their own priorities within the guidelines provided by the U.S. Department of Justice. This freedom may result in greater job satisfaction for the attorneys who occupy these positions, as well as the needed flexibility for federal prosecutions to be concentrated on the types of crime characteristic of

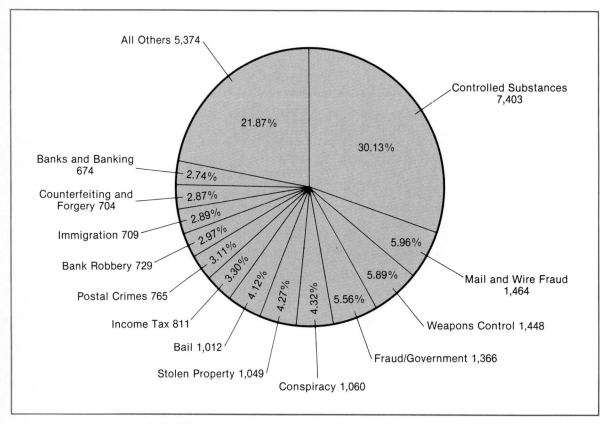

FIGURE 9.1
Criminal Cases Pending, by Offense, in United States Attorneys' Offices as of September 30, 1987 (total 24,568). *Source:* U.S. Department of Justice, *United States Attorneys' Statistical Report: Fiscal Year 1987* (Washington, D.C.: Office of Management Information Systems and Support Staff of the Executive Office for U.S. Attorneys, 1988).

specific areas. But it also results in different types of law enforcement throughout the federal system, which in turn can lead to charges of unjust practices.

Problems also may exist when state and federal authorities have jurisdiction to prosecute in a particular case. Overlapping jurisdiction occurs when the alleged crime is a violation of state and federal law. Congress has not provided a clear standard to aid U.S. attorneys in deciding when to prosecute in such cases; so the responses may differ among the federal districts. One authority has concluded that U.S. attorneys should continue to have the discretion to "decide in advance, on a subject-by-subject rather than a case-by-case, which areas most need the special resources they can bring to bear in the service of public interest." Limiting this discretion to a subject-by-subject rather than a case-by-case basis reduces the chances that particular types of individuals will be discriminated against in prosecutorial decisions. "At the same time, a general preference for declining to act in areas that can indeed be left to state and local prosecution does appear to be wise."[5]

THE PROSECUTOR'S ROLE

Throughout the pretrial and trial stages of a criminal case, the specific functions performed by the prosecutor will be discussed as each stage of the process is detailed in the next two chapters. The purpose of this discussion is to give an overview of the general function of the prosecution in the United States. The prosecutor is the person primarily responsible for bringing charges against persons accused of committing crimes. The prosecutor may be the most influential person in the United States in the power that he or she has over the lives of citizens.[6]

The prosecutor in most jurisdictions has virtually unlimited **discretion** in deciding whether to bring formal charges against the accused. Statutes vary among the states, but generally they provide that the prosecutor or assistant prosecutors of a particular jurisdiction shall appear at all trials and shall prosecute all actions for crimes committed in their jurisdictions. But these statutes have been interpreted to mean that prosecutions must be brought by prosecutors or their assistants and not that *all* crimes brought to the attention of the prosecutor must be prosecuted. Consequently, prosecutors have the discretion to refuse to prosecute; this decision is virtually unchecked, as the following excerpt indicates.[7]

State v. *Mitchell*

Fundamentally, a prosecutor is vested with broad discretion in selecting matters for prosecution. A decision to prosecute or not to prosecute is to be accorded judicial deference in the absence of a showing of arbitrariness, gross abuse of discretion or bad faith. . . .

It is fundamental that the mental processes of public officials by means of which governmental action is determined is generally beyond the scope of judicial review.

Providing prosecutors with unchecked discretion to determine not to prosecute may be abused. According to Kenneth Culp Davis, a recognized legal authority on discretion in the criminal justice system, "A startlingly high proportion of all official discretionary action pertaining to administration of justice is illegal or of doubtful legality."[8]

It is clear, however, that, for whatever reasons, most people accused of crime are not prosecuted; and of those who are prosecuted, most do not proceed through all stages of the criminal justice system. Figure 9.2 indicates what happens to 100 typical arrests. Note that six are diverted or referred, which means the prosecutor refers them to another agency, such as a drug treatment facility.

Of each 100 cases, 23 are "rejected at screening," meaning that the prosecutor refuses to prosecute those cases. Almost one-half, 49, are carried forward, but most of those will be disposed of by plea bargaining, discussed in Chapter 10. The focus here is on the reasons prosecutors decide whether to prosecute, and if so, how they do so.

The Decision Not to Prosecute

Many times the prosecutor will either refuse to prosecute or, after deciding to prosecute and bring formal charges against the suspect, will petition the court to drop the charges. Prosecutors are criticized frequently for these decisions, the allegation being that the decisions are made for political reasons, for example, refusing to prosecute white-collar or corporate crimes. However, a recent study indicated that prosecutors who do not prosecute white-collar or corporate crimes indicate that the main reason is that they do not have sufficient resources for successful prosecution of these cases, which generally are quite complex and expensive to prosecute. The researchers also found, however, that "Prosecutors in small districts

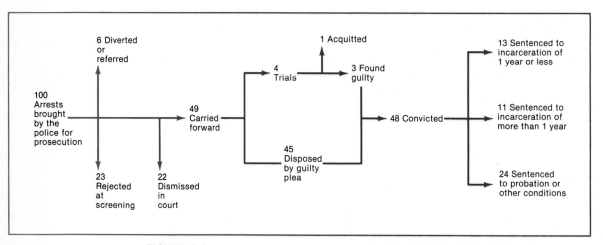

FIGURE 9.2
Typical Outcome of 100 Felony Arrests Brought by the Police for Prosecution.
Source: U.S. Bureau of Justice Statistics, *The Prosecution of Felony Arrests, 1981* (Washington, D.C.: U.S. Department of Justice, 1986), p. 2.

were more constrained by the potential impact that a corporate prosecution might have on the local economy than their counterparts in large districts."[9]

It therefore is important to understand that practical reasons such as lack of resources may lead to a refusal to prosecute, especially cases that involve a lot of time and thus are costly. Other reasons are summarized in Table 9.1. These reasons may also apply to a prosecutor's decision to request a dismissal after a case has officially begun. Table 9.2 contains data from two cities, indicating the percentages in each category of reasons for dismissing cases after they have been filed. This table contrasts the situation in Louisville, Kentucky, with that of Manhattan, New York, two extremes in the 1981 study conducted by the Bureau of Justice Statistics. Note, for example, that 26 percent of the dismissals in Manhattan were due to insufficient evidence, compared to only 11 percent in Louisville.

The Decision to Prosecute

Once the prosecutor decides to prosecute, he or she must decide the appropriate charge(s) to bring against a particular suspect. Criminal statutes often overlap. Some offenses are defined by degrees of seriousness, such as first-degree murder or second-degree murder. There may be sufficient

---

TABLE 9.1 _____

Reasons for Prosecutorial Rejection or Dismissal of Some Criminal Cases

Many criminal cases are rejected or dismissed because of

- **Insufficient evidence** that results from a failure to find sufficient physical evidence that links the defendant to the offense
- **Witness problems** that arise, for example, when a witness fails to appear, gives unclear or inconsistent statements, is reluctant to testify, is unsure of the identity of the offender or where a prior relationship may exist between the victim/witness and offender
- **The interests of justice,** wherein the prosecutor decides not to prosecute certain types of offenses, particularly those that violate the letter but not the spirit of the law (for example, offenses involving insignificant amounts of property damage)
- **Due process problems** that involve violations of the Constitutional requirements for seizing evidence and for questioning the accused
- **A plea on another case,** for example, when the accused is charged in several cases and the prosecutor agrees to drop one or more of the cases in exchange for a plea of guilty on another case
- **Pretrial diversion** that occurs when the prosecutor and the court agree to drop charges when the accused successfully meets the conditions for diversion, such as completion of a treatment program
- **Referral for other prosecution,** such as when there are other offenses, perhaps of a more serious nature in a different jurisdiction, or deferral to Federal prosecution.

Source: Report to the Nation on Crime and Justice, 2d ed. (Washington, D.C.: U.S. Department of Justice, 1988), p. 73.

TABLE 9.2

Reasons for Dismissal of Cases After Filing or Indictment:
A Comparison of Two Cities

Most Serious Charge	Total	Insufficient Evidence	Witness Problems	Due Process Problems	Interest of Justice	Plea on Another Case	Referral to Diversion	Referral for Other Prosecution	Other
				Cases Dismissed due to					
Louisville, Kentucky, 1981									
Percent of dismissals	100%	11%	10%	3%	28%	3%	15%	3%	24%
Homicide and manslaughter	100	30	10	0	50	0	0	0	10
Sexual assault	100	6	12	0	35	6	0	0	41
Robbery	100	9	12	9	26	9	0	0	35
Assault	100	11	28	0	28	0	6	0	28
Burglary	100	13	11	5	27	8	14	2	21
Larceny and auto theft	100	10	13	0	27	0	33	3	13
Stolen property	100	0	4	4	36	4	24	0	28
Fraud	100	12	6	0	24	6	12	18	24
Drugs	100	20	0	5	45	5	5	10	10
Weapons	—	—	—	—	—	—	—	—	—
Other	100	15	15	8	15	8	0	8	31
Manhattan, New York, 1981									
Percent of dismissals	100%	26%	24%	1%	17%	4%	0%	1%	26%
Homicide and manslaughter	100	35	15	0	7	2	0	2	40
Sexual assault	100	10	53	—	12	1	0	2	21
Robbery	100	17	38	0	8	3	0	4	30
Assault	100	10	49	0	19	2	0	—	21
Burglary	100	17	23	1	24	5	0	1	29
Larceny and auto theft	100	17	22	—	32	8	0	1	19
Stolen property	100	26	12	1	33	7	0	1	20
Fraud	100	17	8	0	39	14	0	0	23
Drugs	100	51	2	3	11	4	0	—	30
Weapons	100	47	6	5	9	2	0	—	32
Other	100	15	21	—	38	3	0	1	22

Source: Bureau of Justice Statistics, *The Prosecution of Felony Arrests, 1981* (Washington, D.C.: U.S. Department of Justice, 1986), p. 57.

evidence that the suspect has committed a number of crimes. The prosecutor must decide which charges to make in each case, and there is no requirement that the suspect be charged with all possible crimes.

Once the prosecutor has decided on specific charges, formal charges must be made. The law will specify where and how those charges are to be filed with the court. The prosecutor will prepare an **information,** a document that formally names a specific person and the specific charges against that person. The information is only one method by which formal charges are made. The second method is an **indictment** by a **grand jury,** which will be discussed in more detail in the next chapter.

There are cases in which the law requires a formal grand jury indictment. But even then, the prosecutor often will have considerable influence over the grand jury. Although the grand jury is viewed as a safeguard against unfounded criminal charges, and thus serves as a check on the prosecutor, most grand juries follow the recommendation of the prosecutor.[10]

Goals of Charging Decisions What goals should prosecutors strive for when they decide whether to charge a suspect? When charging decisions are made, most prosecutors have scant evidence about the defendant or the alleged crime. Charging decisions, therefore, may be based on intuition, personal beliefs about the usefulness of punishment, the relation of the crime to the possible penalty, or even personal bias or prejudice. Most prosecutors must make charging decisions without adequate guidelines or established goals. Where goals and guidelines exist, they differ from one jurisdiction to another. However, some general goals of prosecution are commonly accepted.

One goal for charging decisions is crime reduction. Prosecutors attempt to control crime by prosecuting and therefore incapacitating offenders and deterring potential criminals. Charging practices may be affected by decisions to concentrate on cases involving repeat offenders and the use of habitual criminal statutes with enhanced penalties. During the 1970s, the Law Enforcement Assistance Administration (LEAA) initiated a program called Career Criminal Prosecution (CCP), designed to establish programs that concentrated prosecution on habitual or career criminals. Some of the programs focused on armed robbers; others included other criminals, but all concentrated on criminals with a long record of criminal activity. Prosecutors had different criteria for determining what would be included in their programs, but the following features were typical of the programs:

1. A special unit was established within the prosecutor's office to handle career criminal cases.
2. The CCP unit might become involved in a case earlier than normal in order to assist the police with arrest and investigation procedures.
3. A special investigator might be attached to the CCP unit to help expedite case preparation.
4. A single deputy prosecutor was assigned responsibility for each case from start to finish, rather than the normal assembly-line processing.
5. Plea bargaining was highly circumscribed, if permitted at all.[11]

The Supreme Court recognizes a right to refuse counsel. Ted Bundy, pictured here with Leon County (Florida) Sheriff Ken Katsaris reading a murder indictment to him, refused counsel through much of the proceedings. Bundy was executed in 1989. (George Kochaniec/Sygma)

The purpose of these programs was to increase convictions of repeat offenders, decrease the amount of time it took to process those cases, increase the strength of the convictions, and increase the severity of sentencing. Analysis of the results indicated that some programs accomplished one or more of these goals; others did not. Various explanations for the conflicting results have been suggested, but evaluators did conclude that

> in those sites where the prosecutors play a prominent role in determining the severity of sentencing, extra attention devoted to specific types of cases can increase the severity of dispositions.[12]

Another goal for charging decisions is the efficient use of resources in the prosecutor's office. Funds and staff limit the number of cases that can be processed. The cost of prosecuting some cases may be too great, and charging decisions must emphasize early case disposition in offices that cannot afford many full trials.

Still another goal may be the rehabilitation of the defendant. The prosecutor may set the level of charge for a defendant with the goal of moving that person into an alternative treatment program, such as job training or alcohol or drug rehabilitation rather than incarceration in prison.

Empirical Evidence on Prosecutorial Decision Making

We have already seen, in Tables 9.1 and 9.2, that several factors are involved in prosecutorial decision making, all of which may be legitimate as well as practical. Decisions may be made for other reasons as well. The prosecutor, for example, may decide whether to prosecute a particular case based on a perception of the prospects of personal career enhancement. There is evidence that prosecutorial decisions may be based on one or more of the following factors:

1. Pressure from the public;
2. Pressure from the media;
3. The promotion of other investigations;
4. The desire to get rid of a suspect who is a particular problem to the community;
5. The belief that provision of social services would be more beneficial to the suspect and society than formal prosecution;
6. The belief that new evidence would be discovered and that such evidence would be favorable to the suspect.[13]

Research also indicates that the relationship between the victim and the suspect may be important in the decision whether to prosecute. This is particularly true in cases of homicide, assault, sexual assault, and robbery. One study found that two types of cases were turned down for prosecution twice as often as other cases: instances involving victim provocation and cases in which the victim had a known history of alcohol abuse. The victim's arrest record or age had no effect on the decision to prosecute, but cases with female victims were rejected more often than cases with male victims.[14]

Cases are more likely to be prosecuted if the victims are white, male, employed, and older than average. The reasons may be related to the type of witness needed for successful prosecution. The testimony of the victim, particularly in crimes against the person, may be crucial to the case. The victim must be able to withstand severe cross-examination by the defense attorney. The victim's life-style, moral character, honesty, and trustworthiness as a witness are important. The victim's appearance is critical, as is the victim's gender, race, neighborhood, job, and ability to communicate. Victims who lead questionable life-styles may not be credible witnesses. In rape cases, for example, female victims who have met the alleged rapist at a bar and gone away with him voluntarily are not the best witnesses in convincing a judge or jury to convict the defendant.[15]

The most serious offenses leave the least discretion for prosecutors in charging decisions. Crimes such as murder, rape, arson, armed robbery, kidnapping, and serious drug crimes receive the most attention from the public. Since the majority of prosecutors are elected officials, they seldom ignore public attitudes when charging suspects for these crimes.[16]

Middle-level offenses, such as thefts without violence or bribery, are publicized less often. In these types of cases, prosecutors have greater latitude. Prosecutors may be more likely to reduce or drop charges if the defendant agrees to participate in a diversion program or to make restitution to the victim. The greatest latitude is available when the suspect has been charged with a minor offense. There are large numbers of arrests for crimes such as purse snatching, shoplifting, disorderly conduct, or loitering. Usually the harm is slight, and the prosecutor declines to prosecute.[17]

Controlling the Prosecutor's Discretion

This discussion has indicated that prosecutors have great discretion in the criminal justice system. Prosecutors have even greater discretion than police. The arrest power of the police can be minimized by prosecutors who refuse to file formal charges against those arrestees. Although the prosecutor has no direct control over the police, this power to decline prosecution may affect the way police operate. If the prosecutor often refuses to prosecute certain types of cases, the police may stop making arrests when suspects appear to have violated those offenses. On the other hand, vigorous prosecution of some kinds of offenses might encourage police to be more diligent in arresting for those offenses.

Previous discussions of discretion have indicated that discretion is a basic characteristic of the U. S. system of criminal justice. It is not possible to anticipate all possible circumstances that might be reasonably considered in making a decision to arrest or to prosecute. But efforts must be made to establish guidelines and policies regarding the exercise of discretion.

Prosecutorial Innovations and Guidelines   One way to control prosecutorial discretion is for the prosecutor's office to establish guidelines and policies. This has been done in some offices in recent years as prosecutors have realized the need for innovative practices. As new situations arise in the criminal justice system, frequently there is a need for significant reform of procedures and standards. In Chapter 11 the significant stages of a trial will be discussed. The problems of prosecuting defendants accused of child abuse, especially sexual abuse, already have been noted. The combination of the rules of trials and the unique situation of children has presented prosecutors with the need to reform their procedures.

Children frequently are terrified to appear in court and testify against their alleged abusers. By definition children are immature in their emotional, cognitive, and physical development. They usually do not understand the interview process, particularly repeated interviews and cross-examination. The National Institute of Justice (NIJ) examined many proposed reforms that might be applied at trial when the victim is a child. Some of these are controversial; others, as noted in our previous discussion, have been accepted by some courts. A summary of the proposed reforms is reproduced in Spotlight 9.3. Notice the frequency with which it is necessary to permit the prosecutor (or judge; some of the decisions must be made by the trial judge) to use discretion, once again emphasizing the importance of discretion in the criminal justice system.

Statutory Guidelines   Prosecutorial discretion also may be controlled by establishing statutory guidelines. Recognizing that the power to decide whether to prosecute could lead to abuse of discretion, the state of Wash-

SPOTLIGHT 9.3
SUMMARY OF PROPOSED REFORM MEASURES IN THE PROSECUTION OF SEXUAL ABUSE OF CHILDREN CASES

CAUSE OF STRESS	SUGGESTED PROCEDURE	NECESSARY CONDITIONS
Pretrial Period		
Repeated interviews	Videotaping of first statement	Discretion
	Coordination of court proceedings	Discretion
	Joint interviews/one-way glass	Discretion
Time to disposition	Priority scheduling	Discretion, statute
Repeated schedule changes	Limitation of continuances	Discretion
Removal of child from home, retaliation	No contact orders or removal of offender	Statute
Fear of unknown	Thorough preparation	Discretion
	Tour of courtroom	Discretion
Victim/family exposed in media	Media cooperation in suppressing identifying information	Discretion
Court Proceedings		
Physical attributes of courtroom	Alternative setting for child's testimony	Statute
	Tour of courtroom	Discretion
	Small witness chair	Discretion
	Judge sitting at witness' level	Discretion
Audience, jury	Exclusion of spectators	Statute
	Videotaped deposition	Statute
	Closed circuit television	Statute
	Spectators asked to leave	Discretion
Defendant's presence	Closed circuit television	Statute
	Blackboard as screen	Case law
	Alternative seating arrangements	Case law
	Instruction to child to look elsewhere, to tell the judge if the defendant "makes faces"	Discretion
Description of events	*Res gestae*	Case law
	Expert witnesses to explain apparent lapses in child's testimony	Case law
	Presence of victim advocate	Statute, discretion
	Dolls, artwork	Discretion

Source: Debra Whitcomb, "Prosecuting Child Sexual Abuse—New Approaches," *National Institute of Justice Reports* (Washington, D.C.: U.S. Department of Justice, May 1986), p. 6.

ington, in its 1981 Sentencing Reform Act, specified reasons for which prosecution may be declined.

A Prosecuting Attorney may decline to prosecute, even though technically sufficient evidence to prosecute exists, in situations where prosecution would serve no public purpose, would defeat the underlying purpose of the law in question or would result in decreased respect for the law.[18]

Recognizing the vagueness of those categories of reasons, the legislature included commentary that illustrates what is meant by each of nine specific reasons that might be used to decline prosecution. Those include such instances as when the violation is slight or only technical and when no public purpose would be served by prosecution; when statutes are rarely enforced or most people act as if they do not exist; when prosecution would be clearly contrary to the intent of the legislature; when the cost of prosecution is disproportionately high; when the defendants already are charged with more serious offenses involving lengthy sentences; and when victims request that prosecution be declined.

Washington state, like many other jurisdictions, recognizes the right of the prosecutor to decline prosecution in cases in which immunity has been granted to the suspect. This means that in exchange for testimony aiding in the conviction of another person, the suspect gets a promise from the prosecutor that no charges will be filed or that only some of several possible charges will be filed. Although this practice is controversial, sometimes it is the only way police and prosecutors can get the evidence needed in criminal cases.

As of 1988, nine states had attempted to reduce the possibility of prosecutorial abuse at this stage by enacting legislation that would permit private individuals to challenge prosecutorial inaction. In the words of one authority, this would

> provide a signal that the prosecutor has been "unfaithful" in the execution of his duties. Ultimately the scheme should promote broader public confidence in the criminal justice system.[19]

The Washington state attempt to control prosecutorial discretion was preceded by efforts in the federal system. The U.S. Department of Justice has for some years had the *United States Attorney Manual*, which contains some guidance for prosecutorial decision making. But, not until a 1980 directive from the attorney general of the United States did we see "the first public pronouncement of prosecutorial policies ever issued by the Department of Justice." The attorney general stated that publication of these policies would

> serve two important purposes: ensuring the fair and effective exercise of prosecutorial responsibility . . . and promoting confidence on the part of the public and individual defendants that important prosecutorial decisions will be made rationally and objectively on the merits of each case.[20]

Establishing guidelines for prosecutorial discretion embodies the principle that discretion should be controlled not eliminated. Such guidelines will become increasingly critical as prosecutors become even more important in the criminal justice system. In subsequent chapters, we will study the recent movement toward abolishing discretion in sentencing, as well as reducing the use of parole. Both are measures aimed at getting tough with crime, and they are often combined with longer statutory sentences. This may mean that discretion is removed from judges and parole boards but shifted to prosecutors. Prosecutors retain the power to decline prosecution; and they may choose to do so in ever-increasing numbers if the stiffer laws are viewed as too harsh or if the prisons and jails continue to be so overcrowded that processing more defendants through the system would create severe problems.

Judicial Review   One final way that prosecutors might be controlled is by the exercise of judicial review. Defendants who think they have been unfairly treated might appeal their convictions on the basis of prosecutorial misconduct. This is possible but difficult. The landmark case using the equality principle to overturn a prosecutor's decision is a century old. In *Yick Wo v. Hopkins,* the Supreme Court held that if the prosecutor uses a law that is fair and impartial as written and applies it to a defendant with "an evil eye and an unequal hand" so that the prosecutor creates discrimination, the defendant has been denied equal protection of the laws. The defendant has been denied the right of an individual to be treated with equal regard, and the decision may be overturned.[21] Related to the equality principle is the rule that, under our Constitution, charging decisions cannot be based on categories such as race, religion, or sex.

The legal principle of rationality means that prosecution under any law must be related to the goal of that law. For example, a woman argued that she was denied equal protection of the law when she was prosecuted for prostitution but her male customers were not prosecuted. The court, however, said that the prosecutor's decision could not be challenged as long as there was "some rational relationship between the city's objective of controlling prostitution and the practice of arresting chiefly women violators."[22]

These legal principles of equality and rationality are difficult to enforce in the courts because intentional disparate treatment or discrimination is difficult to prove. In response to a defendant who argued that the prosecutor had engaged in selective enforcement when he was charged under a habitual criminal statute whereas other defendants with similar criminal records were not prosecuted under that law, the Supreme Court said, "The conscious exercise of some selectivity in enforcement is not in itself a federal constitutional violation." The defendant did not win because he could not show that the disparate treatment was intentional.[23]

Overcharging is another kind of prosecutorial abuse for which judicial review may be a remedy. Prosecutors abuse their discretion when they file charges that are not reasonable in light of the evidence available at the time the charges are filed. Overcharging may be done on purpose to coerce the defendant to plead guilty to a lesser charge.

Allegations of overcharging often are difficult to prove, however. Prosecutors may legitimately charge a suspect with any crime for which there is sufficient evidence to connect that suspect. If the prosecutor decides not to file the most serious charges that could be filed and if the defendant refuses to plead guilty to the lesser charges, the prosecutor may then file the more serious charges. This is not an abuse of discretion.

Prosecutorial misconduct also involves legally withholding evidence that would be favorable to the defense. The landmark Supreme Court case of *Brady v. Maryland*, decided in 1963, held that prosecutors who suppress evidence favorable to defendants are violating the due process rights of those defendants.[24] More recent Supreme Court decisions have adhered to the *Brady* rule in principle but

> confined its application to only the most self-evident violations. This area is an outstanding example of the Court's insensitivity to prosecutorial misconduct and the right of defendants to a fair trial.[25]

Prosecutors may abuse discretion in their choice of words used at trial. Neither prosecutors nor defense attorneys have unlimited discretion in the way they describe events, defendants, witnesses, or anyone else connected with the trial. When defendants challenge these statements, courts will analyze them in light of the Supreme Court's decisions requiring that (1) the words be read in context and (2) the effect of the words is to deny the defendant a fair trial.[26]

The same test also is used in other allegations of prosecutorial misconduct. But the prosecutor's actions must be interpreted, and appellate courts normally will defer to trial courts in deciding whether the conduct constituted a violation of the defendant's rights. Consider the following excerpt from *Darden v. Wainwright*. Do you think these words would so prejudice the jury that the defendant could not have gotten a fair trial?[27]

Darden v. *Wainwright*

Petitioner next contends that the prosecution's closing argument at the guilt–innocence stage of the trial rendered his conviction fundamentally unfair and deprived the sentencing determination of the reliability that the Eighth Amendment requires. . . .

The prosecutors then made their closing argument. That argument deserves the condemnation it has received from every court to review it, although no court has held that the argument rendered the trial unfair. Several comments attempted to place some of the blame for the crime on the Division of Corrections, because Darden was on weekend furlough from a prison sentence when the crime occurred.[9] Some comments implied that the death penalty would be the only guarantee against a future similar act.[10] Others incorporated the defense's use of the word "animal."[11] Prosecutor McDaniel made several offensive comments reflecting an emotional reaction to the case.[12]

[To give you more facts in making a decision, here are the respective footnotes referred to above. Citations are omitted.]

9. "As far as I am concerned, there should be another Defendant in this courtroom, one more, and that is the division of corrections, the prisons. . . . Can we expect him to stay in a prison when they go there? Can we expect them to stay locked up once they go there? Do we know that they're going to be out on the public with guns, drinking? . . .

10. "I will ask you to advise the Court to give him death. That's the only way I know that he is not going to get out on the public. It's the only way I know. It's the only way I can be sure of it. It's the only way anybody can be sure of it now, because the people that turned him loose—"

11. "As far as I am concerned, and as Mr. Maloney [defense counsel] said as he identified this man as an animal, this animal was on the public for one reason."

12. "He shouldn't be out of his cell unless he has a leash on him and a prison guard at the other end of that leash. I wish [Mr. Turman] had had a shotgun in his hand when he walked in the back door and blown his [Darden's] face off. I wish I could see him sitting here with no face, blown away by a shotgun. . . .

Do those words, taken alone, strike you as sufficient to decide the defendant did not get a fair trial? If so, recall that they must be interpreted in context, which in this case, according to the Supreme Court, involved defense arguments that "blamed the Polk County Sheriff's Office for a lack of evidence, alluded to the death penalty, characterized the perpetrator of the crimes as an 'animal,' and contained counsel's personal opinion of the strength of the state's evidence."

The crime involved in this case also was a particularly heinous one. Darden was attempting the armed robbery of Mrs. Turman in a furniture store in 1973. When Mrs. Turman's husband unexpectedly came in the back door, Darden shot him. As Mr. Turman was dying, Darden attempted to force Mrs. Turman into a sexual act. A young neighbor entered the store and tried to help Mr. Turman but was shot three times by Darden who then fled. In his rush to escape, Darden had an automobile accident. A witness to that accident testified that he was zipping his pants and buckling his belt. Officers traced the car, and with this evidence, charged Darden with the crimes against the Turmans.

During the trial the prosecutor repeatedly said he wished Darden had used the gun to kill himself. Other comments are reported in the excerpt. Under these circumstances, the Supreme Court held that although the prosecutor's comments were improper, they were not sufficient to deny Darden a fair trial. Four justices strongly dissented in this case. In 1988 Darden was executed in Florida's electric chair (see Spotlight 9.4 later in this chapter).[28]

One of the most effective ways to control prosecutorial misconduct is by providing adequate defense counsel for those accused of crimes. The second half of this chapter focuses on the right to counsel and the role of the attorney as defense counsel in our system of criminal justice.

DEFENSE AND THE RIGHT TO COUNSEL

The defense of a criminal case is extremely important in the adversary system. If the prosecutor tries to prove the case against the defendant by introducing evidence that has been seized or a confession that has been

Defense attorneys are responsible for protecting the constitutional rights of their clients. Ernesto Miranda, whose case resulted in the Miranda warning that police must give before they may question a suspect, is shown here with his attorney. Miranda was later stabbed to death. (UPI Bettmann Newsphotos)

elicited in violation of the defendant's rights, the defense attorney should ask the court to exclude that evidence. If the prosecutor files charges for which there is insubstantial evidence, the defense attorney should ask the court to dismiss those charges.

The basic purpose of the defense attorney is to protect the legal rights of the defendant and thereby preserve the adversary system. It is not the function of the defense attorney to judge the guilt or innocence of the defendant; that is an issue to be decided by the judge or jury. Rather, the defense attorney is to make sure that all of the defendant's rights are observed. The defense attorney also gathers and presents evidence and witnesses that support the defense and examines the evidence and witnesses produced by the prosecutor.

It is important to understand this basic function of the defense. In our adversary system we require that, for a person to be convicted of a criminal offense, all the elements of that offense must be proved by the prosecutor and the question of guilt decided by a jury or judge. The evidence must be strong enough for a person to determine **beyond a reasonable doubt** that the defendant is guilty. This burden of proof is much stronger than that required in a civil case because the repercussions of a criminal conviction are much greater than those in a civil case.

The drafters of the U.S. Constitution recognized that, in a criminal trial, the state's powers would be immense compared to those of the defendant. They therefore established a right to counsel in criminal trials. This right to counsel is the key to maintaining the adversary system, for many of the rights of due process have little value if defendants do not have legal counsel to defend those rights. We begin with a close look at the right to counsel and then consider the role of the attorney in implementing that right.

The Sixth Amendment to the U.S. Constitution provides that "in all criminal prosecutions, the accused shall enjoy the right . . . to have the Assistance of Counsel for his defense." Many scholars consider the **right to counsel** the most important of all the defendant's due process rights. The use of counsel by those who can hire attorneys has seldom been questioned, but the right to have counsel appointed at the expense of the state (or federal government in a federal trial) has been the subject of considerable litigation.

It is important to an understanding of this emerging right to counsel to note that the Bill of Rights, the first 10 amendments of the U. S. Constitution, originally applied only to the federal government. They were included to restrain the federal government's power. Today most of those rights have been applied to the states through the Due Process Clause of the Fourteenth Amendment, which specifies that states may not deny "life, liberty, or property" without "due process of law." But it took the Court over a century to apply most of the rights contained in the Bill of Rights to the states. The evolution of the right to appointed counsel is a good example.

The Right to Appointed Counsel

Historical Developments   The right to appointed counsel, which means counsel provided at government expense, has not always been recognized in the United States. In 1932 in *Powell v. Alabama*, the Supreme Court gave limited recognition to the right.[29] *Powell* was appealed from a state court and thus technically did not involve the Sixth Amendment right to counsel. In *Powell*, nine black youths were charged with the rape of two white women in Alabama. Eight of the defendants were convicted and sentenced to death. Several issues were raised on appeal; two of them related to the lack of counsel.

In *Powell*, the Court first considered the issue of whether the defendants had been given adequate opportunity to retain private counsel. But the Court then focused on the issue of whether appointed counsel should have been provided since the defendants could not have afforded to retain counsel even if they had been given the opportunity to do so.

In discussing the right to counsel, the Court in *Powell* emphasized that the right to be heard would have little meaning unless accompanied by a right to counsel. The Court held that there was a right to appointed counsel but limited that right to the facts of *Powell*, in which the crime committed carried the death penalty. Specifically, the Court said there is a right to appointed counsel "in a capital case, where the defendant is unable to employ counsel and is incapable adequately of making his own defense because of ignorance, feeble-mindedness, illiteracy, or the like." At the time *Powell* was decided almost half the states already provided a right to appointed counsel in capital cases. In federal trials that right was provided by a congressional statute.

In 1938 the Supreme Court decided a case under the Sixth Amendment, holding in *Johnson v. Zerbst* that there is a right to appointed as well as to retained counsel and that this right is not limited to capital

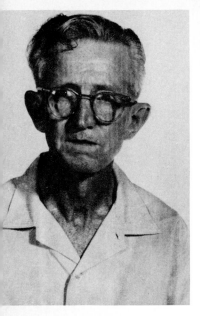

Clarence Earl Gideon, representing himself at trial, saw his case go to the Supreme Court and establish the right for defendants in felony trials to have appointed counsel if they could not afford to retain attorneys. (AP Wide World)

cases.[30] *Johnson* was a federal case, and during the next 25 years, the Court refused to extend the right to appointed counsel to all criminal cases tried in state courts.

In 1942 the Supreme Court specifically refused to apply the right to appointed counsel to states. In *Betts v. Brady*, the Court established a fundamental fairness test, holding that an indigent defendant in a state trial would be entitled to appointed counsel in a noncapital case only where it could be shown that circumstances necessitated appointed counsel for the defendant to receive a fair trial.[31] *Betts v. Brady* was a controversial case, but it remained the law until 1963 when it was specifically overruled.

The *Gideon* Case On January 8, 1962, the Supreme Court received a large envelope from prisoner no. 003826 in Florida. Clarence Earl Gideon, a pauper who had been in and out of prison most of his life, had printed his request in pencil. He was not a violent man, just one who frequently committed nonviolent crimes. He was charged with breaking and entering a poolroom with the intent to commit a misdemeanor, which was a felony under Florida law. Gideon requested that the state appoint an attorney for him. The judge responded that he was sorry but that the laws of Florida did not provide for appointed counsel except in capital cases. Gideon responded, "The United States Supreme Court says I am entitled to be represented by Counsel." Gideon conducted his own defense. He was convicted and sentenced to five years in the state prison.

Gideon appealed to the U.S. Supreme Court, which agreed to hear the case and appointed a prestigious law firm in Washington, D.C., to defend Gideon. The result was one of the few occasions in which the Court has specifically overruled an earlier decision. In *Gideon v. Wainwright*, the Court reversed its ruling in *Betts v. Brady* and applied the right to appointed counsel to state cases. The following excerpt is from the case.[32]

Gideon v. *Wainwright*

Since 1942, when *Betts v. Brady* was decided by a divided Court, the problem of a defendant's federal constitutional right to counsel in a state court has been a continuing source of controversy and litigation in both state and federal courts. . . . Upon full reconsideration we conclude that *Betts v. Brady* should be overruled . . .

In our adversary system of criminal justice, any person haled into court, who is too poor to hire a lawyer, cannot be assured a fair trial unless counsel is provided for him. This seems to us to be an obvious truth. . . . A defendant's need for a lawyer is nowhere better stated than in the moving words of Mr. Justice Sutherland in *Powell v. Alabama*: "The right to be heard would be, in many cases, of little avail if it did not comprehend the right to be heard by counsel. Even the intelligent and educated layman has small and sometimes no skill in the science of law. If charged with crime, he is incapable, generally, of determining for himself whether the indictment is good or bad. He is unfamiliar with the rules of evidence. Left without aid of counsel he may be put on trial without a proper charge, and convicted upon incompetent evidence or evidence irrelevant to the issue or otherwise inadmissible. He lacks both the skill and knowledge adequately to prepare his defense, even though he may have a perfect one. He requires the guiding hand of counsel at every step in the proceedings against him. Without it, though he be not guilty, he faces the danger of conviction because he does not know how to establish his innocence." . . .

The Court in *Betts v. Brady* departed from the sound wisdom upon which the Court's holding in *Powell v. Alabama* rested. Florida, supported by two other States, has asked that *Betts v. Brady* be left intact. Twenty-two states, as friends of the Court, argue that Betts was "an anachronism when handed down" and that it should now be overruled. We agree.

Scope of the Right to Appointed Counsel Gideon was convicted of a felony; consequently his case extended the right to appointed counsel in felony cases. In 1972 the Supreme Court extended the right to misdemeanors when the conviction of a particular misdemeanor would result in the "actual deprivation of a person's liberty." In *Argersinger v. Hamlin*, the Court held "that absent a knowing and intelligent waiver, no person may be imprisoned for any offense, whether classified as petty, misdemeanor, or felony unless he was represented by counsel at his trial."[33]

The Court clarified *Argersinger* in *Scott v. Illinois*, decided in 1979. Scott was fined but not given a prison sentence although the statute under which he was convicted for shoplifting provided for either punishment. In ruling that Scott was not entitled to appointed counsel, the Court emphasized the difference between *actual imprisonment* and any other form of punishment. A key paragraph from the opinion emphasizes this point.[34]

Scott v. Illinois

Although the intentions of the *Argersinger* Court are not unmistakably clear from its opinion, we conclude today that *Argersinger* did indeed delimit the constitutional right to appointed counsel in state criminal proceedings. Even were the matter *res nova* [a new case not decided; a new matter], we believe that the central premise of *Argersinger*—that actual imprisonment is a penalty different in kind from fines or the mere threat of imprisonment—is eminently sound and warrants adoption of actual imprisonment as the line defining the constitutional right to appointment of counsel. *Argersinger* has proved reasonably workable, whereas any extension would create confusion and impose unpredictable, but necessarily substantial, costs on 50 quite diverse States. We therefore hold that the Sixth and Fourteenth Amendments to the United States Constitution require only that no indigent criminal defendant be sentenced to a term of imprisonment unless the State has afforded him the right to assistance of appointed counsel in his defense.

Of course, states may extend the right to appointed counsel beyond those limits set by the Supreme Court. Six states (Colorado, Kansas, New

Mexico, Oklahoma, Utah, and Wyoming) had extended the right to *civil* cases that might result in a jail term when the issue was appealed to the Supreme Court. The Court refused to hear the case of *Walker v. McLain*, decided by the United States Court of Appeals of the Tenth Circuit. When the Supreme Court refuses to hear a case, the lower court's decision remains the law in that jurisdiction.[35]

Gideon, *Argersinger*, and *Scott* concern the right to appointed counsel at trial. The scope of this right is more extensive, however, and although the Court continues to deal with application problems, the rule was set down by the Court in 1967 in *United State v. Wade*. The Sixth Amendment right to counsel, said the Court, applies during "critical stages" in criminal proceedings.[36]

Although the extent of the Court's rulings on these issues is complex

SPOTLIGHT 9.4
THE GIDEON CASE 25 YEARS LATER

This Friday marks the 25th anniversary of Gideon v. Wainwright, one of the most popular decisions ever handed down by the United States Supreme Court.

Prior to *Gideon,* a person too poor to hire a lawyer had an unqualified constitutional right to appointed counsel only when charged with a crime punishable by death. In noncapital cases, he had no such absolute right. If forced to defend himself without a lawyer and convicted of a serious crime, he could obtain relief only if he could show specifically that he had been "prejudiced" by the absence of a lawyer, or that "special circumstances" (his lack of intelligence or education, or the gravity and complexity of the offense charged) rendered criminal proceedings without the assistance of defense counsel "fundamentally unfair."

The trouble was that application of this test was inherently speculative and problematic. When a layman defends himself, the resulting record usually makes him look overwhelmingly guilty and the case look exeeedingly simple. Such a record does not reflect what defenses or mitigating circumstances a trained advocate would have seen or what lines of inquiry might have been pursued.

The *Gideon* Court deemed it an "obvious truth" that a person "too poor to hire a lawyer cannot be assured a fair trial unless counsel is provided for him." Thus, the Court established an absolute right to appointed counsel in all serious criminal cases. (A decade later, the Court applied *Gideon* to misdemeanor defendants sentenced to prison.)

Most of the Warren Court's leading criminal procedure cases evoked sharp dissents on the Court and produced much unhappiness, even anger, in law enforcement circles and in the public. *Gideon* is a striking exception.

It was a unanimous decision. It was supported by a broad ethical consensus. It was widely applauded by the legal profession, press and public. It was the subject of a book by Anthony Lewis and a stirring television movie that was based on the book.

But this is no time for congratulation. On death row are some 2,000 prisoners, 99 percent of whom cannot afford a lawyer. *Gideon* is small comfort to them. Why? For one thing, in the years since *Gideon,* the Court has made it clear that the constitutional right to assigned counsel does not apply to litigation beyond the first appeal. And too many lawyers consider their job done when the highest court of any state has affirmed the conviction.

In such an event, so far as the Constitution is concerned, a prisoner who seeks Supreme Court review or other post-conviction relief is left to his own devices. And many death row inmates cannot read or write.

Some states have tried to fill the gap. For example, Florida, where the *Gideon* case arose, has established a state agency to represent death row inmates in post-conviction proceedings. Since it started up in October 1985, this agency has won 60 stays of executions. Yesterday, after seven dates with the executioner, Willie Jasper Darden, an inmate at Florida State Prison, at Starke, went to the electric chair for the 1973 murder of a furniture store owner

and cannot be discussed in detail here, it is possible to articulate some general conclusions. The right to counsel does not apply to all pretrial stages, although it has been applied to most.[37] The application of the right to appointed counsel at sentencing, probation hearings, and during incarceration will be discussed in subsequent chapters.

The right to appointed counsel applies to some but not to all appeals, as indicated by the discussion in Spotlight 9.4, an essay by law professor Yale Kamisar. States may extend constitutional rights beyond those mandated by Supreme Court interpretations of the federal constitution, as indicated earlier; but, if they do not do so in appeals that the Court considers discretionary rather than mandatory, the fact that one person may retain private counsel does not mean the state must provide appointed counsel for indigents.

in Lakeland. Mr. Darden had lived longer on death row than any condemned inmate in the United States.

In other states, such as Texas, where more than 250 people are on death row, there is no state support for counsel beyond the first round of appeals.

True, every person on every death row was represented by a lawyer at his trial and at the penalty phase—the part of the trial at which the jury determines whether to sentence the person convicted of a capital offense to life imprisonment or death.

But because the emotional and physical strain is so great and the compensation so low, most private lawyers shy away from capital-punishment cases. Unfortunately, not infrequently the lawyers who do represent capital defendants in the first instance make mistakes that not even the most skilled appellate lawyers can overcome.

As Prof. Welsh White of the University of Pittsburgh School of Law points out in a recent book, the best way to be successful at the penalty stage "is to present a dramatic psychohistory of the defendant to the jury" (to show, for example that the defendant was abused as a child or abandoned by his parents), so that the jury can see and understand him as a human being.

But a significant number of trial lawyers in capital cases either do not adequately understand the importance of the penalty stage or lack the time, resources or commitment to gather the necessary information about the defendant's background.

In theory, an appellate lawyer can overturn a death sentence by demonstrating that the defendant was the victim of "ineffective" trial counsel. But this is a herculean task. An appellate lawyer must

not only show that trial counsel was deficient but that his unprofessional performance "prejudiced" the defendant—that but for trial counsel's subpar performance, the outcome would have been different.

It is tempting to conclude—and many a busy court reviewing a death sentence has yielded to this temptation—that even if trial counsel had gathered together a massive amount of material pertaining to the defendant, and even if he had presented the mitigating factors discovered as a result, the defendant would still have received the death penalty.

This state of affairs led Justice Thurgood Marshall last year to voice concern that lower courts may be getting the impression that the right to counsel "guarantees no more than that a person who happens to be a lawyer is present at trial alongside the accused."

Justice Hugo L. Black, who wrote the opinion for the Court in *Gideon,* observed in another case involving the rights of indigent defendants that "there can be no equal justice where the kind of trial a man gets depends on the amount of money he has."

That is a nice saying. And the *Gideon* Court thought it had gone a long way toward achieving "equal justice" in the administration of criminal justice. But death row lawyers—almost all of whom can tell horror stories about capital cases bungled by trial counsel—have another saying: "People with money don't get the death penalty."

Source: Yale Kamisar, "The Gideon Case 25 Years Later," *New York Times* (16 March 1988), p. 27. Copyright © 1988 by The New York Times Company. Reprinted by permission.

In 1987, in *Pennsylvania v. Finley*, Chief Justice Rehnquist, writing for the Court, said, referring to an earlier case:

> We also concluded that the equal protection guarantee of the Fourteenth Amendment does not require the appointment of an attorney for an indigent appellant just because an affluent defendant may retain one. "The duty of the State under our cases is not to duplicate the legal arsenal that may be privately retained by a criminal defendant in a continuing effort to reverse his conviction, but only to assure the indigent defendant an adequate opportunity to present his claims fairly in the context of the State's appellate process."[38]

As Professor Kamisar indicates in Spotlight 9.4, the lack of appointed counsel on appeal is most critical in capital punishment cases.

The Supreme Court will continue to face many questions on the right to counsel, and as Spotlight 9.4 indicates, there is still a serious question as to whether recognition of this right has eliminated the concern that people with money receive greater justice.

The Right to Effective Assistance of Counsel

The right to effective assistance of counsel is not specifically mandated by the Constitution, but it has been held to be implied by that document. After all, the right to counsel would have little or no meaning without *effective* counsel. The Court used the terms "effective and substantial aid" in *Powell v. Alabama* and in several subsequent cases referred to effective assistance of counsel.[39]

The definition and application of the terms *effective assistance of counsel* were left to the lower courts. In 1945 the District of Columbia Circuit Court articulated the standard that counsel would not be considered ineffective unless counsel's actions reduced the trial to a "farce or mockery of justice." Other lower courts adopted this standard; some courts developed higher standards, such as "reasonably effective assistance."[40] In 1984, the Supreme Court faced the issue of defining *effective assistance of counsel*. The Court adopted the "reasonably effective assistance" standard then used by all the lower federal courts and stated that no further definition was needed than the establishing of a two-prong test, explained in this brief excerpt from *Strickland v. Washington*.[41]

Strickland v. *Washington*

A convicted defendant's claim that counsel's assistance was so defective as to require reversal of a conviction or death sentence has two components. First, the defendant must show that counsel's performance was deficient. This requires showing that counsel made errors so serious that counsel was not functioning as the "counsel" guaranteed the defendant by the Sixth Amendment. Second, the defendant must show that the deficient performance prejudiced the defense. This requires showing that counsel's errors were so serious as to deprive the defendant of a fair trial, a trial whose result is reliable. Unless a defendant makes both showings, it cannot be said that the conviction or death sentence resulted from a breakdown in the adversary process that renders the result unreliable.

Analysis of cases holding that a defendant did or did not receive effective assistance of counsel requires an extensive knowledge of procedural criminal law, but such knowledge is not required to understand some cases that deal with the issue. For example, a lower federal court in 1970 held that a defendant was not denied effective assistance of counsel when his attorney fell asleep during the trial. The trial judge, noting this problem, did not awaken the attorney because he did not think he was missing anything important. The appellate court held that counsel's action did not make a "farce or mockery of justice" out of the trial![42]

This case, like others, illustrates the need to look more carefully at all the facts before drawing a conclusion. It is, of course, possible to conclude that anytime an attorney falls asleep during trial, the trial becomes a "farce or mockery," or under the *Strickland* guidelines, defendant was denied "reasonably effective assistance of counsel," and the two-prong test was met. It is also possible, however, that nothing important happened during that brief period of sleep. Perhaps this issue could best be analyzed in light of your experiences with class lectures or reading a text!

The Right to Refuse Appointed Counsel

Defendants may choose to give up their right to counsel and represent themselves. The Supreme Court has said that the

> question is whether a State may constitutionally hale a person into its criminal courts and there force a lawyer upon him, even when he insists that he wants to conduct his own defense. It is not an easy question, but we have concluded that a State may not constitutionally do so.[43]

The **waiver** of the right to counsel must be voluntarily and knowingly made. Judges know that the trial process is complicated, and they guard against the possibility that defendants will create an unfair disadvantage by appearing **pro se** (representing themselves). Judges question defendants carefully about their knowledge of criminal law and procedure and their understanding of the advantages of having counsel present.

Some judges require standby counsel to be present with the defendant to explain the basic rules, formalities, and etiquette in the courtroom.[44] Nevertheless, defendants who represent themselves at trial may create serious problems for the court and for victims, as illustrated by the case discussed in Spotlight 9.5.

Some defendants who represent themselves try to appeal their convictions by complaining that they did not have effective assistance of counsel. In such cases, the reviewing court will examine whether the defendant

A man who served as his own attorney and confronted victims on the witness stand at his trial has been sentenced to 376 years in prison on 14 counts of rape and burglary.

Judge Lynne Hufnagel of Denver County Court imposed the sentence Friday on Quintin Keith Wortham, 27 years old, for six counts of sexual assault and eight counts of burglary and theft. A jury found him guilty on all counts Tuesday after deliberating two hours. Judge Hufnagel imposed consecutive terms ranging from 16 to 32 years.

District Attorney Norm Early said the sentence was the longest in the history of Colorado. Mr. Early's office said Mr. Wortham would not be eligible for parole for 60 years, if at all.

Of Mr. Wortham's rapes of young professional women in 1985 and 1986 and the manner in which he committed them, Judge Hufnagel said: "No terrorist could have conceived a more effective torture. He teased, he threatened all with death, he forced each to hear an unceasing banter about themselves, about him and about his life. The possibility is remote at best that Quintin Wortham will ever be anything but a savage parasite."

A public defender had been appointed to act as Mr. Wortham's counsel, but the defendant never called on that lawyer in the four-week trial.

Mr. Early said he had no doubt that Mr. Wortham was responsible for all 11 reported cases of rape in 1984 and 1985 in the historic residential area behind the State Capitol. Mr. Early said the style of the rapes also fitted a pattern of 30 to 50 other rapes in the area in that period and that he believed Mr. Wortham was responsible for many of those as well.

This was Mr. Wortham's second trial on the rape and burglary charges. His first trial last year attracted attention when the defendant served as his own attorney. The courtroom atmosphere was raucous as Mr. Wortham badgered witnesses, in some cases the rape victims, to bolster his contention that the police had railroaded him and that the victims had misidentified him.

The first trial was declared a mistrial after prosecutors contended that Mr. Wortham's behavior made a fair trial impossible. At one point, Mr. Wortham was banned from the courtroom and a public defender was appointed; Mr. Wortham later dismissed the lawyer. The defendant refused to obey the judge's order not to discuss evidence that was deemed inadmissible.

He was accused of trying to tamper with evidence by attempting to remove hair from the band of a hat that the rapist wore in each attack.

In attempting to defend himself at the second trial, he called to the stand rape victims in cases in which he had not been charged, to testify that they could not identify him.

But in one case he called a rape victim who had failed to identify Mr. Wortham in the initial lineup. When he asked if she could identify him now when she could not do so earlier, she told Mr. Wortham she had recognized his voice at a hearing months after the lineup. When the victim heard Mr. Wortham's voice in court, she said, "An icy chill took hold of me and it was very clear to me that you were the person who did such a horrible thing."

made a knowing and intelligent waiver of the right to counsel and, if so, the conviction will stand. As one court said, "[the defendant] represented himself by his own choice. He cannot complain now that the quality of his *pro se* defense amounted to denial of the effective assistance of counsel."[45]

Before looking at the methods of providing defense attorneys for indigent defendants, a brief look at private defense counsel is appropriate.

Private Defense Counsel

Many defendants prefer to retain their own defense counsel, and they must do so if they are not eligible for an attorney provided at public expense. It is a common belief that the defense attorney with the best reputation for winning cases is one who works privately and charges very high fees. These attorneys are easily recognizable, but their fees preclude many defendants from retaining their services.

Finding a good defense attorney who is not so widely known is more difficult. Few standards exist for measuring the competency of attorneys in criminal defense work. Some are selected by references from former clients. Others may be selected from advertising on radio or television. In some cities, the local bar association will make referrals upon request. Defendants should choose an attorney who is a competent trial lawyer, but the personality and style of the attorney also might be important.

Some systematic attempts have been made to categorize private attorneys who are engaged in criminal defense work. One classification system notes the percentage of time of the lawyer's total practice that is spent on criminal defense work. Another distinguishes between attorneys whose major skills are in courtroom practice or trial work and those who specialize in negotiation with prosecutors over a bargain that will involve a plea without a trial. A third system separates attorneys who handle special types of nonviolent crimes in federal courts from attorneys who handle crimes of violence (murder, rape, assault), victimless crimes (prostitution, narcotics addiction, sexual offenses), or minor property crimes (burglary and larceny) in state courts.[46]

Alan Dershowitz, a noted Harvard law professor and defense attorney, says there are two rules for selecting private defense attorneys. The first "is to be certain that he or she is interested *only* in achieving the best legal result for the client." The defendant should be sure the attorney is not attempting to gain media exposure, further a personal cause, (such as opposition to capital punishment or police brutality), or maintain a good relationship with the prosecutor and the courts. The second rule is to choose a well-rounded attorney. Lawyers who concentrate on plea bargains and avoid trials may not be in the best position to help the defendant. Defendants also should avoid attorneys who are lazy or too busy and those who guarantee positive results.[47]

ORGANIZATION AND STRUCTURE OF DEFENSE SYSTEMS FOR INDIGENTS

Three models have been used for organizing and providing defense counsel for indigent defendants: the public defender, assigned counsel, and the contract models. The map of the United States in Figure 9.3 indicates the states in which a majority of counties provide counsel for indigents, along with the type of defense system each state favors.

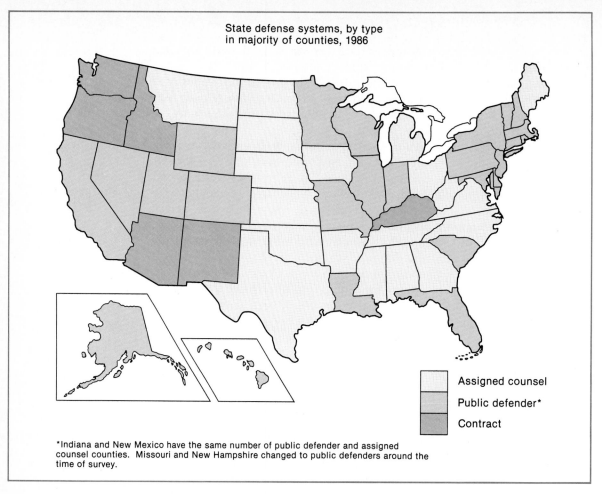

State defense systems, by type
in majority of counties, 1986

Assigned counsel

Public defender*

Contract

*Indiana and New Mexico have the same number of public defender and assigned counsel counties. Missouri and New Hampshire changed to public defenders around the time of survey.

FIGURE 9.3

Public Defense Systems in the United States (*Source:* Bureau of Justice Statistics, *National Criminal Defense Systems Study: Final Report* (Washington, D.C.: U.S. Department of Justice, 1986), front cover.)

Public Defender Systems

Since the *Gideon* case, most counties have met the need to provide counsel for indigents by establishing **public defender** systems. The public defender system is actually a public law firm whose mission is to provide counsel in criminal cases for defendants who cannot afford to retain private counsel. The size of the system will vary.

Most public defender systems are located in metropolitan areas. They are publicly supported and administered by an attorney who usually is called the *public defender.* That person will be assisted by other attorneys who usually are called *assistant public defenders.* The system also will be staffed by the usual support personnel. In larger offices, law students may work as interns. The public defender system may be statewide or local.

Like prosecutors, public defenders have the advantage of specializing in criminal cases. This increases their expertise and efficiency, but it may also contribute to professional burnout. Also like prosecutors, many public defenders work with tremendous caseloads, leaving them insufficient time to devote to any particular case. Inadequate budgets often result in a lack of support staff and equipment.[48]

Public defenders enjoy the excitement and competition of trial work, but they also point to the many disadvantages of public defense work: most cases are lost instead of won; some clients are hostile and arrogant and others are very demanding; they constantly work with "the raw nerve ends of society, man's inhumanity to man." Public defenders must also work against the popular image that they are less qualified than private attorneys.[49]

Several suggestions have been made for improving the public defender system. Larger budgets would permit the programs to add attorneys and cut caseloads. Part-time law students should be employed to conduct initial interviews, make eligibility determinations, verify client information, develop alternate sentencing plans, and do basic criminal law research. Some of these tasks also may be performed by **paralegals,** who are not attorneys but have some legal training and can work under the supervision of attorneys.

Better recruitment and more adequate training of attorneys would also improve public defender programs. Training programs should be continuous, with an emphasis on efficiency and ethical standards as well as negotiating and trial skills. If the office does not have a formal training program, efforts should be made to assign new personnel to a more experienced attorney for a period of observation or to contract with private agencies or other public defender offices for training programs.

The burden of improving public defender services rests in two places. Both the legal profession and society must assume the responsibility for protecting our constitutional guarantees. The image of public defender services as politically unpopular, and therefore having a low priority for criminal justice funds, needs to be replaced. Criminal defendants will never be popular, but the public must provide the money and resources necessary to make the system work as a protective device to ensure that no one is denied the constitutional right to be defended by counsel.[50]

Assigned Counsel

Almost two-thirds of the counties in the United States have an **assigned counsel** system. Under this model, attorneys are assigned to defend particular indigent defendants. The assignments usually are made by the judge who will preside over that trial, but some jurisdictions have moved to a more formal and organized system in an attempt to coordinate assignments throughout a jurisdiction. Assignments normally are made from lists of attorneys who have volunteered to participate in the program, although in some jurisdictions all attorneys are expected to participate in the assigned counsel program. A minority of jurisdictions have some procedures for assessing qualifications of attorneys who participate in assigned counsel cases, but the majority have no qualifications beyond a license to practice law. Most areas that have assigned counsel systems do not have formal provisions for removing names from the list of participating attorneys.

Assigned counsel are paid on a fee schedule that may be determined by state statute or by local bar regulations. In some jurisdictions, however, the requirement is that attorneys assigned to represent indigent defendants must receive "reasonable compensation" for their work. This gives judges wide discretion in determining fees for assigned counsel. Attorneys have complained about different fees for the same types of cases. In general the money received by assigned counsel is less than the average fees paid to private attorneys, and in most jurisdictions, considerably less. Maximum fees are frequently established, making it impossible for assigned counsel to be paid an adequate fee for all hours worked in a complicated case.[51]

In large jurisdictions assigned counsel systems have the advantage of involving more attorneys in the criminal court process. This may help expose problems and lead to reforms in the court system. The assigned counsel system may serve as a check on the informal system of interaction among prosecutors, defense attorneys, and judges. If the same people are always involved in criminal cases, there may be a greater tendency to cooperate with each other to the detriment of defendants. However, most assigned counsel systems are in small counties; and in many of these jurisdictions the attorneys, prosecutors, and judges are well known to each other.

There also are some problems. Only a few attorneys may volunteer to accept criminal cases, and the list of attorneys may not be rotated enough, thus allowing favoritism in the assignment process. Defense counsel who cooperate with judges and prosecutors are selected more often. Aggressive attorneys who fight for their client's rights may not be asked to handle future cases. Furthermore, it may be difficult for the judge to select a lawyer competent to handle an unusual or complex case. On the other hand, if all attorneys must participate in the assigned counsel system, there is a greater chance of appointing counsel who are experienced in the practice of criminal law.

Contract Systems

A national survey of publicly supported defense systems disclosed that 6 percent of the counties provide representation for indigent defendants through a contract system. Most of these counties are small (less than 50,000 people). In the contract system, a bar association, private law firm, or individual attorney contracts with a jurisdiction to provide legal assistance for indigent defendants.[52]

The contract system has the advantage of allowing attorneys and the funding source some flexibility in negotiating terms. For attorneys, a contract to provide legal services can establish a definite income and all the security that goes with it. This system may present problems, too. For example, the most common type of contract system arrangement is the block grant, in which the attorney (or bar association or law firm) contracts for a set fee to cover that attorney's representation of all indigent defendants in that jurisdiction. If the number of cases exceeds expectations, the attorney must continue to represent indigent defendants until the end of the contract period. A significant increase in the number of cases could create extremely heavy caseloads for attorneys, resulting in inadequate pay for the attorneys and inadequate control for the defendants.

Comparison of Defense Systems

Some prosecutors prefer assigned counsel because they are less experienced in criminal matters than public defenders. Assigned counsel may be guided by a practical concern: the profit motive. Since assigned counsel normally have full-time practices in other areas of the law, where they could be earning higher fees, they often prefer early dispositions or quick dismissals in criminal cases. Prosecutors therefore may be able to settle more cases without trials. This may be efficient for prosecutors, courts, and society, but it does not always result in the best defense for defendants.

Some argue that indigent defendants represented by public defenders may be in a better position than those with appointed counsel. Because public defender offices provide a regular salary, they may attract better-qualified attorneys than the appointed counsel system. Compensation is very low for appointed counsel and most attorneys cannot afford to take time away from their private practices to engage in criminal defense work. Public defenders generally have more money available for investigative work than assigned counsel. Public defenders have more experience negotiating with the prosecutor and may be more knowledgeable in criminal law and procedure.[53]

How does the use of publicly funded counsel compare to private defense? In explaining the reason for providing defense counsel for the poor, the Supreme Court said, "There can be no equal justice where the kind of trial a man gets depends on the amount of money he has."[54] Despite this recognition of the right to defense counsel, some argue that indigents receive less adequate counsel than defendants who hire a private attorney.

One study found that the middle group of private attorneys and public defenders were equally competent but that the best private attorneys were superior to the best public defenders. However, the worst public defenders clearly were better than the bottom group of private attorneys.[55]

Others claim that there is no significant difference in the outcome of cases defended by public defenders and assigned or contract counsel as compared with those defended by private attorneys. One study found that the probability of conviction was not related to the type of attorney conducting the defense. The small differences generally work in favor of those represented by public defenders. It may be that if most cases went to trial, private counsel would obtain better results; but in most cases a plea is negotiated between the prosecution and the defense, a system in which the better trial skills of the private attorney often are outweighed by the public defender's greater skills in negotiating with the prosecutor.[56]

Counsel provided for indigent defendants may be as effective as private defense attorneys, but many indigent defendants do not believe that. A comparison found that all clients of private lawyers believed the attorneys were on their side, but only 20 percent of those represented by public defenders felt the same way. Another study disclosed that the use of private counsel resulted in more positive prisoner attitudes than did the use of either appointed counsel or public defenders. However, it also showed that prisoners who receive lesser punishment "will perceive fair, diligent, and open legal and factual investigation on the part of their lawyer."[57]

In evaluating the cynical attitudes toward public defenders as compared with private attorneys, it is important to consider the factors that might influence such attitudes. The public defender's clients are poor. They are less likely to speak effectively, to be able to aid in their own defense, or to understand the criminal process and their constitutional rights. They also are more likely to remain in jail pending trial. In addition to the trauma of being incarcerated while awaiting trial, they do not have the opportunity to select their own attorneys.[58]

In addition, defendants may distrust public defenders because they distrust the government and they do not believe in the possibility of equal justice for all. They may have the attitude that money determines the worth of legal services. Defendants may believe that public defenders get paid for guilty pleas or have to meet quotas of guilty pleas in order to keep their jobs in the system.[59]

There are suggestions for improving the defendant's perception of counsel. The first is a program of defendant education and awareness so that clients would have the information necessary to judge realistically whether their counsel conducted an adequate representation. The second is to change the parts of the indigent defense system that create or reinforce negative perceptions. One possibility is for attorneys to increase their attention to the client by spending more time conversing during the initial interview and less time filling out forms, by not appearing overly friendly to prosecutors or other court personnel, and by not having two clients in the same courtroom at the same time. One final suggestion is that indigent defendants should have the same ability to hire and fire public counsel as those who can afford to hire private attorneys.[60]

One final problem with providing counsel for indigent defendants is that all of the models are expensive. And with cutbacks in federal and state funding for many programs, indigent defense systems are facing serious funding problems, which may be expected to continue for some time. Local, state, and federal governments, however, must find ways to continue financing defense systems for indigent defendants in order to comply with constitutional requirements concerning the right to counsel.

THE DEFENSE ATTORNEY'S ROLE

Defense attorneys are charged with the responsibility of protecting the constitutional rights of defendants. In this chapter we focused on the right to counsel, but we noted that this right does not exist only at trial. What, then, is the role of the defense attorney in implementing his or her responsibility to represent a defendant in the criminal justice system?

The first encounter that a defense attorney has with a client will often be at the jail. A suspect, after arrest and booking, will be permitted at least one phone call. That call is often to a lawyer or to a friend, requesting that the friend find a lawyer. If the suspect cannot afford an attorney, counsel will be appointed by the judge at the first court appearance. Those who can afford to retain attorneys, however, often will be visited by their attorneys before that court appearance.

The first responsibility of the defense attorney is to interview the client and obtain as many facts as possible. The attorney must gain the confidence of the client to the extent that the defendant will be willing to disclose the important facts. The attorney should explain that this information is confidential between the attorney and the defendant. It will often be necessary for the defense attorney to begin an investigation by interviewing witnesses or friends, going to the scene of the alleged crime, and securing physical evidence. The attorney also will talk to the prosecutor to see what information the police and prosecution have secured against the defendant.

The initial interview with the defendant is a very important one. Defendants may be confused about the law. They may have little or no recognition of their constitutional rights. They may not understand the importance of certain facts to the defense. The attorney must be able to elicit the needed information while maintaining a sense of perspective and understanding.

As soon as the defense attorney has enough information, he or she should advise the defendant concerning the strategy that might be used in the case. It might be reasonable for the defendant to plead guilty rather than go to trial. Negotiating pleas before trial is a frequent and very important procedure, which will be discussed in the next chapter. The defense attorney should explain to the defendant the pros and cons of pleading guilty, but the attorney must be careful about encouraging a guilty plea when the evidence is strong that the defendant is not guilty. Even in those cases, a particular defendant, because of his or her prior record or the nature of the alleged offense, might be well advised to plead guilty to a lesser offense rather than risk conviction on the more serious charge. All these issues involve trial strategy, which includes knowing what to expect from the prosecutor as well as trying to predict what the judge and jury will do should the case go to trial.

In some cases defense attorneys will need to talk to the families of their clients and inform them of what to expect during the initial stages of the criminal justice process. Families and friends also might be valuable sources of information useful to the attorney in preparing a defense and in preparing sentencing recommendations if the defendant is found guilty. Getting the facts from defendants and their families and friends is a difficult problem in many cases. It also is emotionally draining, and it is a process for which most defense attorneys are not trained. Defense attorneys devise many strategies to elicit information from clients. Some use sworn police statements to shock the defendant into being honest. Others appear nonjudgmental and use hypothetical questions to allow clients to save face. Some attorneys admit they browbeat the clients by being tyrannical. Others try to be friendly, but they may resent the time required to discover the facts. One attorney who quit legal services after three years explained,

> I was trained in law, but not in how to work with people . . . it was that
> difficulty in dealing with people and their personal problems, with having
> to be a psychiatrist instead of a lawyer, that became the problem for
> me—not the legal matters per se.[61]

Defending guilty defendants may be a problem for some attorneys. Those considering criminal defense work as a career should understand that they will be representing many guilty clients. Many attorneys would rather defend the guilty than the innocent because there is less pressure to obtain a dismissal or an acquittal, and they do not face the extreme emotional strain of seeing an innocent person receive an undeserved prison sentence. However, the attorney whose client is acquitted or found not guilty might feel responsible if that client commits another crime. For some attorneys, the fear that their clients might terrorize society if they are freed creates tension, although they may rationalize it by convincing themselves that the prosecutor may be blamed for losing the case or that it is better to release a guilty person than to convict an innocent one.

After the initial interviews and investigation, the defense attorney must keep track of the scheduled procedures for the remainder of the time the case is in the criminal justice system. Defense attorneys are criticized frequently for missing deadlines, being unprepared for hearings, or attempting to delay the proceedings by asking for a **continuance.** Sometimes continuances are justified because there has not been sufficient time to prepare for the hearing. Other times the delays are unreasonable and may even be requested to obstruct justice.

Private defense attorneys also have been known to attempt to delay proceedings because they have not been paid by their clients. It is difficult to collect fees after a case has ended, particularly when the defendant is not pleased with the result. Some attorneys handle this problem by requiring that defendants pay in advance. They require a retainer fee, and when that amount of money has been exhausted by the time and expenses of the attorney, another fee will be required before the attorney continues with the case.

It is important for the defense attorney to keep the defendant informed of what is happening in the case. This, however, is a function neglected by many attorneys. Defendants often complain that they have not been told what is happening in their cases; some do not even know when they will go to court for the pretrial hearing or for the trial until shortly before time for their appearance.

Even while obtaining facts and other forms of evidence from defendants and others, defense attorneys should begin preparing the case for trial should that occur. Trial strategy is important, and an unprepared attorney will do a great disservice to the defendant. In recent years there has been great controversy in the United States over the competency of trial lawyers, particularly defense attorneys. Former chief justice Warren E. Burger led the allegations of lawyer incompetency. Bar associations have appointed commissions to study the problem. The results vary, but the lack of adequate training in trial skills is a frequently mentioned problem. Law schools have felt the pressure to increase training in trial advocacy; but it is an expensive process, and not all professors are dedicated to the belief that it is a major function of legal training.

DEFENSE AND PROSECUTION: A CONCLUSION

The function of prosecution has been proclaimed the most important in the criminal justice system. The defense of a criminal case also is recognized as the most important, since the constitutional rights are of no consequence unless they are recognized in individual cases. Defense attorneys are there to protect the legal rights of defendants.

Regardless of the conclusion on which is more important, prosecution or defense, it is clear that these two functions are critical to the criminal justice system. The defense attorney and the prosecuting attorney have tremendous impact on the individual defendants and all other processes of the system. If the prosecutor refuses to prosecute in certain types of cases, the police may refuse to arrest for those violations. If the prosecutor abuses the discretion of the office, defendants who are improperly brought into the system may justifiably react with anger and hostility, and the rights of everyone may be jeopardized. Vigorous and fair prosecution that results in more convictions will increase the number of people in our already overcrowded jails and prisons.

Inadequate defense by attorneys creates dissension among defendants and jeopardizes the adversary system. But adequate defense that results in acquittals may anger the public, police, prosecutors, and victims. Overburdened prosecution attorneys often must compromise the system; but that is also true of overburdened defense attorneys. Hostility between prosecution and defense attorneys may endanger defendants' rights to fair treatment; too much cooperation between them could have the same result, as we will see in the next chapter's discussion of the most extensive interaction between prosecution and defense: the process of negotiating for a guilty plea before trial.

The strain between the due process and the crime control models of criminal justice runs throughout any analysis of prosecution and defense. The extreme of crime control might lead the prosecution to violate the due process rights of defendants. But if defense attorneys are vigorous in their efforts to preserve these due process rights, crime control will be more difficult. The problem, then, is to develop the system to the point of achieving some compromise between the two models.

SUMMARY

This chapter focused on the prosecution and the defense of criminal cases, beginning with an overview of the relationship of these two important functions to the philosophy of the adversary system. Each then was discussed in detail.

In discussing prosecution, we looked at the historical emergence of public prosecution, contrasting that approach with the method of private prosecution that was its predecessor in the United States and that still exists in some other countries. Although private prosecution might work in simple societies, where most people know each other and often know who commits the criminal offenses, this system is not effective in large and complex societies. Victims in larger societies often do not know who commits crimes against them. Victims also may abuse their private powers of prosecution. Thus, in the United States a system of public prosecution emerged.

Public prosecution systems in the United States are varied. Although most prosecutors are elected officials, their functions and the structures of their offices will differ depending on the size of the jurisdiction and the complexities of local needs. State systems of prosecution, like those at the federal level, may be quite large. They differ from local systems in some respects. State and federal prosecutors may issue opinions on the constitutionality of their respective state and federal statutes. But they are also charged with the prosecution of state and federal crimes, and like local prosecutors, they must make important decisions on which cases to prosecute and which charges to bring in each case.

This power to determine who to prosecute and which charges to bring when there are several options gives prosecutors at all levels tremendous power. Choosing not to prosecute usually will end the case. Once the initial decision to prosecute has been made, prosecutors may drop charges. Charges may be dropped for a lack of evidence or for political or personal reasons. This power is virtually unchecked. Even when the prosecutorial decision to drop charges occurs after the defendant has made a court appearance and the judge must approve the prosecutor's decision, the prosecutor still has immense power in the final determination. Judges often defer to prosecutors who insist that they are overworked, their resources are limited, and there just is not enough evidence to continue this prosecution.

Such extensive power may lead to abuse, of course. Prosecutors may abuse their discretion in many ways. They may overcharge defendants, with crimes for which they have little or no evidence, to coerce the defendants to plead guilty to crimes for which they have sufficient evidence. This avoids trials and reduces the prosecutors' caseload while providing them with "victories."

These and other possible examples of prosecutorial misconduct have led to the development of methods to control prosecutorial discretion. Departmental policies within the prosecutor's office may provide sufficient guidelines to prevent serious abuses of discretion, but legislative guidelines and judicial review have become necessary in many jurisdictions.

The second focus of the chapter was on the constitutional right to counsel and the meaning of defense. The right to appointment of counsel for indigents was traced historically, culminating with the critical *Gideon* decision in 1963, in which the Court held that the right to appointed counsel for indigents was not limited to capital cases, but applied to other felonies as well. In 1972 the right to appointed counsel for indigents was extended. In *Argersinger v. Hamlin*, the Court held that no one may be sentenced to incarceration, even for a short time for a petty offense, without having had benefit of counsel at trial.

The right to appointed counsel, however, does not exist at all pretrial and posttrial stages, although it does exist at "critical stages." *Actual imprisonment*, not the mere threat of imprisonment, appears to trigger the right to appointed counsel in criminal cases. The right to counsel implies a right to effective counsel, which has been defined by the Supreme Court in *Strickland v. Washington* as involving a two-prong test. The defendant must show that counsel was deficient and that deficiency resulted in prejudice to the defendant who, as a result, did not get a fair trial. This standard is very difficult to prove.

The right to counsel also involves a right to refuse counsel. Defendants may serve as their own attorneys provided they have knowingly and intelligently waived their right to outside counsel. If they wish counsel and cannot afford to retain an attorney, one must be provided for them. Several systems provide such counsel. We looked closely at the public defender system, the assigned counsel system and the contract system, noting how they differ from each other and from the use of privately retained defense counsel. In discussing which type of defense is most effective, we saw that the studies vary in their conclusions, but that, no matter what the studies indicate, defendants generally believe that they get a better defense with private attorneys.

The role of the defense attorney in relationship to the client and the responsibility of that attorney to provide adequate assistance of counsel are both very important aspects of the defense system. To provide an adequate defense, the attorney must be able to relate to his or her client in such a way as to secure needed evidence and to gain the assistance of the client should the decision be made to put the defendant on the witness stand. The interaction of the defense attorney and prosecutor is important, too. The specifics of that interaction will be discussed in detail in the next chapter in the context of pretrial procedures.

STUDY QUESTIONS

1. What is the difference between public and private prosecution? Which system do you think is best?

2. Compare and contrast the different types of prosecution systems in this country.

3. What is the main function of the prosecutor? Why is the prosecutor allowed so much discretion in fulfilling that role? What are the problems with allowing such discretion?

4. How can prosecutorial discretion be kept within reasonable limits?

5. What is meant by the *right to counsel*? Describe briefly what that right means today compared to its historical meaning in this country.

6. What is the importance of the *Gideon* case?

7. What is the scope of the right to appointed counsel? Should it be expanded, as for example, in the case of *Scott v. Illinois*?

8. What does the Supreme Court mean by *effective assistance of counsel*? If you had the opportunity to define that term for the Court, what would you include?

9. If you were a defendant in a criminal case, would you prefer to be represented by private counsel, a public defender, or assigned counsel? What are the reasons for your decision?

10. What ways would you suggest for improving the availability and quality of legal defense counsel?

11. Would you prefer to be a defense attorney or a prosecuting attorney? Why would you choose one over the other?

12. What is the relevance of the due process model and the crime control model to the discussion in this chapter?

ENDNOTES

1. See Abraham S. Goldstein, "Prosecution: History of the Public Prosecutor," in Sanford H. Kadish, ed., *Encyclopedia of Crime and Justice* (New York: Macmillan Publishing Co., 1983), vol. 3, pp. 1286–89. See also Allen Steinberg, "From Private Prosecution to Plea Bargaining: Criminal Prosecution, the District Attorney, and American Legal History," *Crime and Delinquency* 30 (October 1984): 568–92.

2. Philip Revzin, "For the People: Richard McQuate Has Prestige, Little Crime as a Rural Prosecutor," *Wall Street Journal* (6 May 1976). For further information on rural prosecutors, see James Eisenstein, "Research on Rural Criminal Justice: A Summary," in Shanler D. Cronk et al., eds., *Criminal Justice in Rural America* (Washington, D.C.: U.S. Department of Justice, 1982), Chapter 7, pp. 105–45. See John Hagan and Marjorie S. Zatz, "The Social Organization of Criminal Justice Processing: An Event History Analysis," *Social Science Research* 14 (June 1985): 103–25 for a discussion of the differences between rural and urban courts.

3. Joan E. Jacoby, *The American Prosecutor: A Search For Identity* (Lexington, Mass.: D.C. Heath and Co., 1980), pp. 55–61, 277.

4. Ibid., pp. 64–65, 71–74, 275, 277, 278.

5. Mark F. Pomerantz, "Prosecution: United States Attorney," in Kadish, ed., *Encyclopedia of Crime and Justice,* vol. 3, p. 1295.

6. For a journalistic account of prosecutors and their work, based on interviews with famous prosecutors, see James Stewart, *The Prosecutors* (New York: Simon and Schuster, 1987), reviewed and criticized by noted law professor and trial attorney Alan M. Dershowitz of Harvard, in the *American Bar Association Journal* (1 October 1987), pp. 144–46.

7. State v. Mitchell, 395 A.2d 1257 (Sup. Ct., N.J., App. Div., 1978).

8. Kenneth C. Davis, *Discretionary Justice: A Preliminary Inquiry* (Baton Rouge: Louisiana State University Press, 1969), p. 12.

9. Michael L. Benson et al., "District Attorneys and Corporate Crime: Surveying the Prosecutorial Gatekeepers," *Criminology* 26 (August 1988): 505.

10. See Abraham S. Goldstein, *The Passive Judiciary: Prosecutorial Discretion and the Guilty Plea* (Baton Rouge: Louisiana State University Press, 1981), p. 9.

11. Peter W. Greenwood, "The Violent Offender in the Criminal Justice System," in Marvin E.

Wolfgang and Neil Alan Weiner, eds., *Criminal Violence* (Beverly Hills, Calif.: Sage Publications, 1982), p. 334.

12. Ibid., p. 335.
13. Michael R. Gottfredson and Don M. Gottfredson, *Decision Making in Criminal Justice: Toward the Rational Exercise of Discretion* (Cambridge, Mass.: Ballinger Publishing Company, 1980), pp. 152–53. For a more recent empirical study indicating that prosecutorial decisions are often made in terms of predictions of career enhancement, see Celesta A. Albonetti, "Criminality, Prosecutorial Screening, and Uncertainty: Toward a Theory of Discretionary Decision Making in Felony Case Processings," *Criminology* 24 (November, 1986): 623–44.
14. For further discussion, see K. Williams, *The Role of the Victim in the Prosecution of Violent Offenses*, Institute for Law and Social Research, Publication No. 12 (Washington, D.C.: U.S. Government Printing Office, 1977); and Martha A. Myers and Gary D. LaFree, "Sexual Assault and Its Prosecution: A Comparison with Other Crimes," *Journal of Criminal Law and Criminology* 73 (Fall 1982): 1282–1305. See also Albonetti, ibid.
15. For a study indicating racial differences in the decision whether to prosecute, see Cassia Spohn et al., "The Impact of the Ethnicity and Gender of Defendants on the Decision to Reject or Dismiss Felony Charges," *Criminology* 25 (February 1987): 175–91, finding a "pattern of discrimination in favor of female defendants and against black and Hispanic defendants. Hispanic males are most likely to be prosecuted fully, followed by black males, Anglo males, and females of all ethnic groups." Ibid., p. 175.
16. James Vorenberg, "Decent Restraint of Prosecutorial Power," *Harvard Law Review* 94 (May 1981): 1526.
17. Ibid., pp. 1526–27, 1531.
18. REV. CODE WASH., Section 9.94A 440(1).
19. Stuart P. Green, "Private Challenges to Prosecutorial Inaction: A Model Declaratory Judgment Statute," *Yale Law Journal* 97 (February 1988): 507.
20. U.S. Department of Justice, *Principles of Federal Prosecution*, 1980; quoted in David Boerner, *Sentencing in Washington: A Legal Analysis of the Sentencing Reform Act of 1981* (Seattle: Butterworth Legal Publishers, 1985), pp. 12–18.
21. Yick Wo v. Hopkins, 118 U.S. 356 (1886). In the *Yick Wo* case, a public board that was authorized to issue laundry licenses denied licenses to Chinese applicants and granted licenses to nearly all white applicants.
22. City of Minneapolis v. Buschette, 240 N.W. 2d, 500, 505 (Minn. 1976).
23. Oyler v. Boles, 368 U.S. 448, 456 (1962).

24. Brady v. Maryland, 373 U.S. 83 (1963).
25. Bennet L. Gershman, "The Burger Court and Prosecutorial Misconduct," *Criminal Law Bulletin* 21 (May–June 1985): 219. See Moore v. Illinois, 408 U.S. 786 (1972); Giglio v. United States, 405 U.S. 150 (1972). See also Bennett L. Gershman, *Prosecutorial Misconduct* (New York: Clark Boardman Co., 1985).
26. See Greer v. Miller, 107 S.Ct. 3102 (1986).
27. Darden v. Wainwright, 477 U.S. 168 (1986), *reh'g denied*, 107 S.Ct. 24 (1986), *remanded*, 803 F.2d 613 (11th Cir. 1987).
28. For more information on prosecutorial misconduct, see Bennett L. Gershman, *Prosecutorial Misconduct* (New York: Clark Boardman Company, 1985). For information on prosecutorial misconduct regarding the grand jury, see "Prosecutorial Misconduct in the Grand Jury: Dismissal of Indictments Pursuant to the Federal Supervisory Power," *Fordham Law Review* 56 (October 1987): 129–50. For a discussion of the Darden case and the implications of that decision for controlling prosecutorial misconduct, see "Prosecutorial Misconduct during Closing Argument after Darden v. Wainwright: The Guilty Need Not Complain," *Houston Law Review* 25 (January 1988): 217–44.
29. Powell v. Alabama, 287 U.S. 45 (1932). See Wayne R. LaFave and Jerold H. Israel, *Criminal Procedure* (St. Paul, Minn.: West Publishing Co., 1985), pp. 473–75. The source will be used for this historical background of the right to counsel.
30. Johnson v. Zerbst, 304 U.S. 458 (1938).
31. Betts v. Brady, 316 U.S. 455 (1942).
32. Gideon v. Wainwright, 372 U.S. 335 (1963). For a detailed account of this case, see Anthony Lewis, *Gideon's Trumpet* (New York: Random House, 1964).
33. Argersinger v. Hamlim, 407 U.S. 25, 37 (1972).
34. Scott v. Illinois, 440 U.S. 367 (1979), footnotes omitted.
35. Walker v. McLain, 768 F.2d 1181 (10th Cir. 1985), *cert. denied*, 474 U.S. 1061 (1986).
36. United States v. Wade, 388 U.S. 218 (1967).
37. For example, it does apply to the preliminary hearing, Coleman v. Alabama, 399 U.S. 1 (1970); it does not apply to a show-up identification that occurs before the suspect has been formally charged with a crime, Kirby v. Illinois, 406 U.S. 682 (1972), although even after a formal stage, the right may not always be applied. It has not been applied to a photographic identification that took place without the defendant, United States v. Ash, 413 U.S. 300 (1973).
38. Pennsylvania v. Finley, 481 U.S. 551 (1987), quoting Ross v. Moffitt, 417 U.S. 600, 616 (1974).
39. Powell v. Alabama, 287 U.S. 45 (1932); Avery v. Alabama, 308 U.S. 444 (1940); Glasser v. United

States, 315 U.S. 60 (1942); Michel v. Louisiana, 350 U.S. 91 (1955); McMann v. Richardson, 397 U.S. 759 (1970).

40. Diggs v. Welch, 148 F.2d 667 (D.C. Cir. 1945); *cert. denied*, 325 U.S. 889 (1945). Rummel v. Estelle, 590 F.2d 103 (5th Cir. 1979), *remanded* 498 F.Supp. 793 (W.D. Tex 1980), *aff'd.* 445 U.S. 263 (1980).

41. Strickland v. Washington, 466 U.S. 668 (1984). See also United States v. Cronic, 466 U.S. 648 (1984), and Burger v. Kemp 107 S.Ct. 3114 (1987).

42. United States v. Katz, 425 F.2d 928 (2d Cir. 1970).

43. Faretta v. California, 422 U.S. 806, 807 (1975).

44. McKaskle v. Wiggins, 465 U.S. 168 (1984).

45. United States v. Brown, 591 F.2d 307, 310–311 (5th Cir. 1979), *cert. denied*, 442 U.S. 913 (1979). See also United States v. Thibodeaux, 758 F.2d 199 (7th Cir. 1985).

46. Paul B. Wise, *Criminal Lawyers: An Endangered Species* (Beverly Hills, Calif.: Sage Publications, 1978), pp. 32–38.

47. Alan M. Dershowitz, *The Best Defense* (New York: Random House, 1982), pp. 404–405, 414–15.

48. For a recent account of the job of public defender based on a study of Cook County, Illinois, see Lisa J. McIntyre, *The Public Defender: The Practice of Law in the Shadows of Repute* (Chicago: University of Chicago Press, 1987).

49. William Hoffer, "This Lawyer Is Guilty of Doing Good," *Barrister* 12 (Spring 1985): 9–12, 50–51.

50. For a discussion of effective assistance of counsel for indigent defendants, see *New York University Review of Law & Social Change*, 14, no. 1, which contains a colloquium on the topic, "Effective Assistance of Counsel for The Indigent Criminal Defendant: Has the Promise Been Fulfilled?"

51. Bureau of Justice Statistics, *National Criminal Defense Systems Study: Final Report* (Washington, D.C.: U.S. Department of Justice, 1986), p. 18.

52. Ibid., p. 19.

53. Herbert Jacob, *Justice in America: Courts, Lawyers, and the Judicial Process*, 2d ed. (Boston: Little, Brown and Co., 1972), pp. 65, 66.

54. Griffin v. Illinois, 351 U.S. 12 (1956).

55. Wise, *Criminal Lawyers*, pp. 210–212.

56. Robert Hermann et al., *Counsel for the Poor: Criminal Defense in Urban America* (Lexington, Mass.: D.C. Heath and Co., 1977), p. 166.

57. Geoffrey P. Alpert, "Inadequate Defense Counsel: An Empirical Analysis of Prisoners' Perceptions," *American Journal of Criminal Law* 7 (March 1979): 18.

58. Jerome H. Skolnick, "Social Control in the Adversary System," in John A. Robertson, ed., *Rough Justice: Perspectives on Lower Criminal Courts* (Boston: Little, Brown and Co., 1974), p. 104. See also Dershowitz, *The Best Defense*, p. 416.

59. Hermann et al., *Counsel for the Poor*, pp. 168–69.

60. Alpert, "Inadequate Defense Counsel," p. 21.

61. Christina Maslach and Susan E. Jackson, "Lawyer Burn Out," *Barrister* 5 (Spring 1978): 53.

Pretrial Procedures

Jennifer, a 15-year-old high school student, was very active in her local church and school activities. About a month after the opening of school in the fall, Jennifer's mother began to notice that Jennifer was losing interest in her church and schoolwork and that she shunned her friends. After a long talk about the problems, Jennifer confessed to her mother that for the past year she had been having sexual relations with one of her teachers, Mr. Jones. Mr. Jones had just told her that he was terminating the relationship because he did not want to get a divorce and his wife was getting suspicious about his behavior.

Jennifer's mother called the police and reported what Jennifer had told her. Sexual relations with a female under 16, even with her consent, constitutes the crime of statutory rape, a felony. In this jurisdiction, conviction of statutory rape carries a penalty of from 5 to 20 years in prison. The police secured a proper arrest warrant, and Mr. Jones was arrested, taken to the police station, and booked.

Jones has no prior criminal record. He is an excellent teacher, and there is no evidence that he has been involved sexually with any of his other students. He is married and has three children. His wife has agreed to go with him if he will seek professional counseling. Jennifer's parents do not want her to be subjected to the rigors of being a witness in a criminal trial, thinking the experience would make it even more difficult for her to recover emotionally from the relationship.

INTRODUCTION

The facts in the CJA are presented to the prosecutor, who must make a decision whether to charge Jones with statutory rape, with a lesser offense, or to decline prosecution. For purposes of analysis, we will assume that Jones is prosecuted and that his case proceeds through all of the pretrial stages. Even though this chapter will examine each of those stages, we must understand that the stages in the criminal justice process are not discrete. They do not always happen one after the other; some stages overlap. Nor are the functions of the police, prosecutors, defense attorneys, and judges limited to particular stages. Citizens, as victims and witnesses as well as members of juries, also function at different levels.

STEPS IN THE CRIMINAL JUSTICE PROCESS

Figure 1.1 in Chapter 1 diagrams the steps in the criminal justice process. References to that figure will be made in this chapter because the diagram aids in visualizing the processes discussed here. The specific stages occurring before trial are enumerated in Figure 10.1 for easy reference in this chapter.

The stages in the criminal justice process are very important for two reasons. First, most people who are arrested will not be tried in a criminal court. Figure 9.2 points out how the system loses cases before trial. After initial investigation, there may not be sufficient evidence for an arrest.

Steps in the Criminal Justice Process before Trial

1. Report of a crime
2. Investigation prior to arrest
3. Arrest
4. Booking
5. Postarrest investigation
6. Prosecutor's decision to charge suspect with a crime
7. Initial appearance
8. Preliminary hearing
9. Grand jury review
10. Arraignment
11. Pretrial motions
12. Pretrial conferences

FIGURE 10.1
Steps in the Criminal Justice Process Before Trial

There may be sufficient evidence, but the police may not be able to locate the suspect, or for some other reason the police may not arrest. Those who are arrested may not be prosecuted for any number of reasons, as was discussed in Chapter 9. After the prosecutor files charges, those charges may be dismissed by the judge or they may be dropped by the prosecutor. This action may occur at any of the court sessions before trial. The charge also may be dropped or the case dismissed even after the trial begins.

This process of case reduction results in what has been called the *funnel effect*. As we move from the initial reporting of a crime through all the stages of the system, there is a significant reduction of cases. It has been estimated that of 5,000 felonies that come to the attention of police through their own observation or through citizen complaints, only 1,500 arrests will be made. Of those, 400 arrestees will be juveniles, who are processed through the juvenile court system. Prosecutors will file formal charges against only 600 of the 1,100 adult arrestees. That 600 will be reduced to 500, with approximately 50 being dismissed by magistrates during early pretrial procedures and another 50 cases being dropped by the prosecution.

Of the 500 remaining cases, 400 will be disposed of by a guilty plea, although many of those pleas will be to a misdemeanor not a felony. The remaining 100 adult defendants will go to trial; 70 percent will be convicted, although in some cases the conviction will be for a lesser offense than that charged, perhaps even a misdemeanor. The final result is that of 5,000 reported felonies, only about 250 adults will be sentenced to incarceration. Most of those will spend only a short term in jail. Many will be placed on probation or receive a short jail term followed by probation. Only about 100 will be sentenced to prison.[1]

From Reporting a Crime to Filing Charges: An Overview

Earlier chapters have dealt with the ways that criminal activities come to the attention of the police; the police processes of arrest, search and seizure, interrogation, and formal booking; and the prosecutor's decision whether to prosecute. In those discussions, the roles of police and prosecutor were emphasized. Also emphasized were the constitutional rights of due process involving the procedures and the responsibility of the defense attorney to make certain that those rights are not violated.

More attention, however, should be given to the specific methods by which police and prosecution investigate alleged criminal activity. The statutory and case law in these areas is extensive and complex. Only a sample will be examined here.

Investigation of a Criminal Case

In the discussions of police activities, we noted that early police investigation of a reported crime is very important. Evidence may be lost or destroyed. Witnesses may disappear. Thus, police will often question potential witnesses at or near the scene of a crime as soon as they can do so. They will check for physical evidence. In cases involving auto accidents, police probably will be required to include in their report a labeled diagram of how the accident apparently occurred. Diagrams are particularly important if the accident involved a drinking driver and serious injury or death of the victim and resulted in the possibility of felony charges being filed.

In the case of Mr. Jones, as soon as Jennifer's mother called the police and reported what Jennifer told her about her relationship with Mr. Jones, the police questioned Jennifer and her mother to see whether there is

Securing physical evidence is very important in a criminal case. (Jim Schaffer/ PhotoEdit)

sufficient evidence to believe that Mr. Jones did engage in sexual relations with Jennifer. If they found sufficient evidence, they would be able to secure an arrest warrant, and Mr. Jones could be arrested.

Securing Physical Evidence from the Accused Securing physical evidence that a crime has occurred may involve searching the automobile, home, or person of the suspect. It may involve getting a blood sample or breath test from the suspect in the case of a DWI arrest. In many cases, the police will interrogate someone but not file charges. Even in those cases, however, a report may be filed.

Police also may be required to file detailed reports when they investigate a crime, particularly a felony. Usually the reports will be filed on a printed form that contains questions about the offense, location, description of vehicle, weapons, injuries, and location of the injured parties.

These initial investigations at the time of a crime or right after a crime has been reported may be followed by more intensive investigations by the police or prosecution. In either case, the investigations often will be conducted by persons specially trained in investigatory processes. Fingerprints, weapons that might have been used in the crime, or any other physical evidence may be sought.

Medical examinations will be required of some victims, particularly rape victims. In a case involving statutory rape, however, where the female has consented to sexual intercourse, it is unlikely that such evidence will be available. For example, in this chapter's CJA, because Jennifer did not complain about the alleged sexual acts, any sexual activity that occurred might not have been recent enough to secure evidence of semen that could be compared to the semen of the accused.

Examinations may also be required for victims of any violent crime. Psychological examinations of victims may be given to obtain evidence

Physical evidence may also be secured from the accused; here an officer obtains fingerprints. (W. Marc Bernsau/Image Works)

that might be useful to the prosecution. Psychological or psychiatric examinations of defendants may be ordered at some point before trial in order to determine whether the defendant is mentally competent to stand trial.

Evidence also may be secured from the accused. For example, police may obtain body fluid or hair samples from the suspect. The police, however, cannot compel a suspect to testify against himself or herself. That would be a violation of the Fifth Amendment, discussed earlier in connection with police interrogation. The law in this area is complicated, but clearly the Supreme Court has held that some forms of evidence may be secured from suspects without violating their due process rights.[2]

Lineups, Showups, and Pictures One frequently used method of obtaining eyewitness identification of a suspect is to conduct lineups or showups. A **lineup** involves several people. The witness (who also may be the victim) is asked to look at all of the people in the lineup and decide whether he or she can identify the person(s) who allegedly committed the crime. Lineups are permissible provided they are conducted properly.[3] It would be improper to place five men in a lineup with only one dressed in a peculiar type of jacket, like the one reportedly worn by the armed robber.

Usually it is improper to ask a witness to identify the suspect in a showup which involves only that suspect. This kind of identification procedure has been widely condemned by courts but allowed under very restricted circumstances. It was permitted in a case in which a suspect was arrested when keys found at the scene of a murder were identified as his. The police took him, handcuffed to two police officers, to the hospital room of the wife of the murder victim two days after the murder. She had been stabbed by the man who killed her husband. Although this type of showup would not be permitted in most circumstances, the Supreme Court ruled that it was permissible in this case since the injured wife was the only person who could exonerate the defendant and it was not known how long she would live.[4]

Pictures also may be shown to witnesses for identification of suspects although restrictions are placed on this procedure, too. Among other requirements, it must be shown that the witnesses had a good opportunity to view the suspect. The pictures must be viewed soon after the alleged crime, while the memory of the witnesses is still clear. Multiple witnesses may not view the pictures in the company of each other. The police may not make suggestive comments regarding the pictures and the suspect.[5]

There also may be occasions in which crime suspects want a lineup and police refuse to conduct one. Figure 10.2 is an example of the form that may be filed when the defendant asks the court to compel the state to conduct a lineup. Notice in that form the statements that indicate why defendants might want to participate in a lineup. In some cases, a lineup is not necessary. Mr. Jones, for example, has been identified as the suspect; so a lineup would serve no purpose.

Electronic Surveillance and the Use of Informants One of the most controversial methods for obtaining evidence is the use of electronic surveillance. The first case of wiretapping that came before the Supreme Court involved the

IN THE DISTRICT COURT IN AND FOR _____ COUNTY
STATE OF

THE STATE OF _____   No. _____
                    Plaintiff,

    —vs—

_____
                    Defendant.

MOTION TO COMPEL THE STATE TO CONDUCT A LINEUP

COMES NOW the Defendant and respectfully moves this Honorable Court to compel the State to conduct a lineup prior to preliminary hearing with the Defendant in participation wherein any potential identification witness would be requested to make, if possible, a positive identification of the person alleged to have committed the offense(s) set forth in the preliminary information in this cause.

Defendant so moves on the following grounds:

1. The case(s) is set for preliminary hearing on

2. Defendant alleges that at said preliminary hearing he would be required to be present behind the bar at counsel table. Only counsel for the State and counsel for the Defendant will be in the immediate vicinity. From this situation, any complaining witness is made obviously aware of who the Defendant is.

3. The prior opportunity of the complaining witness to observe the alleged criminal act and its alleged perpetrator was extremely limited.

4. There have been no lineups or showups to the Defendant's knowledge prior to this time where the complaining witness had an opportunity to observe the subject accused of the crimes in the instant case(s). Given the placement of the Defendant in the preliminary hearing, there arises an impermissible innuendo for the complaining witness that the Defendant is a person who committed the offense(s) charged.

5. The above-mentioned placement of the Defendant at the preliminary hearing amounts to a pre-trial one-man showup, wherein the complaining witness is confronted with the Defendant.

6. The practice of showing the suspect singly to persons for the purposes of identification, and not as part of a lineup, has been widely condemned. *Stovall* v. *Denno*, 388 U.S. 293, 87 S.Ct. 1967, 19 L.Ed. 1199 (1967).

7. The above-mentioned placement of the Defendant at the preliminary hearing is so impermissibly suggestive that the Defendant will be denied due process as provided by the Fourteenth Amendment of the United States Constitution. *U.S.* v. *Caldwell*, 481 F.2d 487 (D.C., Cir., 1973).

WHEREFORE, Defendant respectfully requests this Court for an Order requiring the District Attorney to conduct a pre-trial lineup with the Defendant in participation and viewed by the complaining witnesses. Further, Defendant respectfully requests this Court to continue the preliminary hearing until after such time as the above-mentioned lineup can be held.

                                        _____
                                        ATTORNEY FOR DEFENDANT

CERTIFICATE OF DELIVERY

This is to certify that on the ___ day of _____ , 19 ___ , a true and correct copy of the above and foregoing Motion was delivered to the District Attorney in and for _____ County, [State name].

                                        _____
                                        ATTORNEY FOR DEFENDANT

FIGURE 10.2
Motion to Compel the State to Conduct a Lineup

use of a telephone line to intercept messages. A divided Court (5–4 decision) held that the surveillance was permissible.

The Fourth Amendment prohibition against unreasonable searches and seizures contains a statement that search warrants shall not be issued except on probable cause and under oath, "and particularly describing the place to be searched, and the persons or things to be seized." In *Olm-*

stead v. United States, the Court read that amendment literally, emphasizing that, because the method for surveillance did not involve an entry to the houses or offices of the defendants, there was no search of a "place" and no "things" were taken.[6] Justice Oliver Wendell Holmes, in a strong dissent in *Olmstead*, referred to wiretapping as dirty business and took the position that "it is a less evil that some criminals should escape than that the government should play an ignoble part."

Later cases, however, have applied the Fourth Amendment to wiretapping and some other forms of electronic surveillance. Relying on a right to privacy, the Court in *Katz v. United States* held that obtaining evidence by attaching a device to a public telephone booth and listening to the conversation of the defendant was a violation of the Fourth Amendment.[7] The Omnibus Crime Control and Safe Streets Act passed by Congress in 1968, however, permits some forms of electronic surveillance, when the proper official of the United States Department of Justice obtains a court order for the surveillance. The order will be granted in specified types of cases involving alleged violations of federal laws. Under some circumstances, states also may apply. Further, it is permissible for the president of the United States to order electronic surveillance under conditions that threaten national security.

The right to privacy that the Court recognized is not violated in some cases involving electronic surveillance when a person is wired for sound. The **informant,** usually a friend or acquaintance of the suspect, is wired by the police. The informant engages the suspect in conversation, and their words are monitored by police. The evidence then may be used in the trial of the suspect.[8]

It is also permissible for police to pose as individuals who wish to engage in criminal activity, to infiltrate situations in which such activities might occur, and to arrest those who commit a crime. This process is used frequently in attempts to get evidence of drug-law violations and to get information on persons suspected of engaging in illegal sexual activities. The police frequently are criticized for such actions; and if they go too far in them, the evidence they secure may not be used against the suspects. Although the police may provide the opportunity for individuals to commit crimes, they may not induce people to commit crimes they would not otherwise commit.[9] This is known as **entrapment.** The acquittal of John DeLorean, famous auto maker accused by the government of being involved in illegal drugs, is an example of a case in which the jury found that the federal agents went too far in their activities and actually entrapped the suspect.

The Supreme Court has also recognized an exception to the *Katz* right to privacy. In 1984 in *Oliver v. United States*, the Court recognized an "open fields" exception. In *Oliver*, police were tipped off by an informant that the suspect was growing marijuana in his fields. Two police officers drove to the farm, which had a "No Trespassing" sign on the locked gate. They found a footpath and walked into the fields, in which they found marijuana growing.[10]

Recall the earlier discussions of search and seizure, indicating that the Fourth Amendment right to be free of *unreasonable* searches and seizures has been interpreted by the Court to extend to the home and its *curtilage*, meaning the area immediately surrounding the home. Within this area, a person has a reasonable expectation of privacy.

But, in *Oliver* the Court said that reasonable expectation of privacy does not extend to "open fields." In a lengthy opinion, the Court said, "open fields do not provide the setting for those intimate activities that the Amendment is intended to shelter from government interference or surveillance." The "No Trespassing" sign did not establish a reasonable expectation of privacy. Finally, the Court said that even if the police committed a trespass on the suspect's property, they did not violate the Fourth Amendment prohibition against unreasonable search and seizure.

In a subsequent case, *California v. Ciraolo*, decided in 1986, the Court held that an individual who erects fences (one 6 feet and the other 8 feet) around the curtilage of his yard to prevent public viewing is not protected from aerial surveillance. The Court upheld a search from 1,000 feet above the curtilage, reasoning that since any member of the public could fly in that space, the suspect had no reasonable expectation of privacy from aerial surveillance; thus the search was not unreasonable.[11]

Initial Appearance

If the investigation indicates to the prosecutor that sufficient evidence is available to lead a reasonable person to think that a particular suspect committed the crime and if the prosecutor decides to file formal charges against the suspect, in most cases that suspect must be taken before a magistrate for an **initial appearance.** The initial appearance is for the purpose of having the court determine whether there is probable cause to charge this suspect with this crime.

A suspect who has been retained in custody must be taken before the magistrate without unreasonable delay. The time involved in processing the suspect at the police station will probably mean that the initial appearance cannot take place until the following day. If the suspect is booked on a weekend, the initial appearance cannot take place until the following Monday unless special provisions have been made. In some metropolitan areas, because of the high volume of arrests on weekends, magistrate's courts hold special sessions on weekends to permit initial appearances earlier than usual and thus decrease the amount of time defendants will spend in jail.

The initial appearance usually is quite brief. Magistrates verify the names and addresses of the defendants and inform defendants of the formal charges and of their constitutional rights, including the right to remain silent and to know that anything they say may be held against them. Where applicable, the right to counsel will be discussed. Although the procedures differ among jurisdictions, at this stage in many areas the process of appointing counsel at least will be started. Defendants who have retained counsel usually will have their attorneys with them at this initial appearance.

If the defendant is charged with a minor offense, the determination of guilt or innocence might be made at the initial appearance. If not, the defendant will be informed of the next stage in the proceeding. Defendants who have been charged with serious offenses will probably still be in custody. In those cases, magistrates usually make determinations whether to release or retain them in custody pending trial. If defendants have been released by the police after booking, magistrates will review the terms of those released and decide whether they were properly made under the circumstances.

In the case of Mr. Jones, because the police have secured no evidence that he is involved with other students and therefore is a threat to others, they probably will release him after booking even though he is charged with a serious offense.

Preliminary Hearing

In many cases, the initial appearance is followed by a **preliminary hearing,** at least in cases involving felonies. This hearing usually occurs between 1 and 2 weeks after the initial appearance. During the interval between these two stages, prosecutors often drop charges as they discover that there is insufficient evidence to proceed with the cases. If cases are not dropped, the preliminary hearing is held to determine whether there is probable cause to continue with those cases. A preliminary hearing is not required in all states. If it is not required, prosecutors may take the case directly to a grand jury (discussed later) where that is required. If a grand jury is not required, prosecutors may proceed on their own.

If a preliminary hearing is held, the prosecution and the defense will present sufficient evidence to enable the magistrate to decide the issue of probable cause. The preliminary hearing may not be closed to the public unless the court specifically finds that closure is essential to preserve higher values than the First Amendment right of the press to cover and of the public to know about such hearings. To close the preliminary hearing, then, a defendant would have to show that he or she could not get a fair hearing without closure.[12]

Defendants may waive the preliminary hearing, and many choose to do so, but that **waiver** must be a knowing and intelligent one. A preliminary hearing will probably be required (unless waived by the defendant) in the case of Mr. Jones, because he is charged with a felony. If Mr. Jones does not waive his preliminary hearing, at this stage the prosecution will present evidence they have secured from their investigations, and the defense will present evidence in favor of the accused. The magistrate or judge will decide whether there is sufficient evidence to establish probable cause that Mr. Jones had sexual relations with Jennifer. If so, the case will be presented to a grand jury.

Grand Jury Review

In the United States, the official accusation of a felon begins in one of two ways. The prosecutor may initiate the proceedings by returning an **information.** That may be done in cases not requiring action by the **grand jury** or when the grand jury review is waived. Some states require a grand jury

indictment in felony cases, although states differ in the crimes for which that is required. Some limit the requirement to serious felonies.

In federal courts, grand jury indictments are required for prosecution of capital or otherwise infamous crimes with the exceptions noted in the Fifth Amendment.

> No person shall be held to answer for a capital, or otherwise infamous crime, unless on a presentment or indictment of a Grand Jury, except in cases arising in the land or naval forces, or in the Militia, when in actual service in time of War or public danger; . . .

The grand jury is composed of private citizens, usually 23, although some states have reduced the number. Originally a majority of the votes was required, but today some states, particularly those with a grand jury smaller than 23, require more than a majority vote. The grand jury review differs from the initial appearance and the preliminary hearing in that evidence is presented only by the prosecutor. The defendant does not have a right to present evidence or even to be present. The grand jury is not bound by all the rules of evidence required at trial. The deliberations are secret.

The basic function of the grand jury is to hear the evidence presented by the prosecutor and to decide whether there is probable cause to return the indictment presented by the prosecutor. If they return the indictment, that is called a **true bill.** The indictment is the official document stating the name of the accused, the charge, and the essential facts supporting that charge. In returning that indictment, the grand jury is not bound by the decision of the magistrate at the preliminary hearing.

The grand jury indictment is usually not required in misdemeanor or petty offense cases. Those are begun officially when the prosecutor returns an information. In this chapter's CJA, formal proceedings against Jones could begin with a prosecutorial information if the charge is lewd behavior, a misdemeanor; but a charge of statutory rape, a felony, would probably require a grand jury indictment.

Once it is in session, the grand jury may initiate investigations. This is often done when there are allegations of widespread corruption in public agencies. The grand jury also may be used to investigate organized crime. When the grand jury begins an official prosecution in this manner—that is, by action on its own knowledge without the indictment presented by the prosecutor—it returns a **presentment.** A presentment is an official document, an accusation asking for the prosecutor to prepare an indictment. This function of the grand jury is illustrated in Spotlight 10.1.

The grand jury serves as a check on prosecutorial discretion. The Supreme Court recognized this important function when it said that the grand jury

> serves the invaluable function in our society of standing between the accuser and the accused, whether the latter be an individual, minority group, or other, to determine whether a charge is founded upon reason or was dictated by an intimidating power or by malice and personal ill will."[13]

SPOTLIGHT 10.1
OUR INVALUABLE GRAND JURIES

The grand jury, an institution some would abolish, has again proved itself a powerful instrument of social reform.

A Manhattan grand jury that recently investigated the death of an 18-year-old woman at a Manhattan hospital did not find enough evidence to return an indictment. But it did find that serious problems in the way the hospital delivered health care may well have contributed to the young woman's death.

This, in turn, led the grand jury to recommend drastic changes in the way interns and residents are trained and supervised, including a limitation on the exhausting 36-hour shifts they are required to work, as well as new standards regulating the use of physical restraints and the prescribing of drugs.

At the recommendation of a panel of prominent physicians, the grand jury's ideas then became a central part of sweeping changes in hospital regulations proposed by the New York State health commissioner.

This grand jury was hardly an aberration. Grand juries have traditionally aroused the public to rally around significant causes.

For centuries, the grand jury in England was authorized to issue "presentments"—reports of nonindictable or objectionable misconduct. And in colonial America, grand juries also undertook the task of protecting citizens from the tyranny of royal rulers.

The most prominent example was the case of Peter Zenger, a New York newspaper publisher who printed a personal attack on the English Governor. In 1734, the Governor twice sought to have Zenger indicted by a grand jury for criminal libel and twice Zenger's fellow citizens refused to charge him. It was only through executive fiat that Zenger was brought to trial. Ultimately, his fellow citizens acquitted him.

In the very first draft of the Bill of Rights, James Madison included a provision requiring criminal cases to be prosecuted by grand jury and authorized the grand jury to return "presentments" concerning social problems that went beyond the question of simple criminal liability. This provision was incorporated into the Fifth Amendment of the Federal Constitution.

New York State's Constitution codified the right of citizens to be charged with committing a felony only by indictment by a grand jury of their peers. Under the state's Constitution, grand juries also continued the practice of investigating public corruption. In 1872, a grand jury probing New York City corruption helped end the reign of Boss William Marcy Tweed and his associates. In the 1930's, grand juries did much to assure the prosecution of racketeering and political corruption.

In 1938, the Constitution was amended so that a grand jury's power to inquire into the willful misconduct by public officers "shall never be suspended or impaired by law." Again in the 1950's, grand juries in New York investigating crimes and official misconduct routinely issued reports dealing with such topics as organized crime's involvement with the waterfront, gambling and police corruption.

In 1961, however, New York State's highest court sought to end the practice of releasing grand jury reports that called attention to official misconduct and recommended reforms—even though that practice had long been recognized as one of the grand jury's most valuable functions.

There was an immediate public outcry, and in time the Legislature restored the grand jury's power to make "presentments" and even broadened the scope of the reports. The Legislature also included safeguards to protect from unfounded charges those persons whose conduct was described in the reports.

In this age of widespread public and private corruption and the mistrust it engenders, grand juries continue to be a vital means not only for leveling criminal accusations but also for identifying and remedying social problems. A grand jury system that can trigger sweeping changes in the system of medical care that affects millions of people must itself be a healthy one.

Source: Robert M. Morgenthau (former district attorney of New York City), "Our Invaluable Grand Juries," *New York Times* (23 June 1987), p. 27. Copyright © 1987 by The New York Times Company. Reprinted by permission.

In reality, however, the grand jury frequently is an arm of the prosecution. In fact, in most cases presented by prosecutors to grand juries, the indictment is returned as a true bill. The California Supreme Court has noted that the grand jury is independent only in the sense that it is not formally attached to the office of the prosecutor. Grand jurors are free to vote independently of the prosecutor's recommendations, but they rarely do. After noting that there is strong empirical data for this conclusion, that court referred to the comment of a former prosecutor: "Today, the grand jury is the total captive of the prosecutor who, if he is candid, will concede that he can indict anybody, at any time, for almost anything before any grand jury."[14] Of course, some procedures must be observed by the grand jury, and the body of case law is extensive and at times conflicting. For example, like trial juries (discussed in the next chapter), the composition of the grand jury may not discriminate against racial groups.[15]

When the case against Mr. Jones is presented to the grand jury, the jury could decide not to return an indictment based on their belief that Jennifer is close enough to the age of consent that the alleged sexual activity should not be prosecuted. If the grand jury does not return an indictment and this jurisdiction requires an indictment for a charge of statutory rape, the case will be dropped. The prosecutor, however, may be able to return an information for a lesser offense such as lewd behavior, which may not require a grand jury indictment.[16]

Arraignment on the Information or Indictment

After the indictment or information is officially filed with the court, a time can be scheduled for the **arraignment.** At that hearing, judges or magistrates formally read the indictments or informations to defendants, inform them of their constitutional rights, and ask for a plea to the charges. If the defendant pleads not guilty, a date will be set for trial. If the defendant pleads guilty, a date will be set for formal sentencing unless that takes place at the arraignment, as is often the case with less serious offenses.

In some jurisdictions a defendant is also permitted to plead ***nolo contendere,*** which literally means, "I do not contest it." That plea in a criminal case has the legal effect of a guilty plea. The difference is that that plea cannot be used against that defendant in a civil case. Thus, if the defendant pleads *nolo contendere* to felony charges of driving while intoxicated and leaving the scene of an accident, that plea cannot be used by a victim who suffered injuries and property damage in the accident when that person files a civil case to recover damages for personal injury and property damage.

If Mr. Jones pleads *nolo contendere*, he could then be sentenced in criminal court, but that plea could not be used against him if Jennifer or her parents filed any number of tort actions that they might bring against him in civil cases. Assume, however, that he pleads not guilty so that we can proceed with his case through all the pretrial stages.

Lawyers may argue pretrial motions before the judge. (Peter Menzel/Stock Boston)

Pretrial Motions

A **motion** is a document submitted to the court asking for a rule or an order. Some motions are obviously inappropriate before trial; a motion for a new trial is an example. But several other types of motions might be made before the trial begins.

The defense might make a motion to suppress evidence on the allegation that the evidence was secured in violation of the defendant's rights. This is usually a very simple motion, as indicated by the form in Figure 10.3. Defendants might also make a motion to dismiss the case because of insufficient evidence. There could be other reasons: the defense might attack the technical sufficiency of the charging document, question the composition of the grand jury, or claim alleged prosecutorial misconduct.

It is also common for the defense to file a motion requiring the prosecutor to produce evidence, a process called **discovery.** Because of the importance of this type of motion, an example of a form used for its filing is reproduced, in part, in Figure 10.4. If the court grants any or all of those requests, the prosecutor would have to produce the information to avoid surprises at trials and enable the defense attorney to prepare an adequate defense.

Discovery procedures are defined by court rules and procedural statutes, but the nature of the discovery rules varies from permitting extensive discovery to rather limited discovery. Discovery is a two-way street. The prosecution and the defense are entitled to certain information that the other side plans to use at trial. Lists of witnesses, prior statements obtained from those witnesses, and the nature of physical evidence are the kinds of information that the prosecution and defense might wish to obtain.

IN THE DISTRICT COURT IN AND FOR   COUNTY,
STATE OF

THE STATE OF   )   Case No.
)
            Plaintiff,)
)
—vs—   )
)
)
           Defendant.)

MOTION TO SUPPRESS STATEMENTS

COMES NOW the Defendant, by and through his/her attorney, and moves this Honorable Court to issue its order directing that the alleged statements taken in the above-entitled cause(s) be suppressed upon the grounds and for the reasons that the said statements were taken in violation of the Defendant's rights under the Constitutions of the State of   and of the United States.

_____
Attorney for Defendant

CERTIFICATE OF DELIVERY

This is to certify that on the _____ day of _____ 19 , a true and correct copy of the above and foregoing Motion was delivered to the District Attorney in and for   County, [State name].

_____
Attorney for the Defendant

FIGURE 10.3
Motion to Suppress Statements

IN THE DISTRICT COURT IN AND FOR   COUNTY
STATE OF

THE STATE OF   )   No.
)
            Plaintiff,)
)
—vs—   )
)
)
           Defendant.)

MOTION TO PRODUCE

Defendant moves that the State be required to disclose and, if a tangible item is involved, to produce for inspection and/or copying by the Defendant all material in the possession and control of the State which may be favorable to the Defendant or exculpatory or which could reasonably affect the determination of the Defendant's guilt or innocence, reduce punishment, or is relevant to the subject matter of the charge, or which may in any manner assist the Defendant. Disclosure and production of the material herein requested is to be made without regard to whether the material to be disclosed and produced is considered by the State to be admissible at the trial, and whether or not the State feels the material is exculpatory in nature.

Defendant requests that disclosure and production of said material include, but not be limited to, the following:

1. Statements of all persons who have been interviewed by an agent of the State of
an investigator or member of the   Police Department or the   County Sheriff's Office

FIGURE 10.4
Motion to Produce

FIGURE 10.4
(Cont.)

or any other governmental agency in connection with the subject matter of this case, whether or not the State intends to call them to testify at trial, . . .

2. Stenographic recordings or transcriptions of any oral statement made by *any* person to an agent of the State, an investigator or police officer of the _____ Police Department, a member of the _____ County Sheriff's Office, or a member of any other governmental agency in connection with the subject matter of the case . . .

3. The transcript of any statement given to the District Attorney's Office during their investigation concerning the subject matter herein by any persons, whether or not the State intends to call them at the time of the trial, and whether or not the statements were recorded.

4. The names and addresses of all persons who may have some knowledge of the facts involved in the instant case.

5. The prior criminal record of all persons the State intends to call at time of trial, including indictments, convictions, acquittals, or pending charges. This information is required by the defense to determine whether bias or prejudice exists on the part of the State witnesses and to impeach the credibility of said witnesses if any of them has been convicted of a felony or a misdemeanor involving dishonesty.

6. Any material relating to the competency of witnesses to be called by the State, such as a history of mental illness or psychiatric care or civil or criminal commitment to a State or private mental hospital.

7. Written or recorded statements or a summary of any such statements made by the Defendant in this case or copies of any statements, admissions, confessions, or declarations against interest verbatim or otherwise, which may have been made by the Defendant and the names of the persons taking such statements.

8. The original report of the arresting officer(s) in this case.

9. Any and all other evidence now in the custody of the District Attorney's Office, the _____ Police Department, the _____ County Sheriff's Office, or any other agency of the State which may be exculpatory, material or otherwise favorable to the Defendant.

10. All reports of a scientific nature, and the subject matter of those reports, which have been prepared by an expert, technologist, identification officer, or other scientific authority pertaining to any instrument, substance or means allegedly used in the commission of the crime and any report made or which may be made which relates to any fingerprints, ballistics reports, handwriting exemplars, or photographs of the crime scene together with the prints, exemplars, photographs or any other scientific material relating to this case which may be exculpatory in nature or favorable to the Defendant.

11. Any physical or tangible objects in the possession of the District Attorney's Office, the _____ Police Department, the _____ County Sheriff's Office, or any other governmental agency including, but not limited to, items taken from the Defendant's person or his property, relating to the pending charge(s).

12. Disclosure of the identity of any informant used by the _____ Police Department or expected to be used in the procurement of or use of evidence expected to be used against the Defendant.

13. Any and all oral statements made to any member of the _____ Police Department or District Attorney's staff or any other law enforcement official, relating to the pending charge(s).

14. Any inconsistencies between the testimony of State's witnesses at the preliminary hearing or trial of the case and statements or reports of statements included within the District Attorney's case file.

The Defendant therefore respectfully requests this Honorable Court to require the State of _____ to produce all material now known or which may become known, or which through the exercise of due diligence may be learned from the investigating officers or witnesses in the case, which is exculpatory in nature or favorable to the accused, or which may lead to exculpatory material or which tends to negate the guilt of the accused as to the offense charged or would tend to reduce the punishment therefore.

Defendant further moves this Court to conduct an *in camera* inspection of the District Attorney's file in order that a neutral and detached judicial officer may determine the existence or nonexistence of such material.

_____
Attorney for Defendant

CERTIFICATE OF DELIVERY

I hereby certify that on the _____ day of _____, 19 _____, a true and correct copy of the above and foregoing Motion to Produce was delivered to the District Attorney in and for _____ County, [State name].

_____
Attorney for Defendant

Under some circumstances, both the prosecution and the defense may obtain oral statements from witnesses outside of court and before trial. These statements are called **depositions,** and the person from whom they are taken is the deposed. They are taken under oath, recorded verbatim (usually by a court reporter), and may be used in court. They are permitted when there is a court order or rules of procedure that permit depositions. Attorneys for both sides will be present. Depositions often take place in the office of one of the attorneys. Witnesses or other parties also may be given **interrogatories,** a series of questions that are to be answered truthfully, with the respondent signing a statement of oath that the answers are correct.

The defense might also file a motion for a change of **venue.** Venue refers to the place of trial. If the case has received considerable media attention, the defense might succeed with the argument that the defendant could not get a fair trial in that jurisdiction, and therefore a change of venue should be granted.

Although many defense motions might be filed before trial, these motions do not often result in dismissals. The prosecutor might also file motions. Once formal charges have been filed, prosecutors may not drop or change those charges without the permission of the court. The prosecutor frequently files a motion to drop or lower charges as the result of plea bargaining, discussed later.

Mr. Jones's attorney will probably file a motion to produce, asking for specified evidence that the prosecution has acquired. If the alleged sexual acts occurred in a small town where Mr. Jones is well known, he might ask for a change of venue on the grounds that he could not obtain a fair trial in a small town where everyone knows him and the alleged victim.

Pretrial Conferences

At various times during the pretrial period, prosecution and defense may have conferences. Judges might also be involved in these conferences. These conferences are not necessarily for negotiating a plea, although that is frequently the purpose. In addition to motions that the prosecution and defense might wish to make individually or other issues they want to discuss with the judge, there will be times when both sides will want to ask for more time to secure evidence or to negotiate a plea.

Pretrial conferences are sometimes referred to as status conferences. They may be quite informal, with the prosecution and the defense discussing the status of the case. They will enumerate the issues on which they agree so that no time is wasted in court arguing issues that are not in dispute. The judge will probably want each attorney to give an estimate of the time he or she expects to take to present the case.

Both the prosecution and the defense will be using the pretrial period to prepare for trial. Preparation may include further investigations of physical evidence, repeated attempts to locate witnesses who have not yet been found, interviews with witnesses, obtaining depositions of expert and other witnesses, and reviewing those depositions, along with all other in-

formation pertinent to the trial. Attorneys might spend time with their own witnesses, making sure they know what information the witness will give at trial and preparing the witness for the types of questions that might be asked by opposing counsel.

Attorneys will be involved in keeping a record of the expenses of trial preparation, which will include costs of their own time (even if they are public defenders, paid by the case and not by the hour, or prosecutors on salary, they probably will keep an hourly record of their activities) as well as out-of-pocket costs for investigations, depositions, interrogatories, and expenses for expert witnesses.

Lists of witnesses who will be called for trial must be prepared, and the proper papers for notifying those witnesses must be filed. If the witnesses do not want to appear, it will be necessary to get a court order to **subpoena** the witnesses. A subpoena is an order to appear in court at a particular time and place and to give testimony on a specified subject or issue. As a precautionary measure, subpoenas might be issued to all potential witnesses to make it more difficult for them to change their minds and refuse to appear in court to testify. Witnesses also may be ordered to produce documents or papers that are important to the trial.

The pretrial conferences will be very important, perhaps decisive, in this chapter's CJA. Jennifer's parents do not want her to be a witness in court. Without her testimony the prosecution will have a very weak case. During pretrial conferences the defense attorney and the prosecution may decide that the best course is either to plea bargain (discussed later) or to dismiss the case.

RELEASE OR DETENTION: BAIL OR JAIL?

Once a person has been charged with a crime, the decision whether to release or detain that individual pending trial is an important one. For the defendant it is a time "when consultation, thoroughgoing investigation and preparation . . . [are] vitally important."[17] During this period, the defendant either retains an attorney or is assigned counsel by the court. The defense counsel and the prosecutor negotiate and consider the possibility of plea bargaining. Witnesses are interviewed and other attempts are made by both sides to secure evidence for the trial. Uncovering additional evidence may change the nature of the case and can even result in dropping or reducing charges before trial.

For society, the issue of whether the defendant is released or detained before trial also is critical. Public outcries, accusing courts of coddling criminals, are common when persons charged with serious crimes are released. When those released before trial commit crimes during that release, the response is even more critical.

The Bail Decision

The procedures by which the **bail** decision will be made vary among jurisdictions, but a hearing is required and the defendant is entitled to the benefit of counsel at that hearing. In the federal system, the hearing must take place within 24 hours of arrest. In some jurisdictions there are statutes specifying what types of offenses are bailable. In others there are specifications concerning what the magistrate should consider in making the decision. In many cases, however, the magistrate has wide discretion in the bail decision, and there is virtually no check on this decision. The case of Mr. Jones is an example of a case in which most judges would grant bail. Mr. Jones has no prior record. He has not been involved in a crime using force, and he is not likely to be dangerous to other people.

The magistrate also has wide latitude in setting the amount of bail. In the federal system, the factors most closely related to the level of bail, in order of importance, are the seriousness of the current charge, the district in which the bail hearing occurs, and the criminal record of the offender.

Only a small percentage of arrestees are detained in jail awaiting trial. A defendant who is detained in jail later may petition the court to reduce the amount of bail or grant bail if it were previously denied. Sometimes judges grant these motions, particularly when the defense has had more time to gather evidence that favors pretrial release of the defendant.

History of the Bail System

The bail system developed for very practical reasons. It began in England, probably before 1000 A.D. Before urbanization and the development of modern courts, judges traveled from jurisdiction to jurisdiction to hold

Professional bondsmen offer their bail services at all hours. (David Hall)

court sessions. They could not get to any one place often; consequently, it was necessary to devise a way of detaining the accused before the judges arrived. The bail system developed because the detention facilities used were recognized as horrible places of confinement and were expensive to maintain.

Sheriffs began to ask other people, usually relatives of the defendant, to serve as sureties who assumed custody of defendants and guaranteed that they would appear for trial. If the defendants did not appear, the judge could try the surety for the crime with which the defendant was charged. The surety actually had the power of a jailer, charged with making sure the defendant did not flee before trial. The practice of using private sureties was followed in this country but was later replaced by a system of posting bond to assure the presence of the accused at trial.

The Bail Bond System

An opportunity to make money resulted in the development of the bail **bond** system. The bail bondsman, in return for a fee, posts the bond for the defendant. If the defendant does not appear at trial, the bond money must theoretically be forfeited to the court. In reality the forfeiture is almost never enforced, but since some bondsmen post bond without actually having the money available, some jurisdictions require bondsmen to prove that they could pay the forfeiture should that be necessary.

Analysis of the Bail Bond System

The bondsman system has been highly criticized. Bondsmen have considerable power over defendants, for not only can they determine the fee they charge but also whether they accept certain defendants. For example, they might reject people they consider to be bad business risks just because they do not know them. On the other hand, bondsmen may agree to post bond for professional criminals at a low fee because they consider them to be good business risks.

One investigator, in his study of the criminal courts of two cities, found that the bail bondsman business is very competitive and that the main devices employed by bondsmen to get more business are illegal. These devices are reciprocal referrals between bondsmen and criminal lawyers and collusion with jail personnel. He noted that for some defendants the bondsman actually engages in the unauthorized practice of law.[18]

Criticism of the bail bondsman system has led some states to place legislative restrictions on the practice of bondsmen or to eliminate the system entirely. In 1976 Kentucky passed a statute making it "unlawful for any person to engage in the business of bail bondsman." The system was replaced by a network of pretrial service agencies that offer other forms of pretrial release procedures. Oregon retained the bail bond system but adopted procedures that have made it very difficult for the business to continue profitably. The Oregon statute provides that the judges "shall impose the least onerous condition" necessary to assure that the defendant will appear at trial.[19]

Alternatives to the Bail Bond System

Dissatisfaction with the bail bond system has led to the development of other forms of pretrial release. Spotlight 10.2 defines the various release methods in use today. Both financial and nonfinancial methods are used, ranging from requiring the defendant to post the full amount of bail to releasing defendants on their own assurance that they will appear at trial. This method is called **Release on Recognizance** (ROR or OR).

Under ROR, defendants are released after signing an oath that they will appear at trial. ROR may be used with or without conditions. If there are conditions and defendants do not meet them, they may be charged with bail violation. Conditions may range from not leaving the jurisdiction at any time before trial, to restrictions on the types of people with whom the defendant may associate, to setting a curfew. Spotlight 10.2 also indicates that defendants may be released to the custody of a third person, often an attorney.

Early Bail Reform: The Manhattan Bail Project

In the 1960s a New York industrialist, Louis Schweitzer, became concerned about the poor youths who could not make bail and therefore were detained while awaiting trial. He established the Vera Foundation, which, along with the New York University School of Law and the Institute of Judicial Administration, conducted an experiment on bail. The experiment was based on the hypothesis that "more persons can successfully be released...if verified information concerning their character and roots in the community is available to the court at the time of bail determinations."[20]

The project was begun in 1961. New York University law students interviewed defendants for information that would be relevant to pretrial release: (1) present or recent resident at the same address for six months or more, (2) current employment or recent employment for six months or more, (3) relatives in New York City with whom the defendant was in contact, (4) no previous conviction of a crime, (5) resident in New York City for ten years or more.

After the interviews, the staff would decide whether to recommend release. If they decided to do so, the recommendation would be sent to the arraignment court, where defendants would be assigned randomly to experimental or control groups. For the control group, the recommendation was not given to the court. For the experimental group, copies of the recommendation were given to the judge, prosecutor, and assigned counsel. The judge would make the decision whether to grant release.

Of those recommended for release by the staff, 60 percent were released by the judge, compared to only 14 percent of those the staff did not

SPOTLIGHT 10.2
METHODS OF PRETRIAL RELEASE

Both financial bonds and alternative release options are used today

FINANCIAL BOND

Fully secured bail—The defendant posts the full amount of bail with the court.

Privately secured bail—A bondsman signs a promissory note to the court for the bail amount and charges the defendant a fee for the service (usually 10 percent of the bail amount). If the defendant fails to appear, the bondsman must pay the court the full amount. Frequently, the bondsman requires the defendant to post collateral in addition to the fee.

Deposit bail—The courts allow the defendant to deposit a percentage (usually 10 percent) of the full bail with the court. The full amount of the bail is required if the defendant fails to appear. The percentage bail is returned after disposition of the case, but the court often retains 1 percent for administrative costs.

Unsecured bail—The defendant pays no money to the court but is liable for the full amount of bail should he or she fail to appear.

ALTERNATIVE RELEASE OPTIONS

Release on recognizance (ROR)—The court releases the defendant on the promise that he or she will appear in court as required.

Conditional release—The court releases the defendant subject to his or her following specific conditions set by the court, such as attendance at drug treatment therapy or staying away from the complaining witness.

Third party custody—The defendant is released into the custody of an individual or agency that promises to assure his or her appearance in court. No monetary transactions are involved in this type of release.

Citation release—Arrestees are released pending their first court appearance on a written order issued by law enforcement personnel.

Source: Bureau of Justice Statistics, *Report to the Nation on Crime and Justice: The Data,* 2d ed. (Washington, D.C.: U.S. Department of Justice, 1988), p. 76.

---

recommend. Thus, because of the project, four times as many persons were released pending trial. For those who were released and did not appear for trial, the staff reported that various factors—"illness, ignorance of legal processes, family emergencies, and confusion about when and in what court to appear"—had accounted for nearly all the nonappearances, and this was usually corrected by a phone call to their home, place of work, or relatives.

Other cities have adopted bail reform plans that involve release of defendants on their own recognizance pending trial or some other method. The National Advisory Commission on Criminal Justice Standards and Goals indicated in its 1973 report that ROR had become a significant alternative to money bail bonds. The commission concluded that, although the system of using other-than-money bail for releasing defendants before trial is a sound one, it has experienced some serious administrative problems.[21]

SPOTLIGHT 10.3
THE FEDERAL BAIL REFORM ACT OF 1984

Under the Bail Reform Act of 1966, the judicial officer was generally required to impose the minimal conditions of release necessary to assure only that the defendant appear in court. Further, while an individual might be held for failure to post bail, detention without bail was permitted only in cases involving capital crimes.

The Bail Reform Act of 1984 materially changed these provisions. In particular, the Act provides that, in reaching decisions on bail and release, the court shall give consideration not only to ensuring the defendant's appearance in court but also to protecting the safety of individuals and the community.

The pretrial detention provisions of the Act make special reference to particular categories of offenses and offenders. The Act authorizes pretrial detention for defendants charged with crimes of violence, offenses with possible life (or death) penalties, major drug offenses, and felonies where the defendant has a specified serious criminal record.

Additionally, the Act creates a rebuttable presumption that no conditions of release will assure the appearance of the defendant and the safety of the community under the following circumstances: the defendant committed a drug felony with a 10-year maximum sentence; the defendant used a firearm during the commission of a violent or drug trafficking offense; or the defendant was convicted of specified serious crimes within the preceding 5 years while on pretrial release.

The Act does not require that prosecutors request pretrial detention for all defendants in these groups.

The Act also provides for temporary detention (up to 10 working days) of illegal aliens or persons under pre- or posttrial release, probation, or parole at the time of the current offense. This provision was added for the purpose of allowing time for other law enforcement or immigration officials to take appropriate action.

Source: Bureau of Justice Statistics, *Pretrial Release and Detention: The Bail Reform Act of 1984* (Washington, D.C.: U.S. Department of Justice, February 1988), p. 2. The Bail Reform Act is codified in UNITED STATES CODE 18, Sections 3141–56.

Federal Bail Reform

In 1966 Congress passed the federal Bail Reform Act. Its major purpose was to ensure that persons arrested for crimes in the federal system would not be needlessly detained when detention was not necessary. The approach was followed by many states, but within the last decade the public has exerted pressure to be more conservative in granting bail.

In 1984 Congress passed a major revision of the criminal code. That statute contained provisions on bail that supersede the 1966 act. Spotlight 10.3 contrasts these two reform measures. The major change is the use of preventive detention, a practice that must be examined in light of the historical purpose of bail.

The Purpose of Bail and Preventive Detention

The Eighth Amendment to the United States Constitution prohibits requiring excessive bail. The provision has been interpreted to mean that when bail is used, its amount may not be excessive but there has been no clear definition of what that means. In 1951, in *Stack v. Boyle*, the Court considered this issue.[22]

Stack v. *Boyle*

From the passage of the Judiciary Act of 1789, to the present...
federal law has unequivocally provided that a person arrested for a non-capital offense shall be admitted to bail. The traditional right to freedom before conviction permits the unhampered preparation of a defense, and serves to prevent the infliction of punishment prior to conviction. . . . Unless this right to bail before trial is preserved, the presumption of innocence, secured only after centuries of struggle, would lose its meaning.

The right to release before trial is conditioned upon the accused's giving adequate assurance that he will stand trial and submit to sentence if found guilty. . . . Like the ancient practice of securing the oaths of responsible persons to stand as sureties for the accused, the modern practice of requiring a bail bond or the deposit of a sum of money subject to forfeiture serves as additional assurance of the presence of an accused. Bail set a figure higher than an amount reasonably calculated to fulfill this purpose is "excessive" under the Eighth Amendment.

Earlier cases made it clear that the only legitimate purpose of bail was to assure the presence of the accused at trial. It was not to be used to punish defendants or to protect public safety. By federal rules and some statutes, bail could be denied in capital cases. Bail could also be denied in noncapital cases in which the defendant had a history of flight to avoid prosecution. The reason in both instances was consistent with the original purpose of bail, that is, to secure the presence of the accused at trial.

Until recently, the only legitimate purpose of bail was to secure the presence of the defendant at trial, although there was evidence that bail had actually been used for preventive detention, especially in connection with people who are considered dangerous or who have been involved in riots and demonstrations.[23]

In 1970, with the passage of the District of Columbia Court Reform and Criminal Procedure Act, **preventive detention** was recognized as a legitimate purpose of bail. This statute permits judges to deny bail to defendants charged with dangerous crimes if the government has clear evidence that the safety of others would be endangered if the accused were released. Bail could also be denied, among other situations, in cases involving persons who had been convicted of a violent crime while on probation or parole. Other jurisdictions followed Washington, D.C., in passing statutes or changing their constitutions to permit the denial of bail for preventive detention. The most controversial change, however, occurred in the new federal statue, as indicated in Spotlight 10.3.

The federal statute permits judges to deny bail if they have sufficient reason to think a defendant poses a dangerous threat to the community. The defendant, however, is entitled to a hearing on that issue. But if there is sufficient evidence to charge the defendant with a serious drug offense or certain other serious offense, there is a "presumption of dangerousness." This means that the defendant will be considered dangerous, and therefore bail may be denied unless the defendant can prove to the court that he or she is not dangerous. This burden may be a difficult one to sustain.

Problems with Preventive Detention   In most cases preventive detention has been adopted without consideration of the administrative costs and problems it entails. For example, preventive detention provisions, if used extensively, may significantly increase the costs of prisons and jails as large numbers of persons who otherwise might not be detained are detained. This is particularly true in a state where the jails already are overcrowded. Preventive detention has led to increased litigation on the issue of whether the suspect is dangerous; it has also been challenged on constitutional grounds. In 1981 the District of Columbia Court of Appeals upheld the District of Columbia preventive detention statute.[24]

Pretrial detention for preventive reasons is permitted in some jurisdictions today. (Stephen Crane)

Constitutionality of the Federal Statute   Some lower federal courts upheld the constitutionality of the Federal Bail Reform Act of 1984; others declared it unconstitutional. The Supreme Court in 1984 in *Schall v. Martin* upheld preventive detention of juveniles. That case will be discussed in Chapter 17.[25]

Not until 1987, however, did the Court decide a case challenging the preventive detention of dangerous persons provision of the Bail Reform Act. *United States v. Salerno* involved the detention of Anthony Salerno and Vincent Cafaro, who were charged with numerous crimes associated with organized crime. At the pretrial detention hearing, the government presented evidence that both defendants were in high positions of power in organized crime families. The government contended that the only way to protect the community was to detain these persons pending trial. Pertinent parts of the Supreme Court's decision in the case follow.[26]

United States v. *Salerno* _____

We have repeatedly held that the government's regulatory interest in community safety can, in appropriate circumstances, outweigh an individuals's liberty interest.... Given the well-established authority of the government, in special circumstances, to restrain individual's liberty prior to or even without criminal trial and conviction, we think that the present statute providing for pretrial detention on the basis of dangerousness must be evaluated in precisely the same manner that we evaluated the laws in the cases discussed above.

The government's interest in preventing crime by arrestees is both legitimate and compelling.... The Bail Reform Act ... narrowly focuses on a particularly acute problem in which the government interests are overwhelming. The Act operates only on individuals who have been arrested for a specific category of extremely serious offenses. Congress specifically found that these individuals are far more likely to be responsible for dangerous acts in the community after arrest. Nor is the Act by any means a scattershot attempt to incapacitate those who are merely suspected of these serious crimes. The government must first of all demonstrate probable cause to believe that the charged crime has been committed by the arrestee, but that is not enough. In a full-blown adversary hearing, the government must convince a neutral decision-maker by clear and convincing evidence that no conditions of release can reasonably assure the safety of the community or any person. While the government's general interest in preventing crime is compelling, even this interest is heightened when the government musters convincing proof that the arrestee, already indicted or held to answer for a serious crime, presents a demonstrable danger to the community. Under these narrow circumstances, society's interest in crime prevention is at its greatest.

On the other side of the scale, of course, is the individual's strong interest in liberty. We do not minimize the importance and fundamental nature of this right. But, as our cases hold, this right may, in circumstances where the government's interest is sufficiently weighty, be subordinated to the greater needs of society. We think that Congress' careful delineation of the circumstances under which detention will be permitted satisfies this standard.

The Court's decision in *Salerno* does not answer all questions about the constitutionality of preventive detention.[27] And lower federal courts disagree on its consitutionality, whereas supporters of the *Salerno* decision argue that bail was never intended to be an absolute right; that the community's interest in safety permits preventive detention; and that the Bail Reform Act of 1984 has sufficient procedural protections to ensure that defendants' rights are protected[28]

Extensive litigation can be expected to continue on the constitutionality of the Bail Reform Act of 1984, but it seems clear that at least some forms of preventive detention will be recognized, and state legislatures will continue to pass statutes or amend their constitutions to provide for preventive detention. In 1986, for example, the people of Illinois voted overwhelmingly to amend their constitution to provide for preventive detention. The stated reason was the "spiraling crime rate."[29]

THE GUILTY PLEA

The guilty plea is very important in the U.S. criminal justice system since most defendants plead guilty. Bureau of Justice (BJS) studies indicate that 89 percent of defendants accused of serious felonies (homicide, rape, robbery, aggravated assault, burglary, larceny, and drug trafficking) plead guilty rather than go to trial. BJS data also indicate the following:

- Jury trials occur more frequently with violent than with nonviolent offenses.
- Of the 11 percent convicted at trial, only 4 percent were convicted by juries.

- Very few trials occurred with nonviolent offenses of burglary, larceny, and drug trafficking.
- How a defendant is found guilty has a significant relationship to sentence, with those found guilty by juries receiving prison terms at a rate (82 percent) twice as high as those who pled guilty (43 percent).
- The average prison term is substantially longer for defendants found guilty by a jury compared to those who entered a guilty plea.[30]

Defendants may choose to plead guilty without any negotiation between the prosecution and the defense. Various reasons may account for this decision. Defendants may think that they have no chance to be acquitted at trial. They may not want to engage in any kind of plea bargaining because that, like a trial, might take more time than they are willing to devote to the process. Some defendants want a quick decision. This may be particularly true if they have been denied bail and must wait in jail until a plea bargain is reached or the trial occurs.

In cases involving minor offenses, defendants are often placed on probation. That means they will not have to serve time in jail or prison. They might prefer to plead guilty and get on with their lives. Pleading guilty may save the family money in the case of defendants who do not qualify for publicly supported counsel. Getting back to work will enable defendants to continue supporting their families and to reduce the stress placed on everyone by an indecisive situation.

Defendants who decide not to plead guilty (either with or without plea bargaining) are most often charged with serious crimes that involve long sentences. They apparently prefer to take their chances at being acquitted at trial rather than agree to a certain prison term.

Defendants who plead guilty may already know the court process and the reputation of the prosecutor in that jurisdiction. If the prosecutor has a reputation for recommending stricter sentences for defendants who insist on trials compared to those who plead guilty, the defendant may be willing to enter a guilty plea. Juries in that jurisdiction might also have a reputation for being tough on defendants, and that reputation might lead the defendant to plead guilty.

The defense attorney might encourage the defendant to plead guilty. This advice is often the best advice that the attorney can give the defendant and should not be viewed as a dereliction of the defense attorney's duty to the client. It may also be bad advice in some cases; but if the defendant has little chance of acquittal at trial, the attorney should explain that to the defendant. The attorney should also explain what will be involved financially and otherwise if the case goes to trial. In all cases, however, the final decision whether to plead guilty should be the defendant's.

In deciding whether to plead guilty, the defense should consider carefully the implications of studies indicating that defendants who plead guilty are less likely to be sentenced to prison than defendants who go to trial and are convicted. Those who plead guilty also generally receive shorter sentences. The difference in sentencing between pleading guilty and being found guilty after a trial may be related to the nature of the offense or to other factors that are not in themselves related to whether guilt is determined by a guilty plea or by a trial.

The Process of Pleading Guilty

How does a defendant plead guilty? Jurisdictions will vary in their processes. Figure 10.5 is an example of the Record of Plea form used in one jurisdiction. By signing this form, defendants swear that they are of sound mind, that they are not under the influence of drugs or alcohol, that they fully understand they are waiving the rights associated with a trial, and that nothing has been promised in return for their signature on this form. The form contains an indication of the sentence recommended by the prosecutor (in this case, the district attorney). The judge does not have to abide by that recommendation, but often does.

After the form is completed, the defendant, the defense attorney, and the prosecutor will appear before the magistrate or judge for formal entering of the plea. At that time the judge will question the defendant. Before the plea is accepted, the judge must be convinced that the plea is a knowing and intelligent one and made voluntarily. The Supreme Court has made it clear that, since a defendant who pleads guilty gives up several constitutional rights, including the right to a trial by an impartial jury, that guilty plea requires "an intentional relinquishment or abandonment of a known right or privilege," and must be declared void if it is not a knowing and intelligent plea.[31]

If the judge decides that the plea is a knowing and intelligent one, the judge may accept that plea, in which case a formal record will be made with the court. As Figure 10.5 indicates, the defendant in that jurisdiction has ten days during which an appeal can be made on any sentence imposed by the court.

Defendants who change their minds and wish to withdraw their guilty pleas may petition the court to do so. If that request is made prior to sentencing, the judge will often grant the request; motions to withdraw a guilty plea after sentencing usually are not granted. There is no absolute right to withdraw a guilty plea at any time.[32]

PLEA BARGAINING

A Brief History

One of the most controversial practices in the U.S. criminal justice system is **plea bargaining,** a process in which the prosecution and the defense attempt to negotiate a plea. The negotiation may involve reducing charges, dropping charges, or recommending a sentence. Plea bargaining became a part of the U.S. system after the Civil War but was not widely practiced until this century. Little attention was paid to the process until crime commissions began their studies in the 1920s. Factors that may have contributed to the increased use of plea bargaining are

1. The increasing complexity of the trial process (which may have led to the greater use of nontrial procedures, both for economic reasons and because officials sought to avoid the technicalities of trial);

IN THE DISTRICT COURT OF _____ COUNTY
STATE OF _____

STATE OF _____

          Plaintiff,

vs.

_____ ,

          Defendant.

CR __-_____-_____

_____

DOB: _____

RECORD OF PLEA

I am the defendant in this case and I have signed my name at the end of this statement. My lawyer has also signed at the end of this statement. I have received and read a copy of the written charge against me which my lawyer now has. My lawyer and I have talked about this charge. I have told my lawyer what I did and what I know about the crime I am accused of. My lawyer has told me what he has learned about the witnesses and evidence against me. I have talked to my lawyer as much as I want to and we both agree it would be best that I plead _____ to the charge of _____

I believe that the witnesses and evidence against me can prove this charge and establish facts to support my plea.

My lawyer has told me what the minimum and maximum punishment is for this crime and has also told me the District Attorney recommends that the court give me the following sentence:

_____

_____
                                               (D.A.'S INITIALS)

I understand the court does not have to follow this recommendation.

I understand I can appeal any sentence the court gives me on this plea by filing a notice of appeal within 10 days.

I know that by pleading to this charge I give up my right to have a fair, speedy and public trial and all the other rights that go with a trial. I now give up my rights and plead by signing this Record of Plea. I also understand I waive any motions or defects in the proceedings to date.

I want the court's record to show that my lawyer has explained to me my rights and that I understand my rights. I know that the purpose of a trial is to decide whether I am guilty or innocent of the crime I am accused of. I know that I have the right to choose whether I want a jury of _____ citizens to hear my case and make this decision, or to have a judge without a jury hear my case and make this decision. I know that I do not have to prove either to the judge or the jury that I am innocent, because the law gives me the right to remain silent and the law presumes I am innocent. I also know the District Attorney must prove that I am guilty beyond a reasonable doubt. I know that before I can be found guilty at trial, the witness against me must appear in court and testify under oath before the judge and the jury. I also know I can be in court at all times during the trial, that my lawyer can be there with me, and that my lawyer and I can participate in selecting the jury. I know my lawyer and I can see and hear the witnesses and evidence against me, that we can object to certain evidence, and cross examine the witnesses against me. I know I can call witnesses who can testify for me and the court will order witnesses to attend court on my behalf. I also know that if I want to give up the right to remain silent I can tell the judge and the jury my side of this case, and that myself and my lawyer can make arguments to the judge and the jury. I understand *all* jurors must agree I am guilty beyond a reasonable doubt before I can be found guilty.

I fully understand these rights and I make a free choice at this time to give up these rights and plead. I was not promised anything, or threatened or forced against my will to give up these rights and plead. I am fully competent and am not under the influence of any drugs, medication or alcohol.

_____   _____
      Defendant   Attorney for Defendant

DATE: _____   DATE: _____

                    Court's Minute

_____

_____

FIGURE 10.5
Recording Defendant's Plea

2. Expansion of the substantive criminal law (particularly the enactment of liquor-prohibition statutes);
3. Increasing crime rates;
4. The frequent political corruption of urban criminal courts at and after the turn of the twentieth century;
5. The greater use of professionals in the administration of criminal justice (police, prosecution, and defense).[33]

The Supreme Court Approves Plea Bargaining

Not until the 1970s did the Supreme Court recognize the process of plea bargaining as appropriate and even essential to the criminal justice system. In 1971 the Court approved plea bargaining as a means of managing overloaded criminal dockets, referring to the process as "an essential component" of the criminal process, which "properly administered . . . is to be encouraged."[34] The Court does require, however, that the process not involve threatened physical harm or mental coercion that might result in an involuntary plea by the defendant.[35]

There is no right to plea bargaining. According to the Supreme Court, states and Congress may abolish plea bargaining; but where it does exist, it is not improper to offer leniency "and other substantial benefits" to defendants in exchange for a guilty plea.[36] In 1984 the Court upheld a prosecutor's withdrawal of an offer that had been accepted by the defendant. In *Marbry v. Johnson*, the defendant, after accepting the prosecutor's offer, was told that the offer was a mistake and therefore was being withdrawn. The defendant appealed; the federal appellate court agreed with the defendant that the withdrawal was not permissible. The Supreme Court disagreed, reversed the lower federal court, and stated that an agreement to a plea bargain is merely an "executory agreement that does not involve the constitutional rights of the accused until it is embodied in the formal pleas." In upholding the prosecutor's withdrawal of the plea, the Court said, "The Due Process Clause is not a code of ethics for prosecutors" but rather is concerned "with the manner in which persons are deprived of their liberty."[37]

The reasons for allowing plea bargaining, as well as some of the prosecutorial activities permissible in the process, are articulated by the Supreme Court in *Bordenkircher v. Hayes*, decided in 1978. This case involved a defendant who was indicted by a grand jury on the charge of uttering a forged instrument (passing a hot check), an offense carrying a prison term of 2 to 10 years. After the arraignment on the charge, the prosecutor offered to recommend a 5-year sentence if the defendant would plead guilty to the indictment. If he did not do so, the prosecutor said that he would return to the grand jury and ask for an indictment under the Kentucky Habitual Criminal Act (since repealed). Conviction under that act would result in a life term in prison because the defendant had two prior felony convictions.

Defendant Hayes did not plead guilty. The prosecutor did get the indictment under the Habitual Criminal Act. The jury found Hayes guilty of uttering a forged instrument and in a separate proceeding found that he had two prior felony convictions. As required by statute, upon conviction under that act, he was sentenced to life in prison. Here is an excerpt from the Supreme Court's decision in holding that the prosecutor's actions were permissible.[38]

Bordenkircher v. Hayes

We have recently had occasion to observe: "Whatever might be the situation in an ideal world, the fact is that the guilty plea and the often concomitant plea bargain are important components of this country's criminal justice system. Properly administered, they can benefit all concerned." . . .

To punish a person because he has done what the law plainly allows him to do is a due process violation of the most basic sort, and for an agent of the State to pursue a course of action whose objective is to penalize a person's reliance on his legal rights is "patently unconstitutional." But in the "give-and-take" of plea bargaining, there is no such element of punishment or retaliation so long as the accused is free to accept or reject the prosecution's offer.

Plea bargaining flows from "the mutuality of advantage" to defendants and prosecutors, each with his own reasons for wanting to avoid trial. . . .

While confronting a defendant with the risk of more severe punishment clearly may have a "discouraging effect on the defendant's assertion of his trial rights, the imposition of these difficult choices [is] an inevitable"—and permissible—"attribute of any legitimate system which tolerates and encourages the negotiation of pleas." . . .

To hold that the prosecutor's desire to induce a guilty plea is an "unjustifiable standard," which, like race or religion, may play no part in his charging decision, would contradict the very premises that underlie the concept of plea bargaining itself. Moreover, a rigid constitutional rule that would prohibit a prosecutor from acting forthrightly in his dealings with the defense could only invite unhealthy subterfuge that would drive the practice of plea bargaining back into the shadows from which it has so recently emerged.

Four justices dissented in *Bordenkircher*, arguing that the facts of the case constituted prosecutorial vindictiveness which the Court had earlier held was impermissible. In his dissent, Justice Powell said, "In this case, the prosecutor's actions denied respondent due process because their admitted purpose was to discourage and then to penalize with unique severity his exercise of constitutional rights."[39]

The Process of Plea Bargaining

Plea bargaining may occur during any stage of the criminal process, but defense attorneys prefer to begin negotiations as soon as possible. The longer a defendant has been in the system, the less likely prosecutors are to plea bargain because of the time and effort already spent on the case. The prosecutor also may want to initiate plea bargaining early to dispose of a heavy caseload. On the other hand, he or she might stall on the process, thinking that defendants will be more cooperative the longer they have to wait, especially if they are being detained in jail.

The process of plea bargaining may be initiated by the prosecution or the defense, but the defendant has no right to a plea bargain. The prosecutor may refuse to discuss any kind of bargain and insist on a trial. Likewise, the defendant may refuse to bargain and insist on a trial.

Normally the process of plea bargaining will begin early in the pretrial procedures and be completed before the date set for trial. It is possible for the parties to negotiate a final plea even after the trial has begun, but a defendant's guilty plea cannot be withdrawn merely because he or she chose the wrong strategy.[40]

Once the plea bargain is reached, the defense and prosecution will submit formal papers to the judge, who must accept or reject the plea. The judge is not required to abide by any promise made by the prosecution. Thus, it is possible for the defendant, after plea negotiations, to enter a guilty plea with the understanding that a particular sentence will be imposed and be faced with a different, even harsher sentence.[41]

Judges generally may not participate in plea negotiations in federal cases, although some state and local jurisdictions do permit this practice. When judges do participate, they may directly or indirectly indicate the sentence that might be imposed in the case, encourage defense attorneys and prosecutors to reach a settlement, nudge defendants to accept the plea negotiation decision, or actively intervene in the negotiations. Whether or not they participate in plea negotiations, judges may engage in a pattern of **implicit bargaining** by imposing lesser sentences on defendants who plead guilty rather than insist on a trial.

The participation of judges in the plea negotiation process has been criticized. Defendants may feel that if they refuse an offer that has involved the judge, they will face harsher punishment if convicted after a trial. If judges participate in this pretrial process, they may lose their ability to serve as a check on the possibility that in plea negotiations prosecutors and defense attorneys will accommodate each other to the detriment of the defendants and society. On the other hand, participation of judges in the negotiation process might lessen the possibility of surprise at the final hearing on sentencing. It might also reduce the problem of judges accepting guilty pleas without adequately considering whether the plea really was intelligent and voluntary.[42]

The process of plea bargaining does not always involve active participation by the defendant. Sometimes this is because the defense attorney chooses not to involve the defendant actively. In other cases the defendant may not want to be involved in the initial negotiations but prefers to wait until there is a plea offer and then discuss that with defense counsel.

Some defendants just do not understand the process, and their attorneys do not adequately explain to them what is going to happen. This lack of understanding may lead to such injustice as the following example. A defendant who heard his name called in court approached the bench and entered a plea of guilty. When asked why he pleaded guilty to the charge of statutory rape when he had been charged with grand theft, he replied, "Well, I thought maybe my attorney had made a deal for me."[43]

Others argue that defendants are the most powerful participants in the plea bargaining process because they could break the system if they all insisted on trials. But since such a unified effort is unlikely to occur, they really do not have much power as individual defendants.

One final participant in plea bargaining should be mentioned. It is not common in some jurisdictions to permit victims to be a part of the negotiations if they choose to do so. Some victims do not want to participate; others may be too vindictive or too lenient, but at a minimum victims should be kept informed of the proceedings at all stages in the pretrial procedures. Whether they should participate actively in plea negotiations is controversial. Some argue that it would give defendants a chance to begin some rehabilitation by being confronted with the victim. It would give victims an opportunity to see the defendant as a whole person. Others take the position that the participation of victims would be disruptive to the system and have negative effects on victims.[44]

Types of Plea Bargains

There are two basic types of plea negotiations. In **charge bargaining,** the defendant agrees to plead guilty to a specific charge, and the prosecutor agrees to dismiss any other charges, or to prosecute only for a lesser offense. An armed robbery charge might be dropped in exchange for a plea of guilty to common-law robbery, a lesser offense. A rape charge might be dropped in favor of aggravated assault.

In the case of Mr. Jones in this chapter's CJA, a charge of statutory rape, a felony, might be replaced by a charge of lewd behavior, a misdemeanor, with a stipulation that Mr. Jones seek professional counseling. The plea bargain may include an agreement that the prosecutor will not file any other available charges, such as habitual criminal charges, use of a gun in connection with a crime, or possession of drugs during the commission of a crime.

A second type of plea bargaining is **sentence bargaining.** In this type, the defendant wants the prosecutor either to recommend a more lenient sentence than would be normal for the crime or not to oppose the recommendation made by the defense. The latter bargain may include lesser forms of sentencing such as making payment to the victim rather than being incarcerated.

Charge bargaining and sentence bargaining cannot be completely separated. A lesser charge may have a lower sentence or may allow probation. Thus, when a charge is reduced from a felony to a misdemeanor, not only is the length of the sentence reduced, but the defendant may serve the time in a local facility rather than a state institution, be fined, placed on probation, or given a work assignment—all lesser penalties.

Analysis of Plea Bargaining

The necessity for plea bargaining has been noted by the Supreme Court as well as by most scholars. If from 75 to 90 percent of all cases in which prosecution proceeds beyond the arraignment do not go to trial and, as

SPOTLIGHT 10.4
PLEA BARGAINING: THE CASE OF ROBERT C. CHAMBERS, JR.

The highly publicized trial of Robert C. Chambers, Jr., 21, a New York "preppie" from a wealthy family, provides an excellent example of a plea bargain that apparently was satisfactory to the defendant and to the victim's family.

Chambers was charged with murdering his girl friend, 18-year-old Jennifer Levin. Throughout the 13-week trial, Chambers claimed that he did not mean to hurt Jennifer when he placed his hands on her neck that night in New York's Central Park. He said he struck only one blow to her after she squeezed his testicles during a sex act.

The Chambers' trial brought reaction from fem-inist groups who referred to his "blame-the-victim" defense. A plea bargain was reached after it became clear that after eight and one-half days of deliberating, the jury might not reach a verdict. The result would be a mistrial and a new trial.

Levin's family did not want another trial and agreed to the plea bargain over which they had veto power. The defendant entered a guilty plea to first-degree manslaughter, admitting that he had intended to bring great bodily harm to Levin and thereby cause her death. He expressed his remorse and was sentenced to from 5 to 25 years in prison. He will be eligible for parole in 5 years.

we have seen, the court dockets are already jammed, we can imagine what will happen if all defendants are tried. We would need to increase public expenditures significantly to provide more courts, judges, prosecutors, defense attorneys, court support staff, and facilities. Plea bargaining is necessary not only from a practical standpoint; it is also a viable option for many defendants, as well as for victims and society, as Spotlight 10.4 indicates.

But if prosecutors are allowed to negotiate pleas, abuse might occur. This is a main concern of those who advocate the abolition of plea bargaining. Innocent defendants might be induced to plead guilty; guilty defendants might be induced to plead guilty to charges of crimes they did not commit. Allegations that prosecutors use the system for their professional benefit without considering the best interests of society and allegations that defense attorneys show little interest in their clients and are eager to plead them guilty to end the case are also common complaints. Prosecutorial vindictiveness and defense apathy, along with the lack of sufficient judicial attention to cases at the plea hearing, are also problems.

Abolition of Plea Bargaining

Criticisms of plea bargaining have led in some jurisdictions to its abolition. The most extensive studies of its elimination are from Alaska, where the attorney general instructed prosecutors not to engage in plea bargaining after August 15, 1975. Five years after the ban, a federally funded study indicated that plea bargaining had been effectively curtailed but that there had been a 30 percent increase in the number of trials. Despite that increase, a substantial majority of convictions continued to be the result of guilty pleas rather than trials. Another change in Alaska was a reduction in court delays. The evaluators of the plea bargaining ban suggested that previous court delays had been related to the plea bargaining process. They also reported increased sentence severity for some crimes.[45] That finding was questioned, however, by Albert W. Alschuler, who has written widely on the subject of plea bargaining.[46]

An analysis of plea bargaining in El Paso, Texas, gives more insight to the difficulties of banning it. In El Paso, the fourth largest city in Texas, the local judges initiated a ban on plea bargaining in felony cases. The study found that prosecutors and defense attorneys engaged in covert bargaining despite the judicial ban and that some judges enforced the bargains.

The El Paso study did not appear to indicate that resumption of plea bargaining was not done to ease case pressures but "was the result of an irrepressible tendency to cooperate among members of the courtroom work group." According to the researcher, the study "reinforces the notion that plea bargaining is a permanent component of American criminal process."[47] The tendency of prosecutors and attorneys toward accommodation deserves more attention.

PRETRIAL PROCEDURES, THE COURT, AND ACCOMMODATION: AN ANALYSIS

All the subjects in this chapter, particularly that of plea bargaining, raise questions concerning the organization and structure of courts in the real day-to-day working relationships of the professionals who participate in criminal cases. What relationship does that organization have to the adversary system? Has the adversary system been replaced by a system of accommodation?

Earlier studies were critical of the work environment of the courthouse, pointing out that defense attorneys and prosecutors are on a first-name basis; that they know all the police officers who arrest the defendants and would not think of embarrassing those officers in court by the questions they ask; that defense and prosecution negotiate deals that are beneficial to them but not necessarily to their clients; and that both the prosecution and the defense assume that defendants are guilty. Certain offense patterns are categorized and stereotyped, enabling defense attorneys to react quickly to their clients and spend very little time with them. But, said the researchers, these reactions may be necessary in order for the prosecution and defense to process the cases with the resources and personnel available to them.[48]

Abraham S. Blumberg, an often-cited critic of the court system, went even further. In his observations of a court that he referred to only as Metropolitan Court, Blumberg found that many of the cases were handled by a few defense attorneys whom he called the courthouse regulars. These attorneys were able to get the best court assignments with the most favorable judges because of their connections.

Blumberg described the system as violating due process, justice, and the rule of law, arguing that those goals have been replaced by "concerns of secularism and rationality, based on modern values of efficiency, maximum production, and career enhancement." The result is a system in which the accused is visualized as "possessed of a self which is ideal for organizational purposes—one which is vulnerable to manipulation and capable of manipulating others." Blumberg suggests that the court is not a democratic institution. If the professionals question the directives of the court, they will soon find that sanctions are employed.[49]

Other scholars have disagreed with Blumberg's conclusion that the bureaucratic structure of the court is necessarily disruptive to the adversary process. Jerome Skolnick's analysis of court structure and process puts a different interpretation on the cooperation between prosecution and defense. After 18 months of observing the working relationships of the attorneys in two felony courts in a California city of about 400,000, Skolnick concluded: there is a reciprocal relationship between prosecutor and defense attorney in the American system of criminal justice; this relationship creates a strain toward cooperation; the relationship extends beyond the immediate parties before the court; public defenders do not differ significantly from other cooperative defense attorneys; and, ironically, this cooperation does not seriously hinder the system of justice or the quality of representation.[50]

Albert W. Alschuler also examined the roles of defense attorney, prosecutor, and judge in the criminal court system. He concluded that the system operates for the convenience of these professionals, with little concern for justice and defendants. One of his primary concerns is with the possibility that the functioning of the system at least implicitly encourages defendants to plead guilty rather than exercise their constitutional right to a trial. This implicit bargaining may occur when it becomes known that defendants who go to trial get more severe sentences than those who plead guilty without a trial.[51]

More recent studies of courthouse work groups have been conducted by James Eisenstein and Herbert Jacob, who observed felony courts in three cities: Chicago, Detroit, and Baltimore. Although the procedures for processing cases differed, Eisenstein and Jacob found that the primary factor in explaining the processes in each city was the interrelationship of the courthouse work groups. For example, more plea negotiations took place when the regulars in the courthouse were familiar with each other; fewer took place when these professionals were not well acquainted.[52]

Other recent researchers have not agreed. A study of plea bargaining in robbery and burglary cases in California revealed that, although local environments do develop distinctive patterns of plea bargaining, "the major criteria (i.e., defendant's criminal records) affecting the severity of sentencing in negotiated cases remain relatively stable across jurisdictions." The author concluded that the advantage of this organizational approach to studying courtroom interaction is that it reveals the complexity involved in the various decision-making processes in the criminal justice system.[53]

These analyses of the interaction of professionals in the court, particularly in the process of plea bargaining, illustrate the importance of analyzing any aspect of the criminal justice system by the goals of the system and the total system effect. Once again, we must recall the due process and the crime control models. If we wish to continue to recognize rights of due process, some elements of crime control will be incompatible with the system. If we consider all the other elements of the system, it becomes easier to understand why plea bargaining occurs.

This is not to suggest that plea bargaining or other aspects of the pretrial procedures have no problems, but that we not dwell on the abuses to the extent that we abolish the system without considering the alternatives. One of the best analyses in recent years was written by Malcolm M. Feeley, who considered the process of plea bargaining and the criminal court structure in light of its historical background. Feeley concluded that

> plea bargaining is a product of the very nature and structure of the modern criminal process rather than a result of extra-legal factors or organizational pressures that have caused the criminal process to deviate from its true purposes.

Feeley does not suggest that plea bargaining is desirable or inevitable, but rather that it is "intertwined with a host of factors that are generally regarded as highly desirable. In our quest for perfect justice, we have constructed an elaborate and costly criminal process." He does not believe that plea bargaining can be eliminated without diminishing prosecutorial discretion to reduce or enhance charges and recommend sentencing or without realizing the standards of due process recognized in our criminal justice system. He emphasizes that most of the policies restricting and banning plea bargaining have taken place in a vacuum, without considering the effect that action would have on the rest of the system. "This no doubt goes a long way in explaining why so many policies banning plea bargaining have had such short lives."[54]

It is important in analyzing studies of plea bargaining to look at the basis for those studies. For example, a conclusion that cooperation between prosecution and defense results in cooptation of the defendant's rights may be based only on an analysis of case outcome. Most cases involving cooperation result in a conviction. But most cases probably would involve a conviction anyway, and it may be that cooperation between prosecution and defense attorneys results in greater benefits than harmful results to the defendant.

One researcher found cooperation "to be instrumental in the sense of facilitating daily interaction in ways that benefit defendants." These findings, says the author, are preliminary and should be investigated further. But this study emphasizes the need to be very careful in analyzing any aspect of the system.[55]

SUMMARY

In this chapter we have encountered some of the most critical issues and most difficult procedures in the entire criminal justice system. All of the pretrial court hearings are crucial, for at any stage failure to find probable cause must result in the release of the defendant. If any rights of the accused are violated during arrest, interrogation, investigation, or search and seizure, the evidence secured as a result of those violations must be excluded from the trial. Without the illegally seized evidence, many cases must be dismissed for lack of probable cause. The initial appearance, the preliminary hearing, the grand jury review, and the arraignment are all concerned with the issue of determining whether there is sufficient evidence to continue the case.

The critical roles of the prosecution and the defense in these stages cannot be overemphasized. Prosecutorial discretion to drop the charges after the police have arrested a suspect can easily negate the crime control efforts of police. However, that discretionary power can serve as a check on overzealous police officers. Even after the formal charges are filed with the court, either through a prosecutorial information or a grand jury indictment, the prosecutor has considerable influence in getting those charges dismissed. This dismissal may be done for good reasons, such as lack of evidence; or for wrong reasons, such as discrimination or political pressure. Prosecutors also have great power at the stage of grand jury review, because grand juries usually return a true bill on indictments submitted by the prosecution.

The role of the defense attorney is to protect the rights of defendants at all pretrial stages and to plan the defense strategy should the case go to trial. The role of the judge is also important. He or she presides over all formal court hearings and has the power to grant or deny motions, to grant or deny bail, and to accept or reject guilty pleas. To a great extent, the judge also controls the timing of all the stages, because he or she sets dates for the court hearings and for the trial. If a guilty plea has been accepted, the judge usually has the power to impose sentencing at that time.

Two critical procedures discussed in this chapter raise controversial issues in our system of criminal justice: the decision whether to release or detain defendants pending trial and the practice of plea bargaining. The decision whether to release a defendant on bail or to allow some other alternative requires the judge to predict whether that person, if released, would appear for trial. With recent legislation in some jurisdictions permitting pretrial detention for preventive purposes, some judges now have the power to detain if they think the defendant will be dangerous to society. These are not easy decisions in a world in which predicting human behavior is frequently inaccurate. Yet, the decision to detain imposes great burdens on defendants, who are not only inconvenienced but may lose their jobs, suffer the indignities and embarrassments of a jail term, and in some cases suffer physical attacks by other inmates. For those who are later found innocent of the crimes for which they are charged, pretrial detention may seem to be an incredible injustice. For society, pretrial release may mean more crime; but pretrial detention creates the need for more facilities, thus increasing the cost of the criminal justice system.

Plea bargaining is another procedure that raises many issues. The practice is necessary as long as we have high crime rates and insufficient facilities and personnel to try all cases. The practice allows the flexibility necessary if the system is to respond with any degree of concern for circumstances of individual cases. But that flexibility also may lead to abuse of discretion, resulting in bitter defendants, some of whom have reasonable justification for believing that they have been treated unfairly by the system. Plea bargaining may entice defendants to plead guilty to crimes they did not commit rather than risk their constitutional rights to trial. Such a choice might, and usually does, result in conviction.

All these procedures in the pretrial stages raise the issue of the interrelationships of the participants at the courthouse and the effect of those relationships on decision making. It is often argued that prosecutors and defense attorneys accommodate each other and the system; and there is some evidence of accommodation. But there is also evidence that the predictable patterns of interaction are beneficial for the criminal justice system and for some defendants.

This chapter has focused on pretrial procedures and the issues raised by them but many of the pretrial procedures also may occur during trial. Plea bargaining may continue. Many of the motions made at pretrial may be made during the trial as well. The issue of whether the defendant should be released from jail is always open; likewise, the decision to release a defendant pending trial can be revoked when changes in the circumstances warrant that decision. Both prosecution and defense may, and often do, continue investigation to secure more evidence to present at trial, particularly during a long trial. The stages in the criminal justice system are not always separable. Some procedures and issues, however, are peculiar to the criminal trial. To that subject we devote the next chapter.

STUDY QUESTIONS

1. What restrictions are placed on the securing of physical evidence from a suspect?

2. What legal issues are involved in the use of line-ups?

3. Briefly describe the legal use of electronic surveillance and informants to obtain evidence of a crime.

4. What is meant by the *open fields exception* to the right of privacy?

5. Describe the main purposes of the initial appearance, preliminary hearing, and arraignment.

6. What is meant by a *waiver of rights by the defendant*? How do we know when that has properly been done?

7. What is a *grand jury review*? How does that process differ from a prosecutor's information?

8. What are *motions* and *discovery*?

9. Distinguish between *depositions* and *interrogatories*.

10. Why and how did the bail bond system develop? Why is it controversial today?

11. Which of the alternatives to a bail bond system do you think is most feasible? Why?

12. What is the purpose of bail? Should bail be eliminated?

13. What is meant by *preventive detention*? What are the legal issues surrounding this process?

14. What has research revealed about the interrelationships of the prosecutor, the defense attorney, and the judge? Are these relationships good or bad for the criminal justice system? For the defendant?

15. Describe the process of pleading guilty before trial. Does it make any difference whether the plea is a negotiated one?

16. Most European countries do not permit plea bargaining. Why is it permitted in this country? Do you think it should be abolished? Why? If it is, what might be the results?

17. What is the difference between *charge bargaining* and *sentence bargaining*?

ENDNOTES

1. Wayne R. LaFave and Jerold H. Israel, *Criminal Procedure* (St. Paul, Minn.: West Publishing Co., 1985), pp. 19–20. This source provides an excellent overview of the pretrial stages and was used for this discussion.

2. See, for example, Holt v. U.S., 218 U.S. 245 (1910), upholding the requirement that the defendant model a blouse. Holt was referred to in 1966 as the "landmark case." In Schmerber v. California, 384 U.S. 757, 761 (1966), the Court permitted securing blood samples from the defendant.

3. See, for example, U. S. v. Wade, 388 U.S. 218 (1967).

4. Stovall v. Denno, 388 U.S. 293 (1967).

5. See Simmons v. U.S., 390 U.S. 377 (1968).

6. Olmstead v. U.S., 277 U.S. 438 (1928).

7. Katz v. U.S., 389 U.S. 347 (1967).

8. See On Lee v. U. S., 343 U.S. 747 (1952); and Lopez v. U.S., 373 U.S. 427 (1963).

9. See Sherman v. U.S. 356 U.S. 369 (1958).

10. Oliver v. U.S., 466 U.S. 170 (1984), *remanded* 485 A.2d 952 (Me. 1984).

11. California v. Ciraolo, 476 U.S. 207 (1986). See also Dow Chemical Co. v. U. S., 476 U.S. 227 (1986), decided the same day.

12. Press-Enterprise Co. v. Superior Court of California, 478 U.S. 1 (1986).

13. Wood v. Georgia, 370 U.S. 375, 390 (1962).

14. Hawkins v. Superior Court, 22 Cal. 3d 584, 589–90 (Cal. 1978). For more information on the grand jury, see Marvin E. Frankel and Gary P. Naftalis, *The Grand Jury: An Institution on Trial* (New York: Hill and Wang, 1977).

15. See, for example, Vasquez v. Hillery, 474 U.S. 254 (1986); and U. S. v. Mechanik, 475 U.S. 66 (1986).

16. For an extensive discussion of the law regarding grand juries and practice before them, see Sara Sun Beale and William C. Bryson, *Grand Jury Law and Practice* (Wilmette, Ill.: Callaghan and Company, 1986).

17. Powell v. Alabama, 287 U.S. 45, 57 (1932).
18. Forrest Dill, "Discretion Exchange and Social Control: Bail Bondsmen in Criminal Courts," *Law and Society Review* 9 (Summer 1975): 647–67.
19. See KY. REV. STAT., Sections 431, 510 et seq. This statute was upheld in Benboe v. Carroll, 625 F.2d 737 (6th Cir. 1980). See also OR. REV. STAT., Sections 135, 230 et seq. For a recent discussion of the Oregon system see "Oregon's Ten Percent Deposit Bail System—Rethinking the Professional Surety's Role," *Oregon Law Review* 66, no. 3 (1988): 661–84.
20. Charles E. Ares et al., "The Manhattan Bail Project," *New York University Law Review* 38 (January 1963): 68.
21. National Advisory Commission on Criminal Justice Standards and Goals, *Corrections* (Washington, D.C.: U.S. Government Printing Office, 1973), p. 103.
22. Stack v. Boyle, 342 U.S. 1 (1951).
23. See Jerome Skolnick, "Judicial Response in Crisis," in Skolnick, ed., *The Politics of Protest* (New York: Simon and Schuster, 1969); and Frederic Suffet, "Bail Setting: A Study of Courtroom Interaction," *Crime and Delinquency* 21 (October 1966): 329.
24. U.S. v. Edwards, 430 A.2d 1321 (D.C. Ct. App. 1981), *cert. denied*, 455 U.S. 1022 (1982).
25. Schall v. Martin, 467 U.S. 253 (1984).
26. U.S. v. Salerno, 107 S. Ct. 2095, 2102, 2103 (1987), *remanded* 829 F.2d 345 (2d Cir. 1987), cases and citations omitted.
27. See "Eighth Amendment—Pretrial Detention: What Will Become of the Innocent?" *Journal of Criminal Law and Criminology* 78 (Winter 1988): 1048–79.
28. See "Pretrial Detention of Dangerous Individuals: Constitutional Challenges to the Bail Reform Act of 1984," *Stetson Law Review* 27 (Spring 1988): 463–90.
29. See "Preventive Detention: Illinois Takes A Tentative Step towards a Safer Community," *John Marshall Law Review* 21 (Winter 1988): 389–408, referring to Article I, section 9, of the Illinois Constitution.
30. Bureau of Justice Statistics, *Sentencing Outcomes in Twenty-Eight Felony Courts 1985* (Washington, D.C.: U.S. Department of Justice, July 1987), pp. 25, 26.
31. McCarthy v. U.S., 394 U.S. 459 (1969), quoting the waiver standard established in Johnson v. Zerbst, 304 U.S. 458, 464 (1938).
32. See U.S. v. Buckles, 843 F.2d 469 (11th Cir. 1988), *cert. den.*, 109 S. Ct. 2450 (1989).
33. Albert W. Alschuler, "Plea Bargaining," in Sanford H. Kadish, ed., *Encyclopedia of Crime and Justice* (New York: Macmillan Publishing Co., 1983), vol. 2, p. 830. For a brief history, see Joseph B. Sanborn, Jr., "A Historical Sketch of Plea Bargaining," *Justice Quarterly* 3 (June 1986): 111–38.
34. Santobello v. New York, 404 U.S. 257, 260–61 (1971).
35. Brady v. U.S., 397 U.S. 742 (1970).
36. Corbitt v. New Jersey, 439 U.S. 212, 219, 223 (1978).
37. Mabry v. Johnson, 467 U.S. 504 (1984).
38. Bordenkircher v. Hayes, 434 U.S. 357, 360–65 (1978), footnotes and citations omitted.
39. Bordenkircher v. Hayes, 434 U.S. 357, 372–73 (1978), Justice Powell dissenting.
40. Brady v. U.S., 397 U.S. 742, 757 (1970).
41. Although the case involves complications not discussed here, the Supreme Court in Rickets v. Adamson, 107 S. Ct. 2680 (1987) held that defendant's rights not to be tried twice for the same offense were not violated under these facts. Defendant, one of three charged with first-degree murder, entered a guilty plea in return for a specific prison term and his testimony against codefendants. He complied with that agreement and received a prison term. But he refused to testify when the codefendants were retried after their first convictions were overturned on appeal. Defendant was then tried for first-degree murder, convicted, and sentenced to death.
42. James A. Cramer, ed., *Plea Bargaining* (Beverly Hills, Calif.: Sage Publications, 1981), p. 193.
43. Martin Mayer, *The Lawyers* (New York: Harper and Row, 1966), p. 160.
44. For a detailed discussion, including legal issues, of permitting victims to participate in plea bargains, see Sarah N. Welling, "Victim Participation in Plea Bargains," *Washington University Law Quarterly* 65, no. 2 (1987): 301–56.
45. Michael L. Rubinstein et al., *Alaska Bans Plea Bargaining* (Washington, D.C.: U.S. Government Printing Office, 1980).
46. Albert W. Alschuler, "The Changing Plea Bargaining Debate," *California Law Review* 69 (1981): 652–730.
47. Robert A. Weninger, "The Abolition of Plea Bargaining: A Case Study of El Paso County, Texas," *UCLA Law Review* 35 (December 1987): 265–313, quotations on pp. 312 and 313.
48. See Edwin M. Shur, *Law and Society: A Sociological View* (New York: Random House, 1968), as an example of the earlier works.
49. Abraham S. Blumberg, *Criminal Justice* (Chicago: Quadrangle Books, 1967), pp. 104–6, 78. Second edition published in 1979 by New Viewpoints, New York.
50. Jerome H. Skolnick, "Social Control in the Adversary System," *Journal of Conflict Resolution* 11 (March 1967): 59–60.
51. Albert W. Alschuler, "The Prosecutor's Role in Plea Bargaining," *University of Chicago Law Review* 36 (Summer 1968): 50–112.
52. James Eisenstein and Herbert Jacob, *Felony Jus-*

tice: An Organizational Analysis of Criminal Courts (Boston: Little, Brown and Co., 1977).

53. J. Fred Springer, "Burglary and Robbery Plea Bargaining in California: An Organizational Perspective," *Justice System Journal* 8 (Summer 1983): 157–85, quotation on p. 157.

54. Malcolm M. Feeley, "Plea Bargaining and the Structure of the Criminal Process," *The Justice System Journal* 73 (Winter 1982): 352–53.

55. Michael J. Lichtenstein, "Public Defenders: Dimensions of Cooperation," *The Justice System Journal* 9 (Spring 1984): 102, 110.

Trial and Appeals

Susan, a 20-year-old black college student, is arrested for shoplifting $75 worth of merchandise. Because the amount is over $50, she is charged with grand larceny, a felony. Susan is the daughter of the president of the university that she attends. The community is shocked by her alleged crime, and the media publicity of the crime is extensive. Susan's defense attorney tries unsuccessfully to get the prosecutor to plea bargain the case to a misdemeanor of petty theft and recommend probation. The prosecutor has decided to make an example of Susan; she thinks that a conviction in this case will reduce shoplifting by college students.

Susan's case goes to trial. At jury selection, there are 30 prospective jurors: 5 are black; 10 are women; none is under the age of 30. The final jury of 12 includes only one woman and no blacks. Susan's attorney conducts an excellent defense, but the jury returns a verdict of guilty of grand larceny. The prosecutor recommends the maximum sentence of 5 years in prison, and the judge assesses that penalty.

INTRODUCTION

Susan's case raises only a few of the procedures that take place in a criminal trial, but the facts raise some of the most important and controversial issues in the criminal justice system. Our system guarantees the right to a public trial by an impartial jury of one's peers. In Susan's case, the extensive media publicity of the alleged crime raises the issue of whether she can get a fair trial in her community. Her race and the absence of black jurors raises the question of whether there has been any systematic or purposeful exclusion of blacks from the jury. The lack of young adults on the jury raises the question of what is meant by a jury of Susan's peers.

This chapter describes each stage of a criminal trial. Because all aspects of a trial are governed by the due process rights of the defendants and by rules of procedure, the chapter begins with a discussion of the constitutional rights of defendants at trial. The final section of the chapter focuses on an analysis of the use of juries in criminal trials.

CONSTITUTIONAL RIGHTS OF DEFENDANTS AT TRIAL

The beginning of this text discussed the adversary system and looked briefly at the due process and equal protection rights of defendants in the criminal justice system. Subsequent chapters have discussed specific rights where applicable. The legitimate police practices of reasonable searches and seizures, as well as interrogation of suspects, were discussed in light of the constitutional prohibition against unreasonable searches and seizures and the right of defendants not to be compelled to testify against themselves. The right to counsel at all critical stages in the criminal justice process was discussed, along with the right to effective assistance of counsel and the right to refuse counsel. All these rights are important at trial. They were discussed earlier because they are also important during pretrial procedures. This discussion of the constitutional rights of defendants at **trial** is not meant to be exclusive; it must be understood in the context of the other discussions. It focuses on the rights that have not been discussed and that pertain mainly to the criminal trial.

The Right to a Speedy Trial

The right to a speedy trial can be traced to the twelfth century, and it was a recognized right in the early days of this country's development. The right is embodied in the Sixth Amendment:

> In all criminal prosecutions, the accused shall enjoy the right to a speedy and public trial, by an impartial jury of the State and district wherein the crime shall have been committed, which district shall have been previously ascertained by law, and to be informed of the nature and cause of the accusation; to be confronted with the witnesses against him; to have compulsory process for obtaining witnesses in his favor, and to have the Assistance of Counsel for his defence.

The Supreme Court has held that the right to a speedy trial also applies to defendants in state trials and that this right "is as fundamental as any of the rights secured by the Sixth Amendment."[1]

Some defendants, however, are not brought to trial quickly. Indeed, that is not always a positive goal. Some cases are very complex and require more time for trial preparation. Defense and prosecution may ask for and be granted continuances beyond the originally established trial date, and there are circumstances under which those continuances should be granted. But under normal circumstances, defendants must be brought to trial within the requirements of the statutory and procedural provisions of the various jurisdictions.

The Speedy Trial Act of 1974   In 1974 Congress passed the Speedy Trial Act, which was amended in 1979. The act with its amendments provides that, for suspects in federal cases, an indictment or an information must be filed within 30 days of the arrest or of the time when the defendant is served with a summons on the charge. That period may be extended for 30 days in a felony charge if the grand jury was not in session during that time. Trial is to

> commence within seventy days from the filing date (and making public) of the information or indictment or from the date the defendant has appeared before a judicial officer of the court in which such charge is pending, whichever date last occurs.[2]

It is possible, of course, that the defendant could be tried so quickly that there would not be adequate time for preparing a defense. The Speedy Trial Act therefore provides that, without the consent of the defendant, "the trial shall not commence less than thirty days from the date on which the defendant first appears through counsel or expressly waives counsel and elects to proceed pro se."

As might be expected, there has been litigation on the meaning of the Speedy Trial Act. All of the legal details cannot be discussed here, but Spotlight 11.1 is included to give an example of the litigation. The case was a highly publicized murder trial involving a doctor who was convicted of the murders of his wife and children. The case also is included to give an example of the kind of evidence that may be crucial in a criminal trial.

SPOTLIGHT 11.1
UNITED STATES V. JEFFREY R. MACDONALD

The facts in this case are not in issue: a jury heard and saw all the witnesses and saw the tangible evidence. The only point raised here by petitioner involves a legal issue under the Speedy Trial Clause of the Sixth Amendment. Accordingly, only a brief summary of the facts is called for. On the night of February 17, 1970, respondent's pregnant wife and his two daughters, aged 2 and 5, were brutally murdered in their home on the Fort Bragg, North Carolina, military reservation. At the time, MacDonald, a physician, was a captain in the Army Medical Corps stationed at Fort Bragg. When the military police arrived at the scene following a call from MacDonald, they found the three victims dead and MacDonald unconscious from multiple stab wounds, most of them superficial, but one a life-threatening chest wound which caused a lung to collapse.

At the time and in subsequent interviews, Mac-Donald told of a bizarre and ritualistic murder. He stated that he was asleep on the couch when he was awakened by his wife's screams. He said he saw a woman with blond hair wearing a floppy hat, white boots and a short skirt carrying a lighted candle and chanting ''acid is groovy; kill the pigs.''[1] He claimed

that three men standing near the couch attacked him, tearing his pajama top, stabbing him and clubbing him into unconsciousness. When he awoke, he found his wife and two daughters dead. After trying to revive them and covering his wife's body with his pajama top, MacDonald called the military police. He lost consciousness again before the police arrived.

Physical evidence at the scene contradicted MacDonald's account and gave rise to the suspicion that MacDonald himself may have committed the crime.[2] On April 6, 1970, the Army Criminal Investigation Division (CID) advised MacDonald that he was a suspect in the case and confined him to quarters. The Army formally charged MacDonald with the three murders on May 1, 1970. In accordance with Article 32 of the Uniform Code of Military Justice, 10 U.S.C. § 832, the Commanding General of Mac-Donald's unit appointed an officer to investigate the charges. After hearing a total of 56 witnesses, the investigating officer submitted a report recommending that the charges and specifications against MacDonald be dismissed. The Commanding General dismissed the military charges on October 23, 1970. On December 5, 1970, the Army granted MacDonald's request for an honorable discharge based on hardship.

At the request of the Justice Department, however, the CID continued its investigation. In June

[1]A woman generally within this description was apparently seen by the military police as they rushed to answer respondent's call. During the course of this case, considerable suspicion has been focused upon Helena Stoeckley. Stoeckley was 19 at the time and a heavy user of heroin, opium, mescaline, LSD, marijuana and other drugs; within days after the crime she began telling people that she was involved in the murder or that she at least had accompanied the murderers and watched them commit the crimes. She also wore mourning dress and displayed a funeral wreath on the day of the victims' funeral. The investigation confirmed that she had been seen returning to her apartment at 4:30 that morning in the company of men also generally fitting the descriptions given by MacDonald. Stoeckley testified at trial that she had no memory of the night in question because she was ''stoned'' that night. She did, however, admit that at the time of the crime she owned and frequently wore a blond wig and a pair of white boots and that she destroyed them within a few days after the crime because they might connect her with the episode.

[2]Threads from MacDonald's pajama top, supposedly torn in the living room, were found in the master bedroom, some under his wife's body, and in the children's bedroom, but not in the living room. There were 48 puncture holes in the top, yet MacDonald had far fewer wounds. The police were able to identify the bloodstains of each victim, and their location did not support MacDonald's story. Blood matching the type of MacDonald's children were found on MacDonald's glasses and pajama top. Fragments of surgical gloves were found near the bodies of the victims; the gloves from which those fragments came were found under a sink in the house.

Notice the references in the spotlight footnotes to the evidence that was contradictory to the testimony of the defendant.

Even under the Speedy Trial Act, some delays are permissible. Several are listed in the act, including the obvious reasons, such as delays caused by examinations to determine whether the defendant is competent to stand trial; delays caused by the defendant's mental incompetence to

1972, the CID forwarded a 13-volume report to the Justice Department recommending further investigation. Additional reports were submitted during November 1972 and August 1973. Following evaluation of those reports, in August 1974, the Justice Department presented the matter to a grand jury. On January 24, 1975, the grand jury returned an indictment charging MacDonald with the three murders. . . .

MacDonald was then tried and convicted on two counts of second-degree murder and one count of first-degree murder. He was sentenced to three consecutive terms of life imprisonment. . . .

The Sixth Amendment right to a speedy trial is thus not primarily intended to prevent prejudice to the defense caused by passage of time; that interest is protected primarily by the Due Process Clause and by statutes of limitations. The speedy trial guarantee is designed to minimize the possibility of lengthy incarceration prior to trial, to reduce the lesser, but nevertheless substantial, impairment of liberty imposed on an accused while released on bail, and to shorten the disruption of life caused by arrest and the presence of unresolved criminal charges."

. . . Once charges are dismissed, the speedy trial guarantee is no longer applicable. At that point, the formerly accused is, at most, in the same position as any other subject of a criminal investigation. Certainly the knowledge of an ongoing criminal investigation will cause stress, discomfort and perhaps a certain disruption in normal life. This is true whether or not charges have been filed and then dismissed. . . . But with no charges outstanding, personal liberty is certainly not impaired to the same degree as it is after arrest while charges are pending. After the charges against him have been dismissed, "a citizen suffers no restraints on his liberty and is [no longer] the subject of public accusation: his situation does not compare with that of a defendant who has been arrested and held to

answer." . . . Following dismissal of charges, any restraint on liberty, disruption of employment, strain on financial resources, and exposure to public obloquy, stress and anxiety is no greater than it is upon anyone openly subject to a criminal investigation.

. . . In this case, the homicide charges initiated by the Army were terminated less than a year after the crimes were committed; after that, there was no criminal prosecution pending on which MacDonald could have been tried until the grand jury, in January 1975, returned the indictments on which he was tried and convicted. During the intervening period, MacDonald was not under arrest, not in custody and not subject to any "criminal prosecution." Inevitably, there were undesirable consequences flowing from the initial accusation by the Army and the continuing investigation after the Army charges were dismissed. Indeed, even had there been no charges lodged by the Army, the ongoing comprehensive investigation would have subjected MacDonald to stress and other adverse consequences. However, once the charges instituted by the Army were dismissed, MacDonald was legally and constitutionally in the same posture as though no charges had been made. He was free to go about his affairs, to practice his profession, and to continue with his life.

The Court of Appeals acknowledged, and MacDonald concedes, that the delay between the civilian indictment and trial was caused primarily by MacDonald's own legal manuevers and, in any event, was not sufficient to violate the Speedy Trial Clause. Accordingly, the judgment of the Court of Appeals is reversed, and the case is remanded for further proceedings consistent with this opinion.

Reversed and remanded.

Source: United States v. Jeffrey R. MacDonald, 456 U.S. 1 (1982), some footnotes omitted, citations omitted.

stand trial; and delays caused by deferred prosecution when that is agreed upon by the prosecutor, the defendant, and the court. The act permits delays caused by continuances granted to the defense or the prosecution when these are granted to serve the ends of justice.

The Speedy Trial Act applies only to prosecutions in federal courts, but most states have constitutional provisions for the right to a speedy trial. Those provisions are similar to the Sixth Amendment. Most states also have procedural or statutory rules indicating specifically how many days may elapse between arrest and trials, ranging from 75 days to 6 months.

Felony Case–Processing Time

The importance of a speedy trial, both to the defendant and to society, has led to concern about the actual time that elapses between initial apprehension of the offender and final disposition of the case. The Bureau of Justice Statistics (BJS) studied the felony case–processing time in 12 jurisdictions. The results of that study are reported in Table 11.1.

As Table 11.1 indicates, the median time for processing felony cases is 3.5 months, although those cases indicted (by a grand jury) and bound over (by an indictment) for trial average 4.5 months. Table 11.1 also con-

TABLE 11.1

Felony Case–Processing Time In 12 Jurisdictions

	Average Elapsed Time from Arrest to Disposition For:	
	Cases Filed In Court	Cases Indicted and Bound Over For Trial
Total (mean)	3.5 mos.	4.9 mos.
Type of disposition		
Dismissal	2.8	5.3
Guilty plea	3.4	4.5
Trial	7.1	7.4
Most serious charge		
Homicide	6.2	7.1
Sexual assault	4.2	6.0
Robbery	3.5	4.4
Burglary	3.2	4.1
Larceny	3.2	4.7

Note: Data are derived from 12 different jurisdictions and represent median case processing times within jurisdictions averaged using the mean across all jurisdictions with available data. Data for "total" and "type of disposition" were available from all 12 jurisdictions; data for "most serious charge" were available for 9 jurisdictions. The elapsed time in months was computed by dividing the elapsed time in days by 30.4 (the average number of days per month in a nonleap year).

Source: Bureau of Justice Statistics, *Felony Case–Processing Time* (Washington, D.C.: U.S. Department of Justice, August 1986), p. 2.

tains case–processing time by crime, indicating that the more serious crimes require longer for processing.

The Right to a Public Trial

The Sixth Amendment guarantees the right to a public trial. This right does not mean that the defendant may be tried by the media. If it can be shown that the defendant cannot get a fair trial because of publicity in the jurisdiction where the case is to be tried, the trial should be moved to another jurisdiction.

Media publicity in criminal cases raises a delicate problem: the conflict between the First Amendment free speech right of the press and the right of the public and the defendant to a trial by an impartial jury, a jury not biased by media information. The Supreme Court has had several occasions to consider this conflict.

In a 1966 case, the Court overturned the conviction of Dr. Sam Sheppard, who had already served 10 years in prison after his conviction for murdering his wife. On retrial Sheppard received an **acquittal,** but he was not allowed to return to the practice of medicine. He tried to begin a new life in France after suffering intense rejection in this society. He subsequently committed suicide. In overturning Sheppard's conviction, the Court said:[3]

Sheppard v. *Maxwell* _____

Murder and mystery, society, sex and suspense were combined in this case in such a manner as to intrigue and captivate the public fancy to a degree perhaps unparalleled in recent annals. Throughout the preindictment investigation, the subsequent legal skirmishes and the nine-week trial, circulation-conscious editors catered to the insatiable interest of the American public in the bizarre. . . . In this atmosphere of a 'Roman holiday' for the news media, Sam Sheppard stood trial for his life.

_____

In a highly controversial decision in 1979, the Court held that the press may be excluded from a pretrial hearing on the issue of whether to suppress or admit certain evidence at the subsequent trial. *Gannett v. DePasquale* reopened the power struggle between the press and the Court and between the rights of the public and the rights of the defendant.[4]

Public and press reactions were predictably critical. The *New York Times* lead editorial, with the headline, "Private Justice, Public Injustice," stated,

> Now the Supreme Court has endorsed secrecy in language broad enough to justify its use not only in a pretrial context but even at a formal trial. . . . The power to make public business private is a dangerous power, far in excess of the supposed benefit.[5]

Time referred to the decision as a "stunning shock" to the press. "It is also by far the court's sharpest blow to the press in a long string of such adverse rulings."[6]

In subsequent cases the Court has continued to wrestle with the rights of defendants versus the First Amendment free speech right of the press and of the public. The Court has held that under some circumstances the former must give way to the latter.[7] Later cases have examined what some of those circumstances might be. For example, in *Globe Newspaper v. Superior Court*, the Court held invalid a Massachusetts statute that had been interpreted to mean exclusion of the press from *all* trials when under-18-year-old victims of sexual offenses were testifying. It stated that each case must be examined in terms of its own facts, such as the "the minor victim's age, psychological maturity and understanding, the nature of the crime, the desires of the victim, and the interests of parents and relatives."[8]

The Use of Cameras During the Trial   With respect to the media, the use of television in trials should also be mentioned. In 1977 Florida began an experimental program of permitting television coverage of criminal trials. The experiment lasted for 1 year, after which the Florida Supreme Court reviewed evidence concerning the effects of such coverage. The court concluded that on balance the advantages were greater that the disadvantages and specified guidelines for subsequent use of media coverage of trials.[9]

Many jurisdictions now permit the use of cameras in the courtroom. Cameras are not permitted in federal courtrooms; the use was barred in 1946. Former chief justice Warren E. Burger, calling television in the courtroom "the most destructive thing in the world," said, "There will be no cameras in the Supreme Court of the United States while I sit there."[10]

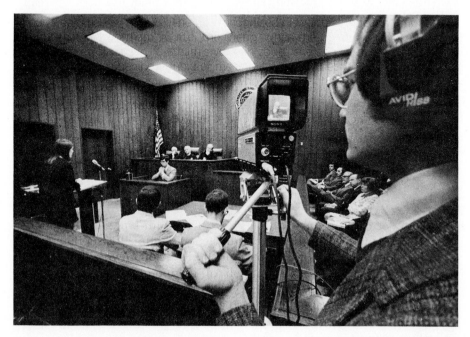

Most U.S. trials are open to the public, but not all jurisdictions permit televising of the proceedings. (Ellis Herwig/Stock Boston)

The Right to a Trial by Jury

History of the Jury System   The Sixth Amendment guarantees the defendant a right to a trial by a **jury.** The jury system is a relatively modern development. It may be traced to the *fiscus*, "which was related to the royal revenue jurisdiction in imperial Rome." The Franks continued this concept, referring to the royal lands as *fiscal lands*.

One of the frequent problems concerned disputes over royal lands, which the king would attempt to settle by directing an *inquisito*, or inquiry. Private citizens and royal representatives would discuss the dispute, which usually led to a settlement. Later the *inquisito* was extended to include asking a group of leading citizens to give opinions to the king's representatives. The group of citizens was called a *jurata*. Its report to the king's representatives was known as a *veredictum*. Thus, the foundation for a jury system, the rendering of a verdict, evolved.

The system was taken by the Normans to England in 1066, where the royal inquisition became known as an *assize*. Later, courts of assize developed. Later still, a number of citizens would be summoned and asked whether they knew any people in the area who had committed crimes. Twelve had to agree on a particular person for royal action to be taken. This, of course, was the beginning of the grand jury system.

The trial jury did not develop until after Pope Innocent III condemned the ordeal in 1215. At first the grand jury also served as the trial jury, but the system gradually evolved into separate juries.[11] The trial jury is sometimes called the **petit jury.** The word *petit* literally means minor, small, or inconsequential, but in this context it is used simply to distinguish the trial jury from the grand jury.

The trial jury is an important aspect of the U.S. system of criminal justice; it is neither small, minor, nor inconsequential. Compared to the grand jury, however, the trial jury has fewer jurors. It is less important in the sense that most serious crimes require an indictment by a grand jury for prosecution; if the grand jury does not return the indictment, there will be no need for a trial jury because the case will be dropped.

The U.S. Jury System   The trial jury is an integral part of the U.S. system of criminal justice. It is also a feature that today distinguishes this system from most others. Spotlight 11.2 gives an example of a different type of jury system. A recent magazine article estimated that "we conduct eight times as many criminal jury trials as does the rest of the world combined." Why do we continue to use a system that is not common in other countries? We still believe it is important in a criminal trial to have the representation of community values. The jury in our system today "serves the same intangible purpose it served in 12th century England: to express as closely as possible the will of the community, to embody shared concepts of justice."[12]

The importance of the right to a jury trial, along with a brief history of its evolution, was emphasized by the Supreme Court in *Duncan v. Louisiana*. This case involved a defendant who was charged with simple battery, a misdemeanor punishable by a maximum of two years' imprison-

SPOTLIGHT 11.2
TRIAL BY JURY IN OTHER COUNTRIES

In many European countries, trial by jury means that the defendant is tried before a judge and two lay jurors. Various methods are used for selecting the lay jurors. The judge conducts the trial and may ask questions; but the decision of guilt or innocence, as well as the sentence (unless a specific sentence is required by statute for that offense), are decided by a vote of the professional judge and the two lay jurors. This picture was taken at a trial in Oslo, Norway. The people sitting directly to the right and left of the judge are lay jurors.

Source: Sue Titus Reid

ment and a $300 fine. Duncan's request for a trial by jury was denied by the trial court in Louisiana. At that time, the Louisiana Constitution granted jury trials only in cases in which, upon conviction, defendants could be sentenced to imprisonment at hard labor or to capital punishment. Duncan was convicted of the crime charged, sentenced to 60 days in the parish prison, and fined $150. The supreme court of Louisiana denied his request for appeal. Duncan appealed to the U.S. Supreme Court, alleging that he had been denied his constitutional right to a jury trial.[13]

Duncan v. *State of Louisiana*

The history of trial by jury in criminal cases has been frequently told. It is sufficient for present purposes to say that by the time our Constitution was written, jury trial in criminal cases had been in existence in England for several centuries and carried impressive credentials traced by many to Magna Carta. Its preservation and proper operation as a protection against arbitrary rule were among the major objectives of the revolutionary settlement which was expressed in the Declaration and Bill of Rights of 1889. . . .

A right to jury trial is granted to criminal defendants in order to prevent oppression by the Government. . . . Providing an accused with the right to be tried by a jury of his peers gave him an inestimable safeguard against the corrupt or overzealous prosecutor and against the compliant, biased, or eccentric judge . . . [T]he jury trial provisions in the Federal and State Constitutions reflect a fundamental decision about the exercise of official power—a reluctance to entrust plenary powers over the life and liberty of the citizen to one judge or to a group of judges. . . . The deep commitment of the Nation to the right of jury trial in serious criminal cases as a defense against arbitrary law enforcement

qualifies for protection under the Due Process Clause of th[...]
Amendment, and must therefore be respected by the States.

Procedures for Selecting the Jury Pool Jurisdictions differ in their procedures for selecting potential members of the grand and petit juries. The specific processes are illustrated here by a look at the federal system. The federal system is governed by the Federal Jury Selection and Service Act of 1968, designed to ensure that potential jurors are selected randomly from a cross section of the community. The federal act specifically provides that no citizen "shall be excluded from service as a grand or petit juror in the district courts of the United States on account of race, color, religion, sex, national origin, or economic status." The various district courts are free to develop their own jury selection procedures within that statutory mandate.

Once the names of potential jurors are selected, jury qualification forms are sent to each person selected. Upon receipt of those completed forms, the district judge is to determine whether a potential juror is qualified to serve. The statutory reasons for disqualification in the federal system are reprinted in the first section of Spotlight 11.3. Those who initially qualify may be excused for any of the reasons indicated in the second section of Spotlight 11.3.

If any of the procedures are violated in the selection of the jury pool, the attorney general may petition the court to stay all proceedings involving that jury pool, and another selection must be made. This action must be taken within a specified time. According to the Federal Jury Selection and Service Act, the defendant (also under time restrictions), upon discovery of improper selection of the potential jurors, may move to have the indictment dismissed "on the ground of substantial failure to comply with the provisions of this title in selecting the grand or petit jury."

After the names of qualified jurors are available, from time to time there will be a public drawing of those names from a jury wheel. Jurors selected will be notified by means of a **summons,** a formal document issued by the court to notify a person that his or her presence is required for a particular reason in a particular court at a specified time and day. The potential juror, after arriving at the specified place, may sit all day and not be picked for a jury. If that happens, he or she must return for jury selection in the next case. This procedure can go on for days. Some but not all states have limits on how long a person must serve on jury duty.

The problems created when a person has to sit in court waiting to be questioned for a jury panel and the time consumed by actual jury duty make this service less than desirable for many people. Some people, however, find jury duty interesting and challenging.

Legal Requirements in Jury Pool Selections Despite the acceptance of the process of excusing some potential jurors, our statutes and court decisions place limitations on exclusions that can be made in the composi-

SPOTLIGHT 11.5

THE FEDERAL JURY SYSTEM

Qualifications for Jury Service

. . . In making such determination the chief judge of the district court, or such other district court judge as the plan may provide, shall deem any person qualified to serve on grand and petit juries in the district court unless he—

(1) is not a citizen of the United States 18 years old who has resided for a period of 1 year within the judicial district;
(2) is unable to read, write, and understand the English language with a degree of proficiency sufficient to fill out satisfactorily the juror qualification form;
(3) is unable to speak the English language;
(4) is incapable, by reason of mental or physical infirmity, to render satisfactory jury service; or
(5) has a charge pending against him for the commission of, or has been convicted in a State or Federal court of record of, a crime punishable by imprisonment for more than 1 year and his civil rights have not been restored. . . .

Reasons for Excluding Potential Jurors from the Jury Pool

. . . [A]ny person summoned for jury service may be

(1) excused by the court, upon a showing of undue hardship or extreme inconvenience, for such period as the court deems necessary, at the conclusion of which such person shall be summoned again for jury service . . ., or

(2) excluded by the court on the ground that such person may be unable to render impartial jury service or that his service as a juror would be likely to disrupt the proceedings, or
(3) excluded upon peremptory challenge as provid[ed] by law, or
(4) excluded pursuant to the procedure specified [in] law upon a challenge by any party for good cause shown, or
(5) excluded upon determination by the court tha[t] his service as a juror would be likely to threate[n] the secrecy of the proceedings, or otherwise adversely affect the integrity of jury deliberatio[n]

No person shall be excluded under clause (5) of th[is] subsection unless the judge, in open court, determines that such is warranted and that exclusion of the person will not be inconsistent with section[s] 1861 and 1862 of this title. The number of person[s] excluded under clause (5) of this subsection shall not exceed 1 per centum of the number of persons who return executed jury qualification forms during the period. . . . (Note: Sections 1861 and 1862 specify the policy of jury selection which is to recognize the right to an indictment by a grand jury and trial by a petit jury, to avoid discrimination against citizens because of race, color, religion, sex, national origin, or economic status.)

Source: Sections 1865 and 1866 of The Jury Selection and Service Act of 1968, (2 U.S.C.A., Chapter 28, Section 1861, as Amended, 2 November 1978).

tion of juries.[14] Juries must be representative of the community, but that does not mean that the Court is imposing a requirement that

> juries must mirror the community and reflect the various distinctive groups in the population. Defendants are not entitled to a jury of any particular composition, but the jury wheels, pools of names, panels, or venires from which juries are drawn must not systematically exclude distinctive groups in the community and thereby fail to be reasonably representative thereof.[15]

There also are some size requirements for juries. Although 12 is the usual number of petit jurors, some jurisdictions permit a smaller number. The U.S. Supreme Court has upheld smaller juries in some cases. In 1978 the Court considered the case of a theater manager who was convicted in a county criminal court on misdemeanor counts of distributing obscene materials. He was convicted by a five-person jury, permitted in the state in which he was convicted (Georgia), as well as in Louisiana and Virginia. The Court, after reviewing studies showing that smaller juries are less objective and less accurate than larger ones, held that juries of fewer than six (a number approved by the Court in a noncapital state case) are constitutionally impermissible.[16]

The following term the Court held that although a six-person jury is permissible, conviction by a less than unanimous vote of that size jury "presents a similar threat to the preservation of the substance of the jury trial guarantee and justifies our requiring verdicts by six-person juries to be unanimous."[17] The Court had already held that a unanimous vote is not required in a 12-person jury trial.[18]

The Right to Trial by an Impartial Jury

The Sixth Amendment provides for the right to trial by an impartial jury. This means that the jury may not be unduly prejudiced by media publicity before the jury deliberations. It also means that in the jury selection process, the jury cannot be stacked against the defendant to ease the state's burden in proving its case. The issue frequently arises in selecting juries for cases in which a conviction could result in a capital punishment sentence.[19]

In addition to the right to trial by an impartial jury, the defendant also has a right to have the proceedings conducted by an impartial judge.

(Wayne Stayskal/Tampa Tribune)

This is of course true when the case is tried without a jury (in some cases, a defendant may waive the right to a jury trial), in which case the judge will determine guilt or innocence, but it also refers to the requirement for an impartial judge at all judicial proceedings.

The Supreme Court in 1927 acknowledged that it would be a violation of the defendant's due process rights for the proceedings to be presided over by a judge who has a "direct, personal, substantial pecuniary interest in reaching a conclusion against him in his case."[20] The defense or prosecution may challenge a particular judge's ability to be objective and impartial, but judges are not to assume that it is always permissible for them to preside over a judicial proceeding if they are not challenged by the parties. If there is a conflict of interest, judges should remove themselves by a process called **recusal.**

In some cases, although qualified to preside, during the course of the trial, the judge may become unable to continue presiding. In those cases it is permissible to have a substitute judge, provided that he or she first becomes familiar with all the proceedings to that point in the case.

The Right to Trial by a Jury of Peers

The Sixth Amendment also guarantees the right to a trial by a jury of peers. This right has been interpreted by the Supreme Court to mean that people may not be *systematically* excluded from jury pools for reasons of race, sex, ethnic origin, religion, or socioeconomic status. That does not mean, however, that once the actual jury is selected it will reflect the composition of these groups in the community.

The list of categories of persons against whom the jury selection process may not discriminate does not include age. What does that mean

The U.S. Constitution provides for the right to a jury trial in most cases. (Jim Pickerell/ Stock Boston)

to a young person convicted of a crime and tried in an adult court? Juries characteristically include very few young people. In 1985, a federal court reversed its earlier decision and held that a young defendant did not have a right to a new trial because young adults from ages 18 to 34 were underrepresented on the jury. The court held that a "mere statistical disparity in the chosen age group" is not sufficient to establish a violation of the Sixth Amendment right to a jury of peers. The defendant must show that the underrepresented group is defined and limited by a factor or characteristic that can be easily defined, that the group may be characterized by a common thread of similarity in attitude, ideas, or experience, and that the group has a community of interest.

Consider the implications of this decision. If you were a defendant and thought you should be entitled to a jury consisting of some persons of your age, how would you prove the criteria required by the federal court? If you are 19 years old, could you show that 19-year-olds have a community of interest and a common thread or similarity in attitudes, ideas, or experience that distinguish them from 30-year-olds? If so, what would you say about the right of other groups to be tried by a jury of their peers? The court warned that "if the age classification is adopted, surely blue-collar workers, yuppies, Rotarians, Eagle Scouts and an endless variety of other classifications will be entitled to similar treatment."[21]

Susan, in this chapter's CJA, is tried before a jury consisting of women and blacks with some black women; but they are all over 30, and Susan is only 20. She would probably not succeed in challenging the jury selection in her case.

Other Constitutional Rights of Defendants at Trial

Some constitutional rights of defendants discussed earlier in connection with the police or with pretrial procedures may also be applicable during the trial of a criminal case. A confession obtained or evidence secured in violation of the defendant's rights should be excluded from the trial under the exclusionary rule, also discussed earlier. As noted, there are exceptions to the exclusionary rule, but illegally obtained evidence normally is excluded.

Some rights discussed earlier take on their fullest meaning during the trial. For example, defendants must be notified of the charges against them. That notice must occur during the early pretrial stages, but formal charges must also be read to the defendant at the trial. Defendants have the right to compel witnesses to testify on their behalf and the right to confront and cross-examine witnesses who testify against them. These rights and others have been interpreted to mean that defendants have a right to be present at the trial. The right to be present at the trial is, however, subject to the defendant's good behavior, as illustrated by the classic case of *Illinois v. Allen*.[22]

Illinois v. Allen involved a defendant, Allen, who appealed his conviction for armed robbery on the grounds that he was improperly excluded from his own trial. At the beginning of the trial, Allen insisted on being his own lawyer, rejecting the services of his court-appointed counsel.

When Allen began questioning prospective jurors, the judge interrupted him and asked him to confine his questions to the matters relating to the qualifications of prospective jurors. Allen responded in an abusive and disrespectful manner. The judge asked appointed counsel to proceed with the examination of prospective jurors. Allen continued to talk, "proclaiming that the appointed attorney was not going to act as his lawyer. He terminated his remarks by saying, 'When I go out for lunchtime, you're [the judge] going to be a corpse here.'"

Allen took a file from his attorney, tore it, and threw it on the floor. The judge warned Allen that he would remove him from the trial if he continued in this manner, but the warning had no effect on Allen's conduct. Allen was removed from the courtroom, and the examination of the jury continued in his absence. He was later returned to the court but, after another outburst, was again removed. During the presentation of the state's case, he was occasionally brought to the courtroom for identification, but during one of those visits Allen again used vile and abusive language in responding to a question from the judge. After assuring the court he would behave, Allen was permitted to be in the courtroom while his attorney presented the case for the defense.

Justice Black, in delivering the opinion for the Court, upheld the right of the trial judge to exclude Allen from his own trial. Black pointed out that Illinois had three constitutionally permissible options in this case. They could cite Allen for **contempt of court,** exclude him from the trial, or bind and gag him and leave him in the trial. Each option was discussed, with the Court noting the possible prejudicial effect binding and gagging might have on the jury.

> Not only is it possible that the sight of shackles and gags might have a significant effect on the jury's feelings about the defendant, but the use of this technique is itself something of an affront to the very dignity and decorum of judicial proceedings that the judge is seeking to uphold.

It also prevents the defendant from meaningful contact with his attorney. For that reason, the Court refused to hold that the state must use this method in lieu of excluding the defendant from trial. In the following excerpt, Justice Black explains the importance of maintaining decorum in the courtroom.[23]

Illinois v. Allen

It is essential to the proper administration of criminal justice that dignity, order, and decorum be the hallmarks of all court proceedings in our country. The flagrant disregard in the courtroom of elementary standards of proper conduct should not and cannot be tolerated. . . .

It is not pleasant to hold that the respondent Allen was properly banished from the court for a part of his own trial. But our courts, palladiums of liberty as they are, cannot be treated disrespectfully with impunity. Nor can the accused be permitted by his disruptive conduct indefinitely to avoid being tried on the charges brought against him. It would degrade our country and our judicial system to permit our courts to be bullied, insulted, and humiliated and their orderly progress thwarted and obstructed by defendants brought before them charged with crimes. As guardians of the public welfare, our state and federal judicial systems strive to administer equal justice to the rich and the poor, the good and the bad, the native and foreign born of every race, nationality, and religion. Being manned by humans, the courts are not perfect and are found to make some errors. But, if our courts are to remain what the Founders intended, the citadels of justice, their proceedings cannot and must not be infected with the sort of scurrilous, abusive language and conduct paraded before the Illinois trial judge in this case.

THE TRIAL PROCESS

In this section the stages or steps of a criminal trial are discussed in the order that they occur. Spotlight 11.4 lists those steps, and the discussion follows the order in that list. These stages are not always distinct, and some of the procedures may occur at various stages. For example, motions might be made throughout the trial; an obvious motion is one to dismiss or to declare a mistrial made by defense counsel after the prosecutor or a prosecution witness has said something improper. A defense motion for change of **venue** (place of trial) might be made before and during the trial as increased media attention to the trial leads the defense to argue that it is impossible for the defendant to have a fair trial in that area.

All participants in the trial must abide by proper rules and etiquette in order for the trial to proceed. This includes defendants, as we have seen, but it also includes attorneys (both defense and prosecution), witnesses, and spectators. Anyone in the courtroom may be admonished by the judge for improper conduct which, if it continues, could lead to sanctions that might even include contempt of court—an act that embarrasses, humili-

SPOTLIGHT 11.4
STAGES IN THE TRIAL AND APPEAL OF A CRIMINAL CASE IN THE UNITED STATES

1. Opening of the court session
2. Jury selection
3. Opening statement by the prosecutor
4. Opening statement by the defense attorney
5. Presentation of evidence by the prosecutor
6. Cross-examination by the defense
7. Redirect examination by the prosecutor
8. Cross-examination by the defense
9. Presentation of the defense's case by the defense attorney
10. Cross-examination by the prosecutor
11. Redirect by the defense
12. Cross-examination by the prosecutor
13. Rebuttal proof by the prosecutor
14. Closing statement by the prosecutor
15. Closing statement by the defense
16. Rebuttal statement by the prosecutor
17. Submitting the case to the jury
18. The verdict
19. Postverdict motions
20. Sentencing
21. Appeals and writs

ates, or undermines the court's authority. Contempt of court could result in a jail term and removal from the courtroom.[24]

Opening the Court Session

When it is time for the court session to begin, the bailiff arrives and calls the court to order with such words as "Hear ye, hear ye, the court of the Honorable Judge Smith is in session—all rise." At that point everyone in the courtroom should rise. The judge, usually dressed in a robe, enters the courtroom and sits. Then everyone else may sit. The judge will announce the case, "The State of California versus John Jones, Case No. 45629-16." The judge will then ask whether the prosecution is ready; if so, he or she asks whether the defense is ready. If both are ready, the case will begin with jury selection. After the jury has been selected and sworn, the judge will read the indictment or information, inform the court that the defendant has entered a plea of not guilty (or not guilty by reason of insanity if that is permitted), and the trial will begin with the opening statements.

Jury Selection

Usually the members of the jury pool are seated in the courtroom before the judge enters. After the formal opening of the court session, the judge instructs the jury pool about procedure. The minute clerk begins by selecting names from a jury wheel, drawing names out of a fish bowl, or using some other similar procedure. As each name is drawn, the minute clerk reads and spells the name. The first person selected will sit in the first seat in the jury box, and so on until the jury box is filled. Questioning of the jury follows, a process called **voir dire,** which literally means "to tell the truth." The defense attorney and the prosecuting attorney voir dire the jury; that is, they question each potential juror and then decide whether or not they would approve the selection of that person. Judges may also question potential jurors. In the federal system, judges have discretion to permit or to deny attorneys to question prospective jurors. In the federal system, jury selection takes an average of 3 hours; in some states, the process may take weeks or even months.

After they are questioned, potential jurors may be excused from jury duty in two ways. If they are excused for cause, they are presumed to be biased in the case because of answers that indicate bias. Bias may also be presumed on the basis of the potential juror's association with or knowledge of the defendant or some other person involved in the trial, because of their personal financial interest in the case, or because of some particular background that might prejudice them. For example, a person whose spouse has been murdered might be presumed to be prejudiced against a defendant on trial for murder. Attorneys are entitled to an unlimited number of challenges for cause.

The second way a potential juror may be excused is by **peremptory challenge,** which means that the attorneys may excuse without cause. No reason need be given, that is the purpose of the challenge. In the federal

Judge listening to witness testify at trial. (Charles Steiner/ Sygma)

system, the prosecution and the defense each have 20 peremptory challenges in a capital case and 3 in a misdemeanor case. In a felony case, the prosecution has 6; the defense has 10.

Some attorneys use scientific selection of jurors. Through empirical studies, social scientists have provided information on characteristics that are related to opinions and therefore may influence the decision of a juror. Scientific selection of juries has gone beyond the stage of social scientists conducting research to identify characteristics that might assist attorneys in jury selection. Professional consultants are hired by some attorneys to assist in the questioning and selection of jurors.

Jury Selection and Racism   As noted earlier, no reason need be given by attorneys who use peremptory challenges to excuse potential jurors. But there are some legal restrictions on the peremptory challenges. Racism will serve as an example. In 1880 the Supreme Court held that a statute permitting only white men to serve on juries was unconstitutional. And although in 1965, in *Swain v. Alabama*, the Court held that it was permissible to exclude *individual* blacks through peremptory challenges, the Court left open the possibility that *systematic* exclusion of blacks would not be legally acceptable.[25] Other decisions were made in the intervening years, but the key decision did not come until 1986 in *Batson v. Kentucky*. Relevant portions of that decision are excerpted.[26]

Batson v. Kentucky

Petitioner, a black man, was indicted in Kentucky on charges of second-degree burglary and receipt of stolen goods. On the first day of trial . . . the judge conducted *voir dire* examination of the venire, excused certain jurors for cause, and permitted the parties to exercise peremptory challenges. The prosecutor used his peremptory challenges to strike all four black persons on the venire, and a jury composed only of white persons was selected. . . .

Exclusion of black citizens from service as jurors constitutes a primary example of the evil the Fourteenth Amendment was designed to cure. . . .

The Equal Protection Clause guarantees the defendant that the State will not exclude members of his race from the jury venire on account of race, or on the false assumption that members of his race as a group are not qualified to serve as jurors. . . .

Racial discrimination in selection of jurors harms not only the accused whose life or liberty they are summoned to try. Competence to serve as a juror ultimately depends on an assessment of individual qualifications and ability impartially to consider evidence presented at a trial. A person's race simply "is unrelated to his fitness as a juror."

. . . The harm from discriminatory jury selection extends beyond that inflicted on the defendant and the excluded juror to touch the entire community. Selection procedures that purposefully exclude black persons from juries undermine public confidence in the fairness of our system of justice. . . .

Although a prosecutor ordinarily is entitled to exercise permitted peremptory challenges "for any reason at all, as long as that reason is related to his view concerning the outcome" of the case to be tried, the Equal Protection clause forbids the prosecutor to challenge potential jurors solely on account of their race or on the assumption that black jurors as a group will be unable impartially to consider the State's case against a black defendant.

[The Court then discussed procedures for challenging the peremptory challenges and concluded that the conviction in this case should be reversed.]

Since *Batson* lower courts have dealt with variations in fact patterns in which the case might apply, and further litigation can be expected. In 1988, for example, the Supreme Court of Utah, in *State v. Cantu*, examined the implication of *Batson* in an allegation that the prosecutor used the peremptory challenge improperly to exclude a Hispanic in the jury selection process of a Hispanic defendant.

The Utah Supreme Court, in sending the case back for further action based on the court's instructions, enumerated the proof required of defendants who raise a challenge under *Batson*. The defendant must show

1. That he is a member of a recognizable racial group;
2. That the prosecution exercised peremptory challenges to remove from the panel members of the defendant's race; and
3. That all the relevant facts and circumstances raise an inference that the prosecution used its peremptory challenges to exclude the veniremen from the petit jury on account of their race.[27]

Opening Statements

After the jury is selected, attorneys may make opening statements. They may also waive the opening statement. The prosecutor makes the first opening statement. This is the prosecution's chance to outline briefly what he or she intends to prove during the trial. The opening statement is very important; it should be planned carefully and delivered convincingly.

The opening statement should be brief but long enough to present an adequate statement of the facts the prosecution intends to prove. It should be interesting but not overly dramatic. The prosecutor must be certain not to overstep his or her boundaries and raise the ire of the judge, the defense, and the jury. Statements designed to be inflammatory or that are too prejudicial are not permitted.

The defense is permitted to follow the prosecution with an opening statement, and many defense attorneys will do so. The same principles apply to the defense as to the prosecution. The opening statement should raise the interest of the jury to listen further but should not be too long or too dramatic. A defense attorney has the option of waiving the opening statement until the prosecution has presented its evidence. Some do so in order to hear that evidence before revealing what the defense will be. Prosecutors, knowing that this may occur, may make comments in their opening statements that would lead the jury to expect the defense to make a statement or to be suspicious if the defense does not do so.

Presentation of the Evidence

Before looking at the types of evidence that might be presented by the prosecution and then by the defense, it is necessary to understand some general rules of evidence and to look at the categories of evidence that apply to both the prosecution and the defense.

Rules of Evidence   The rules of evidence in criminal cases are contained in statutory and case law. They are complex, and they may differ from one jurisdiction to another. No attempt will be made here to cover those rules; however, a few general rules are important to a basic understanding of the criminal trial.

Any evidence presented must be relevant, competent, and material to the case. The meaning of those words has been litigated in many cases because the meaning may differ depending on the type of case being heard. In rape cases, historically the defense was permitted to ask the victim about her prior sexual experiences, to imply that the sexual relationship was by choice, not force. If she had had sexual relationships with other men, particularly if it could be inferred that she was promiscuous, a rape conviction was unlikely. Today many jurisdictions have changed that rule. Some will not permit any questions about the victim's sexual experiences other than with the defendant. This change in what is defined as material evidence may not only affect the outcome of the case, but it makes it much more likely that victims will report rapes and that they will be willing to testify at trial.

Attempts by either the prosecution or defense to introduce evidence or to ask questions thought by the opposing side to be incompetent, irrelevant, or immaterial may be reacted to by raising an objection: "Your Honor, I object to the admission of that evidence (or to the answering of

Demonstrative evidence consists of such items as the police have secured here from a search of the accused. (Sygma)

that question) on the grounds that it is incompetent, irrelevant, and immaterial." The attorney who raises the objection may be asked to be more specific concerning the reasons for the objection. If the objection is sustained, the evidence will not be admitted. If the objection involves a question posed to the witness, the judge will tell the witness not to answer the question. If the question has already been answered, the judge will instruct the jury to disregard the answer, unless the information is so prejudicial that the judge declares a **mistrial,** which means the case will have to begin again with a new jury.

Demonstrative Evidence Some evidence may be competent, relevant, and material to the case but still be excluded because it has been secured in violation of the defendant's rights or because it is considered to be too prejudicial or inflammatory.

Consider the following scenario: A shoots and kills B, but while B is still alive and conscious, A tortures B by beating B and finally removing B's ear. Should the amputated ear be admitted as evidence? Clearly, it is material to the issue of the circumstances surrounding the killing and therefore may be relevant to the elements required to prove first-degree murder in that jurisdiction. But would showing the ear be too inflammatory? Or suppose that B does not die, but B's leg is amputated as a result of the beating. Clearly, B can be present in court as a witness, but would it be proper to show the amputated leg, or for that matter, have B crawl in front of the jury rather than move about in a wheelchair or on crutches?

This kind of evidence is called **demonstrative evidence,** or real evidence: the kind of evidence that is real to the senses in contrast to evidence presented by the testimony of other people. Demonstrative evidence can be quite powerful.

Consider this example from a recent case in which a defendant was on trial for killing a police officer. Another police officer who was wounded testified in the case. The shirt he was wearing the night of the shootings was introduced as evidence; he was asked to model the shirt, dirty and smelly though it was (it had been six months since the trial, and of course the shirt had not been washed). The jury could then see the bullet holes and more easily understand the details of the shooting. This demonstrative evidence was considered appropriate.

Deciding which evidence to admit and which to exclude is a great responsibility of the trial judge. He or she may be overruled on appeal, but many of the decisions made at trial will stand, and they will be critical to the outcome of the case.

The Hearsay Rules and Its Exceptions Some testimonial evidence that is relevant, material, and competent may be excluded because it is **hearsay evidence.** Hearsay evidence is evidence offered by the testifying witnesses, but it does not refer to what that witness has heard, seen, felt, or otherwise experienced. Rather, it refers to what someone else has told that witness. Such evidence is generally not admissible. Here is an example.

A child is the victim of an alleged act of forcible rape. The child has told her parents out of court her version of what happened when the act allegedly took place, but the parents do not want the child to testify in court. The parents fear that the child will be further damaged psychologically by having to recall the experiences. Furthermore, the child will be subjected to the rigors of cross-examination by the defense. However, if the child's testimony is not presented, there probably will not be a conviction. The parents will not be permitted to testify in court to what the child told them. That would be hearsay evidence.

There are some exceptions to the hearsay rule; they, too, are rather technical, but two hypothetical cases will serve to illustrate exceptions that have been made to the hearsay rule. The first exception has been made quite recently and is not widely recognized. In some courts the doctor or nurse who examined the child after the alleged sexual molestation will be permitted to testify to what the child told them at that time and to give their own medical testimony based on their examination of the child. This exception has been criticized, particularly in light of what some believe is increasing evidence that some, perhaps many, children do not tell the truth about alleged sexual molestation.

The second hypothetical case is related to a long-recognized exception to the hearsay rule: the dying declaration. Mrs. Jones is dying. The demonstrative evidence indicates foul play but is not sufficient to link a particular suspect to the murder. While the police are talking to her, she says, "John Jones tried to kill me." She then dies. The police officer (or anyone else who heard that statement) will be permitted to repeat that statement in court. Dying declarations are permitted because it is assumed that a person who is dying will not tell a lie. Whether that is true is open to speculation, but the law does make interesting assumptions!

However, there are some restrictions on admitting a dying declaration as an exception to the hearsay rule. It must be shown that the dying person had reason to know the facts about which the statement was made and that the person knew that death was imminent. In most jurisdictions, the evidence will be admitted only in homicide cases concerning the death of the person who made the statement.[28]

Testimony of Witnesses

Witnesses may also present testimonial evidence. They may be called by the prosecution or by the defense, and they will be sworn in before they are permitted to testify. If they do not tell the truth, they could be prosecuted for perjury. There are several types of witnesses.

The testimony of a *victim-witness* is often a preferred type of testimonial evidence. In many cases, prosecutors will drop charges if victims will not agree to testify against the accused. *Eyewitnesses* are also prime candidates for being called to testify in criminal cases. Psychologists, however, have seriously questioned the use of eyewitnesses, finding evidence that some jurors place too much weight on their testimonies.[29]

Expert witnesses may also be called by the defense or the prosecution. Expert witnesses have some special expertise not common to the average person on the subject about which they are testifying. Experts in ballistics might be called to testify about the specifics of when and where the gun was fired and what kind of gun was used. Medical experts might testify to the cause of death in a murder case. Psychiatrists might testify concerning the insanity or sanity of the defendant at the time the alleged crime took place.

Experts must be admitted to the court as experts before they can testify. The attorney who introduces the expert will first offer evidence to qualify the discipline or area of expertise. That will not be a problem with some experts, such as most doctors. It is a problem when attempting to qualify a geneticist for testifying about the relationship between chromosomes and criminal behavior. U.S. courts have held that the science of genetics is not sufficiently advanced to be able to make accurate predictions about the effect of the XYY chromosomal abnormality on human behavior. Judges therefore have refused to admit genetics expert witnesses on the issue of the effect of the XYY chromosomal abnormality on human behavior.[30]

After the discipline is qualified, the particular expert must be qualified. Experts are typically asked where they received their training, how much experience they have had, and whether they have ever testified in these kinds of cases. Opposing counsel will try to discredit the expert during cross-examination. Both the prosecution and the defense might present experts from the same field. If they disagree, it is the jury's responsibility to determine credibility.

Witnesses must testify to facts, not opinion, although in some instances opinion will be allowed. But witnesses are never permitted to testify to the ultimate question of fact in a criminal case: the guilt or innocence of the defendant. One way for counsel to get around the requirement of factual, not opinion, testimony is to ask hypothetical questions concerning facts similar to those in the case on trial.

Direct and Circumstantial Evidence

One further distinction important to the presentation of evidence is the difference between direct and circumstantial evidence. Evidence offered by an eyewitness is **direct evidence.** Evidence that may be inferred from a fact or series of facts is **circumstantial evidence.**

Direct evidence might show that A owned the gun. A had possession of the gun the day of the shooting. The shot was fired from that gun, but no direct evidence is offered that A fired that gun. The jury might be permitted to infer that from the direct evidence offered. Circumstantial evidence is crucial in many criminal cases.

Examination of the Evidence

After each side, beginning with the prosecution, presents its witnesses, they may be questioned by the opposing attorney. The prosecution will question its witnesses in a process called **direct examination.** The defense may then **cross-examine** that witness or reserve the right to do so later. If the defense cross-examines, the prosecutor may again ask questions of the prosecution witness in a process called *redirect examination*. If that occurs, the defense may cross-examine the witness again. The same process occurs in reverse after the defense has presented its evidence.

The Prosecution's Case

The prosecution is the first to present evidence. The prosecution's case may include the presentation of demonstrative evidence as well as the testimony of the victim, other witnesses, and experts. Police officers involved in either the arrest or the investigation of the case also usually will be called to testify.

The Defense Attorney's Case

After the prosecution has presented its case and all cross-examination and redirect examination has occurred, the defense presents its case. Some special issues arise here.

The Defendant as a Witness The defendant has a right not to testify. The reason is that even innocent persons might appear guilty if they take the stand. If the defendant does not testify, neither the prosecution nor the judge may make unfavorable comments on that refusal. The prosecutor may not suggest to the jury that the defendant's refusal implies guilt.[31]

In early English law, from which much of U.S. law is derived, defendants were not considered competent to testify because they had a vested interest in the outcome of the case. This approach became part of our early common law, but today the defendant by statute is allowed to take the stand in his or her own behalf. Some choose to do so. If they

The prosecutor gives her summary arguments to the jury. (Billy E. Barnes/Stock Boston)

testify, defendants must also be sworn in; they may be prosecuted for perjury if they testify to falsehoods.

Defendants who take the stand may be cross-examined by the prosecutor. Rules vary, but generally whatever rules apply to other witnesses will apply to the defendant. In most jurisdictions this means that the cross-examination may cover only those subjects covered on direct or redirect examination. Where that is the case, the defense attorney has the ability to limit the subject matter on which the prosecution can ask questions to the subjects covered on direct examination. Some jurisdictions, however, permit the prosecution to go beyond those subjects once the defendant takes the stand.

Character Witnesses   The defense may also call *character witnesses*, who testify about the defendant's character. If the defense calls character witnesses, the prosecutor may then call witnesses to testify to the defendant's bad character, but the prosecutor may not begin this line of evidence. Character witnesses, like all other witnesses, may be subjected to stringent cross-examination. This is difficult for many people, and it therefore is important that attorneys who plan to call character or other kinds of witnesses spend time with those witnesses preparing them for trial.

Defenses   Commission of a criminal act, even with the required criminal intent, is not sufficient for a verdict of guilty if the defense can adequately prove a legally accepted reason why the law should not be applied in this case to this defendant. Many defenses might be raised. Infancy, intoxication, duress, involuntary action, entrapment, public duty, legal impossibility, self-defense or defense of others, acting under authority of law (for example, a justifiable killing by a police officer), and insanity are some common defenses. Not all of these defenses are always acceptable; jurisdictions differ in which ones they will accept and the conditions under which they are acceptable. Differences also exist in the type of proof required to prove the defenses.

These defenses can easily be overemphasized, particularly after a highly publicized case such as the successful use of the insanity defense in the case of John Hinckley, Jr., accessed of attempting to assassinate then President Ronald Reagan and others. The insanity defense is not used often. When it is used, it is rarely successful, leading a widely recognized legal scholar and professor to conclude, "In a world filled with crime and the inability to cope with it, focusing on insanity is like worrying whether the violin is out of tune in the band playing on the deck of the Titanic."[32]

Rebuttal Proof by the Prosecution

After the defense has rested its case, the prosecutor has the option of presenting additional proof to rebut the case presented by the defense. Not all prosecutors choose to exercise this option. Where it is exercised, the prosecution may call or recall police officers to testify regarding facts that have been in dispute among witnesses at the trial.

Closing Statements

The closing statement is first given by the prosecution, then the defense; this is followed with rebuttal by the prosecutor. Both attorneys must be careful not to go beyond the evidence and reasonable inferences from the evidence offered in the case. The prosecutor in particular must be careful about the role as advocate, as the following statement from a Supreme Court opinion indicates. This case involves a federal prosecutor, but the same principle applies to state and local prosecutors.[33]

Berger v. United States

The United States Attorney is the representative not of an ordinary party to a controversy, but of a sovereignty whose obligation to govern impartially is as compelling as its obligation to govern at all; and whose interest, therefore, in a criminal prosecution is not that it shall win a case, but that justice shall be done. As such, he is in a peculiar and very definite sense the servant of the law, the two-fold aim of which is that guilt shall not escape or innocence suffer. He may prosecute with earnestness and vigor—indeed, he should do so. But, while he may strike hard blows, he is not at liberty to strike foul ones. It is as much his duty to refrain from improper methods calculated to produce a wrongful conviction as it is to use every legitimate means to bring about a just one.

Some comments that would be improper for the prosecution to make are noted in Spotlight 11.5. If the prosecutor goes too far in the closing

---

SPOTLIGHT 11.5
IMPROPER COMMENTS FOR THE PROSECUTOR TO MAKE IN CLOSING ARGUMENTS

1. "Misstate the evidence or mislead the jury as to the inferences it may draw from the evidence, or to refer to specific evidence which was never introduced at the trial or which was excluded from evidence by the court;" . . .
2. "Express his personal belief or opinion as to the truth or falsity of any testimony or evidence or the guilt of the defendant, such as by stating that he is vouching for the truthfulness of certain witnesses. . . ."
3. Making any argument that would "divert the jury from its duty to decide the case on the evidence, such as by injecting issues broader than the guilt or innocence of the accused under the controlling law or by making predictions of the consequences of the jury's verdict."
4. "Arguments calculated to inflame the passions or prejudices of the jury, such as comments which appeal to racial, religious or class prejudice, personal attacks upon defense counsel, or uncomplimentary characterizations of the defendant which lack a reasonable foundation in the evidence or the charge."

Source: Wayne R. LaFave and Jerold H. Israel, *Criminal Procedure* (St. Paul, Minn.: West Publishing Co., 1985), p. 886.

statements, the judge must then determine whether the statements are so prejudicial or so erroneous that they might have undue influence on the jury's determination of guilt. If so, they are considered **prejudicial errors,** and the judge will order a mistrial. If not, they are considered **harmless errors.**

Harmless errors are minor or trivial errors not deemed to be sufficient to harm the rights of the parties who assert the errors. Chapter 9's discussion of *Darden v. Wainwright* indicated that although the Supreme Court found that the prosecutor's comments were improper, it held that they were not sufficient to deny Darden a fair trial. Harmless errors and prejudicial errors may be committed by defense or prosecution and may refer to actions or comments made at various stages in the criminal process.

The defense will offer a closing statement after that of the prosecutor unless the defense chooses to waive this step. The defense should also be careful not to go beyond the evidence or to be too emotional, but as a practical matter closing statements by defense attorneys are rarely the subject of appeal. This is because the prosecution may not appeal if the defendant is acquitted; if the defendant is convicted and the defense appeals, that appeal will be concerned only with alleged errors made by the prosecution or rulings made by the judge.

Why would the defense ever waive the closing argument? One defense attorney explains why in an example of interesting trial strategy. The defendant was a 23-year-old, slim, handsome, clean-cut man. He was charged with a fourth count of driving while intoxicated (DWI) and could upon conviction have received 90 days in jail, the maximum penalty.

After the prosecution's presentation of evidence, the defense did nothing. As the attorney said, "All I had was the defendant, and I certainly did not want to put him on the stand. He had no defense, and I did not want to give the prosecution a chance to cross-examine him. So I rested the case before I started."

The prosecution then gave his closing argument. Usually in that jurisdiction the prosecution's closing statement is presented in two parts. In the first part the prosecution will review the case and emphasize the evidence and inferences from the evidence that should lead the jury to convict. After the defense's closing statement, the prosecution will use the rebuttal to recommend penalty. This prosecutor apparently planned to follow that customary procedure. But the defense attorney waived his closing argument, which meant that the prosecution did not get a rebuttal. He therefore had no opportunity to recommend that the jury impose the maximum penalty of 90 days. The jury returned a verdict of guilty but assessed a penalty of only 5 days in jail and a large fine!

Submitting the Case to the Jury

After all of the preceding steps have been completed, the case is submitted to a jury (unless the case is tried by the judge). The judge may not direct the jury to return a guilty verdict, but in many jurisdictions trial judges, on their own or by granting a motion from the defense, may direct the jury to return a verdict of not guilty. This is called a **directed verdict,** and the defense may make a motion to that effect.

Why would a trial judge have that power? If the evidence is so weak that it is unreasonable to conclude that the defendant is legally guilty, it would be a travesty of justice to let the case go to the jury, let the jury return a verdict of guilty, and then make the defendant wait for an appeal to get justice. The trial judge thus has the responsibility of weighing the evidence before submitting the case to the jury.

Instructions to the Jury   The judge also has the responsibility of charging the jury, which means to instruct the jury on matters of law relating to the case it must decide. In most jurisdictions, patterned jury instructions are given for the most commonly raised issues. The judge also accepts suggested instructions from the prosecution and the defense and will then usually have a conference with them on the suggested instructions. The judge determines the final instructions and presents them orally to the jury.

In many cases the jury instructions are determined before the closing arguments. The judge gives those instructions to the attorneys, who may want to take them into consideration in preparing their final arguments. The charge of the judge is very important, for it can be influential, perhaps determinative in the jury's decision.

The jury charge should be as clear and simple as possible without distorting the meaning of the law. The law as applied to many cases is complicated and difficult to understand, especially for people who are not legally trained. Yet, it is the responsibility of the jury to apply that law to the case they are hearing. It is the responsibility of the trial judge to explain the law in terms that the jury can understand. If the judge's charge is too complicated or is an inaccurate interpretation of the law in the case, the defense may appeal that issue. In some instances the case will be reversed and require a new trial.

The charge must explain to the jury the law that applies to the case, and it must clarify what the jury may do. If, for example, the defendant has been charged with first-degree murder but the law permits the jury to return a verdict of guilty of second-degree murder, that must be explained, along with the elements that must be proved for conviction on both of those charges. The judge should explain the meaning of evidence and distinguish the types of evidence. If conflict exists in the testimonial evidence, the jurors need to understand that they are the final determiner of whose testimony is most credible. This is particularly true when expert opinions conflict. Jurors may expect conflict between the testimony of a victim and a defendant but be very confused when two physicians, testifying on the same case, have different statements. Experts do differ; the jury is to decide whom to believe. The jury also may ignore the testimony of all experts if it so chooses.

The judge may instruct the jury to disregard certain evidence that has been admitted but that for some reason should not be considered. Recent research has indicated that in these cases juries do not disregard the evidence and may even unconsciously use it to create "facts" that were not presented but which they may need for their decision. The results of this study, which was conducted by American Bar Foundation researcher Jonathan Casper, raise the critical questions of whether a mistrial should always follow the admission of such evidence.[34]

In the federal system and in some states, the judge is permitted to summarize and comment on the evidence when the charge is given to the jury. This is an immense responsibility, for the obligation of the judge to be a neutral party continues throughout the trial unless the right to a jury trial is waived and the judge is to determine guilt or innocence.

Many areas of law might be covered by the judge in the instructions. The nature of each charge will depend on the nature of the case being tried. Two issues, however, deserve further attention: the presumption of innocence and the burden and standard of proof.

Presumption of Innocence and Standard of Proof   In the U.S. criminal justice system, the defendant is presumed innocent. The **presumption of innocence** is an important principle. It means that the prosecution has the responsibility of proving every element required for conviction and that the defendant does not have to prove innocence. The defendant can do nothing and still be acquitted if the government does not prove its case. Despite the importance of this presumption, former attorney general Edwin Meese said, "If a person is innocent of a crime, then he is not suspect." To that statement, Laurence Tribe, a noted Harvard law professor and scholar of constitutional law replied, "Mere accusation does not transform one into a criminal. Civilized society could not long survive if Mr. Meese's views became prevalent."[35]

The presumption of innocence is essential in protecting those who are falsely accused of crime. Innocent people are convicted (although perhaps rarely), but as Spotlight 11.6 indicates, the conviction of innocent persons can be devastating to their personal and professional lives. The criminal justice system is also impaired when the rights of innocent persons are violated, particularly when that violation leads to a conviction.

The standard of proof in a criminal case is **beyond a reasonable doubt.** That burden is a heavy one; it means essentially that when jurors look at all the evidence, they are convinced, satisfied to a moral certainty, that guilt has been established by the facts. Some judges refuse to define *beyond a reasonable doubt* on the assumption that not much more can be said. We all understand those words, and any attempt to define them further might be confusing or misleading. The jury is simply told that it must find the defendant guilty beyond a reasonable doubt.

The *presumption of innocence* perhaps is more difficult to understand. Judges usually instruct on that presumption, although the U.S. Supreme Court held that it is not constitutionally required that an instruction on the presumption of innocence be given. According to the Court, all circumstances must be examined to determine whether the defendant had a fair trial without an instruction on the presumption. If so, the case will not be reversed for failure to give the instruction.[36]

The Verdict   After the charge is read to the jury, the bailiff will take the jury to the jury room to deliberate. These deliberations are to be conducted in secret. It is the bailiff's responsibility to be sure that no one talks to the

SPOTLIGHT 11.6
CONVICTION OF THE INNOCENT

Case 1

In 1983 Lenell Geter, a 26-year-old black engineer who had no criminal record, was given a life sentence after his conviction for an armed robbery of a Kentucky Fried Chicken restaurant in Balch Springs, Texas. Geter was identified by five eyewitnesses who picked him out of a police lineup. But nine of his co-workers from the electronics firm where he worked testified that he was at work at the time of the robbery. His fingerprints were never found at the scene of the crime; no physical evidence was found to link him with the crime.

After Geter ran out of money, his privately retained attorney quit the case. His court-appointed attorney tried to get him to plea bargain, and reportedly was not prepared for trial. Several witnesses who would have assisted in the defense were not located in time for the trial. After national attention was focused on the case, a Dallas County court awarded Geter a new trial and he was released on $10,000 bond. He was retried and found innocent.

Case 2

In 1985 a federal judge freed Rubin "Hurricane" Carter, who had served almost 20 years in prison after being convicted of a triple murder. Prosecutors claimed that the former middleweight boxing contender was a dangerous and violent man; the judge found that the original conviction was based on racism and concealed evidence. According to the judge, "if my ruling is correct, Mr. Carter's past imprisonment may have been a travesty. To continue it would be even a greater one."

---

jurors; nor are the jurors permitted to seek advice. If they need further instruction, they may send the bailiff to ask the judge. That instruction may or may not be given, depending on the nature of the request.

During long and highly publicized trials, the jury may be sequestered, which means they will be escorted by the bailiff not only in and out of the courtroom but to all meals and to the hotel rooms where they will be staying. Access to television and newspapers will not be permitted.

When the jurors deliberate, they usually have access to the demonstrative evidence that has been introduced during the trial. If they have been permitted to take notes during the trial, they may have their notes for the deliberation. Generally it is left to the discretion of the trial judge whether jurors may take notes.

Many judges will not permit note taking for a number of reasons. Taking notes may distract the juror and others; too much emphasis may be placed on one juror's notes; the notes may even be falsified. Jurors may be taking notes on less important points and miss more important points; consequently, many judges will not allow note taking but rather will require the jury to rely on the summaries of the case made by each attorney and on the instructions of the judge.

The jury may be given a copy of the charges against the defendant. Some judges will also give them a written copy of the judge's instructions or charge to the jury, but some judges only charge the jury orally. In some trials the jury deliberates for hours and does not reach a verdict. They report to the judge, who may tell them to go back and try again. How many times the judge can send them back and how long they must deliberate is a matter of jurisdictional rules, but the judge cannot require them to deliberate for an unreasonable period of time. The definition of reasonable will depend on the complexity of the trial. If they cannot reach a verdict, the jury is deadlocked, and the judge must declare a mistrial.

Mistrials may also be declared under other circumstances, such as the death of a judge or one of the attorneys. Mistrials may be declared during the trial as the result of a prejudicial error made by one of the parties involved in the trial. Other reasons may include prejudicial media publicity that comes to the attention of the jury or efforts of someone to bribe some or all of the jurors.

If the jury is not deadlocked and does return a verdict, the verdict may be not guilty. In that case the judge may order a verdict of acquittal, and the case is over. The judge cannot reverse a verdict of not guilty. The judge may, but rarely does, reverse a verdict of guilty. This may happen if the judge believes the evidence was not sufficient to support the verdict of guilty.

Postverdict Motions

If the jury returns a guilty verdict, the defense may make a motion for a judgment of acquittal. That motion may also be made before the case goes to the jury and probably is more appropriately done at that time. The motion is based on the argument that the evidence is not sufficient to support a guilty verdict. The court may be more likely to grant that motion before the jury has returned a verdict, particularly in a close case.

The more common motion made by the defense after a guilty verdict is a motion for a new trial. This motion may be made on several specific grounds or on general grounds; that is, a new trial is in the interest of justice. Court rules or statutes may also enumerate specific grounds on which this motion may be based.

Sentencing

After a verdict of guilty, either the judge or the jury will impose sentence. The process often takes place at a later hearing to allow time for presentence reports. It is an important stage; the next chapter is devoted to sentencing and the concepts of punishment underlying sentencing.

APPEALS AND WRITS

Spotlight 11.7 explains the appeal process, along with what might happen to a case after appeal. A successful appeal does not necessarily mean that the case is over and the defendant is free from the criminal justice system. A successful appeal usually means that the case is retried, and the defendant is once again convicted. A successful appeal on a sentence, for example the death penalty, may result in another death sentence. The difference is that in the retrial, the state must not commit the errors made in the first trial. As Spotlight 11.7 indicates, it is also possible that on appeal a defendant may be successful on some issues and not on others.

Defendants may also petition for writs. **A writ** is an order from the court. It gives permission to do whatever was requested or orders someone to do something specific. A common writ filed for offenders is a writ of **habeas corpus.** *Habeas corpus* literally means "you have the body." Originally a writ of habeas corpus was an order from the court to someone like a sheriff or a jailer to have the body in court at a specified time and to indicate the legal theory under which the body was being held. Today it is more extensive, and its use is governed by statutes that differ from jurisdiction to jurisdiction. Basically it is a means by which an inmate may question the legality of confinement. It does not question the issue of

SPOTLIGHT 11.7
THE APPEAL PROCESS

An appeal occurs when the defendant in a criminal case (or either party in a civil case) requests that a court with appellate jurisdiction rule on a decision that has been made by a trial court or administrative agency.

Appellate courts receive two basic categories of cases, appeals and writs. Appeals, by far the most time-consuming and important, occur when a litigant's case receives a full-scale review after losing at the trial level (or, in several States, after losing in certain administrative proceedings).

The appeal begins when the party losing the case in the trial court, the "appellant," files a notice of appeal, usually a month or two after the trial court decision. Then within a few months the appellant files the trial court record in the appellate court. The record, often bulky, consists of the papers filed in the trial court along with a transcript of the trial testimony. Next the appellant and the opposing party, the "appellee," file briefs that argue for their respective positions. The briefs are usually followed by short oral presentations to the judge. Finally, the judges decide the case and issue a written opinion. An increasing number of courts, but still a minority, decide some appeals without written opinions.

State supreme court decisions are usually issued by the full court; intermediate court decisions are generally issued by three-judge panels. The whole decision process takes roughly a year, although it ranges from 6 months in some courts to several years in courts with large backlogs.

In making its final disposition of the case, an appellate court may

- "affirm," or uphold, the lower court ruling.
- "modify" the lower court ruling by changing it in part, but not totally reversing it.
- "reverse," or set aside, the lower court ruling and not require any further court action.
- "reverse and remand" the case by overturning the lower court ruling but requiring further proceedings at the lower court that may range from conducting a new trial to entering a proper judgment.
- "remand" all or part of the case by sending it back to the lower court without overturning the lower court's ruling but with instructions for further proceedings that may range from conducting a new trial to entering a proper judgment.

Thus, the termination of an appellate court case may or may not be the end of the case from the perspective of the parties involved in the case. They may be required to go back to the lower court for further proceedings. If Federal law is involved, a party can petition for review in the U.S. Supreme Court. In criminal cases, defendants can file further petitions in a Federal court or a State court.

Source: Bureau of Justice Statistics, *Trends: The Growth of Appeals, 973–83* (Washington, D.C.: U.S. Department of Justice, February 1, 1985), p. 3.

guilt or innocence but asserts that some due process rights of offenders are being violated or have been violated.

Under some circumstances, sentences may be appealed. Occasionally they will be reversed and the case sent back for resentencing. In practice, this rarely occurs. Appellate courts have given judges wide discretion in sentencing. As long as the sentence is within the statutory provisions and the sentencing judge has not abused his or her discretion or shown undue prejudice, it is difficult for defendants to challenge a judicial sentence effectively. In rare cases, courts may declare a legislatively determined sentence to be in violation of the defendant's rights.

ANALYSIS OF TRIAL BY JURY

Why should we permit a trial by jury? The lack of expertise of most jurors concerning the cases they decide has led many to question this method of deciding cases.

> Why should anyone think that twelve persons brought in from the street, selected in various ways, for their lack of general ability, should have any special capacity to decide controversies between persons?[37]

It is clear that a jury may acquit a defendant even when the evidence clearly indicates beyond a reasonable doubt that the defendant is guilty of the crime charged. There is some negative reaction to this possibility. The reason for allowing juries to acquit in the face of evidence to the contrary is that "the very essence of the jury's function is its role as spokesman for the community conscience in determining whether or not blame can be imposed."[38]

That juries do exercise this power was clearly demonstrated by the American jury system study. That study involved a composite analysis of 3,576 criminal jury trials, including 1,063 instances in which the judge and jury arrived at different conclusions concerning the application of law to the case. The study indicated that in cases where the jury might empathize with the defendant or in cases in which the jury did not consider the behavior of the defendant so bad as to be worthy of condemnation, the jury would acquit or convict on a lesser charge.[39] But is this desire to have community input into the system justifiable in light of the costs of a jury trial? Former Chief Justice Warren E. Burger proposed the elimination of jury trials in complicated civil cases; Justice John Paul Stevens of the U.S. Supreme Court has advocated that, although he has "great faith in the jury system," it may well be a "luxury we cannot afford."[40]

And although some people enjoy jury duty, the fact that most people called for jury duty try to get excused, led defense attorney F. Lee Bailey to assert that "most people put jury duty in a class with measles and root canal work."[41] But despite this and the hue and cry that comes from the press and the public when a jury makes an unpopular decision, there is still strong support for the system. A recent popular magazine article, "Jury System Not Perfect, but It Works," may have hit on the most appropriate reason for maintaining the right to a trial by jury in criminal cases.[42]

SUMMARY

This chapter focused on the criminal trial. The procedures and issues surrounding the criminal trial in the U. S. system of criminal justice are extensive and complicated. Numerous statutes and court decisions govern these issues and procedures throughout the system. It is not possible to state "the law" in many of these areas, since the justices of state courts and lower federal courts often differ in their analysis of how statutes and constitutions apply to the facts before them.

Even when the Supreme Court agrees to hear and decide some of the controversies, we often do not know exactly how these decisions will be applied in similar cases. Some of the Court's decisions are close. Many of the criminal procedure cases have been decided by a 5–4 vote. Thus, a change of one member of the Court could alter the direction of what has often been called the revolution in criminal procedure of the past two decades.

It is possible, however, to state generally what happens in the trial of a criminal case and how the constitutional guarantees apply to any or all of the stages of that trial. This chapter therefore began with a brief overview of those constitutional rights discussed earlier in the text and gave closer attention to the rights that are more specific to the trial stages. The right to a speedy trial, the right to a public trial by a jury of one's peers, and the rights to confrontation and cross-examination of witnesses, along with defendants' right to remain silent and not be forced to testify against themselves, are crucial to understanding the implementation of the various stages of the trial. Although states have considerable freedom in establishing the procedures by which they will conduct criminal trials, they may not violate these basic constitutional rights.

In that sense, every stage of the trial must be understood and analyzed in light of the constitutional requirements to which all defendants are entitled. The right to a public trial by an impartial jury thus precludes selection of the jury in secret. It also precludes systematic exclusion of people because of their race, sex, religion, ethnic origin, or socioeconomic status. That exclusion may not occur either implicitly or explicitly. Yet, understanding the right to a jury of one's peers may seem elusive to most people who use this text; for juries are not generally representative of young adults, and the court has held that lack of representation to be permissible in most cases.

The importance of constitutional rights that apply to the trial is underscored by the fact that when those rights are violated, with only a few exceptions, the demonstrative or testimonial evidence secured as a result of those violations must be excluded from the trial. In many cases, it is not possible to prove guilt beyond a reasonable doubt without this tainted evidence; thus, the case must be dismissed. This use of the exclusionary rule has led to considerable controversy concerning the U. S. system of criminal justice. Its implications for the entire system are extensive. Police may become discouraged and refuse to arrest in certain situations, thinking the case will not result in a conviction anyway. Society may become critical of a system that lets the guilty go free. Potential criminals may decide to commit crimes, thinking they will not be convicted even if arrested. On the other hand, those protections are to ensure that, when people are convicted of crimes, those convictions occurred only after proper procedures were followed and constitutional safeguards were observed.

In this chapter, each stage of the criminal trial was explained and discussed, beginning with the opening of the court session in which charges against the defendant are formally read, through jury selection, the presentation of evidence, the final arguments, and the verdict. In all of these stages the defense, the prosecution, and the judge are primary figures in assuring that proper procedures are followed. But following proper procedures does not end the matter. It is important to consider and reconsider the issues involved in the U.S. system of criminal justice.

In this chapter some of those important issues have been raised. The conflict between the right of the public to know and of the media to tell, frequently conflicts with the right of the defendant to be tried fairly and impartially. Which right should give way when that occurs? The right of the defendant to a trial by jury creates enormous expenses and consumes considerable time of all participants in the criminal trial. At what point, if ever, should that right of the defendant give way to the realities of cost?

The criminal trial has an enormous effect on the rest of the criminal justice system. Long trials increase the backlog in the courts and result in a greater likelihood that defendants will be denied their right to a speedy trial and society will have to spend even more money to keep the system operating. Mistrials increase the amount of time and money devoted to trials. Failure to convict in numerous cases might lead the public to question the effectiveness of the system. Conviction of the inno-cent undermines the entire system. Repeated appeals lead many to question whether there is any finality in the law.

Throughout this discussion of the procedures and issues of the trial, however, it should be remembered that the vast majority of defendants do not go to trial. It therefore is important not to let the issues of the trial overshadow the need to give attention to the pretrial stages of the criminal justice system. But it is also important to understand and analyze what happens after defendants either plead guilty or are found guilty at trial. Sentencing is a critical stage of the system. It will be the subject of the next chapter.

STUDY QUESTIONS

1. What is the purpose of the Speedy Trial Act of 1974? What kinds of delays does it permit?

2. Why is the right to a public trial important to defendants? What are the legal problems and issues with public trials as far as the media are concerned?

3. Briefly explain the history of the jury system and why it is considered important in this country. Should it be abolished? Why or why not?

4. What are the requirements for jury size and the selection of names for the jury pool? What is meant by an impartial jury? A jury of peers?

5. What is the role of the judge in controlling the conduct of defendants at trial?

6. Should people who are chosen for the jury pool be permitted to be excused from jury duty at their own request or should all persons called be required to serve? If you think personal requests should be honored, for what reasons should they be honored? What reasons should not be considered?

7. What is the significance of *Batson v. Kentucky*?

8. How do opening statements differ from closing statements? Are both required for the prosecution and the defense?

9. What is the hearsay rule? What are some of the exceptions?

10. What is the difference between direct and circumstantial evidence?

11. What is meant by direct examination, cross-examination, and redirect?

12. What are defenses? Should they be allowed?

13. Describe the role of the judge in presenting the case to the jury.

14. Describe the role of the jury in a criminal trial.

15. What are postverdict motions?

ENDNOTES

1. Klopfer v. North Carolina, 386 U.S. 213 (1967).
2. U.S.C., Ch. 18, Sections 3161–74.
3. Sheppard v. Maxwell, 384 U.S. 333, 356 (1966), quoting 135 N.E. 2d, 340, 342 (1956).
4. Gannett Co., Inc., v. DePasquale, 443 U.S. 368 (1979).
5. "Private Justice, Public Injustice," *New York Times* (5 July 1979), p. A 16.
6. "Slamming the Courtroom Doors," *Time* (16 July 1979), p. 66.
7. See, for example, Richmond Newspapers, Inc., v. Virginia, 448 U.S. 555 (1980), a case concerned with trial, rather than pretrial procedures.
8. Globe Newspaper Co., v. Superior Court, 457 U.S. 596 (1982). See also Press-Enterprise Co. v. Superior Court, 464 U.S. 501 (1984), involving a sexual abuse trial. The Court said it would be appropriate to close the process of questioning potential jurors. In Press-Enterprise Co. v. Superior Court, 478 U.S. 1 (1986), the Court listed

three circumstances that must be met before a pretrial proceeding could be closed to the public.

9. "Cameras in the Courtroom: Florida's Bundy Case Tests the Fairness of Televising Trials," *Time* (23 July 1979), p. 76.

10. News Brief, *Arkansas Gazette* (13 November 1984), p. 1.

11. For a history of the jury system, see Harry Elmer Barnes, *The Story of Punishment: A Record of Man's Inhumanity to Man*, 2d rev. ed. (Montclair, N.J.: Patterson Smith, 1972), pp. 25–33; and Jon M. Van Dyke, "Jury: Jury Trial," in Sanford H. Kadish, ed., *Encyclopedia of Crime and Justice* (New York: Macmillan Publishing Co., 1983), vol. 3, pp. 932–41.

12. Irving R. Kaufman, "The Verdict on Juries," *New York Times Magazine* (1 April 1984), pp. 42, 44.

13. Duncan v. Louisiana, 391 U.S. 145, 149 (1968).

14. Smith v. Texas, 311 U.S. 128, 130 (1940).

15. Taylor v. Louisiana, 419 U.S. 522, 523 (1975), footnotes and citations omitted.

16. Ballew v. Georgia, 435 U.S. 223 (1978). See also Williams v. Florida, 399 U.S. 78 (1970). In Colgrove v. Battin, 413 U.S. 149 (1973), the Court held that a six-person jury is permissible in federal cases.

17. Burch v. Louisiana, 441 U.S. 130, 138 (1979).

18. Apodaca v. Oregon, 406 U.S. 404 (1972).

19. See Witherspoon v. Illinois, 391 U.S. 510 (1968); and Wainwright v. Witt, 469 U.S. 412 (1985).

20. Turney v. Ohio, 273 U.S. 510 (1927).

21. Barber v. Ponte, 772 F.2d 982 (1st Cir., 1985), *cert. denied* 475 U.S. 1050 (1986).

22. Illinois v. Allen, 397 U.S. 337 (1970).

23. Illinois v. Allen, 397 U.S. 337, 343, 346–47 (1970).

24. For a discussion of the trial stages, along with pertinent examples from court cases, see Wayne R. LaFave and Jerold H. Israel, *Criminal Procedure* (St. Paul, Minn.: West Publishing Co., 1985).

25. Swain v. Alabama, 380 U.S. 202 (1965).

26. Batson v. Kentucky, 476 U.S. 79 (1986), citations and footnotes omitted.

27. State v. Cantu, 750 P.2d 591, 595 (Utah 1988). In 1987 the U.S. Supreme Court held that *Batson* applies to all cases still pending on direct review. Griffith v. Kentucky, 479 U.S. 314 (1987). For a discussion of cases since *Batson*, see "Discrimination by the Defense: Peremptory Challenges after *Batson v. Kentucky*," *Columbia Law Review* 88 (March 1988): 355–68.

28. See *McCormick's Hornbook on Evidence*, student ed., 3d ed. (St. Paul: West Publishing Co., 1984).

29. See Elizabeth F. Loftus, *Eyewitness Testimony* (Cambridge, Mass.: Harvard University Press, 1979).

30. See People v. Yukl, 372 N.Y.S. 2d 313 (N.Y. 1975).

31. See Griffin v. California, 380 U.S. 609 (1965).

32. Harvard Law School Professor Arthur Miller, quoted in *American Bar Association Journal* 70 (March 1984): 44.

33. Berger v. U.S., 295 U.S. 78 (1935).

34. See "Juries Often Disregard Judge's Word," *New York Times* (28 March 1988), p. 12; and " 'The Jury Will Disregard . . .' But New Study Suggests that by Then It's Too Late," *American Bar Association Journal* (1 November 1987), p. 34.

35. Quoted in *American Bar Association Journal* 71 (December 1985): 35.

36. Kentucky v. Whorton, 441 U.S. 786 (1979), *remanded* 585 S.W. 2d 388 (Ky. 1979), *reh. denied* 444 U.S. 887 (1979).

37. Erwin Griswold, United States solicitor general, quoted in "Jury System Not Perfect, but It Works," *U.S. News and World Report* (1 November 1982), p. 45.

38. U.S. v. Dougherty, 473 F.2d 1113, 1142 (D.C. Cir. 1972). Chief Judge David Bazelon, concurring in part and dissenting in part; *reh. denied*, 473 F.2d 1147.

39. Harry Kalven and Hans Zeisel, *The American Jury* (Boston: Little, Brown and Co., 1966). For more recent analyses of the jury system, see the following: Lawrence S. Wrightsman, *In The Jury Box: Controversies in the Courtroom* (Beverly Hills, Calif.: Sage Publishers, 1987); and F. P. Hans and N. Vidmar, *Judging the Jury* (New York: Plenum Press, 1986).

40. "Juries May Be Luxury in Future, Says Stevens," *American Bar Association Journal* 65 (September 1979): 1292.

41. F. Lee Bailey, *The Defense Never Rests* (New York: Stein and Day, 1971), p. 257.

42. "Jury System Not Perfect," p. 45.

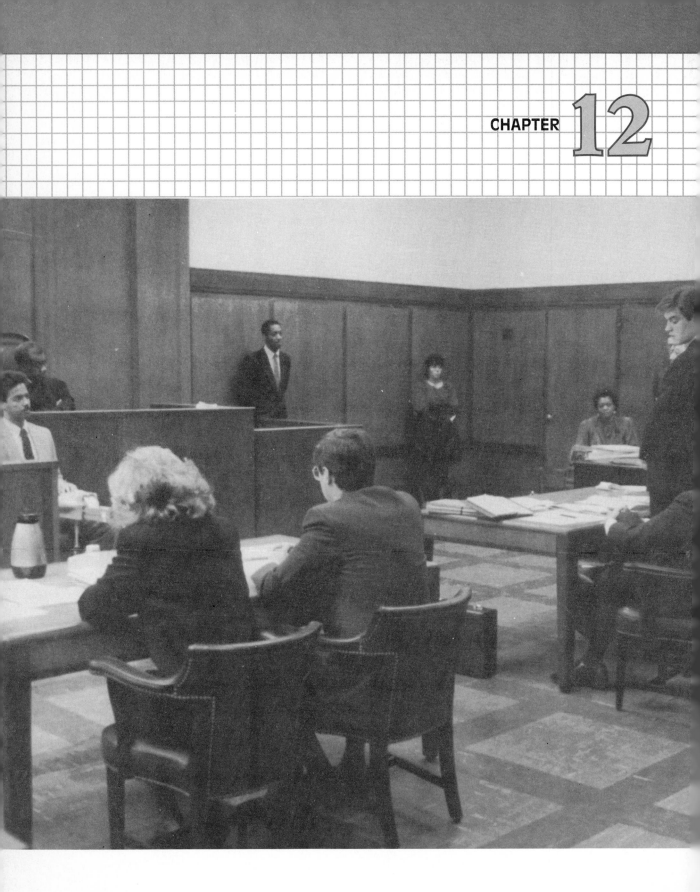

Sentencing

CRIMINAL JUSTICE IN ACTION

Peter and Jane, two college students, were living together in an apartment near campus. Someone tipped the police that these two students were involved in drug transactions. Proper arrest and search warrants were secured; police arrived at the apartment; Peter and Jane were arrested, and the apartment was searched. The rooms of the apartment were littered with marijuana leaves in various stages of drying. Quantities of crushed, packaged marijuana were stored at various places throughout the apartment. The stove boiler contained marijuana leaves and apparently had been used as a dryer.

Both Peter and Jane were convicted of illegal possession of marijuana, a felony in that jurisdiction. Only recently had the legislature changed the designation of that crime from a misdemeanor to a felony. It was argued at the time of the change that increased penalties would deter this illegal behavior. Conviction carried a penalty of 5 to 10 years in prison, although with proper reasons, the judge could suspend the sentence.

The judge sentenced Peter to 10 years in prison without suspending the sentence. Jane received a 5-year suspended sentence. She was placed on probation and required to perform 100 hours of community service in a drug rehabilitation center.

The judge cited as his reasons for the differential sentencing that the presentence investigations indicated that Peter was the instigator of the crime, that he had previously been in minor trouble with the law although he had never been formally charged with a crime, and that he was not cooperative with authorities when arrested. He showed no remorse. Indeed, he continued to brag about his criminal behavior.

Jane had never been in trouble with the law. She was an excellent student, and the evidence indicated that she did not smoke marijuana. Jane had already begun professional counseling. Pctcr had refused to go to a counselor.

INTRODUCTION

The cases of Peter and Jane illustrate some of the procedures and issues in sentencing. Two of the most discussed topics involve the apparent disparity in sentencing and the increased penalties for certain crimes thought to represent a threat to the welfare of society. These are closely related to historical concerns about punishment and sentencing.

Increasing concern with rising crime rates in this country, particularly the incidence of personal, violent crimes in which victims appear to be chosen randomly, has precipitated a get-tough policy in sentencing that closely resembles the mechanical and harsh philosophy of Beccaria, who argued successfully in the eighteenth century that punishment should fit the crime. It was a philosophy that made sentencing easy. The legislature determined the sentence for each offense, and the court's only function was to determine whether the accused had committed the offense. That system was soon abolished in many countries because it did not take into account mitigating circumstances, which were emphasized by the neoclassical school.

In the United States during this century, a philosophy of individualized treatment developed. Supported by legislatures and recognized by the courts, the philosophy reached its most extreme form in the indeterminate sentence. Recently this philosophy has come under attack. Some states have already returned legislatively to a determinate sentencing structure, combined in some cases with the abolition of parole and based on the belief that the philosophy of rehabilitation was a failure. Treatment does not work, the argument goes. Let's try incarceration for longer periods of time. "Lock 'em up and throw away the key! Crudely put, that increasingly is the rallying cry in an America fed up with violent crime."[1]

The trend toward harsher sentencing has included decreasing the discretion of sentencing judges and parole boards. This discretion, it is argued, has led to sentencing disparity, which would be reduced significantly if more definite sentencing provisions are established by the legislature. The assumption is that such provisions will significantly reduce sentencing disparity, reduce or eliminate the early release of inmates from prison, and eventually reduce the crime rate. Such assumptions, however, must be analyzed carefully in light of the total system of criminal justice. This chapter will examine the procedures of sentencing and the trends in sentencing. It will also consider the effect that current reforms are having and might continue to have on the overall crime problem.

THE CONCEPT OF PUNISHMENT

Two Cases of Murder: A Punishment Problem

A young woman driving a Chevrolet Caprice along Interstate 57 in southern Cook County, Illinois, on the night of June 3, 1973, was forced off the highway by a car occupied by four men. With one of the men pointing a gun at her, she was ordered to remove her clothing and climb through a barbed-wire fence at the side of the road. Henry Brisbon, Jr., responded to her pleas for life by thrusting a shotgun in her vagina and firing. She agonized for several minutes before her assailant fired the fatal shot at her throat. In less than an hour Brisbon had committed two more murders.

Brisbon's next victims, also riding in their car along I57 when forced off the road, were planning to be married in 6 months. They too pleaded that their lives be spared. Brisbon told them to lie on the ground and "kiss your last kiss," after which he shot each in the back. Brisbon took $54 in cash, two watches, an engagement ring, and a wedding band from his victims. He was later arrested and convicted of these crimes; but because the death penalty in Illinois had been invalidated, he was given a term of from 1,000 to 3,000 years. While serving that term he killed an inmate and was sentenced to death under the new death penalty statute of Illinois.

During an earlier incarceration, Brisbon was involved in 15 attacks on guards and inmates and was responsible for beginning at least one prison riot. He hit a warden with a broom handle and crashed a courtroom during a trial. Despite these acts of violence, Brisbon, now on death row says, "I'm no bad dude. . . . Just an antisocial individual." He blames his problems on the strict upbringing of his Muslim father who taught him

Henry Brisbon, Jr. (left), convicted of random multiple murders, was sentenced to from one to three thousand years. While in prison he killed an inmate and received a death sentence. Roswell Gilbert (right) was sentenced to life on conviction of murdering his wife who was suffering from Alzheimer's disease and who begged for mercy killing. (AP Wide World; Robert Azmitia/UPI Bettmann Newsphotos)

to dislike white people. The result: "I didn't like nobody." How does he feel about his victims? "All this talk about victims' rights and restitution gets me. What about my family? I'm a victim of a crooked criminal system. Isn't my family entitled to something?"[2]

How should society react to the crime of Henry Brisbon? At his trial that resulted in the death sentence, the prosecutor described Brisbon as "a very, very terrible human being, a walking testimonial for the death penalty." The prosecutor who prosecuted him for the I57 murders said, "On the day he dies in the chair at Statesville, I plan to be there to see that it's done. Nobody I've heard of deserves the death penalty more than Henry Brisbon."[3]

The sentences of Brisbon and Hans Florian should be compared. In March 1983 Florian, 79, went to the hospital to visit his 62-year-old wife, who was suffering from a disease that would eventually make her senile and helpless. Florian had earlier placed his wife in a nursing home because he was unable to care for her; but when she became too ill to be cared for properly in that facility, she was hospitalized. While she was hospitalized her husband, Hans Florian, went every day, placed her in a wheelchair, and wheeled her around the floor of the hospital to give her a change of scenery. On the day in question, he wheeled her into a stairwell and shot her in the head, quickly ending her life. According to a neighbor, "He's no murderer. He did it out of love because she was suffering so much."[4] Florian was charged with first-degree murder. Should he be convicted of that charge? His act was apparently premeditated and without legal justification. If convicted, should he be sentenced to death?

Most people will have no difficulty contrasting the case of Hans Florian with that of Henry Brisbon, Jr., in view of the atrocity of the killings Brisbon committed. But at the same time, the legal elements of first-degree murder may be present in both cases. The Supreme Court has made it clear that capital punishment cannot be imposed without considering the mitigating and aggravating circumstances. So, perhaps Florian should not be executed but should he be convicted and sentenced either to life or a long term of years?

The grand jury refused to indict Hans Florian, but similar cases have resulted in indictments, trials, convictions, and incarcerations. How is the problem to be solved? Does Florian deserve to be free while others who kill in situations similar to that of Florian are convicted and sent to prison? Should Brisbon be executed?

A Historical Overview of Purposes

Throughout history various reasons have been given for punishment and sentencing. Four basic objectives are generally recognized: **deterrence, rehabilitation, incapacitation,** and **retribution.** These objectives are defined in Spotlight 12.1, which also mentions other factors that might be considered in punishment and sentencing: the concerns for fairness, equity, and the social debt that the offender owes to society because of prior crimes. The debate over which one of these objectives ought to be the basis for punishment and sentencing continues. Chapter 3 examined the classical and neoclassical recognition of deterrence as the basic reason for punishment. The cry of that period was to "let the punishment fit the crime."

That period was followed by the positivists, who were influential in developing the philosophy of rehabilitation, a punishment philosophy that now can be considered historical, for its influence on sentencing has been severely diminished. The philosophy of rehabilitation has been described as the rehabilitative ideal, characterized by the juvenile court, probation, parole, and the indeterminate sentence. The ideal is based on the premise that human behavior is the result of antecedent causes that may be known by objective analysis and that permit scientific control of human behavior. The assumption is that the offender should be treated, not punished. Social scientists strongly endorsed the rehabilitative ideal and began developing treatment programs for institutionalized inmates. The ideal was incorporated into some statutes, proclaimed by courts, and supported by presidential crime commissions.

The demise of this rehabilitative ideal was headlined in *Time* magazine in 1982: "What Are Prisons For? No Longer Rehabilitation, But to Punish—and to Lock the Worst Away." The article referred briefly to the original purpose of U. S. prisons: not only to punish, but also to transform criminals "from idlers and hooligans into good, industrious citizens." The article concluded, however, that

> no other country was so seduced for so long by that ambitious charter. The language, ever malleable, conformed to the ideal: when a monkish salvation was expected of inmates, prisons became penitentiaries, then reformatories, correctional centers and rehabilitation facilities.[5]

The simple fact is that prisons did not work as intended.

The backbone of the rehabilitation philosophy was the indeterminate sentence. No longer would a court at the time of sentencing give an offender a definite term, for a judge could not possibly predict how much time would be needed for the treatment and rehabilitation of that offender. Consequently, in most jurisdictions the legislature established minimum and maximum terms for each offense, with judges showing wide discretion in setting the sentence. Treatment personnel would then evaluate the person and recommend and implement treatment. The parole board would decide when that individual had been rehabilitated and could safely be released back into society. The punishment was fitted to the criminal, not to the crime. In short, the philosophy was that criminals should be incarcerated until they were cured or rehabilitated.[6]

The 1970s brought cries that treatment does not work and that the indeterminate sentence was poorly administered with no guidelines. These criticisms resulted in harsh feelings by offenders, who claimed that it created psychological problems for them. Others saw the system as one that coddled criminals while crime rates soared. Americans demanded a get-tough policy in sentencing. The result has been a movement toward more severe and definite sentences.[7]

Modern Justification for Punishment: The Justice Model

The current philosophy of punishment is generally called the *justice approach* or the **just deserts** model. It is based on two philosophies: deterrence and retribution. The retribution basis assumes that offenders will be assessed the punishment they deserve in light of the crimes they have committed. It is also assumed that appropriate punishments will deter those criminals from engaging in further criminal acts and deter others from committing crimes.

The justice model emerged as dissatisfaction with the philosophy of rehabilitation increased. In 1976 Andrew von Hirsch represented the position of the report of the Committee for the Study of Incarceration. Indicating their basic mistrust of the power of the state, the committee members rejected rehabilitation and the indeterminate sentence and turned to deterrence and just deserts as reasons for punishment. But in their rejection of rehabilitation as a reason for punishment, the committee advocated shorter sentences and sparing use of incarceration.[8] The rehabilitative model has also been rejected by Ernest van den Haag, who emphasizes just deserts and the utilitarian aspect of punishment.[9]

The person most often cited as responsible for the current popularity of the justice model is David Fogel. Fogel formulated 12 propositions on which he believes the justice model may be tested. He argues that punishment is necessary for implementing the criminal law, a law based on the belief that people act as a result of their own free will and must be held responsible for their actions. Prisoners should be considered and treated as "responsible, volitional and aspiring human beings." All the processes of the agencies of the criminal justice system should be carried out "in a milieu of justice."[10]

Discretion cannot be eliminated, but under the justice model it would be controlled, narrowed, and subject to review. The emphasis is shifted from the processor (the public, the administration, and others) to the consumer of the criminal justice system, a shift from what Fogel calls the *imperial* or *official perspective* to the consumer of justice perspective. Justice for the offender must not stop with the process of sentencing but must continue throughout the correctional process.

Under Fogel's justice model, an incarcerated person should be allowed to choose whether to participate in rehabilitation programs. The only purpose of incarceration is to confine for a specified period of time, not to rehabilitate the criminal. The offender receives only the sentence he or she deserves, and that sentence is implemented according to fair principles.

THE CONCEPT AND PROCESS OF SENTENCING

Sentence refers to some form of punishment imposed on a convicted offender. It encompasses "all decisions and decision-makers resolving who will, and will not, be punished and the nature and amounts of punishment."[11] Sentencing is perhaps the most complex of the processes in our criminal justice system. It involves numerous people, ranging from legislators who formulate sentencing laws to probation officers who compile the presentence reports that may be used by judges in making a final sentencing decision. Sentencing also involves prison administrative authorities who often have considerable discretion and power in determining how long inmates will be incarcerated. They determine the extent of good-time credits inmates will receive for their behavior while incarcerated. Likewise, they determine the removal of good-time credits for unacceptable behavior. These administrative authorities may be extremely influential with the parole boards, which have the power to determine whether inmates will be released early.

Sentencing may also be affected by the prosecutor's recommendations and by the reactions of victims or other witnesses who may testify at the trial or who may be permitted to engage in discussions concerning the appropriate sentence.

A study of sentencing is further complicated because it differs significantly from state to state, from court to court within a state, and even from county to county. Attitudes toward what is and is not appropriate in sentencing also differ significantly.

Sentencing Strategies

Four main strategies are used for sentencing: indeterminate, determinate, presumptive, and mandatory sentences. Most states use a combination of these strategies. An **indeterminate sentence** involves legislative specifications of ranges of sentences that permit judges to exercise discretion in determining actual sentences. In its purest form, the indeterminate sentence would be from 1 day to life. In actuality, it usually involves legislative specification of a maximum and minimum term for each offense. The legislative sentence for armed robbery might be not more than 25 nor less than 10 years. Judges would then be free to set the sentence at any point in between.

Another sentencing model involves the **presumptive sentence.** In presumptive sentencing the normal sentence is specified for each offense, but judges are permitted to deviate from the normal sentence. Some jurisdictions, however, require that any deviation from a presumptive sentence be accompanied by written reasons for the deviation. The law also may specify which conditions and circumstances can be considered for deviating from the presumptive sentence.

Mandatory sentences are sometimes confused with determinate sentences. A *mandatory sentence* means that the sentence must be imposed upon conviction. Mandatory sentences are specified by legislatures (or by Congress), and they usually involve a prison term. The mandatory sentence leaves the judge no discretion concerning incarceration. If the sentence specifies a prison term, the judge may not impose probation as an alternative nor suspend the sentence.

In a **determinate sentence** structure, although the legislature specifies a fixed term of incarceration for conviction of a particular offense, the judge may have the option of suspending that sentence or imposing probation rather than a jail or prison term. But once that sentence is imposed, the parole board does not have the discretion to reduce the sentence by offering early parole. The determinate sentencing scheme, however, may involve a provision for mandatory parole after a specified portion of the determinate sentence has been served. It also may include a provision for sentence reduction based on good-time credits earned by the prisoner.

Determinate sentences may include a provision for raising or lowering the sentence if there are mitigating or aggravating circumstances. For example, the determinate sentence for rape might be 15 years; but if a weapon is used to threaten the victim, there may be a provision for increasing the penalty. Likewise, if there are circumstances that reduce the moral culpability of the offender, the sentence might be reduced. An example would be extreme passion in a homicide, as when the accused finds his or her spouse in bed with another and in a fit of anger kills that person.

In any of the sentencing models, the power to determine sentence length may be altered by other factors. Power may be given to the governor to commute a sentence of life to a specified term of years or to commute a death sentence to a life sentence. The governor also may have the power to pardon an offender. (In the case of a federal crime, the pardoning power would reside in the president of the United States.) It also is possible that sentence length may be reduced in accordance with a good-time policy. In such cases legislatively or judicially imposed sentences may be reduced because of the good behavior of the inmate.

In recent years, many states, faced with severe prison overcrowding and federal court orders concerning acceptable prison capacity, have enacted legislation that enables the governor to order early release of some inmates to make room for new ones. This policy has come under increasing criticism, particularly when early releasees commit additional crimes.

The Sentencing Hearing

For less serious offenses, particularly when the case is not tried before a jury, the judge may pronounce sentence immediately upon finding the defendant guilty or upon accepting a guilty plea. Sentencing may also be immediate when the judge has no option but to assess the statutory penalty. Sentencing may be set for a future date but not involve any special investigations. The judge will take recommendations from the defense and prosecution. The trend, however, is toward having a separate sentencing hearing. After the verdict at trial, the judge will usually set a formal date for sentencing, leaving sufficient time to conduct appropriate presentence investigations.

Some jurisdictions *require* a separate sentencing hearing. Washington state is an example. Washington's sentencing reform statute requires a sentencing hearing in every case. It must be held within 40 court days following conviction, although that period may be extended by the court on its own or upon a motion by the prosecutor, provided there is a good reason for the extension. The reason for requiring a sentencing hearing after the conviction is to permit time for securing information that might be pertinent to the sentencing decision. Many judges prefer to obtain this information from presentence investigations.

The **presentence investigation (PSI)** should include information based on interviews with the defendant, family, friends, employers, or others who might have information pertinent to a sentencing decision in that defendant's case. Medical, psychiatric, or other reports from experts might also be included. Prior offenses, work record, school record, associates, pastime activities, attitudes, willingness to cooperate, and problems with alcohol or drugs are other kinds of information that might be included.

If the PSI is conducted thoroughly, it is a time-consuming job. In some jurisdictions the reports are prepared by the Department of Corrections (DOC). These departments usually have diagnostic facilities and perhaps are better equipped to conduct the investigations than probation officers, who conduct the PSI in many jurisdictions.

The PSI is usually conducted by a probation officer. A study in California indicated that probation officers spend half their time engaged in this activity. That study also found that courts do not necessarily follow these recommendations. The researchers suggested that refusal to follow the reports may reflect the judges' beliefs that the PSIs are not accurate in their predictions of which offenders will be good risks on probation. The evidence from that study, as indicated in Figure 12.1, indicates that

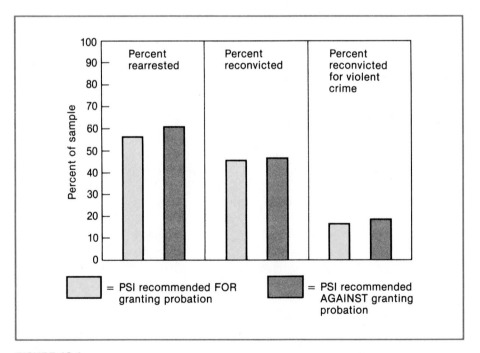

FIGURE 12.1

Relationship Between Presentence Investigations (PSI) and Recidivism: A Study of California Offenders. *Source:* Joan Petersilia, *Probation and Felony Offenders* (Washington, D.C.: U.S. Government Printing Office, National Institute of Justice, March 1985), p. 5.

persons recommended for probation were rearrested and reconvicted about as frequently as those recommended for incarceration.

The Sentencing Decision

Judges decide most sentences (unless the legislature has removed all judicial discretion), but in some cases (usually in serious offenses such as first-degree murder) juries have some sentencing power. The judge is not always required to follow the jury's recommendation. Where the jury does have sentencing power, the judge instructs the jury concerning the law and its application to sentencing.

As the discussion of the PSI indicates, many factors might be considered in the sentencing decision. Recently, however, some states have attempted to formalize and restrict the factors that may be considered. One method is the use of sentencing formulas. The Washington Sentencing Reform Act is an example. That statute specifies, in addition to requiring a hearing that the defendant has a right to attend, the nature of factors that may be considered in the sentencing decision. The process is illustrated by the worksheet reprinted in Figure 12.2. Once the offender's score

FIGURE 12.2
Worksheets for Determining Appropriate Sentence, State of Washington. *Source: Sentencing Worksheet and Scoring Form prepared by the Sentencing Guidelines Commission of the State of Washington.*

EXAMPLE CASE # 3

Defendant's birthdate: October 15, 1944

CIRCUMSTANCES OF CRIME:	The defendant burglarized an office at a used car lot on June 13, 1985. He had been complaining about being "ripped off" on a car deal and had vowed to "get even". The defendant had been drinking heavily the night of the burglary.
BACKGROUND OF DEFENDANT:	The defendant is 41 years old and has a long history of alcohol abuse. This is the first contact with law enforcement since his last felony sentence.
CONVICTIONS:	Pled guilty to the following crime: Burglary, Second Degree (RCW 9A.52.030)

PRIOR ADULT RECORD:

Date	Offense
1-11-77	Robbery, Second Degree (2 counts, consecutive sentences)

PRIOR JUVENILE RECORD: None

Date	Offense
1-11-77	Robbery, Second Degree (2 counts, consecutive sentences)

PRIOR JUVENILE RECORD: None

Comments on scoring this case:
- In 1977, the two counts of Second Degree Robbery received consecutive sentences; thus, they each count as criminal history in the Offender Score.

FIGURE 12.2
(Cont.)

BURGLARY, SECOND DEGREE
(RCW 9A.52.030)
BURGLARY 2

I. OFFENDER SCORING (RCW 9.94A.360 (7))

ADULT HISTORY: (All adult offenses served concurrently count as ONE offense; those served consecutively are counted separately)

Enter number of Burglary 1 convictions . . . . 0 × 2 = 0

Enter number of Burglary 2 convictions . . . . 0 × 2 = 0

Enter number of other felony convictions . . . . 2 × 1 = 2

JUVENILE HISTORY: (All adjudications entered on the same date count as ONE offense)

Enter number of Burglary 1 felony adjudications . . . . 0 × 2 = 0

Enter number of Burglary 2 adjudications . . . . 0 × 1 = 0

Enter number of other felony adjudications . . . . 0 × ½ = 0

OTHER CURRENT OFFENSES: Other current offenses which do not encompass the same criminal conduct count in offender score)

Enter number of other Burglary 1 convictions . . . . 0 × 2 = 0

Enter number of other Burglary 2 convictions . . . . 0 × 2 = 0

Enter number of other felony convictions . . . . 0 × 1 = 0

Total the last column to get the TOTAL OFFENDER SCORE 2
(round down to the nearest whole number)

II. STANDARD SENTENCE RANGE

A. OFFENDER SCORE:	0	1	2	3	4	5	6	7	8	9 or more
STANDARD RANGE: (Seriousness Level II)	0–90 days	2–6 months	3–9 months	4–12 months	12+–14 months	14–18 months	17–22 months	22–29 months	33–43 months	43–57 months

B. The range for attempt, solicitation, and conspiracy is 75% of the standard sentence range for the completed crime (RCW 9.94A.410)

C. Add 12 months to the entire standard sentence range with a special verdict/finding that the offender or an accomplice was armed with a deadly weapon and burglary was of a building other than a dwelling (RCW 9.94A.310, 9.94A.125)

D. Financial obligations may be added: fines, restitution, court costs, attorney's fees, assessments (SHB 1247 Section 23, RCW 9.94A.140, 9.94A.120 (9), 9.94A.270 (1))

III. SENTENCING OPTIONS FOR SECOND DEGREE BURGLARY

A. If "First-time offender" eligible: 0–90 days confinement and up to two years of community supervision with conditions (RCW 9.94A.120 (5))

B. If sentence is one year or less: the statute directs the court to consider and give priority to alternatives to total confinement. One day of jail can be converted to one day of partial confinement or eight hours of community service (up to 240 hours) (RCW 9.94A.380)

C. If sentence is one year or less: community supervision may be ordered for up to one year (SHB 1247, Section 22)

D. Exceptional sentence (RCW 9.94A.120 (2))

THIS OFFENSE REFERENCE SHEET IS FOR USE WITH THE BURGLARY 2 SCORING FORM

is figured, the standard sentence range may be obtained from the scale. A prior conviction for the same offense as the current one will result in more points than will convictions on other felonies.

Formal Sentencing

If the defendant has been convicted of more than one offense, the judge usually will have the authority to determine whether the sentences are to be imposed concurrently or consecutively. With **concurrent sentences,** the defendant satisfies the terms of all sentences at the same time. For example, if the defendant is sentenced to 20 years for each of three counts of armed robbery, the total number of years served will be 20 if the sentences are concurrent. With **consecutive sentences,** the defendant will have to serve 60 years (unless the term is reduced by parole or good time). Most multiple sentences are imposed concurrently. In a recent study, only about one out of nine defendants who were convicted of multiple charges received consecutive sentences. Their average prison term was 18.9 years, compared to 8.9 years for offenders with multiple convictions who received concurrent sentences.[12]

After the sentence is determined, the judge reads the sentence to the defendant. The sentence then is officially recorded in court records. If the sentence involves incarceration, the defendant is usually taken immediately into custody (or returned to custody if he or she had not been released before trial). The judge may allow the defendant some time to prepare for incarceration, but that occurs very rarely and generally applies only in the cases of government officials or other people who might, in the eyes of the judge, need time to get their affairs in order and who would not be a danger to society or flee the jurisdiction.

TYPES OF SENTENCES

Spotlight 12.2 defines the major types of sentences. Each will be discussed in this section.

Fines

The **fine** is a type of punishment in which the offender is ordered to pay a sum of money to the state in lieu of or in addition to other forms of punishment. Fines have generally been used in cases involving traffic violations or other nonviolent offenses. Recently, with the increasing interest in victim compensation, including compensation for violent and property crimes, some jurisdictions have begun to assess fines to offenders convicted of violent crimes.

Historically fines were frequently used as punishment, and those unable to pay fines were usually incarcerated. Fines are also used in conjunction with incarceration, with the latter being extended beyond the original sentence if the fine has not been paid. The Supreme Court faced

SPOTLIGHT 12.2
TYPES OF SENTENCES

Death penalty—In most States for the most serious crimes such as murder, the courts may sentence an offender to death by lethal injection, electrocution, exposure to lethal gas, hanging, or other method specified by State law.

Incarceration—The confinement of a convicted criminal in a Federal or State prison or a local jail to serve a court-imposed sentence. Confinement is usually in a jail, administered locally, or a prison, operated by the State or Federal Government. In many States offenders sentenced to 1 year or less are held in a jail; those sentenced to longer terms are committed to a State prison.

Probation—The sentencing of an offender to community supervision by a probation agency, often as a result of suspending a sentence to confinement. Such supervision normally entails specific rules of conduct while in the community. If the rules are violated a sentence to confinement may be imposed. Probation is the most widely used correctional disposition in the United States.

Split sentences, shock probation, and intermittent confinement—A penalty that explicitly requires the convicted person to serve a brief period of confinement in a local, State, or Federal facility (the "shock") followed by a period of probation. This penalty attempts to combine the use of community supervision with a short incarceration experience. Some sentences are periodic rather than continuous; for example, an offender may be required to spend a certain number of weekends in jail.

Restitution and victim compensation—The offender is required to provide financial repayment or, in some jurisdictions, services in lieu of monetary restitution, for the losses incurred by the victim.

Community service—The offender is required to perform a specified amount of public service work such as collecting trash in parks or other public facilities.

Fines—An economic penalty that requires the offender to pay a specified sum of money within limits set by law. Fines often are imposed in addition to probation or as alternatives to incarceration.

Source: Bureau of Justice Statistics, *Report to the Nation on Crime and Justice: The Data*, 2d ed. (Washington, D.C.: U.S. Department of Justice, 1988), p. 96.

the issue of whether this practice is constitutional and, in 1970 in *Williams v. Illinois*, held that it was a denial of equal protection to confine an indigent person longer than the terms of the maximum legislative sentence for a particular crime because that indigent was unable to pay a fine.[13]

Williams involved a person who, upon conviction of petty theft, received the maximum sentence provided by state law: 1 year in prison and a $500 fine plus $5.00 court costs. The judgment directed that if, at the end of the sentence, the defendant had not paid the fine, his period of incarceration should continue until he had "worked off" the fine. Under Illinois law, the rate for working off a fine by serving jail time was $5 a day. Under this plan, Williams would have served 101 days beyond the maximum 1 year provided for conviction of petty theft. The Supreme Court held that this was not permissible under the federal constitution.

In 1970, in *Tate v. Short*, the Court also held that an indigent defendant could not be imprisoned for failure to pay a traffic violation fine when a fine was the only punishment provided for that offense.[14] In 1983, in

Bearden v. Georgia, the Court held that when a defendant is placed on probation and ordered to pay restitution (discussed later) but cannot pay the full restitution, probation cannot automatically be revoked and the probationer incarcerated. The court must consider alternatives to incarceration. This brief excerpt explains some of the Court's reasoning.[15]

Bearden v. Georgia

We hold, therefore, that in revocation proceedings for failure to pay a fine or restitution, a sentencing court must inquire into the reasons for the failure to pay. If the probationer willfully refused to pay or failed to make sufficient bona fide efforts legally to acquire the resources to pay, the court may revoke probation and sentence the defendant to imprisonment within the authorized range of its sentencing authority. If the probationer could not pay despite sufficient bona fide efforts to acquire the resources to do so, the court must consider alternate measures of punishment other than imprisonment. Only if alternate measures are not adequate to meet the State's interests in punishment and deterrence may the court imprison a probationer who has made sufficient bona fide efforts to pay. To do so otherwise would deprive the probationer of his conditional freedom simply because, through no fault of his own, he cannot pay the fine. Such a deprivation would be contrary to the fundamental fairness required by the Fourteenth Amendment.

Fines are used frequently: they are most often imposed on first-offender defendants who are able to pay; they are not confined to nonviolent, petty offenses. A survey of 120 jurisdictions, conducted by the U.S. Department of Justice, disclosed that in many jurisdictions a fine is often imposed for more serious offenses. Table 12.1 contains the total number of the 126 jurisdictions in which it was reported that fines are commonly imposed for each crime listed.

Restitution and Community Work Service

The use of **restitution,** requiring offenders to reimburse victims financially or with services, has had a long history in the United States. Restitution was approved by the U.S. Supreme Court as early as 1913.[16] It has received the support of most crime commissions. The primary rationale for restitution is compensation of the victim. Another is that the state should assist crime victims. It is also argued that there is a greater chance of reducing the number of **recidivists** if offenders participate in some form of restitution, either financial or work services. A final rationale is retribution.

Restitution may be combined with work assignments. The work assignments may be designed to benefit only the victim or a larger group, as in the case of **community service** work assignments. Offenders have been sentenced to the following activities: coaching Little League, tutoring students, working with retarded children, restoring abandoned cemeter-

TABLE 12.1

Types of Offenses for Which Fines Are Commonly Imposed

	Total N = 126
Driving while intoxicated/DUI	78
Reckless driving	39
Violation of fish and game laws and other regulatory ordinances	27
Disturbing the peace/breach of the peace/disorderly conduct	41
Loitering/soliciting prostitution	19
Drinking in public/public drunkenness/carrying an open container	19
Criminal trespass	13
Vandalism/criminal mischief/malicious mischief/property damage	15
Drug-related offenses (including sale and possession)	44
Weapons (illegal possession, carrying concealed, etc.)	9
Shoplifting	20
Bad checks	16
Other theft	36
Forgery/embezzlement	7
Fraud	6
Assault	48
Burglary/breaking and entering	14
Robbery	4

Source: Sally T. Hillsman et al., National Institute of Justice, *Fines as Criminal Sanctions* (Washington, D.C.: U.S. Department of Justice, September 1987), p. 3, footnote omitted.

ies, repairing government buildings, and erasing graffiti. A juvenile who stole from a farmer was required to raise a pig and a calf for the farmer. A father of nine children, convicted of drunken driving, was required to chop firewood and deliver it to charitable organizations. He was also required to attend an alcohol treatment program. A man convicted of selling pornographic material was sentenced by a Chicago judge to donate 3,000 clean books to the library in the county jail. A newspaper publisher in California, convicted for driving while intoxicated, was required to write and publish three editorials on the dangers of alcoholism.

Here is one final example. A 400-pound man who pleaded guilty to passing hot checks in the amount of $2,169 was given a sentence of 6 months' probation and ordered to make restitution and pay the $600 in court costs and attorney fees. When he failed to meet the financial requirements, indicating that he could not get a job because of his weight, the judge informed him that he could lose weight and get a job or he would be sent to jail, where he could lose weight on jail food and become "a mere shadow of the man you are."[17]

Restitution and community work service programs have a long history, but not until the 1960s was much attention paid to these sentencing alternatives. The increasing emphasis on rehabilitation, especially of juveniles, gave restitution and community work service a much needed push in the 1960s and 1970s.[18] Many programs were developed in the past two decades. Some were aimed at juveniles, with a recent survey report indicating that at least 500 to 800 restitution and community service programs for juveniles are in existence. Despite the lack of data on programs for adults, the National Institute of Justice estimates that there are 250 to 500 programs. Many of these are for persons with alcohol and drug problems.[19]

Restitution and community work service programs also have been utilized in recent years as one method of reducing jail and prison populations. There are some problems with these programs, however. Victims may overestimate or underestimate losses. Problems of enforcement also exist. What should be done when an offender refuses to pay or cannot pay because of a lack of resources? What if the offender steals to meet the restitution obligations? If the offender is assigned to work services, supervision may be required, and that is costly. The victim may not want any contact with the offender. The community may react negatively to having offenders work in certain types of services.

Additional problems involve decisions regarding which losses are to be included in the restitution program. Should the offender have to pay the victim for pain and suffering or only for economic losses? Should offenders have to share the cost of their apprehension and conviction, or should they be responsible only for their victims' losses? Should restitution be combined with other penalties, or is it sufficient in itself in some cases? Restitution might not be a penalty at all for those who are in a financial position to pay without feeling hardship.

Many of the administrative questions are left open by the statutes providing for restitution or work service as a punishment for crime. Many statutes are ambiguous about the kind of work that may be assigned. Others require work programs or restitution of a nature that aids the victim but also fosters rehabilitation of the offender.

Restitution is also permitted in the federal system. Chapter 4 noted that Congress passed the Victim and Witness Protection Act of 1982 (VWPA). The victim-compensation portion of that statute was mentioned in that discussion, but the act also contains a restitution provision. That provision has been controversial, however, with some lower federal courts requiring trial judges to have hearings on the extent of the victim's damages before ordering restitution.[20]

Other courts have upheld the constitutionality of VWPA. For example, in *United States v. Atkinson*, the United States Court of Appeals for the Second Circuit took the position that the VWPA only requires that a judge "consider" specific factors before ordering restitution. It does not require a hearing on those factors. The *Atkinson* court emphasized that "like other aspects of sentencing, restitution orders require an exercise of discretion." That discretion may at times even be based on a "hunch" or guesswork.[21]

Probation

In 1979 in California, a 48-year-old nurse, convicted for involuntary manslaughter in the fatal shooting of her husband, was placed on **probation** under house arrest. She was required to report to the probation department every morning and evening, seven days a week. She was permitted to retain her job and care for her child. She was part of a program designed to place felons on probation when the probation department had concluded that those offenders were not dangerous to society.

The defendant in this case had shot her husband in a scuffle over his pistol. She told her probation officer that her husband had been drinking and that when he was under the influence of alcohol, he was physically abusive to her, often threatening her with his gun. The defendant was described as a "hard-working, God-fearing first offender" who was a "devout member of a fundamentalist church." The county supervisor said no purpose would be served by sending this woman to jail. She would lose her job and would be unable to care for her child, who would be placed in a foster home at the expense of the county. She would mix with career criminals and probably leave prison in far worse condition. The supervisor also emphasized the added cost of incarceration. The already overcrowded county jail housed inmates at a cost of $7,000 a year to the taxpayers.[22]

This case is unusual only in that it involves the use of probation for a serious felon, a practice becoming more common as jails and prisons become more overcrowded and the cost of incarceration soars. These reasons appear to be more important than the earlier purpose of probation to allow rehabilitation of the offender. Probation is a sentence imposed by the judge at sentencing. It permits the offender to remain in the community, usually under supervision, for a specified period of time during which the offender must observe specified rules and regulations. Violation of those rules may result in incarceration. Probation is a form of sentencing, but because the result is to place the offender in the community, usually under supervision, it will be discussed in more detail in Chapter 16.

Corporal Punishment

Corporal punishment is not a legal sentence in the United States. The last statute to be repealed was the Delaware whipping statute in 1973. Recently, however, some scholars have argued for a return to corporal punishment as a less expensive, and more humane, punishment than incarceration. Graeme Newman, in his provocative argument for a return to corporal punishment, suggests that the "acute punishment of electric shock is easily demonstrated to be superior in every respect to our current punishment practices."

Newman describes a "typical occurrence in today's courtroom," involving a mother who was convicted of a third offense of shoplifting. The judge imposed a sentence of from 6 months to 1 year in a penitentiary and informed the defendant that her 3-year-old daughter would be "turned over to the care of the Department of Youth, since the presentence report indicates that you have no husband or relatives who could care adequately for her." Thus, an innocent child is punished along with her guilty mother. This, says Newman, is typical of our current system in that "literally thousands of people are punished for other people's crimes." In contrast, he suggests that in many cases the most effective and appropriate form of

Corporal punishment, once induced by the cat o' nine tails, could lead to death. (Bettmann Archive)

punishment is corporal, particularly electric shock. In Spotlight 12.3, Newman describes how this type of punishment might be implemented.

Newman's system involves two parts. First, acute corporal punishment would be administered for the punishment of *crimes* as opposed to *criminals*. The same amount of punishment would be assessed for each offense. Thus, we would be punishing that criminal act. Additional corporal punishment would not be given just because the offender to be punished also has been convicted of other criminal acts. On the other hand, we do need a system for punishing people who repeatedly commit criminal acts, and for those, Newman develops the second part of his plan: a prison-intensive system for criminals. In the prison-intensive system, the only possible prison sentence would be a long one, for example, 15 years. This sentence would be reserved for *criminals*, people who repeatedly break the law, although Newman does not specify what that involves. The decision, he says, would be made by each community.

Newman advocates the return to corporal punishment because he believes it to be a better method of punishment. We can, through modern technology, control the intensity and duration of electric shock. But we do not have such control over prisons. "Prisons work on a person's mind as well as his body." Newman believes that his system would deemphasize prison as a form of punishment yet maintain a system of appropriate punishment. The result would be a decreased need for prisons, resulting in a tremendous savings in the amount of money we spend on incarceration. Most important, we would have a system of punishment that allows us to concentrate punishment not on criminals per se, but on "free citizens who have exercised their right to break the law. In this way the most basic of all freedoms in society is preserved: the freedom to break the law."[23]

Now, an example of what punishment of the future could be like.

Twenty-year-old John Jefferson stands along with his lawyer, the public defender.

"John Jefferson," says the judge, "the court has found you guilty of burglary in the first degree. Because this is your first offense, but the damage you did was considerable, I sentence you to . . ." The judge pushes a few buttons at his computer console. The average sentence for similar cases to Jefferson's flashes on the display: it is five shock units.

"You will be taken immediately to the punishment hall to receive five shock units. Court dismissed."

The victim of this crime is sitting at the back of the court. He approaches the court clerk, who directs him to the punishment hall where he will be able to watch the administration of the punishment.

Jefferson's wife and child are ushered to the waiting room where they will await Jefferson's return after he has been punished.

Meanwhile, in the punishment hall, Jefferson is seated in a specially designed chair. As part of the arrest procedure he has already received a medical examination to establish that he was fit to receive punishment.

In addition to the victim, a few members of the press are seated on the other side of the glass screen. The punishment technician, having settled the offender in the chair, returns to an adjoining room where he can observe the offender through a one-way screen. A medic is also present.

The technician sets the machine at the appropriate pain level, turns the dial to "5," and presses the button.

Jefferson receives five painful jolts of electricity to his buttocks. He screams loudly, and by the time the punishment is over, he is crying with pain.

The technician returns and releases the offender. "Stand and walk a little," he says.

Jefferson walks around, rubbing his buttocks. A shade drops over the spectators' screen.

"Do you still feel the pain?" asks the medic.

"Goddam, I sure do! But it's getting better. Can I go now?"

"Just sign here, and you've paid your dues."

Jefferson sighs happily and asks, "Which way to the waiting room?"

"Straight down the passage and second left."

Jefferson enters the waiting room where his wife rushes into his arms, crying, "I'm so glad it's over! Thank goodness you weren't sent to prison."

Source: Graeme Newman, *Just and Painful: A Case for the Corporal Punishment of Criminals* (New York: Macmillan Publishing Co., 1983), pp. 42–43.

Capital Punishment

Another type of sentence that has been used extensively in the past is **capital punishment.** Over the years the use of capital punishment has changed, with abolition movements beginning in the eighteenth century, gaining momentum in the late 1800s, and leading to actual abolition of the penalty in many states during this century, only to be returned recently.

In 1972 in *Furman v. Georgia*, the U.S. Supreme Court held that although capital punishment is not per se cruel and unusual punishment, it constitutes such when, in its application, it involves unconstitutional discrimination. The Court, however, left the door open for new legislation providing for capital punishment if it is applied without violating the constitutional rights of defendants. By 1976, 36 states had responded with new capital punishment statutes, but some of those were also challenged in the courts. In 1977 the constitutional issues were satisfied in the case of the Utah statute; Gary Gilmore became the first person executed since 1967.[24] Figure 12.3 indicates the status of the death penalty by states as of 1987.

Data on Capital Punishment   In May 1979, after a long and complicated legal battle, John Spenkelink, convicted of murdering a man with a hatchet, was the first involuntary victim (Gilmore refused to appeal his sentence and asked that it be carried out) of capital punishment in the United States since 1967. Spenkelink was executed in Old Sparky, the electric chair in Florida. In recent years, the pace of executions has quickened. Compared to only 6 executions between 1976 and 1982 and only 5 in 1983, in 1984 21 people were executed. In 1985 the number dropped to 18. Use of the death penalty increased in 1986, with 297 persons sentenced to death and 18 executed. In 1987, 25 inmates were executed, but the number dropped to 11 in 1988. By the end of June, 1989, a total of 114 individuals had been executed since 1976, and the death row population had risen to 2,160. Of those, only 25 are females. Fifty-two percent are white; 40 percent are black; 6 percent are Hispanic, and 2 percent are American Indian. (See Figure 12.4 for the growth rate of death row populations from 1953–1987.)

The death penalty received widespread national attention in late 1988 and early 1989 before, during, and after Florida executed notorious serial murderer, Ted Bundy.

Gary Gilmore was executed by firing squad in Utah in 1976. (Akhtar Hussein/ Woodfin Camp)

Expressions of a convicted killer: Ted Bundy, executed in 1989 for the murder of Kimberly Diane Leach, but wanted for numerous other murders. He confessed to some of those murders before his execution. (Mark Foley/AP Wide World; AP Wide World)

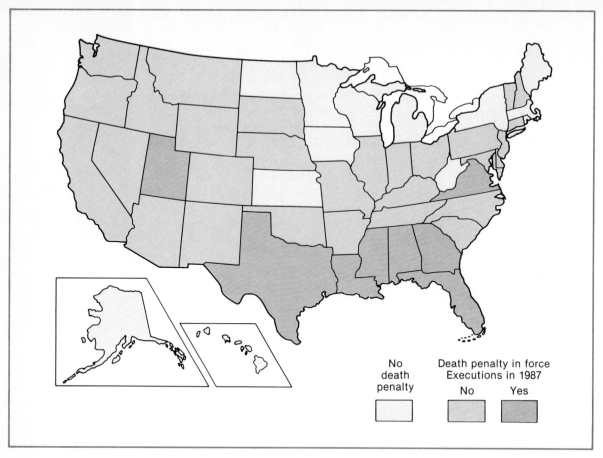

FIGURE 12.3
Status of Death Penalty as of December 31, 1987, and 1987 Executions. *Source:*
Bureau of Justice Statistics, *Capital Punishment, 1987* (Washington, D.C.: U.S.
Department of Justice, July 1988), p. 1.

The states with the largest death row populations in 1987 were as
follows: Florida (277), Texas (256), California (200), Georgia (116), and
Illinois (108). Most inmates are relatively uneducated, with 1 in 10 having
no more than a seventh grade education. The median level of education
was almost 11 years.[26]

Methods of Capital Punishment   People have been executed in many ways:
by ax, by rope, by drawing and quartering, by boiling, by gas, by electricity, and by firearms. Execution by firing squad is a frequently used
method in other countries today. In the United States the most popular
methods have been hanging, electrocution, and the gas chamber. Recently
attention has been focused on death by lethal injection. Oklahoma was
the first state to adopt this method, but it has not had any executions since
its adoption. Some states provide alternative execution methods, with

Two "modern" methods of execution: the gas chamber and the electric chair. Also popular today is lethal injection. (UPI Bettmann Newsphotos; David Burnett/Woodfin Camp)

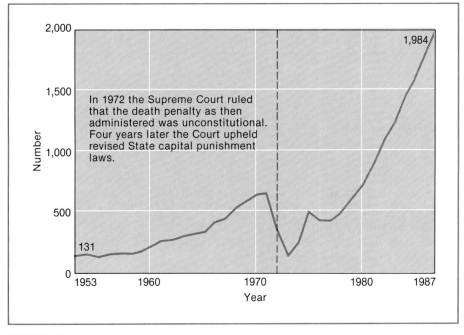

FIGURE 12.4

Persons Under Sentence of Death, 1953–1987. *Source:* Bureau of Justice Statistics, *Capital Punishment, 1987* (Washington, D.C.: U.S. Department of Justice, July 1988), p. 2.

TABLE 12.2

Method of Execution, by State, 1987

Lethal Injection	Electrocution	Lethal Gas	Hanging	Firing Squad
Arkansas	Alabama	Arizona	Montana	Idaho[1]
Delaware	Connecticut	California	Washington[1]	Utah[1]
Idaho[1]	Florida	Colorado[4]		
Illinois	Georgia	Maryland		
Mississippi[2]	Indiana	Mississippi[2]		
Montana[1]	Kentucky	Missouri[5]		
Nevada	Louisiana	North Carolina[1]		
New Hampshire[3]	Nebraska			
New Jersey	Ohio			
New Mexico	Pennsylvania			
North Carolina[1]	South Carolina			
Oklahoma	Tennessee			
Oregon	Vermont			
South Dakota	Virginia			
Texas				
Utah[1]				
Washington[1]				
Wyoming				

[1]Authorizes two methods of execution.
[2]Mississippi authorizes lethal injection for those convicted after 7/1/84; executions of those convicted prior to that date are to be carried out with lethal gas.
[3]Lethal injection authorized effective 1/1/87.
[4]Lethal injection authorized effective 7/1/88.
[5]Lethal injection authorized effective 7/29/88.
Source: Bureau of Justice Statistics, *Capital Punishment, 1987* (Washington, D.C.: U.S. Department of Justice, July, 1988), p. 5.

some permitting the inmate to select the method. Table 12.2 indicates the current legal methods by state.

Texas made history with lethal injection for execution. In the late evening of December 6, 1982, Charlie Brooks, Jr., one of two men convicted of kidnapping and killing a young auto mechanic, was strapped to a roll-away bed (called a *gurney*) and covered with a white sheet. After the prison physician examined Brooks' veins to see whether a catheter could be inserted, a technician inserted a tube through which lethal drugs were injected, resulting in Brooks' death.

Problems with a 1985 execution by lethal injection in Texas led the Department of Corrections to review procedures for this method. It took technicians about 45 minutes of repeated pricking of the inmate's arms and legs before they found a vein that was not damaged by drug abuse. Such problems underscore the belief that lethal injection is not painless. Others take the position that lethal injection is not painful enough. "It's too lenient," said one of the students who demonstrated the night of one Texas execution. "They've got to go out painfully."[27]

Incarceration or Confinement

A final type of punishment is confinement or **incarceration.** Offenders may be incarcerated in a jail or a prison or confined in a community treatment center. These facilities, along with the issues surrounding confinement and incarceration, will be discussed in subsequent chapters. It is important to this discussion of the sentencing process, however, to keep in mind that the sentence imposed is rarely the sentence served. This is because the U.S. system incorporates several types of discretionary release.

Release on parole is discussed in Chapter 16. Another method of release is a **pardon.** Although infrequently used, a pardon may be granted by the president (federal cases) or state governor (state cases). Pardons differ from parole (granted by a parole board) not only in the method by which they are extended but also in the legal effect on the inmate. Paroles usually are accompanied by conditions; violation of which may result in reincarceration. Parole is granted only after some time has been served in jail or prison; a pardon may be granted prior to incarceration.

A pardon may also be granted prior to conviction. Although this practice has been questioned, former president Gerald Ford pardoned former president Richard M. Nixon with regard to the Watergate scandal. In late 1988, President Ronald Reagan refused to pardon Oliver L. North, the former White House aide who was indicted and convicted of charges associated with the Iran-contra affair that occurred during the Reagan administration.

Another form of discretionary release is the use of **good-time credits.** These credits are earned for good behavior during incarceration and reduce the time served from the actual sentence imposed by the trial court. Although the amount of time reduced may be specified by law and thus not be discretionary, some discretion is always involved in awarding good-time credits.

Recall also that some states now permit the governor (or another designated official) to release inmates early when a designated population cap is reached. This is to permit confinement of new inmates without violating federal court limits on prison populations.

Among those requesting, but not receiving, pardons before President Reagan left office was Patricia Hearst, heiress who was kidnapped by the Symbionese Liberation Army in 1974. She served part of her prison term for an armed robbery in which she participated with the SLA. Today she is a private citizen, married to her former bodyguard and the mother of two children. (Don Spaek/Gamma Liaison)

TRENDS AND ISSUES IN SENTENCING

Two major trends have taken place in sentencing, and they are related. The first is the trend to reduce judicial discretion in the sentencing decision. The second is the trend toward determinate sentencing. Both are the result of a concern over the crime rates and concern with alleged disparity in sentencing. Both are controversial.

Sentencing Disparity

There is great concern about **sentence disparity,** but its meaning is not clear. Some use the term to refer to any differences that they think are unfair or inappropriate. Thus, the differences between legislatively determined sentences in two jurisdictions might be viewed as disparate. Others, who limit the term to the differences in sentences imposed by judges, might argue that the different sentences of Peter and Jane in this chapter's CJA illustrate sentence disparity. Some include any differences; others look to the circumstances surrounding the crime before determining whether sentences are disparate and take the position that the sentences of Peter and Jane are different but not disparate.

Sentencing disparity may stem from legislative, judicial, or administrative decisions. Sentence length may vary from jurisdiction to jurisdiction because legislatures establish different terms for the same crime. Legislatures also may differ in how they figure the time served; for example, whether they give credit for time spent in jail before trial or begin the sentence term at the sentencing stage. Furthermore, they may differ in whether a defendant with multiple sentences serves them concurrently or consecutively.

Legislative sentences may be disparate if within a system there are sentences that are considered unfair. Sentencing disparity may also result from decisions made by administrators. Prosecutors may have influence over the sentence imposed. In the plea bargaining process, the prosecutor may offer a deal that involves a lesser penalty for one offense if the offender will plead guilty to another or to several others.

Juries also have considerable discretion, even when they are not empowered to determine sentences. If they think that the judge will be too harsh or if they perceive that the legislative sentence is too harsh, the jury may refuse to convict. In that case juries have the ultimate power to decide sentences. Although the system of parole has been abolished in some states, where it does still exist, parole authorities have great latitude in deciding actual sentence length. Even when the legislature specifies by statute the percentage of a term that must be served before an offender is eligible for parole, the parole board still has the power to determine when, if ever, that person will be released before the end of the actual sentence.

Judicial sentences also are a source of disparity. Most of the recent changes in sentencing laws have been aimed at controlling or removing judicial sentencing discretion. But before we discuss these measures, it is important to consider the accuracy of the allegations of sentencing disparity.

Analysis of Sentencing Disparity   Numerous studies have been conducted on sentencing disparity, although the studies, certainly the earlier ones, did not always examine the variables closely enough to permit a distinction between differences and disparity.[28] Some researchers, however, were quick to argue that extralegal variables—such as race, ethnicity, sex, and socioeconomic status—determine sentence differences and, therefore, the differences represent sentencing disparity. The two variables most frequently considered have been race and sex.

Sol Rubin, in an earlier article, discussed several studies of differential sentencing and concluded that it was clear that blacks and whites are treated differentially when convicted of the same offense. Blacks are more likely to get longer sentences, more likely to be sentenced to capital punishment, and more likely to be executed.[29] In contrast, Edward Green concluded that, although variation in sentencing by race does exist,

> it is a function of intrinsic difference between the races in patterns of criminal behavior. The Negro pattern is a product of the isolative social and historic forces that have molded the larger Negro subculture.[30]

Other investigators have found substantial race differences in sentencing outcomes and concluded that the differences originate in the early stages of the sentencing process.[31]

In a more recent study of racial discrimination and sentencing, blacks were found more likely than whites to receive prison terms, to be represented by a public defender rather than a private attorney, to have high bail set, to be detained before trial, and to engage in plea bargaining. The investigators noted that sentencing differentials may occur because blacks are less likely to be released pending trial and are less likely to have a private attorney. Blacks also are more likely to face a more serious current charge and a more serious prior record. But, even when controlling for both legal and extralegal factors, claimed the investigators, there is a statistically significant relationship between race and incarceration.[32]

Not all scholars agree, and the debate continues on whether race is a factor in sentencing disparity. Researchers have also pointed out that even when the results do not indicate discrimination by race in sentencing, discrimination may occur at any of the stages before sentencing.[33] It also is argued that sentence disparity is related to the sex of the offender.[34] Some researchers say that women are treated differently at every stage in the criminal justice system and that this treatment is clearly sexist; that is, women are discriminated against because of their sex. Others say the system is more lenient toward women. Women get lighter sentences for the same offenses as men.

Darrell J. Steffensmeier, who has written extensively on the subject of women in the criminal justice system, reviewed the empirical evidence concerning differential sentencing of women and concluded that, although preferential treatment exists, it is of small magnitude. He argued that the "changing sex role definitions and the contemporary women's movement have had little impact on sentencing outcomes of either male or female defendants" and that the differentials by sex have been diminished recently.[35]

Solutions to Sentencing Disparity   Many solutions to sentencing disparity have been proposed, but most of the reform efforts have centered on two approaches: controlling judicial discretion and removing judicial discretion from the sentencing process.

Sentencing Guidelines   Some control might be exercised over judicial sentencing by establishing guidelines or requirements. Sentencing guidelines are seen as a way to control discretion without abolishing it, while correcting the extreme disparity that can result from individualized sentencing.[36]

Basically, guidelines work as follows. A judge has an offender to sentence. The judge may consider the offender's background, the nature of the offense, or other variables without any guidelines. The difference, when sentencing guidelines are used, is that the relevance of these variables may have been researched. The judge also has a benchmark of a reasonable penalty in these circumstances. The judge may decide it is reasonable in a given case to deviate from the guidelines; in that situation, reasons should be given.

This approach is based on an empirical analysis of what has been done in the jurisdiction, not a philosophy of what ought to be done. Researchers who reported on their evaluation of the use of sentencing guidelines in Cook County, Illinois, concluded,

> In the final analysis, sentencing guidelines based only on past experiences may merely reify past biases. . . . In fact, then, sentences have been altered according to a design that is untested by law and unverified by science.

But if judges do not change their sentencing practices in accordance with the guidelines, then what good are they?[37]

Sentencing Guidelines in the Federal System   After years of attempts, Congress finally revised the criminal code in 1984. Part of the revised code provided for the establishment of a federal sentencing commission, appointed by the president and charged with the responsibility of establishing sentencing guidelines. The commission appointed by President Reagan issued a preliminary report in 1986 and a final report in April 1987. The statute provided that if the Congress did not enact changes prior to November 1, 1987, the recommendations of the Sentencing Commission would become law on that date.

Despite serious controversy over the proposed sentencing guidelines, leading many federal judges as well as others to ask Congress to delay implementation of the guidelines, a delay was not granted; and the law went into effect as scheduled. In the few months following, several lawsuits were filed, challenging the guidelines. Some federal judges refused to enforce the guidelines. Others complained that the guidelines give the appearance of precision but only succeed in removing important judicial discretion. They do not achieve either of their goals: removing disparity and establishing sentences that are in proportion to the crimes for which they are assessed.[38]

More critical, however, are the constitutional challenges to the federal sentencing guidelines. Lower federal courts have split on the issues, but in early 1989, the Supreme Court by an 8–1 vote upheld the 1984 federal sentencing reform act.[39]

Sentencing Councils   Another proposal for controlling judicial sentencing is the use of sentencing councils. First used in 1960 in the Eastern District of Michigan, the sentencing council has been adopted by other courts. A study of sentencing councils in New York and Chicago indicated how they functioned. The councils in both cities met weekly. For each offender to be sentenced, the presentence reports were circulated. Each judge recommended a sentence, and judges met to discuss the case. After the discussion, the sentencing judge in each case made his or her decision. The recommendation of the sentencing council was advisory, not mandatory.

The New York and Chicago systems differed in that for New York all sentencing cases were considered and each case was brought before a panel of three judges. For Chicago, participation in the council was voluntary and each case went before the entire council of judges who participated. The researchers concluded:

> In each court the council is able to reduce about ten percent of the sentence disparity in the cases that come before it. In Chicago, since only one-third of the cases are brought before the council, the reduction in all cases is under four percent.[40]

Another study of sentencing councils, however, arrived at a different conclusion: for some offenses disparity increased and for others it decreased.[41] But one authority, after questioning the assumptions on which they were based, has warned that these two studies should "be accepted only with caution." The councils might not be expected to result in great reductions in sentencing differentials because they are advisory, not mandatory, he explained. But they might still be considered successful in that judges generally react positively to sentencing councils and find the experience to be valuable.[42]

Appellate Review of Sentences   Some jurisdictions have increased the process of appellate review of sentences, and some require that trial judges issue written reasons for their sentences. These reasons could assist appellate courts in reviewing the trial courts' decisions. Appellate courts, however, have traditionally deferred to trial courts on sentencing, and it is not likely that extensive changes will be made in that practice.

Determinate Sentencing

The second major proposed solution to sentencing disparity is the reduction or removal of judicial sentencing discretion, clearly the most popular approach today. It is manifested primarily in the adoption of determinate sentencing, although a brief look at the California approach indicates that discretion and flexibility remain in the determinate sentencing provisions.

One of the most rigid of the new determinate sentencing statutes is that of California, the state that pioneered in the indeterminate sentence and that used it most extensively. The California statute removes the rehabilitation philosophy and substitutes punishment as the reason for incarceration. It specifies that sentences are not to be disparate and that individuals charged with similar offenses should receive similar sentences. The judge may decide on the basis of aggravating or mitigating circumstances to raise or lower the presumed sentence, but written reasons must be given for deviating from the presumed sentence.

The California statute abolishes the parole board with its discretion to determine release, but it also provides that all releasees be placed under parole *supervision* for 1 year upon release. Good-time credits for good behavior in prison are still available to reduce sentence length. The law permits sentencing judges to add up to 3 years to a sentence imposed on a defendant whose crime results in great bodily injury to the victim.[43]

Analysis of the Return to Determinate Sentencing

Before passing determinate sentencing statutes, politicians and researchers expressed concern about the effects of the proposed statutes. It was argued that the perceived negative effects of wide discretion in sentencing would not be eliminated. Discretion (and possibly disparity) would still exist but would be more hidden, "through the informal manipulation of prosecutorial charges and the evaluation of inmate behavior through the allocation of credit time."[44]

Perhaps even more important, the public would be misled into thinking the system is more harsh than it actually is, that discretion and sentencing disparity have been abolished, and that crime is being deterred. This belief would give them an excuse to ignore the criminal justice system for another 10 years. As Norval Morris said in commenting at the State-wide Governor's Conference on the Indiana code, "Of course, no one expects these provisions to be enforced in the way they're written—they are simply for public reactions."[45]

Studies of the effects of the earlier tough drug laws in New York provide empirical evidence of the assumption that determinate sentencing laws may result in the use of wider discretion. When the discretion of judges in determining sentence length in New York was reduced, judges reacted with more dismissals, and judges and juries reacted with a higher acquittal rate.[46]

Some jurisdictions have attempted to remedy the displacement effect of discretion; others have tried to anticipate the problem and cope with it in the legislation for determinate sentencing. One example has been the attempt to eliminate or block plea bargaining as a mechanism for escaping the strict, determinate penalties. New York tried that approach by prohibiting plea bargaining for the more numerous, less serious offenses, but retaining it for the more serious offenses. The result was that, with less incentive to bargain, defendants more often demanded trials.

> The lesson from this experience was that rigid restrictions on plea bargaining could not feasibly be enforced without much greater disruptions to the criminal justice system than the state was prepared to tolerate.[47]

Another concern was that determinate sentencing would increase the actual time defendants spend in prison, creating problems in already overcrowded facilities. Research in California indicates that although there has been an increase in the use of imprisonment, the length of sentence has not been affected significantly by the determinate sentencing statute. Sentence length has increased during recent years, but researchers say the increase in sentence length began before the determinate sentencing statute was passed, so it is not the direct result of that statute.[48]

In Indiana, initial research found an increase in the length of prison term served,[49] but later research found a slight decline.[50] In North Carolina, preliminary estimates were that there would be "a slight overall decrease in prison time served for felonies with an increase for certain violent felonies being counteracted by a decrease for other more common felonies."[51]

Another concern with determinate sentencing is the long-term effect it might have on inmates. To the extent that prison populations increase, we can expect a significant negative effect on prisons and prison inmates. Most prisons already are overcrowded, and the results of that situation will be magnified by any increase in the number of prisoners that results from determinate sentencing.

Determinate sentencing might have other negative effects on inmates as well. If the reform efforts merely shift but do not remove discretion and if the use of that discretion by prosecutors (for example) is viewed as disparate and unfair, we can expect the same reactions from defendants and inmates as with their perceived judicial sentencing disparity. If good-time credit remains or if inmates may still be released on parole, with determinate sentencing these administrative decisions may become even more important and even more disparate.

On the other hand, to the extent that determinate sentencing is viewed as more just and fair, we may expect defendants and inmates to react more positively to their experiences in the criminal justice system. Lynne Goodstein and John Hepburn, in their analysis of determinate sentencing, found some evidence that inmates have a greater perception of fairness and equity under determinate as compared to indeterminate sentencing. As long as the determinate sentences are not longer than the actual time an inmate would serve under an indeterminate structure, many inmates prefer determinate sentences since it gives them the security of a more definite release time.

Goodstein and Hepburn, after emphasizing the importance of refraining from using determinate sentencing to enact other reforms (such as longer sentences and reduction or elimination of good-time credits), conclude:

> and given that determinacy is preferred by most prisoners and has been demonstrated to lead to no ill-effects on inmate behavior, it would be unreasonable to abandon it as another correctional failure. It has succeeded in providing management with better planning capabilities and inmates with a feeling of greater sentencing equity and release certainty. These limited impacts may be all that realistically should be expected.[52]

One final controversy over determinate sentencing centers around whether it will have a deterrent effect on crime. Many argue that it will, but this conclusion is questioned by the extensive research of Joan Petersilia and Peter W. Greenwood at the Rand Corporation: "Our analysis indicates that for a one-percent reduction in crime, prison populations must increase by three to ten percent, depending on the target population to be sentenced."[53] Nor is it at all clear that sentencing revision will affect the rates of recidivism once the inmates serving those longer terms are released.

Some methods of punishment have been held unconstitutional in the United States. Delaware was the last state to abolish corporal punishment at the whipping-post. (Bianca Adams Miller/ Culver Pictures)

LEGAL ISSUES IN SENTENCING AND PUNISHMENT

It is also important to understand the constitutional limitations placed on sentencing. The Eighth Amendment of the U.S. Constitution prohibits the imposition of **cruel and unusual punishment:** "Excessive bail shall not be required; nor excessive fines imposed; nor cruel and unusual punishments inflicted." Courts have decided many cases interpreting the phrase *cruel and unusual*. Only a few areas will be examined to illustrate the development of law in this area.

Methods of Punishment

Some methods of punishment are considered cruel and unusual regardless of how they are imposed. The Supreme Court has upheld capital punishment when imposed by "modern" methods such as electrocution or hanging. But the Court has also said that burning at the stake, crucifixion, or breaking on the wheel are not permissible. The Court has stated that punishments are cruel "when they involve torture or a lingering death."[54]

Proportionality

The Court has held that punishment is cruel and unusual if it is disproportionate to the crime for which it is imposed. This issue has been raised regarding the method of punishment and the length of sentence imposed. In *Coker v. Georgia*, the Court held that capital punishment is disproportionate to the offense of raping an adult woman.[55] The Court also held that the Eighth Amendment prohibition against cruel and unusual punishment means that the length of sentence must be proportionate to the offense for which it is imposed.[56]

The proportionality issue generally arises in cases of capital punishment and habitual offender or recidivist statutes that provide for an increased penalty once a defendant has been convicted of a number of offenses. The U.S. Supreme Court faced the issue in 1980 when the justices looked at the Texas statute permitting a life sentence to be imposed under the recidivist statute.

Rummel v. Estelle involved a defendant who had previously been convicted in Texas state courts and sentenced to prison on two separate occasions for two separate felonies. William James Rummel had been convicted of fraudulent use of a credit card to obtain $80 worth of goods or services and on another occasion of passing a forged check in the amount of $28.36. Upon conviction of his third felony, obtaining $120.75 by false pretenses, he received a mandatory life sentence. The Supreme Court held that the life sentence was not disproportionate to the offenses committed by Rummel and, therefore, did not constitute cruel and unusual punishment.[57]

In *Solem v. Helm*, however, the Court held that it was not permissible to impose a life sentence on a defendant who was convicted of a seventh nonviolent felony, passing a $100 hot check. The Court distinguished *Helm* from *Rummel*. In *Rummel*, the defendant had a chance for parole, but in *Helm*, the defendant was sentenced to life in prison with no possibility of parole.[58]

The Supreme Court held in *Pulley v. Harris* that in the process of sentencing in death penalty cases, a proportionality review is not necessary. This means that the state is not required to attempt to find out whether other similarly situated defendants also received the death penalty.[59]

Consideration of Aggravating and Mitigating Circumstances

In capital punishment cases, the Court has held that aggravating and mitigating circumstances must be considered before imposition of the death penalty. This means that the trial court must consider factors such as the circumstances under which the crime occurred, the propensities and character of the defendant, and the prior record of the defendant. Future predictions must be made on the basis of some objective standard, some concrete criteria. The sentencing body must set forth the reasons and review must be available. The Court thus requires an inquiry into the *causes* of the defendant's behavior before the death penalty is imposed.[60]

The Court continues to look at the implications of the requirement to consider aggravating and mitigating circumstances. More decisions can be expected on this issue, which the Court has also extended to cases involving prior convictions. In *Summer v. Shuman*, for example, the Court held that it is impermissible to have a statute requiring mandatory imposition of the death penalty for a murderer who is already serving a life sentence without parole.[61]

Arbitrary and Capricious Administration of Punishment

Capital punishment, or any other punishment that is not per se cruel and unusual, may become so if it is imposed unfairly. This issue also frequently arises in death penalty cases. In the 1972 landmark capital punishment decision *Furman v. Georgia*, the Court faced the issue of whether the capital punishment statute of Georgia was being imposed arbitrarily and unfairly. The justices described the imposition of capital punishment in Georgia as random, irregular, capricious, excessive, disproportionate, discriminatory, uneven, wanton, and freakishly rare. According to the Court, the death penalty was cruel and unusual because of the arbitrary manner in which it was actually assessed.[62]

The ruling in *Furman* does not preclude sentencing differences. The Supreme Court has specifically stated, "The Constitution permits qualitative differences in meting out punishment and there is no requirement that two persons convicted of the same offense receive identical sentences."[63] It does mean, however, that when differences are made, the government must show that they rest on some reasons other than categories such as race or sex.

Not all allegations of discrimination, however, are accepted by the Court. The issue of alleged racial discrimination arose in *McCleskey v. Kemp*, one of the most controversial sentencing cases before the Court in recent years. McCleskey, a black, argued unsuccessfully that his conviction should be reversed because empirical studies show the death penalty is imposed more frequently on black persons whose murder victims are white.[64]

In rejecting McCleskey's argument, the Court held that the study in question did not establish that the administration of the Georgia capital punishment system violated the Equal Protection Clause. The Court emphasized that in order to prevail McCleskey would have to show that the decision makers in *his* case acted with discriminatory purpose and that he did not do. A brief excerpt from the decision indicates the Court's reaction to the empirical study.[65]

McCleskey v. *Kemp*

[A]t most, the Baldus study indicates a discrepancy that appears to correlate with race. Apparent disparities in sentencing are an inevitable part of our criminal justice system. . . . In light of the safeguards designed to minimize racial bias in the process, the fundamental value of jury trial in our criminal justice system, and the benefits that discretion provides to criminal defendants, we hold that the Baldus study does not demonstrate a constitutionally significant risk of racial bias affecting the Georgia capital-sentencing process.

Criminal Intent and Punishment

Although we have already explored the *mens rea*, or criminal intent requirement for criminal convictions, it is important to note that this element takes on even greater significance in capital punishment cases. In 1982, in *Enmund v. Florida*, the Court held that it was cruel and unusual punishment to impose the death penalty on a person who aided and abetted a crime but who was not present at the murders. Furthermore, there was no evidence that Enmund intended to kill anyone.[66]

In 1986 in *Tison v. Arizona*, however, the Court upheld the death penalty when it was imposed on two brothers who did not actually kill but who watched their father (whom they had helped escape from prison) and another convict murder several members of one family. Although the brothers testified that they were surprised by the murders, they made no effort to assist the victims, and, with the two murderers, they drove away in the victims' car. The Court said the reckless indifference to human life exhibited by the brothers while involved in a crime was sufficient to sustain the death penalty.[67]

In *Tison*, as in many capital punishment cases, several justices issued strong dissents. It can be expected that with the close votes (frequently 5–4) in sentencing cases (particularly those involving capital punishment), the Supreme Court decisions will continue to arouse considerable controversy.

SUMMARY

This chapter began with a scenario followed by an introduction that raised the issue of the purposes of punishment and sentencing. The purposes of punishment were examined historically, emphasizing that rehabilitation is no longer a main reason for punishment in this country. Today the philosophies of retribution, or just deserts, and deterrence are the dominant reasons for punishment. This approach is embodied in the justice model, characterized by the reduction or elimination of judicial sentencing discretion and the reduction in the use of parole release from prison. Sentences are now longer and more definite, with some jurisdictions recognizing only the good-time credits given to inmates for good behavior during incarceration as sufficient reason for reducing sentences.

The sentencing process, ranging from the sentencing hearing to the formal stage of imposing the actual sentence on the convicted defendant, involves numerous procedural issues and problems. Recent criticisms that judicial discretion led to serious sentencing disparity has led some jurisdictions, including the federal, to make significant changes in the sentencing process as well as in the types of sentences imposed.

Sentencing charts that reduce judicial discretion are typical of the changes. The types of sentences imposed remain consistent, but the frequency of use changes over time. For example, fines and restitution or community service are frequently used today even with serious offenses in order to reduce jail and prison populations.

The law concerning types of sentences also continues to evolve. What at first may appear to be a great reform may be questioned legally. For example, increased use of restitution as punishment would appear to be a positive reform, but as the discussion noted, in the federal system at least, there are serious problems concerning implementation of the new restitution provisions. Courts have not agreed on whether the restitution provision is constitutional.

Corporal punishment illustrates changing attitudes about punishments. Corporal punishment was quite common in earlier days but more recently has been held unconstitutional by numerous federal courts faced with the issue, usually in prison environments. Yet, one authority, Graeme Newman, has advocated that a return to some forms of corporal punishment would be beneficial to the society and to criminals.

Capital punishment, however, captures most of the attention given by courts and others to punishment. The use of capital punishment as a sentence has increased, as has the actual carrying out of the sentence. Yet, over 2,000 inmates wait on prisons' death rows, while scholars and judges argue the relative merits of this punishment in a modern society.

Of the sentencing reforms that have occurred in recent years, perhaps the most controversial has been the federal Sentencing Commission's proposed sentencing guidelines, which became law on November 1, 1987. In January, 1989, the U.S. Supreme Court upheld the constitutionality of the statute.

Belief that sentencing guidelines and sentencing councils would be not be sufficient to eliminate perceived sentencing disparity led to a movement toward determinate sentences. The trend toward tougher sentencing may be a needed reform, but it is important to consider all of the arguments, pro and con, regarding this movement and what it can and cannot accomplish. Caleb Foote has concluded that "from a historical perspective, the current flurry of so-called determinate sentiment will turn out to be a fad, a minor and temporary irritant to a system irrevocably wedded to discretion."[68]

Others have concluded that, on many issues, the sentencing reform movement has moved sharply away from the philosophy and intent of the justice model on which it is based and that the "changes that have occurred bear only a superficial resemblance to the principles they purport to embody."[69]

It may be that too much was expected of sentencing reforms. Norval Morris, a noted law professor and authority in many areas of criminal justice, wrote a provocative article in which he warned,

> Sentencing reform is going to make only marginal differences in the incidence of crime and delinquency in this country. Nevertheless, it has large importance because justice and fairness matter greatly to our system.[70]

However, it is crucial that the reforms be evaluated carefully. It is possible that in our rush to change the system, we will institute reforms that do not achieve the purposes for which they are intended while eliminating any progress made by prior approaches. Leonard Orland's prediction might be true: "The new sentencing philosophy won't eliminate sentencing disparity, and it may seriously undermine our efforts to rehabilitate offenders."[71]

The final section of this chapter discussed some of the legal issues that sentencing raises. Sentences may be declared cruel and unusual and therefore a violation of the Eighth Amendment if they are not proportional to the crimes for which they are assessed; if they are imposed without consideration of aggravating and mitigating circumstances; or if they are imposed in an arbitrary and capricious manner to discriminate, for example, against racial minorities.

Capital sentences will be examined more carefully than others. Thus, it is not surprising that, although those who aid and abet others to commit crimes may be assessed the same penalty as that of the principal criminal, this will not always be the case in capital punishment. *Tison v. Arizona*, however, illustrates that when an accomplice is involved with others who commit murder, to the extent that he or she shows a reckless indifference to human life, capital punishment will be upheld.

This chapter concludes our study of what happens in the adult criminal court system. As we have seen, most people accused of crimes do not go through the entire system. But for the small percentage who do, and for a society that needs and deserves protection from property as well as violent offenders, confinement and incarceration have become the solutions. Whether they are adequate solutions will be the underlying issue in the next section.

1. Explain and distinguish *deterrence, rehabilitation, incapacitation,* and *retribution.* Explain how any or all of these philosophies of punishment and sentencing relate to the just deserts or justice model.

2. What is the difference between determinate and indeterminate sentences? How do they compare with mandatory sentences?

3. Is a sentencing hearing necessary? Is it required? What occurs in a sentencing hearing? What is the value of a presentence investigation? Should the PSI be available to the prosecution and the defense as well as the judge? Why or why not?

4. Should fines be used for punishment of violent offenders? Give reasons for your answer.

5. Should persons who cannot pay fines (or restitution) be incarcerated? What do the cases hold on this issue?

6. What are the problems with restitution and community work service?

7. What legal issues have arisen in the implementation of the federal restitution provision?

8. Discuss the trends in the use of capital punishment.

9. What is a *pardon?*

10. What is meant by *sentencing disparity?*

11. What effect will sentencing guidelines and sentencing councils have on judicial sentencing?

12. What problems have arisen with regard to federal sentencing guidelines?

13. Has the return to determinate sentencing been a wise move? Why or why not?

14. Under what authority is there a prohibition against cruel and unusual punishment in the United States?

15. What is *proportionality?* How does the concept apply to sentencing?

16. What is the importance of aggravating and mitigating circumstances for sentencing?

17. Should the Supreme Court in *McCleskey v. Kemp* have found unconstitutional discrimination? Why or why not?

18. Do you believe it is cruel and unusual punishment to impose capital punishment on someone who actually does not commit the murder in question? If you accept the Court's position in *Tison v. Arizona,* where would you draw the line? Under what circumstances would an accomplice *not* be appropriately convicted when he or she was involved in another crime but the principal committed murder?

ENDNOTES

1. "Get-Tough Approach Makes a Comeback," *U.S. News and World Report* (1 November 1982), p. 47.
2. "An Eye for an Eye," *Time* (24 January 1983), p. 30.
3. Ibid.
4. "Husband Faces Murder Charge in Mercy Killing of Wife," *Tulsa World* (20 March 1983), p. B6.
5. *Time* (13 September 1982), p. 38.
6. For a more detailed discussion of the indeterminate sentence, see Sue Titus Reid, "A Rebuttal to the Attack on the Indeterminate Sentence," *Washington Law Review* 51 (July 1976): 565–606.
7. For a discussion of the movement away from rehabilitation, see Philip Jenkins, *Crime and Justice: Issues and Ideas* (Monterey, Calif.: Brooks/Cole Publishing Company, 1984), pp. 169–87; for his discussion of retribution and deterrence, see pp. 143–68.
8. Andrew von Hirsch, *Doing Justice: The Choice of Punishments* (New York: Hill and Wang, 1976).
9. Ernest van den Haag, *Punishing Criminals: Concerning a Very Old and Painful Question* (New York: Basic Books, 1975).
10. David Fogel, ". . .We Are the Living Proof . . ." *The Justice Model for Corrections* (Cincinnati, Ohio: W. H. Anderson, 1975), p. 192, emphasis in the original.
11. Michael H. Tonry, "Sentencing: Allocation of Authority," in Sanford H. Kadish, ed., *Encyclopedia of Crime and Justice* (New York: Free Press, 1983), vol. 4, p. 1432.
12. Bureau of Justice Statistics, *Felony Sentencing in Eighteen Local Jurisdictions* (Washington, D.C.: U.S. Government Printing Office, May 1985), p. 2.
13. Williams v. Illinois, 399 U.S. 235 (1970).

14. Tate v. Short, 401 U.S. 395 (1971).
15. Bearden v. Georgia, 461 U.S. 660 (1983).
16. See Bradford v. U.S., 228 U.S. 446 (1913).
17. See "Fitting Justice?" *Time* (24 April 1978), p. 56; and "Do Not Go Directly to Jail; Pass 'Go'; Collect $200 and Repay Your Victim," *Student Lawyer* 8 (December 1979): 9; and *Student Lawyer* 7 (March 1979): 13.
18. See Richard C. Boldt, "Restitution, Criminal Law, and the Ideology of Individuality," *Journal of Criminal Law and Criminology* 77 (Winter 1986): 969–1022.
19. See Douglas C. McDonald, National Institute of Justice, *Restitution and Community Service* (Washington, D.C.: U. S. Department of Justice, 1986), p. 2.
20. See, for example, U.S. v. Palma, 760 F.2d 475 (3d Cir. 1985), and U.S. v. Johnson, 816 F.2d 918 (3d Cir. 1987).
21. U.S. v. Atkinson, 788 F.2d 900 (2d Cir. 1986). See also U.S. v. Brown, 744 F.2d 905 (2d Cir. 1984), *cert. denied*, 469 U.S. 1089 (1984). For a general discussion of restitution, see Boldt, "Restitution, Criminal Law, and the Ideology of Individuality."
22. "Prisoner Is under House Arrest in Move to Save Funds on Coast," *New York Times* (18 March 1979), p. 39, col. 3.
23. Graeme Newman, *Just and Painful: A Case for the Corporal Punishment of Criminals* (New York: Macmillan Publishing Co., 1983), pp. 42–43, 58–60, 64, 142.
24. Furman v. Georgia, 408 U.S. 238 (1972). For an interesting account of the Gilmore story, see the Pulitzer Prize–winning book by Norman Mailer, *The Executioner's Song* (New York: Warner Books, 1979). For an analysis of capital punishment see Ernest van den Haag, *The Death Penalty* (New York: Plenum Press, 1983).
25. "Society's Conflict on Death Penalty Stalls Procession of the Condemned," *New York Times* (19 June 1989), p. 11, col. 1.
26. Ibid., pp. 1, 5.
27. Quoted in "The First 'Humane' Execution?" *Newsweek* (20 December 1982), p. 41.
28. An excellent review of earlier studies and an analysis of the explanations may be found in an article on the general problem of discrimination in the entire system of criminal justice: Andrew Overby, "Minority Group Discrimination in the Administration of Justice," in Norman Johnston et al., eds., *The Sociology of Punishment and Correction*, 2d ed. (New York: John Wiley and Sons, 1970), pp. 261–70. For a more recent review and analysis of the literature on sentencing disparity, see Martin L. Forst, "Sentencing Disparity: An Overview of Research and Issues," in Martin L. Forst, ed., *Sentencing Reform: Experiments in Reducing Disparity* (Beverly Hills, Calif.: Sage Publications, 1982), pp. 9–34.
29. Sol Rubin, "Disparity and Quality of Sentences—A Constitutional Challenge," *Federal Rules Decisions* 40 (1966): 65–67.
30. Edward Green, "Inter- and Intra-Racial Crime Relative to Sentencing," *Journal of Criminal Law, Criminology and Police Science* 55 (1964): 356–58.
31. James D. Unnever, Charles E. Frazier, and John C. Henretta, "Race Differences in Criminal Sentencing," *The Sociological Quarterly* 21 (Spring 1980): 197–206.
32. Cassia Spohn et al., "The Effect of Race on Sentencing: A Re-Examination of an Unsettled Question," *Law and Society Review* 16 (February 1981): 71–88.
33. Margaret Farnsworth and Patrick M. Horan, "Separate Justice: An Analysis of Race Differences in Court Processes," *Social Science Research* 9 (December 1980): 381–99.
34. See Rita James Simon, "American Women and Crime," *Annals of the American Academy of Political and Social Science* 423 (January 1976): 31–46.
35. Darrell J. Steffensmeier, "Assessing the Impact of the Women's Movement on Sex-Based Differences in the Handling of Adult Criminal Defendants," *Crime and Delinquency* 26 (July 1980): 344–57.
36. See Leslie T. Wilkins et al., *Sentencing Guidelines: Structuring Judicial Discretion: Report on the Feasibility Study* (Washington, D.C.: National Institute of Law Enforcement and Criminal Justice, LEAA, 1978); and Wilkins, "Sentencing Guidelines to Reduce Disparity?" *The Criminal Law Review* 1980 (April 1980): 201–14.
37. John D. Hewitt, Robert M. Regoli, and Todd R. Clear, "Evaluating the Cook County Sentencing Guidelines: A Replication and Extension," *Law and Policy Quarterly* 4 (April 1982): 259–60, 261. For general discussions on state sentencing guidelines, see Cheney C. Joseph, Jr., "Criminal Procedure: Sentencing Guidelines," *Louisiana Law Review* 48 (November 1987): 257–91; and Honorable Daniel E. Wather, "Disparity and the Need for Sentencing Guidelines in Maine: A Proposal for Enhanced Appellate Review," *Maine Law Review* 40, no. 1 (1988): 1–40.
38. For a discussion of the constitutional issues involved in the sentencing commission and its proposals, see Lewis J. Liman, "The Constitutional Infirmities of the United States Sentencing Commission," *Yale Law Journal* 96 (1987): 1363–88.
39. Mistretta v. U.S., Nos. 87-7928 and 87-1904, 1/18/89.
40. Shari Seidman Diamond and Hans Zeisel, "Sentencing Councils: A Study of Sentence Disparity and Its Reduction," in Marcia Guttentag with Shalom Saar, eds., *Evaluation Studies Review Annual* 2 (Beverly Hills, Calif.: Russell Sage, 1977), p. 617.

41. Federal Judicial Center, *The Effects of Sentencing Councils on Sentencing Disparity*, Staff Paper FJC-SP-81-2 (Washington, D.C.: Federal Judicial Center, 1981), pp. 81–95; quoted in Michael H. Tonry, "Sentencing: Sentencing Councils," in Kadish, ed., *Encyclopedia of Crime and Justice*, vol. 4, p. 1484.
42. Tonry, ibid.
43. CAL. PENAL CODE, Section 1170 *et seq.* (1979).
44. Todd R. Clear, John D. Hewitt, and Robert M. Regoli, "Discretion and the Determinate Sentence: Its Distribution, Control, and Effect on Time Served," *Crime and Delinquency* 24 (October 1978): 444.
45. Quoted in ibid.
46. Kenneth Carlson, *Mandatory Sentencing: The Experience of Two States*, Policy Briefs, National Institute of Justice (Washington, D.C.: United States Government Printing Office, 1982).
47. Ibid., p. 15.
48. See David Brewer et al., "Determinate Sentencing in California: The First Year's Experience," *Journal of Research in Crime and Delinquency* 18 (July 1981): 200–31. See also Malcolm Davis, "Determinate Sentencing Reform in California and Its Impact on the Penal System," *British Journal of Criminology* 25 (January 1985): 1–30.
49. Todd R. Clear and John D. Hewitt, "The First Year of the Indiana Penal Code: Some Comments on Its Impact," Mimeographed (Muncie, Ind.: Ball State University, Department of Criminal Justice and Corrections, 1978). Cited in Stevens H. Clarke, "Sentencing: Determinate Sentencing," in Kadish, ed., *Encyclopedia*, vol. 4, p. 1443.
50. Richard Ku, *Supplemental Report: Case Studies of New Legislation Governing Sentencing and Release; American Prisons and Jails*, vol. 4 (Washington, D.C.: U.S. Government Printing Office, 1980); cited in Clarke, ibid., p. 1443.
51. Clarke, ibid., pp. 1445–46.
52. Lynne Goodstein and John Hepburn, *Determinate Sentencing and Imprisonment: A Failure of Reform* (Cincinnati, Ohio: Anderson Publishing Co., 1985), p. 175.
53. Joan Petersilia and Peter W. Greenwood, "Mandatory Prison Sentences: Their Projected Effects on Crime and Prison Populations, *Journal of Criminal Law and Criminology* 69 (Winter 1978): 615.
54. In re Kemmler, 136 U.S. 436 (1890).
55. Coker v. Georgia, 433 U.S. 584 (1977).
56. Weems v. U.S., 217 U.S. 349 (1910).
57. Rummel v. Estelle, 445 U.S. 263 (1980).
58. Solem v. Helm, 463 U.S. 277 (1983).
59. Pulley v. Harris, 465 U.S. 37 (1984).
60. See Baldwin v. Alabama, 472 U.S. 372 (1985); Eddings v. Oklahoma, 455 U.S. 104 (1982); Lockett v. Ohio, 438 U.S. 586 (1978); Zant v. Stephens, 462 U.S. 862 (1983); Barclay v. Florida, 463 U.S. 939 (1983).
61. Summer v. Shuman, 479 U.S. 948 (1987).
62. Furman v. Georgia, 408 U.S. 238 (1972).
63. Williams v. Illinois, 399 U.S. 235, 243 (1970).
64. McCleskey v. Kemp, 481 U.S. 279 (1987).
65. Ibid. For a discussion of the case, see "McCleskey v. Kemp: An Equal Protection Challenge to Capital Punishment," *Mercer Law Review* 39 (Winter 1988): 675–96.
66. Enmund v. Florida, 458 U.S. 782 (1982). The Court further explained this case in Cabana v. Bullock, 474 U.S. 376 (1986).
67. Tison v. Arizona, 481 U.S. 137 (1987).
68. Quoted in Frederick A. Hussey, "Parole: Villain or Victim in the Determinate Sentencing Debate," *Crime and Delinquency* 26 (April 1980): 221.
69. David F. Greenberg and Drew Humphries, "The Cooptation of Fixed Sentencing Reform," *Crime and Delinquency* 26 (April 1980): 221.
70. Norval Morris, "The Sentencing Disease: The Judge's Changing Role in the Criminal Justice Process," *The Judges' Journal* 18 (Summer 1979): 8–13, 50; quotation on p. 12.
71. Leonard Orland, "Is Determinate Sentencing an Illusory Reform?" *Judicature* 62 (March 1980): 381.

4 CONFINEMENT AND CORRECTIONS

After the processes of convicting and sentencing, society is faced with the problem of what to do with offenders. Historically, convicted offenders were treated informally by means of various psychological and physical punishments. Physical or corporal punishments became severe, however, and for humanitarian and other reasons some reformers decided corporal punishment should be replaced with confinement.

Confinement facilities—formerly used primarily for detaining the accused temporarily while they awaited trial or the convicted while they awaited corporal or other forms of punishment—were then viewed as places for punishment and reformation. Although many reformers saw confinement facilities as replacements of corporal punishments, others saw them as an environment in which offenders would be reformed through work, time for reflection, and in some cases corporal punishment.

The history of the emergence of prisons and jails as places of punishment is a fascinating study, but one laced with controversy, idealism,

and unfulfilled promises. This section traces that development from its early beginning through modern times. Chapter 13 focuses on the history and structure of confinement, pointing out the differences between state and federal systems, the different levels of security that characterize confinement, and the emergence of prisons as places for punishment. This chapter provides the background needed for an analysis of some of the procedures and issues surrounding modern correctional facilities.

Chapter 14 examines the administration and inmate life of the modern prison, looking particularly at the ways in which the internal structure of the prison may be used to control inmates. That control is not always successful, however. Prison violence is discussed in Chapter 15, which focuses on the reaction of federal courts to correctional facilities. Unconstitutional conditions of confinement facilities are examined in the context of recent federal court decisions. Part IV closes with a chapter on probation, parole, and community corrections.

Chapter 13. The History and Structure of Confinement
Chapter 14. Life in Prison
Chapter 15. Conditions of Incarceration: The Courts React
Chapter 16. Probation, Parole, and Community Corrections

The History and Structure of Confinement

OUTLINE

KEY TERMS

classification
community-based
  corrections
custody
humanitarianism
inmates
jail
offenders
penitentiary
prison
reformatory
silent system
transportation
warden
workhouse

Doug, a poor white man who grew up in the slums and who dropped out of school at age 12, has never worked a steady job for more than 2 months. He is convicted of his first felony, burglary, and is sentenced to 5 years in prison. Doug has no history of violence.

Steve, a rich white man who grew up in the most exclusive neighborhood of a large city, attended college for two years before committing a burglary, for which he is convicted and sentenced to 2 years. Steve has no prior criminal record but does have a history of violence among his family and friends.

Sonny has a history of convictions for criminal acts, but all were nonviolent. Sonny is a high-school graduate who has held a steady job for years. He is convicted of driving while intoxicated and sentenced to 2 weeks in jail. His wife, Bertha, who has a history of violence and a long criminal record, was convicted of armed robbery of a federally insured bank and sentenced to 10 years in prison.

Richard, vice-president of the local bank, is convicted of embezzling money from his bank, a federal offense and a felony. Richard, a prominent member of the community, is already receiving psychiatric treatment for his problems. He has no prior record. The federal court in which he was convicted sentenced him to 3 years in prison.

INTRODUCTION

The facts about the offenders in this chapter's CJA raise questions concerning how the criminal justice system will respond to their convictions and sentences. In each case it will be necessary to decide where the offender will serve the sentence. These hypothetical cases are designed to illustrate the differences between state and federal systems and the problem of deciding what level of security is needed in each case.

Two of the offenders, Bertha and Richard, were tried in federal courts because they violated federal laws. They will be incarcerated in the federal system unless that system contracts with a state for their incarceration. Richard probably will go to a minimum-security federal prison used mainly for incarcerating white-collar offenders. Placement of Bertha might be a problem because of the limited facilities for women in the federal system. She might be incarcerated in one of the federal co-correctional institutions.

Steve and Doug will probably be incarcerated in state prisons, but in each case a decision must be made concerning the security level required. Doug might be considered for minimum or medium security since he has no history of violence. Steven's case is more difficult since he has manifested some violent behavior but was not convicted of a violent crime. Sonny, who is sentenced to a two-week term, will serve his sentence in a local jail rather than a prison.

The decisions regarding where these offenders will be incarcerated should be related to the purposes for confinement. In the past, offenders were not confined for long periods of time. Lengthy confinements would have been impractical in a less populated world where formal police protection did not exist and where conditions were so unstable that populations moved from one place to another in search of food and shelter. Under those conditions, the punishment of persons who violated the norms of society was usually carried out by quick methods such as corporal punishment, or in extreme cases, capital punishment. Confinement was usually for very short periods while defendants awaited corporal punishment or trial.

If confinement is for holding a person until trial or corporal punishment, little attention need be paid to that confinement except to see that it is secure. The architecture, conditions, and administration will reflect the goal of security. If humanitarian reasons are not important, the conditions of confinement are relatively unimportant. Likewise, if the reason for confinement is to remove offenders from society and punish them for their criminal acts, then programming, treatment personnel, and prison conditions are unimportant. Prison is a place of custody and punishment; being there is the punishment. Prisoners are getting what they deserve as a result of their criminal activities.

However, if the purpose of confinement is to rehabilitate offenders, more attention must be given to the total program of confinement. Location of confinement facilities is important; facilities should be close enough to inmates' homes to enable family members to visit. Conditions of confinement are important because they are related to the rehabilitation of inmates. Treatment programs, educational and work opportunities, fairness in discipline, and many other activities behind the prison walls are important. Administration and management must reflect a treatment-rehabilitation orientation and, at the same time, maintain security within the institution.

This chapter will look at the historical development of the incarceration of offenders in prisons and jails as a method of detention and punishment. Throughout the discussion, the purposes of confinement discussed earlier—retribution, incapacitation, deterrence, and rehabilitation—should be kept in mind. The focus on one or more of these purposes is not necessarily chronological in the history of prisons, but the purpose will be tied to the type of prison that emerges.

THE EMERGENCE OF TOTAL INSTITUTIONS

Historical Development

The transition from corporal punishment to prison as punishment took place in the eighteenth century. In 1704 Pope Clement XI erected the papal prison of San Michele in Rome. In 1773 the prison in Ghent, Belgium, was established by Hippolyte Vilain XIII. In 1776 England was faced with a rising crime rate, the elimination of the need for galley slaves, and decreasing opportunities for **transportation** of criminals to her colonies. England legalized the use of hulks, which were usually broken-down war vessels.

By 1828 at least 4,000 convicts were confined in prison hulks. The ships were unsanitary, poorly ventilated, and vermin infested. Contagious diseases killed many prisoners. Punishments were brutal. There was little work for the prisoners; such idleness was demoralizing. Moral degeneration inevitably set in because of the "promiscuous association of prisoners of all ages and degrees of criminality."[1] This system of penal confinement in England lasted until the middle of the nineteenth century.

The spirit of **humanitarianism** that arose during the Enlightenment was undoubtedly among the reasons for the substitution of imprisonment for transportation, corporal, and capital punishment. People began to realize the horrors inherent in the ways **offenders** were treated. French philosophers such as Voltaire, shocked by what they called judicial murders, sought changes in the criminal justice system.

Voltaire was particularly moved by the execution of Jean Calas, who was convicted of murdering his own son. It was later discovered that the son had in fact committed suicide. Voltaire and his friends challenged the government to reverse the conviction postmortem. They led the fight for criminal justice reform. In 1777, from his own private funds, Voltaire doubled the honorarium to be given to the person who wrote the best essay on a new criminal code. "Voltaire and the Encyclopedists prepared the ground for the later success of Beccaria, who accomplished the most 'effective work in the reform of criminal jurisprudence.' "[2] Beccaria's contributions were discussed in Chapter 3 of this text.

Another important philosophical development in France during the French Revolution was the emphasis on rationalism. This approach was important in the history of prisons because of its influence on social and political philosophy. The philosophers believed that social progress and the greatest happiness for the greatest number would occur only through revolutionary social reform. Such social reform could be brought about only by applying reason.

It was logical that these reform ideas would flourish in the United States because many Frenchmen lived here during the French Revolution and many influential Americans had been to France. Since the Constitutional Convention was greatly influenced by the political philosophy of French philosophers, it is not unreasonable to assume that its members also were aware of the French social philosophy.

There are other important reasons for the rise of the prison system in America. The increasing emphasis on personal liberty meant that deprivation of liberty could be seen as punishment. In addition, after the Industrial Revolution there was an increasing need for labor that could be supplied by prisoners.

John Howard: The Great Prison Reformer   One of the greatest prison reformers of all time was John Howard (1726–1790), an Englishman who is often credited with the beginning of the **penitentiary** system. Howard traveled throughout Europe and brought to the attention of the world the sordid conditions under which prisoners were confined.

Howard's classic work, *State of Prisons*, published in 1777, was extremely influential in prison reform in Europe and in the United States. Among his other ideas, Howard suggested that prisoners should be housed alone in clean facilities and provided clean clothing. Women and children should be segregated. Jailers should be trained and well paid.

Emergence of the Penitentiary in America

The history of correctional institutions can be traced back to Roman, French, and English systems. But the unique contribution of America was the substitution of imprisonment for corporal punishment. In the eighteenth century the Quakers of West Jersey and Pennsylvania substituted imprisonment for corporal punishment. They also combined the **prison** and the **workhouse,** or confinement at hard labor.

This new system, called the Pennsylvania system, can be traced back to 1776 when the First State Constitution of Pennsylvania provided for criminal law reform. As a result, convicts were incarcerated in the Walnut Street Jail in Philadelphia. They worked at hard labor as a substitute for corporal punishment, and they were housed in solitary confinement. This **jail** was a model for the development of the Pennsylvania System, solitary confinement at hard labor; and the jail was visited by many foreigners who copied both the philosophy and the architecture. The Pennsylvania System embodied both theory and practice on such a large scale that it became world famous.

On September 15, 1787, Pennsylvania passed a law that reduced the number of capital crimes, substituted imprisonment for many felonies, and abolished most corporal punishments. A 1794 statute abolished capital punishment except for first-degree murder and substituted fines and imprisonment for corporal punishment in the case of all other crimes. The Pennsylvania criminal code reform set the stage for similar developments in other states.

Walnut Street Jail In 1787 in Pennsylvania, Benjamin Rush, Benjamin Franklin, and others met to discuss punishment. Rush proposed a new system for the treatment of criminals. This system included classification, individualized treatment, and prison labor to make prisons self-supporting. In 1790 a law was passed that established the principle of solitary confinement. The Walnut Street Jail was to be remodeled so that the philosophy could be implemented. Individual cells would be provided for serious felons. Other prisoners would be separated by sex and by whether they had been sentenced or were only being detained. This law was the beginning of the modern prison system in the United States, for it established the philosophy that was the basis for the Pennsylvania system and later the Auburn system.

The prisoners at Walnut Street Jail worked an 8-to-10-hour day and also received religious instruction. They worked in their cells and were paid for the work. Guards were not permitted to use weapons, and corporal punishment was forbidden. Prisoners were allowed to talk only in the nightrooms before retiring. This plan was followed in some other states with variations. But by 1800, problems with the system were obvious. Crowded facilities made work within individual cells impossible; there was not enough productive work for the large number of prisoners, and vice flourished. The Walnut Street Jail ultimately failed because of politics, finances, lack of personnel, and crowding. However, it had gained recognition throughout the world.

The Walnut Street Jail and other early prisons faced serious problems. Despite the thick walls and high security, prisoners escaped. To combat that problem, some **wardens** required **inmates** to wear uniforms; in some prisons the color of the uniform indicated whether the convict was a first-, second-, or third-time offender. Discipline was also a problem. Some wardens reinstituted corporal punishment; others used solitary confinement.

Funding was a problem in these early prisons, and facilities were needed for exercise. To alleviate these problems, work programs such as gardening were devised, but those programs were not effective. The inmates were neither reliable nor efficient, and administrators were not skilled in managing the labor situation. The result was that most prisons operated at a loss.

> By 1820, the viability of the entire prison system was in doubt, and its most dedicated supporters conceded a near total failure. Institutionalization had not only failed to pay its own way, but had also encouraged and educated the criminal to a life in crime.[3]

In response to these problems, two distinct types of prison systems were developed: the Pennsylvania, or separate system, based on solitary confinement, and the New York, or Auburn system, the silent system. These two systems were the subject of intense debate. Tourists flocked to see the prisons; foreign nations sent delegates to examine the two systems. By the 1830s the two American penitentiary systems were famous around the world.

The Pennsylvania System   With the failure of the Walnut Street Jail, solitary confinement at hard labor appeared a failure. Consideration was given to a return to corporal punishment. But in 1817 the Philadelphia Society for the Alleviations of the Miseries of Prisons began a reform movement that eventually led to a law providing for the establishment of the separate system of confining inmates in solitary cells without labor.

The first separate system prison was opened in Pittsburgh in 1826 and later was known as the *Western Penitentiary*. Because of the problems of idleness in this prison, the law was changed to permit work in solitary confinement before the establishment of the Eastern Penitentiary in Philadelphia. The design of its building eventually became the basic architectural model for the Pennsylvania system.

The Eastern Penitentiary, or Cherry Hill as it was called because of its location in a cherry orchard, was established in 1829. It was the first large-scale attempt at implementing the philosophy of solitary confinement at all times with work provided for inmates in their cells. The law that authorized construction of this prison clearly specified that although the commissioners could make some alterations and improvements in the plan used for the Western Penitentiary, the principle of solitary confinement must be incorporated.

John Haviland, the architect for Cherry Hill, was faced with the problem of creating a design that would permit solitary confinement but would not injure inmates' health or permit escapes. His solution was seven wings, each connected to a central hub by covered passageways. Each prisoner had a single inside cell with an outside exercise yard. Prisoners were blindfolded when taken to the prison and were not permitted to see other prisoners. They were not even assembled for religious worship. The chaplain spoke from the rotunda with prisoners remaining in their individual cells.

Before Cherry Hill was completed, it became the focus of discussion among prison reformers around the world. It became the architectural model for most of the new prisons in Europe, South America, and, later, Asia, but the architectural design was not popular in the United States.

The Auburn System   The prison system that became the architectural model for the United States was the Auburn system. In 1796 New York passed a law that provided for the building of two prisons. Newgate in New York City was first occupied in 1797. That prison soon became so crowded that as many prisoners had to be released as were admitted to make room for new inmates.

The Auburn prison was similar to Newgate, with workshop groups during the day and several prisoners to a cell at night. But discipline was a problem; so a new system, which became known as the Auburn system, developed. The Auburn system featured congregate working during the day, with an enforced silent system. The prisoners were housed in individual cells at night. The architecture created a fortresslike appearance with a series of tiers set in a hollow frame, a much more economical system than that of Cherry Hill.

The **silent system** was strictly enforced at Auburn. The prisoners ate face-to-back. They had to stand with arms folded and eyes down so they could not communicate with their hands. They had to walk in lockstep with a downward gaze. Strict regulation of letters and visits with outsiders and few or no newspapers further isolated them. Inmates were brought together for religious services, but each sat in a boothlike pew that prevented seeing anyone other than the speaker.

Discipline was strictly enforced at Auburn. The warden, Captain Elam Lynds, thought that the spirit of a person must be broken before reformation could occur. He was largely responsible for the Auburn punishment philosophy. It is said that he changed the discipline rules without legislative authority, instituted the silent system, fed the prisoners in their cells, and required the lockstep in marching. A committee from the legislature visited the prison, approved of the way it was being run, and persuaded the legislature to legalize the new system.

In 1821 a system of **classification** was instituted. It placed dangerous criminals in solitary confinement. Solitary confinement led to mental illness, death, and inmates' pleadings for work. A commission established to study prisons later recommended abolishing solitary confinement and putting all prisoners to work.

Comparison of the Pennsylvania and Auburn Systems   Architecture is extremely important in distinguishing the Pennsylvania and Auburn systems. The latter emphasized the congregate but silent system, the former solitary confinement. Both emphasized the importance of a disciplined routine and isolation from bad influences. Both reflected the belief that, because the inmate was not inherently bad but rather the product of a defective social organization, he or she could be reformed under proper circumstances. The discussions of crime centered around the advantages and the disadvantages of these two systems, but no one seriously questioned the premise on which both rested: that incarceration was the best way to handle criminals.[4]

The differences in architecture of the two systems resulted in differences in cost: the Auburn system was more economical to build, although the Pennsylvania system probably was more economical to administer. It was also argued that the Auburn system was more conducive to productive inmate labor and less likely to cause mental illness. The silent system continued until recently, not for the original purpose of preventing cross infection, but because it was easier to run an institution if the inmates were not allowed to speak to each other.

Both the Pennsylvania and the Auburn systems sound harsh today, but they must be viewed in historical perspective.

> The most that can be said for this period of American prison history is that, despite all its stupidities and cruelties, it was better than a return to the barbarities of capital and corporal punishment for crime. In the face of public indignation at the chaos existing in early American prisons in 1820, it maintained the penitentiary system.[5]

Emergence of the Reformatory Model

The disagreement over the Pennsylvania and Auburn systems eventually led to a prison system that emphasized reformation, a system characterized by indeterminate sentences, parole, work training, and education. Before looking at the emergence of that system in the United States, it is necessary to look briefly at the European developments that influenced the U.S. system.

European Background: The Contributions of Maconochie and Crofton   We look to the works of Captain Alexander Maconochie, an Englishman, and Sir Walter Crofton, an Irishman, for the beginnings of a reformatory movement. Maconochie began the movement in 1840 when he was placed in charge of the British penal colony on Norfolk Island. Norfolk Island, off the coast of Australia, was used by England for the worst offenders who had been transported from England to mainland Australia, where they committed further crimes. Maconochie was very critical of the system of transportation. England earlier had transported her criminals to the colonies in America. After the American Revolution that no longer was an option, so many were sent to Australia. The conditions of transportation were awful. Prisoners were chained together and in some cases had only standing room on the ships. Fevers and diseases were rampant; food was meager; sanitary conditions were unbelievable; homosexual rape and other forms of violence were rampant.

Upon his arrival at Norfolk, Maconochie began to implement his reformation philosophy. He emphasized that he was not lenient and that society has a right to punish those who break its laws, but

We have no right to cast them away altogether. Even their physical suffering should be in moderation, and the moral pain framed so as, if possible, to reform, and not necessarily to pervert them. The iron should enter both soul and body, but not so utterly to sear and harden them.[6]

Maconochie's reform program was characterized by his advocacy of the indeterminate sentence. He also believed that prisoners should work, improve their conduct, and learn frugality of living before they were released. While in prison, they should earn everything they receive. Their work served to remove the required number of "marks" each had to earn. When they were qualified by discipline to do so, they should work in small groups of about six or seven, with all of the prisoners answerable for the behavior of the entire group as well as of each member. Before they were released, while still required to earn their daily tally of marks, prisoners should be given a proprietary interest in their labor. They also should be subjected to less rigorous discipline in order to be prepared to live in society without the supervision of prison.

Maconochie was never given the authority that he thought he would have when he went to Norfolk. His ideas were controversial and not greatly appreciated by the British authorities, but he made many changes in the penal colony, and it was more humane when he left.

Maconochie described his accomplishments as follows: "I found a turbulent, brutal hell, and left it a peaceful well-ordered community." Evidence proved him right. But the controversy over his methods and philosophies led to his recall in 1844.

> He was replaced by Major Childs, an incompetent who sought to carry out instructions to restore the previous evil methods in place of Maconochie's reforms. This led, on July 1, 1846, to a revolt by some of the convicts, and four of the penal staff were murdered.[7]

Sir Walter Crofton, a disciple of Maconochie, applied Maconochie's reform ideas to the Irish prisons where he served as chairman of the Board of Directors. The Irish system was widely recognized for the following emphases:

1. A reward system—all advantages, including release, were based on rewards for good behavior.
2. Individual influence of the prison administrators on the prisoners—prison populations were to be kept small (300 in ordinary prisons, 100 in intermediate prisons) to permit this influence.
3. Gradual release from restrictions—restrictions were gradually removed until during the last stage, the intermediate prison, one-half of the restrictions were removed.
4. A parole system involving strict supervision after release and revocation for infractions of the rules.[8]

The American Reformatory: Elmira Sets the Stage   American reformers visited the Irish prison system in the 1860s and returned with great enthusiasm for their reformation philosophy. On October 12, 1870, a meeting, led by the penologist Enoch C. Wines, was held in Cincinnati, Ohio, to settle the dispute between the Pennsylvania and the Auburn systems. This meeting led to the organization of the American Correctional Association, then called the *National Prison Association*. The group drew up 37 principles calling for indeterminate sentences, cultivation of inmate's self-respect, classification of prisoners, and advancement of the philosophy of reformation not punishment.

The Elmira Reformatory, established in 1876, emerged from this meeting. This institution became the model for **reformatories** designed for young offenders. The architecture was similar to that of the Auburn system, but greater emphasis was placed on educational and trade training. Indeterminate sentences with maximum terms, opportunity for parole, and the classification of inmates according to conduct and achievement were the greatest achievements of this new institution.

It was predicted that Elmira would dominate the U.S. prison system. Elmira was established at the same time that other reforms, such as the juvenile court, probation, parole, indeterminate sentences, and others were emerging.[9]

From Reformation Back to Custody   The great contribution of the Elmira reformatory system was its emphasis on rehabilitation through education, which led to greater prison discipline, indeterminate sentences, and parole. But the system eventually declined, mainly because of the lack of trained personnel to conduct the education system and to carry on the classification system adequately.

A great increase in the prison population in the late 1800s resulted in overcrowding. New prisons were built, including Attica (New York) in 1931 and Statesville (Illinois) in 1925. Most of these followed the Auburn architectural plan and were characterized by increasing costs per inmate, Sunday services, a chaplain on duty most of the time, and insufficient educational and trade training. Trade training was based on the needs of the institution, not the interests or needs of the inmate. Insufficient funds were available for adequate personnel.

Those institutions did provide work for inmates, and the prison products were sold on the open market. This industrial period of prison history, however, irritated those in private industries, who complained that competition from prisons was unfair because of the low wages. In 1929 the Hawes-Cooper Act was passed, followed in 1935 by the Ashurst-Summers Act to restrict the sale of prison goods. These in turn were followed by state laws designed to do the same.

> With the passage of these laws, the Industrial Prison was eliminated. In 1935 for the great majority of prisoners the penitentiary system had again reverted to its original status: punishment and custody.[10]

MODERN PRISONS: AN OVERVIEW

U.S. prisons emerged as a substitute for corporal punishment; however, as pointed out in the next chapter, corporal punishment continued. Supposedly prisons emerged as places in which prisoners could be reformed.[11]

The early reform approach also was abandoned. According to David Rothman, reform was abandoned for several reasons. The change was not inherent in prison designs. Some disappointment was to be expected because of the great expectations the founders had for the success of the prison movement. Change also came about because of the resources drained from prisons during the Civil War. Additionally, the rehabilitation goal promoted but also disguised the shift from reform to custody. Too often, the administration of the prison assumed that incarceration was reformation, and no one recognized that reformation was lacking. The administrators would then relax their reformative efforts, and abuses of power arose within the prisons.

The nature of the inmate also affected the change from a rehabilitative to a custodial emphasis. The silent, segregated systems were not designed for hardened criminals serving long-term or life sentences. The founders who envisaged reformation of the offender had not contemplated what to do with the hardened criminal or the juvenile already committed to a life of crime. When the situation arose, **custody** seemed the best answer. The public accepted that approach because of the need for safety and security.[12]

The custodial institution also seemed the best way to handle changes in the composition of the inmate population. As cities became larger and their populations became more heterogeneous, including an influx of immigrants as well as distinct social classes, traditional methods of social control became ineffective. When those persons entered prison, custody seemed the best approach.

By the late 1800s it was clear that reformation was no longer a major goal of prisons. Later reports revealed corruption between guards and inmates, cruel punishment of inmates, overcrowded prisons with financial problems, and severe criticism of both the Pennsylvania and the Auburn systems. But prisons remained long after the original goals were abandoned. As hardened criminals were placed in prison for long periods of time, prisons turned into holding operations with wardens content if they could prevent riots and escapes.

Some reformers began to express dissatisfaction with incarceration per se, criticizing long sentences as counterproductive and large expenditures on prisons as foolish and unnecessary. Probation and parole were advocated but slow to be adopted. Most seemed content to incarcerate for the sake of security.

Why did the public stand for the decline of the original prison philosophy? Rothman suggests that part of the explanation might be that it usually is easier to capture public interest "with predictions of success than with the descriptions of corruption." Some may have believed that incarceration was synonymous with rehabilitation. But, said Rothman, the reasons went deeper. Many persons saw the prison as performing an important social function, for they noted that the majority of inmates were from the lower social class and many were immigrants. Few upper- or upper-middle-class persons were incarcerated.[13]

In recent years reformation or rehabilitation has been dealt a severe blow by researchers who claim that empirical evidence indicates that rehabilitation has failed. As previous discussions have indicated, some evidence of the rehabilitative ideal remains, but it is no longer the dominant purpose for punishment. It has been replaced by the just deserts model, with its emphasis on deterrence and retribution as the main reasons for punishment.

Many aspects of modern U.S. prisons will be examined in the next two chapters, which will demonstrate that "modern" prisons are characterized by disruption, violence, monotonous daily routine, lack of work opportunities, and unconstitutional living conditions. Many prisons are facing federal court orders to improve inmates' living conditions or be closed. Some readers will question whether these modern prisons are an improvement over the earlier ones. Others will say the question is not relevant; prisoners should be punished—just what the system is doing.

TYPES OF CONFINEMENT INSTITUTIONS

Offenders may be confined in various types of institutions. These institutions are classified in several ways.

Jails, Prisons, and Community Corrections: A Brief Comparison

Although the terms *jail* and *prison* are often used interchangeably and although the two types of institutions have many common characteristics, they may be distinguished by their purposes. Jails and detention centers are used for the detention of persons awaiting trial. They are also used for short-term detention of persons in need of care when no other facilities are immediately available. For example, a public drunk might be detained until sober or until arrangements are made for admittance to a treatment facility. Jails are also used to detain witnesses to a crime if it is thought that they might not otherwise be available for testimony at the trial. Jails are used for incarceration of persons sentenced to short terms, usually less than 1 year.

Prisons are used for the incarceration of offenders sentenced for lengthy terms, usually over 1 year, and for more serious offenses, usually felonies. A third type of facility is also used for confinement: a **community-based corrections** facility that houses offenders but permits them to leave during part of the day to work, attend school, or engage in treatment programs. Offenders may also be confined in special-purpose facilities such as treatment centers for abusers of alcohol or drugs, sex offenders, or the mentally ill.

Prison Security Levels

Prison security levels may be divided into three main categories: maximum, medium, and minimum security, as Spotlight 13.1 indicates. The federal government and most states have all three types; most prisoners are in maximum-security prisons. Characteristics of the security levels

SPOTLIGHT 13.1
PRISON SECURITY LEVELS

- Maximum- or close-custody prisons are typically surrounded by a double fence or wall (usually 18 to 25 feet high) with armed guards in observation towers. Such facilities usually have large interior cell blocks for inmate housing areas. In 1984, according to self-reports of superintendents, about 1 in 4 State prisons was classified as maximum security, and about 44% of the Nation's inmates were held in these facilities.
- Medium-custody prisons are typically enclosed by double fences topped with barbed wire. Housing architecture is varied, consisting of outside cell blocks in units of 150 cells or less, dormitories, and cubicles. In 1984, according to self-reports of superintendents, 40% of all prisons were medium security and 44% of the Nation's inmates were held in such facilities.
- Minimum-custody prisons typically do not have armed posts and may use fences or electronic surveillance devices to secure the perimeter of the facility. More than a third of the Nation's prisons are graded by superintendents as minimum-security facilities, but they house only about 1 of 8 inmates. This is indicative of their generally small size.

Source: Bureau of Justice Statistics, *Report to the Nation on Crime and Justice: The Data,* 2d ed. (Washington, D.C.: U.S. Department of Justice, 1988), p. 107.

---

will differ from one jurisdiction to another. As Spotlight 13.1 indicates, levels also differ in outside security and in architecture.

Many of the maximum-security prisons are old; 41 percent were built before 1925. During the first quarter of this century, most prisoners therefore were housed in maximum-security prisons, although many of the inmates did not require that security level. Unfortunately, this still occurs in some jurisdictions. Maintenance of these old maximum-security facilities is difficult and costly; many of the complaints about prison conditions

Security levels differ, but it is often difficult to distinguish prisons just by outward appearances. The prison on the left is a medium-security prison in Rhode Island. The one on the right is the Texas maximum security prison. (Bryce Flynn/Stock, Boston; David Woo/Stock, Boston)

The guard tower is deceiving. This prison in Connecticut is a minimum-security prison, with no guards in the tower and no guards on patrol. Inmates housed in this prison are serving sentences of under five years. (Norman Y. Lono/UPI Bettmann News)

that will be discussed subsequently are related to the problems of maintaining such old facilities. Maximum-, medium-, and minimum-security prisons differ in the emphasis on treatment and related programs and in the freedom permitted inmates. In maximum-security prisons, inmates are detained in their cells for longer periods of time and given less freedom of movement within the cell blocks than in the other security levels.

One further type of prison occasionally used is the open prison. Open prisons make use of the natural environment for security. An example is Alcatraz Island, located in San Francisco Bay. Called "the Rock" because the island is mainly rock, Alcatraz has been used for numerous purposes, including a military prison and a maximum-security federal prison. It officially became a federal prison on January 1, 1934, and its purpose was to incarcerate the most dangerous federal criminals.

The U.S. attorney general at that time described the prison as one that would make no pretense at rehabilitation. Rather, it would be a place for "the ultimate punishment society could inflict upon men short of killing them; the point of no return for multiple losers." Alcatraz was described by one writer as "the great garbage can of San Francisco Bay, into which every federal prison dumped its most rotten apples."[14]

Alcatraz incarcerated some of the most notorious federal prisoners, men such as George "Machine Gun" Kelly, a college-educated man from a prosperous family, convicted of bootlegging; and Robert F. Stroud, a young pimp who killed a customer after he attacked one of Stroud's prostitutes. Stroud became known as the "Birdman of Alcatraz" because of his knowledge of diseases of birds.

Men such as Kelly and Stroud were sent to Alcatraz because it was considered the most secure prison in the United States. It was assumed that no one could survive in the icy waters and current long enough to swim to San Francisco. There are no records of successful escapes, although on June 11, 1962, three convicts escaped and their bodies were never found.

The cost of keeping a prisoner at Alcatraz was three times as high as at any other federal prison. Major capital improvements were needed, and those would have been prohibitively costly. In early 1963 the U.S. attorney general, Robert F. Kennedy, flew to Alcatraz and announced that it would be closed as a federal penitentiary. On March 21, 1963, the prison was closed. Inmates were transferred to other federal prisons. After a period of occupation by Indians between 1969 and 1971, Alcatraz became a tourist attraction. Today it is the most frequently visited tourist attraction in the San Francisco area.

Alcatraz illustrates some of the problems with open prisons. They may be more secure, but they are costly and inconvenient. Land is scarce and it is difficult to find appropriate places for prison colonies. It thus is unlikely that the open prison will be used extensively in the future.

Women's Prisons

Until the late nineteenth century, women, men, and children occupied the same dungeons, almhouses, and jails. The institutions were plagued with physical and sexual abuses. Prison reform led to segregating women into areas of the existing institutions. There were few women inmates, however, and that was used to justify not providing separate facilities. Some women's sections did not even have a female matron. Vocational training and educational programs were not even considered. In 1873 the first separate prison for women, the Indiana Women's prison, was opened, with an emphasis on rehabilitation, obedience, and religious education. Other institutions followed: in 1877 in Framingham, Massachusetts; a reformatory for women in 1891 in New York; the Westfield Farm in 1901; in 1913 an institution in Clinton, New Jersey.

In contrast to institutions for men, institutions for women are generally more aesthetic and less secure. Women inmates generally are not considered high security risks. They usually are not as violent as male inmates. There are some exceptions, but on the whole the institutions are built and maintained with the view that the occupants are not great risks to themselves or to others. Women inmates usually also have more privacy than men while incarcerated.

Co-Correctional Institutions

Some jurisdictions have developed co-correctional institutions. One of the reasons for this development is the realization that women may not be receiving equal treatment in correctional facilities. Women's prisons are less secure and physically more attractive and comfortable; but they are

Compared to prisons for men, those for women are usually not as crowded; nor is inmate life as structured. But they also do not usually have as many programs and work opportunities. (David E. Kennedy/TexaStock)

A few prisons are co-educational. Here female and male inmates attend worship services together. (Michael D. Sullivan/TexaStock)

also geographically more isolated than institutions for men and have fewer facilities for educational and vocational training, as well as for medical, psychological, and psychiatric treatment facilities.

It has also been suggested that the sex roles exhibited in male and female institutions (aggressive macho in the former and family related in the latter) might be counteracted by a co-correctional institution. Some of the institutions were developed primarily to meet problems of overcrowding in existing facilities.[15]

Some states have opened co-correctional prisons. The most frequent reason for going coed is that prisons for men are overcrowded whereas only a small percentage of total prisoners are women. Spotlight 13.2 indicates that women constitute less than 5 percent of the national prison population but their numbers are increasing more rapidly than those of male inmates. Spotlight 13.2 also relates some of the positive results experienced in Illinois' coed prison.

SPOTLIGHT 13.2
COEDUCATIONAL PRISON EXPERIENCES IN ILLINOIS

Officials and inmates were wary when this state prison began housing women, as well as men, earlier this year. But of all the potential problems that crossed their minds, there is one that no one anticipated: how difficult it would be for the prison store to keep men's cologne in stock.

"We're acting more gentlemanly," said Charles Johnson, a 27-year-old inmate serving time for murder at Logan Correctional Center. "We want to look nice and smell nice, too."

72 Women Among Inmates

Logan, which began taking women in March to relieve overcrowding at the Illinois penitentiary for women, now has 72 women among 842 prisoners. While women have been imprisoned with men at work camps and minimum-security facilities, Logan is the nation's only coed medium-security prison.

In the last five years, the number of women in the nation's prisons has increased at a rate double that of men. And the number of coed prisons has more than doubled, to 89, in the last 10 years, said Charlotte Nesbitt, a spokeswoman for the American Corrections Association. Still, she said, women account for less than 5 percent of the nation's prison population.

"At first, I didn't like the idea of being in prison around men," said Marcia Kelly, who is serving time for a forgery conviction, as she sat in a library lounge next to Mr. Johnson. "But it's more normal this way."

So far, the biggest change at Logan has been improved behavior among the men, officials said, though there has been some grumbling from both men and women.

'Cleaned Up Their Act'

"The presence of women has seemed to have a calming effect on the men," said Stephen McEvers, the warden at Logan. "Most of the men have really cleaned up their act."

The presence of women among male prisoners has given guards new responsibilities as they patrol the grounds. At Logan, guards issue tickets to men and women observed holding hands or touching in a sexual manner.

At Logan, both men and women have complained that the guards are too restrictive.

"We've haven't caught anybody, per se, involved in sexual relations," said Mr. McEvers. But some inmates have been seen leaving bathrooms together. In those cases, the offenders have been transferred to more restrictive quarters in another prison.

"What would happen if somebody gets pregnant? — I don't know," said Michael Lane, the director

STATE AND FEDERAL PRISONS

Most of the prisons in this country are state institutions, but the federal government also has a large prison system.

The Federal System

The previous discussion of the emergence of U.S. prisons referred to state-supported prisons. The federal government contracted with states to incarcerate federal prisoners. The federal government did not have prisons until the 1900s, but one of the first acts of Congress was to pass a statute encouraging states to permit the incarceration of federal prisoners, at the federal government's expense, in state prisons. Federal prisoners with less than a year to serve or those awaiting trials were usually kept in local jails.[16]

(David Zalaznik/NYT Pictures)

of the Illinois Department of Correction. "I'm the last person to say it can't or couldn't happen."

Men Talk of New Problems

In some states, correction officials have turned to coed prisons to remedy inequities in programs. Prisons for men generally offer more educational programs than do those for women.

At Logan, some of the male inmates complain that the presence of women, with the extra scrutiny of guards, has made prison life more difficult.

"You put us into prison with women, and then tell us we can't be too close to them," said James Rich, who is serving his second sentence at Logan for

burglaries. "It's getting people into more trouble than they were in to begin with."

Homosexuality Seen Decreasing

Before women entered this prison, guards told officials they feared being "set up" by inmates claiming they were being sexually harassed. No such incidents have occurred here. Guards say their responsibilities have increased now that they must closely watch male and female inmates together. However, they pointed out that infractions for homosexual behavior have decreased since the introduction of women.

In training sessions for guards, prison officials stressed that "an inmate's an inmate's an inmate, no matter whether they're male or female," Mr. McEvers said.

But the men here contend that women are treated preferentially. Males must wear only prison issued undershirts and jeans, for example, while women are allowed to keep personal wardrobes.

At the women's prison in Dwight, inmates selected for transfer to Logan were initially unhappy about the move. "But now we're actually getting some volunteers," said Gwen V. Thornton, assistant warden at Dwight.

"Some of the men here treat you with respect, and others are ignorant jerks," said Elizabeth Ramirez, an inmate. "It's not that different than it is on the outside."

Source: "Women Blend in with Men at Illinois Prison," by Dirk Johnson. Copyright © 1987 by The New York Times Company. Reprinted by permission.

The Federal
Correctional Institution
in Pleasanton,
California. (AP/Wide
World Photos)

In 1870 Congress established the Justice Department, which had a general agent in charge of the federal prisoners in local jails and state prisons. That position was later called *superintendent of prisons*. The superintendent was in charge of the care and custody of federal prisoners and reported to an assistant attorney general in the Department of Justice.

Overcrowding in state prisons after the Civil War led some states to become reluctant to house federal prisoners; some states would accept only federal prisoners from within their borders. Transporting federal prisoners to other states was expensive. In 1891 Congress passed a statute authorizing the purchase of land for three federal prisons.

The first federal prison was taken over from the War Department at Fort Leavenworth, Kansas. The facility had been used to house military prisoners. It was quickly found to be inadequate for the federal system, and Congress authorized the building of a prison on the Fort Leavenworth military reservation. Federal prisoners housed at Fort Leavenworth built the prison. On February 1, 1906, inmates were moved to the new prison, and Fort Leavenworth was returned to the War Department. Final work on Leavenworth was not completed until 1928. Leavenworth was followed by the construction of federal prisons in Atlanta, Georgia, and McNeil Island, Washington, all prisons for men. These prisons followed the architecture and philosophy of the Auburn system.

The Federal Bureau of Prisons   Prison overcrowding, poor conditions, and inconsistent administration of prisons that were run primarily by local wardens led to the need for more organization in the federal system. On May 14, 1930, President Herbert Hoover signed the law that created the Bureau of Prisons. As Figure 13.1 indicates, that bureau is today a complex system, headed by a director who reports to the U.S. Justice Department. The bureau has a prison industries division as well as a research arm, the

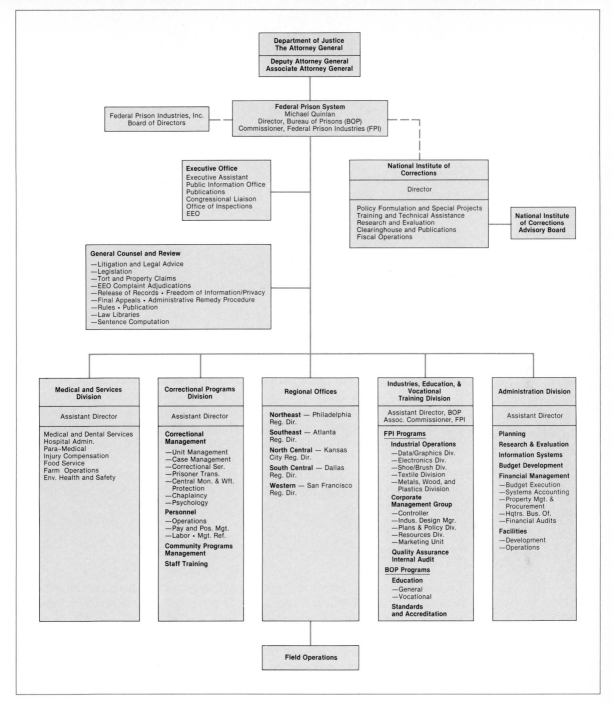

FIGURE 13.1

Federal Bureau of Prisons: Organizational Structure. *Source:* U.S. Department of Justice, Federal Bureau of Prisons, *Facilities 1984* (Washington, D.C.: U.S. Government Printing Office, 1985), p. 112.

National Institute of Corrections. The five regional offices of the bureau are located in Philadelphia, Atlanta, Kansas City, Dallas, and San Francisco. The bureau has an extensive legal department, as well as divisions overseeing programming, medical services, and administration.

In 1927 the federal system opened a prison for women in Alderson, West Virginia. Women federal prisoners also are incarcerated in the Federal Correctional Institution at Morgantown, West Virginia. Women with special medical problems are assigned to the Federal Correctional Institution in Lexington, Kentucky. The Federal Correctional Institution at Pleasanton, California, has a Children's Center and Pregnant Women's Shelter Home program for women who give birth while incarcerated in federal prisons.[17]

State Systems

All states have correctional systems, which generally are centralized and headed by a director who reports to the governor. The director is responsible for overseeing all correctional facilities. Most states have all three levels of security—maximum-, medium-, and minimum-security prisons—in addition to separate institutions for juveniles and women and treatment centers in the communities. Not all levels of security are available for women, however, because of the smaller number of female inmates.

States may contract with other states for the incarceration of some inmates. After a riot, it is not uncommon for inmates to be transferred to another state until the riot-damaged facilities are remodeled, repaired, or replaced. Such transfers may occur to remove the leaders of the riot. States may also contract with other states to house prisoners whose lives might be in danger in their own states. Such arrangements also might be made between a state and the federal system.

State prison systems differ considerably in size and complexity, as well as in conditions within prisons and administrative problems. Most of the procedures and issues discussed in the following two chapters will concern state prisons. State prisons also differ in the cost of maintaining prisoners.

Populations of State and Federal Prisons

In the past decade, federal and state prisons have experienced dramatic growth in population, as indicated in Figure 13.2. The 627,402 prisoners in 1988 represented a 76 percent growth in prison populations over the previous 8 years and a 7.2 percent increase over 1987. The state growth rate was highest in Rhode Island, Colorado, New Hampshire, Michigan, and California, in that order. Women inmates increased at a faster rate than men but still constituted only a small percentage (5.2 percent) of the total inmate population in 1988.[18]

J. Michael Quinlan, Director of the Federal Bureau of Prisons.

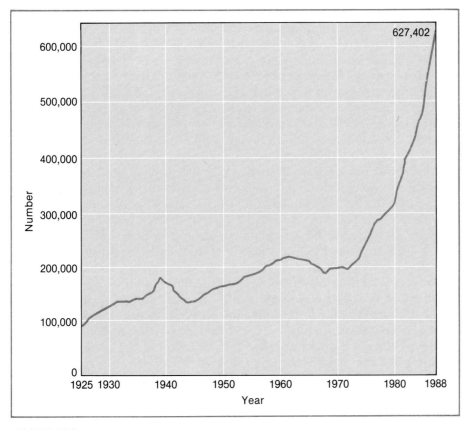

FIGURE 13.2
Number of Sentenced State and Federal Prisoners, Yearend 1925–1988. *Source:* Bureau of Justice Statistics, *State and Federal Prisoners, 1925–88* (Washington, D.C.: U.S. Department of Justice, October 1986). The 1986 data are from Bureau of Justice Statistics, *Prisoners in 1986,* published in May 1987.

LOCAL SYSTEMS: THE JAIL

Jails may be defined as "local (usually county) institutions used to confine individuals awaiting trial or other legal disposition, adults serving short sentences, or some combination of both." There are approximately 3,500 jails in the United States.[19] Jails are the most important facilities in the system of criminal justice because they affect the most people. The "jail is a major intake center not only for the entire criminal justice system, but also a place of first or last resort for a host of disguised health, welfare, and social problems cases."[20]

Jails can be traced far back into history when they made their debut "in the form of murky dungeons, abysmal pits, unscaleable precipices, strong poles or trees, and suspended cages in which hapless prisoners were kept."[21] The purpose of those jails, also called *gaols*, was mainly to detain people awaiting trial, transportation, the death penalty, or corporal punishment. The old jails were not particularly escape proof, and the person in charge often received additional fees for shackling prisoners. Inmates were not separated according to classification; physical conditions were terrible; food was inadequate; and no treatment or rehabilitation programs existed.

These early detention centers were followed in the fifteenth and sixteenth centuries in Europe by facilities characterized by work and punishment. These institutions were called *workhouses*, or *houses of corrections*. After the breakup of the feudal system, all of Western Europe experienced a significant increase in pauperism and public begging. In 1557, to combat this problem, a workhouse called the *Bridewell*, was established in London. The dominant philosophy at the Bridewell was a belief that if people had to work at hard and unpleasant tasks, they would abandon their wantonness and begging. The sordid conditions of jails and workhouses in Europe were brought to the attention of the world by John Howard, the great prison reformer mentioned earlier. After his tour of European institutions, Howard said in 1773 that more inmates died of jail fever than of execution.[22]

The first jails in the American colonies were places of confinement used mainly to hold those awaiting trial, those who could not pay their debts, and convicted persons waiting to be taken to prison. Jails only rarely were used as punishment. Most of the offenses for which people can be sentenced to jail or prison today were handled in other ways then: by corporal punishment, capital punishment, fines, or publicly humiliating activities such as sitting in the stock or pillory so people could jeer at the offenders. When the stocks were used, the victim's ankles were chained to holes in a wooden frame. The pillory was a device of varying shapes and sizes to which the offender was secured in several ways, one of which was to be nailed to boards. The pillory was often driven through town so that people could throw rotten eggs or vegetables at the offenders.

In the 1600s, to replace such severe punishments, Pennsylvania Quakers suggested what they considered to be a more humane form of treatment, the use of jails as punishment. Jails in this country thus came to be used not only for the confinement of those awaiting trial but also as places for those serving short-term sentences.

Whether jails are more humane than corporal punishment, however, is another issue. A federal court examining the facilities of a jail in Boston in 1974 ordered that it be closed because it imposed unconstitutional conditions upon the inmates. The court concluded that after familiarizing itself with modern correctional facilities, a serious argument could be made for returning to the system of corporal punishment, which at least ended at some point. There is serious doubt whether the harmful effects of prisons and jails ever can be erased from the lives of those who have been forced to endure this "modern, humane treatment."[23]

The horrible conditions of American jails have continued to develop over the years. In 1923 Joseph Fishman, a federal prison inspector, investigator, and consultant in the United States wrote a book, *Crucible of Crime*, in which he described the jails of the United States. He based his descriptions and evaluations on visits to 1,500 jails. He said that some of the convicted would ask for a year in prison in preference to 6 months in jail because of the horrible conditions of the jails.

According to Fishman most jails were characterized by the lack of space, adequate meals, bathing facilities, hospital, and separate facilities for juveniles. Although Fishman said jail conditions were terrible nationwide, the facilities were worse in the South. Fishman's conclusion might be summarized by his definition of jails as

> an unbelievably filthy institution. . . . Usually swarming with bedbugs, roaches, lice, and other vermin; has an odor of disinfectant and filth which is appalling; supports in complete idleness thousands of able-bodied men and women, and generally affords ample time and opportunity to assure inmates a complete course in every kind of viciousness and crime. A melting pot in which the worst elements of the raw material in the criminal world are brought forth, blended and turned out in absolute perfection.[24]

Jail Populations

National jail surveys were not conducted until 1972; they are not conducted yearly; and the analyses of the data are not published quickly. The national jail survey that followed the 1978 survey did not occur until 1983. The next jail census was scheduled for 1988, but the data were not published in time for this text. Some preliminary data through 1987, however, were available.

The 233,251 persons held in U.S. jails on June 30, 1983 represented 98 persons jailed for every 100,000 in the population, a 29 percent increase over 1978. "The 1978–83 jail population increase was more than three times larger than any prior change between censuses." The growth rate for women inmates was higher than that for men, a 65 percent increase versus a 40 percent increase. The largest jail populations were in California (which had over two-and-one-half times the population of any other state), New York, Texas, and Florida, in that order.

Approximately 50 percent of those detained in jail in 1983 had not yet been to trial, in contrast to those already convicted and serving a jail

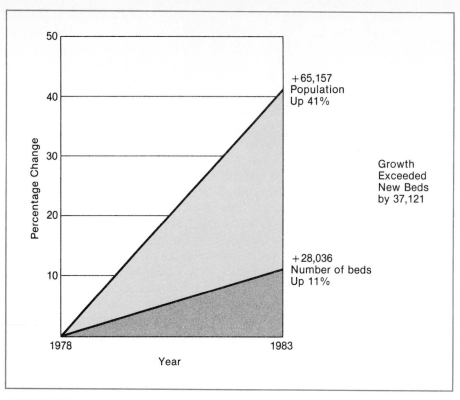

FIGURE 13.3

Jail Inmates: Population Growth v. New Beds, 1978–1983. *Source:* Charles B. DeWitt, National Institute of Justice, *New Construction Methods for Correctional Facilities* (Washington, D.C.: U.S. Department of Justice, March 1986), p. 3.

term. That figure was higher than the 1972 data, when only 42 percent of the inmates were pretrial detainees. Of jailed inmates, 7 percent were women, with 28 percent of those women incarcerated in California.[25]

Data available on jail inmates as of the end of 1987 indicate that 92 percent were men; 57 percent were white, 42 percent were black, and 52 percent were pretrial detainees awaiting their trials and thus not yet convicted. The average daily jail population was 290,300, which represented a 28 percent increase since 1983.

Approximately 26 percent of jail inmates were in jail only because the institutions to which they had been sentenced were overcrowded. They thus were waiting for space for their longer-term incarcerations.[26]

The growth of jail populations has far exceeded the growth of bed space for incarcerating these inmates, as illustrated by Figure 13.3, which compares figures between 1978 and 1983. As the following discussion will indicate, the cost of providing additional facilities is enormous.

Administration of Jails and Jail Standards

The typical jail in the United States is small (see Figure 13.4), built before 1970, and in need of renovation. It is located in a small town, usually the

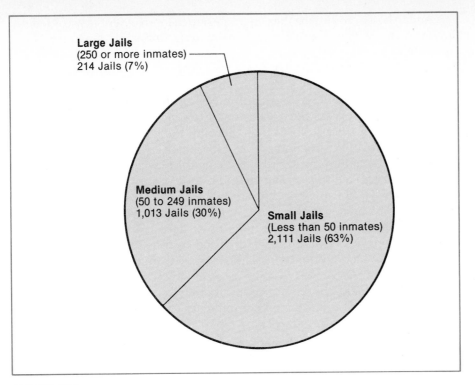

FIGURE 13.4
Jails by Size (total 3,338 jails in 1983) *Source:* Charles B. DeWitt, National Institute of Justice, *New Construction Methods for Correctional Facilities* (Washington, D.C.: U.S. Department of Justice, March 1986), p. 4.

county seat of a predominantly rural county. These small rural jails constitute the majority of jails but house a minority of the jail population. Some of these jails are seldom used; many are not crowded, in contrast to jails in urban areas. The typical jail is locally financed and administered.

Some states have assumed partial control of their jails and established statewide minimum standards. Professional organizations also have been involved with jail standards. In the 1980s, the American Correctional Association sponsored the organization of the Commission on Accreditation for Corrections. That commission has developed standards for jails. The commission certifies jails that meet those standards.

The Role of the Federal Government in Local Jails

Supervision or evaluation by states or professional organizations may not be sufficient to raise jail standards to an acceptable level. Federal courts have already become involved, and their actions will be discussed in a subsequent chapter in conjunction with court orders concerning jail and prison conditions.

The influence of the federal government on jails is also seen in other areas: federal technical assistance, financial assistance, and the imposing of standards. Three approaches characterize the movement toward federal involvement in local jails: the contractual, financial, and regulatory approaches.

In the contractual approach, the federal government provides services to local jails on a contract basis. This approach takes several forms. First, the federal government makes agreements with local governments to supply excess federal commodities such as extra blankets and other supplies for use in local jails. Second, the government has reduced the red tape involved in contracting with localities to arrange for federal prisoners to be held in local jails while awaiting space in federal prisons. Localities have liked this arrangement because of the money they received for temporarily housing the inmates. Third, the government has made available some money for local jails, under federal court order, to renovate their facilities. "In return, such jails must agree to guarantee to house federal prisoners for some specified period of time." Fourth, the government has provided technical assistance and training for jail personnel; some of which is free. Fifth, in some cases in which local jails face lawsuits by federal prisoners, the federal government will provide attorneys for the jails, provided those jails are in compliance with the Department of Justice's prison and Jail Standards.[27]

The financial approach began with the 1965 declaration of President Lyndon Johnson that crime was no longer a local problem; it was a national problem, needing infusion of national funds. Johnson created a presidential commission on crime. Congress passed the Law Enforcement Assistance Act and later passed legislation that provided for the establishment of the Law Enforcement Assistance Administration (LEAA). LEAA ceased to exist in 1982 after spending $7.7 billion.

During its existence, however, LEAA provided funds for improvement of jails; and the dissolution of LEAA "brought with it a rather abrupt end to anything approximating a substantial federal financial commitment to local corrections." Today the role of the federal government in local jails is continued on a much smaller level through the National Institute of Corrections (NIC), an agency created in 1974 "to help advance the practice of corrections at the state and local levels." NIC provides some grant money for research and development, but "its major direct link to individual jails is in training, technical assistance, and information dissemination."[28]

The third type of federal involvement in local jails is illustrated by the regulatory approach. Despite the reduction in federal funds to local jails, the federal government still maintains influence over the administration of local correctional facilities. This is done primarily through federal legislation, mandating requirements that must be met if local governments are to receive financial or other assistance from the federal government.

Other legislation may have an indirect effect on jails. In 1982 Congress passed the Alcohol Traffic Safety and National Driver Register Act, which, among other provisions, authorizes the Secretary of Transportation to "make grants to those states which adopt and implement effective programs to reduce safety problems resulting from persons driving while under the influence of alcohol."[29]

Many states have changed their statutes to provide stiffer penalties—in some cases, automatic penalties—for traffic violations involving the abuse of alcohol. In many cases the result has been a swelling of jail populations, leading some jurisdictions to resort to such methods as reservations for weekend jail time, use of motels or other facilities for serving jail time, or a backlog of months before convicted defendants are able to serve their sentences.

In 1980 the Department of Justice established detailed minimum standards for adult correctional facilities, including local jails. Those standards were interpreted as extremely important by the Justice Department of the Carter administration. Fulfilling the voluntary standards was a prerequisite to receiving certain federal funds and assistance. The Reagan administration, however, treated the guidelines only as suggestions.

The federal government has also provided states and local governments with assistance in building new facilities and remodeling existing correctional facilities. Coping with overcrowding, however, presents several problems.

PROBLEMS IN PROVIDING ADDITIONAL CORRECTIONAL SPACE

A survey of state and local correctional administrators, conducted by the National Institute of Justice, indicated that prison and jail overcrowding was seen as by far the most pressing problem for criminal justice systems.[30] Providing additional facilities, however, is a very costly measure. Some jurisdictions have responded to overcrowding by building new facilities; others have remodeled existing facilities, resulting in a corrections business that is one of the fastest growth industries in the United States.

Construction costs, of course, are not the only expenses to be considered. Operational costs of jails and prisons are high, and they continue to increase, outstripping the ability of many jurisdictions to cover the cost. Construction time also is a factor. Because many jurisdictions are under federal court order to reduce their prison and jail populations, they need immediately available space to solve the problem. Some jurisdictions therefore have sought faster construction plans and methods.

Location of new facilities is frequently a problem. Many residents do not want prisons, jails, or even community treatment facilities in their neighborhoods. A few years ago in York City residents complained so vigorously about a proposed jail in their areas that the term *nimby*, standing for "not in my back yard," was coined. Sometimes community resistance can be eased or eliminated by involving residents in the planning phase of the facility.

CORRECTIONS AND THE PRIVATE SECTOR

We have seen that prisons and jails are financed by federal, state, and local governments, and we have noted some of the problems in providing, maintaining, and operating these facilities. Costs of new facilities are prohibitive in many areas; renovations are quite costly, too. Many jails and prisons are overcrowded, but others are underused. They are located in very small areas, and they are outmoded. They are seldom needed, but when they are needed, they are essential. Many suggestions have been made for solving these and other problems. The most recent, and perhaps the most controversial, is to involve the private sector.

In March 1988, a White House commission recommended that the federal government turn over the operation of prisons, air traffic control facilities, mail delivery, and many other services to private businesses.[31] The chair of the President's Commission on Privatization described the agencies that now administer such services as "muscle-bound to the point of paralysis." But he also correctly predicted that it was unlikely that the recommendations of the 13-member commission appointed by President Reagan in September 1987 would be put into effect before Reagan's presidency ended.[32]

Correctional facilities have often had to rely on outside agencies to provide certain goods and services for the institutions, particularly jails and juvenile and adult community correctional facilities. Studies indicate this practice to be more cost-effective than would be the case if every institution provided every service and product that it needed. Medical service contracts are mentioned most frequently as more cost-effective than in-house medical services.[33]

Research by the National Institute of Justice indicates that the involvement of the private sector in corrections exists in three main areas: (1) prison work programs, (2) financing construction, and (3) managing facilities. The first, probably the one with the most promise, will be discussed in a later chapter. The second and third areas are important to this discussion.

In the past, jail and prison construction normally has been financed by governments with their current operating revenues and general obligation bonds. With decreasing government budgets and revenues and the increasing need for facilities, coupled with the rising costs of construction, this is no longer possible in many areas. Governments have in some instances thus turned to the private sector. The most popular method of private financing is the *lease-purchase*. Private investors gain tax advantages by underwriting the leases; they also get some cash flow from payments, along with an opportunity to transfer to the lessee some of the risks, such as insurance on the facility. It therefore is possible that private financing will be less expensive than bond financing. The practice is criticized because it enables governments to get around the debt ceilings and the requirements of referenda for the bonds to finance construction of new facilities. It therefore decreases citizen involvement.[34]

A second kind of private-sector involvement is the *confinement service contract*, in which the private sector locates the site for the facility, leases or constructs the facility, and provides the staff and services necessary for operating the facility. The costs per inmate are figured; that rate is paid by the government to the private vendor. This arrangement is used at all levels of government. Some facilities handle more than one type of service.

498

For jails, combining several small jurisdictions to use regional facilities also is a solution to some of the jail problems.

The involvement of the private sector in corrections raises many questions. Politically, it is argued that corrections is a government function that should never be delegated. To do so will increase problems, leading to lobbying for programs that might not be in the best interests of the public or corrections. The profit motive will reduce the incentive to decrease the number of people incarcerated. The profit incentive will encourage larger and larger private prisons. To make a profit, those facilities must be occupied. When the incentive for full prisons is combined with the public's call for longer and harsher sentences, the result may be more inmates serving more time.

Critics also believe that the government will not realize long-term cost savings. In addition to paying the per-day fee for more inmates and for more days in confinement, the government eventually will be forced to pay increased daily fees. If the government does not have its own prisons, it may have no alternative but to pay the fees set by the private firms.

Many other questions arise concerning private correctional facilities. If an inmate sues, will the government be held liable along with the private business? Should the government be involved in internal discipline or staff training? Will the short-term relief offered by private prisons turn into long-term, costly government obligations? Will public employees accept the presence of private staff? Will corrections administrators allow transfer of inmate control to private business? Will the public lose its voice in determining the location of private prisons?[35]

Although we do not yet know whether private prisons can exist successfully with traditional government programs, some believe there are definite advantages. The private sector can concentrate on special offenders. This may include women, juveniles, illegal aliens, or inmates who are at risk in the general prison population, such as child molesters, former law enforcement officials, or prison informants.

The private sector may provide an invaluable service simply by showing jail and prison officials that efficient and flexible management is possible in corrections, too. In most government facilities, competitive business principles, creative use of staff, adaptation of existing buildings and programs to meet changing needs, and experimentation with new ideas all seem to lag behind the private sector. Private involvement in corrections may encourage correctional administrators to modernize management styles, staff relations, and inmate care.[36]

SUMMARY

This chapter sets the stage for the next chapters, which discuss life in prisons, legal issues of prisons, and community corrections. It is important to understand the history of jails and prisons to evaluate what is happening today. The chapter therefore began with the European background of incarceration, emphasizing the reform efforts of John Howard. Howard was influential in America, but the Quakers led the movement toward incarceration, intended as a form of punishment to replace the horrible methods of corporal and capital punishment widely used here.

Two systems that emerged in the United States, the Pennsylvania system with its emphasis on solitary confinement and the Auburn system with its emphasis on the silent system, competed for recognition both in the United States and in Europe. The influence of the systems is still seen today; many of our maximum-security prisons, built in the late 1800s and early 1900s, reflect an architecture typical of the Auburn system. In Europe, many prisons built on the architectural model of the Pennsylvania system are still in use. The Elmira Reformatory did not survive long as a place of reformation, but it set the stage for the movement toward rehabilitation and established the reformatory model that became characteristic of institutions for juveniles.

It is impossible to talk about a prison system in the United States, because states have their own unique systems, local communities differ widely in their jail systems, and the federal government has its own system. The federal system generally is considered the most efficient and effective, and often provides a model for state systems. State prisons have been the sites of most of the riots and overcrowded conditions that will be discussed in later chapters. But many local jails also face problems of overcrowding and inadequate facilities, leading to the establishment of jail standards by the federal government, the American Correctional Association, and some states.

Problems of cost in building new facilities to handle the overcrowding of jails and prisons, coming at a time when many government budgets were being cut, has led to the involvement of the private sector in the financing and management of jails and prisons. This is a very recent and highly controversial innovation.

Inadequate conditions, overcrowding, and problems of management in jails and prisons increase the problems of living behind the walls, as we will see in the next chapters.

STUDY QUESTIONS

1. Trace the development of prison reform in Europe.

2. What characterized the emergence of prisons in the United States?

3. Compare and contrast the Pennsylvania and the Auburn systems.

4. What is a *reformatory*? Why were they developed?

5. What is the difference between prisons centered on a philosophy of custody and those on rehabilitation?

6. Distinguish between the state and federal prison systems.

7. How does the purpose of jail today compare to its historical place?

8. What are the problems associated with improving jail and prison overpopulation?

9. What is the place of the private sector in jails and prisons?

ENDNOTES

1. Harry Elmer Barnes, *The Story of Punishment* (Boston: Stratford Co., 1930), pp. 117, 122. The introductory material on the history of prisons is based on this source unless otherwise noted.
2. Stephen Schaefer, *Theories in Criminology* (New York: Random House, 1969), pp. 104, 105.
3. David J. Rothman, *The Discovery of the Asylum: Social Order and Disorder in the New Republic* (Boston: Little, Brown and Co., 1971), pp. 92–93.
4. Ibid., p. 83.
5. "State Prisons in America 1787–1937," in George C. Killinger and Paul F. Cromwell, *Penology* (St. Paul: West Publishing Co., 1973), p. 41.
6. Quoated in John Vincent Barry, "Alexander Maconochie," in Hermann Mannheim, ed., *Pioneers in Criminology*, 2d enlarged ed. (Montclair, N.J.: Patterson Smith, 1972), p. 90.
7. Ibid., pp. 91, 95, 96, 97.

8. Ibid., pp. 99–100.
9. Orlando G. Lewis, *The Development of American Prisons and Prison Customs* (1922); reprinted (Montclair, N.J.: Patterson Smith, 1967), p. 7.
10. "State Prisons in America," p. 53.
11. See Michel Foucault, *Discipline and Punish: The Birth of the Prison*, trans. Alan Sheridan (New York: Pantheon Books, 1977).
12. Rothman, *The Discovery of the Asylum*, pp. 238–39.
13. Ibid., pp. 243–53.
14. Francis J. Clauss, *Alcatraz: Island of Many Mistakes* (Menlo Park, Calif.: Briarcliff Press, 1981), p. 35. The brief history of Alcatraz comes from this source.
15. J. G. Ross et al., National Evaluation Program, Phase I Report, *Assessment of Coeducational Corrections*, National Institute of Law Enforcement and Criminal Justice (Washington, D.C.: U.S. Government Printing Office, 1978). Unless otherwise indicated, the material in this section on coeducational institutions comes from this publication, which was based on the first nationwide assessment of such institutions.
16. This history of the federal prison system comes from a publication by Norman A. Carlson, who at the time was director of the Federal Bureau of Prisons. See *The Development of the Federal Prison System*, supplied by the Federal Bureau of Prisons upon request.
17. Norman A. Carlson, *Federal Bureau of Prisons: 1984* (Washington, D.C.: U.S. Government Printing Office, 1985), p. 10.
18. Bureau of Justice Statistics, *Prisoners in 1988* (Washington, D.C.: U.S. Department of Justice, April 1989), pp. 1, 3.
19. Advisory Commission on Intergovernmental Relations, *Jails: Intergovernmental Dimensions of a Local Problem: A Commission Report* (Washington, D.C.: U.S. Government Printing Office, May 1984), p. 2.
20. Hans Mattick, "The Comtemporary Jails of the United States: An Unknown and Neglected Area of Justice," in Daniel Glaser, ed., *Handbook of Criminology* (Skokie, Ill.: Rand McNally, 1974), p. 781.
21. Edith Elisabeth Flynn, "Jails and Criminal Justice," in Lloyd E. Ohlin, ed., *Prisoners in America* (Englewood Cliffs, N.J.: Prentice-Hall, 1973), Chapter 2, p. 49.
22. Jerome Hall, *Theft, Law and Society* (Boston: Little, Brown and Co., 1935), p. 108. See also John Howard, *State of Prisons*, 2d ed. (Warrington, England: Patterson Smith, 1792).
23. Inmates of the Suffolk County Jail v. Eisenstadt, 360 F. Supp. 676 (D. Mass. 1973), *aff'd*, 494 F.2d 1196 (1st Cir. 1974) *cert. denied*, 419 U.S. 977 (1974).
24. Joseph F. Fishman, *Crucible of Crime: The Shocking Story of the American Jail* (New York: Cosmopolis Press, 1923), pp. 13–14.
25. Bureau of Justice Statistics, *The 1983 Jail Census* (Washington, D.C.: U.S. Department of Justice, November 1984).
26. Bureau of Justice Statistics, *Jail Inmates 1987* (Washington, D.C.: U.S. Department of Justice, December 1988), pp. 1, 3.
27. *Jails: Intergovernmental Dimensions of a Local Problem*, pp. 151–52.
28. Ibid., p. 154.
29. U.S.C., Chapter 23, Section 402, as amended.
30. Stephen Gettinger, National Institute of Justice, *Assessing Criminal Justice Needs* (Washington, D.C.: U.S. Department of Justice, June 1984), p. 1.
31. For a brief description of recent developments in privatization of prisons, see John J. Dilulio, Jr., National Institute of Justice, *Private Prisons* (Washington, D.C.: U.S. Department of Justice, 1988).
32. "Panel Urges Broad Privatization," *Dallas Morning News* (19 March 1988), p. 3A.
33. See Camille G. Camp and George M. Camp, *Private Sector Involvement in Prison Services and Operations*, Criminal Justice Institute for the National Institute of Corrections (Washington, D.C.: U.S. Government Printing Office, February 1984); cited in Joan Mullen, *Corrections and the Private Sector*, National Institute of Justice (Washington, D.C.: U.S. Government Printing Office, March 1985), p. 2.
34. Mullen, ibid., pp. 2–3.
35. Ibid., pp. 2–8. See also "Private Prisons," *Emory Law Journal* 36 (Winter 1987): 253–83, and "Privatization of Corrections: Is the State Out on a Limb when the Company Goes Bankrupt?" *Vanderbilt Law Review* 41 (March 1988): 317–41.
36. See Anthony P. Travisono, "Is 'For-Profit' a Wolf at the Door?" *Corrections Today* 47 (July 1985): 4.

Life in Prison

Karl, a 22 year-old college student from an upper-class family, is sentenced to prison for violating drug laws. Because of the extent of his involvement, he is sent to a maximum-security prison, although he has no prior record. Karl does not know anyone in prison. Karl weighs only 135 pounds and is 5 feet 6 inches tall.

On his second day of incarceration, Karl is approached by three inmates who rape him repeatedly. Karl reports these acts to officials who refuse to place him in protective custody. The next day, one of the inmates who raped him approaches him with a "deal." If you become my "sexual property," I will protect you from the other inmates. Karl agrees, believing he has no other alternative for protection from homosexual rape.

Anthony, 20, grew up in the slums of a major city, where he belonged to a gang of youths who frequently engaged in violent and other antisocial behavior. Anthony is given a 10-year sentence on his second conviction for aggravated assault and battery. Several of his gang members are already in the maximum-security prison in which he is incarcerated. Although this is his first incarceration, Anthony adjusts quickly to prison life, for his gang-member friends provide him with pro-

tection from other inmates. They also provide him some ties to the outside and a social group with whom he can spend his prison time.

Susan, a young mother of three minor children, is convicted of three counts of illegal drug possession. Susan is pregnant, but neither she nor prison officials know that; she became pregnant while in jail awaiting her trial. She is sentenced to 15 years in prison; but because the state in which she is convicted does not have a maximum-security prison for women, that state contracts with another state for her incarceration. She is 1,000 miles from her children while she is incarcerated.

Susan missses her children and feels inadequate because of her inability to care for them. She worries about giving birth in prison, and she is concerned about how this baby, fathered by a jail guard, will be cared for after birth. She has been told that she will be forced to give the baby up for adoption, but as the time of birth draws near, she knows that will be a very painful requirement. In her distress over her family, Susan, a very feminine person, is comforted by a woman inmate who is very masculine. The two develop a "family," consisting of a "husband" and "wife."

INTRODUCTION

The cases of Karl, Anthony, and Susan raise problems and issues similar to those raised by the hypothetical offenders in the CJA of the previous chapter. In that discussion, the concern was with categorizing the offenders to decide where they would be incarcerated. This chapter goes further and looks at what might happen to the offenders once they are incarcerated.

In a maximum-security prison, Karl's size and inability to protect himself make him a prime target for homosexual rape. One way to avoid that, however, is to succumb to the sexual advances of one inmate, who in turn agrees to protect Karl from others.

Anthony's previous connections with a gang, some of whom also are incarcerated and who already have adapted to prison life, provides him with social life and status. His gang friends provide Anthony with protection from other inmates. Susan, like most inmate mothers, must adjust to her frustration at not being able to see and care for her children. Susan faces the added problem of pregnancy and childbirth in prison. In her attempts to adjust to these and other problems, Susan turns to another inmate for comfort. They form a relationship that, unlike those of men inmates, may or may not be sexual but that simulates the family relationships they so desire.

Karl, Anthony, Susan, and other inmates must adjust to life inside prison. From the point of view of prisoners, imprisonment is a series of "status degradation ceremonies" that serve two functions: to destroy their identities and to assign them new identities of a lower order.[1] The way prisoners are treated when they enter prison exemplifies society's rejection; they are stripped of most of their personal belongings, given a number, searched, examined, inspected, weighed, and documented. To the prisoners, these acts represent deprivation of their personal identities. The actions may be conducted in a degrading way that further emphasizes their diminished status. They face the guards, who have contacts and families in the outside world but who are there to make sure the inmates conform to the rules of the institution.

Gresham M. Sykes has referred to the psychological and social problems that result from the worst punishment, deprivation of liberty, as the "pains of imprisonment." In his classic study of men in a maximum-security prison, Sykes discussed the moral rejection by the community, which is a constant threat to the self-concept of the inmate; the deprivation of goods and services in a society that places a high emphasis on material possessions; the deprivation of heterosexual relationships and the resulting threat to his masculinity; and the deprivation of security in an inmate population where he faces threats to his safety and sometimes to his health and life.[2]

In their attempts to adjust to the pains of imprisonment, inmates devise ways of manipulating their environment. Sometimes this manipulation creates serious problems of control, thus presenting the guards, staff, and administrators with their greatest problem: control of the population. Regardless of their views on retribution, just deserts, rehabilitation, or deterrence, prison officials are charged with the ultimate responsibility of maintaining safety and order within the prison and keeping inmates from escaping. This is not an easy charge, and the problems are becoming more serious.

This chapter examines the roles of prison administrators and guards, charged with the responsibility of maintaining prisons. It discusses the interaction of their roles with those of inmates. We begin by examining the administration of prisons, both in historical context and in view of more recent developments. The main focus of this chapter, however, is on the people who live behind the walls twenty-four hours a day.

ADMINISTRATION OF PRISONS

Prison systems have a director, who reports to the governor or a corrections board. In the federal system, the director reports to the United States

Attorney General's Office. The average period of service for a corrections director is 4 years and 7 months. This is a high-pressure job, with the director responsible for all adult institutions within the system.

Prison directors hire and fire wardens or superintendents of the various institutions and manage the correctional agency's central staff. Preparing and managing a budget is one of the most important functions of the director. He or she has to justify to the legislature the need for additional funds for running the prisons; a difficult problem today, with so many states facing budget cuts while prison populations continue to increase.

The job of director or head of the state (or federal) department of corrections is a very important one, but the day-to-day administration of adult prisons is the responsibility of the warden or superintendent of each institution. It therefore is important to consider the position of warden.

Historical Background: The Authoritarian Warden

In the early prisons, **wardens** had great power. Although some exercised control as the result of strong personalities, most of the wardens controlled their institutions with the authority that came from their positions. The strict chain of command from the warden down to the inmates was emphasized by the military atmosphere of most institutions: the wearing of uniforms, the use of job titles, lock-step marching, and total deference to the warden and his staff. Strict discipline, and in some cases, corporal punishment, were part of that traditional, authoritarian management style.

The authoritarian warden of earlier prisons also exercised an authoritarian management style in his interaction with his staff. He had total authority to hire and fire the staff, and he required their undivided loyalty. Loyalty was more important than competence in determining who worked for the warden. The warden also controlled the resources of the institution. Most wardens lived on the grounds of the institution, and the warden's household budget was included in that of the prison.

The authoritarian style of management may be found in some prisons today, but it is more difficult for wardens to manage in this way because of the recognition of the legal rights of guards and inmates. This, however, was the predominant style of prison management until the middle of this century. The earlier classic studies of prisons emphasized this style of management, the warden with the iron hand, who saw as his mission keeping order, social control, and respect.[3]

The authoritarian method of prison administration is illustrated by James B. Jacob's sociological study of Illinois' Stateville prison.[4] For 30 years, Joseph E. Ragen was Stateville's warden. A former sheriff of a small Illinois town, Ragen had only a ninth-grade education. Ragen personally exercised control over even minute details of prison life and administration. Ragen established a prison so orderly and efficient that it became known throughout the world. Ragen demanded absolute loyalty from those who worked for him. Their reactions and feelings were characterized

Alcatraz, separated from land by the bitter cold waters and strong current of San Francisco bay, symbolized the early American prison system of high security and authoritarian wardens. (UPI Bettmann News)

as ranging from love and respect to fear and deep resentment, from intense loyalty to a feeling that Ragen was arbitrary and authoritarian.

Ragen imposed severe rules on inmates and guards. For the inmates, the **silent system** was enforced in dining halls and wherever they were marching. When the emphasis on prison reform and concern for inmates began spreading across the country in the mid-1950s, Ragen simply redefined his system of total control by calling it *rehabilitation*. Contact with the outside world was carefully monitored. Inmates who defied the warden, and especially those who tried to complain to the outside world, were beaten or placed in solitary confinement or segregation, sometimes for years.

In 1961 Ragen left Stateville to become the director of public safety in Illinois. In that position, he was in charge of managing the entire Illinois prison system. He appointed many of his people from Stateville to high positions in the system. His loyal assistant warden became warden at Stateville. Ragen left behind him a 132-page rule book that codified his system, and until 1965 that book still ruled the institution. Ragen himself spent considerable time there, in essence still controlling the prison.

In 1965 Ragen became ill and apparently had a mental breakdown. He had to resign and was replaced by a rival of several years, Ross Randolph, who relaxed prison rules considerably. Shortly after Randolph took over Stateville, changes within the prison began to affect the ability of officials to continue managing the prison successfully under the traditional authoritarian model of management. The 1962 revision of the Illinois Criminal Code resulted in shorter sentences and thus greater turnover of inmates. The proportion of minority inmates increased significantly. These changes led to the disintegration of the traditional inmate social system, discussed later in this chapter.

Black nationalism and other movements were on the upswing, and inmates were less willing to accept the authoritarian system they had experienced earlier. The institution became more bureaucratic. Problems developed between the prison administrators and those of the newly created state department of corrections. Conflict also arose between the security-oriented guards and the new treatment-oriented personnel.

When Jacobs completed his study of Stateville, he indicated that the last stage of the institution, which he called the *stage of restoration*, was characterized by a strengthening of security, improved services, and improved morale of guards. A later report concluded that the internal problems at Stateville were not solved. In 1978, 2,000 inmates at the institution held a Christmas party in violation of prison rules. Inmates drank homemade liquor, smoked marijuana, and roamed freely about the institution. According to one report,

> No guard dared to stop them. To many observers, this Christmas party symbolized the ultimate degradation of Stateville, one of the world's most famous prisons and once an international model for discipline. It marked the administration's defeat in a ten-year battle to control the institution, a period of struggle that had left the prison a hellhole for both inmates and staff.[5]

The Modern Prison: A Need to Reassess Methods of Administration and Management

During the 1970s, significant changes took place at Stateville and other American prisons. First, there were demographic changes. Harsh drug laws led to the incarceration of more young people (some from the middle class) with drug problems. The percentage of prison population that was poor, black, and urban increased.

Attempts to crack down on gang activity resulted in greater numbers of gang members in prison. These gang members maintained close ties to their members outside prison. Increased politicalization within prisons occurred as the younger, more radical prison population viewed incarceration as a political process. They looked with disdain upon the traditional rewards the guards might offer in exchange for their cooperation.[6]

A second factor that precipitated change during the 1970s was the warden's decreased power. Inmates and guards no longer were willing to accept the authoritarian style of governance, and their rejection of that style has been supported by federal court orders. Court decisions that required changes in the physical conditions of prison, as well as provision of due process in some correctional proceedings, reduced the traditional power of prison administrators.

There are numerous obstacles to significant changes in prison management, however. First, each social group within the prison has its own set of values, which often are in conflict. Second, the conflict between the goals of custody and rehabilitation still exists. Third, there are insufficient facts on which to base decisions. Part of this results from a lack of research, a lack of evaluation of treatment programs, and a lack of knowledge about applicability of new management techniques to prison settings. With a lack of knowledge of treatment and management, the prison administrator tends to fall back on rule books and manuals, which are likely to produce a more rigid and authoritarian type of organization.

Finally, prisons continue to be faced with serious financial problems, which have reduced expenditures for management training programs and resulted in an inability to recruit trained persons at competitive salaries. The result is that the person who becomes a correctional manager without being professionally trained in management often is afraid to take the risks necessary for significant change. This type of manager, who has been described as "bureaucratically impotent," has learned over the years how to manipulate those who are in a position to judge the manager and the prison's programs. Consequently, few people ever learn what is really going on in prison until there is a real crisis, such as a riot.[7]

Some signs of progress are evident in the area of corrections management. First, more institutions are implementing research techniques to measure the success of programs and evaluation strategies for personnel. Therefore, an increasing amount of information is available to correctional managers. Second, professional organizations are developing standards for criminal justice administration, including corrections. These standards reflect a general concern with effective management. More important, the standards being developed by correctional managers in the field may be more responsive to problems and more acceptable to administrators.[8]

A third and most important reform in prison administration is the increased attention to professionalism. Recent attention has been given to attracting more highly educated people to the correctional field. Management also has sought to improve correctional training and introduce new management techniques. A problem arises, however, when professionalism is viewed as the *solution* to organizational problems, resulting in a better image of the organization, without sufficient attention to underlying problems.

For example, research indicates that more highly educated correctional officers do not have more positive and humane attitudes toward inmates than less educated officers. Furthermore, the more highly educated officer may be more frustrated in the job. Thus, the appearance of professionalism may be only that, unless adequate prior and on-the-job training programs are implemented to prepare correctional officers for the problems they will face. Important organizational changes must be made, too. If, in fact, the recruitment of a new breed of professionals is no more than "window-dressing" on the same abusive, warehouse-oriented institutions that have characterized our correctional system for the past century, then the current crisis in corrections is likely to continue well into the future.[9]

The life of a correctional officer is dangerous, and it may be monotonous. These and other problems lead to heavy turnover in these positions. (Buddy Mays/Black Star)

CORRECTIONAL OFFICERS

The goals of the correctional institution and the management style of the warden are very important in determining the success or failure of the institution, but the individuals with the most extensive contact and perhaps the greatest effect on inmates are the **correctional officers,** or **guards.** Despite their importance, little empirical evidence exists about the 126,592 custodial staff members employed by 51 correctional agencies in this country in 1988.[10] The two earlier classic studies of prison communities, conducted by Donald Clemmer and Gresham M. Sykes, mentioned the role of guards in the prison community but were not addressed to the career of the guard or even to a systematic sociological analysis of the guard's role.[11]

Correctional officers in maximum-security prisons spend almost all of their work days behind bars in close contact with inmates. It is impossible to generalize the working conditions or the reactions of all guards, but normally the job is monotonous, filled with routine. That routine may be to walk, and walk, and walk, just staring, making sure no one is violating the rules. As one guard said, "We're all doing time, some of us are just doin' it in eight-hour shifts."[12] Salaries are low. Fringe benefits are not great; the risk is tremendous. Stress is high. The result is a high rate of turnover in most institutions.

Function of Correctional Officers

The primary function of guards today is to maintain internal security and discipline. They are responsible for keeping inmates from injuring themselves and others and for making sure that inmates follow the rules of the prison. How do they do that? In previous days, when corporal punishment was allowed, guards could control inmates by brute force. There is evidence that some use that method today, although it is not constitutionally permitted. As Spotlight 14.1 indicates, the prohibition against the use of physical force for routine control of inmates is frustrating to many guards, particularly when it is combined with increased violence by prison inmates.

Another method guards have used to control inmates is to manipulate the inmate's **social system,** discussed later. Guards permit selected inmates to have positions of authority and control over other inmates. These powerful inmates in turn keep other inmates under control. In recent years, federal courts have prohibited the use of inmates in positions of power over other inmates. Such inmates are often called **building tenders.** In some cases, the changes in power have occurred quickly, without the addition of more guards to fill the power void. Inmates gaining control of institutions for at least temporary periods has lead to some of the riots discussed in the next chapter.

Guards' use of inmates to help control other inmates has also led to corruption, including guards accepting bribes from inmates or bringing **contraband** into the prison for inmates. Contraband is any forbidden material, such as drugs, alcohol, and weapons. Contraband may be smuggled into the prison by inmates' visitors or brought in by guards (or other prison personnel).

Although it is argued that only in an isolated number of instances do guards smuggle drugs into prisons, these incidents receive considerable

SPOTLIGHT 14.1
CHANGES FRUSTRATE GUARDS

The typical officer in the Texas Department of Corrections (TDC) has strong conservative beliefs and grew up in a rural setting. Some became correctional officers because they wanted to work in law enforcement or wanted the security of a government job; others say prison provided the only employment in their small towns. The TDC officers belong to a tight-knit society made up of their peers, and most believe that others do not understand them.

After the court ordered TDC to discontinue using inmate building-tenders, increased violence resulted in the prisons. Correctional officers now feel unprotected and betrayed by the system; they continue to believe that inmates only understand threats

of violence and corporal discipline. "They have a really simplified view of what's going on. They can't take a 2-by-4 and get inmates' attention anymore. You can imagine their level of frustration and confusion. For years they have been told it's OK to beat inmates over the head with that 2-by-4. Now they can't, and they don't know what else to do." A former TDC prison captain agrees, saying "You go into a place every day that could blow up any minute, and you can't control it. It's pure frustration when an officer comes to you with urine all over him and all you can tell him is go dry off."

Source: Summarized from John Toth and Frank Klimko, "Changes Frustrate TDC Guards," *Houston Chronicle* (21 November 1984), p. 1.

publicity. In January 1988, the *New York Times* reported that four senior correctional officers at New York's Sing Sing prison were demoted and transferred after an investigation produced evidence that they failed to stop drug smuggling by guards who reported to them. Two of the four guards who reportedly brought in the drugs for resale to inmates resigned, and two were suspended pending further investigation. The *Times* also reported that women guards were involved in sexual relations with inmates and that the senior officials had failed to stop these illegal activities.[13]

In October, 1988, officials began arresting Philadelphia prison guards after an intensive investigation, called "the most extensive criminal investigation of its type in the nation's history." Guards have been charged with smuggling money, guns, and drugs into the prison and helping inmates escape. Some have been charged with accepting bribes "to turn one unit into a social club for reputed mobsters." One of the officials reported that "Every kind of criminal activity that occurs outside also occurs inside the prison—and it is generally more profitable inside."[14]

One of the methods officials have proposed for eliminating drug smuggling by guards is compulsory drug testing. In September 1987 President Reagan issued an executive order directing drug testing for all federal employees who occupy sensitive positions. The Bureau of Prisons was one of the first to take steps to implement testing for the 13,000 federal prison employees; but in June 1988 a federal judge in San Francisco prohibited this testing, saying that there was no justification for testing "innocent, law-abiding and wholly competent" workers.

During its 1988–1989 term, the U.S. Supreme Court decided the issue of compulsory drug testing in the context of other cases that have previously been decided and appealed. Controlling correctional officers through random searches and drug testing may or may not be effective, even if the Supreme Court upholds the policy. Perhaps a better method of control is to improve the recruitment and training of correctional officers.*

Recruitment and Training of Correctional Officers

Usually a high-school diploma is sufficient for the entry-level officer, although it would be difficult today for someone without college training to advance to an administrative position. Good health is required, of course, for the duties of a correctional officer may involve strenuous physical work, particularly during a riot or other prison disturbance. Mental and emotional health also are important, although many jurisdictions provide inadequate testing and training in this area.

Stress management is becoming an important element of officer training. The American Correctional Association (ACA) now provides numerous publications to assist officers in dealing with the daily problems they face. The ACA also provides correspondence courses; criminal justice institutes provide continuing-education programs. Some prison systems are giving correctional officers a taste of life as an inmate by sending them to prison to be treated as inmates for a short period of time, but these programs are expensive and not widely used.

Training of correctional officers usually is conducted at a central place within the prison system, and the nature of that training varies from one system to another. Of necessity, it covers security; but guards also must learn how to protect themselves from inmates who attack them physically, and how to react when inmates curse, spit, or even urinate on them.

Editor's note. The Court upheld drug testing in two cases in 1989. Skinner v. Railway Labor Executives Assoc., 109 S. Ct. 1402 (1989); and National Treasury Employees Union v. VonRaab, 109 S. Ct. 1384 (1989).

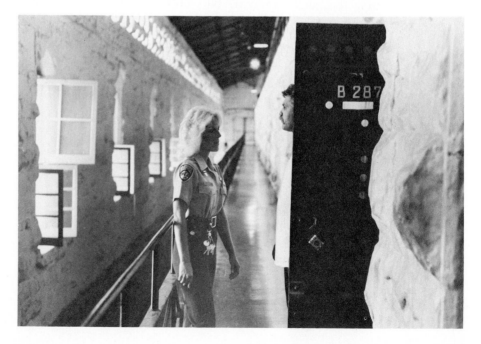

Recruitment efforts have resulted in more women working as correctional officers. (Bernard Charlon/ Gamma-Liaison)

Recruits are taught the rules and regulations that govern inmate behavior in the prisons, and they must learn the rules and constitutional provisions that govern the behavior of guards in relation to inmates.

The agency average for training recruits in 1988 was 198 hours of preservice training, and 37 hours of annual inservice training thereafter.[15] In recent years prison systems have made significant improvements in the working conditions, salaries, and fringe benefits of correctional officers. Spotlight 14.2 indicates some of the changes in the Florida system.

Correctional Officers: Recent Research

Although until relatively recently little social science research had been conducted on guards or correctional officers, in the past few years this situation has changed. Social scientists have become interested in many aspects of the job and the attitudes of those who guard inmates.

The effect of increased professionalism on the attitudes guards have toward inmates is one topic of focus. One reason for higher education and more sophisticated training is to decrease the cynicism of guards toward inmates. Robert M. Regoli and his colleagues have found, however, that the relationship between professionalism and cynicism is rather complex and that most aspects of professionalism do not decrease cynicism. In one study, they found

> that only one professionalism dimension—sense of calling to the field—reduced a prison guard's cynicism. Effects of other professionalism dimensions on cynicism ranged from negligible to moderate.[16]

Regoli and Eric D. Poole have also reported that guards feel they no longer are in control within the prison. The changes, most of which were brought about by developments discussed in the next chapter of this text, have resulted in working conditions that guards find frustrating. "With their traditional status and role altered by institutional reform policies, guards feel threatened by inmates, misunderstood by superiors, and unsupported by fellow officers." Deteriorating working conditions, as perceived by guards, have resulted in a feeling of "normlessness, isolation, and self-estrangement."[17]

Female Correctional Officers

Several court cases established the right of women to work in correctional institutions for men and affected their hiring and promotion, but these changes have occurred only recently.[18] Women constitute only 14.4 percent of correctional officers.[19] Female correctional officers face resistance from the prison administration and some of their male colleagues. One study found that female guards were tested more often by male officers than by inmates; that male officers were uneasy and unaccepting of female officers in prisons for men; and that male officers believed women were not physically strong enough for the job. Women who listened to these comments came to believe that acting like men would win acceptance. Men, however, then complained that women officers went too far.[20]

Female guards have commanded respect among their male colleagues as well as the inmates they confine, although some report that gaining the confidence of their colleagues was the more difficult task! (Max Gutierrez/UPI Bettmann News)

SPOTLIGHT 14.2
FLORIDA'S CORRECTIONAL CHIEF VIEWS THE FLORIDA SYSTEM AND CORRECTIONAL OFFICERS

The correctional officer is the unsung hero of the criminal justice profession. The public has always related better to other law enforcement professionals—the highway patrol, the city police, the marine patrol officer. Correctional officers have usually been the underdog. The current trend, however, indicates people are now beginning to realize correctional officers are an invaluable part of law enforcement.

For example, the Florida Department of Corrections is making positive efforts to enhance correctional officers' image within the criminal justice system. The Florida Department of Corrections has 12,000 employees in 32 major institutions, 55 smaller facilities, and 100 probation and parole offices. More than 6,000 of these employees are line correctional officers. Our overriding concern has always been to have correctional officers fully integrated into the criminal justice picture, not only in the minds of other members of the profession, but, just as important, in the perception of the public as well. The public should learn to see that the officer is the counselor, the advisor, the regulator, the authority figure, and it is the correctional officer who most frequently influences inmates' attitudes.

The correctional officer has been frequently viewed as the low man on the totem pole in education, training, and professionalism. However, correctional officers are without a doubt the most valuable change agents affecting incarcerated offenders by virtue of their direct contact with inmates. A highly skilled and trained psychologist may work with an inmate on a scheduled basis—one, or maybe two hours per week—but it is the correctional officer who is in constant, day-to-day contact. . . .

Toward Parity

Like correctional departments in many states, the Florida Department of Corrections has come a long way in recent years in achieving correctional officer parity with other beginning law enforcement officers. The starting salary of a Florida correctional officer has been increased five times since 1979, from $8,623 to $13,650 (58.3 percent); however, the current salary is still $319 (2.3 percent) below the $13,969 starting salary of a highway patrolman, campus policeman, or marine patrol officer. . . .

Better Training

The Correctional Training Institute at Raiford, Florida, was established in 1973 to meet the growing de-

In spite of the negative attitudes in their work environment, it appears that female correctional officers are able to establish and maintain personal authority in a prison setting; they are not manipulated by inmates any more often than male officers. A recent study indicates that "the authority of women correctional officers is as legitimate as that of their male colleagues."[21]

The presence of women in prisons for men creates a more normal environment in the institution, allows inmates to relax, and encourages better dress and behavior among inmates. One study concluded that female officers may be able to capitalize on this and "redefine modes of officer-inmate relations so that tensions are reduced and the prison environment is improved generally."[22]

Despite the problems they have encountered, many women find the position of correctional officer to be rewarding and challenging. In Spotlight 14.3 a female correctional officer in the federal system indicates why she continues to enjoy her job.

mands of minimum standards certification for all correctional officers. The institute conducts courses in basic and specialized training programs throughout the year.

The Criminal Justice Standards and Training Commission was established by the legislature to provide a vehicle for uniform basic training for both correctional and law enforcement personnel. This action has been a boon to our training efforts, and we are now turning out better trained and more qualified officers.

Today, all newly hired Florida correctional officers must receive 320 hours of basic recruit training during the first year of employment. Our Bureau of Staff Development continues to encourage advanced career development and specialized training throughout the year. Special incentives are offered, which often include tuition costs and fees for special career development courses or college work. . . .

Toward the Future

We in corrections have come a long way in a relatively short time, and we are on the threshold of complete parity with law enforcement. We continue to make adjustments and to fine tune our operations, and we are beginning to see the benefits of our hard work and patience. Florida's correctional officer turnover rate has decreased from 63 percent to 24 percent annually. (It is still considerably higher, however, than law enforcement turn-over, which is under 10

percent.) Decreased correctional officer turnover has significantly improved the operating climate of our institutions by providing a larger number of experienced and trained officers to effectively supervise and control the inmate population.

For the future, correctional systems nationwide will continue efforts to expand correctional horizons and to look for new, innovative ideas that will enhance the professional stature of the nation's correctional officers.

There are many resources that we have just begun to use, such as the exploration, testing, and expansion of computer technology in the delivery of in-service training.

Correctional officers are an invaluable mechanism of the criminal justice system, and we have already gained valuable ground in our quest for professional equality with our peers in law enforcement. The key to professionalism is a well-trained, dedicated staff. I am proud that Florida has been fortunate enough to unlock some of the doors that have hindered our progress. I hope our accomplishments and innovations can be a source of encouragement for correctional officers throughout the nation. Professional equality is a reality, and officers should be proud to wear their uniforms.

Source: Louis L. Wainwright, former Secretary of the Florida Department of Corrections, "Correctional Officer: Agent of Change," Copyright 1985 by the American Correctional Association from *Corrections Today* 47 (July 1985): 50–54. All rights reserved. Used with permission.

SPOTLIGHT 14.3
A CORRECTIONAL OFFICER DESCRIBES
HER ATTITUDES TOWARD HER JOB

I don't think of my job as simply a way to make a living. Rather, it is something to pursue with the object of accomplishing things for society and for offenders.

I am proud of my role in corrections. It is gratifying to me to be part of making difficult situations better and of showing offenders there really is a better way of life for them once they realize they were wrong. I have always wanted to know why people do the things they do, even when what they do is an unfortunate blight on mankind. The progression to psychology and criminal justice was a natural one. Duty as a correctional officer, I thought, could give me the absolute straight-to-the-core knowledge of behavior.

As a correctional officer, my primary concern is with security, including constant surveillance of fences, inmate activities, and control of contraband. Supervision of inmate activities includes keeping watch during recreation, meal times, visits, and educational programs. . . .

Fellow Human Beings

Interaction with the inmates is second in my scale of things only to institutional security. Living as they do in a vastly different society, inmates meet many difficulties that the correctional officer may be able to help them with: family problems, for example, or problems of adjustment to life in the institution. It's in this area that the correctional officer may be able to make the most positive contribution to an inmate's life.

I believe that whether we're inmates or officers, we are fellow human beings; no matter what set of circumstances brought us where we are, we deserve fairness and a reasonable amount of compassion. The officer who practices these qualities can make a real contribution and can make the difference between lives lived in vain and lives filled with renewed hope.

Being a good correctional officer demands many skills. Dedication to the job is necessary. Being a worthwhile citizen in your own right is important. Living by the rules is necessary if you are to govern others properly. Constant alertness, decisiveness, wisdom in the face of the unexpected, sound

knowledge—all are needed. Proper bearing is important because it shows confidence and alertness and knowledge of duties. The ability to adjust to adverse circumstances is valuable. I think that the following are also important: being willing to perform in areas outside your primary duties, being a team worker and contributing knowledge and constructive ideas, supporting the institution's morale programs, and doing all these things with an altruistic desire.

No matter what set of circumstances brought us where we are, we deserve fairness and compassion.

A corrections officer can gain a wealth of knowledge. People outside penal institutions do not realize what the job is; working inside, with inmates of all races and from all walks of life, is a revelation. It is a task of major proportions—housing, feeding, accommodating personal wants, beliefs, needs, attempts to rehabilitate, as well as causing inmates to understand that they broke the law and that we sincerely want to prepare them for freedom, if possible.

Anyone thinking of entering this challenging profession should have a number of important qualities:

- A desire to help people
- Ability to work without showing fear or anxiety
- Knowledge of human behavior
- Ability to live under discipline and to obey orders
- Good health and an organized life-style

Once on the job, newcomers should react favorably to on-the-job training, should be willing to start on probation, should accept constructive criticism, should accept shift duty graciously and occasionally add assignments.

We all need to start with a positive attitude, knowing that good work is rewarding. Our job is a full-time one that demands that we be ever alert. There is always more to learn to make our jobs and our performance better. I hope to contribute to this cause for this institution, for our country, and for my personal satisfaction.

THE BEGINNINGS OF INCARCERATION

Characteristics of Prisoners

The typical prison inmate is from the lower socioeconomic class, has a turbulent family background, is unemployed, relatively uneducated, and not married at the time of incarceration. Spotlight 14.4 gives additional data on prison inmates.

Going to Prison

After the offender has been sentenced, official papers will be prepared to turn him or her over to the **custody** of the State Department of Corrections (or the Federal Bureau of Prisons in the federal system). The offender may be transported to prison immediately or retained in jail for a short period. In some states the offender will be sent to a diagnostic center for a physical

SPOTLIGHT 14.4
PROFILE OF STATE PRISON INMATES

[Based on a survey of the 1986 state inmates, the Bureau of Justice Statistics researchers have reported the following:]

- Over four-fifths of State prison inmates were recidivists—they had previously been sentenced to probation or incarceration as a juvenile or adult. More than 60% had been either incarcerated or on probation at least twice; 15%, three or more times; and nearly 20%, six or more times.
- Two-thirds of inmates in 1986 were serving a sentence for a violent crime or had previously been convicted of a violent crime. Most of these— 55% of all inmates—had a current violent offense.
- The 11% of inmates whose current offense was nonviolent but who had previously been convicted of a violent crime had the longest prior records of all recidivists—72% had three or more prior convictions.
- More than half (53%) of all inmates were recidivists with a record of at least one violent conviction.
- Of the one-third of inmates with no record of violence, 84% (29% of the total State inmate population) were recidivists. Only 5% of State prison inmates in 1986 were nonviolent offenders with no previous convictions. Over half of these were convicted of drug trafficking or burglary.

- About 13% of the inmate population were first-time offenders in for a violent crime. Over half of these had been convicted of murder (including nonnegligent manslaughter) or robbery.
- Just over a third (35%) of all inmates said they were under the influence of a drug at the time of their offense, and 43% said they were using drugs daily in the month before the offense.
- More than half of inmates (54%) reported that they were under the influence of drugs and/or alcohol at the time of the offense.
- Most of the victims of State prison inmates incarcerated for a violent crime were male, about two-thirds were white, and over one-fourth were well known to the offender.
- One-third of murderers and nearly half of those convicted of negligent manslaughter said their victims were well known to them. Similarly, a third of rapists and almost two-thirds of those sentenced for other types of sexual assault reported that their victims were well known to them.

Source: Bureau of Justice Statistics, *Profile of State Prison Inmates, 1986* (Washington, D.C.: U.S. Department of Justice, January 1988), p. 1.

Entering prison may be the most frightening experience of the entire process. (James L. Shaffer/PhotoEdit)

exam, psychological testing, and orientation. Assignment to a particular institution will be made after a thorough evaluation of the various test results. In others, the decision regarding placement may be made according to the seriousness of the offense, the age and sex of the offender, and whether the offender has a prior record (and, if so, the extent and nature of that record). In the case of women, there may be no choice; the state may have only one institution, which will have to accommodate all security levels unless the state contracts with another state or the federal system.

If the state has a central diagnostic unit, inmates must be transported from that unit to their individual assignments for **incarceration.** Where large numbers are involved, transportation may present a security problem. In the Texas Department of Corrections (TDC) system, those who are not escorted to prison by a Texas Ranger or a sheriff must ride the bus provided by TDC for this purpose. The bus has been described as follows:

> Three steel slab benches run the length of the bus. These steel slabs are designed to hold 40 to 60 inmates, but often as many as 90 to 100 are packed into the bus. An inmate, handcuffed and shackled, is given no opportunity to relieve himself during the entire trip.[23]

Upon arrival at the assigned institution, the inmate probably will be isolated from the general population for several days or even a week or longer. During that period the inmate will be told the rules or given a rule book to read. Physical exams will be given. In more secure facilities, the inmate will be strip-searched for drugs and weapons. The inmate may be required to take a special bath and use a special shampoo. Urine samples may be taken to determine whether the inmate is on drugs. Laxatives may be given to determine whether the inmate is smuggling drugs.

The inmate's clothing may be taken and special prison clothing issued. In less secure institutions and often in women's prisons, inmates are permitted to wear their own clothing. Table 14.1 indicates the articles of clothing and personal possessions that may be taken into Texas prisons. These provisions will differ from state to state and even within states, depending on the security needs of the institution. When inmates are not allowed to keep personal clothing, they may be required to pay to have the clothing shipped home or find that it has been donated to the Salvation Army. When the inmate is released, most prisons will issue one new set of clothing.

During the orientation period the inmate will be required to complete numerous forms concerning his or her background, medical history, and lists of persons who might be visiting. The inmate might be asked whether he or she fears any persons in the prison; in some cases it will be necessary to place the inmate in protective custody for protection from the rest of the population. Other inmates and correctional officials may test the inmate during the orientation period; most inmates advise that it is wise to be respectful to the officers and be careful about making friends among other inmates.

Generally the inmate will not be permitted to have visitors during this orientation period. Phone calls will be prohibited or limited. It thus

TABLE 14.1

Items That an Inmate May Take to Prison in the Texas System

1. Watch—one, no batteries available at commissary
2. Ring—one, not expensive
3. Cigarette lighter—one, not butane
4. Prescriptive glasses—no shades
5. Bible—one
6. Religious medal—one
7. Tennis shoes—one pair; no boots or large heels
8. Personal pictures—no Polaroid hardbacks; none larger than 8" × 5"
9. Legal material—addresses, medical papers
10. Cash—no more than $200

A list for female offenders adds the following items:
11. New, unsharpened pencils
12. Bras—several
13. Panties
14. Slips
15. Scarves
16. Pantyhose—two to three dozen pairs
17. Men's "T" shirts—no writing
18. Simple combs—no brushes

Source: William T. Habern, "Going to Prison," mimeographed, Texas Department of Corrections.

is a lonely, frustrating time and can be quite stressful for many inmates. Inmates may be interviewed for job assignments or educational programs in an effort to determine placement within the institution.

Inmates will usually be permitted to buy limited personal items from the **commissary,** but times for purchases and frequency of purchases will be limited. Money may not be kept by inmates in most institutions; it will be placed in a trust fund against which the inmate may draw for purchases. Money that can be received from family will be limited.

Life in Prison: A Brief Look

Life in prison is monotonous and routine. In maximum-security prisons, inmates are regulated for most of each day, beginning with the time for rising in the morning. Meal schedules are often unusual; for example, in some prisons inmates eat breakfast at 3 or 4 A.M. and then go back to bed for naps before beginning the regular work day. This is done because of the long time period required to feed a large population in a secure facility. Dinner may be served as early as 3 P.M. Some inmates are fed in their cells. During lock-down, when there has been internal trouble among inmates, and particularly after riots, inmates may be confined to their cells most of the day, with all meals served in their cells.

Most prisons do not have sufficient jobs for all inmates to work an 8-hour day; so many inmates must find ways to fill their time. The security needs of the institution will determine how free they are to do so, but in some prisons they will be permitted to move about rather freely within certain areas of the prison. Inmates may be out of their cells (or rooms, in the case of more modern facilities) and permitted to mingle with other inmates.

Some inmates live in rooms rather than cells and are permitted to keep a limited amount of personal items to make their confinement more liveable. (Jeff Albertson/The Picture Cube)

Recreational facilities may be available in the prison's common areas. Ping-pong is an example. Some prisons have gyms, but hours of use will be limited. Others have weight rooms or a provision for outdoor recreation such as baseball or basketball. Some books will be available for inmates to take to their cells or rooms.

In large prisons, particularly maximum-security institutions, inmates will be limited to a specified number of showers per week, for example three, and they will be marched to and from and supervised while showering. Privacy is nonexistent in most prisons. During the hours of the regular work week, inmates may be assigned to jobs or be permitted to attend educational or vocational classes. Others may have no organized activities.

After dinner, inmates may be permitted to socialize with other inmates in common areas. The institution may provide activities such as movies, Alcoholics Anonymous meetings, drug abuse seminars, or other self-help programs. Most institutions will have television available; many will permit inmates to have a television and radio in their cells, provided that they purchase them from the commissary to avoid the problem of contraband being brought into the institution by this means.

Part of the inmate's day may be spent writing letters to friends and family, although he or she will be limited in the number that can be sent and received; gifts also will be limited or excluded. Inmates may spend time taking care of their personal or prison-issued clothing and working at institutional assignments.

In minimum-security institutions, some inmates may be permitted to leave the institution from time to time for various purposes. But for the most part, inmates will be confined day and night for the duration of their sentences. During confinement, particularly in the maximum-security prisons for men, inmates may be subjected to homosexual advances or even rape; some live in constant fear of violence and may find that their only "freedom" comes from an alliance with a stronger man who will protect them in exchange for sexual or other favors.

ADAPTATIONS TO PRISON: THE MALE INMATE

How do inmates adapt to the prison environment? In earlier prisons they were not allowed to interact with other inmates. With the end of the segregated and silent systems came the opportunity for inmates to interact. One result of this interaction has been the opportunity for prisoners to form a prison **subculture** or community. The new inmate encounters this subculture through the process of socialization or, as it is called in prison, **prisonization.**

In 1940 Donald Clemmer reported his study of the male prison community of Illinois' maximum-security prison at Menard. The book has become recognized as one of the most thorough studies of a prison setting. Many of the more recent studies of prisons have been conducted as tests of Clemmer's theories, the most important of which was his concept of prisonization.

Clemmer defined *prisonization* as "the taking on, in greater or lesser degree, of the folkways, mores, customs, and general culture of the penitentiary." The process begins as the new inmate learns his or her status as a prisoner. The most important aspects of prisonization are "the influences which breed or deepen criminality and antisociality and make the inmate characteristic of the ideology in the prison community."

The degree to which prisonization is effective in a given inmate depends on several factors: (1) the inmate's susceptibility and personality; (2) the inmate's relationships outside the prison; (3) the inmate's membership in a primary group in prison; (4) the inmate's placement in the prison such as which cell and cellmate; and (5) the degree to which the inmate accepts the dogmas and codes of the prison culture.

Clemmer contended that the most important of these factors is the primary group. Clemmer saw prisonization as the process by which new inmates became familiar with and internalized prison **norms** and values. He argued that once the inmates became prisonized they were, for the most part, immune to the influences of conventional value systems.[24]

Other scholars have tested Clemmer's conclusions. Stanton Wheeler, in a study at the Washington State Reformatory, found strong support for Clemmer's position on prisonization. Wheeler also found that the degree to which inmates became involved in the process of prisonization varied by the length of time the inmate is in prison. Inmates were more receptive to the institutional values of the outside world during the first and the last 6 months of incarceration. During their middle period of incarceration, they were more receptive to values of the inmate subculture.[25]

In comparing prisonization among men as compared to women inmates, researchers have questioned the Wheeler hypothesis. Geoffrey P. Alpert and others found that although time spent in prison was significantly related to prisonization among women inmates, this was not the case among men inmates. In their study of inmates in the Washington State prison system, these researchers also found that other variables were predictive of prisonization. Among women, attitudes toward race and the police were significant. Among men, the variable of age was significant, as were attitudes toward law and the judicial system.[26]

The Inmate Subculture: Models for Analysis

Scholars have analyzed the emergence and development of the inmate subculture and developed two models for explaining the phenomenon: deprivation and importation. In the **deprivation model,** the inmate's pattern of behavior is an adaptation to the deprivations of his or her environment. The inmate social system is functional for inmates; it enables them to minimize the pains of imprisonment through cooperation. For example, inmate cooperation in the exchange of favors not only removes the opportunity for some to exploit others but enables inmates to accept material deprivation more easily. Their social system redefines the meaning of material possessions. Inmates come to believe that material possessions, so highly valued on the outside, result from connections instead of hard work and skill, which enables them to insulate their self-conceptions from failure in work and skill.

In addition, those goods and services that are available can be better distributed and shared if the inmates have a cooperative social system. Because of the pains of imprisonment and the degradation of inmates, which result in a threat to their self-esteem, inmates repudiate the norms of the staff, administration, and society and join forces with each other, developing a social system that enables them to preserve their self-esteem. By so rejecting their rejectors, they can avoid having to reject themselves.[27]

The more traditional approach to an understanding of the inmate subculture, according to John Irwin and Donald R. Cressey, is that patterns of behavior are brought with the men to prison, constituting the **importation model.** Irwin and Cressey argued that social scientists have overemphasized inside influences as explanations for the prison inmate culture. The prison subculture is really a combination of several types of subcultures brought by inmates from past experiences and used within prison to adjust to the deprivations of prison life.[28]

Research on the deprivation and importation models was conducted by Charles W. Thomas at a maximum-security prison. Thomas' research was designed to show the importance of both importation and deprivation variables. When an inmate arrives at prison, both the formal organization and the inmate society compete for his allegiance; these two represent conflicting processes of socialization. Thomas calls the efforts of the formal organization *resocialization*, and those of the inmate society *prisonization*. The success of one requires the failure of the other. The prison is not a closed system.

In explaining the inmate culture, one must examine all of these factors: preprison experiences, both criminal and noncriminal; expectations of prison staff and fellow inmates; quality of the inmate's contacts with persons or groups outside the walls; postprison expectations; and the immediate problems of adjustment that the inmate faces. Thomas found that the greater the degree of similarity between preprison activities and prison subculture values and attitudes, "the greater the receptivity to the influences of prisonization." Thomas also found that inmates from the lower as compared to the upper social class are more likely to become highly prisonized; those who have the highest degree of contact with the outside world had the lowest degree of prisonization; and those with a higher degree of prisonization were among those who had the bleakest postprison expectations.[29]

Other researchers have found support for one or the other of the models. Leo Carroll, in his study of race relations in a maximum-security prison, found some support for the importation model, although he concluded that the model needed refinement. Carroll criticized the deprivation model as diverting attention from important factors within prison, such as racial violence.[30] Support for both the importation and the deprivation models also has been found in studies of prisons in other countries.[31]

Studies of jail inmates are important in determining whether the inmate subculture is imported into the institution or results from adaptations to the institutional setting. James Garofalo and Richard D. Clark, in reporting their findings of support for both approaches, stated the following:

> Experienced inmates—who are already familiar with the inmate subculture—enter the jail, assess how long they will be in, and readapt readily to the inmate subculture. "Carriers" of the subculture bring their knowledge of its norms into the jail, consistent with an importation viewpoint. But readapting to the subculture is most likely a functional response to the confinement situation [which supports the adaptation theory].[32]

Adaptation to prison life was perhaps not so difficult in earlier days for those who considered themselves to be career criminals. George "Machine Gun" Kelly, infamous criminal of the 1930s, poses in front of his cell. (Bettmann Archive)

Social Roles and Terminology of the Inmate System

The inmate social system is characterized by social roles and often involves the development of a special vocabulary. The special language is not developed primarily for secrecy nor as a symbol of the inmates' loyalty to each other (the guards use the language, too) but rather as a distinguishing symbol. Special terms designate inmate social roles. Although these words differ somewhat from institution to institution, the roles they designate remain the same. Some of the special terminology used in prisons is defined in Spotlight 14.5.

SPOTLIGHT 14.5
SELECTED INMATE SLANG AND DEFINITIONS

Bum rap	Unjust conviction or charge	Ice	Segregation
Fall partners	Two or more inmates convicted for same offense	"Keep my name out of your mouth"	Quit talking about me
Meditation	Solitary confinement		
Wall-time	Inmates assessed minor punishment by standing with face to the wall for one or more hours	Run	Walk area in front of cells
		The hole	Solitary
		Ketch-out	Inmate who stays out of cell or dorm because of fear of other inmates
Shelling peas or peanuts	Inmates assessed minor punishment of shelling one or more gallons of peas or peanuts		
		Punch it	Escape or attempt to escape
		Head running	Conversation, bull session
Punk or brownie	Anal sodomy, homosexual takes female role	Rap with	More serious conversation with inmate or employee
Hot lips, girl, or old lady	Oral sodomy, homosexual takes female role	Snitch, stoolie, stool pigeon	Giving information to employees concerning other inmates
Stud, daddy, or wolf	Aggressive homosexual taking the male role	Jigger	Stop activity, someone is coming
Switch engine	Two individuals trading off on anal sodomy	Look out	Expression to get attention, as in "Hey, you"
Turn-out	Inmate who becomes a punk after incarceration, either by choice or force	Kite or kiting	Sending out or receiving letters illegally
		Hang it on me	Give me some of your . . .
Writ writer	Inmate who writes writs concerning his sentence or treatment	Drive-up	Newly arrived inmate
		Pour it out	To relieve one's kidneys
		Aggie	Large farm hoe
Jailhouse lawyer	Inmates who assist others in writ writing	Shank, spike, shiv	Some kind of knife or sharp, pointed weapon
Free world	World outside the prison	The man	The warden
Pill line	Sick call	Running a store	Inmates who trade or sell commissary goods
Chain	Group of inmates arriving or departing		
		One on the ground	When an inmate has escaped
Raisin jack or chock	Homemade alcoholic beverage	Rabbit	Inmate who has escaped before, or has tried to escape
Snitch jacket	Reputation for being a snitch		
Ace	Best friend	Boss	Correctional officer

An example of the special terminology used by inmates to designate social roles may be seen in Leo Carroll's study of a small Eastern institution for men. Carroll found that black compared to white inmates had a different set of social roles and a different form of organization of their lives while in prison. Their main focus was racial identification. Most blacks were united in a solidarity group based on two ideological perspectives. One, which Carroll calls *soul*, emphasized the historical black American culture and affirmed the importance of acceptance and perseverance. The other, black nationalism, valued African culture and emphasized revolution against racism, colonialism, and imperialism. According to Carroll, both were imported into the prison from the outside. Blacks were not totally unified within the prison, but they were far more unified as a group than the white inmates.[33]

The Inmate System as an Agency of Social Control

The inmate social system may create problems for guards and other prison personnel; the resulting social roles also may create problems for inmates upon release and even for society. It is clear, however, that the inmate social system also serves as an agency of social control within the prison. The inmate society wields a powerful influence over the inmate because it is the only reference group available. It is powerful because, while incarcerated, people need status; in addition, they may be more susceptible than usual to peer-group pressure and more prone to look to the peer group than to authority figures for social support. Inmates therefore will permit themselves to be controlled by the social system of their peers, a form of social control that is functional to the prison when it maintains order within the institution. To understand this system of control, we must look more carefully at the problems of control faced by the institution.

Within the prison two powerful groups seek to control one another: the guards, who are mainly interested in custody and security, and the inmates, who are interested in escaping as much as possible from the pains of imprisonment. Richard Cloward has studied the power struggle between these two groups. Cloward notes that in most institutions, force can be converted into authority because people usually recognize the legitimacy of authority and are motivated to comply. In prison, however, the inmates have rejected the legitimacy of those who seek to control them. A real problem of social control is the result. In many ways the job of the custodian in prison is an impossible one. He or she is expected to maintain control and security within the institution but has had to give up traditional methods of doing this—force. The new, more liberal philosophy of recognizing due process and other rights of inmates has increased problems of social control for guards.[34]

Under the authoritarian regime of prison administration and management, inmate cooperation was necessary to maintain peace within institutions. The few guards could not possibly have kept a disorganized body of inmates under control. Inmates actually ran the institutions, and the guards cooperated. For example, guards would permit the leaders to take the supplies they needed. When a "surprise" search was to be conducted, they would let the inmate leaders know in advance. The leaders would then spread the word as a form of patronage. The guards thus were aiding certain inmates in maintaining their positions of prestige within the inmate system; in return, inmate leaders maintained order. The system was a fairly stable one with little disorder.

Federal court orders to abolish inmate positions of power over other inmates have changed the traditional system of inmate-guard interaction and altered the role of the inmate social system in social control. The results are illustrated by the Texas prison system. Texas, with the nation's highest number of violent deaths of inmates in 1985 (a total of 27), has been plagued with attempts of the administration to maintain order within the nation's second largest prison system.

After a disturbance in late 1985, during which eight inmates were killed in 8 days, Texas prison officials announced that they were declaring war on the prison situation. They locked down 17,000 inmates in 13 prisons. Sociologists studying the Texas prison system earlier had reported that the use of inmates as building tenders had kept racial tension in check, and little violence existed.[35] Inmates were removed from those powerful positions as the result of a federal court order. The result was a power vacuum, and gangs filled much of that vacuum.

The power of the inmate subculture to control inmates also may be altered by significant changes in the inmate population. In his classic study of Stateville, James Jacobs found that population changes in the late 1960s, involving an increased number of inmates who belonged to Chicago gangs, altered the nature of the inmate social control system. The norms that once solidified most of the inmates became less important. Inmates did not have allegiances as inmates but rather as members of certain organizations outside the prison.

Jacobs concluded that these changes in the inmate social structure increased the problems of controlling inmates. At Stateville the inmates were more politicized and more willing to make demands on institutional authority than in the past. They attacked guards more frequently and refused to obey guards' orders more often. The resulting crisis in control was characterized by the first escapes since the 1940s, the first guard killed in 30 years, and the first hostages taken since the 1920s. The presence of the four gangs in the institution precipitated the problems, says Jacobs, "but the underlying cause was the failure of the reform regime to find a new equilibrium to replace the authoritarian regime of personal dominance."[36]

The Economic System and Inmate Control   Inmate social control can be seen in the economic system of the prison subculture. In every prison there is a legitimate economic system. Inmates may earn money in prison work, receive money from home, or bring a limited amount of money when they enter prison. Although they are not totally free to spend that money in any way, they do have commissary privileges. The money is kept in a trust for them, and expenses are deducted from their account.

In the prison community, however, an economic system, which John Irwin called a **sub-rosa economic system,** develops. Irwin is referring to the informal economic system in which contraband dealings and gambling exist under a strict set of inmate-created rules. Irwin argued that this sub-rosa economic system in prison also has undergone changes in recent years. Affluence has increased in prison as in society. Inmates are not allowed to have cash, but many acquire it, having it smuggled in by friends on the outside.

According to Irwin, gambling and distributing contraband are the main forms of prison economic activity. Wheeling and dealing are frequent and extremely important. Rules for wheeling and dealing develop. These are violated frequently and hostility increases. Stealing and cheating are acceptable under the theory that might makes right. An inmate who engages in these sub-rosa economic activities has to be able to protect himself. Since individuals on their own usually cannot protect themselves, gangs and cliques develop.[37]

Vergile Williams and Mary Fish, in their extensive discussion of prison sub-rosa economic systems, argued that administrators must look at the illicit economic transactions as a network, a system, not as individual acts. For example, suppose a guard finds out that inmate John, who wanted to change his cell assignment, made an illicit arrangement with inmate Steve, who was in a position to influence the change. John paid Steve two cartons of cigarettes for this transaction. The guards probably would react only to this transaction and not consider the total economic system. But if John and Steve were not caught, the following transactions might result. Steve gives the cigarettes to Paul, whom he owes a debt for another illicit activity. Paul has a bad debt outstanding, and he uses the cigarettes to hire Roger to beat up Dick, who owes the debt. The transactions can continue, with the same two cartons of cigarettes involved as payment in each transaction, perhaps eventually being returned to the first inmate in the series of transactions.

It is important, to the goals of both custody and treatment, that guards understand the system nature of illicit economic transactions. As inmates gain power through these illicit economic transactions, they may gain access to contraband, facilitate escapes, and gain power over other inmates, any one or all of which may lead to violence. Treatment may be affected in those cases in which inmates engaging in the illicit activities are motivated primarily by their rebellion against society rather than by their desire to solve an immediate economic need. For those inmates, success in the illicit prison ventures may convince them that such activities are worthwhile and should be continued in society upon release.[38]

Gangs, Race, Fear, and Social Control   Discussions of prison inmate subcultures, particularly the element of social control through power and fear, often involve implications of conflicts between races. Many of the gangs are aligned on the basis of race. In earlier prisons, racial problems were avoided through strict segregation and the lack of contact between inmates.

In the 1960s, however, the climate of prisons began to change. Contact among inmates was already permitted, but the demography of prisons also changed. The prison population shifted to minorities, mainly blacks and Hispanics, who brought with them the black nationalistic and militant organizations from the society outside the prison. The rising development of racial pride and activism among Chicanos also spread to prisons. In California, for example, Chicano inmates became more hostile to whites and developed closer relationships to black inmates. Meanwhile, white prisoners developed a deep sense of the injustices of prison conditions, especially the indeterminate sentence. "In 1969 the 'political' activities in the prisons were fused with the outside radical movement, and the 'prison movement' came into being."[39]

The prevalence of gangs and the extent to which they control inmate life in prison is illustrated by the following excerpt from a 1988 federal case in Illinois. The procedural issues of this case are beyond the scope of this discussion, but the court's description of prison gangs is illuminating.[40]

David K. v. Lane

Pontiac Correctional Center, located in Pontiac, Illinois, is one of four maximum security facilities in Illinois. On the average, Pontiac houses 2,000 inmates. At the time the district court made its findings, there were approximately 1,800 inmates in Pontiac's general population and 260 inmates in the Pontiac protective custody unit. The protective custody unit is designed "to ensure the safety of inmates determined to be vulnerable to attack and intimidation." . . .

Only 12 percent of the total inmate population at Pontiac is white, yet 40 percent of the total white inmate population is in protective custody while only 9 percent of the total black population and 13 percent of the Hispanic population are in protective custody. The inordinately high number of white inmates in protective custody is directly related to the predominately black gang-activity at Pontiac.

At the hearing on the motion for a preliminary injunction, it was estimated that anywhere from 75 percent to 99.5 percent of the total inmate population at Pontiac are gang members. Although the district court found that the number was probably closer to 75 percent, defendant-appellee, Michael Lane, the director of the Illinois Department of Corrections, testified that about 90 percent of all Pontiac inmates are gang members or are gang-affiliated. A portion of the inmates entering Pontiac, who are not gang members, ultimately "choose" to affiliate or, in the vernacular, "ride" with or "aid and assist" a gang. Inmates, who ride with gangs are offered protection by the gang but must pay for that protection literally and figuratively by performing any number of deeds, ranging from carrying weapons to performing a "hit" for gang members.

Virtually all gangs are black or Hispanic. White inmates do not normally become members of the black or Hispanic gangs but may only "ride" the non-white gangs. All inmates, who are not gang members, are "strongly urged" and, more often than not, physically coerced to affiliate with a gang. . . .

Gang activity, including extortion, possession of contraband, intimidation, and physical and sexual abuse, is expressly prohibited by Pontiac prison rules. Further, the administration, as a matter of departmental policy, does not officially recognize the existence of various prison gangs. The fact is, however, that the existence of those gangs is a reality with which the administration is confronted daily. In an attempt to realistically deal with gang-related problems, prison officials discipline gang "activity" but do not discipline non-violent displays of gang "membership." However, these non-violent exhibitions of gang membership create an environment in which the gangs flourish and as a consequence, an environment in which prohibited gang activities can and do take place with alarming intensity and frequency. It is not an overstatement that the gang "situation in Illinois prisons" has reached "the crisis stage."

Sex in Prison

Isolation from the opposite sex implies abstinence from the satisfaction of heterosexual relationships at a time when, for many inmates, sex drives are quite strong. Many may turn to homosexual behavior not by preference but because they need some sexual outlet. It is impossible to get accurate data on the degree to which homosexual acts take place within a prison or jail. Earlier studies reported that between 30 and 40 percent of male inmates had some homosexual experiences while in prison. These estimates were discussed at a conference on prison homosexuality in the early 1970s. Peter C. Buffum wrote a synthesis of the five working papers presented at that conference, and he concluded that the evidence suggests that many of the beliefs about prison homosexuality are myths.

According to Buffum, among the important myths are that there is a high incidence of homosexual rape in prisons and that rape is the main form of prison homosexuality. Finally, the belief that we can solve the problem by establishing outlets for sexual drives is a myth.[41] Others have not agreed, and the subject thus deserves greater attention.

Male Homosexuality: An Overview Male homosexuality in prison seldom involves a close relationship between the parties. In some cases, a man who is particularly vulnerable to homosexual attacks will enter into a relationship with another man who agrees to protect him from the attacks of others, as indicated in this chapter's Criminal Justice in Action.

Earlier studies found that homosexual acts of male prisoners seemed to be a response to their sexual needs coupled with their background of socialization. Men are taught to be aggressive, and it has been argued that for some, playing the male role (the wolf) in a homosexual act enables them to retain this self-concept. Such men are usually from the lower class, where a man's masculine self-concept is based more on sexual activity than on any other activity (in contrast to the middle-class man, who may gain his masculinity from his job status, family, or both).

It is very important to the wolf's self-concept that he retain the only measure of masculinity he has. Playing the male role allows him to continue thinking that he is masculine because he is the aggressor and the penetrator. Although he also may be looking for a meaningful emotional relationship to replace those outside the prison, he is more likely to be looking for the release of physical tension.

Many inmates see a prison homosexual relationship as

> little more than a search for a casual, mechanical act of physical release. Unmoved by love, indifferent to the emotions of the partner he has coerced, bribed, or seduced into a liaison, the wolf is often viewed as simply masturbating with another person.

The effeminacy associated with the male homosexual in the outside world is removed because the role the wolf plays is stripped "of any aura of 'softness', of sentiment or affection . . . his perversion is a form of rape and his victim happens to be a man rather than a woman, due to the force of circumstance."[42]

Leo Carroll's study of male inmates is consistent with earlier findings, which emphasize the sometimes violent and mainly physical nature of the sexual relationships in men's prisons as compared to the predominantly family nature of such relationships in women's prisons. Among male inmates, prostitution is the most frequent type of homosexual relationship, and it usually is an interracial relationship. Carroll also found that aggressive and violent sexual behavior was often explained not as an attempt to prove one's masculinity, but as the result of racial problems. "The prison is merely an arena within which blacks may direct aggression developed through 300 years of oppression against individuals perceived to be representatives of the oppressors."[43]

This discussion of male homosexuality and the forms it takes in prison should be considered in light of our previous discussion of the importation versus deprivation theories advanced to explain the inmate community. Clearly, prison presents the inmate with a problem of sexual deprivation, but according to Buffum (speaking of the options the inmate faces—nocturnal sex dreams, self-masturbation, and sexual contact with the same sex), "the meaning, amount, and character of these adjustments will be strongly dependent on the meaning that these same behaviors had for the inmate before he or she was incarcerated."[44]

Homosexual Rape   Susan Brownmiller supports the importation theory of homosexual rape and argues that rape in prison is a power play. She analogizes homosexual rape in a male prison to the rape of a woman by a man in society—it is the result of a need to dominate, to control, to conquer.[45]

Daniel Lockwood, who reported on his analysis of men in New York prisons, interviewed men designated as targets of sexual propositions or **sexual abuse,** as well as men who were identified as sexual aggressors. He found that many verbal threats of sexual aggression did not result in actual aggression.[46]

Most prison victims of homosexual rape do not report the act to officials, mainly because of the fear of reprisal by other inmates. As Spotlight 14.6 indicates, some inmates fear for their lives if they cooperate with officials in trying to solve an act of violence. These fears perhaps are not unreasonable. In 1987, 87 inmates were killed in prison, and many more were injured as the result of the violence of other inmates.[47]

Self-Inflicted Violence

According to the latest data, the suicide rate was higher than the homicide rate in prisons. In 1987, 135 suicides occurred in prisons (this figure excludes jail suicides), representing a 9.8 percent increase over 1986. Homicides, however, were down by 25 percent in 1987 compared to 1986.[48] The decrease in homicides may be attributed to the increased lockdowns in some systems, for example, Texas.[49]

The reasons for self-inflicted violence and suicide in prison are various. They have been linked to overcrowded institutions, the extended use of solitary confinement, and the psychological consequences of being a

"His skin is pale, his hands often tremble and his eyes look blurry. 'I don't sleep at night if I can help it. I just stay up until I pass out from exhaustion'," says the inmate. "For the last five months, the . . . inmate has been afraid to shut his eyes for fear he may never open them again." He says two prison gangs have a contract out on his life, and gang members have boasted that he "will leave TDC in a coffin."

What happened? The inmate gave prison administrators the name of the man who stabbed his cellmate to death. "To prisoners, a snitch is consid-

ered worse than a murderer and often can get into a lot more trouble." Today, the inmate worries about survival because "somehow, word has leaked out that he talked with prison officials."

The inmate is now in protective custody. His wife says, "He's one man against an underground army." His mother says, "It's not fair. My son is in the terrible position that he is because he cooperated when officials asked for his help."

Source: "Helping Prison Authorities Puts Convict's Life at Risk," *Houston Chronicle* (18 November 1984). Reprinted with permission.

---

victim in prison. Inmates who are threatened with rape or other violence often become depressed and desperate about their physical safety, because their only options are fight or flight. If they submit to violence, they will be branded as weak and forced to face even further violent attacks from aggressive inmates. If they seek help from the prison administration, they will be branded as snitches or rats. Furthermore, the inmate social system rewards violence against weaker inmates.[50]

Jail suicides are even more frequent than prison suicides. Suicide is

Loneliness in prison can lead to self-inflicted violence. (David Powers/Stock, Boston)

the highest cause of jail deaths, with approximately 1,000 inmates taking their lives each year. The average jail suicide victim is

> a white male, 22, who has been arrested for public intoxication—the only offense leading to his arrest. Most likely he would have no prior arrests or history of attempted suicide or mental illness.[51]

ADAPTATIONS TO PRISON: THE FEMALE INMATE

How does the female inmate adapt to prison? Characteristics of the female offender may help to explain the nature of the woman's adaptation to prison life and the differences between her methods of adapting and those of the typical male offender. Women constitute less than 5 percent of the inmates in state and federal prisons. Data from a national study of women in corrections disclose that female prisoners are relatively uneducated, young, have had contact with social welfare, and have worked at some time in their lives. Married offenders were not living with their spouses when convicted; most had dependent children at home. Of the women, 50 percent were black, although only 10 percent of the total female population is black.

Female inmates serving terms of 1 year or less were convicted of the following offenses: 41 percent for property crimes such as shoplifting, forgery, and fraud; 20 percent for drug offenses; and 11 percent for violent crimes such as assault, battery, or armed robbery. Of those serving longer sentences, 43 percent were convicted of violent crimes such as murder and armed robbery; 29 percent for property crimes, and 22 percent for drug offenses.[52]

Adjustment to prison can be particularly difficult for women, many of whom have children to care for. (Pamela Price/Picture Cube)

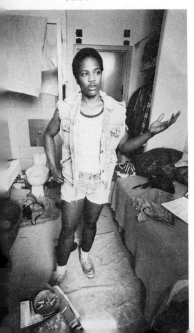

The Female Inmate Subculture

We began our discussion of the ways that male inmates adapt to prison life by looking at the process of prisonization and the development of a subculture. The same processes occur among female inmates, but there are some differences.

Rose Giallombardo, in her study of the Federal Reformatory for Women, considered the issue of whether the female prison subculture is an adaptation to the pains of imprisonment or whether it is imported from the woman's experiences in the outside world. Giallombardo concluded that the prison inmate culture or social system cannot be explained solely as a response to prison deprivations, although they may precipitate its development. Giallombardo illustrates her point primarily by looking at sex roles within correctional institutions for women and girls. Those sex roles reflect the roles women play in society. Her point is that not only attitudes and values but also roles and statuses are imported into the prison system. The deprivations of prison then provide the structure in which these roles may be played.[53]

The evidence seems to suggest that although the roles within the inmate systems of men and women differ, they reflect the difference in attitudes, values, and roles that traditionally have distinguished men and women in this culture. For example, in his study of a men's prison, Sykes suggested that loss of security is the greatest problem the male prisoner faces. For the woman this appears not to be the case. The loss of liberty and autonomy are the major deprivations felt by women in prison. They miss the lack of freedom to go and come and resent the restrictions on communications with family and friends. They may be frustrated because they have no control over things that happen in the outside world: their children may be neglected, a loved one may become sick or die, or their husbands may be unfaithful. In the institution everything is planned for them.

For some, depending on their lives outside, the prison is a deprivation of goods and services to which they are accustomed. As soon as they enter the institution, they are stripped of most of their worldly possessions.

> In this single act, a kind of symbolic death of the individual takes place. In the performance of this stripping and mortifying process, the prisoner is brought to terms with society's rejection of the criminal.

After new inmates are fingerprinted and photographed, they must take a supervised bath in a room with no door. After the bath

> comes the most embarrassing admission experience, a rectal and vaginal examination by a nurse in a room with other women present—an examination not for medical reasons, but for the discovery of contraband.[54]

Their self-images may be further damaged by the removal of their personal clothes and issuance of a prison uniform that often is faded, unattractive, and probably does not fit. Nor will they be allowed any individuality in dress in many institutions.

Like male prisoners, female inmates develop a special language to designate social roles. Although some of the same social roles are designated, the language differs from that of male inmates. The language differences relate mainly to the different function that the inmate subculture seems to serve for women and men inmates. For women the inmate subculture mainly is a substitute for the family, as indicated in this chapter's CJA. Women will take on special family roles for which they have special prison terms. The woman who plays the male role in the family is called the *stud*, as contrasted to the female, who is called the *femme*. They may refer to each other as daddy or mommy. Their family relationship takes on sexual and economic dimensions.

The prison family is the basic economic unit. The members of the family share in the legal and illegal goods. The economic and sexual relationships are closely related. In fact, some women may become involved in homosexuality in order that the stud may get items for her, or the latter may seduce the former with economic goods and services. Gifts are given to show fidelity, love, and concern.[55]

Female Homosexuality

Homosexuality among female inmates usually develops out of mutual interest and to alleviate the depersonalization of the prison and gain status.

> The overriding need of a majority of female prisoners is to establish an affectional relationship which brings in prison, as it does in the community, love, interpersonal support, security and social status. This need promotes homosexuality as the predominant compensatory response to the pains of imprisonment.[56]

The homosexual relationship for the woman may take the place of the primary group relationship of some male prisoners. Talk of loyalty, sharing, trust, and friendship among female prisoners thus refers to the homosexual relationship not primary groups per se. These homosexual relationships attempt to stimulate the family found outside the prison and therefore are not primarily for sexual gratification. This relationship, according to Giallombardo's study, is the most important among the relationships of women in prison. Many of the women form a relationship that is recognized as a marriage, based on the belief that one cannot do time alone.[57]

For female inmates, pseudofamilies compensate for the lack of the close family environment on the outside. They also permit the exercise of dominant and submissive roles that the women have learned outside of prison. Within these pseudofamilies there is an opportunity for homosexual behavior, but the primary reason for forming family relationships appears not to be for that purpose.

> The primary source is the deprivation of the emotionally satisfying relationships with members of the opposite sex and the desire to create the basis for a community of relationships that are stable and predictable.[58]

Another characteristic of the homosexual behavior of female inmates distinguishes their behavior from that of male prison homosexual involvement. Whereas male homosexuality, especially homosexual rape, usually is manifested in actual physical sexual contact (oral or anal sex), for women, sexual relationships in prison may actually involve only a strong emotional relationship with some bodily contact that would be legitimate outside prison (for example, embracing upon seeing one another). It does not always involve sexual intercourse, as one normally thinks of male homosexuality. Some women may hold hands or fondle breasts whereas others engage in more serious forms of sexual contact such as oral-genital contact and bodily contact that attempts to simulate heterosexual intercourse.[59]

The 1986 publication of *Stranger in Two Worlds*, written by Jean Harris, focused national attention on the problems of women in prison. At that time, Harris had served 5 years for her conviction of murdering her lover, a physician noted for the "Scarsdale Diet." Harris, the former headmistress of a prestigious Virginia school, claimed unsuccessfully that she did not go to her lover's home to kill him; rather, she intended to talk to him and then commit suicide. She was distressed over the fact that the doctor broke off their relationship.[60]

Harris described inmate life from her view and those of other inmates, in her hope to bring about prison reform. She is also campaigning, along with her son and others, for her own early release. Her son has secured thousands of signatures asking that Harris, already the victim of one heart attack, be released from prison because of her health. Thus far, however, authorities have refused to do so.[61]

Mothers in Prison

Most female inmates have children, and most were living with their children at the time they were incarcerated. Care for their children is a primary concern of inmate mothers, and separation from their children is one of the greatest pains of their imprisonment.

Mothers who are incarcerated must, in addition to the loss of self-esteem that may come with incarceration, face their inadequacy to care for their children. They must cope with the problems of readjustment they and their children will face when the mothers are released from prison. They must deal with the lack of visitation opportunities for children and the problems of telling those children what is happening with their mothers. Some may face lawsuits over the legal custody of the children. All these problems may affect the ways that incarcerated mothers adapt to prison life.[62]

Some prisons have recognized the need to provide facilities and programs for inmates' children, and a growing number are permitting women inmates to keep their children in prison. Some have instituted programs designed to assist men inmates with their family problems, especially with children. This can have negative as well as positive results, of course, particularly among children old enough to understand the meaning of prison.[63]

SUMMARY

This chapter looked into the roles of those who live and work in prisons. The security goals of prisons are decided by how these people interact. In the earlier days, authoritarian prison wardens and guards maintained security by keeping inmates separate, not permitting them to talk to each other, or by using fear and force, often involving corporal punishment. Those methods are no longer permitted; new management techniques are necessary.

The guards, or the keepers, as they are often called, are crucial to prison management. They have primary responsibility for maintaining internal discipline, order, and security. Their jobs are difficult and at times boring, but they also are challenging and rewarding to many who have chosen the profession of correctional officer.

When we think of life behind bars, however, we think mainly of inmates serving time in those facilities. We began our discussion of inmate life by looking briefly at what happens after sentencing: how offenders get to prison and what may be expected during testing and orientation. This chapter's brief look at the routine of daily life in prison will be expanded in the next chapter, when we look more closely at prison programs and activities. Here, however, we were concerned mainly with how inmates adjust to prison life through the process of prisonization. The resulting subculture was discussed in view of its origin: whether inmates developed the subculture as a method of adapting to the deprivations of prison, or whether they already had the values of the subculture and imported them into prison.

The male inmate subculture is characterized by social roles that assist inmates in maintaining some self-esteem and positive self-concepts. Unfortunately, some accomplish these goals at the expense of other inmates: social control through economics, through racial and gang violence, and through homosexual attacks.

Some inmates adjust to prison life by inflicting violence on themselves rather than on others, and in some cases, suicide is the result.

Female inmates also develop patterns of adaptation to prison life, but their adaptations are less violent than those of males. Their sexual adjustments may involve homosexuality or just close friendships that simulate the family. Their social roles also mirror the roles they have played in society. Women face many of the same deprivations as male inmates, but they face the additional problems of adjusting to life without the daily care of their children. Mothers behind bars only recently have become a subject of research, and even today few provisions are made for them to interact with their children.

Adaptations to prison are made more difficult by the lack of activities, the lack of educational and vocational opportunities, and the conditions in which prisoners must live. All of these aspects of prison life have become the subjects of federal court orders; we now turn to a closer examination of the relationship between what goes on in prison and court intervention.

STUDY QUESTIONS

1. What were the characteristics of the authoritarian warden? What do you think would be the characteristics of the ideal warden?

2. What changes have occurred within prisons within the past two decades that have forced changes in prison administration?

3. How did early prison guards control inmates? If allowed, would those techniques be effective today?

4. What is the significance of prison gangs? What could be done to lessen their influence in prisons?

5. What is *prisonization*? How does it occur?

6. What is a *subculture*? How do prison subcultures develop? Are there differences between male and female subcultures or in the way they develop?

7. Distinguish male and female prison homosexuality.

8. What provisions do you think should be made for incarcerated women who have children at home or for women who give birth during incarceration?

ENDNOTES

1. See Harold Garfinkel, "Conditions of Successful Degradation Ceremonies," *The American Journal of Sociology* 61 (March 1956): 420–24.
2. Gresham M. Sykes, *The Society of Captives* (Princeton, N.J.: Princeton University Press, 1958), pp. 63–83.
3. Norman Holt, "Prison Management in the Next Decade," *The Prison Journal* 57 (Autumn–Winter 1977): 17–19.
4. James B. Jacobs, *Stateville: The Penitentiary in Mass Society* (Chicago: University of Chicago Press, 1977).
5. Kevin Krajick, "At Stateville, the Calm Is Tense," *Corrections Magazine* 6 (June 1980): 6.
6. This discussion is based on Holt, "Prison Management."
7. Alvin W. Cohn, "The Failure of Correctional Management," pp. 49–60; in Edward Sagrin and

Donal E. J. MacNamara, eds., *Corrections: Problems of Punishment and Rehabilitation* (New York: Holt, Rinehart and Winston, 1973).

8. Alvin W. Cohn, "The Failure of Correctional Management—Revisited," *Federal Probation* 43 (March 1979): 13, 14.

9. Nancy C. Jurik and Michael C. Musheno, "The Internal Crisis of Corrections: Professionalization and the Work Environment," *Justice Quarterly* 3 (December 1986): 477. See also James B. Jacobs, *New Perspectives on Prisons and Imprisonment* (Ithaca, N.Y.: Cornell University Press, 1983).

10. George Camp and Camille Camp, *Corrections Yearbook* (South Salem, N.Y.: Criminal Justice Institute, 1988), p. 43.

11. Donald Clemmer, *The Prison Community* (New York: Holt, Rinehart and Winston, 1958); and Sykes, *Society of Captives*. For an excellent publication of materials on prison guards, see Ben M. Crouch, ed., *The Keepers: Prison Guards and Contemporary Corrections* (Springfield, Ill.: Charles C. Thomas, 1980).

12. Quoted in Edgar May, "Prison Guards in America: The Inside Story," *Corrections Magazine* 2 (December 1976): 3.

13. "Four Correction Officers Demoted at Sing Sing," *New York Times* (31 January 1988), p. 33.

14. "A Web of Crime Behind Bars," *Time* (24 October 1988), p. 76.

15. Camp, *Corrections Yearbook*, p. 45.

16. Robert M. Regoli, Eric D. Poole, and Roy Lotz, "An Empirical Assessment of the Effect of Professionalism on Cynicism among Prison Guards," *Sociological Spectrum* 1 (1981): 53.

17. Eric D. Poole and Robert M. Regoli, "Alienation in Prison: An Examination of the Work Relations of Prison Guards," *Criminology* 19 (August 1981): 268. For other studies of guards and their problems regarding power to control inmates, see John R. Hepburn, "The Exercise of Power in Coercive Organizations: A Study of Prison Guards," *Criminology* 23 (February 1985): 145–64; Nigel Long et al., "Stress in Prison Staff: An Occupational Study," *Criminology* 24 (May 1986): 331–45; Crouch, *The Keepers*; and Jacobs, *New Perspectives on Prisons and Imprisonment*.

18. See, for example, Dothard v. Rawlinson, 433 U.S. 321 (1977); and Washington v. Gunther, 452 U.S. 161 (1981). For recent analyses of women guards in men's prisons, see Lynn Zimmer, *Women Guarding Men: A Study of Female Guards Who Work in Prisons for Men* (Chicago: University of Chicago Press, 1986); Joycelyn M. Pollock, *Sex and Supervision: Guarding Male and Female Inmates* (Westport, Conn.: Greenwood Press, 1986).

19. Camp and Camp, *Corrections Yearbook*, p. 43.

20. Barbara A. Owen, "Race and Gender Relations among Prison Workers," *Crime and Delinquency* 31 (January 1985): 156. For an analysis of the problems associated with women correctional officers, see Jacobs, *New Perspectives on Prisons and Imprisonment*, Chapter 9, "Female Guards in Men's Prisons," pp. 178–201.

21. Rita J. Simon and Judith D. Simon, "Female COs: Legitimate Authority," *Corrections* 50 (August 1988): 132.

22. Ben M. Crouch, "Women Guards in Men's Prisons: Problems and Prospects," paper presented at the Law and Society Association Annual Meetings, Denver, Colorado, 1983, p. 19. See also Geoffrey P. Alpert, "The Needs of the Judiciary and Misapplications of Social Research: The Case of Female Guards in Men's Prisons," *Criminology* 22 (August 1984): 441–56.

23. William T. Habern, "Going to Prison," mimeographed, Texas Department of Corrections, p. 10.

24. Clemmer, *The Prison Community*, pp. 298, 300, 301.

25. Stanton Wheeler, "Socialization in Correctional Communities," *American Sociological Review* 26 (October 1961): 697–712.

26. Geoffrey P. Alpert, et al., "A Comparative Look at Prisonization: Sex and Prison Culture," *Quarterly Journal of Corrections* 1 (Summer 1977): 29–34.

27. See Sykes, *The Society of Captives*; and Gresham M. Sykes and Sheldon L. Messinger, "The Inmate Social System," in Richard A. Cloward et al., eds., *Theoretical Studies in Social Organization of the Prison* (New York: Social Science Research Council, 1960).

28. See John Irwin and Donald R. Cressey, "Thieves, Convicts and the Inmate Culture," *Social Problems* 10 (Fall 1962): 142–55.

29. Charles W. Thomas, "Prisonization or Resocialization: A Study of External Factors Associated with the Impact of Imprisonment," *Journal of Research in Crime and Delinquency* 10 (January 1975): 13–21.

30. Leo Carroll, "Race and Three Forms of Prisoner Power Confrontation, Censoriousness, and the Corruption of Authority," in C. Ronald Huff, ed., *Comtemporary Corrections: Social Control and Conflict* (Beverly Hills, Calif.: Sage Publications, 1977), pp. 40, 41, 50–51.

31. Ronald L. Akers et al., "Prisonization in Five Countries: Type of Prison and Inmate Characteristics," *Criminology* 14 (February 1977): 538.

32. James Garofalo and Richard D. Clark, "The Inmate Subculture in Jails," *Criminal Justice and Behavior* 12 (December 1985): 431.

33. Leo Carroll, *Hacks, Blacks, and Cons: Race Relations in a Maximum Security Prison* (Lexington, Mass.: D. C. Heath and Co., 1974).

34. Cloward, "Social Control in the Prison," in Cloward et al., *Theoretical Studies*.

35. James W. Marguart and Ben M. Crouch, "Coopting the Kept: Using Inmates for Social Control in a Southern Prison," *Justice Quarterly* 1, no. 4 (1984): 491–509. The use of building tenders in the Texas prison system is discussed in numerous places in the recently published book about that system. See Steve J. Martin and Sheldon Ekland-Olson, *Texas Prisons: The Walls Came Tumbling Down* (Austin: Texas Monthly Press, 1987).

36. Jacobs, *Stateville*, pp. 46, 159, 172.

37. John Irwin, "The Changing Social Structure of the Men's Prison," in David F. Greenberg, ed., *Corrections and Punishment*, Sage Criminal Justice System Annuals (Beverly Hills, Calif.: Sage Publications, 1977), vol. 8, pp. 21–40.

38. Vergile Williams and Mary Fish, *Convicts, Codes and Contraband* (Cambridge, Mass.: Ballinger Publishing Company, 1974), pp. 137–42.

39. Irwin, "The Changing Social Structure of the Men's Prison," p. 27.

40. David K. v. Lane, 839 F.2d 1265, 1267–68 (7th Cir. 1988), footnote omitted. For recent information on prison gangs, see the following: C. G. Camp, *Prison Gangs—Their Extent, Nature and Impact on Prisons* (Washington, D.C.: U.S. Department of Justice, 1985); Lester H. Baird, "Prisons Gangs: Texas," and Roger W. Crist, "Prison Gangs: Arizona," *Corrections Today* 48 (July 1986): 12, 13, 18, 11, 25–27; and Steve Daniels, "Prison Gangs: Confronting the Threat," *Corrections Today* 49 (April 1987): 66, 126, 162.

41. Peter C. Buffum, *Homosexuality in Prisons* (U.S. Department of Justice et al., Washington, D.C.: U.S. Government Printing Office, 1972), p. 13.

42. Sykes, *Society of Captives*, p. 97.

43. Carroll, *Hacks, Blacks, and Cons*, p. 194.

44. Buffum, *Homosexuality in Prisons*, p. 9.

45. Susan Brownmiller, *Against Our Will: Men, Women and Rape* (New York: Simon and Schuster, 1975), p. 258.

46. Daniel Lockwood, *Prison Sexual Violence* (New York: Elsevier Science Publishing Co., 1980), p. 21.

47. See Camp and Camp, *Corrections Yearbook*, p. 19.

48. Ibid.

49. For additional information on prison violence, see Michael Braswell et al., *Prison Violence in America* (Cincinnati: Anderson Publishing Co., 1985.

50. See Garvin McCain et al., *The Effect of Prison Crowding on Inmate Behavior* (Washington, D.C.: U.S. Government Printing Office, 1980), pp. 113–15.

51. "Preventing Jail Suicides," *On The Line* (publication by the American Correctional Association) 2 (May 1988), p. 6. See also Bobbie Hopes, "Jail Suicide Prevention: Effective Programs Can Save Lives," *Corrections Today* 48 (December 1986): 64, 66, 70; and L. Thomas Winfree, Jr., "Toward Understanding State-Level Jail Mortality: Correlates of Death by Suicide and by Natural Causes, 1977 and 1982," *Justice Quarterly* 4 (March 1987): 56–76.

52. Ruth M. Glick and Virginia V. Neto, "National Study of Women's Correctional Programs," in Barbara Raffel Price and Natalie J. Sokoloff, eds., *The Criminal Justice System and Women* (New York: Clark Boardman Co., 1982), pp. 141–54.

53. Rose Giallombardo, *The Social World of Imprisoned Girls: A Comparative Study of Institutions for Juvenile Delinquents* (New York: John Wiley and Sons, 1974).

54. David A. Ward and Gene G. Kassebaum, "Women in Prison," in Robert M. Carter, Daniel Glaser, and Leslie T. Wilkins, eds., *Correctional Institutions* (Philadelphia: J. B. Lippincott, 1972), p. 215.

55. Williams and Fish, *Convicts, Codes, and Contraband*, pp. 99–122.

56. Ward and Kassebaum, "Women in Prison," pp. 217–18, 219.

57. Rose Giallombardo, *Society of Women: A Study of a Woman's Prison* (New York: John Wiley and Sons, 1966).

58. John Gagnon and William Simon, "The Social Meaning of Prison Homosexuality," *Federal Probation* 32 (March 1968): 27, 28.

59. David Ward and Gene Kassebaum, "Sexual Tensions in a Women's Prison," in Leon Radzinowicz and Marvin E. Wolfgang, eds., *Crime and Justice: The Criminal in Confinement* (New York: Basic Books, 1971), pp. 146–55. For other studies of women in prison, see Nicole Hahn Rafter, *Partial Justice: Women in State Prisons, 1800–1935* (Boston: Northeastern University, 1985); and Estelle B. Freedman, *Their Sisters' Keepers: Prison Reform in America, 1830–1930* (Ann Arbor: University of Michigan Press, 1981). See also James G. Fox, "Women in Prison: A Case Study in the Social Reality of Stress," in Robert Johnson and Hans Toch, eds., *The Pains of Imprisonment* (Beverly Hills, Calif.: Sage Publications, 1982), pp. 205–20. For other studies of women in prison, see Nicole Hahn Rafter, *Partial Justice: Women in State Prisons, 1800–1935* (Boston: Northeastern University, 1985).

60. Jean Harris, *Stranger in Two Worlds* (New York: Macmillan Publishing Co., 1986).

61. See "A Book from the Pen: Will Her Powerful Critique Help Free Jean Harris?" *Newsweek* (28 July 1986), p. 24.

62. Phyllis Jo Baunach, "You Can't Be a Mother and Be in Prison . . . Can You? Impacts of the

Mother-Child Separation," in Price and Sokoloff, eds., *The Criminal Justice System and Women*, pp. 155–69.

63. For a new book that describes programs for inmates and their children, see James Boudouris, *Prisons and Kids: Programs for Inmate Parents* (Laurel, Md.: American Correctional Association).

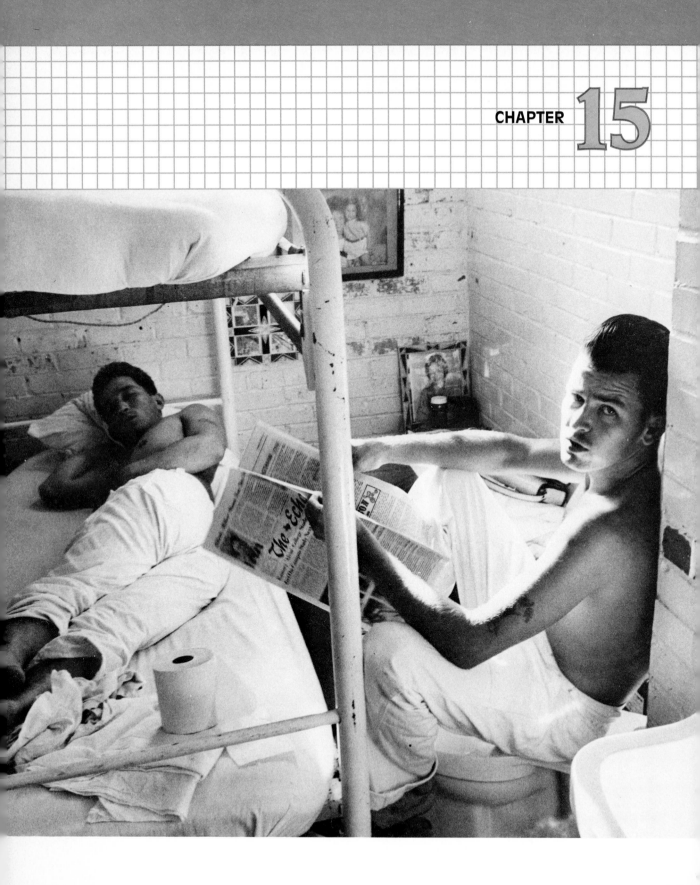

Conditions of Incarceration: The Courts React

KEY TERMS

civil death
civil rights
conjugal visiting
contempt of court
contraband
double celling
due process
equal protection
Free Venture Program
good-time credits
habeas corpus
hands-off doctrine
writ

Amy and John, a married couple completing their final year in college, are convicted of the felony of selling drugs and sentenced to 3 years in prison. Because they are in a state that has only one prison for women, Amy is incarcerated 600 miles from her husband and her parents. The facility is uncrowded and located in a beautiful remote area of the state 200 miles from a large city. The prison has a nurse on duty 24 hours a day, but doctors and dentists are hired on a contract basis and are available only two mornings a week. Amy is pregnant; she has special medical needs that are not met at the prison. She wants to continue her college education, but there are no provisions for college courses at the prison or for correspondence courses.

John is classified as a medium-security inmate; but although he is incarcerated at the medium-security facility, he gets into a fight when another inmate tries to force him into a homosexual act. The Discipline Committee considers John a risk, reclassifies him, and sends him to the maximum-security prison. Conditions there are far worse than those in the medium-security prison. John has less freedom. He is constantly worried about threats of violence and brutality from the gang members who are incarcerated at the prison. The situation gets out of hand; the prison officials prohibit all correspondence with inmates located in other institutions. This is a large prison system, and gang members from other prisons are alleged to be ordering assassinations and other types of violence within John's prison.

John and Amy may no longer communicate. John at least has access to college-level programs, however, and he is able to complete his college education. Amy is taken to the hospital 200 miles from her prison to have the baby, but no provisions are made for her to keep the baby in prison. Amy becomes very depressed and needs psychiatric care, but the prison does not have a psychiatrist; she turns to religion. However, the particular religious faith that she practices requires candles and other items for services; prison officials say these are security risks and forbids them.

INTRODUCTION

The cases of John and Amy are hypothetical. Probably all of these circumstances would not occur in any two cases. But the alleged facts illustrate many of the topics that will be discussed in this chapter. Increasingly, inmates are successfully arguing that their constitutional rights are being violated in state and federal prisons. John and Amy have several bases for arguing that their rights are being violated; they will win on some and lose on others. This chapter will discuss these issues: the differences in the locations and types of facilities in which John and Amy are incarcerated, the lack of adequate medical facilities in the women's prison, the transfer of John from medium to maximum security, the absence of any provision for Amy to be with her infant, and the prohibition of correspondence between John and Amy.

The recognition of legal rights of inmates has had a rather short history. In an 1871 case a federal court bluntly expressed the lack of legal rights of prisoners by declaring that the convicted felon has as a consequence of his crime, not only forfeited his liberty, but all his personal rights except those which the law in its humanity accords to him. He is for the time being the slave of the state.[1]

This declaration meant that natural or **civil rights,** such as freedom of religion and freedom of speech, guaranteed by the Constitution, were permitted at the discretion of prison officials. Many jurisdictions imposed **civil death** on convicted persons, meaning that they could not sue or be sued, enter into a contract, vote, hold office, or work. In some cases contracts, including the marriage contract, could be voided without their consent. In some jurisdictions convicted persons lost custody of their children. All or some of the elements of civil death might be continued after inmates were released from prison.

In 1974 the United States Supreme Court said,

> But though his rights may be diminished by the needs and exigencies of the institutional environment, a prisoner is not wholly stripped of constitutional protections when he is imprisoned for crime. There is no iron curtain drawn between the Constitution and the prisons of this country.[2]

Before 1974, lower federal courts had already begun looking into claims by prisoners that they were being denied basic constitutional rights during their confinement. By the 1980s numerous lawsuits had been filed by inmates; federal courts had more closely scrutinized prison conditions, particularly regarding overcrowding; and entire prison systems had been placed under federal court orders to reduce populations and make other changes in prison conditions.

Litigation on prisoners' rights is extensive; no attempt can be made in an introductory book to cover that vast body of law. However, it is possible to get a very good overview of the way courts have responded to the issues raised by prisoners. A few words of warning are in order.

In our discussion of courts we saw that the decisions of lower courts do not apply to courts in other jurisdictions. In this chapter, many of the decisions cited are from lower federal courts. Courts faced with similar facts may, and often do, decide issues differently. Only when the U.S. Supreme Court decides the issue is the case binding on all courts, and the Supreme Court has not decided very many prisoners' rights cases.

Another important point is that the law of prisoners' rights is changing rapidly. In all probability, some of the cases discussed in this chapter will be overruled while the book is in production. Because of the rapidly changing law, many of the cases cited will be cases decided in 1987 or 1988. Exceptions will be the Supreme Court cases that are important regardless of their date of decision, if they have not been changed by later Supreme Court cases, and lower federal courts cases that are important for historical reasons or because they are critical cases in a particular area and are still good law. All cases have been checked up to press time to make sure no changes have occurred, such as a higher appellate court overruling the cited case.[3]

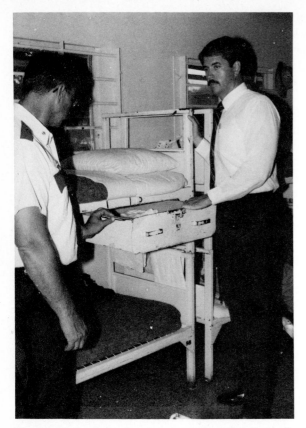 

States and the federal system have established standards for jails. In these pictures, Florida State Jail and Prison Inspector Jimmy Kean checks to see whether this jail's kitchen and cells meet minimum state standards.

HISTORICAL OVERVIEW

Historically in the United States, administration of state prisons has been considered off-limits for federal courts. Federal courts would not hear cases from state courts because no federal rights were considered to be involved. In addition, federal courts observed a hands-off policy toward federal prisons, reasoning that prison administration is a part of the executive, not the judicial, branch of government.

Likewise, state courts have traditionally not heard complaints from prisoners concerning conditions within state prisons. State courts have heard cases mainly involving postconviction remedies that attacked the confinement itself, as opposed to the conditions of confinement. Conditions were considered to be within the realm of prison administration and thus not a proper sphere for judicial interference.

This unwillingness of federal courts to interfere with the daily administration of prisons was called the **hands-off doctrine.** The general reluctance of courts to interfere in the daily administration of prisons also is seen in Supreme Court decisions. In 1979 in *Bell v. Wolfish,* the Court emphasized that prison administrators should be accorded wide-ranging deference in the adoption and execution of policies and practices that in their judgment are needed to preserve internal order and discipline and to maintain institutional security.[4]

The Beginnings of Federal Court Intervention

If federal courts defer to prison officials for the daily administration of prisons, on what basis are those courts involved today? What suddenly brought prisoners to their attention? The civil rights activism of the 1960s included, among other issues, the treatment of prisoners, and during that period federal courts did begin to look at what was happening inside prisons. Many of the earlier cases involved allegations of physical brutality.

One of the most publicized of the earlier accounts of corporal punishment within a modern prison came from two prisons in Arkansas. Among other punishments was the inflicting of electric shock through a device wired to the genitals and to one of the big toes of the inmates. Arkansas inmates also alleged that prisoners had been murdered at the prison and buried in the prison yard. In 1967 the governor of Arkansas released a prison report that had been ordered and then suppressed by the former governor. That report

> painted a picture of hell in Arkansas. To maintain discipline, prisoners were beaten with leather straps, blackjacks, hoses. Needles were shoved under their fingernails, and cigarettes were applied to their bodies.[5]

In January 1968, Thomas O. Merton, superintendent appointed by the governor of Arkansas to reform the prison system, exhumed the bodies of three inmates who had allegedly been murdered by inmates or prison officials. National attention to this process was apparently too much for the governor; Merton was fired. A movie, *Brubaker*, portrayed the attempts of Merton to reform the Arkansas Prison System. His own accounts are found in his book, *The Dilemma of Prison Reform*.[6]

The federal district court, after hearing evidence on the prison conditions in Arkansas, concluded that inmates were living under degrading and disgusting conditions and found the prison system unconstitutional. The need for judicial intervention into the administration of prisons was emphatically stated by the federal court. "If Arkansas is going to operate a Penitentiary System, it is going to have to be a system that is countenanced by the Constitution of the United States."[7]

MODERN LITIGATION: AN INTRODUCTION

During the 1970s and 1980s, federal courts heard many cases on the conditions of prisons. More recently, federal intervention has been extended to jails. Some facilities have been ordered closed until conditions are corrected; others have included orders to change specific conditions. Courts still defer to prison authorities concerning the day-to-day operations of prisons. They will intervene, however, when federal constitutional rights are violated. It is necessary to look more closely at those rights.

In analyzing prisoner's rights, prison officials historically spoke of the difference between *rights* and *privileges*. *Rights* require constitutional protection; *privileges* are there by the grace of prison officials and may be withdrawn at the discretion of officials. In 1971 the Supreme Court rejected the position that "constitutional rights turn upon whether a governmental benefit is characterized as a 'right' or a 'privilege.' "[8]

It is clear, however, that a hierarchy of rights is still recognized. Some rights are considered more important than others and therefore require more extensive due process before they may be infringed upon. A prisoner's right to be released from illegal confinement is more important than the right to canteen privileges. Some of the other rights high in the hierarchy are the right to protection against willful injury, access to courts, freedom of religious belief, freedom of communication, and the right to be free of cruel and unusual punishment.

The recognition of the rights of inmates and of the hierarchy of rights does not mean that the government (or prison officials acting as government agents) may not restrict those rights. Rights may be restricted if prison officials can show that the restriction is necessary for security or for other recognized penological purposes such as discipline and order.[9]

Substantive Legal Rights of Inmates

The rights of inmates stem from the Bill of Rights to the federal Constitution. Previous chapters have analyzed some of those rights: the right to counsel, the right to be free of unreasonable searches and seizures, the right to a public trial by a jury of one's peers, and the right to be confronted with witnesses.

Some of those rights also apply to prisoners; others have not been applied to inmates. One very important area of rights that has not yet been discussed in the text is the basis for considerable litigation on prison issues. Those are First Amendment rights including freedom of speech, of assembly, of the press, of religion, and the right to address the government when rights are being violated.

The Fourteenth Amendment rights to due process and equal protection, discussed previously, also are important to the rights of inmates. Certain elements of due process must accompany disciplinary decisions such as rescinding an inmate's acquired good time or placing inmates in solitary confinement. Equal protection will become an issue in our discussion of the differences between treatment, work opportunities, and medical care provided for men as compared to women inmates.

Many inmate lawsuits will also be argued on the basis of a violation of the Eighth Amendment right to be free of cruel and unusual punishment, or of the Fourth Amendment right to be free of unreasonable search and seizure. (See Appendix A.)

Inmate Civil Actions

Thus far the text has focused on criminal cases. The legal actions discussed in this chapter involve civil cases. Not all constitutional rights that exist at the pretrial, trial, and appellate stages of criminal cases will apply to civil cases and some of the rules of evidence will differ. The distinction between criminal and civil cases is important for another reason. The number of civil cases filed in the past decade has increased even more dramatically than the number of criminal cases. Between 1973 and 1983 civil filings increased by 114 percent compared to 107 percent for criminal filings.[10] Prisoners have accounted for many of these filings, and their filings have increased significantly since 1961. The resulting backlog in civil courts means that prisoners (and others) may face a long wait before a case is decided.[11]

Civil actions brought by inmates usually are over the conditions of confinement or to the actions of prison officials. They involve one of two types of legal actions: habeas corpus or a Section 1983 action. Each will be discussed briefly.

Habeas corpus literally means "you have the body." There are several types of habeas corpus actions, but the one that is relevant to this chapter's discussions is the action brought by the inmate who is asking the court to grant a **writ** of habeas corpus, directing prison officials to release that inmate.

When prisoners request a writ of habaes corpus, they are arguing that they are not legally confined. They may make this argument because prison conditions are alleged to be unconstitutional, or because they have been disciplined improperly or without proper procedures being observed. The habeas corpus action says, "I am being held illegally in this prison because my rights have been violated. Therefore, I should be released." Few inmates are successful in their *habaes corpus* petitions.

A second and more frequently used method for petitioning federal courts is a Section 1983 action. The name comes from the section number of the federal statute, United States Code, Title 42, Section 1983, under which the action may be brought. It is a section of the Civil Rights Act, and it provides that:

> Every person who, under color of any statute, ordinance, regulation, custom, or usage, of any State or Territory, subjects or causes to be subjected, any citizen of the United States or the person within the jurisdiction thereof to the deprivation of any rights, privileges, or immunities secured by the Constitution and laws, shall be liable to the party injured in an action at law, suit in equity, or other proper proceeding for redress.

To come within this statute, inmates must show that prison officials have deprived them of their rights protected by the United States Constitution or by a federal statute. Section 1983 claims may cover almost every aspect of an inmate's life, and litigation under this statute is complex.

If the Section 1983 action is successful, inmates may be awarded damages for the deprivations they have suffered. The federal court also may order prison officials to change the conditions that led to the constitutional violation. In cases of extreme violations, courts have ordered jails or prisons closed until conditions are corrected. In cases of overcrowded facilities, judges may order that the population be reduced.[12]

Prison Conditions: The Total View

Although the various constitutional rights of inmates will be considered separately, it is important to understand that courts do not usually look at these rights in isolation. The concern of the court generally will be with the overall conditions of incarceration. For example, although the Supreme Court has held in two cases that **double celling** or double bunking of inmates was not unconstitutional, that does not necessarily mean the Court would consider double celling constitutional under any circumstances.

In the first case, *Bell v. Wolfish*, involving the housing of two inmates in the same cell in a modern jail facility, the Court noted that the inmates were not required to remain in their cells for long periods of time; thus, double celling might not be expected to have the negative effect that it might have under other circumstances when inmates do not have the freedom to move in and out of their cells.

In 1981 the Court, in *Rhodes v. Chapman*, considered double celling in an Ohio prison. But again, the Court was looking at a relatively new facility. The Southern Ohio Correctional Facility has several workshops, gymnasiums, schoolrooms, day rooms, two chapels, a hospital ward, a

Prison conditions are generally analyzed in their totality before courts decide whether they are unconstitutional. This crowded area may not be unconstitutional if inmates are not required to spend unusually long hours in such confinement. (UPI Bettmann News)

commissary, a barber shop, and a library. It also has a recreation field, a visitation area, and a garden. Cells are reasonably comfortable, with 63 square feet of space and bunk beds, a wall-mounted sink, a toilet, a cabinet, a shelf, a high nightstand, and a radio. Cells are ventilated and well heated; many even have windows that can be opened. Noise has not been a serious problem, and as in the *Bell v. Wolfish* case, most inmates are allowed considerable time outside their cells.[13]

It is also necessary, in considering what conditions are unconstitutional, to distinguish types of facilities. Prisons are classified as maximum, medium, and minimum security. Conditions that might be justified for security in a maximum-security prison may not be permitted in those designed for inmates who need only limited supervision. Likewise, conditions considered constitutional for convicted persons serving a sentence in prison or jail may not be appropriate for pretrial detainees, who are in jail awaiting trial but have not yet been convicted.

FIRST AMENDMENT RIGHTS

One of the most important rights in this country is the right to express ourselves, to communicate with other people. The First Amendment of the United States Constitution, cited earlier, includes some of our most precious rights. These rights also are very important to inmates. The difficult adjustment problems in prison may be eased by communication with family and friends. Injustices within the prison unfortunately are usually changed only by courts; thus the right of inmates to petition the courts is critical. Freedom of religion involves not only the right to think and believe, but the right to engage in religious practices.

Mail

Prisoner correspondence has produced considerable litigation, partly because of the importance of contact with the outside world and partly because this right also involves the rights of persons outside the prison. In the past, prison officials refused to mail letters, refused to give letters to inmates, censored mail, deleted comments from outgoing and incoming letters, removed articles considered to be detrimental to the inmate, and decided who could correspond with particular inmates. Prison officials claimed that these actions were necessary to maintain prison security.

The Supreme Court considered prison censorship of personal mail in a case involving inmates who were not permitted to write letters in which they complained unduly or magnified grievances. They were forbidden to express any inflammatory views whether political, racial, or religious or to send letters that pertained to criminal activity. Letters that were lewd, obscene, defamatory, or that contained foreign matter were also forbidden. All incoming and outgoing mail was screened for violations of these regulations. When officials found a violation of these rules, the letter was returned to the inmate, who then received a disciplinary report and punishment. In *Procunier v. Martinez*, the Court held that censorship of a prisoner's mail is constitutional "if that is necessary to maintain security, order, rehabilitation. Even then, the censorship may be no greater than is necessary to protect those legitimate governmental interests."[14]

An example of the type of censorship that was not permitted by a federal court is found in *McNamara v. Moody*, in which prison officials refused to mail a letter written by an inmate to his girlfriend. The letter was returned to the inmate with a note indicating that it was

> in poor taste and absolutely unacceptable for mailing from this institution. . . . The next time you write a letter such as the one attached, you may be sure that you will meet with the disciplinary team.

The letter in question alleged that the censors lead such blah lives that they "must masturbate themselves while they read other people's mail." The letter also alleged that another inmate told the writer that the censor "has a cat and that he is suspected of having relations of some sort with his cat."

Prison officials argued that it was necessary to censor this mail for security reasons and that censorship was permissible because the words were obscene. The Court disagreed, holding that the words were not obscene ("Vulgar it is; obscene it is not") and that prison officials had not demonstrated that censorship was necessary for prison security and discipline. The Supreme Court refused to hear the case, thus allowing the lower court decision to stand.[15]

In a later case, decided by the Second Circuit Court in 1987, Judge Irving R. Kaufman, widely cited for his judicial opinions, emphasized the importance of distinguishing between the security needs of the institution (for which censorship is permitted) and the unpopular political beliefs of the inmate (for which censorship is not permitted). In *Hall v. Curran*, Judge Kaufman remanded the case for further consideration of the evidence, a procedural matter. But his opinion is important here for its concise statement of the importance of constitutional rights, even in prison, combined with his recognition of the difficulties of prison administration, the need for security and discipline, and the need for deference to prison administration.[16]

Hall v. *Curran*

The preservation of social order and the enforcement of our laws is one of the most basic tasks of government, and prisons are one essential means of accomplishing that task. The maintenance of safety and discipline in our penal institutions is best secured through the kind of professional administrative expertise that can be forged only in the crucible of day-to-day experience. Managing a prison is both a science and an art. Optimal penal environments are created slowly and individually. They do not spring whole from judicial decrees. For this reason, judges traditionally and wisely accord considerable discretion to corrections officials; . . . Nevertheless, our usual judicial restraint in this area must be tempered at times by the mandates of the Constitution. When an inmate alleges violations of his First Amendment freedoms, we are bound to afford him a meaningful opportunity to prove his claim. [The inmate in this case has been denied that right through a procedure called *summary judgment*. The court ordered the case back for a trial]. . . .

A prisoner is not stripped of his First Amendment rights at the cellblock door. Rather, he "retains those First Amendment rights that are not inconsistent with his status as a prisoner or with the legitimate penological objectives of the corrections system." Similarly, the prisoner's correspondent, whether author or intended recipient, "derives from the First and Fourteenth Amendments a protection against unjustified governmental interference with the intended communication." . . .

Examples of mail that might threaten institutional security and that could properly be censored were cited by one court as follows: brochures telling prisoners how to "saw prison bars with utensils used in the mess hall or how to provoke a prison riot;" magazines "detailing for incarcerated drug addicts how they might obtain a euphoric 'high' comparable to that experienced from heroin, by sniffing aerosol or glue available for other purposes within the prison walls." Even in those cases where censorship is proper, however, officials must follow reasonable standards in the methods of censorship, the timing, and the notice given to persons to whom the mail is addressed.[17]

Categories of Mail Limitations that prison officials may place on the right of inmates to communicate by mail with the outside world vary according to the type of mail. Correspondence falls into two categories: privileged and general. Privileged mail is mail between an inmate and attorneys or other persons connected with the courts or treatment of the inmate. General mail is between an inmate and anyone not in the privileged category.

These two categories of mail involve different rules and regulations; there are fewer restrictions on privileged correspondence than on general correspondence. To assist prison officials in drafting procedures and rules that will be constitutional, the American Correctional Association (ACA) has drafted model procedures. Spotlight 15.1 contains the model procedures for regulating general correspondence.

Packages may be categorized as privileged or general mail. The Supreme Court has upheld the right of prison officials to prohibit the receipt by inmates of hardcover books unless they were mailed directly from the publishers, book clubs, or bookstores. The Court considered that regulation to be a security measure. Correspondents might send **contraband** such as money and drugs, even weapons, into prison inside the hardback books. Officials could open packages to determine whether there is contraband, of course, but prisons are also given discretion in limiting, or in some cases prohibiting, receipt of packages because of the time required for these checks.

The correspondence that causes the greatest concern for prison officials is correspondence between inmates in different prisons. In early 1986 officials of the Texas prison system requested the federal court to permit them to prohibit all correspondence of this nature. Texas had to get permission from the federal court because part of the agreement in the set-

SPOTLIGHT 15.1
AMERICAN CORRECTIONAL ASSOCIATION'S PROCEDURES FOR REGULATING GENERAL CORRESPONDENCE OF INMATES

B. Outgoing General Correspondence
1. Inmates shall be allowed to send letters to whomever they wish, including inmates at other institutions, except when clear evidence related to institutional security, order, or rehabilitation exists to justify a limit. Any limitation shall be appealable to the warden or his designee. The number of letters sent shall not be limited.
2. Outgoing mail is not to be opened, inspected or censored in any manner except as is necessary to enforce the requirements of § 11-B of these rules.
3. Indigent inmates shall receive postage and stationery sufficient to send at least three letters of general correspondence per week.

C. Incoming General Correspondence
1. There shall be no limit on the amount of incoming mail an inmate is allowed to receive.
2. All incoming general correspondence may be opened and examined for cash, checks, money orders or contraband.
3. In cases where cash, checks or money orders are found, they shall be removed and credited to the inmate's account.
4. When contraband is found, it shall also be removed.
5. The Director of the Department of Corrections shall establish guidelines for determining when incoming mail is to be read. If a letter is read which the reader believes meets any of the criteria for censorship, the letter shall promptly be referred to the Warden's designee for review and decision as to whether censorship of all or part of the letter is required.
6. In each case where it is deemed necessary to read an inmate's mail, a written record shall be made which shall include the following:
   a. The inmate's name and number.
   b. Name of the sender.
   c. The date the letter was received and read.
   d. The reason for reading the letter, if the decision to read the letter was discretionary.
   e. The signature of the officer who read the mail.
   f. This rule shall not apply if all incoming mail is read.

7. Letters shall not be censored unless there is evidence that the correspondence contains one or more of the following:
   a. Plans for sending contraband in or out of the institution.
   b. Plans for criminal activity.
   c. Instructions for manufacture of weapons, drugs or drugs paraphernalia, or alcoholic beverages.
   d. The letter threatens blackmail or extortion.
   e. Plans for escape or unauthorized entry.
   f. The letter is in code which is not understood by the reader.
   g. The letter contains plans for activities in violation of institution rules.
   h. The letter contains information which, if communicated, would create a serious danger of violence and physical harm to a human being.
   i. The letter contains other material which would, if communicated, create a serious danger to the security of the institution.
8. If a letter is censored, a written notice, signed by the official authorizing the censorship and stating the reason(s) for censorship shall be given to the sender and the inmate.
   a. The sender and/or the inmate may appeal the decision to the warden or his designee who may not be a person involved in the original decision to censor.
   b. Either the original or a legible copy of censored correspondence shall be retained.
9. The written records of reading and censorship shall be reviewed each month by the Director of the Department of Corrections or his designee to determine if:
   a. There were sufficient grounds to censor the mail.
   b. The censorship was no more extensive than necessary to meet the criteria for censorship.
   c. Mail that is selected for reading is chosen in accordance with established policy.

tlement of the prison lawsuit in that state was that officials would permit inmates to correspond.

Texas prison officials argued that sophisticated codes were being sent between inmates and that these codes contained orders for assassinations from leaders of inmate gangs. If only correspondence between gang members was prohibited, argued the officials, those inmates might get non-gang members to send the letters. Lawyers argued that the total prohibition would prevent inmates from getting the only legal advice that was available to some: the services of an inmate law clerk in another institution. In late April 1986, an out-of-court settlement was agreed to by prison officials and attorneys for the inmates. Mail between inmates is allowed as long as the letters are not used to promote violence or break other prison rules.

In 1987 in *Turner v. Safley*, the Supreme Court upheld the Missouri Division of Corrections' ban on mail between inmates in different institutions. The Missouri provisions permitted mail between "immediate family members who are inmates in other correctional institutions" and correspondence between inmates "concerning legal matters." Any other correspondence between inmates was permitted only if "the classification/treatment team of each inmate deems it in the best interest of the parties involved."[18]

The Right to Profits from Publicity One final issue on the right of inmates to communicate with the outside world is whether they should be permitted to receive profits when articles or books about their criminal activities are published. The New York statute, called the *"Son of Sam" statute*, was the result of public concern that Sam Berkowitz, who murdered six young people in New York in the late 1970s, would make millions from his writings about the killings.

The statute, which has been the model for many of the subsequently enacted statutes, provides that any proceeds from "the accused or convicted person's thoughts, feelings, opinions, or emotions regarding [the] crime" must be turned over to the Victim's Compensation Board. The statute covers reenactment "by way of a movie, book, magazine, article, tape recording, phonograph, radio or television presentation, [or] television presentation" and requires that the person contracting with the criminal must also turn over proceeds to the Victim Compensation Board.[19] The New York statute also contains provisions for victims to bring civil actions against their perpetrators and subsequently recover from the victim's compensation fund. No court has yet held that these "Son of Sam" statutes are unconstitutional as a violation of the prisoner's First Amendment right to free speech.

The constitutionality of the New York statute was upheld in 1979;[20] and in 1987 the New York Crime Victims Compensation Board ruled that convicted murderer Jean Harris, author of *Stranger in Two Worlds*, must turn over her $45,000 advance for that book. If she does not still have that money, the publisher must pay that amount to the board. Any profits above that advance must be turned over to the family of the man Harris murdered.

Visitation

Visits with Family and Friends   The Supreme Court has recognized the importance of permitting inmates to see their families and friends, suggesting that such visits might be "a factor contributing to the ultimate reintegration of the detainees into society." But that statement comes from a case involving pretrial detainees in detention in the largest jail in the country, the Los Angeles County Central Jail, with a capacity of 5,000 inmates. The court in *Block v. Rutherford* upheld the total prohibition against visitations in that jail. The Court emphasized that security is a crucial problem in a population that large and that even small children may be used by family and friends to smuggle contraband into the jail.[21]

The position taken by the Supreme Court in *Block v. Rutherford* must be limited to the facts of the case. The Court emphasized that pretrial detainees, who are there because they have been denied bail or were unable to make bail, are likely to be charged with serious offenses. The large size of the population, which would create tremendous administrative problems if visits were permitted, and the short period of confinement are also factors. In other situations, the Court might not uphold a total prohibition on contact visits. Some lower courts have taken that position. Some prison officials maintain that contact visits reduce tensions in the prison and aid in the rehabilitation of inmates.

The ACA emphasizes the importance of visitation between inmates and their families and friends. The ACA Model Procedures suggest that visitation be permitted in an informal atmosphere in which the inmate may have physical contact with visitors. Contact visits are to be distinguished from conjugal visits, discussed later, in which sexual relationships are permitted. In contact visits inmates usually will be permitted to hug and embrace the family member or friend; in some institutions that will be the extent of the contact permitted, and guards will monitor the visits. In other institutions inmates may have limited contacts with visitors throughout the visits. Visits may be particularly important when children are involved.

Security is always a problem, and the ACA Model Procedures, as indicated in Spotlight 15.2, provide restrictions for security. In some situations, where inmates are dangerous to themselves or others or where the risk of contraband is high, inmates may not be permitted to have contact visits. In these situations, the inmate and the visitor will usually be separated by glass; they may talk over a phone or through a screened hole in the glass, but they may not touch each other. One final arrangement is to permit a dangerous inmate to be in the same room with the visitor, but restrain the inmate by handcuffs, body chains, or both.

Conjugal visiting refers to the system administrators have employed in some jurisdictions for providing prisoners with opportunities for sexual and other social contacts with their spouses in a relaxed, unsupervised, special area of the prison community. During the visit the couple may engage in sexual intercourse, just be alone together, or use the time in any other way they choose. In some cases, the visit has been expanded to

SPOTLIGHT 15.2
AMERICAN CORRECTIONAL ASSOCIATION'S PROCEDURES FOR
REGULATING SECURITY DURING VISITATION OF PRISON INMATES

B. Security
1. The visiting room and procedures shall be devised so as to insure the security of the institution.
2. Prior to the visit, all visitors shall be:
   a. Registered as guests and identified.
   b. Checked to determine that they have been approved for visitation.
   c. Advised of all visiting regulations by the placing of such rules in a conspicuous place for all to see.
   d. Searched by a scanning device or frisked. If after these methods have been used, there is still a reasonable suspicion that the person is carrying contraband, a further consensual search may be undertaken. Visitors shall be requested to submit to such further searches only following the approval of an official designated by the superintendent, who shall be of the rank of lieutenant or above, who shall evaluate the grounds asserted to justify the search. A report shall be made following each such search which shall contain the names of the searching officers and the official who approved the

search, the reasons for the search, the extent of the search, and what, if anything, was found.
   e. No body cavity (anal or genital) searches shall be conducted by correctional personnel. If a search less intrusive than such a body cavity search is insufficient to allay suspicions that the visitor is smuggling, the visitor shall be denied access to the contact visiting area or denied admission to the institution, as appropriate.
3. All inmates shall be frisked prior to entering the visiting room.
4. All inmates shall be frisked or strip-searched upon leaving the visiting room to prevent the introduction of contraband into the institution.
5. The institution shall post a large sign in the lobby or other entrance stating that "ALL VISITORS ARE SUBJECT TO SEARCH PRIOR TO BEING ALLOWED TO VISIT ANY INMATE."

include the entire nuclear family, not just the spouse. Some involve a live-in weekend instead of a few hours on visiting day.

Conjugal visiting is common in many European prisons; it is very seldom permitted in this country, and American courts have not been willing to hold that inmates have a constitutional right to marry and engage in conjugal relations.[22] In *Turner v. Safley* the Supreme Court held that states may place substantial restrictions on inmate marriages, but those restrictions must be "reasonably related to legitimate penological objectives," one of which would be institutional security.[23]

In February 1988 the Fifth Circuit responded to the argument of an inmate's wife that she has a constitutional right to conjugal visits with her incarcerated husband and that denial of that right constitutes cruel and unusual punishment. This brief excerpt illustrates the court's reaction.[24]

Davis v. *Carlson* _____

Mrs. Davis's [the inmate's wife] . . . third claim is a complaint of the denial of conjugal visits. No such constitutional right exists; nor are we cited to any common-law or statutory authority supporting one. Finally, Mrs. Davis asserts that Davis's incarceration violates *her* rights against cruel and unusual punishment. It may be, of course, that the incarceration of Davis causes inconvenience, even hardship, to Mrs. Davis; and this is, of course, most unfortunate. There is, however, no intent to punish Mrs. Davis; and unless we were empowered and prepared to declare that because of the effect on the spouse a married person cannot be punished by incarceration, her claim is doomed. We are neither, and it is.

One final point concerning family visits is important in light of the rapid spread of the deadly virus AIDS (Acquired Immunity Deficiency Syndrome). In December 1987 New York's highest court upheld prison officials' decision to prohibit conjugal visits between an inmate infected with AIDS and his wife. The court held that this refusal was not an unreasonable interference with the rights of the inmate or of his spouse.[25]

Visits with the Press   One final type of visit important to inmates is the right to visit with the press. In *Pell v. Procunier*, the Supreme Court upheld a California statute providing that "press and other media interviews with specific individual inmates will not be permitted." The Court said internal security required that some restrictions be made on face-to-face contacts with outsiders. The restriction on visits with the media must be viewed in perspective with alternatives. Inmates may communicate with the press through prison-approved visits and also through the mail. The Court concluded that as long as reasonable and effective means of communications are available and there is no discrimination in the contents of those communications, the prison must be given great latitude in regulating visits with the press.[26]

The Supreme Court has also held that there is no

right of access to government information or sources of information within the government's control, and the news media have no constitutional right of access to a county jail, over and above that of other persons, to interview inmates and make sound recordings, films, and photographs for publication and broadcasting by newspapers, radio and television.[27]

Religious Worship

Numerous court cases have arisen over the First Amendment right to freedom of religion and what that means in the prison setting. The general rule was announced by the U.S. Supreme Court in 1972 in *Cruz v. Beto*. An inmate must be given "a reasonable opportunity of pursuing his faith comparable to the opportunity afforded fellow prisoners who adhere to conventional religious precepts." This does not mean that all religious sects or groups must have identical facilities or personnel. "But reasonable opportunities must be afforded to all prisoners to exercise the religious freedom guaranteed by the First and Fourteenth Amendments without fear of penalty."[28]

In its 1987–1988 term, in *O'Lone v. Estate of Shabazz*, the Court was asked to declare unconstitutional one of the policies of prison officials at New Jersey's Leesburgh State Prison. The details are lengthy and will not be recited, but the essence of the problem was that prison officials, in order to maintain security, had "prohibited inmates assigned to outside work details from returning to the prison during the day except in the case of emergency."

Jumu'ah is a Muslim service, commanded by the Koran, which must be held every Friday "after the sun reaches its zenith and before the Asr, or afternoon prayer." Inmates on outside work detail could not, as the result of the prison official's order, attend this service. The Court, in looking at all the facts, decided that prison officials had acted reasonably. The Court reaffirmed its refusal,

> even where claims are made under the First Amendment, to "substitute our judgment on . . . difficult and sensitive matters of institutional administration" for the determinations of those charged with the formidable task of running a prison.[29]

An inmate may claim a right to practice religious beliefs only if the religion is a recognized one and if the inmate is a sincere believer in that religion. The question may then arise as to whether the inmate may observe all aspects of that religion. As *Shabazz* indicates, some observances may not be permitted for security reasons or because of the time and personnel required to secure the prison during those observances. Other issues may involve diet, grooming, and dress. Some inmates' requests for special food and diet compatible with their religious beliefs have been successful. Some courts have upheld the request of Jewish inmates for kosher food; other courts have refused. Requests of Muslims to have a diet free of pork usually are upheld.[30]

The following case illustrates the problem that courts face in balancing the delicate issues of the need for security within prison against the basic right of inmates to practice their religious beliefs. In *Dettmer v. Landon*, the appellate court recognized the religion as an established one, gave cognizance to the security concerns of officials, and disagreed with the lower court's alternative of permitting the items in question to be used by inmates for religious purposes; however, the items were not allowed to be kept in prison cells.[31]

Dettmer v. Landon

In 1982 Herbert Dettmer began studying witchcraft in a correspondence course provided by the Church of Wicca. Within a year he started meditating, following ceremonies for private meditation described in the correspondence course and in other writings that he had gathered. Dettmer decided that he needed the following items to aid and protect him while meditating: a white robe with a hood, sea salt or sulfur to draw a protective circle on the floor around him, candles and incense to focus his thoughts, a kitchen timer to awaken him from short trances, and a small, hollow statute of "one of the gods or goddesses of the deity," to store spiritual power called down during meditation.

[The lower court had held that the inmate should be permitted to order the items, but they would be kept by prison officials in a secure place and given to the inmate when he wanted to worship. This court, in refusing to permit the use of these items, cites with approval this list of reasons provided by the prison's security chief.]

> A white hooded robe could conceal a prisoner's face, and its resemblance to a Ku Klux Klan robe would likely provoke adverse reaction from other prisoners;
> Candles can be used as timing devices and to make impressions of keys;
> A hollow statue can be used to conceal contraband;
> Sulphur can be used to make an explosive;
> Incense can be used to disguise the odor of marijuana; and
> A kitchen timer can be used as a detonation device. . . .

[This court concluded] that the security officer's concern about inmates' unsupervised possession of candles, salt, and incense is reasonable. There is no substantial evidence indicating that prison officials exaggerate the difficulties in supervising individual inmates' use of contraband articles in religious rites. . . .

The restrictions imposed on Dettmer must be viewed in context of the accommodations officials have made to allow him to observe his religious beliefs. Considered in this manner, the restrictions do not infringe the rights secured to him by the First and Fourteenth Amendments.

Providing recreational opportunities, such as weightlifting (left) and art work permit inmates to spend their time creatively while socializing with each other. (Michael Iscaro/Black Star; Ulrike Welsh/Photo Researchers)

Freedom of Assembly and Self-Government

The First Amendment guarantees the right of assembly. Inmates have argued that they too have that right and the right to engage in self-government to some extent. In 1977 in *Jones v. North Carolina Prisoner's Union, Inc.*, the Supreme Court upheld the right of prison officials in North Carolina to restrict the activities of prison unions, a decision described by two dissenting justices as a "giant step backward" in prisoner's rights.[32] In *Jones* the Court also talked about the right of inmates to associate with each other and the restrictions officials could place on this right. This passage from *Jones* was quoted in a 1986 case in Washington in which the federal court upheld denying a death row inmate the right to associate with other inmates.[33]

Jeffries v. Reed

Prisoners retain those First Amendment protections that are not inconsistent with their status as inmates and, thus, institutional policies which impinge upon these rights must be examined in light of the legitimate policies and goals of the correctional system.

> First Amendment associational rights, while perhaps more directly implicated by the regulatory prohibitions, likewise must give way to the reasonable considerations of penal management. . . . [N]umerous associational rights are necessarily curtailed by the realities of confinement. They may be curtailed whenever the institution's officials, in the exercise of their informed discretion, reasonably conclude that such associations, whether through group meetings or otherwise, possess the likelihood of disruption to prison order or stability, or otherwise interfere with the legitimate penological objectives of the prison environment. . . . "[C]entral to all other corrections goals is the institutional consideration of internal security within the corrections facilities themselves."

Access to Courts

The right of access to courts, recognized by the Supreme Court in *Ex Parte Hull* in 1941, is a prisoner's most important right.[34] Without access to courts, most other rights will have limited meaning. In 1969 in *Johnson v. Avery*, the Supreme Court invalidated a Tennessee prison regulation that forbade inmates to assist one another in preparing legal cases. Because many institutions do not provide legal services, the effect of that law was to deny some inmates access to courts. *Johnson* recognized the right of an inmate to the services of a jailhouse lawyer. However, the Court restricted the use of such services to inmates in institutions that provided no reasonable alternative.[35] In 1977 in *Bounds v. Smith*, the Court presented some guidelines concerning the meaning of the right of access to courts.[36]

Bounds v. Smith

[This] fundamental constitutional right of access to the courts requires prison authorities to assist inmates in the preparation and filing of meaningful legal papers by providing prisoners with adequate law libraries or adequate assistance from persons trained in the law. . . .

Among the alternatives are the training of inmates as paralegal assistants to work under lawyers' supervision, the use of paraprofessionals and law students, either as volunteers or in formal clinical programs, the organization of volunteer attorneys through bar associations and other groups, the hiring of lawyers on a part-time consultant basis, and the use of full-time staff attorneys, working in either new prison legal assistance organizations or as part of public defender or legal services offices.

The meaning of *Bounds* has been litigated. Frequently the cases involve inmates who are on death row or in some other segregated area and either are not permitted to go to the law library or have only indirect access to the library. Courts usually uphold these restrictions because of the threat to security posed by death row inmates.

In upholding a policy of permitting death row inmates access to the law library only through a paging system in which requested books are delivered to them in their cells, a federal court in Pennsylvania emphasized that court decisions "like the decisions of the prison administrators, must not be made in a vacuum, but rather must give due consideration to the depraved nature of the crimes committed and the "character of the inmates." To illustrate his point, the judge included as an appendix to his opinion the information contained in Spotlight 15.3.[37]

Prison law libraries assist inmates in preparing their own appeals. (Alan Carey/ Image Works)

SPOTLIGHT 15.3
COURTS MAY RESTRICT DEATH ROW INMATES' ACCESS TO LAW LIBRARY

In upholding the prison policy of restricting death row inmates' access to the law library to a paging system in which inmates' written requests would be given to pagers who would later bring the library books to the inmates' cells, a federal judge emphasized the threat of institutional security posed by death row inmates. In *Peterson v. Jeffes*, the judge said:

    The following list illustrates the history and proclivity for violence of twenty-two death row inmates at Graterford and Huntingdon [prisons in Pennsylvania.]

INMATE	FACTS OF CASE
Alfred Albrecht	Set house on fire killing wife, mother, and daughter.
Robert Atkins a/k/a Clifford Smith	Shot pharmacist in head at point blank range during armed robbery.
George E. Banks	Shot and killed thirteen people with semi-automatic rifle, twelve of whom were women and children family members.
Leslie Beasley	While at large for one murder, killed police officer attempting to apprehend him.
Roger Buehl	Murdered elderly couple and housekeeper, shooting man in heel, abdomen, and cheek, shooting wife in elbow and eye, and shooting housekeeper in head while tied to chair.
James H. Carpenter	Stabbed man in heart on public street without provocation.
Charles E. Cross	Murdered coworker's wife and two children, mutilating the bodies.
Robert Perry Dehart	After escaping from prison, ambushed victim, killing him with two shotgun blasts to head.
Henry P. Fahy	Raped and brutally murdered young neighbor.
Roderick Frey	Hired man to execute estranged wife.
Rodney Griffin	Shot college student in head for agreeing to testify against friend.
Charles P. Holcomb	Kidnapped, raped, and stabbed victim in neck multiple times.
John C. Lesko	Murdered three people and police officer.
Frederick Maxwell	Invited salesman into home, robbed him, and shot him twice in head.
Otis Peterkin	Murdered two former coemployees, shooting one fifteen times.
Simon Pirela	Injected victim with battery acid, then strangled him.
Alan Lee Pursell	Viciously beat, burned, and mutilated 13 year old boy.
Richard Stoyko	Shot wife three times with shotgun, then murdered man because "his car was in the middle of the road and he wouldn't move it."
Joseph Szuchon	Kidnapped girlfriend, then shot her twice in back with rifle.
Michael Travaglia	Murdered three people and police officer.
Raymond Whitney	Stabbed man during robbery 28 times.
Keith Zettlemoyer	Shot young man twice in neck and twice in chest while handcuffed and lying face down. Victim had agreed to testify against Zettlemoyer in pending felony trial.

Source: Peterkin v. Jeffes, 661 F. Supp. 895, 928–29 (E.D. Pa. 1987), Appendix A, citations omitted, *affd. in part and vacated in part,* 855 F. 2d 1021 (CA3 Pa. 1988).

The right of inmates to access to courts also involves a right to visit with attorneys, although inmates do not have a right to have appointed counsel for their civil actions. But if they have retained attorneys, inmates have a right to reasonable visits with them. Prisons must provide reasonable visitation policies and adequate facilities for inmate visits with attorneys. Inmates also must be permitted to communicate by mail with their attorneys. The Supreme Court allows prison officials to open all letters from attorneys and search for contraband as long as it is done in the presence of the inmates to whom the letters were addressed. This action is not censorship since the mail is not read. Prisons also may require attorneys to indicate on the outside of the envelope that the mail is from a legal office.[28]

FOURTH AMENDMENT RIGHTS

The Fourth Amendment prohibits unreasonable searches and seizures. The key word is *unreasonable*. In the prison setting, the need for security has highest priority; that need will enable prison officials to conduct searches and seizures that would not be permissible in other settings. In 1984 in *Hudson v. Palmer*, the Supreme Court considered the application of the Fourth Amendment to prison cell searches. With an emphasis on the difficult problems of maintaining security in a prison setting, the Court reviewed the recent history of violence in prisons and in that context issued its holding.[39]

Hudson v. Palmer

[T]he Fourth Amendment proscription against unreasonable searches does not apply within the confines of the prison cell. The recognition of privacy rights for prisoners in their individual cells simply cannot be reconciled with the concept of incarceration and the needs and objectives of penal institutions.

Prisons, by definition, are places of involuntary confinement of persons who have a demonstrated proclivity for antisocial criminal, and often violent, conduct . . .

Within this volatile "community," prison administrators are to take all necessary steps to ensure the safety of not only the prison staffs and administrative personnel, but visitors. They are under an obligation to take reasonable measures to guarantee the safety of the inmates themselves. They must be ever alert to attempts to introduce drugs and other contraband into the premises . . .

Virtually the only place inmates can conceal weapons, drugs, and other contraband is in their cells. Unfettered access to these cells by prison officials, thus, is imperative if drugs and contraband are to be ferreted out and sanitary surroundings are to be maintained.

Hudson was decided on a 5–4 vote by the Court. Justice John Paul Stevens, who wrote an opinion in which he concurred in part and dissented in part, took the unusual step of reading his opinion from the bench when the decision was announced.

> By telling prisoners that no aspect of their individuality, from a photo of a child to a letter from a wife, is entitled to constitutional protection, the Court breaks with the ethical tradition that I had thought was enshrined forever in our jurisprudence.

Hudson v. Palmer was brought by an inmate who alleged that the guard who searched his cell did so for malice, not for security, and that the guard destroyed his personal property. Justice Stevens agreed with the Court that random searches are necessary and permissible, but he disagreed with the Court's conclusion that

> no matter how malicious, destructive or arbitrary a cell search and seizure may be, it cannot constitute an unreasonable invasion of any privacy or possessory interest that society is prepared to recognize as reasonable.

According to Justice Stevens, the small amount of possessions and limited privacy that an inmate might have in a cell are little compared to what the rest of society has, but "that trivial residuum may mark the difference between slavery and humanity."

According to the Model Rules promulgated by the ACA, a cursory inspection of an inmate's cell or room may be conducted at any time for any reason. But a more thorough search should only be conducted when prison officials have reasonable cause to believe that contraband will be found, or when the search is authorized by a shift supervisor, or when it is part of a routine security inspection. Inmates may be present if security does not prohibit their presence; they should be given a receipt for any items taken from their rooms or cells. In contrast, in *Block v. Rutherford*, the Supreme Court upheld routine searches of cells while inmates were absent.[40]

Searches of the person are more intrusive. But even here there are degrees of intrusiveness. According to the ACA, searches by means of mechanical devices may be conducted at any time without prior authorization of a supervisor. A casual search of the person or frisk of the inmate may also be conducted at any time and is routinely conducted before and after the inmate has contact visits with family and friends.

The most intrusive search is the body search, which may involve a strip-search or a manual search of body cavities. The Supreme Court has upheld body-cavity searches after inmates have had contact visits.[41] Strip searches of inmates are permitted because of the practice of secreting contraband inside the body, as this excerpt from *State v. Palmer* indicates. This case also illustrates the issues frequently associated with strip searches: the manner and place in which they occur and who conducts the search.[42]

State v. Palmer

All 12 inmates, including appellant, in appellant's "pod" of Cell Block Six were to undergo body cavity searches. The intelligence officer testified that he authorized an initial digital rectal search and, if that search revealed the presence of an object, the inmate would be X-rayed. Finally, if the inmate did not voluntarily give up or excrete the object, it would be removed. An initial digital rectal search was performed on appellant by a correctional medical assistant. Appellant was then escorted to a medical examining room where a medical doctor performed a second digital search. During the search, the doctor felt the presence of an object and ordered an X-ray of appellant's pelvic area. The X-ray revealed the presence of a foreign object believed to be a shotgun shell.

Following the X-ray, appellant was transported to the central unit hospital's emergency room. A second doctor, trained in sigmoidoscopy examinations, first performed a rectal examination which consisted of the insertion of a small scope to determine the nature of the foreign object. Appellant refused to submit to that examination and, eventually, was forced to lay on the table by corrections officers. Appellant finally agreed to position himself on the table so that the item could be removed, and the doctor removed the shotgun shell which had been wrapped in tissue paper in a condom. During the procedure, appellant testified that he suffered severe pain and discomfort and, following the removal he suffered some bleeding.

Searches of other inmates revealed balloons filled with gunpowder and a detonation cord, and subsequent searches led to the discovery of blasting caps and a homemade rip gun capable of shooting a shotgun shell. Other inmates had consented to voluntarily pass or remove the contraband they possessed. One other inmate, who did not immediately excrete his contraband, was placed in an isolation cell and eventually passed a balloon filled with gunpowder.

[The appellate court discusses the dispute between the appellant and the prison officials over the method in which these searches occurred; the appellate court sees no reason to disturb the trial court's findings that the procedures were appropriate under the circumstances.]

Many factors must be considered in determining whether a search is reasonable. They include the crime allegedly being committed, society's interest in punishing the act, and the reliability of the means employed to conduct the search. They also include the strength of law enforcement suspicions that evidence of crime will be revealed, the importance of the evidence sought, and the possibility that the evidence may be recovered by less intrusive means. . . . We acknowledge that the search and removal probably resulted in discomfort, pain and humiliation, however, the removal resulted from the method by which appellant chose to hide the contraband and by appellant's refusal to voluntarily pass it. . . .

The immediate methods employed in this case were reasonable. . . . In view of all the facts and circumstances surrounding this case, we do not find that the search and seizure violated appellant's Fourth Amendment right.

Strip-searches, however, have been held unconstitutional when conducted on a person who visits an inmate, unless the prison official has reasonable cause to think that visitor is attempting to smuggle contraband into the jail or prison.[43] Some courts have also held that it is unconstitutional to have a policy of strip-searching all persons brought to jail, even those charged with minor offenses.[44]

EIGHTH AMENDMENT RIGHTS

The Eighth Amendment prohibits cruel and unusual punishment. Court decisions have made it clear that corporal punishment of inmates violates this clause. It is also clear that inmates have a right to protection from the physical assaults of other inmates to the extent that prison officials reasonably may prevent such assaults.

The issue of what constitutions cruel and unusual punishment, however, goes even further, extending to nonphysical types of punishment, medical care, and general conditions of the prison. Thus, some courts have held that the totality of conditions within prisons are so bad that they constitute cruel and unusual punishment. Those conditions may include overcrowding; unsanitary conditions; methods of discipline; food that is not properly prepared or nutritious, or that contains foreign matter; and about any other condition that threatens the welfare of inmates. Here we focus on medical treatment or the lack of such treatment.

Prison officials have broad discretion in determining what medical care will be provided for inmates. It is difficult if not impossible for courts to make such determinations. The Supreme Court has articulated a standard for care, stating in *Estelle v. Gamble* that "deliberate indifference to serious medical needs of prisoners constitutes the kind of cruel and unusual punishment that is prohibited by the Eighth Amendment."[45]

In 1982 in *Ruiz v. Estelle*, a federal court looked at the Texas prison system (TDC) and concluded that the Eighth Amendment was being violated. The court found a "continuous pattern of harmful, inadequate medical treatment" which led to "anguish and inexpedient medical treatment to inmates on a large scale."[46] In *Ruiz*, the court ordered substantial changes, including more medically qualified staff, elimination of inmate labor in medical and pharmacological functions, improvement of physical facilities, establishment of diagnostic and sick-call procedures and work classification procedures, and a complete overhaul of the record-keeping system. Improvements were made in the Texas system as indicated in Spotlight 15.4, leading in 1985 to the end of court monitoring of TDC. The system, however, must abide by the terms of the settlement.[47]

AIDS: A Special Prison Medical Problem

AIDS (acquired immune deficiency syndrome) has become a household word in the United States, as educational efforts to alert people to the

SPOTLIGHT 15.4
IMPROVEMENTS IN THE TEXAS PRISON SYSTEM
AFTER FEDERAL COURT ORDER

David Ruiz's new home was built to specs.

When the crusading convict returned to the Texas prison system earlier this month after a decade in federal facilities, he was assigned to a new unit with his name written all over it.

Completed last September, the Michael Unit in Palestine is the first prison built under federal court orders in the Texas prison reform suit that began 15 years ago with Ruiz's handwritten complaints about life behind bars. Ruiz, other long-term inmates and even prison officials agree that a lot has changed since then.

"This unit was built to comply with Ruiz, and for the most part we have," said Warden Jack Garner, referring to the long-running suit that bears the inmate's name.

The suit eventually brought improved medical care, outlawed the use of inmate guards who frequently brutalized their fellow convicts and led to a host of other reforms.

Garner said "everything has improved" since Ruiz first filed his complaints in 1973, including significant increases in staffing, vastly improved morale among both staff and inmates and a physical plant that he said "looks more like a college campus."

"I'm sure Ruiz had some bearing on it," Garner said.

Texas' most famous inmate returned to prison in his home state May 26 on the orders of U.S. District Judge William Wayne Justice after Ruiz requested that he be moved closer to his family in Austin.

In an interview last week, Ruiz said that changes wrought by the reform suit during his 10-year absence were gratifying. He said improved conditions there benefit those outside as well as inside the prison walls.

"If you lock up a dog in your back yard and you feed the dog but you whip him every day, one day he'll attack his master," he said. "Or when he gets out, he'll run out to the street and attack an innocent child or a lady or an old man."

Longtime inmates in four prisons cited the demise of the system of building tenders, or inmate guards, and an improvement in medical services as the two most significant changes of the last decade. They said guards are less abusive than in the old days.

And they cited more humane conditions in solitary confinement, such as regular meals, baths, and clean uniforms.

But Ruiz and other inmates said that although violence has decreased dramatically, the Corrections Department deserves lower marks in areas such as enforcing standardized disciplinary procedures and addressing sanitation problems like moldy showers and rat infestations.

Department officials gave little credence to complaints about the system, saying a court-approved plan to phase out monitoring by a special master in two years is proof that prisons are already righting past wrongs.

But officials mirrored the inmates in their assessment of the positive changes since the first Ruiz case settlement in 1981. The most recent and comprehensive settlement in the case came in 1985.

"The health care delivery system went from being one of the worst in the country to being one of the best," said department attorney Kirk Brown.

Brown said replacing inmate guards who performed a variety of functions with professional prison staffers has meant massive hirings. "It takes 5.2 correctional officers to replace one building tender," he said.

"Even in the last couple of years," Brown said, "there have been some pretty remarkable changes."

Ruiz said that in his first two weeks back in a Texas prison he had been able to see for himself the fruits of his long-running legal battle.

Staff members "talk to me like a human being now, not like it used to be," Ruiz said.

And he said a routine physical administered when he returned to Texas prison convinced him that medical care had improved.

"When I was here, none of them was a doctor," he said. "They would look at you, say, 'You all right?' and then decide you would be a good field worker. When I was here before people were afraid to go to sick call."

"I never thought TDC would get this far," Ruiz said.

Source: Melinda Henneberger, "Inmates, Wardens Agree Prison Life Has Improved," *Dallas Morning News* (20 June 1988), p. 1. Reprinted with permission of The Dallas Morning News.

deadly and rapidly spreading disease have been successful. Thousands of people have already died of AIDS, and to date there is no known cure. There is evidence however, that AIDS is spread primarily through sexual contacts (primarily although not exclusively homosexual contacts) and intravenous drug use. Because many inmates have a history of drug abuse and, to a lesser extent, at least while in prison, homosexual contacts, jails and prisons face acute problems concerning the spread of AIDS. Concern with the problem led the National Institute of Justice and the American Correctional Association to sponsor a joint study, resulting in the publication of *AIDS in Prisons and Jails: Issues and Options*, by Theodor M. Hammett. Portions of that report are included in Spotlight 15.5.

SPOTLIGHT 15.5
AIDS IN PRISONS AND JAILS: ISSUES AND OPTIONS

AIDS in the Correctional Population

Responses to the study questionnaire reveal that, since 1981, there have been a cumulative total of 455 confirmed AIDS cases in 25 State and Federal prison systems. Twenty large city and county jail systems reported 311 cases of AIDS among inmates. These figures represent *cumulative* total cases since the responding jurisdictions began keeping records.

As of the period November 1985 to January 1986, there were 144 cases of AIDS among State and Federal inmates in 19 systems and 35 cases among city and county inmates in 11 systems.

No known AIDS cases have occurred among correctional staff as a result of contact with inmates. Questionnaire respondents reported nine cases of AIDS among current or former staff, but none of these individuals had been involved in an incident with an inmate in which transmission of the AIDS virus might have occurred. Indeed, most were known or suspected to have been in AIDS risk groups.

The distribution of AIDS cases across correctional systems is highly skewed. Fifty-one percent of the prison systems have had *no* cases and 80 percent have had fewer than four cases. Among responding city and county jail systems, 39 percent have had no cases and 70 percent have had fewer than four cases.

At the other extreme, two State prison systems and only one of the responding city and county jail

systems have had more than 50 cases. The regional distribution is also highly uneven. Over 70 percent of the cases, both in State prison systems and in city and county jail systems, have occurred in the mid-Atlantic region, with all other parts of the United States contributing much smaller percentages.

The vast majority of correctional AIDS cases, particularly in jurisdictions with large numbers of cases, are believed to be associated with prior intravenous drug abuse. There is substantial debate, but little hard data, on the extent to which the AIDS virus is being transmitted within correctional institutions. The two primary means of transmission are prohibited behavior in all corrections systems. However, logic and common sense suggest that, even in the best-managed correctional facilities, there may be at least some transmission of the infection occurring among inmates.

Correctional Policy Issues and Options

The major policy areas involved in the correctional response to AIDS are education and training; HTLV-III antibody testing; and medical, legal, and correctional management issues.

Source: Theodore M. Hammett, National Institute of Justice (Washington, D.C.: U.S. Department of Justice, February, 1986), pp. 1, 2, 3.

FOURTEENTH AMENDMENT RIGHTS

Due Process

The Fourteenth Amendment prohibits the denial of life, liberty, or property without **due process** or **equal protection.** The due process clause frequently arises in the disciplining of inmates. Such claims involve decisions regarding **good-time credits,** deprivation of freedom and privileges within the prison environment, segregated housing or solitary confinement, and transfers for disciplinary reasons. The focus in due process claims is on the procedures by which these decisions are made.

The due process claims of inmates must pass a two-part test. First, they have to show that the claim involves a liberty or property interest within the Fourteenth Amendment. If so, the test then is to determine what process is due in that situation. If there is no liberty or property right, decisions may be made without giving reasons to inmates. Further, the Court has held that the freedom of prisoners does not fall within the meaning of liberty. That right is extinguished when they are convicted. Thus, an inmate sentenced to 10 years in prison has no liberty interest in getting out sooner. States may create liberty interests by statute; if they do, due process must be provided when that liberty is denied. A state's passing statutes that limit discretion of prison officials in particular areas concerning inmate freedom creates a liberty interest.

In *Olim v. Wakinekona*, the Supreme Court held that the inmate had no liberty interest. Wakinekona was serving a life sentence without possibility of parole, as well as other sentences. He was incarcerated in the Hawaii State Prison. When problems erupted in the maximum-security control unit to which Wakinekona had been assigned after he was classified as a maximum-security risk, a committee held hearings to determine who caused the disturbance. Testimony was taken from other inmates, and the discipline committee concluded that Wakinekona and another inmate were the troublemakers.

Wakinekona was later notified of a hearing to determine whether he should be reclassified within the prison and whether he should be transferred to another prison. That hearing was held by the same committee that found him to be the troublemaker. Wakinekona attended the hearing with his retained counsel. He was told that despite his progress in vocational training in that prison and his desire to continue that training, he was a security risk and a threat to the staff. Since Hawaii had no other maximum-security facilities, he was being transferred 4,000 miles to Folsom State Prison in California.

Wakinekona sued, alleging that his right to due process was denied because the same committee that labeled him a troublemaker also decided on the transfer. He claimed he was entitled to an unbiased tribunal in the latter decision. The Supreme Court held that Wakinekona did not have a liberty interest in remaining in Hawaii and therefore was not entitled to an unbiased tribunal. The Court emphasized that it is often necessary to transfer the prisoners from one prison to another, even from one state to another, and that they have no liberty interest against such transfers.[48]

568

Even if the inmate can show that there is a liberty interest, the due process requirements are limited. In *Hewitt v. Helms,* inmate Helms, serving a term in a state correctional institution in Pennsylvania, sued prison officials on the claim that he was placed in administrative segregation without due process of law. Helms had been given a misconduct report for his alleged part in a riot in which guards were injured. The Court agreed that he had a liberty interest in remaining in the general population. That interest derived from the state statutes and therefore does not necessarily apply in other cases. But, said the Court, that liberty interest does not entitle the inmate to more than a nonadversary and informal hearing.[49]

The Court's holding in *Helms* illustrates why it is so important to read carefully the facts of cases and the reasoning of judges and justices. The Supreme Court had earlier decided *Wolff v. McDonnell,* a case involving reducing the good-time credits of an inmate. In *Wolff,* the Court required that inmates who faced disciplinary charges for misconduct must be given 24 hours advance written notice of the charges against them; a right to call witnesses and present documentary evidence in defense, unless doing so would jeopardize institutional safety or correctional goals; the aid of a staff member or inmate in presenting a defense, provided the inmate is illiterate or the issue complex; an impartial tribunal; and a written statement of reasons relied on by the tribunal. *Wolff* did not, however, require all elements of due process. The court did not require that inmates be provided with an attorney at disciplinary hearings and it limited the right to call and cross-examine witnesses. Prison officials may cut the list of witnesses without giving reasons.[50]

In *Helms* the Court emphasized that its holding in *Wolff* involved procedures that affected the length of time the inmate would be incarcerated. *Wolff* involved good-time credits, which in effect cut the prison sentence. Prison officials had revoked those credits. That, said the Court, is different from changing the status of a prisoner within a prison or transferring one to another prison. In 1985 the Supreme Court held that, when states provide for good-time credits, revocation of those credits may occur only when sufficient evidence has been presented for that revocation. In *Superintendent, Massachusetts Correctional Institution v. Hill,* the Court said,

> We now hold that revocation of good time does not comport with the "minimum requirements of procedural due process," unless the findings of the prison disciplinary board are supported by some evidence in the record.[51]

In another 1985 case, *Ponte v. Real,* the Court held that due process requires that, when prison officials refuse to call witnesses requested by an inmate at a disciplinary hearing, the officials must give reasons for their refusal, but they do not have to give written reasons.[52]

Equal Protection

The Fourteenth Amendment also guarantees equal protection of the laws. Equal protection suits are usually brought by female inmates who do not have the same access to vocational and educational opportunities as male inmates. A study of jails disclosed that female inmates rarely have equal access to programs available for males, even when they are occupying the same general facilities. Females less frequently are allowed to participate in work-release programs. Jails seldom have the medical care that may be needed by all females or the special care needed by pregnant women. Females have unique problems that may not be met within jail facilities, problems such as child care, particularly when infants are involved.[53]

On the other hand, females are more likely to have private rooms, which in some cases are more like dormitory rooms than cells. Females may have greater freedom of movement within the prison. Their prisons do not have the kinds of violence characteristic of many maximum-security prisons for males.

The critical issue, then, is determining at what point female, as compared to male, inmates (or vice versa) are denied equal protection. As a class, are they being discriminated against? The Supreme Court has not ruled on this issue; thus, the cases in the lower courts must be analyzed carefully. It is important to remember that the issue here is not whether a particular service, such as educational programs, must be provided; but rather, if it is provided for one sex whether it must also be provided for the other.[54] The American Correctional Association has adopted a policy of equal opportunity for female and male inmates. This policy is reprinted in full in Spotlight 15.6.

PRISON PROGRAMS AND LEGAL RIGHTS

The rights discussed thus far are guaranteed by the Constitution. But what about activities and programs that are not required by that document? If inmates do not have a constitutional right to an education, to vocational training, and to work opportunities, should those activities be provided?

The lack of educational or work opportunities, combined with a lack of other opportunities, may be cited by courts as evidence that the prison system does not meet minimum constitutional requirements. Courts have not ruled that inmates have a right to any educational opportunities they may choose, however, and some courts have ruled that inmates do not have a right to a free college education.[55]

Although education and work opportunities may be therapeutic for inmates while they are incarcerated, prisons do not have sufficient jobs to keep all inmates busy, nor are they required to do so. Nationwide estimates are that only about 10 percent of inmates are employed, and their wages are very low.

Earlier statutes that prohibited the sale of prison-made goods across state lines severely restricted the nature and type of work available in prisons. Since prison-made products could be sold only to other state institutions, most prison labor was geared to the production of soap, clothing, office furniture, license plates, road signs, and other products needed by states in public institutions.

Some improvements have occurred. The federal prison system has been expanding vocational training and work opportunities for inmates.

Some prison systems permit inmates to sell products made in prison. These children are holding parole pals made especially for them by Texas inmates. (David Hall)

SPOTLIGHT 15.6
EQUAL OPPORTUNITIES FOR INMATES

In August 1984, the American Correctional Association ratified a National Correctional Policy concerning female offenders. The policy, which follows, speaks directly to the issue of parity for male and female offenders.

American Correctional Association National Correctional Policy on Female Offender Services

Correctional systems must develop service delivery systems for accused and adjudicated female offenders that are comparable to those provided to males. Additional services must also be provided to meet the unique needs of the female offender population.

Policy Statement:
  Correctional systems must be guided by the principle of parity. Female offenders must receive the equivalent range of services available to other offenders, including opportunities for individualized programming and services that recognize the unique needs of this population. The services should:

A. Assure access to a range of alternatives to incarceration, including pre-trial and post-trial diversion, probation, restitution, treatment for substance abuse, halfway houses, and parole services;

B. Provide acceptable conditions of confinement, including appropriately trained staff and sound operating procedures that address this population's needs in such areas as clothing, personal property, hygiene, exercise, recreation, and visitation with children and family;

C. Provide access to a full-range of work and programs designed to expand economic and social roles of women, with emphasis on education, career counseling, and exploration of nontraditional as well as traditional vocational training; relevant life skills, including parenting and social and economic assertiveness; and pre-release and work/education release programs;

D. Facilitate the maintenance and strengthening of family ties, particularly those between parent and child;

E. Deliver appropriate programs and services, including medical, dental, and mental health programs, services to pregnant women, substance abuse programs, child and family services, and provide access to legal services; and

F. Provide access to release programs that include aid in establishing homes, economic stability, and sound family relationships.

This Public Correctional Policy was unanimously ratified by the American Correctional Association Delegate Assembly at the 114th Congress of Correction, San Antonio, August 23, 1984.

Under the direction of Federal Prison Industries (FPI), the federal system operates about 100 workplaces producing such items as shoes, boots, paint brushes, textiles, canvas, mattresses, clothing, parachutes, furniture, cable assemblies, wiring harnesses, printed circuits, computer services, drafting, printing services, and signs. The FPI has been criticized because inmates receive low wages and are trained for jobs that may not exist outside penal institutions.[56]

Some developments in prison labor have also occurred at the state level. The Prison Industries Enhancement (PIE) Act passed in 1979 allows prison-made goods in specified pilot projects to be shipped interstate, provided certain requirements are met. Inmates who produce the goods must be paid fair wages for the area in which the prison is located. Deductions of up to 80 percent of the inmate's wages must be used to support the inmate's family, to pay taxes, to provide for restitution to the victim, and to cover the cost of the inmate's room and board in prison. Prisoners may not be forced to work in the programs covered by PIE; all work is voluntary.[57]

In an effort to improve state prison labor programs, the federal government developed the **Free Venture Program** to assist states in applying free world business practices and principles to prison industry and labor. Originally, grants were provided to states that wanted to remodel their prison industries. Private consultants were used in setting up the program, and the initial responses were positive. Inmates were positive about the work opportunities, although they complained that working often prevented their participation in other programs, such as education and counseling.[58]

SPOTLIGHT 15.7
NEW YORK'S PRISON WORK PROGRAMS

At a time when some states are turning their prison workshops over to private managers, New York State prison officials are taking a different course: They are hunting for new products, new customers and new ways to put inmates to work.

The search is part of an effort to treat the factories at 15 state prisons like businesses with 3,000 workers — inmates — who make a lot more than license plates.

Items being shipped from a State Department of Correctional Services warehouse here include sheets and pillow cases for shelters for the homeless in New York City, lockers for New York City public schools and modular furniture for state offices. All carry the prison system's brand name Corcraft.

Like record albums and kitchen knives advertised on television, these products are not sold in stores. By law, they can be sold only to state or local governments, in part because of union objections to what is considered unfair competition.

Even so, Corcraft has become a money maker. Nine years ago it had sales of $9 million and a loss of $8 million. Last year it reported sales of $60 million and a profit of $7.1 million.

Partnerships Arranged

Now Corcraft is arranging partnerships outside prison walls with companies that can design new products for inmates to make. Corcraft has signed agreements with a Canadian company to design

office furniture and with Burlington Industries to design fitted sheets for hospitals.

"In the same way that General Motors established a partnership with Toyota, Chrysler with Mitsubishi, I.B.M. with Microsoft and so on, we, too, have developed partnerships with our private colleagues," said Susan E. Butler, an assistant correction commissioner who is in charge of Corcraft. To find new markets for such products — and bigger profits — the Cuomo administration is preparing legislation that would allow Corcraft to do business with nonprofit organizations and Federal agencies.

At the same time the correction department is creating nonmanufacturing jobs for prisoners.

Telephone Calls Handled

In one program, inmates answer questions from motorists who call the Department of Motor Vehicles to ask about license and registration renewals. The calls are forwarded to a bank of telephones at the Bayview prison for women in Manhattan, where they are answered by inmates trained in telephone etiquette and drilled in the 100 most frequently asked questions.

Ms. Butler said the telephone bank was already answering 7,500 calls day. But 10,000 calls are coming in, so she plans to set up a second phone bank at the Arthur Kill Correctional Facility on Staten Island.

She contends that prison industry programs have something to offer business. Inmates who have worked on the telephone banks, for example, often

Although wages are generally low, inmates in Free Venture shops receive higher wages than inmates in traditional prison work programs. Inmates believe wages should be tied to productivity and job performance to provide an incentive to work. They also say their self-esteem is enhanced when they earn money to purchase family presents, to pay for family visits, and to buy their own supplies from the prison commissary. More research is needed on the effect of prison industry programs on inmates and the institution. These programs may be able to change the atmosphere in prisons.[59] States also are expanding prison work programs, as illustrated by Spotlight 15.7, which contains information about New York prison labor programs.

seek telephone jobs when they are released. At the same time, she said, prison work has much to offer prisons because it can help offset the cost of incarceration.

But that view is not universal. "By moving business from the private sector to prisons, we are transferring income and opportunity for law-abiding businesses to prisoners who demonstrably have harmed society," said Paul Caggiano, president of the Coalition for Common Sense in Government Procurement, a nonprofit group in Washington that represents more than 100 companies and monitors Federal purchasing.

Not a New Idea

The idea of putting prisoners to work is not new. State correction officials say the nation's first prison work program began at the state prison in Auburn, N. Y., 160 years ago. Until the late 19th century—when reformers and unions complained that the work was exploitative—the leasing of convicts to private businesses was common.

Under Ms. Butler, Corcraft increasingly functions like a private corporation. She is so determined not to be seen as a bureaucrat that she describes herself as the president of Corcraft, and she has been pressing to make products that are more attractive than those usually turned out by prisons.

One product that has just made its debut is Ultraframe, a modular office system that will soon replace the battered metal desks in some state offices. With wood-and-chrome desks and fabric-covered wall panels in taupe, aquamarine or mauve,

Ultraframe is what Ms. Butler thinks state offices should look like.

"Working for New York State, you felt like a second-class citizen, always comparing your office to the private sector," she said. "State employees shouldn't feel that way anymore."

95-Cents-an-Hour Pay

A state correction spokesman, James Flateau, said wages paid to the prisoners were typically 95 cents an hour.

Paul Cole, the secretary-treasurer of the New York State A.F.L.-C.I.O., said his group would oppose any expansion of prison work that threatened union jobs. "Inmates need to do things that are productive, but the goal should not be to compete with union labor on the outside," he said.

Like automobile and steel makers, Corcraft has also been pushing for productivity increases. To keep maximum-security inmates on the job longer, guards now conduct roll calls in the workshops rather than walking the inmates back to their cells four times a day and calling out their names there.

The result, Ms. Butler said, is an increase in work time from three hours in 1984 to about 6½ hours now.

"It didn't take an M.B.A. to figure out if your workers are working three hours and you're paying your supervisors for eight hours, you are not going to break even," she said.

Source: "New York's Prisons Find New Work for Inmates," by James Barron. Copyright © 1988 by The New York Times Company. Reprinted by permission.

ANALYSIS OF PRISON REFORM

Despite changes that have been made in prison conditions, the fact remains that today many jails and prisons remain under federal court orders, and this situation will continue until specified changes are made. Two particular concerns remain to be solved: jail and prison overcrowding and inmate violence, especially riots. These two problems are related to all other issues discussed in this chapter.

Overcrowding: The Major Issue of the 1980s

Overcrowding is the main problem faced by prisons and jails today.[60] A 1985 publication of the American Correctional Association and the National Coalition for Jail Reform indicated that 81 percent of jail inmates in this country "live in less than 60 square feet of cell space each, the accepted minimum standard; that is about the size of two double bed mattresses." Of the hundred largest jails, 70 percent were under court order to reduce populations, to improve other conditions, or both. Almost 8 percent of all jails are under court order regarding some conditions found to be unconstitutional.[61] Part of jail overcrowding results from holding those sentenced to prison until space is available in state and federal prisons.

Jail overcrowding has increased the problems of jail administrators; some have dramatically indicated their disapproval of the policy by taking their inmates to the appropriate prisons and handcuffing them to the chain-link fences surrounding those institutions. In some cases, the jailers have been ordered by court to take back the inmates; in other cases the inmates have subsequently been admitted to the already overcrowded

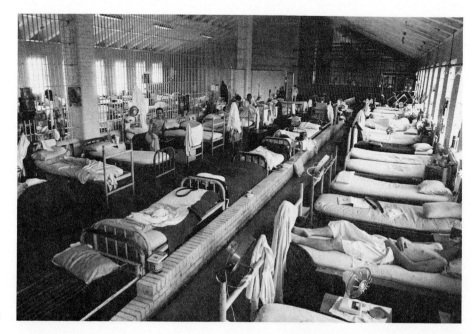

Overcrowded prisons leave little room for comfort or privacy. (Alan Pogue/TexaStock)

574

prisons. Many prisons are under federal court orders to reduce their populations.

What effect does overcrowding have on jail and prison inmates? Research on the effects of overcrowding has been conducted for some years, but only recently has attention been given to the serious effects it might have on inmates. Federal courts have accepted the position that overcrowding has negative effects on inmates. The following excerpt from the 1980 federal court case involving the Texas prison system (TDC) is an example. In *Ruiz v. Estelle*, nearly every aspect of the TDC operation was found to be unconstitutional, and the prison was placed under court order to develop plans for bringing the system into compliance with constitutional standards.[62] As indicated in Spotlight 15.4, living conditions in the Texas prisons have been improved in recent years although overcrowding remains a daily concern.[63]

Ruiz v. *Estelle*

The overcrowding at TDC exercises a malignant effect on all aspects of inmate life. Personal living space allotted to inmates is severely restricted. Inmates are in the constant presence of others. Although some degree of regimentation and loss of privacy is a normal aspect of life in any prison, the high population density at TDC leaves prisoners with virtually no privacy at any time of the day or night. Crowded two or three to a cell or in closely packed dormitories, inmates sleep with the knowledge that they may be molested or assaulted by their fellows at any time. Their incremental exposure to disease and infection from other inmates in such narrow confinement cannot be avoided. They must urinate and defecate, unscreened, in the presence of others. Inmates in cells must live and sleep inches away from toilets; many in dormitories face the same situation. There is little respite from these conditions, for the salient fact of existence in TDC prisons is that inmates have wholly inadequate opportunities to escape the overcrowding in their living quarters.

Even when they are away from the housing areas, inmates are confronted with the inescapable reality that overcrowding is omnipresent within the prison confines . . .

Many, if not most jail and prison problems are related to overcrowding. Perhaps the most serious is violence, as illustrated by riots and escapes. In late 1987 and early 1988, internal violence and escapes at Riker's Island, one of New York City's jails, focused attention on the issue. Riker's Island, the world's largest jail complex, processes nearly 100,000 inmates a year and houses approximately 2,400 inmates at any given time.

In February 1988, 550 inmates, apparently to protest the administration's search and seizure policies, barricaded themselves in their dormitories, armed with homemade weapons. No hostages were taken, but considerable damage was done to the jail. New York City jails at that time were operating at 103 percent of capacity.[64]

In September, 1988, New York City's most recent jail opened. Located on the St. Lawrence Seaway about 240 miles from New York City, the Cape Vincent Correctional Facility was built to help relieve the overcrowding of New York City's jails. This new institution was quickly overcrowded. In October 1988, the 700-bed jail had 710 inmates. Fifty-six more beds were added to the jail's dormitories, but they also were quickly filled, leaving New York's latest facility overcrowded.[65]

Prison Riots

Inmates may protest prison conditions in several ways in addition to filing lawsuits. Peaceful strikes or attempts to develop inmate councils that might have a voice in the governing policies of the institution occasionally are used as the avenues for improving prison conditions. Prison riots command the serious attention of the public and the media. Although few in number, prison riots are serious in their destruction of property and their injuries to humans, injuries that in some cases result in death.

Two of the most destructive and highly publicized riots in America occurred in 1971 in Attica, New York, and in 1980 in Santa Fe, New Mexico. The riot in Attica has been summarized in the 1985 opinion of a federal judge whose court heard the most recent allegations of violations of constitutional rights in that facility. The following brief excerpt states the relevant facts.[66]

Abdul Wali v. *Coughlin*

Attica Correctional Facility is a maximum security prison in upstate New York. In September 1971, an uprising at the institution resulted in the deaths of forty-three persons—thirty-two inmates and eleven correctional employees. In the words of the Special Commission appointed by the Governor to investigate the incident: "[T]he State Police uprising which ended the four-day prison uprising was the bloodiest one-day encounter between Americans since the Civil War."

In the aftermath of the riot, the very word "Attica" became symbolic of all that was wrong with America's maximum security prisons. . . . [T]he Attica of 1971 was a squalid, degrading and dangerous place for convicts and guards alike. The prison's physical plant was vastly overtaxed. Built to house some 1,700 inmates, the facility was then home to more than 2,200. Emphasis was placed not on rehabilitation, but only on confinement and security. There were no meaningful educational or vocational training programs; idleness became the prisoners' principal occupation. An all-white staff of correction officers ruled an inmate population that was fifty-four percent black and nine percent Puerto Rican. Levels of personal hygiene and available medical care were scandalously low.

It would be comforting to believe that Attica was somehow different—that it was an exceptionally bad institution. Perhaps its archaic architecture was somehow to blame. After all, the thirty-foot-high wall and endless rows of six-foot by nine-foot by seven-foot cells were designed in another era. Or perhaps the tensions in Attica were the result of inner-city criminals being policed by officials familiar only with the rural life of northern New York State. The sad

This was the scene in a cellblock at the New Mexico State Penitentiary after 36 hours of rioting ended. (Joe Marquette/UPI Bettmann News)

truth, however, was that the Attica of 1971 was little better or worse than other maximum security prisons of that time. That the riot broke out there had more to do with chance than with any idiosyncrasy of the particular institutions. The words of the Special Commission made it hauntingly clear: "Attica is every prison; and every prison is Attica."

We recite these sad facts of our recent history not to suggest that the situation at Attica has remained unchanged in the thirteen years since the bloody uprising, but rather to emphasize the institution's history of tension and violence. Indeed, we are given to believe that some beneficial innovations have been effected since that time, although it appears that by 1982, much remained to be done.

On February 2, 1980, a riot as devastating as the Attica riot occurred at the state prison in Santa Fe, New Mexico. Estimates of damage ranged from $20 million to repair to $60 or $80 million to replace the prison. At least 90 persons required hospitalization, and 33 inmates were killed. Characteristic of the killings was the torture and incredible brutality of inmates toward inmates, which led national guardsmen to regurgitate on the scene and firemen who had fought in Vietnam to proclaim that they had never seen such atrocities during that war.[67]

Several recent prison riots are featured in Spotlight 15.8. Again we see brutality, physical injury, death, and destruction of property. We see inmates protesting prison conditions and dramatically demonstrating their anger at prison officials who have not changed those conditions.

The West Virginia prison has been under a federal court order since 1983, but before the 1986 riot, only a few steps had been taken toward compliance with the 1983 court order. According to a state senator who visited the prison,

> Sewage was just lying on the passageway between the cells. It was like a cesspool. I'm not one who likes to coddle prisoners, but conditions at that prison are beyond anything you ought to do to human beings.

Said the governor, "The constitutional officers of the state will reform the institution, not the courts."[68]

Aftermath of Riots: Attica in 1985

What happens after the riots? Do they result in substantial reform of prison conditions? A 1983 study of conditions at Attica, ordered by the state after a work strike by inmates, reported that although conditions at Attica had improved, many of the inmate grievances that led to the strike were justified. The report concluded:

> Until a meaningful and substantive effort is undertaken to revamp the operation of the Attica facility and to address the problems cited in this report, the underlying tension and frustration that culminated in the strike will continue to pose a serious threat to the stability of the institution.[69]

The commissioner of corrections blamed the strike on overcrowding, which he blamed on the federal court. After the 1971 riot, prison officials had administratively capped the population at Attica; but in 1981, in view of overcrowding at another correctional facility in New York, a federal court chose to release the cap at Attica and ordered that more prisoners be incarcerated there.

Another study of Attica, published in 1983, was also critical of the conditions. The inmates, upon hearing about the study, requested copies, but their requests were refused. They sued, and the federal court, in a 1985 opinion, held that correctional officials had not shown sufficient reasons for withholding the report and that it should be made available to the inmates. The 1983 report challenged the conclusion of correctional offi-

SPOTLIGHT 15.8
SELECTED RIOTS IN AMERICAN PRISONS, 1985–1988

McAlester, Oklahoma – Oklahoma State Penitentiary, 17 December 1985

Three guards stabbed, in serious condition; another guard, a woman, was in good condition; seven guards taken hostage; prison under inmate control for 20 hours. Estimated property damage: $375,000. Prison's capacity is 496; population at the time of the riot was 610. Immediate precipitating factor, according to the warden, was his firing of five inmates in chief work positions. These inmates had considerable control over other inmates; the warden was trying to get the control back in the hands of the administration. Twenty inmates were transferred to prisons in other states; inmate freedom inside the prison was greatly restricted; many are still in lockdown 22 hours a day.

The OSP was the scene of a major riot in 1973. At that time, the prison was overcrowded. A later court order found conditions unconstitutional and placed the prison under court order to eliminate those conditions. Considerable progress was made. The prison was removed from the order in 1984, but some claimed that it was slipping back into unconstitutional conditions.

Moundsville, West Virginia – West Virginia Penitentiary, 1 January 1986

Inmates, wielding homemade weapons, took guards hostage and seized control of the prison; 3 inmates killed; 16 hostages taken; prison held by inmates for 43 hours. Guards taken hostage were forced to watch inmates brutalize, torture, and then kill inmates thought to be snitches. The body of one inmate, a convicted murderer and child molester, was dragged up and down a cellblock as other inmates spat on him. The riot was triggered by inmate anger over restrictions on contact visits with family and friends, and the cancellation of a Christmas open house.

Officials in the state blamed each other for the problems. The current governor and the former governor "traded charges of accusing each other of cowardice and misguided policies." The current governor said the inmates killed were accused of being informants for the administration; and that the informant policy was started by the previous governor, who retorted that during the 3-day crisis the current governor was nowhere to be found. "For reasons known only to himself, the governor chose to leave the hard negotiating in Moundsville to his press secretary." On 16 January 1986, inmates began a work strike to protest continued restrictions of their activities since the riot. In February, 25 inmates who had been placed in isolation since the New Year's Day riot broke out of their cells. Guards quickly persuaded 23 of the inmates to surrender and then captured the other 2. Sixty-eight inmates were in isolation as a result of the riot.

The West Virginia Penitentiary was placed under court order in 1983 after the court found unconstitutional conditions, including maggot-infested food

cials that the problems at Attica were the result of overcrowding and that therefore new prisons should be provided. According to the report, the problems at Attica stemmed from two sources: "The negative attitude exhibited by Attica officials towards the inmates in their charge, and the failure to provide adequate resources." Citing racist practices on the part of guards, physical abuse of some inmates, violation of regulations concerning proper treatment of inmates in solitary confinement cells, lack of exercise facilities, uneven enforcement of the large number of rules inmates must follow, idleness, inadequate medical care, inadequate facilities in the law library, and problems regarding visitation privileges, the report concluded with a commendation of the inmates who staged a peaceful strike in protest of such conditions.

and raw sewage in living areas. The prison at that time was overcrowded and officials were ordered to reduce the population.

Federal Prisons in Atlanta, Georgia, and Oakdale, Louisiana, 1988

On 21 November 1987, the federal penitentiary at Oakdale, Louisiana exploded into flames as Cubans reacted to news that United States officials were about to sign with Cuban officials providing for the repatriation of more than 2,500 Cubans who were being held in U.S. prisons. Although investigations later indicated that precautionary measures might have prevented the spread of the riots, such measures were not taken. On November 23, Cuban inmates in the Atlanta penitentiary took 75 hostages and burned three buildings.

These two riots resulted in millions of dollars of damage, the death of 1 inmate, and the seizure of more than 120 hostages. The uprisings ended on December 4, when the Atlanta inmates and government officials came to terms. They agreed that there would be no reprisals against the inmates except for major misconduct or specific violent assaults against others. Loopholes in the agreement, however, may permit prosecuting some inmates.

The U.S. government agreed to delay deportation proceedings. Immediately after the riot, the inmates were moved to other prisons. By spring 1988, some Cubans had been released to relatives or halfway houses; others were approved for release from prison and were awaiting sponsors.

Stringtown, Oklahoma, 14 May 1988

Inmates at the Alford Correctional Center, a medium-security prison near Stringtown, Oklahoma, took eight prison guards hostage, and burned two buildings. The ordeal lasted 62 hours. It was the eighth Oklahoma prison riot since the McAlester riot of 1973, discussed earlier, which led to a landmark federal case that placed the Oklahoma Prison System under court orders to improve.

Oklahoma prison officials estimated they would need $7.7 million to rebuild the facility, and legislators adjourned in late June without appropriating the money. However, they did allocate one day in July to decide what to do about the prison system, already overcrowded prior to losing this facility.

An Oklahoma Department of Public Safety report on the riot concluded that it could have been avoided. The report indicated that a "lack of detention cells, non-compliance with prison policies, a slow response and not enough emergency keys" contributed to the riot, and ACLU attorney Louis Bullock, who has handled the landmark decision that has been in the courts for 16 years, declared Oklahoma's prison system as the most violent of the past decade. According to Bullock,

We simply cannot afford to lose a prison every two years. . . . They've got to break the cycle of violence in Oklahoma prisons. . . . Our approach to corrections is bankrupt. . . . It doesn't work. They've got to start on a very fundamental level to change.[1]

[1] "Riot Further Strains Resources of Prison System," *Tulsa World* (22 May 1988), p. A7. Among other suggestions Bullock made was to expand the use of community-based facilities, discussed in the next chapter.

A footnote at the end of the report said,

> Inmates we have interviewed since the general strike ended have informed us that Superintendent Smith's chief response to the strike thus far, announced by him through the public address system in early November, has been to change the flavor of ice cream available for sale in the commissary.

The report ended with an observation of the lessons to be learned from the peaceful strike in contrast to the earlier bloody riot.

> The challenge now faced by state and Attica officials is to acknowledge the severity of the conditions at Attica, and to take immediate and decisive steps to correct them. It would be a tragedy of immense proportions if the administration's response is to pretend that the crisis has passed, and to walk away from the fundamental problems. Surely, the painful lesson to be drawn from such a response would be that more than individual grievances or peaceful public protests are necessary to improve the unbearable conditions.[70]

SUMMARY

Prisoners must retain reasonable opportunities to exercise basic human rights while they are incarcerated. According to the U.S. Supreme Court,

> The continuing guarantee of these substantial rights to prison inmates is testimony to a belief that the way a society treats those who have transgressed against it is evidence of the essential character of that society.[71]

But the Court has made it clear that some rights are forfeited by inmates and that security needs may permit restriction of rights normally recognized in prison. This chapter has surveyed the historical and current approaches to the legal rights of inmates.

The chapter began with a look at the traditional hands-off doctrine, in which federal courts refused to become involved in the daily administration and maintenance of prisons. As a result of recognized abuse of prisoners and the civil rights movement that brought the nation's attention to the problems not only of minorities in society but also of the conditions under which inmates lived, courts began to abandon the hands-off policy. Courts still defer to prison officials, but they no longer tolerate violations of basic rights.

An introduction to the procedures for filing lawsuits was followed by an overview of the First, Fourth, Eighth, and Fourteenth Amendments of the Constitution. The importance of mail and other communication began the discussion of the First Amendment rights of inmates. Visitation, religious worship, freedom of assembly and self-government, and access to courts—all rights within the First Amendment—were analyzed, followed by the Fourth Amendment right to be free from unreasonable searches and seizures, the Eighth Amendment right to be free from cruel and unusual punishment, and the Fourteenth Amendment rights to due process and equal protection. All of these rights may be restricted if prison officials are able to show the action is necessary to maintain a legitimate prison goal such as security and safety.

We then looked at prison education and prison labor. Both are important for many reasons, but the reality is that prisons do not have enough meaningful jobs to keep all inmates busy during the work day, and educational programs are limited.

Many of the problems of incarceration are related to overcrowding. There are two basic ways to solve this problem. We can build more facilities, a prospect discussed in an earlier chapter. However, costs are overwhelming; perhaps even more important, if we build them, we fill them. The second solution is to reduce the populations in prison. This has been done in some states by passing a statute that permits the governor to declare an emergency situation when notified that the prison population has reached 95 percent (or some other figure) of legal capacity.

Other jurisdictions have kept jail populations at reasonable levels by not jailing arrestees. In 1986, criticism of the only woman ever to be chief of police in a major U.S. city was aimed at Penny E. Harrington of Portland, Oregon. She and the mayor were under fire because the city's burglary rate was increasing. It was the highest in the nation for the third year in a row. Harrington replied that local police were arresting more burglars than ever before; but because of the crowded jails, the police gave them citations and did not put them in jail. Some were arrested for another burglary within minutes after they left the police station.[72] Harrington resigned in June 1986, after only 17 months in office and shortly before the release of a report concluding that her administration was a failure.

The Oregon and Texas situations illustrate the system effects of incarceration. If inmates are released early or are not detained or imprisoned after conviction, they may commit additional crimes. But if more people are sent to jail and prison, the system will become more costly; facilities will be even more crowded; and there will be an even greater probability that the rights of inmates will be violated.

The final section looked at the major prison riots of recent times. The Attica riot of 1971, examined in the context of prison conditions in 1985, clearly illustrates not only the devastation of riots regarding personal injury, death, and property damage, but also shows the slowness with which meaningful changes are made. Recent reactions of Attica inmates indicate the continuing frustration of prisoners and demonstrate that a peaceful protest by inmates may not be sufficient for prison reform. The 1986 riot in West Virginia illustrates the torture and brutality of which inmates are capable.

This chapter has focused on the rights of inmates, but these rights must be viewed in the context of the needs of society. How can prisons achieve a balance between the rights of inmates and the needs of safety? One problem with the recognition of the rights of inmates is that there is not always public support for the approach; nor is there public support for spending more money on facilities. But the courts have made it clear that an unwillingness or even a financial inability to improve prison conditions will not be acceptable. Courts, however, have given prison systems reasonable time to bring their facilities up to constitutional standards. Prison officials who defy court orders may find themselves held in **contempt of court,** a criminal offense for which they may be incarcerated. They also may find their facilities closed by federal court order.

Inmates, on the other hand, can expect only a negative reaction from society when they protest prison conditions by rioting. Those who file frivolous lawsuits are finding strong reactions not only from prison officials and the public, but also from judges who are devising ways to reduce frivolous appeals.

The courts, public, inmates, and prison officials may all be expected to continue the struggle of finding a reasonable balance that will permit society to be protected and to exercise its right to punish those who offend while providing a system of punishment that does not demean and degrade inmates.

STUDY QUESTIONS

1. What is the *hands-off doctrine* and to what extent (and why) has it been abandoned?

2. What is meant by a *hierarchy of rights*?

3. Compare and contrast a writ of habeas corpus and a Section 1983 action.

4. What restrictions may prison officials place on the correspondence, visitation, and religious rights of inmates?

5. Why is access to courts so important and what is meant by *access*?

6. How does the Fourth Amendment prohibition against unreasonable searches and seizures apply in prison?

7. How does the Eighth Amendment prohibition against cruel and unusual punishment apply to inmates?

8. What is meant by *due process* and how does that apply to prison disciplinary hearings?

9. May male and female inmates be treated differently in the same prison system?

10. If most prisoners are relatively poorly educated, why do we not make a greater effort to provide education classes in prisons?

11. Should prisoners have to work? If there is a lack of jobs, how should that problem be solved?

12. How are prison and jail overcrowding problems interrelated?

13. Do you think prison riots result in prison reform? What evidence does the chapter offer on this question?

ENDNOTES

1. Ruffin v. Commonwealth, 62 Va. 790, 796 (1871).
2. Wolff v. McDonnell, 418 U.S. 539 (1974).
3. For an overview on the law of prisoners' rights, along with case excerpts, see Sheldon Krantz, *The Law of Corrections and Prisoners' Rights*, 3d ed. (St. Paul, Minn.: West Publishing Co., 1986). The supplement that updates that text was published in 1988.
4. Bell v. Wolfish, 441 U.S. 520, 547–48 (1979), citations omitted.
5. *Time* (9 February 1968), p. 14.
6. Thomas O. Merton, *The Dilemma of Prison Reform* (New York: Holt, Rinehart and Winston, 1976).
7. Holt v. Sarver, 309 F. Supp. 362 (E.D. Ark. 1971). This case has a long history of remands and reversals leading to the Supreme Court case, Hutto v. Finney, 437 U.S. 678 (1978), *reh'g denied*, 439 U.S. 1122 (1979). A good source for the history up to 1977 is found in Finney v. Hutto, 548 F.2d 740 (8th Cir. 1977).
8. Graham v. Richardson, 403 U.S. 365, 375 (1971).
9. See O'Lone v. Estate of Shabazz, 482 U.S. 342, 345 (1987).
10. Bureau of Justice Statistics, *The Growth of Appeals: 1973–83 Trends* (Washington, D.C.: U.S. Department of Justice, February 1985), p. 2.
11. Bureau of Justice Statistics *Special Report: Federal Review of State Prisoner Petitions: Habeas Corpus* (Washington, D.C.: U.S. Dept. of Justice, March 1984), p. 2.
12. For an extensive analysis of 1983 actions, see H. E. Barrineau, III, *Civil Liability in Criminal Justice* (Cincinnati, Ohio: Anderson Publishing Co., 1987). For a recent case involving a 1983 claim, see Molton v. Cleveland, 839 F. 2d 240 (6th Cir. 1988), *Cert. denied*,—U.S.—(1989).
13. Bell v. Wolfish, 441 U.S. 520, 545 (1979); Rhodes v. Chapman, 452 U.S. 337 (1981).
14. Procunier v. Martinez, 416 U.S. 396, 413, (1974), *overruled in part* by Thornburgh v. Abbott, No. 87-1344 (May 15, 1989). After the text was in press, the Court decided Thornburgh v. Abbott, in which the Court overruled Martinez to the extent that Martinez covered incoming mail. Regulations concerning incoming mail must now be analyzed under the standard set forth in Turner v. Safley, 482 U.S. 78 (1987), and will therefore be valid if they are "reasonably related to legitimate penological interests." The result in Abbott is that the Court has now approved more stringent rules for the regulation of incoming prison mail. The Procunier test is that limitations of First Amendment freedoms "must be no greater than is necessary or essential to the protection of the particular governmental interest involved."
15. McNamara v. Moody, 606 F. 2d 621 (5th Cir. 1979), *cert. denied*, 447 U.S. 929 (1980).
16. Hall v. Curran, 818 F. 2d 1040, 1043–44 (2nd Cir. 1987), case names and citations omitted.
17. Sostre v. Otis, 330 F. Supp. 941, 944–946 (S.D. N.Y. 1971).
18. Turner v. Safley, 482 U.S. 78 (1987).
19. N.Y. EXEC. LAW, Section 632-a.
20. Matter of Johnson, 430 N.Y.S.2d 904 (N.Y. Sup. Ct. 1979). For a discussion of the New York and other state statutes, see "Criminals Selling Their Stories: The First Amendment Requires Legislative Reexamination," *Cornell Law Review* 72 (September 1987): 1331–55.
21. Block v. Rutherford, 468 U.S. 576 (1984). On May 15, 1989, the Supreme Court ruled in Kentucky Department of Corrections v. Thompson, No. 87-1815, that Kentucky prison regulations on visitation do not create a "liberty interest" entitling inmates to hearings or other due process protections when a visitor is denied entry.
22. See McCray v. Sullivan, 509 F. 2d 1332 (5th Cir. 1975), *remanded*, 399 F. Suppl. 271 (S.D. Ala. 1975), *cert. denied*, 423, U.S. 859 (1975).
23. Turney v. Safley, 482 U.S. 78 (1987).
24. Davis v. Carlson, 837 F. 2d 1318 (5th Cir. 1988), cases and citations omitted.
25. Doe v. Coughlin, 523 N.Y.S.2d 782 (N.Y. Ct. App. 1987), *reargument denied*, 71 N.Y.2d (1987), *cert. denied*, 102 L. Ed. 166 (1988).
26. Pell v. Procunier, 417 U.S. 817 (1974).
27. Houchins v. KQED, Inc., 439 U.S. 812 (1978).
28. Cruz v. Beto, 405 U.S. 319, 322, text and n. 2 (1972), *appeal after remanded*, Cruz v. Estelle, 497 F. 2d 496 (5th Cir. 1974).
29. O'Lone v. Estate of Shabazz, 482 U.S. 342, 345 (1987), cases and citations omitted.
30. See generally David L. Abney, " 'Our Daily Bread'—Prisoners' Rights to a Religious Diet," *Case and Comment* 90 (March–April 1985): 28–38.
31. Dettmer v. Landon, 799 F. 2d 929, 930, 933, 934 (4th Cir. 1986), *cert. denied*, 483 U.S. 1007 (1987).
32. Jones v. North Carolina Prisoner's Union, Inc., 433 U.S. 119 (1977).
33. Jeffries v. Reed, 631 F. Supp. 1212, 1217 (E.D. Wash. 1986), quoting Jones v. North Carolina Prisoners' Unions, 433 U.S. 119, 132 (1977), also referring to Pell v. Procunier, 417 U.S. 817, 822 (1974).
34. Ex Parte Hull, 312 U.S. 546 (1941), *reh'g denied*, 312 U.S. 716 (1941).
35. Johnson v. Avery, 393 U.S. 483 (1969).
36. Bounds v. Smith, 430 U.S. 817, 821, 828, 831 (1977), citations omitted.
37. Peterkin v. Jeffes, 661 F. Supp. 895, 928 (E.D. Pa.

1987), *aff. in part* and *vacated in part*, 855 F. 2d 1021 (CA3 Pa. 1988).

38. Wolff v. McDonnell, 418 U.S. 539 (1974).
39. Hudson v. Palmer, 468 U.S. 517, (1984), citation omitted, *remanded*, Palmer v. Hudson, 744 F. 2d 22 (4th Cir. 1984).
40. Block v. Rutherford, 468 U.S. 576 (1984).
41. Bell v. Wolfish, 441 U.S. 520 (1979).
42. State v. Palmer, 751 P. 2d 975, 976, 977 (Ariz. App. 1987), *reh'g denied*, 12 April 1988.
43. See Hunger v. Auger, 672 F. 2d 668 (8th Cir. 1982).
44. Giles v. Ackerman, 746 F. 2d 614 (9th Cir. 1984), *cert. denied*, 471 U.S. 1053 (1985).
45. Estelle v. Gamble, 429 U.S. 97 (1976), *reh'g denied*, 429 U.S. 1066 (1977), *remanded*, 554 F. 2d 653 (5th Cir. 1977).
46. Ruiz v. Estelle, 679 F. 2d 1115 (5th Cir. 1982), *amended in part, vacated in part*, 688 F. 2d 266 (5th Cir. 1982), *cert. denied*, 460 U.S. 1042 (1983).
47. For an extensive analysis of the Texas Prison System in recent years, see Steve J. Martin and Sheldon Ekland-Olson, *Texas Prisons: The Walls Came Tumbling Down* (Austin: Texas Monthly Press, 1987).
48. Olim v. Wakinekona, 461 U.S. 238 (1983), *remanded*, 716 F. 2d 1279 (9th Cir. 1983).
49. Hewitt v. Helms, 459 U.S. 460 (1983), *remanded*, 712 F. 2d 48 (3rd Cir. 1983).
50. Wolff v. McDonnell, 418 U.S. 539, 563–72 (1974).
51. Superintendent, Massachusetts Correctional Institution v. Hill, 472 U.S. 445 (1985).
52. Ponte v. Real, 471 U.S. 491 (1985), *remanded*, Real v. Superintendent, Massachusetts Correctional Institution, Walpole, 482 N.E. 2d 1188 (Mass. 1985).
53. *Jails in America: An Overview of Issues* (College Park, Md.: American Correctional Association in cooperation with the National Coalition for Jail Reform, 1985), p. 24.
54. For a general discussion, see Charlotte A. Nesbitt, "Female Offenders: A Changing Population," *Corrections Today* 48 (February 1986): 76–80.
55. See Hermandez v. Johnston, 833 F. 2d 1316 (9th Cir. 1987).
56. For recent developments in FPI, see Gerald M. Farkas, "Prison Industries: Working with the Private Sector," *Corrections Today* 47 (June 1985): 102–3. For a critique, see General Accounting Office, *Report to the Attorney General: Improved Prison Work Programs Will Benefit Correctional Institutions and Inmates* (Washington, D.C.: U.S. Government Printing Office, 1982), pp. 16, 17. See also Federal Prison Industries, Inc., *Schedule of Products Made in Federal Penal and Correctional Institutions* (Washington, D.C.: U.S. Government Printing Office, 1984).
57. U.S. CODE, Ch. 18, Section 1761.
58. See Sharon Goodman, "Prisoners as Entrepre- neurs: Developing a Model for Prison-Run Industry," *Boston University Law Revew* 62 (November 1982): 1163–95.
59. Grant R. Grissom, *Impact of Free Venture Prison Industries upon Correctional Institutions* (Washington, D.C.: U.S. Government Printing Office, January 1981). See also Gail S. Funke et al., *Assets and Liabilities of Correctional Industries* (Lexington, Mass.: D. C. Heath and Co., 1982).
60. For a brief overview of prison crowding, see Sandra Evans Skovron, "Prison Crowding: The Dimensions of the Problem and Strategies of Population Control," in Joseph E. Scott and Travis Hirschi, eds., *Controversial Issues in Crime and Justice* (Beverly Hills, Calif.: Sage Publications, 1988), pp. 183–98.
61. *Jails in America*, pp. 11–13, 18–19.
62. Ruiz v. Estelle, 503 F. Supp. 1265 (S.D. Tex. 1980), *aff'd in part, rev'd in part*, 679 F. 2d 1115 (5th Cir. 1982), *amended in part, vacated in part*, 688 F. 2d 266 (5th Cir. 1982), *cert. denied*, 460 U.S. 1042 (1983).
63. For a brief overview of prison crowding, see Sandra Evans Skovron, "Prison Crowding."
64. "Inmate Uprising at Riker's Island," *Corrections Today* 50 (April 1988): 204. See also "New York Jails: Escapes and Strife Fuel Turmoil," *New York Times* (12 December 1987), p. 13. For more detailed analyses of jail and prison overcrowding and their effects, see the following recent publications: Stephen D. Gottfredson and Sean D. McConville, eds., *America's Correctional Crisis: Prison Populations and Public Policy* (Westport, Conn.: Greenwood Press, 1987); and Paul B. Paulus, *Prison Crowding: A Psychological Perspective* (New York: Springer Verlag, 1988).
65. "New York's Country Jail Now Like the City: Filled, *New York Times* (3 October 1988), p. 16.
66. Abdul Wali v. Coughlin, 754 F. 2d 1015, 1018–19 (2d Cir. 1985), citations omitted.
67. Cited in Joseph W. Rogers, "Postscripts to a Prison Riot," paper presented at the Annual Meeting of the Academy of Criminal Justice Sciences, Louisville, Ky., 25 March 1982.
68. Quoted in "Guards Losers Too, in Riot-Torn Prison," *Tulsa World* (5 January 1986), p. 14A.
69. Cited in Abdul Wali v. Coughlin, 754 F. 2d 1015, 1020 (2d Cir. 1985).
70. This report, based on a study of the Prisoner's Legal Services (PLS) of New York, a public interest law firm that represents inmates, is published by PLS and entitled *Attica: A Report on Conditions, 1983*. It is reprinted in its entirety as Appendix A in Abdul Wali v. Coughlin, 754 F. 2d 1015, 1036–48 (2d Cir. 1985), *disapproved* by O'Love v. Estate of Shabazz, 482 U.S. 342 (1987).
71. Hudson v. Palmer, 468 U.S. 517, 523, 525 (1984).
72. "Police Chief in Rift with Her Officers," *New York Times* (31 January 1986), p. 9.

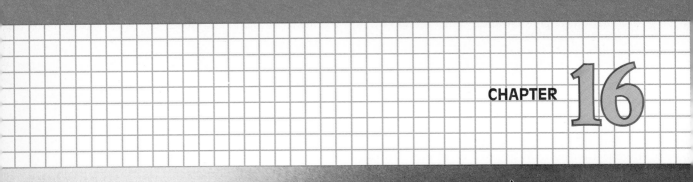

GET READY
FOR TOMORROW

CHAPTER **16**

Probation, Parole, and Community Corrections

Roger and Barbara are both arrested for leaving the scene of an accident in which an injury occurred, a felony in their jurisdiction. After conviction, the judge imposes a 5-year sentence on each but suspends the imposition of those sentences and places the offenders on probation. They are told to report to their probation officers at specified times and to file reports. They are given a list of rules that are to govern their behavior while on probation. Among other rules, they are told that they may not leave the county without the permission of their probation officers; they may not purchase or consume liquor; and they are not to commit further crimes.

After two months of carefully observing the terms of their probation, Roger and Barbara drive across the county line to purchase liquor. They are seen by a police officer who recognizes them and reports their offenses to their probation officers. Barbara and Roger are notified that there will be probation revocation hearings, which they attend. Probation is revoked in both cases; Barbara and Roger are sent to prison.

After serving one-half of their 5-year sentences, Roger and Barbara are eligible for parole. Roger has actively participated in educational and vocational programs while in prison and believes that he is ready for parole. He attends his parole hearing but the parole board, without giving any reasons, tells him he must spend more time in prison.

Barbara has been less active in educational and vocational programs while in prison, but she is granted parole. She is assigned a parole officer and given a list of rules that she must follow while she is on parole. Barbara faces many problems in her adjustment to living within these rules and finding a job upon release from prison. She also may encounter problems in returning to her family.

INTRODUCTION

The cases of Roger and Barbara illustrate many of the procedures and issues discussed in this chapter. Supervision of offenders in the community is a frequent alternative to prison. The conditions of this alternative may be severe for some offenders; violations of the terms of probation or parole are common. Violations may result in revocation of probation or parole, but proper procedures must be followed when revocations occur.

This chapter focuses on probation, parole, and community treatment of offenders. It begins with an overview of **community-based corrections**, noting the historical development and discussing problems offenders face when they enter these programs. It examines how problems might be minimized by preparation before release from prison and by provision of resources in the community.

Probation, the most frequently imposed sentence, and parole, until recently a major form of release from prison, are discussed in their historical contexts and with their modern changes. Both probation and parole have been the focus of considerable attention in recent years. Crimes committed by probationers and parolees frequently receive widespread publicity, leading to public pressure to reduce the use of probation and parole. In some cases, these pressures have been successful.

Like other changes in the criminal justice system, however, changes in the use of probation and parole must be viewed in terms of their effects on the rest of the system. A significant reduction in the use of one or both places severe strains on the correctional system, causing prison overcrowding and all the problems that overcrowding involves. It also may result in the incarceration of offenders who do not need such severe restraints. On the other hand, crimes committed by probationers and parolees reduce the safety and security of society. It is not possible to predict with great accuracy who will harm society while on probation or parole.

SUPERVISION OF OFFENDERS IN THE COMMUNITY: AN OVERVIEW

Earlier discussions described some methods used in the past to permit the accused or the convicted offender to remain in the community. Family members, friends, or attorneys served as sureties to guarantee the presence of the accused at trial. Sureties later were replaced by a variety of methods of posting bond. Early reformers such as John Augustus were successful in their efforts to have convicted persons placed on probation in the community. In the late 1880s in New York City, halfway houses were used to permit inmates a gradual readjustment to the community.

The major impetus for the modern movement toward supervision of the offender within the community was given by the Federal Prisoner's Rehabilitation Act of 1965 and by the President's Crime Commission, which (in its 1967 report) stated that the new direction in corrections recognizes that crime and delinquency are not only failures of the individual offenders; they are also community failures. The commission saw the task of corrections as one of **reintegrating** the offender into the community, restoring family ties, getting the person an education or employment, and securing for the offender a place in the normal functioning of society. That, said the commission, requires changes in the community and in the offender.

Staffers and residents of halfway house for former prison inmates. (Ellis Herwig/Picture Cube)

The president's commission described the traditional methods of institutionalizing offenders as fundamentally deficient. The commission concluded that reintegration is likely to be more successful if we work with offenders in the community rather than confine them in prisons.[1] In 1973 the National Advisory Commission on Criminal Justice Standards and Goals called for an increased emphasis on **probation.** The commission concluded, "The most hopeful move toward effective corrections is to continue to strengthen the trend away from confining people in institutions and toward supervising them in the community."[2]

Reintegration of the offender into the community is not a one-way process, however. The community also must take an active role in the process of treating the offender. It might not be sufficient to try to reintegrate the offender into the community; the latter may need to change more than the offender. For example, if resources for reintegration are not available, they must be developed. The community must provide the resources for offenders.

Many reactions to offenders do not fall within the definition of community-based corrections. Fines and restitution are alternatives to incarceration, but they are not community-based corrections. The important factor in community-based corrections is the relationship between those involved in the program, both clients and staff, and the community. Community-based programs involve an element of supervision aimed at assisting the offender to reintegrate into the community. In some programs supervision may not be adequate, but it is the effort to supervise and improve that distinguishes community-based programs from fines and restitution, both of which, of course, could be combined with community-based corrections.

Community-based corrections should also be distinguished from **diversion,** a process of turning the offender away from the criminal (or juvenile) systems and into other programs. Diversion occurs instead of, not in addition to, criminal court processing. Traditionally it has been used mainly in the processing of juveniles. But diversion may also be used for adult offenders. The alcoholic or drug addict who is apprehended for petty theft might be counseled to enter a drug and alcohol treatment program in the community and might be told that successful completion in that program will result in dropping criminal charges. That program might be a community-based treatment program.

Diversion programs, however, are not the focus of this chapter, in which the term *community-based corrections* refers to that process of involving convicted offenders in supervised programs aimed at reintegrating them into the community. These programs may be offered within prisons to prepare offenders for release. They may be community-based programs outside the prisons to which offenders report on a part-time basis before

On release, inmates may be given a check for a small amount of money, but cashing those checks is not always possible. Some businesses, however, cater to releasees. (David Hall)

their release from prison, or they may be programs provided for convicted offenders who are placed on probation.

The use of community-based programs and supervision provides the common element of procedures like probation and **parole,** which in other respects are quite different, as subsequent discussions will explain. But community-based corrections also include residential programs. Foster homes and group homes may be used for juveniles who do not need specialized treatment programs but who have experienced difficulties living in their own homes.

Halfway houses or community treatment centers for adults also involve residential treatment. The halfway house is usually viewed as a place for the offender to go from prison; it provides a gradual reentry into society, with the offender living in a supervised environment but leaving that facility during the day to work or participate in vocational or educational programs. The community treatment center may serve the same purpose, but it might also be used for persons who have not been to prison, such as those who are on probation and need more supervision that could be provided in a nonresidential environment.

Residential programs may be used for more than halfway programs. Some are viewed as long-term programs for offenders, usually juveniles, who need intensive treatment and supervision. Programs may be designed for offenders with particular needs. For example, some programs are limited to first offenders; others are limited to recidivists who do not appear to be able to function effectively without intensive supervision. Some programs are nonresidential, with offenders living in their own homes but coming to the treatment centers for therapy, either group or individual, and for participation in seminars and other programs designed to assist offenders with adjustment problems.

PROBLEMS OF OFFENDERS ON RELEASE

Before offenders are placed in community corrections after a prison sentence, attention should be given to problems they will face. The problems will vary considerably, but some are common. Inmates need street clothing when they are released from prison. Although most prisons will either provide clothing or permit inmates to receive clothing from home, it is rarely sufficient. The prison may provide only one set of clothing; the inmate may not have family or friends who will provide additional clothing. Even a prearranged job will not be much help, for the inmate will not get a paycheck for a week or longer.

Many prison systems provide inmates with a small amount of money upon release if the inmate does not have any money. That amount varies from state to state but may be as low as $50. Inmates usually get a bus ticket home. Out of these provisions, inmates who have no other financial resources must pay for additional clothing, for room and board, and in many cases, for debts incurred before incarceration and restitution. They also may have a family to support.

Employment is another problem faced by the released offender. Institutions may or may not provide assistance to offenders in seeking em-

Leo J. Nolin, 74, greets youngsters as he was released after serving 50 years in prison on conviction for murder. Inmates have to cope with many changes that have occurred in the world during their incarceration. (AP/Wide World Photos)

ployment. Inmates also face social adjustments upon release from prison. The day of release is characterized by a sense of optimism, the belief that in the beginning and in the long run life will be different and pleasant. Release from prison has been called a positive life change, but people also experience uncertainty, loneliness, depression, and disorganization.[3]

For many ex-offenders, release from prison means frustration and anxiety over how to act and what to say in social situations and on the job. Feelings of helplessness, insecurity, fear, indecision, and depression may result in physical problems such as loss of appetite, chronic exhaustion, problems in sleeping, or sexual difficulties. The fear of the unknown is illustrated by the comments of the inmate in Spotlight 16.1. This fear of the unknown may be particularly acute for the inmate who has not been able to maintain close ties with his or her family during the period of incarceration.[4]

Relationships with family members may also create problems for ex-offenders. Spouses and children suffer as a result of the offender's incarceration; anger and hostility may greet the offender who returns home. Years of absence, with few opportunities for family members to visit their loved ones in prison, may create interpersonal problems that are beyond repair. Financial problems created by the absence of the offender may compound the interpersonal problems.

Financial, economic, social, and other problems that inmates encounter on release from prison may be eased if adequate services are provided for ex-offenders by the community. An example of the kind of programs that might be instituted is provided by the community support services program in Kentucky. This program was started by administrators in the Bureau of Corrections, who felt that it was unreasonable to expect probation and parole officers to provide all services that would be needed for clients on probation and parole. They devised a system

SPOTLIGHT 16.1
AN EX-OFFENDER FACES FREEDOM IN THE OUTSIDE WORLD

I had not slept very well and my thoughts were chaotic. This was it. They were going to turn me loose at last. It did not seem quite real. Nothing is ever certain in prison. . . . I was sweating, nervous, and agitated. . . . The hour I had to wait for the crew to come and unlock the door seemed to last an eternity. . . .

I walked out of the wing slowly—though I really felt like running. . . . I hurriedly dressed, was photographed, and passed into the waiting room. I signed papers which I did not read and can't remember to what they pertained. It didn't matter! All that mattered was getting out! I could think of nothing else.

The guard left . . . an electronically controlled glass door . . . opened. I stood there waiting for a command to leave. None came. Finally, I noticed [the guard's] arm waving at me impatiently to pass through. I hesitated, afraid to make a wrong move, but he motioned again. . . . I stepped through the glass door. . . . That was it. I was free. One world closed and another opened. The world I left was a hell and the one I entered was unknown to me. I looked for a face or a voice to greet me, but no one even saw me. I was a stranger in an alien land.

Source: Quoted in Sheldon Ekland-Olson et al., "Postrelease Depression and the Importance of Familial Support," *Criminology* 21 (May 1983): 263–64.

whereby probation and parole officers are viewed as brokers of services, with many necessary services provided by the community. Figure 16.1 diagrams the services that are available in the Kentucky program for offenders placed on probation and parole.

After their needs are assessed, clients may be referred back to their probation or parole officers, or they may be referred to either one or all of the three major divisions of services: employment, education, or community service. The employment division provides not only placement services but also training, and training may include on-the-job training (OJT), prevocational training (PVT), or training in the living skills necessary for success on the job. Housing, medical, and other needs may be

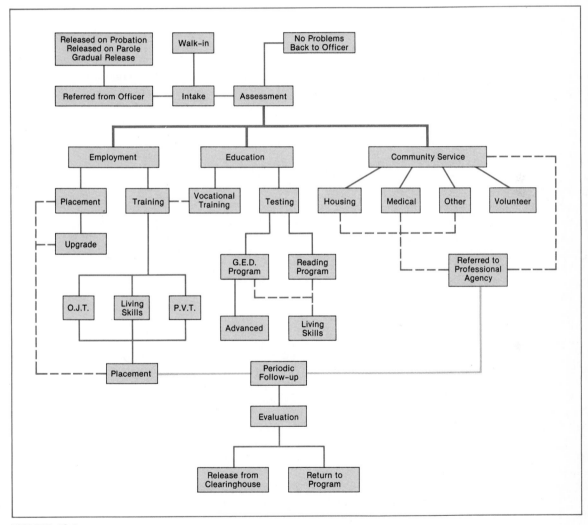

FIGURE 16.1

Services for Offenders on Release to the Community. *Source:* Betsy Coffey and Brett Scott, "Community Support Service: The Kentucky Experience." Reprinted with the permission of the American Correctional Association, *Corrections Today,* American Correctional Association Monographs, Series 1, Number 5. All rights reserved. (Laurel, Md.: American Correctional Association, May 1981), 76.

SPOTLIGHT 16.2
ADJUSTMENT SEMINARS FOR FEMALE OFFENDERS RELEASED TO THE COMMUNITY

A New You—Personal Development Program

This is a self-improvement program coordinated with the Lewis University Personal Development Program of Chicago, Ill., and designed to help participants gain feelings of self-worth and pride.

From the classes, which are concerned with the inner person, the students receive information on how to deal with life in a positive manner. From the classes on feminine development, they learn how to feel and be more attractive. This course is designed to build confidence, and improve the inner and outer person, because as a student watches herself become more physically attractive, her mental attitudes begin to alter; a new person is helped to emerge.

This course consists of 12 weekly sessions, and each person who completes the program will receive a certificate and several cosmetics. To complete the program, the student must attend at least 11 of the classes and meet other class requirements as specified during the first night's session. Excused absences are only those pertaining to illness.

Thirty participants will be chosen on the basis of their ability and commitment to attend all 12 sessions without interruption, their unavailability to a later session, and personality balance.

Below is a tentative course outline for the 12 sessions:

Class 1: Presenting a Confident You—How to stand, walk, and sit correctly; development of poise and physical coordination; tips on guides for everyday living; points of good posture; social interaction and first impressions.

Class 2: How Good and Poor Attitudes Affect Us—Changing attitudes, hang-ups about traditional female roles, etc.

Class 3: Personal Hygiene and Birth Control—Mouth care, internal hygiene; birth control methods; medical safeguards (self-examination for breast cancer). Speaker from Planned Parenthood.

Class 4: What Motivates You—Exercise on motivation; how to motivate yourself; power of the mind; creative thinking.

Class 5: Powers of the Mind—Conscious vs. Subconscious, the six senses, perception, awareness, positive thinking (17 success principles).

Class 6: Cleansing and Care of Hair, Skin, and Nails—Manicures; hair care; dermatology. Speaker: Dr. William Parsley, a dermatologist, on skin disorders.

Class 7: Basic Make-up Techniques—Application of liquid foundations; powder, eye and lip make-up, etc. Fashion coordination. Speaker from Shillito's cosmetic department.

Class 8: Values and Needs that Are Important to You—What are values; the relationship between values and needs; values and motivation; values and perception; "Island Exercise" role expectation—changing roles and values.

Class 9: Personality and Manners—Attitudes and manners in everyday relationships; what makes a pleasing personality; what makes a negative person; social manners; assertiveness; self-evaluation (physical fitness exercise class is an alternative).

Class 10: Guidelines for Setting Goals—What are goals; setting goals is not new; relationship between goals and motivation; managing conflict.

Class 11: Seventeen Success Principles as Applied—Job preparation; choosing a career; your abilities vs. your desires; values and careers; new opportunities for women; child care. Speaker from Female Offender Resource Center; alternatives.

Class 12: Review and Role Playing Exercises—"Bombardment" exercise.

New Ideas

Each participant is required to give a three-minute presentation before completion.

The program begins at 7:00 each evening and usually ends by 8:45.

The sessions that have an outside speaker are devoted almost entirely to their topic.

The participants vote on the most improved persons in: (a) attitude, (b) appearance, and (c) group participation (last session).

We give an "extra mile" award to the participants who we feel put forth extra effort.

Source: Betsy Coffey and Brett Scott, "Community Support Service: The Kentucky Experience," in *Community Corrections,* reprinted with the permission of the American Correctional Association Monographs, Series 1, Number 5 (Laurel, Md.: American Correctional Association, May 1981), pp. 78–79.

handled in the community service division, which has a branch of volunteers ready to help clients.

Educational and vocational programs include testing as well as training and experience. Throughout the process, evaluation and reassessment are important features. For specialized problems such as those that female offenders might face in their readjustment process, the Kentucky program offers special adjustment seminars. Spotlight 16.2 describes one of these programs.[5]

PREPARATION FOR RELEASE

Preparation for release from prison is very important. Preparation may be made in various types of programs; the most frequently used will be discussed briefly. Unfortunately, many prison systems do not provide sufficient preparation for the inmate upon release from prison.

Furlough or Work Release

The first **work release** law was the Huber Law, passed in Wisconsin in 1913. The next statute, that of North Carolina, was not passed until 1957. The first **furlough** program was introduced by legislation in Mississippi in 1918. A few states passed laws providing for work release or furloughs before 1965, but most of the programs in existence today were established by state laws after the 1965 federal law, the Prisoner Rehabilitation Act, was passed.

It is necessary to distinguish work release programs from furlough programs. A furlough usually means permitting the inmate to leave the institution once or occasionally for a specified purpose other than work or study. The offender may be given a furlough to visit a sick relative, to attend a family funeral, or to look for a job. The leave is only temporary, however, and usually is granted for only a short period of time.

In work release programs, the inmate is released from incarceration to work or to attend school. Inmates may participate in work-study, take courses at an educational institution, or work at a job in the community. Work release is also referred to by other names: day parole, outmate program, day work, daylight parole, free labor, intermittent jailing, and work furlough. Work release is used more frequently than study release.

State legislation varies regarding who decides whether an inmate should be put on work release. State legislation also differs as to how the money earned by the inmate is to be used. Most legislation permits states to contract with other political subdivisions for housing of inmates because they cannot always find work near the institution. Some provide halfway houses or work-release centers, and some use county jails. Conditions for employment usually are that inmates cannot work in areas where there is a surplus of labor. They must be paid the same as others doing the same job. If a union is involved it must be consulted, and the releasee cannot work during a labor dispute.

Furlough and work release programs are important for several reasons. Work release programs enable offenders to engage in positive contacts with the community, assuming of course, that work placement is satisfactory. It also permits offenders to provide some support for themselves and their families. This can eliminate the self-concept of failure that may be the result of the loss of the supportive role that is so important in American society. The offender may obtain more satisfying jobs than the prison could provide.

Work release and furlough programs provide a transition for the incarcerated inmate from a closely supervised way of life in prison to a more independent life within society. These programs give the community a transition period to accept offenders back into society. These programs have permitted some states to close one or more correctional facilities, thus decreasing the cost to the taxpayer.

Problems with work release involve the selection process, finding sufficient jobs, gaining community acceptance, and most important, making sure that inmates do not commit further crimes while they are on release. There is no guarantee, of course, that offenders placed on furlough or work release will not commit further crimes; the possibility that they will has led to community action to eliminate these methods of early release.

The Case of Willie Horton   Furloughs became an issue in the 1988 presidential election. Vice-President George Bush raised the issue with regard to Willie Horton, sentenced to life without parole for a murder committed in Massachusetts. Horton was released on weekend passes or furloughs for nine times without incident. But on the tenth pass, he broke into a Maryland home, twice raped the wife and stabbed the husband.

Horton is now serving two life sentences in Maryland, but his Massachusetts record was apparently too much for Bush's opponent, Michael Dukakis, governor of Massachusetts. Bush won the election, and perhaps would have done so without his negative campaign ad about Horton, but there is no question but that the ad seriously damaged Dukakis. And it probably will have an effect on furlough programs despite empirical evidence that most of the 53,000 inmates furloughed in 1987 committed very few crimes.[6] Spotlight 16.3 raises the issue of what will now become of furlough programs, and if they are abolished, how we will handle the Willie Hortons of the future.

Prerelease Programs

All inmates who are to be released should have the opportunity to participate in programs that prepare them for release. It is unreasonable to expect that the problems faced by releasees will be solved by inmates without any assistance from counselors and other professionals. The services offered in the Kentucky community support services program should also be available to inmates before release.

Prerelease centers would probably be the best solution for preparing for release inmates who have serious adjustment problems but who are being released because they have completed their terms. In a residential

SPOTLIGHT 16.3
WHAT DO WE DO WITH WILLIE HORTONS?

Convict Willie Horton was only supposed to strike temporary fear into the hearts of America's citizens and, in that service, help elect George Bush president of the United States.

The Republican effort, tainted as it was with racism and sexual violence, succeeded as an effective TV political message, textbook stuff they'll be using for years as a masterpiece of negative advertising.

But now it turns out that the intensely advertised Horton furlough from a Massachusetts prison and his attack on a Maryland couple has reopened an emotional debate over crime and punishment.

The debate was kicked off when it was learned that Horton and other long-term felons sentenced for brutal crimes—even murder—are routinely let out for short periods to move among us.

As in Horton's case, many have not served even a minimum sentence and the process described as rehabilitation sometimes smells more like experimentation.

For a nation of conscience, there are some troubling facts not often discussed, even when attention is turned to the Willie Hortons and thousands of others who have arrived at that place where justice is dispensed and crime is supposedly paid for by the criminal:

- All but about 2 percent of criminals now serving time will one day be out of prison and out in the streets. As a practical matter, there may be no such thing as a life sentence, not even when a publicity-seeking judge piles a series of life sentences on top of each other and adds another hundred years to that.
- Preparing prisoners for release—deciding who is ready and who is not and setting the terms— holds none of the certainties of the multiplication tables or cake recipes. Mistakes are made.
- The same public inclined to demand tough sentences often as not won't vote for legislators who will raise taxes to build more prisons. The result

can be prisoners squeezed out into society, ready or not, as new prisoners are squeezed into cellblocks.

The prison furlough and work-release plans—the gift that delivered Willie Horton to the Bush presidential campaign—are somewhat new to penology, driven along by the concept of prisoner rehabilitation and the reality of prison overcrowding.

Not too long ago, 50 years or so, in simpler, less violent, more law abiding and unenlightened times, parole from prison was often like seat-of-the-pants flying, judged by intuition, experience and the conduct of the prisoner.

For most prisoners there arrived what old-time wardens and parole officers described as a "now" time, when a convict felt rightfully punished, repentant and honestly anxious to turn his life around.

The trick then, without today's layers of bureaucracy, was to help the prisoner hold onto his "now" time in prison until he qualified for parole.

A lost "now" time, it was said, often produced a hardened, embittered, institutionalized criminal, a certain recidivist, and a potentially dangerous individual when, by law, he had to be turned out. As today's professionals work that larger and infinitely more complicated field, seeking the "now" time and using the techniques of work-release, furloughs, reduced sentences and the rest of it, the failures become famous.

They might even become notorious, as in the case of Willie Horton.

But if the attempts at rehabilitation, even of the cruelest killers, rapists, torturers and all the refuse of society don't serve society and even mock justice, then other solutions are needed.

Could we now look to Bush for those solutions now that he has introduced us to Willie Horton?

Source: Leonard Larsen, a veteran Washington reporter who writes a column twice weekly for Scripps Howard News Service. Reprinted in the *Tallahassee Democrat* (28 December 1988).

---

environment that has more supervision than they would have under probation or parole but less than they experienced in prison, they may be able to make the adjustment to freedom gradually enough to succeed upon final release. In these cases, for a specified period before their release, inmates would be transferred to prerelease facilities to finish their terms.

David E. Johnson waves his parole papers. Johnson was released after serving 18 years in prison. His participation in the Concord Achievement Rehabilitation Volunteer Experience was cited as a major reason for his early release. (AP/Wide World Photos)

Those facilities ideally would provide the full range of services needed to prepare inmates for release, including meaningful work opportunities.

Preparation of inmates for release is not sufficient to assure that they will make adequate adjustments when they leave prison. Their families also need to be prepared for the adjustments that they make upon the return of the inmate to the family. Counseling for families should be provided.

Despite the need for preparing inmates and their families for release, the brutal fact is that many prison systems, already facing severe overcrowding, are releasing inmates early to provide room for others ready for incarceration. Little if any efforts are made to prepare these inmates for release. In Florida in 1988, inmate Charlie Street was released under the early release plan. Street had served 55 percent of his 15-year sentence for attempted murder. Street was later accused of murdering two policemen, leading to severe criticism of Florida's early release plan. The plan remains, however, for Florida, like most other states, cannot build prisons fast enough to contain all those sentenced to prison terms.[7]

PROBATION AND PAROLE: AN OVERVIEW

Probation and parole are the most frequently used alternatives to prison and probably the most controversial. Probation is a sentence that does not involve confinement but may involve conditions imposed by the court, usually under the supervision of a **probation officer.**

The term *probation* is also used to refer to the status of a person placed on probation, to refer to the subsystem of the criminal justice system that handles this disposition of offenders, and to designate a process that refers to the activities of the probation system: preparing reports, supervising probationers, and providing or obtaining services for probationers.

Parole refers to the release of persons from correctional facilities after they have served part of their sentences. It is distinguished from unconditional release, which occurs when the full sentence has been served (or the full sentence minus time reduced because of **good-time credits**). Parolees are placed under supervision and conditions are imposed upon their behavior.

Probation and parole permit a convicted person to live in the community under supervision. Probation and parole are based on the philosophy that the rehabilitation of some individuals might be hindered by imprisonment (or further imprisonment) and will be aided by supervised freedom. The processes differ in that parole is granted after a portion of the prison term is served, whereas probation is granted in lieu of incarceration. Probation is granted by the judge. Parole is usually granted by a **parole board** appointed or elected specifically for that purpose.

In recent years probation and parole have come under severe attack, and despite the extensive use of these procedures, many attempts have been made to reduce the number of people who are permitted to participate. But because of overcrowded prisons and jails, the programs have not been cut back as severely as some had hoped. Problems arise; security of the community and cost are the two biggest. Despite these problems, probation and parole are important elements of the criminal justice system. In 1986, three out of every four offenders were living in the community; of those, a large majority, 64.6 percent, were on probation. Between 1983 and 1986, probation and parole populations increased at a higher rate than prison and jail populations.[8]

PROBATION: AN ALTERNATIVE TO INCARCERATION

Scholars do not agree on the origins of probation, but its use is often traced to English common law. The earliest use of a system that resembled probation was the concept of *benefit of clergy*. The church maintained that only it had jurisdiction over members of the clergy. If the clergy committed crimes, they were not to be subjected to the criminal courts but were to be handled by the church courts.

Henry II objected to this system and insisted that clerics suspected of crimes should be tried in secular courts. The compromise worked out provided that clergy accused of crimes would be tried in secular courts but with benefit of clergy. That meant that their bishops could claim dispensation for them. The charge would be read, but the state would not present evidence against the accused cleric. The accused would be allowed to give his view of the accusation and bring witnesses. With the only evidence coming from witnesses chosen by the accused, it is understandable that most cases resulted in acquittals.

Benefit of clergy was later extended to all church personnel as protection against capital punishment and eventually to all people who could read. The ability to read signified the person's association with the church. To test the clerical character, the accused was given a psalm, usually the fifty-first, to read. Those who demonstrated an ability to read were released from secular courts and turned over to the ecclesiastical courts. The device was used to mitigate the harsh sentences of the criminal law. Because of severe abuse, it fell into disfavor. Parliament later declared that certain acts would be felonies "without benefit of clergy" and finally abandoned the use of the device.

In the United States, probation is traced to John Augustus, a prosperous shoemaker in Boston. He asked that offenders be given their freedom within the community under his supervision. Massachusetts responded with a statute in 1878. By 1900, 6 states had probation statutes; by 1915, 33 states had statutes providing for adult probation; and by 1957, all states had probation statutes. In 1925, a statute authorizing probation in federal courts was passed.[9]

Types of Probation

We have already noted that probation is the most frequently used sentence, but it is important to look more closely at the types of probation.

Felony Probation   Although probation is often considered most appropriate for offenders convicted of minor offenses, it is important to realize that probation is also used for *serious* offenders, a process referred to as *felony probation*. Over one-third of probationers in the United States have been convicted of felonies. The number of **recidivists,** or repeat offenders, is high.

In 1985 the Rand Corporation published the results of its study of 16,000 felons on probation. Over a 40-month period, the research team tracked 1,671 felons; a total of 2,608 criminal charges were filed against these felons. Of the felony probationers, 65 percent were arrested, 51 percent were convicted, and 34 percent were returned to jail or prison. As Figure 16.2 indicates, most of the offenses committed by the probationers were serious.

Joan Petersilia, who directed the Rand study, warned that this information should not be used to abolish probation. Rather, it should be used to assess the problems we have created by rapidly increasing the use of probation without adequate increases in funds and staff. "No single human can adequately evaluate, report on, and supervise 300 criminals at a given time."[10]

The Rand Corporation study concluded that probation is not working as it is currently being used. But the researchers also emphasized that sending these felons to already overcrowded prisons will not solve the problem, either. They suggested alternatives.

> The answer may be intensive surveillance programs that include intense monitoring and supervision, real constraints on movement and action, requirement of employment, mechanisms to immediately punish infractions, and added requirements of community service, education, counseling, and therapy.[11]

House Arrest   One variation on probation is **house arrest**. Offenders are placed under severe restrictions. They may live at home but they may leave only under specified conditions. The process is explained in the following excerpt, from *United States v. Murphy*. This case involved a defendant who had been convicted of mail fraud and obstruction of justice. She faced a maximum penalty of 50 years in prison and a $56,000 fine.

According to the judge, Murphy was not dangerous; so incapacitation was not necessary. Rehabilitation could best occur outside prison. In her case specific deterrence could be accomplished without incarceration. The judge quickly dismissed general deterrence as a reason for incarceration, indicating his belief that we do not know much about that type of deterrence. The maximum fine could not be paid by Murphy "and would accomplish nothing except to make it impossible for the defendant to live and rehabilitate herself." The maximum prison terms were much too long for this young defendant, who had no prior convictions. "The conditions of imprisonment, even in the best prisons for women, are reprehensible."

The judge assessed a fine of $5,000 and imposed three prison sentences of 5 years each to be served concurrently. The imposition of those sentences was suspended, and the defendant was placed on house arrest for 2 years. The judge explained the procedures.[12]

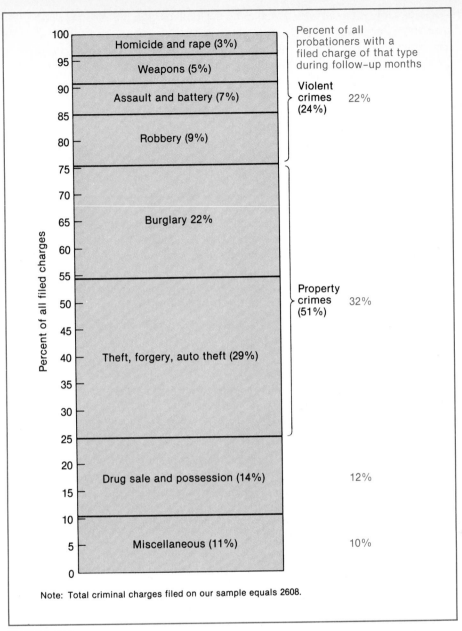

FIGURE 16.2
Types of Charges Filed on Felony Probationers During Their Probation Periods.
Source: Joan Petersilia et al., *Granting Felons Probation: Public Risks and Alternatives* (Santa Monica, Calif.: Rand Corporation, 1985), p. 24.

United States v. *Murphy*

The defendant will be required to remain in her apartment, or other place of abode. She may not change that place without the consent of Probation. She may leave only as permitted by Probation for medical reasons, employment and religious services and essential shopping for food and the life. She may go directly to and from her job and may seek a new job only as permitted by Probation. She is at all times subject to strict supervision, to surprise visits by Probation and strict control. Obviously there is serious danger of depression and worse and Probation will arrange for suitable psychiatric and other appropriate services for defendant . . .

Probation is directed to propose a set of standards for house arrest. These regulations will be used in this and future cases.

Should the defendant get into any further trouble, or should she not comply strictly with Probation's orders, she will be ordered to serve out her prison terms. I remind her that they are now suspended, not cancelled.

In some jurisdictions house arrest is accompanied by electronic monitors. These monitors are attached to the person of the offender, usually to the ankle or the wrist. The devices can be monitored by a probation officer, who will then know if and when the person leaves home during curfew hours. Some research is available on the use of electronically monitored home confinement. One study, funded by the National Institute of Justice, concluded that

The equipment operated successfully.
Monitored home confinement appeared to be acceptable to the local criminal justice community.
The concept did not appear to pose legal problems when used as an alternative to detention.
As compared to detention, monitoring resulted in "substantial savings" to the criminal justice system.[13]

Although electronic monitoring of probationers is relatively new, in the past few years the scholarly literature in the field has increased significantly. Social scientists such as Joseph B. Vaughn emphasize that more time and experience are required for thorough evaluation of the benefits of this approach. He particularly warns against concluding that electronic monitoring will alleviate prison overcrowding.

Although the technology may be a useful tool in the repertoire of the criminal justice system, it is not the sole remedy for the overcrowding problem and cannot serve as a substitute for sound correctional policy making.[14]

After looking at the use of electronic control in Florida, Florida State University criminology professors Thomas G. Blomberg and Gordon P. Waldo, along with researcher Lisa C. Burcroff, suggested that in the future electronic surveillance may be extended to other areas of the criminal justice system and to society as a whole. They conclude that

electronic surveillance may soon become the new strategy of social control without empirical justification for this strategy having been established or some of the potential negative consequences identified.[15]

It is also argued that electronic monitoring is being utilized without sufficient inquiry into the legal implications of this type of surveillance.[16]

Many people raised objections when John Zacarro, Jr., was placed on house arrest after conviction for selling drugs. (AP/Wide World)

One final argument against home arrest (with or without electronic monitoring) is that the sentence is too lenient and may be used to favor socially and politically influential offenders such as John Zaccaro, Jr., son of John Zaccaro and Geraldine Ferraro, the first woman to run for the vice presidency of the United States. Ferraro argued that her son, who was convicted of possessing a small amount of marijuana, was harshly sentenced because of the publicity surrounding her unsuccessful attempt at the second highest office in the country. House arrest, with or without electronic monitoring, is often accompanied by intensive probation supervision.

Shock Probation and Periodic Sentencing   Probation may be combined with house arrest, fines, restitution, or even a term of incarceration. Some statutes permit sending offenders to prison for a short period of time and then placing them on probation. It is assumed that this procedure will shock the offender into appropriate behavior. This process is sometimes called *shock probation*, although that term is technically incorrect since probation is an *alternative* to incarceration. That terminology, however, was used in the Ohio statute passed in July 1965. The Ohio program involves a judge-imposed sentence of a brief period of incarceration, followed by probation.[17]

The purpose of shock probation is to expose offenders to the shock of prison before placing them on probation and to release them before they are negatively influenced by the prison experience. The chief of the Adult Parole Authority in Ohio has summarized the purpose of shock probation as

1. A way for the courts to impress offenders with the seriousness of their action without a long prison sentence.

Electronic monitoring devices, in addition to periodic checks with probation officers, are often used for tracking offenders permitted to remain in the community. (Mary Kate Denny/PhotoEdit)

2. A way for the courts to release offenders found by the institution to be more amenable to community-based treatment than was realized by the courts at the time of sentence.
3. A way for the courts to arrive at a just compromise between punishment and leniency in appropriate cases.
4. A way for the courts to provide community-based treatment for rehabilitable offenders while still observing their responsibilities for imposing deterrent sentences where public policy demands it.
5. A way to afford the briefly incarcerated offender protection against socialization into the inmate culture.[18]

Since 1965 a few other states have adopted shock probation.

Probation may also be combined with a jail term in what is called *periodic sentencing*. The offender may be confined to jail during the night but be permitted to go to work or to school during the day. The jail term might be served on weekends only, with the offender free to move about in the community during the week although under some terms of probation. The weekend alternative has been used frequently for offenders who have been convicted of driving while intoxicated, particularly in jurisdictions in which jails are crowded and the offender has a steady job.

Administration of Probation

Figure 16.3 diagrams the services usually located in a probation department and indicates the organization that a department might use. In this diagram, the administration of probation is a court function, meaning that it is located in the judicial branch of government. In some jurisdictions, various courts may have probation departments, resulting in an overlap of services and other administrative problems. Others have a statewide probation system with branches at the city and county levels.

Probation departments also may be found in the executive branch, reporting to the governor in the case of statewide systems. Probation departments differ greatly in size and complexity and in the extent and quality of services that they provide for clients. Thus, it is not possible to specify a type of probation department, although Figure 16.3 shows one example.

As Figure 16.3 indicates, one division of the probation department includes the services that probation departments provide for courts. The **presentence investigation** usually is prepared by the probation department through interviewing clients and related parties, investigating and compiling materials relevant to each case, and developing recommendations for the sentencing body. The department also provides the court with services for processing and reporting probation cases. This section would keep records of all persons on probation, the status of their probation, whether probation has been revoked, and other pertinent data.

Probation departments also provide services for clients on probation. Those services might assess the client's needs and provide actual services for clients on probation. Counseling, referral to other community sources, and supervision are the most common services provided by probation

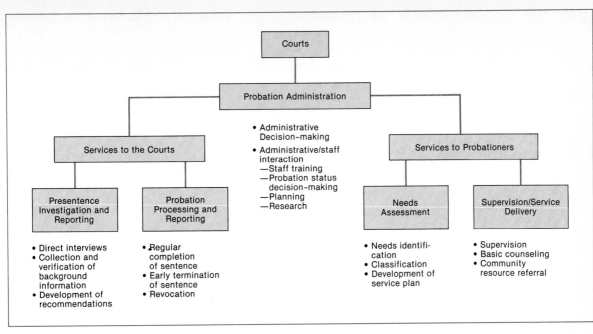

FIGURE 16.3
Service Structure of a County Probation System. *Source:* Donald J. Thalheimer, *Cost Analysis of Correctional Standards: Community Supervision, Probation, Restitution, Community Service* (Washington, D.C.: U.S. Government Printing Office, 1978), vol. 1, p. 6.

departments to their clients. Counseling alcoholics and the families of alcoholics is a frequent service offered by probation departments.[19]

Probation departments are usually headed by a chief probation officer, who has the typical functions of a chief executive officer of an organization. The major responsibility for hiring, training, and firing probation officers and for managing all sections of the probation department will be in the hands of this officer. The chief probation officer will also have public relations functions, working with community leaders, attorneys, police officers, and court personnel.

If the probation department is large enough, it will probably have an assistant chief probation officer, who will report to the chief probation officer and who may be assigned such responsibilities as coordinating volunteer efforts and administering the department. A supervisor might be in charge of coordinating the efforts of those who prepare the presentence investigations, assign cases, and handle other administrative functions.

Probation officers work directly with clients on probation. These officers should have training in the various aspects of probation work, including skills in interpersonal relationships. They provide counseling for probationers and perform the function of surveillance to make sure that their clients are not violating probation conditions.

Probation officers usually do the investigative work in preparing the presentence investigation and may be required to make a sentence recommendation to the judge before sentencing. This function of being involved, at least to some extent, in the sentencing decision and then in supervising the probationer may present problems. Probationers may resent the position the probation officer has in relationship to the judge. Furthermore, it is questionable whether probation officers may be effective counselors while responsible for surveillance as well.

Average beginning salaries for probation officers are not high enough to attract many well-qualified people, particularly if the goal is to attract people who have baccalaureate degrees, as the National Advisory Commission recommended in its report. Efforts must be made to raise salaries and to improve working conditions for probation officers.

Conditions of Probation

The purpose of probation is to assist offenders in making social adjustments and reintegrating into society as law-abiding citizens. Therefore, the policy has been to impose restrictions on the freedom of the offender. Restrictions differ from jurisdiction to jurisdiction, but some are common to all regions.

Figure 16.4 is an example of a probation order. Probationers are required to report to an officer periodically at specified times and places; the officer also may visit the client. Probationers may change residence only with the permission of the supervising officer. They must work (or attend school or some other approved activity); if those plans are changed, the changes must be reported. In some cases they will not be allowed to make changes without prior permission of the supervising officer or court.

Probationers are usually required to submit periodic reports of their activities and progress. They may be restricted in the use of alcoholic beverages and appearance in bars or other questionable places. They are not permitted to use drugs. They are not permitted to own, possess, use, sell, or have under their control deadly weapons or firearms. Their associations are restricted.

In some jurisdictions, probationers will not be permitted to drive an automobile; in others, driving is permitted only with prior permission of the supervising officer. Normally they will not be permitted to leave the county or state without permission. Such permission will probably be granted infrequently and only for extraordinary reasons. Probationers, of course, are required to refrain from violating laws and to cooperate with their probation officers. In some cases curfews or restrictions on where they may live may be imposed. Their civil rights also will be affected. They are not usually permitted to marry, engage in business, or sign contracts without permission.

The American Bar Association has suggested the following restrictions on probation conditions. Generally, every probationer should be required to lead a law-abiding life, but no other conditions should be required by statute. Additional probation conditions should be made by the sentencing court on an individual basis, according to individual needs. It is appropriate to develop standards for such conditions "as long as such conditions are not routinely imposed." The conditions imposed in each case should be for assisting the probationer to lead a law-abiding life.

In the District Court of _____County

STATE OF _____

CASE NUMBER _____

DEFENDANT _____

OFFENSE _____

DATE _____

RULES AND CONDITIONS OF PROBATION:

1. I will until my final release, make a report in writing and in person as directed by the Supervising Authority.

2. I will not use or be in possession of intoxicants or illicit drugs of any kind, or visit places where illicit drugs are unlawfully sold, dispensed or used. I understand that I am not allowed to enter or loiter around beer taverns or clubs.

3. I will not leave the State of _____without written permission of the Supervising Authority. I will not leave _____County without permission of the Supervising Authority.

4. I will not communicate with persons on Parole or inmates of penal institutions, nor will I associate with persons having a criminal record or involved in criminal activity. I understand that it is my responsibility to know whether an associate has a criminal record.

5. I will allow the Supervising Authority to visit me at my home, place of employment or elsewhere. I will notify the Supervising Authority prior to changing residence or employment.

6. I will carry out all instructions the Supervising Authority may give me, including but not limited to, urinalysis, curfew, and treatment.

7. I understand it will be a violation of my Probation to own, carry or possess firearms or ammunition of any type or to be in a vehicle where firearms are located.

8. I will work regularly at a lawful occupation and support my legal dependents without public assistance as long as I am physically able to do so.

9. I will refrain from violating City, State or Federal laws and I will report within 48 hours if I am arrested or questioned by any law enforcement agency.

10. I hereby agree to pay the sum of $10.00 per month for the term of my probation to the Department of Corrections to defray the costs of my supervision.

11. SPECIAL CONDITIONS

( ) TREATMENT/URINALYSIS

( ) DRUG/ALCOHOL COUNSELING

( ) RESTITUTION-EXHIBIT A ATTACHED

( ) PSYCHIATRIC COUNSELING

( ) COMMUNITY SERVICE ___ HOURS

( ) MAIL-IN PENDING INTERSTATE

( ) STAY AWAY _____

( ) WAIVE RULE(S) _____

( ) MEDIATED AGREEMENT

( ) OTHER _____

I understand and agree that the continuance of my probation depends entirely on my conduct. I understand that should I violate the terms and conditions of my probation, the Court may revoke my sentence and I may be required to serve imprisonment of the sentence imposed by the Court.

I hereby certify that I have carefully read or have been read and explained the above Rules and Conditions and fully understand what my obligations are while under supervision of the Department of Corrections. I further acknowledge receipt of a copy of these Rules and Conditions which I agree to study from time to time so that I will be fully informed at all times regarding my obligations while under supervision.

_____
ATTORNEY FOR DEFENDANT

_____
DEFENDANT–PROBATIONER

Department of Corrections, Probation and Parole

FIGURE 16.4
Order for Probation Conditions

They should be reasonably related to his rehabilitation and not unduly restrictive of his liberty or incompatible with his freedom of religion. They should not be so vague or ambiguous as to give no real guidance.[20]

Legal Limits on Probation Conditions   Just as courts have been reluctant to interfere with the daily administration of prisons, they traditionally also have taken a hands-off policy toward the imposition of probation conditions. In recent years, however, courts have rejected some restrictions as constituting improper restrictions on probationers' rights.

Earlier cases often focused on sterilization as a condition of probation. In *People v. Blankenship*, the court upheld the requirement that a defendant undergo a vasectomy as a prerequisite to probation. The defendant, a 23-year-old man, pleaded guilty to the rape of a 13-year-old. Both had syphilis, although there was no evidence that he communicated the disease to her. The court recognized that syphilis could be cured, but "it was not so much concerned with curing the disease with which appellant was afflicted as it was with preventing appellant from transmitting the disease to his possible posterity."[21]

In *People v. Dominguez* the trial court imposed on a 20-year-old mother of two illegitimate children, upon her conviction for armed robbery, a condition of probation that she not again become pregnant out of wedlock. She did, and the court revoked the probation. On appeal the case was reversed. The appellate court noted that, although the trial court has wide discretion in setting the terms of probation, that discretion "must be impartial, guided by 'fixed legal principles, to be exercised in conformity with the spirit of the law.'" When the condition of probation has no relationship to the crime for which the probationer was convicted or to future criminality, and which is not in itself criminal, it is invalid. "Contraceptive failure is not an indicium of criminality."[22]

In *Inman v. State* an appeals court ruled that requiring a young man to cut his hair for 2 years as a condition of probation was unconstitutional.

> We . . . take judicial notice that the rotunda of the State Judicial Building contains busts of three of our most eminent . . . Justices, featuring the magnificent shoulder-length locks of our beloved Chief Justice."[23]

A woman convicted of child abuse was ordered to refrain from having children during her 5-year probationary period. The appellate court struck that order, ruling that it was an unconstitutional violation of the right to privacy and an abuse of judicial discretion.[24]

Earlier discussions indicated that some states have enacted statutes prohibiting criminals from making money on speaking or writing about their criminal activities. This issue was recently litigated with regard to a probation condition. In February, 1988, the Ninth Circuit Court of Appeals upheld two restrictions of the appellant's probation. This excerpt from *United States v. Terrigno* explains the reasons the court found these restrictions proper. The appellant was convicted of embezzling public funds and converting them to her personal use.[25]

United States v. Terrigno

Terrigno was the Executive Director of Crossroads Counseling, a federally funded organization that counseled area residents seeking employment and provided emergency assistance (e.g. rent payments and grocery store gift certificates) for the needy. . . .

A sentencing judge has broad discretion in setting probation conditions. Exercise of this discretion is reviewed carefully where probation conditions restrict fundamental rights, but such restriction is permissible. . . .

Terrigno contends that the probation condition violates her first amendment rights. . . .

In this case, the trial court has not restricted Terrigno's right to speak, it has merely forbidden her to receive money for speaking about her crime during the five-year term of her probation. The trial court simply wanted to assure that Terrigno would not profit from her crime by exploiting her story in the media. The court's concern with this possibility is reasonable in that there had already been considerable media interest in the trial because of Terrigno's prominence as a lesbian and as the first mayor of West Hollywood.

We think this probation condition has a reasonable nexus with the twin goals of probation, rehabilitation and protection of the public. We have indicated before that the standard for determining the reasonable relationship between probation conditions and the purposes of probation is necessarily very flexible precisely because of "our uncertainty about how rehabilitation is accomplished." We certainly cannot say it is unreasonable to think that the rehabilitation of a person convicted of embezzlement and conversion of public funds will be more effective if she is reminded in a very practical sense that "crime does not pay."

[The court then gave reasons for supporting the second condition of probation: that the appellant not obtain any employment in a position in which she would be responsible for administering public funds.]

In 1987 the U.S. Supreme Court ruled that probation officers may search probationer's homes without first securing a search warrant if they have the approval of the probation supervisor and if there is reasonable grounds to believe that the probationer is in possession of contraband. In *Griffin v. Wisconsin*, the probation officer received a tip that his probationer had a gun in his home, in violation of one of the conditions of probation in Wisconsin: probationers may not possess firearms without receiving advance approval from a probation officer.[26]

Probation Supervision

One of the primary functions of the probation officer is to supervise probationers. The type and degree of supervision will vary. In some probation departments it is the probation officer's job to counsel probationers. In other departments probation officers are expected only to supervise the activities of their probationers, and that supervision may be extremely limited. Which of these models will be chosen may depend on the availability of resources, the caseload of probation officers, their professional training, the needs of probationers, and many other factors. Essentially the officer's function is to assist the probationer in making important transitions—from law-abiding citizen to convicted offender, from free citizen to one under supervision, and finally, back to free citizen.

Some probation officers may prefer to have a close interpersonal relationship with the clients they are assisting. The literature contains numerous articles discussing ways in which probation officers may improve their supervisory relationships with their clients. Many articles also discuss the expectation that probation officers will go beyond supervision and actually serve as treatment agents for their clients. Treatment of probationers can be multidimensional. Many probationers need to learn the social skills involved in successful interpersonal relationships. Most offenders have long histories of personal failures, and the probation officer will be a crucial person in helping them to build up their confidence in themselves and to acquire the social skills and habits necessary for successful interpersonal relationships.

When probation officers go beyond supervision of their clients and begin a treatment process, however, some problems may occur. Many officers lack sufficient training in treatment techniques. Even if the probation officer is trained and skilled in treatment techniques and is licensed for such work, the very nature of the position precludes some kinds of treatment. Because of the legal nature of probation work, the probation officer can never promise the confidentiality that an effective treatment relationship needs. In reality, the probation officer has a conflict of interest. The officer represents not only the interests of the state in violations of the probation agreement or of the law but also the interests of the client in treatment and supervision.

Intensive Probation Supervision   In the past, researchers debated the effect of caseload size on the success or failure of probationers. That issue still is not settled, and many factors are important in determining what type of caseload is most efficient. Today the focus of probation has shifted in many jurisdictions. Rehabilitation is no longer the primary purpose of probation. Probation is to divert from prison persons who might not need that intensive security and supervision, and in that diversion process, to reduce the populations that are swelling the prisons.

In Texas, by enacting a statute providing for **intensive probation supervision (IPS),** the legislature specified that the primary purpose of IPS is diversion.[27] This focus on diversion rather than rehabilitation makes it easier to test whether the program is working. Researchers tentatively concluded that IPS accomplished its goal of diversion. Research also indicated that IPS improves the public image about probation since it involves greater supervision of offenders and results in lower recidivism rates. It is more costly than traditional probation, but it is still considerably less costly than imprisonment.[28]

The Georgia IPS system illustrates the supervision that is typical of this new approach. IPS is conducted by teams, consisting of a probation officer and a surveillance officer. Their total caseload is 25 probationers, each of whom is seen at least five times a week; some may be seen twice in one evening. Conditions of probation are strict. In addition to the requirement of a job, paying fines, and restitution, probationers have to fulfill a community service requirement and be home by 7 P.M. every night. Only persons who would otherwise be subject to incarceration are eligible for IPS; thus, it can be viewed as a diversionary measure.[29]

Georgia's IPS program has been declared successful, but scholars such as Joan Petersilia of the Rand Corporation warn against assuming that this program and its success rate can be replicated in other jurisdictions. According to Petersilia, Georgia has two fairly unique characteristics that may account for the success of its IPS program and that might make replication difficult:

1. A high prison commitment rate, which has created an eligible pool of prison-bound offenders convicted of less serious crimes;
2. An extremely supportive and professional local context.[30]

A more optimistic view comes from John P. Conrad, who has written extensively in the criminal justice field. After discussing the long history of disappointments that such measures as

> psychiatric treatment, group therapy, group counseling, shock probation, . . . probation subsidy, and statistical classification have all fallen short of their promised benefits, some of them abysmally so

Conrad expresses his belief that IPS might be "the great exception." Conrad continues:

> The promise is the drastic reduction of incarceration; the strength lies in realism about the punitive nature of the experience of surveillance. We are no longer deceiving ourselves and attempting to deceive the probationers about the therapeutic benefits of the relationship between the officer and the offender. The officer's hot breath may be on the offender's neck; if the offender doesn't like it, he knows what the consequences will be if he strays too far from surveillance.[31]

PAROLE: ADMINISTRATIVE RELEASE FROM PRISON

Parole is an administrative decision to release an offender after he or she has served some time in a correctional facility but prior to the end of the court's sentence. It may be distinguished from other methods of release from prison. Some inmates are released before serving their full sentences because they have accumulated good-time credits given for good behavior during incarceration. The amount of prison time that can be reduced for good-time credits is determined by prison policies or by legislation. Some offenders are not released from prison until they serve the full term imposed at sentencing; at the end of that term, they must be released. Offenders may also be released by means of a **pardon** granted by the governor of the state or the president of the United States.

Charles H. Street (center, grimacing), who was released early from a Florida prison because of overcrowding, is accused of, among other crimes, killing two Florida police officers in late 1988. (AP/Wide World Photos)

Authorities do not agree on the origins of parole, but several historical developments compete in the discussions. Some have claimed that the concept of conditioned liberty was first introduced in France about 1830. It was an intermediary step of freedom with supervision between prison confinement and complete freedom in the community. Others trace the origins of parole to the work of Captain Alexander Maconochie, who began the reformatory movement in 1840.

Among other reforms, Maconochie developed a system of marks, a term used to refer to the wages that he thought should be paid to inmates who worked. Those who worked and behaved could have their sentences reduced or could use their earned marks for buying rations. Sir Walter Crofton, a disciple of Maconochie, took the mark system to the Irish prison system, where he, too, had a policy of permitting prisoners gradual release from supervision and a reduction of sentence if they behaved properly and worked hard. Crofton added supervision to the release system.

In 1870 Crofton was invited to speak before the American Prison Association. At that meeting a "Declaration of Principles" was adopted, including among other reforms the seeds for adoption of a parole system. The actual beginning of parole in this country is traced to the Elmira Reformatory in New York, opened in 1876. All states and the federal government adopted some type of parole; the process gradually became the most frequently used method of release until the late 1970s, when the movement toward determinate sentencing began.

Modern Developments in Parole: The California Experience

The development of parole in California has been studied in detail; it offers an example of the history of this important method of release from prison. In California, parole originally developed as a means to achieve justice in the amount of time prisoners would serve in prison.

> Parole was introduced in California and used for over a decade, primarily to relieve governors of part of the burden of exercising clemency to reduce the excessive sentences of selected state prisoners.

In later years, parole was used to relieve overcrowding in prisons and in that context, came to be viewed as a rehabilitative measure.[32]

California's parole system underwent changes in 1977 when the Uniform Determinate Sentencing Bill became law in that state. The statute abolished the parole release function of the parole board but retained parole supervision. Upon release from prison, most offenders are now placed on parole supervision for 3 years (5 for those convicted of capital crimes), although there are provisions for release from parole supervision after 1 year. The statute established the Community Release Board to administer the provisions of the new statute. This board has several functions, including the power to revoke the parole supervision period when offenders violate parole conditions. The board also reviews the procedures and administration of good-time credits and the revocation of those credits. California thus retains some aspects of parole; the significant change is that there is no longer a parole board that can reduce the prison sentence of offenders by granting parole release before the expiration of the sentence.[33]

Parole: A Policy of the Past?

Rehabilitation, justice, prison overcrowding—these are the three main reasons for parole in the United States, although the reasons have been emphasized in different places at different times. Some systems developed for the primary purpose of relieving prison overcrowding; some were for the purpose of rehabilitation. Ironically, the movement to abolish parole, a movement that paralleled the movement toward determinate sentencing in the late 1970s and 1980s, was propelled by the cry for justice, the disillusionment with rehabilitation, and the argument that the lack of justice in the parole decision process actually hindered rehabilitation. Parole was called the "neverknowing system" by many inmates, who argued that it was granted for arbitrary and capricious reasons.

Parole has come under severe attack in the United States. In 1971 the American Friends Service Committee, after its report on the criminal justice system, called for the abolition of parole.[34] The abolition movement, however, did not gain momentum until 1977 when Massachusetts senator Edward Kennedy, one of the writers and sponsors of the early bill to revise the federal criminal code; the attorney general of the United States; and the director of the federal prison system all argued for the abolition of parole at hearings on the proposed revision of the federal code.[35]

Norval Morris, professor of law and former dean of the University of Chicago School of Law, in his widely read and provocative book, *The Future of Imprisonment*, called for considerable reduction in the power of the parole board, although not for its abolition. According to Morris, parole "was a fine idea having only the defect that it did not work."[36]

Senator Kennedy argued that sentencing disparity has been compounded by parole. In addition to the possible abuse of discretion at parole decisions, Kennedy suggested that the very existence of a parole system may encourage judges in their lengthy sentences. Judges may impose harsh sentences to make the community think they are being tough with offenders, with the expectation that the parole board will release the individuals early. But because judges are not required to state reasons for their sentences, it is possible that parole boards might inadvertently act contrary to the expectations of the judge.

Even when the parole board members know what the judge expects, they are not required to follow those expectations. Kennedy concluded that, with determinate sentencing, parole release would not be needed.

> Under this system of judicially fixed sentences, parole release would be abolished and whether or not a prisoner has been "rehabilitated" or has completed a certain prison curriculum would no longer have any bearing on his prison release date.[37]

After a decade of attempts, the federal criminal code was revised when President Reagan signed the Comprehensive Crime Control Act of 1984. That act abolishes early release by parole in the federal system, and over a 5-year period, phases out the U.S. Parole Commission. Under the new statute, inmates in the federal system may receive only a maximum of 15 percent good-time credit on their sentences. Under the former statute, they were eligible for parole after serving only half of their sentences.

Organization of Parole Systems

The organization of parole is complex. One reason for this complexity is the variety of sentencing structures under which parole systems must operate. Sentencing structure is closely related to the parole system. In jurisdictions where sentences are long with little time off for good behavior, parole may involve a long period of supervision. In jurisdictions where sentences are short, parole may be relatively unimportant as a form of release, and supervision will be for shorter periods.

Models of Parole Systems Despite the wide variety of parole programs, three models of organization may be identified: the institutional, the independent, and the consolidated model. Under the *institutional model*, found mainly in the juvenile field, the decision to release is made by the correctional staff. The assumption is that those who work closely with the offender are in the best position to make a decision concerning his or her release. Arguments against this organization model are that institutions may make decisions in their best interests, not the best interests of the offender or the community. Decisions may be based on institutional overcrowding. Staff members may be less objective in the decisions because they are closely involved with the offender. Abuse of discretion may be a greater possibility under this model than in the model of independent authority.

Because of those two problems, parole boards for adult correctional facilities have usually followed the *independent authority model*, establishing the parole board as an agency independent of the institution from which individuals are paroled. This model also has been severely criticized. The parole board is often composed of people who know little or nothing about corrections. The board is removed from the institution and often does not understand what is taking place there. Decisions may be made for inappropriate reasons, and as a result, parole boards may release those who should not be paroled and retain those who should be.

In the past decade a new model has emerged, a *consolidated model* of organization for parole boards, and there is a trend toward adopting it. This trend accompanies a move toward consolidating correctional facilities into one common administration, usually a department of corrections. Under the consolidated model the parole-granting board is within the administration of the Department of Corrections but possesses independent powers.

It is important for parole board members to have an understanding of the total correctional programs. This understanding is more likely to occur under the consolidated model than under the other two models. The board, however, also should possess independence so that it can act as a check on the rest of the system.

Internal Organization and Administration   With the exception of the institutional model, most parole systems are located in the executive branch of government and usually administered at the state level. Most systems have one parole board, whose members are appointed by the executive branch. In most states that board has final authority to decide who is granted a parole. In other states the board makes recommendations to someone else who has the final decision-making authority. That person might be the governor of the state.

Some parole board members serve full-time; others serve part-time. They may or may not have specific qualifications for the position. As political appointees, they may be appointed for reasons unrelated to expertise in the kind of decision making that is the function of the board. The board may have the authority to revoke parole as well as to grant it.

The parole system usually will provide some parole services at the institutions in which inmates are incarcerated. Often a person will have the responsibility of interviewing all those eligible for parole and then making written recommendations to the parole board. The parole system also will have a division responsible for parole services, which includes parole supervision. Parole services may be delegated to smaller divisions throughout the state.

Parole officers should have the same kind of qualifications as probation officers. Increasingly, professional organizations and commissions are recommending that parole and probation officers hold at least a bachelor's degree, and some recommend that additional education should be required. In-service training is also very important, should be continued throughout the officer's period of work, and should be evaluated periodically. "Aspiring probation and parole professionals should obtain a broad, liberal arts education, augmented with productive employment in the system."[38]

The Parole Process

The parole process is very important, and adequate preparation should be made for the parole hearing. The ability of the inmate to convey an improved self-image and to demonstrate an ability to work with others and stick with a job may influence the decision of the board. Inmates who have maintained strong ties with their families may have an edge in the decision-making process. Inmates who have had successful experiences on work release, education release, or furlough may have an advantage. A good behavior record in the institution may be viewed favorably.

Inmates should be told what to expect regarding timing of the decision and what kinds of questions they might anticipate. Demeanor and behavior are important; some inmates are even put through mock decision-making situations to prepare them for the parole board hearing. It also is important to prepare the inmate for the decision by the parole board. A negative decision may have a tremendous negative effect on an inmate who has not been adequately prepared before that decision.

Eligibility for Parole   The determination of eligibility for parole varies, but there usually will be some statutory specifications such as requiring that inmates must serve a certain percentage of their sentences before they are eligible for parole. Good-time credits may reduce that period of eligibility. Many jurisdictions will require that inmates have job commitments before parole is granted; others may grant parole on the condition that the inmate must have a job by the time of parole release.

The Parole Hearing   The inmate to be considered for parole may appear before the entire board or only a committee of the board. Larger boards may split into smaller groups to process paroles faster. Usually the parole hearing will be held at the institution where the inmate is incarcerated, although if only a few are eligible, those inmates might be transported by the state to a central location for the hearing.

Many parole systems will allow the inmate to participate in the hearings, although that participation might be very short. Participation will give inmates a greater sense of fairness in that they will have opportunities to express to the board members their perceptions of their chances for success on parole.

Spotlight 16.4 lists the major factors that should be considered in a parole decision. Those factors require information from the past, present, and future. They include statements made by the sentencing judge concerning the reasons for sentencing as well as the inmate's plans for the future. They include disciplinary action, if any, while the inmate is incarcerated. Documentation on changes in attitude and ability also are listed. The crime for which the inmate is serving time, along with any prior experience on parole or probation, will be considered, too.

SPOTLIGHT 16.4
FACTORS TO CONSIDER AT A PAROLE HEARING

1. The commission of serious disciplinary infractions
2. The nature and pattern of previous convictions
3. The adjustment to previous probation, parole, and incarceration
4. The facts and circumstances of the offense
5. The aggravating and mitigating factors surrounding the offense
6. Participation in institutional programs that might have led to the improvement of problems diagnosed at admission or during incarceration
7. Documented changes in attitude toward self or others
8. Documentation of personal goals and strengths or motivation for law-abiding behavior
9. Parole plans
10. Inmate statements suggesting the likelihood that the inmate will commit another crime
11. Court statements about the reasons for the sentence

Source: Christopher Dietz, chairman of the New Jersey State Parole Board, "Parole: Crucial to the Criminal Justice System." *Corrections Today* 47 (June 1985): 32. Copyright 1985 by American Correctional Association. All rights reserved. Used with permission.

Discretion of the Parole Board   Historically, parole boards have had almost total discretionary power in determining parole. Parole was viewed as a privilege, not a right. Since parole was not a right, no reasons had to be given for denial. Elements of due process were not required at the time when the decision was made. As stated by a federal court in 1971,

> The Board of Parole is given absolute discretion in matters of parole. The courts are without power to grant a parole or to determine judicially eligibility for parole. . . . Furthermore, it is not the function of the courts to review the discretion of the Board in the denial of the application for parole or to review the credibility of report and information received by the Board in making its determination.[39]

The reasoning of the federal court in ruling that due process was not required at the determination of parole is that parole granting is not an adversary proceeding. Parole granting is a very complicated decision, and the board of parole must be able to use evidence that would not be admissible in an adversary proceeding such as a trial. The general lack of due process at the parole decision stage has resulted in bitter complaints from inmates. One described his observations of fellow inmates who went before the parole board. They would get their hopes up and do all of the right things such as going to church and Alcoholics Anonymous meetings and behaving properly. The parole board would encourage them during the hearing. Then they would wait for a long time, sometimes six weeks, before being informed of a decision.

If their applications for parole were denied, their feelings of despair would later turn to hatred at being rejected with no reasons given for the decisions. This inmate decided not to go for a parole hearing. He did not "wish to go through the very ugly and unpleasant cycles that my fellow inmates have. . . . You, my keepers, have my body, but my mind is somewhat my own. I feel free in the strength of my convictions."[40]

Perhaps the late Justice Hugo Black of the United States Supreme Court best summarized the view of many inmates toward the parole board:

> In the course of my reading—by no means confined to law—I have reviewed many of the world's religions. The tenets of many faiths hold the deity to be a trinity. Seemingly, the parole boards by whatever names designated in the various states have in too many instances sought to enlarge this to include themselves as members.[41]

Due Process and the Parole Hearing   According to the Fourteenth Amendment, we may not be denied life, liberty, or property without due process of law. Claims by inmates for due process at the parole decision are based on their argument that they have a liberty interest in parole. The Supreme Court has held that, although there is no constitutional right to parole, states may by statute create a protected liberty interest that could then not be denied without due process.

How do we know whether a protected liberty interest has been created and therefore due process is required? According to the Court, if the state creates a parole system and states that, if certain conditions are met by inmates, they are entitled to parole, a liberty interest has been created, for the state has created a presumption that inmates who meet certain requirements will be granted parole. But if the statute is general, giving broad discretion to the parole board, no liberty interest is created.

In *Greenholtz v. Nebraska* the Court examined the Nebraska statute, which provided for two hearings before a final parole decision. At the first hearing, an informal one, the inmate would be interviewed and all relevant information in the files would be considered. If the board decided the inmate was not ready for parole, parole was denied and the inmate was given reasons. If the board found evidence that the inmate might be ready for parole, it would notify the inmate of a formal hearing, at which time the inmate could present evidence, call witnesses, and be represented by retained counsel.

In *Greenholtz* the Court found that a liberty interest had been created by the Nebraska statute but that the procedures required by the statute met due process requirements. In the following brief excerpt from the case, the Court explains why it did not agree with the inmates that the parole board should be required, when denying parole, to specify the evidence it used in making that decision.[42]

Greenholtz v. *Nebraska*

The board communicates the reason for its denial as a guide to the inmate for his future behavior. To require the parole authority to provide a summary of the evidence would tend to convert the process into an adversary proceeding and to equate the Board's parole release determination with a guilt determination. The Nebraska statute contemplates, and experience has shown, that the parole release decision is . . . essentially an experienced prediction based on a host of variables. The Board's decision is much like a sentencing judge's choice— provided by many states—to grant or deny probation following a judgment of guilt, a choice never thought to require more than what Nebraska now provides for the parole release determination. The Nebraska procedure affords an opportunity to be heard and when parole is denied it informs the inmate in what respects he falls short of qualifying for parole; this affords the process that is due under these circumstances. The Constitution does not require more.

In 1987, while analyzing the Montana parole statute, the Court reaffirmed its holding in *Greenholtz* that although the existence of a parole system does not by itself give rise to an expectation of parole, states may create that expectation or presumption by the wording of the statute. In *Board of Pardons v. Allen*, the Court held that the Montana statute, like the Nebraska statute examined in *Greenholtz*, creates an expectation of parole provided certain conditions are met. Thus, if those conditions are met, parole must be granted.[43]

In both of these cases, the Supreme Court emphasized that the wording of the language—the use of the word *shall* rather than *may*—created the presumption that parole will be granted if certain specified conditions are met. The Court thus injected some procedural requirements into the parole-granting process in those states that use mandatory language in their parole statutes. In the words of one commentator, "These procedural protections could increase inmate confidence in the fairness of the system: a confidence many inmates give up while trying to survive in a hostile, overcrowded prison."[44]

Control of Parole Decisions   Parole boards have been bitterly criticized by inmates, and many scholars also have found some decisions to be arbitrary and capricious. Criticism of parole decisions has led to the suggestion that some restrictions should be placed on this important decision-making process.

In the 1920s sociologists developed prediction scales that might be used in many situations such as predicting success in marriage. Some of the scales were adapted for the parole decision. Charts involved such factors as age, education, and prior criminal record to predict whether most inmates with those characteristics would be successful if paroled. The application of prediction scales yielded conflicting results, although the various approaches are not easily compared.[45] The only general conclusion that might be drawn from statistical prediction studies is that it may be easier to predict nonviolent crime than violent crime.

Social scientists also have used the clinical approach to prediction, looking at the specific characteristics of a particular inmate and trying to predict whether that person would be successful on parole. This approach generally has led to overprediction of dangerousness, which means that fewer inmates who are thought to be dangerous actually are.[46]

Another method of control over parole is to require written reasons for denying parole. In the past most parole boards did not give reasons for denial, and courts did not require them to do so. Today some jurisdictions that have retained parole require that reasons be given. Although the result may only be a checklist given to the inmate, this information will at least give the inmate some information on what is required for a successful parole hearing in the future.

Parole guidelines are used as a method of control over parole decision making. The use of systemwide guidelines not only gives inmates a feeling of greater fairness in the parole process, but guidelines have had the advantage in some states of being used to reduce prison overcrowding. Critics of objective guidelines for parole decision making argue that they do not result in greater fairness and may actually increase prison overcrowding.

Civil litigation is increased, too. According to one authority, the first year that objective criteria were used in Florida, the Florida Parole Commission reported a 450 percent increase in civil litigation as inmates claimed that the criteria were not applied fairly. Other states have had similar experiences.[47]

Parole Conditions   Parole conditions are an essential element of the release process. The Supreme Court has stated:

The essence of parole is release from prison, before the completion of sentence, on the condition that the prisoner abide by certain rules during the balance of the sentence . . . the conditions of parole . . . prohibit, either absolutely or conditionally, behavior that is deemed dangerous to the restoration of the individual into normal society.[48]

Parole conditions vary from jurisdiction to jurisdiction and usually are similar to probation conditions. Many parole conditions have been challenged in court. They are valid, however, if they are legal and moral and if it is reasonably possible for the parolee to comply with them.

The advisory commission took the position that states should begin immediately to "reduce parole rules to an absolute minimum, retaining only those critical in the individual case, and to provide for effective means of enforcing the conditions established." Conditions of parole should be "as specific as possible and reasonably related to the facts of the specific parole case."[49]

Parole Supervision

When inmates are released from prison, they must report to parole supervisors or **parole officers.** They will be told the circumstances under which they are to report, how often, when and where to file reports, and what to expect regarding visits from parole officers.

Parole supervision has come under attack. The surveillance function of parole officers can be undermined by large caseloads; officers may not have time for anything more than brief contacts with their parolees. Because of this, some argue that home visits and monthly reports are costly and useless devices for control of parolee behavior and that this function would be better left to the police. Changing the conditions of parole supervision is another suggested reform. Conditions that have little or no relevance to criminal behavior could be eliminated. This change would leave parole officers free to concentrate on the service aspect of supervision: helping with employment, housing, and other adjustments in the community.[50]

In Connecticut, where parole release has been abolished and the term *parole supervision* is no longer used, inmates are released to community group homes and residences. The parole staff still carries out the supervision function. In support of continued community supervision, Connecticut reports that, since the program began in December of 1982, 200 releasees have gone into the community and only 3 have been failures.[51] Another study of Connecticut offenders, conducted before parole was abolished, indicated that only 37 percent of parolees returned to crime, whereas 63 percent of inmates who were released to the community without supervision returned to crime.[52]

A survey of criminal justice research on parole supervision yielded the conclusion that "the evidence seems to indicate that the abolition of parole supervision would result in substantial increases in arrest, conviction, and return to prison."[53] It may be that solutions to the problem of unfairness in the parole system should concentrate on release procedures and decisions and that parole supervision should continue in the community. In support of this argument is the cost factor. The cost of parole supervision is significantly less than the cost of incarceration. As budget problems continue to plague the corrections system, community supervision may be the most cost-effective method for controlling criminal behavior.

But even parole supervision is becoming progressively more costly. It has been suggested that spiraling costs might be effectively reduced by more extensive use of volunteers, with a savings of approximately $332,000 annually in salaries that did not have to be paid as a result of an average of 18,000 volunteer hours each year.[54] More intensive parole supervision has also been suggested. The U.S. Parole Commission is considering the feasibility of selecting several pilot programs throughout the country for intensive supervision. Also suggested is the extended use of house arrest.

On the whole, probation and parole are presented with a great challenge. The Comprehensive Crime Control Act clearly changes the nature of community corrections. "This could be a serious dilemma—or it could be the opportunity for probation and parole to play pivotal roles in protecting society."[55]

PROBATION AND PAROLE REVOCATION

Historically, **probation** and **parole revocation** occurred without due process hearings. In probation cases in which the offender had been sentenced to prison but the judge suspended imposition of the sentence and put the offender on probation, violation of the terms of probation would result in incarceration to serve the original sentence.

In 1967 in *Mempa v. Rhay*, the Supreme Court held that when sentencing has been deferred and the offender placed on probation, revocation of that probation and determination of a sentence of incarceration requires the presence of counsel. The Court reasoned that this situation, in which the offender is actually being sentenced, invokes the requirement that "at every stage of a criminal proceeding where substantial rights of a criminal accused may be affected" counsel is required. This case and others pertinent to probation and parole revocation are summarized in Spotlight 16.5. Revocation of probation that does not involve deciding a sentence, however, still does not always require counsel, although there are some due process requirements, which will be discussed.

Historically, parole revocation also was conducted with little concern for due process. Lack of due process was justified on the basis that parole was a privilege, not a right, or that it involved a contract. The inmate contracted to behave in exchange for freedom from incarceration. If that contract were broken, the inmate could be returned to prison. Others argued that parole was a status of continuing custody, during which the offender was subject to prison rules and regulations; revocation therefore required no greater due process than was required for any action against the inmate while incarcerated.

SPOTLIGHT 16.5
DUE PROCESS AND PAROLE AND PROBATION REVOCATION: THE SUPREME COURT RESPONDS

Mempa v. Rhay, 389 U.S. 128 (1967)

A probationer is entitled to be represented by appointed counsel at a combined revocation and sentencing hearing. This is because sentencing is a stage of the actual criminal proceeding, "where substantial rights of a criminal accused may be affected."

Morrissey v. Brewer, 408 U.S. 471 (1972)

Before parole can be revoked, the parolee is entitled to two hearings. The first is a preliminary hearing at the time of arrest and detention, and is for the purpose of determining whether there is probable cause to believe that parole has been violated. The second hearing is a more comprehensive hearing that must occur before making a decision to revoke parole.

Minimum due process requirements at that second hearing are

1. Written notice of the alleged violations of parole
2. Disclosure to the parolee of the evidence of violation
3. Opportunity to be heard in person and to present evidence as well as witnesses
4. Right to confront and cross-examine adverse witnesses unless good cause can be shown for not allowing this confrontation
5. Right to judgment by a detached and neutral hearing body
6. Written statement of the reason for revoking parole, and of the evidence used in arriving at that decision

The court did not decide whether retained or appointed counsel is required at a parole revocation hearing.

Gagnon v. Scarpelli, 411 U.S. 778 (1973)

The minimum due process requirements enumerated in *Morrissey v. Brewer* apply to revocation of probation. A probationer also is entitled to the two hearings before revocation.

The Court considered the issue of whether counsel is required and held that there is no constitutional right to counsel at revocation hearings, and that the right to counsel should be determined on a case-by-case basis. The Court left the matter of counsel to the discretion of parole and probation authorities and indicated in part that an attorney should be present when required for fundamental fairness. An example might be a situation in which the parolee or probationer is unable to communicate effectively.

Bearden v. Georgia, 461 U.S. 660 (1983)

The state may not revoke probation in the case of an indigent who has failed to pay a fine and restitution, unless there is a determination that the probationer has not made a bona fide effort to pay or that there were not adequate alternative forms of punishment. "Only if alternate measures are not adequate to meet the state's interests in punishment and deterrence may the court imprison a probationer who has made sufficient bona fide efforts to pay."

Black v. Romano, 471 U.S. 606 (1985)

The due process clause generally does not require a sentencing court to indicate that it considered alternatives to incarceration before revoking probation. This case did not involve the indigency issue regarding failure to pay a fine and restitution, as did the *Bearden* case.

In 1972, in *Morrissey v. Brewer*, the Supreme Court looked at parole revocation in the case of two offenders, Morrissey and Booher. Morrissey's parole was revoked for these allegations:

1. He bought a car under an assumed name and operated it without permission.
2. He gave false statements to police concerning his address and insurance company after a minor accident.
3. He obtained credit under an assumed name.
4. He failed to report his place of residence to his parole officer.

Booher's parole was revoked because he had allegedly

1. Violated the territorial restriction of his parole without consent
2. Obtained a driver's license under an assumed name
3. Operated a motor vehicle without permission
4. Violated the employment condition of his parole by failing to keep himself in gainful employment.[56]

No hearing was held before parole was revoked in these two cases. In its discussion of the cases, the Court made several findings. According to the Court, the purpose of parole is rehabilitation. Until parole rules are violated, an individual may remain on parole, and parole should not be revoked unless those rules are violated. Parole revocation does not require all due process rights required at a criminal trial, but it does require some elements of due process. Informal parole revocation hearings are proper, and the requirements of due process for parole revocation will change with particular cases.

In *Morrissey* the Court enumerated the minimum requirements; they are reproduced in Spotlight 16.5. The Court also indicated that there should be two hearings before the final decision is made. The first is to determine whether there is probable cause to support a parole violation. At the second and more formal hearing, the final decision is made whether to revoke parole.

One year after *Morrissey*, the Court extended these minimum due process requirements to probation revocation, but in *Gagnon v. Scarpelli*, the Court also discussed the issue of whether counsel would be required at probation and parole revocation. The Court had not decided that issue in *Morrissey*. In *Gagnon*, the Court held that there might be some cases in which counsel would be necessary in order for the offender to have a fair hearing, but that counsel is not constitutionally required in all revocation cases.

Two other cases of significance to revocation hearings are summarized in Spotlight 16.5. Taken together, *Bearden v. Georgia* and *Black v. Romano* indicate that there are some restrictions on probation revocation. In *Bearden* the Court held that it would be improper to revoke the probation of an indigent who had not paid a fine and restitution unless there was a finding that the indigent had not made a sufficient effort to pay. Even then, the court must look at other alternatives before revoking probation and incarcerating the offender. But in *Romano*, when the offender's probation was revoked because he was charged with leaving the scene of an automobile accident (a felony), the Court held that due process did not require that before incarcerating the offender on the original sentence other sentencing alternatives should have been considered.

It is clear from these decisions, read in conjunction with those involving the decision whether to grant parole, that the Court sees a significant difference between granting parole and revoking parole. The Court states it this way:

> The Court has fashioned a constitutional distinction between the decision to revoke parole and the decision to grant or to deny parole. Arbitrary revocation is prohibited by *Morrissey v. Brewer* . . . whereas arbitrary denial is permitted by *Greenholtz v. Nebraska Panel Inmates.*[57]

PROBATION AND PAROLE: A CONCLUSION

Despite the trend toward determinate sentencing of the late 1970s and 1980s, the fact that most prison systems have been or are under federal court orders to reduce populations has resulted in the continued use of parole even among jurisdictions where it is unpopular. Prison overcrowding also has contributed to the rise in the use of probation. Data indicate that the majority of those admitted to prison are recidivists; that is, they had previously been incarcerated for another crime, or most likely, several crimes. Many of those who enter prison without a prior incarceration previously have been convicted and placed on probation.[58]

Despite the problems of acquiring accurate data on recidivism, it is obvious that many people are repeat offenders. It also is obvious that many convicted offenders cannot be incarcerated for long periods today because of prison overcrowding. It is not obvious, however, that even if they could all be incarcerated, this would be the most effective way to handle the crime problem.

The public continues to push for more severe treatment of criminals, however, and they are supported by many legislators and some scholars. This trend is manifested in the increasing number of legislatures that have enacted statutes providing for life-without-parole sentences for some offenders, usually for repeat offenders and for those convicted of aggravated homicide.[59]

Public reaction to some paroles has also been extensive. The most notorious recent case is probably that of Lawrence Singleton, a 60-year-old convicted of the 1978 brutal attack on Mary Vincent, a 15-year-old hitchhiker. Singleton was convicted of raping, sodomizing, and maiming the teenager whom he left for dead. She survived the attack despite the fact that her forearms were chopped off with an ax. In 1987 Singleton was paroled, but after unsuccessful attempts to locate a place to live without threats from townspeople, Singleton returned to San Quentin, where he had been incarcerated for 8 years of his 14-year sentence. He served his parole time living in a trailer on the grounds of that California prison. In

April 1988, however, he was unconditionally free since he had served without problems the terms of his parole.

It was reported in June of 1988 that Singleton had secured a driver's license in Tampa, Florida, but may have violated a state statute requiring felons to register. Two detectives were assigned to locate Singleton, who continues to protest his innocence in the Vincent case. Singleton's brother's home in Tampa was the scene of an explosion of a crude bomb in June 1988. No one was injured, and there were no arrests.

Vincent, who lives in seclusion in the Pacific Northwest, has a child and says she still fears Singleton. Both the offender and the victim of this case indicate that they feel oppressed by the extensive media coverage of the case.

SUMMARY

This chapter covered some critical areas of criminal justice. Despite the current public demand for stricter reactions to criminals, the crisis of overcrowded jails and prisons forces most jurisdictions to use some forms of community corrections. Despite the retreat from rehabilitation as a purpose for punishment and corrections, offenders are (and will continue to be) in the community, usually with limited supervision. The issue is not whether we wish to have community corrections; the issue is how much attention and funding we will provide to make sure the use of community corrections does not impair the goal of security.

This chapter began with an overview of community-based corrections, considering the history of this approach to corrections along with the cost. Financing is a real problem, particularly with the cutbacks in federal and state budgets; but the costs for corrections in the community are far less than the costs of incarceration, and that is true even when intensive supervision is provided for those offenders residing in the community.

The problems that offenders face when they live in the community were discussed, along with the need for services in assisting them to cope with these problems. We looked at the Kentucky example of providing a variety of services for offenders in the community, ranging from educational and vocational training to seminars on how to interview and how to improve self-concepts.

Probation and parole were discussed in greater depth than other community corrections, since they are the methods most frequently used. Probation is the most frequently imposed sentence and is being used today for serious offenders, mainly because of prison overcrowding. The prognosis for success is not great, although it is thought that, with intensive probation supervision, the probability for success improves significantly. House arrest as a condition of probation also is used today.

Parole is the most frequently used method of release from prison, but its use for early release has been restricted. The various methods of organizing parole systems were discussed, along with the parole process, including eligibility for parole and the parole hearing. The due process requirements for the parole decision-making hearings were discussed. Attempts to decrease the perceived arbitrariness of parole decisions have involved the use of parole guidelines. Due process in the revocation of probation and parole also has helped to remove the arbitrariness and unfairness of those important processes.

The movement away from rehabilitation has resulted in problems for community corrections. Perhaps the most bitter criticisms have been hurled at parole, resulting in action in many states to abolish or at least curtail its use. An early example of this trend is seen in New York. In a comprehensive effort to assess the use of parole in that state, the first study of this type since the beginning of parole, it was concluded that both the theory and practice of parole were repudiated by the facts. Human behavior cannot be predicted; the concept of rehabilitation on which parole is based is vague and subjective, and there is no way to measure when it has occurred.

Parole is a tragic failure. Conspiring with other elements of the criminal justice system—unnecessary pre-trial detention, overlong sentences, oppressive prison conditions—it renders American treatment of those who break society's rules irrational and arbitrary.[60]

Despite the call for abolition of parole, the report noted that some form of discretion in the release of offenders must be retained, especially if sentences are long. It was suggested that parole boards be abolished and replaced by review boards of citizens who have some contacts with inmates outside after release, as in work release programs, and who are representative regarding race, class, and occupation. Judicial review of release decisions also was recommended.

No one can say which is the real problem: the failure of parole per se or the abuse of discretion by parole-granting authorities. In 1975 Maurice H. Sigler, chairman of the United States Board of Parole, argued that parole "has now become the scapegoat of all of corrections' ills." He suggested that the system deserves the same objective, dispassionate analysis that its critics demand of parole decisions.

> To those who say "let's abolish parole," I say that as long as we use imprisonment in this country we will have to have someone, somewhere, with the authority to release people from imprisonment. Call it parole—call it what you will. It's one of those jobs that has to be done.[61]

The abolition of parole may result only in shifting discretion to another area, such as prosecution. Prosecutors may refuse to prosecute; juries may refuse to convict in cases involving long mandatory sentences with no chance of parole. Efforts to control discretion within the parole system may be a more reasonable approach than the total abolition of the system.

STUDY QUESTIONS

1. Define *community-based corrections* and give reasons why some argue that it is to be preferred over incarceration of offenders.

2. What problems do offenders face when they return to the community from incarceration? What is being done to assist them in coping with those problems?

3. What is the difference between *probation* and *parole*? Which is used more frequently?

4. What are the arguments for and against the use of house arrest?

5. What is *electronic monitoring*? Should its use be increased?

6. Discuss *shock probation*.

7. What typical restrictions or conditions are placed on probationers? What should be the guidelines, legally or practically, for such restrictions?

8. What is meant by *intensive probation supervision*? How does it compare in effectiveness to traditional methods of supervision?

9. How does the origin of parole compare to the origin of the prison system?

10. Describe and analyze recent trends in parole systems.

ENDNOTES

1. President's Commission on Law Enforcement and Administration of Justice, *The Challenge of Crime in a Free Society* (Washington, D.C.: U.S. Government Printing Office, 1967), p. 121.
2. National Advisory Commission on Criminal Justice Standards and Goals, *A National Strategy to Reduce Crime* (Washington, D.C.: U.S. Government Printing Office, 1973), p. 121.
3. See John Irwin, *The Felon* (Englewood Cliffs, N.J.: Prentice-Hall, 1970).
4. See Sheldon Ekland-Olson et al., "Postrelease Depression and the Importance of Familial Support," *Criminology* 21 (May 1983): 254–57.
5. Betsy Coffey and Brett Scott, "Community Support Service: The Kentucky Experience," in *Community Corrections*, American Correctional

Association Monographs, Series 1, No. 5 (Laurel, Md.: American Correctional Association, May 1981), pp. 71–75.

6. "Study of 53,000 Inmates on Furlough in '87 Finds Few Did Harm," *New York Times* (12 October 1988), p. 12.

7. See "Prison Arithmetic Benefits the Inmates," *The Miami Herald*, (4 December 1988), p. 1.

8. Bureau of Justice Statistics, *Probation and Parole 1986* (Washington, D.C.: U.S. Department of Justice, December 1987), p. 1.

9. For a recent history, reprinted in celebration of the fiftieth year celebration of federal probation, see Sanford Bates, "The Establishment and Early Years of the Federal Probation System," *Federal Probation* 51 (June 1987): 4–9, originally published in 1950.

10. Joan Petersilia, "Rand's Research: A Closer Look," *Corrections Today* 47 (June 1985): 37.

11. *Criminal Justice Research at Rand* (Santa Monica, Calif.: Rand Corporation, January 1985), p. 11.

12. U.S. v. Murphy, 618 F. Supp. 350 (D.C.N.Y. 1985) withdrawn, rereported, supplemented, 108 FRD 437 (E. D. N.Y. 1985).

13. Daniel Ford and Annesley K. Schmidt, "Electronically Monitored Home Confinement," *National Institute of Justice Report* (November 1985): 2.

14. Joseph B. Vaughn, "Planning for Change: The Use of Electronic Monitoring as a Correctional Alternative," in Belinda R. McCarthy, ed., *Intermediate Punishments: Intensive Supervision, Home Confinement and Electronic Surveillance* (Monsey, N.Y.: Criminal Justice Press, 1987), p. 153.

15. Thomas G. Blomberg, Gordon P. Waldo, and Lisa C. Burcroff, "Home Confinement and Electronic Surveillance," in McCarthy, ibid., p. 169.

16. See, for example, a discussion of the Vermont proposal in "Home Confinement as a Condition of Probation: A Proposal for Vermont," *Vermont Law Review* 12 (Spring 1987): 123–55. See also Rolando V. del Carmen and Joseph B. Vaughn, "Legal Issues in the Use of Electronic Surveillance in Probation," *Federal Probation* 50, no. 2 (1986): 60–69; and J. Robert Lilly et al., "Electronic Jail Revisited," *Justice Quarterly* 3 (September 1986): 353–61.

17. OHIO REV. CODE, Section 2947.061.

18. Cited in Joseph E. Scott et al., "Pioneering Innovations in Corrections: Shock Probation and Shock Parole," mimeographed (Columbus: Ohio State University, 1974), p. 41.

19. See, for example, Eric T. Assur et al., "Probation Counselors and the Adult Children of Alcoholics," *Federal Probation* 51 (September 1987): 41–51; and Edward M. Read, "The Alcoholic, the Probation Officer, and AA: A Viable Team Approach to Supervision," *Federal Probation* 51 (March 1987): 11–15.

20. Standard 12–2,3, *ABA Standards Relating to the Administration of Criminal Justice, Sentencing Alternatives and Procedures* (Washington, D.C.: ABA Standing Committee on Association Standards for Criminal Justice, 1979).

21. People v. Blankenship, 61 P.2d 352, 353 (Cal. App. 4 Dist. 1936).

22. People v. Dominguez, 64 Cal. Rptr. 290, 293 (Cal. App. 2 Dist. 1967).

23. Inman v. State, 183 S.E.2d 413, 415 (Ga. App. 1971).

24. Ohio v. Livingston, 372 N.E.2d 1335 (Ohio App. 1976).

25. United States v. Terrigno, 838 F.2d 371, 373, 374–75 (9th Cir. 1988), cases and citations omitted.

26. Griffin v. Wisconsin, 483 U.S. 868 (1987).

27. TEX. CODE CRIM. PRO., Chapter 42.121, Section 1.01.

28. See Frank P. Williams, III, et al., *Assessing Diversionary Impact: An Evaluation of the Intensive Supervision Program of the Texas County Adult Probation Department* (Huntsville, Texas: Sam Houston State University Criminal Justice Center, 1982).

29. Stephen Gettinger, "Intensive Supervision: Can It Rehabilitate Probation?" *Corrections Magazine* 9 (April 1983): 7–8.

30. Joan Petersilia, "Georgia's Intensive Probation: Will the Model Work Elsewhere?" in McCarthy, ed., *Intermediate Punishments*, p. 15. This book also contains several other recent articles that focus on IPS.

31. John P. Conrad, "Research And Development in Corrections," *Federal Probation* 51 (June 1987), p. 62–64.

32. Sheldon L. Messinger et al., "The Foundations of Parole in California," *Law and Society* 19, no. 1 (1985): 69.

33. For a discussion, see Malcolm Davies, "Determinate Sentencing Reform in California and Its Impact on the Penal System," *British Journal of Criminology* 25 (January 1985): 1–30.

34. American Friends Service Committee, *Struggle for Justice: A Report On Crime and Punishment in America* (New York: Hill and Wang, 1971).

35. Bob Wilson, "Parole Release: Devil or Savior?" *Corrections Magazine* 3 (September 1977): 48.

36. Norval Morris, *The Future of Imprisonment* (Chicago: University of Chicago Press, 1974), p. 47.

37. Edward M. Kennedy, "Toward a New System of Criminal Sentencing: Law with Order," *American Criminal Law Review* 16 (Spring 1979): 361.

38. Harry E. Allen et al., *Probation and Parole in America* (New York: Free Press, 1985), p. 165.

39. Tarlton v. Clark, 441 F. 2d 384, 385 (5th Cir. 1971), *cert. denied*, 403 U.S. 934 (1971).

40. Robert Clarence Miller, "Parole," *Fortune News* (October 1972), p. 10.

41. Quoted in Jessica Mitford, *Kind and Usual Pun-*

ishment: The Prison Business (New York: Alfred A. Knopf, 1973), p. 216.

42. Greenholtz v. Nebraska, 442 U.S. 1 (1979), *remanded sub. nom.*, 602 F. 2d 155 (8th Cir. 1979).
43. Board of Pardons v. Allen, 482 U.S. 369 (1987).
44. Linda M. Trueb, "The Expectancy of Parole in Montana: A Right Entitled to Some Due Process," *Montana Law Review* 48 (Summer 1987): 390.
45. See U.S. Department of Justice, *Sentencing and Parole Release Classification Instruments for Criminal Justice Decisions* (Washington, D.C.: U.S. Government Printing Office, 1979), vol. 4, p. 7.
46. See John S. Carroll, "Judgments of Recidivism Risk: The Use of Base-Rate Information in Parole Decision," in Paul D. Lipsitt and Bruce B. Sales, ed., *New Directions in Psycholegal Research* (New York: Van Nostrand Reinhold, 1980), pp. 66–86; and Don M. Gottfredson et al., *Guidelines for Parole and Sentencing: A Policy Control Method* (Lexington, Mass.: D.C. Heath and Co., 1978).
47. Harry E. Allen et al., *Probation and Parole in America* (New York: Free Press, 1985), p. 165.
48. Morrissey v. Brewer, 408 U.S. 471, 477–78 (1972).
49. National Advisory Commission on Criminal Justice Standards and Goals, *Corrections* (Washington, D.C.: U.S. Government Printing Office, 1973), p. 433.
50. Andrew von Hirsch and Kathleen J. Hanrahan, *Abolish Parole?* (Washington, D.C.: U.S. Government Printing Office, 1978), p. 21.
51. "Parole by Any Other Name," *Criminal Justice Newsletter* 14 (29 August 1983): 5.
52. Howard R. Sacks and Charles H. Logan, *Does Parole Make a Difference?* (Hartford: University of Connecticut School of Law Press, 1979).
53. Robert Martinson and Judith Wilks, "Save Parole Supervision," *Federal Probation* 41 (September 1977): 23–27.
54. Tracy Fisk, "Nevada's Growing Attraction: Department of Parole and Probation," *Corrections Today* 48 (February 1986): 42.
55. Rory J. McMahon, "A New Era: Federal Probation and Parole," *Corrections Today* 48 (February 1986): 20.
56. Morrissey v. Brewer, 408 U.S. 471 (1972).
57. Jago v. Van Curen, 454 U.S. 14 (1981).
58. See Bureau of Justice Statistics, *Examining Recidivism* (Washington, D.C.: U.S. Department of Justice, February, 1985); and Joan Petersilia and Susan Turner, *Prison versus Probation in California: Implications for Crime and Offender Recidivism* (Santa Monica, Calif.: Rand Corporation, July 1986).
59. For a discussion of this trend, see Derral Cheatwood, "The Life-without-Parole Sanction: Its Current Status and a Research Agenda," *Crime and Delinquency* 34 (January 1988): 43–59.
60. Citizens' Inquiry on Parole and Criminal Justice, "The Future of Parole," *The Prison Journal* 54 (Spring–Summer 1974): 38. The full report of this study may be found in Diana R. Gordon and David Rudenstine, *Prison without Walls: Report on New York Parole, Citizens' Inquiry on Parole and Criminal Justice, Inc.* (New York: Holt, Rinehart and Winston, 1975).
61. Maurice H. Sigler, "Abolish Parole?", *Federal Probation* 39 (June 1975): 48.

The juvenile court system emerged as a separate system for processing juveniles who engage in criminal and delinquent activities or who are dependent or neglected. It was seen as a system concerned with the welfare of the child; it, therefore, did not need the procedural safeguards characteristic of the criminal court system.

In recent years that orientation has changed. Some but not all procedural safeguards have been extended to the juvenile court. The result is a system that is far less distinguishable from the criminal court than was the original intention. Whether these are positive or negative changes is debatable.

Chapter 17 discusses the early development and the recent changes that have been made in the juvenile court system. Chapter 17 also discusses the development and changes that have occurred in the correctional system for juveniles.

Chapter 17. The Juvenile Justice System

CHAPTER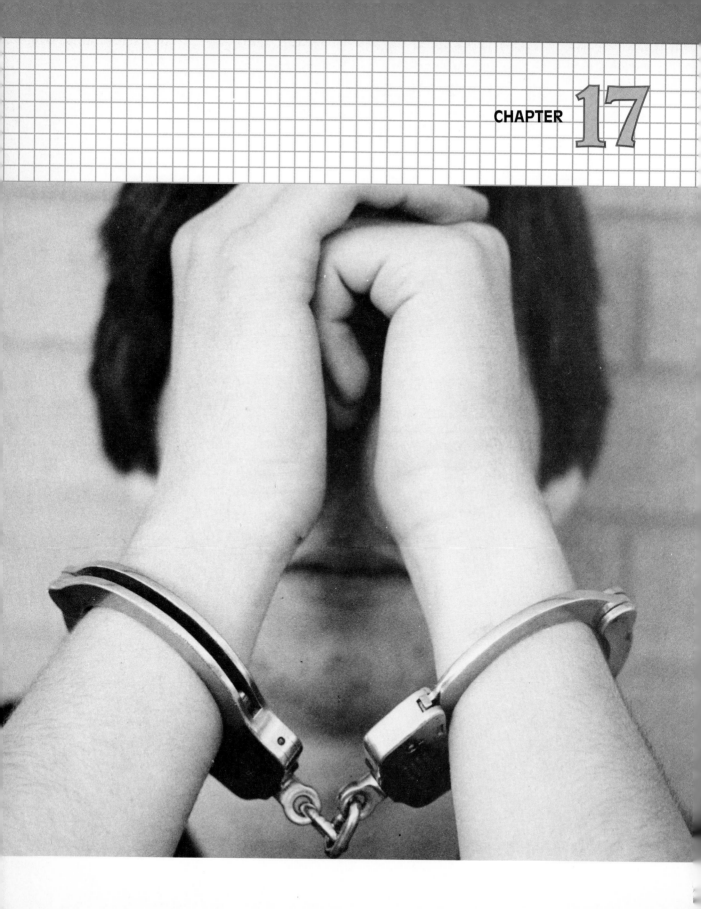

17

The Juvenile Justice System

KEY TERMS

adjudication
aftercare
beyond a reasonable
 doubt
certification
custody
detention
detention center
discovery
disposition
diversion
hearsay evidence
intake decisions
juvenile
juvenile court
juvenile delinquent
parens patriae
petition
status offenses
training school

Doris, 14, and her friend, Chester, 15, had been dating for over a year, although Doris' parents had persistently protested their involvement. The parents argued that Chester was a bad influence on Doris and that both teenagers were a bad influence on Doris' younger sister, Elise, who at 12 was already incorrigible.

One spring day Doris and Chester decided to skip school and drive to the country; they stole an automobile, drove it at high speeds, and had an accident that resulted in the death of a pedestrian. Elise, who adored her older sister, could not deal with the family conflicts that became worse after this accident; so she ran away from home. Her parents requested the police look for Elise, and if they found her, take her to the juvenile authorities because they no longer could control her.

Doris and Chester were apprehended and detained by police. Doris was released to her parents pending her hearing in juvenile court. Chester had been in serious trouble with the law before; so he was detained by the police. At Chester's hearing the juvenile court judge decided that in light of his record and the seriousness of this offense, Chester should be tried as an adult. Under the laws that permit waiver of jurisdiction from the juvenile to the criminal court, Chester's case was transferred to the criminal court. Chester was found guilty of larceny of an automobile and negligent manslaughter and was sentenced to 10 years in prison.

Doris's case was heard by a juvenile court judge who was impressed with her lack of prior trouble with the law and her excellent school record despite her recent truancy. The judge ruled that Doris could remain in her home provided she attended school regularly and did not get into further trouble. The same judge heard the case of Elise after police found her 5 days after she ran away from home. The judge placed Elise in a foster home because of what appeared to be insurmountable problems between Elise and her parents.

INTRODUCTION

The hypothetical cases of Doris, Chester, and Elise illustrate some of the activities that give the juvenile court the legal authority to hear and decide cases involving juveniles. Doris has engaged in criminal activities and is processed through the juvenile court although she is permitted to return to her home. Elise has not committed any act that would be a crime if committed by an adult, but her parents cannot control her. The juvenile court judge decides to place Elise in a foster home. Chester is a juvenile, but the juvenile court judge decides that Chester's prior record and current offenses warrant transferring his case to the criminal court, where he is tried, convicted, and sentenced to prison. These and other procedures will be discussed in this chapter, which focuses on the processing of juveniles in the juvenile and criminal justice systems.

Criminal responsibility in the adversary system is based on the premise that the accused has the ability to understand and control his or her behavior. Most people are presumed to have this ability; but among the exceptions have been persons of tender years. A separate system for them emerged in the late 1800s in the United States. In recent years this separate system has gone through significant changes, including the transferring of

The original intent of the juvenile court was that the judge, acting as a wise father, would counsel the young person. Today the juvenile court observes most procedural safeguards of the criminal court. (James L. Shaffer/PhotoEdit)

some juveniles to the criminal court. For those juveniles who have remained in the juvenile court system, the Supreme Court requires some procedural safeguards.

This chapter begins with a brief historical overview of the background of the juvenile system that emerged in this country. The origin of the juvenile court, along with the dispute over the purposes of this new system for juveniles, are discussed. The chapter then looks briefly at the changes the Supreme Court has required in the traditional juvenile system, before looking more closely at how that system works today. The focus of this chapter is to explain the juvenile system in the same context by using the same approach as in the previous discussions on the processing of the adult offender. Where relevant, contrasts are made to the adult criminal court system.

Although the chapter contains brief discussions of institutionalizing juveniles, juveniles in detention, and juveniles on parole, no attempt is made to discuss these topics thoroughly. The enormous amount of literature in the juvenile field warrants a separate course and a separate text on the subject.[1]

PHILOSOPHY OF THE JUVENILE JUSTICE SYSTEM

The special system of justice for children rests on the belief that they should be treated separately and differently from adults. They need special handling and processing when they engage in delinquent or criminal acts. Children are considered amenable to treatment, to change, and to rehabilitation. This special treatment of children has not, however, always been observed. It is important therefore to look briefly at the historical occurrences that preceded the movement toward a juvenile justice system in this country.

Background and History

Although the first discussion of **juvenile** problems of which we have record dates back 4,000 years to the Code of Hammurabi, the treatment of children in the United States can be traced to the philosophy of the English, who in the eleventh and twelfth centuries developed the practice of treating children differently from adults. A child under 7 was considered incapable of forming the intent required for criminal prosecutions. A child between the ages of 7 and 14 years was presumed to be incapable of forming the intent, but that presumption could be refuted. A child over 14 was treated as an adult.

During this earlier period of English history, when the death penalty was provided for many crimes, children were not legally exempted, although few children were executed. Later in England, the courts of chancery or equity were established for the purpose of avoiding the harshness of some of the strict technicalities of the English common law. Equity courts were to decide cases on the principle of justice and fairness. These courts were also called *chancery courts* because they were under the jurisdiction of the king's chancellor. Equity courts had jurisdiction over many types of cases, including those involving children.[2]

The English king could exercise the power of parent over children and others, a concept called ***parens patriae***, literally meaning the "parent of the country." In time, this concept became so important that England passed statutes permitting the legal rights of parents and other family members to be terminated in the cases of persons who needed the legal guardianship of the king.

Parens patriae was interpreted in England to mean that the sovereign had the responsibility to oversee any children in his kingdom who might be neglected or abused. The court exercised this duty only when it was thought necessary for the welfare of the child, and that rarely occurred. Protection of society and punishment of parents were not considered to be sufficient reasons to invoke the responsibility. Both in the English system and in the system as adopted during the early period of American history, the *parens patriae* doctrine applied only to children who were in need of supervision or help because of the actions of their parents or guardians, not because the children themselves were delinquent. The extension to the juvenile court of jurisdiction over delinquent children was an innovation adopted in Illinois in 1899.[3]

In colonial America, children were initially treated like adults. Capital punishment was permitted but seldom used; however for punishment, many children were deprived of food, incarcerated with adults, or subjected to corporal punishment. Some institutions were established to separate incarcerated juveniles from adults. The New York House of Refuge, established in 1824, was the first and served as a model. These early institutions eliminated some of the evils of imprisoning children with adult criminals, although recent scholars have questioned whether they provided much improvement in the treatment of juveniles.[4]

By the middle 1800s in the United States, probation for juveniles had been established and separate **detention** facilities had been built. The 1800s also saw the evolution of progressive ideas in the care and treatment of dependent and neglected children. Protective societies, such as the Society for the Prevention of Cruelty to Children (developed in New York in 1875), paved the way for the juvenile court. Illinois, however, gets credit for establishing the first **juvenile court** in 1899. Other states quickly followed.

The Juvenile Court: An Overview

Under the *parens patriae* doctrine, the jurisdiction of the juvenile court is extensive. It includes all children who have not yet achieved the age at which the criminal court takes jurisdiction, although that age may differ from state to state. Some states have a minimum age for juvenile court jurisdiction, but as a practical matter courts generally do not decide cases involving very young children.

The establishment of the juvenile court in 1899 extended the doctrine of *parens patriae* to delinquent children. The *parens patriae* doctrine also permits juvenile courts jurisdiction over children who have not committed crimes. Children who need supervision because they have no parents or because their parents are not providing proper supervision are included; they are called *dependent* or *neglected children*.

The juvenile court has historically also had jurisdiction over children who have not violated criminal laws but who violate societal or parental expectations. Some children, for example, Elise in this chapter's CJA, are considered incorrigible because they will not obey their parents, teachers, or other adults. They run away from home; they stay out too late; they refuse to obey their parents or their teachers. These activities are called **status offenses**. The trend in recent years has been to remove status offenses from the jurisdiction of the juvenile court. But when jurisdiction over status offenses remains, the status offender is generally included within the definition of **juvenile delinquent**.

Contrast with Criminal Court   Jurisdiction is not the only factor that distinguishes the juvenile court from the adult criminal court. Spotlight 17.1 lists some of the differences historically.

The juvenile court, with its emphasis on individualized treatment, was visualized as a social agency or clinic not a court of law, a vision that was later to encounter much criticism. The court was to be a social institution designed to protect and rehabilitate the child not a court designed to try the child's guilt. The purpose was to treat not punish. The basic purpose of the juvenile court was to protect the child from the stigma attached to the proceedings in a criminal court.

The vocabulary of juvenile and criminal courts also differed. Children would not be arrested but summoned or apprehended; they would

SPOTLIGHT 17.1
THE CRIMINAL AND THE JUVENILE COURTS:
SOME HISTORICALLY IMPORTANT CONTRASTS

ADULT CRIMINAL COURT	JUVENILE COURT
Court of law	Social institution, agency, clinic
Constitutional rights	*Parens Patriae* approach — supra constitutional rights
Purpose to punish, deter	Purpose to salvage, rehabilitate
Begins with arrest	Begins with apprehension, summons process of intake
Indictment or presentment	Petition filed on behalf of child
Detained in jails or released on bail	Detained in detention centers or released to family or others
Public trial	Private hearing
Strict rules of evidence	Informal procedures
Right to trial by jury	No right to trial by jury
Right to counsel	No right to (or need for) counsel
Prosecuted by state	Allegations brought by state
Plea bargaining	No plea bargaining; state will act in child's best interests
Impartial judge	Judge acting as a wise parent
Pleads guilty, innocent, or *nolo contendre*	Admits or denies petition
Found guilty or innocent	Adjudicated
Sentenced	Disposition of the case
Probation	Probation
Incarcerated in jail or prison	Placed in reformatory, training school, or foster home, etc.
Released on parole	Released to aftercare

not be indicted, but a petition would be filed on their behalf. If detention were necessary, they would be detained in facilities separate from adults not in jails. They would not have a public trial but a private hearing, in which juries and prosecuting attorneys would rarely, if ever, be used. Nor would they usually have counsel.

The juvenile hearing would be informal, for the ordinary trappings of the courtroom would be out of place. Judges would not act as impartial observers, as was their function in the criminal court. Rather, they would act as wise parents disciplining their children in love and tenderness, deciding in an informal way what was best for those children. Juveniles would not be sentenced as the concept is known in the criminal court. Rather, after the hearing they would be **adjudicated**. A **disposition** would be made only after a careful study of the juvenile's background and potential, and the decision would be made in the best interests of the child.

The juvenile court hearing differed from the criminal court in procedure as well as in theory. Rules of evidence required in criminal courts were not applied to the juvenile court. For example, juveniles did not have the right to cross-examine their accusers. Indeed, there was no need for that safeguard since everyone was assumed to be acting in the best interests of the child. **Hearsay evidence,** which would be excluded from the criminal court, would be admitted in the juvenile court. Judges needed all the information they could get for an adequate disposition of cases. The emphasis in the juvenile court was not on what the child did but what the child was. The court was to be concerned with a total diagnosis of the child that would enable the judge to save the child from a criminal career through proper treatment, in contrast with the criminal court's concern with the narrow issue, during trial, of the guilt or innocence of the accused. The juvenile court was to be treatment- not punishment-oriented. The purpose of the court was to prevent children from becoming criminals by catching them in the budding stages and giving them the love and protection that would be provided by parents who believe their children are salvageable.

Early advocates of the juvenile court believed that law and humanitarianism were not sufficient for treatment of the juvenile. They expected juvenile courts to rely heavily on the findings of the physical and social sciences. It was expected that these research findings would be applied scientifically in the adjudication and disposition of juveniles.

The failure of the social sciences to develop sufficient research to implement this philosophy adequately, the failure of the legal profession to recognize and accept those findings that would be of assistance, and the abuse of discretion by correctional officials perhaps are responsible for the tensions that developed over the lack of procedural safeguards in the juvenile court.

Procedural Safeguards   In the juvenile court system, the procedural safeguards of the criminal court were set aside in the interest of treatment and the welfare of children because they were incompatible with those interests. Because the state, in recognizing its duty as parent, was helping not punishing children, no constitutional rights were violated. The child was legally a ward of the state and had no constitutional rights that the court must respect. This philosophy of the juvenile court was summarized in an early court decision, part of which follows. There is clear indication that the juvenile court, always acting in the best interests of the child, was perceived as an institution far more humane than the criminal court.[5]

Commonwealth v. *Fisher* ——————————————————————

[The juvenile court] . . . is not for the punishment of offenders but for the salvation of children. . . . No child under the age of 16 is excluded from its beneficient provisions. Its protecting arm is for all who have not attained that age and who may need its protection. It is for all children of the same class. . . .

To save a child from becoming a criminal, or from continuing in a career of crime . . . the Legislature surely may provide for the salvation of such a child, if its parents or guardian be unable or unwilling to do so, by bringing it into one of the courts of the state without any process at all, for the purpose of subjecting it to the state's guardianship and protection.

The dream of the rehabilitative ideal of the founders of the juvenile court has not been realized. In the blunt words of former Supreme Court justice Abe Fortas,

> There may be grounds for concern that the child receives the worst of both worlds: that he gets neither the protection accorded to adults nor the solicitous care and regenerative treatment postulated for children.[6]

In reality, the juvenile often receives punishment, not treatment. In reality, being processed through the juvenile court rather than the criminal court does not remove the stigma of criminal.

Not only has the juvenile perhaps suffered the "worst of both worlds," but some scholars take the position that that is how it was intended. Disputing the benevolent motives of the founders of the juvenile court, scholars have argued that the juvenile court diminished the civil liberties and privacy of juveniles and that the child-saving movement was promoted by the middle class to support its own interests.[7]

Others have contended that the development of the juvenile court represented neither a great social reform in the treatment of juveniles nor an attempt to diminish their civil liberties and to control them arbitrarily. Rather, it represented another example of the trend toward bureaucratization and an institutional compromise between social welfare and the law. The juvenile court "was primarily a shell of legal ritual within which states renewed and enacted their commitment to discretionary social control over children."[8] Changes have occurred in the juvenile court philosophy and procedures. But before that discussion, it is appropriate to take a brief look at the data on delinquency.

DATA ON JUVENILE DELINQUENCY

It is impossible to get accurate data on the amount of delinquency. Jurisdictions differ in their definitions of delinquency. Theoretically, delinquency does not refer to children processed through the juvenile court because they are in need of supervision, because they are dependent or neglected, or because they are abused. Some jurisdictions, however, include in the delinquency statutes all types of juveniles over which the juvenile court has jurisdiction.

Methods of collecting data on delinquency also vary, and juvenile records usually are considered confidential; some states require that the records be destroyed or sealed. How, then, do we know about juvenile crime? The earlier chapter on crime data discussed the use of self-report studies, in which respondents are asked to indicate what types of offenses they have ever committed and how often they have committed them. From carefully selected samples of the population, predictions can be made on the overall extent of delinquency.

Official arrest rates recorded by age brackets and published by the FBI are another source of data. The official data indicate that in 1987,

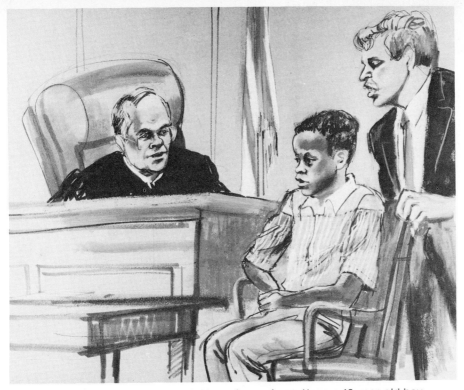

Very young children may be involved in serious crimes. Here, a 10-year-old boy testifies in a New York Court before a Family Court Judge and the boy's lawyer. The boy was convicted of selling crack and was ordered into a home for troubled youngsters. (Drawing by Marilyn Church/AP/Wide World Photos)

persons under 18 accounted for 15.4 percent of the arrests for violent crimes and 32.7 percent of the property crimes in 1987. Figure 17.1 graphs the percentage of total arrests in 1987 of persons under 18 for all serious offenses and several other crimes. The purpose of Figure 17.1 is to demonstrate that, according to official data, juveniles under the age of 18 do not commit most of the violent crimes.

However, if the age is extended from 18 to 25, the picture is different. Those under 25 constituted 46.5 percent of all arrestees for violent crimes in 1987 and 62.1 percent of all arrestees for property offenses. The age group under 21 accounted for 28.5 percent of all arrestees for violent crimes and 48.0 percent of all arrestees for property crimes.[9]

Between 1983 and 1987, the percentage of persons under 18 who were arrested for serious crimes increased in all but three serious crimes. Forcible rape increased by 14.6 percent; murder and nonnegligent manslaughter by 22.2 percent; aggravated assault by 18.6 percent; motor vehicle theft by 67.3 percent, and larceny–theft by 6.5 percent. But the overall percentage of arrests for violent crimes was up by only .3 percent in the age group under 18, and arrests for property crimes were up by 4.4 percent.[10]

Data also indicate that a few juveniles commit a large percentage of the serious crimes committed by juveniles, and these offenders tend to

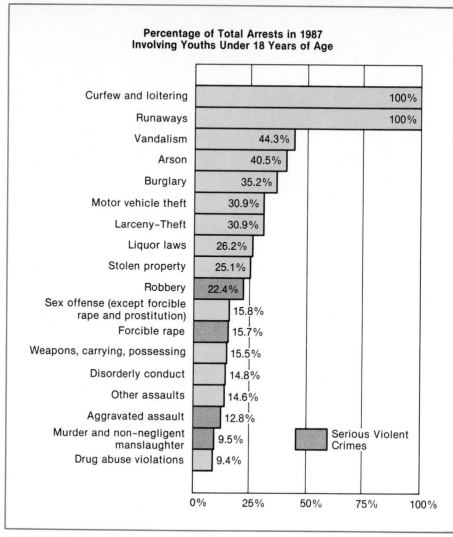

FIGURE 17.1

Percentage of Total Arrests in 1987 Involving Youths Under 18 Years of Age. *Source: Data from Federal Bureau of Investigation, Crime in the United States: Uniform Crime Reports, 1987 (Washington, D.C.: U.S. Government Printing Office, 1988), p. 180.*

continue to commit crimes after they become adults. Recent research has focused on these violent few. This has been done by tracking a cohort, "a complete universe of persons defined by one or more events."

The data in Figure 17.2 come from a cohort of people born between 1956 and 1960, who were arrested for at least one violent offense when they were juveniles in Columbus, Ohio, and who resided in Franklin County, Ohio, during the period of their delinquent activities.

As Figure 17.2 indicates, almost 65 percent of the juvenile arrests involved 30.9 percent of the cohort members, and they were arrested between 5 and 10 or more times. The 1,222 members of the cohort accounted for 4,841 juvenile arrests; the offenses for which they were arrested are indicated in Figure 17.3. Property offenses were slightly higher than vio-

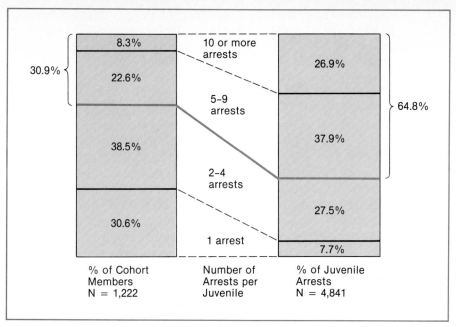

FIGURE 17.2
Number of Juvenile Arrests of Cohort Members. *Source:* Donna Martin Hamparian et al., *The Young Criminal Years of the Violent Few* (Washington, D.C.: U.S. Government Printing Office, June 1985), p. 11.

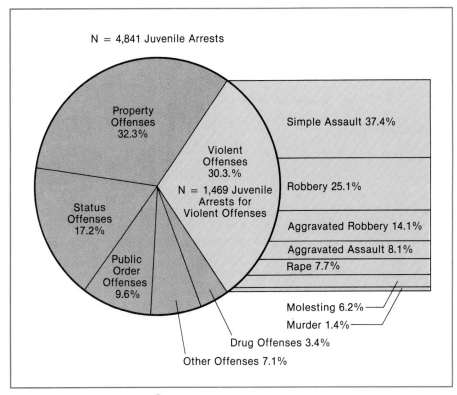

FIGURE 17.3
Juvenile Arrests of Cohort Members by Offense Categories. *Source:* Donna Martin Hamparian et al., *The Young Criminal Years of the Violent Few* (Washington, D.C.: U.S. Government Printing Office, June 1985), p. 12.

lent offenses, and the most frequent arrest for violent offenses was for simple assault. Even with the violent few, murder accounted for only 1.4 percent and rape for 7.7 percent of the total arrests.[11]

CONSTITUTIONAL RIGHTS OF JUVENILES

In recent years, the U.S. Supreme Court has extended to juveniles some but not all of the constitutional rights of adult defendants. In most situations, juveniles have a right to counsel (and to have counsel appointed if they cannot afford private defense counsel), the right not to be tried twice for the same offense, and the right to have the allegations against them proved by the same standard that is used in a criminal trial (beyond a reasonable doubt). They do not have a constitutional right to a trial by jury, although some states provide for that right by statute.

The Supreme Court has not decided the issue of whether juveniles have the right to a public trial, but it has held that the press may not be criminally punished for publishing the name of a juvenile delinquent when the press obtains that name by lawful means.[12] Some states have statutes permitting the press to attend juvenile hearings. Others either leave the decision to the discretion of the judge or prohibit the press entirely. The Supreme Court has not decided the issue of whether juveniles have a right to a speedy trial, but many states have provided by statute for limitations on the period of time a state may take to bring the juvenile case to trial.

U.S. Supreme Court Cases: The Earlier Years of Due Process

The recognition of the constitutional rights of juveniles has occurred in a limited number of cases decided by the U.S. Supreme Court. These cases are discussed briefly.

Kent v. United States   *Kent v. United States*, decided in 1966, does not technically apply to juvenile courts in other jurisdictions because it involved the interpretation of a District of Columbia statute. The case is often cited, however, as an indication of the beginning of the movement to infuse proceedings of the juvenile court with some elements of due process. It also indicates the thinking of the Court on important issues concerning juveniles.

Kent, a 16-year-old, was arrested and charged with rape, six counts of housebreaking, and robbery. The juvenile court in Washington, D.C., in accordance with a statute, waived its jurisdiction over Kent, who was then transferred to the adult criminal court for further proceedings. Kent had requested a hearing on the issue of whether he should be transferred. His attorney requested the social service file used by the court in the transfer decision. Both requests were refused.

Although the D. C. statute required a full investigation prior to waiver of a juvenile to adult court, the juvenile court judge did not state any findings of facts; nor did he give reasons for his decision to transfer Kent to the criminal court, which might lead one to think a full investigation did not occur.

Kent was indicted by a grand jury and tried in a criminal court. A jury found him not guilty by reason of insanity on the rape charge and guilty on the other charges. He was sentenced to serve from 5 to 15 years on each count, for a total of 30 to 90 years in prison. Kent appealed his case. The first appellate court affirmed; the Supreme Court reversed. The Court agreed that juvenile courts need great latitude in juvenile cases; it affirmed the doctrine of *parens patriae*, but with some exceptions, as the following excerpt indicates.[13]

Kent v. United States

We do not consider whether, on the merits, Kent should have been transferred; but there is no place in our system of law for reaching a result of such tremendous consequence without ceremony—without hearing, without effective assistance of counsel, without a statement of reasons. . . . The State is *parens patriae* rather than prosecuting attorney and judge. But the admonition to function in a "parental" relationship is not an invitation to procedural arbitrariness.

While there can be no doubt of the original laudable purpose of juvenile courts, studies and critiques in recent years raise serious questions as to whether actual performance measures well enough against theoretical purpose to make tolerable the immunity of the process from the reach of constitutional guaranties applicable to adults . . . there may be grounds for concern that the child receives the worst of both worlds; that he gets neither the protection accorded to adults nor the solicitous care and regenerative treatment postulated for children.

In re Gault The first juvenile case from a state court to be heard by the United States Supreme Court was *in re Gault*. A brief look at the facts of the case indicate the seriousness of the lack of due process in the juvenile court at that time. The events that led to *Gault* began on June 8, 1964, when 15-year-old Gerald Gault and a friend were taken into custody in Arizona after a Mrs. Cook had complained that two boys were making lewd phone calls to her. Gault's parents were not notified that their son, in effect, had been arrested. When they returned home from work that evening and found that Gerald was not there, they sent his brother to look for him and eventually got the information that he was in police custody.

Gault's parents were never shown the petition that was filed the next day. At the first hearing, attended by Gerald and his mother, Mrs. Cook did not testify; no written record was made of the proceedings. At the second hearing, Mrs. Gault asked for Mrs. Cook, but the judge said that would not be necessary. The decision of the judge was to commit Gerald to the State Industrial School until his majority. When the judge was asked on what basis he adjudicated Gerald delinquent, he said he was not sure of the exact section of the code. The section of the Arizona Criminal Code that escaped his memory defined as a misdemeanant a person who "in the presence or hearing of any woman or child . . . uses vulgar, abusive, or obscene language." For this offense a 15-year-old boy was committed to a state institution until his majority. The maximum legal penalty for an adult was a fine of from $5 to $50 or imprisonment for a maximum of 2 months. An adult but not a juvenile would be afforded due process at the trial.

The case was appealed to the U.S. Supreme Court, which reversed. The late Justice Fortas delivered the opinion for the majority. Counsel had raised six basic rights: notice of the charges, right to counsel, right to confrontation and cross-examination, privilege against self-incrimination, right to a transcript, and right to appellate review. The Supreme Court ruled only on the first four of these issues. The Court also limited the extension of procedural safeguards in the juvenile court to those proceedings that might result in the commitment of juveniles to an institution in which their freedom would be curtailed. Justice Fortas clearly excluded from the Court's decision the preadjudication and the postadjudication, or dispositional, stages. Justice Fortas reviewed the humanitarian philosophy of the juvenile court but said the reality of the juvenile court is an unfulfilled dream. What was designed to be a court that would always act in the best interests of the child had become an institution that was often arbitrary and unfair.[14]

In re Gault

Due process of law is the primary and indispensable foundation of individual freedom. . . . [T]he procedural rules which have been fashioned from the generality of due process are our instruments for the distillation and evaluation of essential facts from the conflicting welter of data that life and our adversary methods present. It is these instruments of due process which enhance the possibility that truth will emerge from the confrontation of opposing versions and conflicting data. "Procedure is to law what 'scientific method' is to science." . . .

Of course, it is not suggested that juvenile court judges should fail appropriately to take account, in their demeanor and conduct, of the emotional and psychological attitude of the juveniles with whom they are confronted.

Ultimately, however, we confront the reality of that portion of the Juvenile Court process with which we deal in this case. A boy is charged with misconduct. The boy is committed to an institution where he may be restrained of liberty for years. It is of no constitutional consequence . . . that the institution to which he is committed is called an Industrial School. The fact of the matter is that, however euphemistic the title, a "receiving home" or an "industrial school" for juveniles is an institution of confinement in which the child is incarcerated for a greater or lesser time. His world becomes "a building with whitewashed walls, regimented routine and institutional hours. . . ." Instead of mother and father and sisters and brothers and friends and classmates, his world is peopled by guards, custodians, state employees, and "delinquents" confined with him for anything from waywardness to rape and homicide.

In view of this, it would be extraordinary if our Constitution did not require the procedural regularity and the exercise of care implied in the phrase "due process." Under our constitution, the condition of being a boy does not justify a kangaroo court.

In re Winship In 1969, in *in re Winship*, the Supreme Court considered whether the proceedings in juvenile court required the same standard of proof as in the adult criminal court, where the requirement is **beyond a reasonable doubt** or whether a lesser standard could be used. The court applied the standard of beyond a reasonable doubt, concluding that "the observance of the standard of proof beyond a reasonable doubt will not compel the States to abandon or displace any of the substantive benefits of the juvenile process."[15]

McKeiver v. Pennsylvania In 1971, the Court refused to extend to juvenile court proceedings the right to a trial by jury. *McKeiver v. Pennsylvania* was a consolidation of several cases from two states, South Carolina and Pennsylvania. The Court emphasized that the underlying reasons for its decisions in *Gault* and *Winship* was the principle of fundamental fairness. When the issue is one of fact finding, elements of due process must be present.

> But one cannot say that in our legal system the jury is a necessary component of accurate fact finding. There is much to be said for it, to be sure, but we have been content to pursue other ways for determining facts.[16]

The Court fully recognized that the juvenile court has not been a great success, but it also concluded that the court should not become a full adversary court like the criminal court. Requiring a jury might put an end to "what has been the idealistic prospect of an intimate, informal protective proceeding." Requiring a jury in juvenile proceedings would not enhance fact finding; nor would it remedy the defects of the system.

> Meager as has been the hoped-for advance in the juvenile field, the alternative would be regressive, would lose what has been gained, and would tend once again to place the juvenile squarely in the routine of the criminal process.

The Court left open the possibility for state courts to experiment, inviting them to try trial by jury in juvenile proceedings, but refusing to require that they do so.[17]

Breed v. Jones In *Breed v. Jones*, decided in 1975, the Supreme Court held that the constitutional provision that defendants may not be tried twice for the same offense applies to juveniles. Breed, 17, was apprehended for committing acts while armed with a deadly weapon. He was adjudicated in the juvenile court, which found the allegations to be true. At the hearing to determine disposition, the court indicated that it intended to find Breed "not . . . amenable to the care, treatment and training program available through the facilities of the juvenile court," as required by the statute. He therefore was transferred to criminal court, where he was tried and found guilty of robbery in the first degree.

Breed argued that the transfer to criminal court after a hearing and decision on the facts in a juvenile court subjected him to two trials on the same offense. The Supreme Court agreed.

> Breed was subjected to the burden of two trials for the same offense; he was twice put to the task of marshaling his resources against those of the State, twice subjected to the "heavy personal strain" which such an experience represents.[18]

Schall v. Martin   In 1984 in *Schall v. Martin*, the Supreme Court upheld the New York statute that provided for preventive detention of juveniles. Preventive detention, said the Court, fulfills a legitimate state interest of protecting society and juveniles by detaining those who might be dangerous to society or to themselves.

In *Schall v. Martin*, the Court reiterated its belief in the fundamental fairness doctrine and the doctrine of *parens patriae*, indicating that it was trying to strike a balance between the juvenile's right to freedom pending trial and the right of society to be protected. The juveniles in *Martin* were apprehended for serious crimes. According to the Court, the period of preventive detention was brief and followed proper procedural safeguards. Three justices strongly disagreed with the Court's decision.[19] Other Supreme Court decisions are discussed later with the issues they involve, such as detention and capital punishment.

THE JUVENILE COURT PROCESS

In this section we look more closely at the way the juvenile system operates. Procedures differ somewhat from jurisdiction to jurisdiction, but this discussion involves the procedures that generally occur. Figure 17.4 diagrams the various steps in the system and should be used as a reference for this discussion.

Prehearing Procedures

Referrals   Juveniles may be referred to the juvenile justice system in various ways. Whereas 84 percent are referred by law enforcement agencies, other referrals come from parents, relatives, schools, probation officers, other courts, and miscellaneous other sources. Of these referrals, although most are for property offenses, 17 percent are for status offenses, as indicated in Spotlight 17.2.

Police Office Investigation   After a referral has been made, the police have observed delinquent behavior, or an offense has been reported and juve-

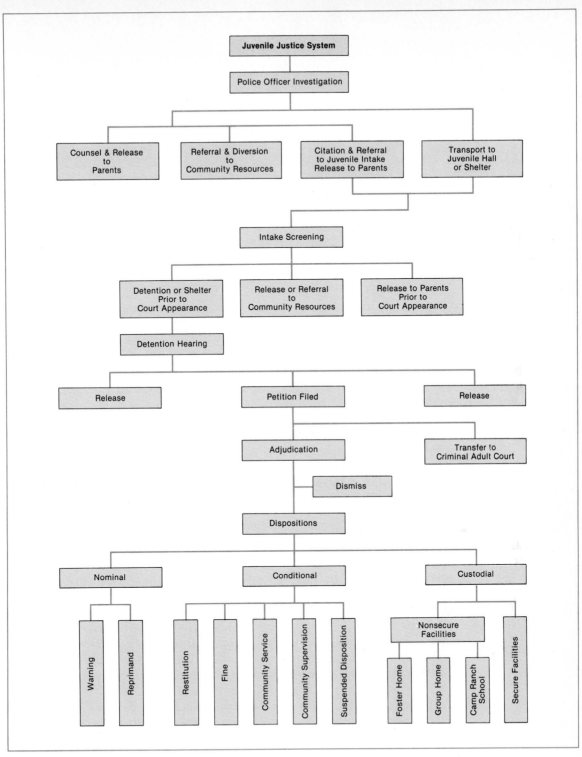

FIGURE 17.4
The Juvenile Justice System. *Source:* National Advisory Committee on Criminal
Justice Standards and Goals, *Juvenile Justice and Delinquency Prevention: Report of
the Task Force on Juvenile Justice and Delinquency Prevention* (Washington, D.C.: U.S.
Government Printing Office, 1976), p. 9.

11% Crimes against persons

Criminal homicide	1%
Forcible rape	2
Robbery	17
Aggravated assault	20
Simple assault	59
	100%

46% Crimes against property

Burglary	25%
Larceny	47
Motor vehicle theft	5
Arson	1
Vandalism and trespassing	19
Stolen property offenses	3
	100%

5% Drug offenses   100%

21% Offenses against public order

Weapons offenses	6%
Sex offenses	6
Drunkenness and disorderly conduct	23
Contempt, probation, and parole violations	21
Other	44
	100%

17% Status offenses

Running away	28%
Truancy and curfew violations	21
Ungovernability	28
Liquor violations	23
	100%

100% Total all offenses

Source: Bureau of Justice Statistics, *Report to the Nation on Crime and Justice*, 2d ed. (Washington, D.C.: U.S. Department of Justice, 1988), p. 78.

niles are suspected, the police may begin surveillance and investigation. There is no way of knowing how many cases are handled by the police without any formal action being taken. Most juveniles will not be taken into custody upon apprehension by police. Police are not the only people who may take children into custody. Officials in child protective services, probation officers, family services, and youth services also may take children into custody in many jurisdictions.

Taking the Juvenile into Custody   Historically, there probably were few guidelines for taking juveniles into **custody.** In the *Gault* case, the Supreme Court specifically excluded prejudicial activities from the due process requirements of that case. Some lower courts have held that taking a juvenile into custody is not an arrest, and therefore the due process requirements that must be observed in the arrest of an adult are not applicable. Most courts appear to consider the process of taking a juvenile into custody an arrest that should be accompanied by due process requirements.

One thing is clear, however: because juvenile proceedings are not regarded as criminal in nature, the police exercise considerably more discretion in dealing with juveniles than they exercise in dealing with adults.[20]

Search and Seizure   Most state courts have interpreted *Gault's* fundamental fairness test to mean that the constitutional prohibition against unreasonable searches and seizures applies to juvenile proceedings. Some states

CAREERS IN CRIMINAL JUSTICE

SUE TITUS REID
Dean and Professor, School of Criminology, Florida State University
PREVIOUS POSITION: Formerly law school associate dean and professor

JAMES D. WHITE
Associate Professor of Criminology, Attorney, Reserve Police Officer

BERNARD R. COHEN
Chief, Bureau of Staff Development, Florida Department of Corrections
PREVIOUS POSITIONS: Deputy Circuit Administrator for Probation and Parole Services; Inmate Classification Supervisor, State Prison

EDDIE LARACUENTE
Case Management Coordinator, Federal Correctional Institute
PREVIOUS POSITIONS: Correctional Officer; Correctional Treatment Specialist; Unit Manager

KENNETH L. BERGSTROM
Bank Director of Security
PREVIOUS POSITION: Police Officer

PEARL VANN
Correctional Officer

CHARLES E. MINER, JR.
Judge, First District
Court of Appeal,
Florida
PREVIOUS POSITIONS:
Prosecutor; Defense
Counsel; Trial Judge;
Police Officer;
Investigator

J. D. LAMER
Warden, Federal Correctional Institute
PREVIOUS POSITIONS: Deputy Regional
Director; Associate Warden;
Correctional Counselor;
Correctional Officer

WINNIE WENTWORTH
Judge, First District Court of Appeal
Florida
PREVIOUS POSITIONS: Commissioner
of Industrial Relations (worker's
compensation appellate body); Assistant
Attorney General, Tax Division Chief;
General Counsel, Department of
Education; Law Clerk, Florida Supreme
Court

PHIL WELSH
Inmate Classification
Administrator,
Department of
Corrections

JOHN R. L. ISAACS XV *(left)*
Reading Teacher, Federal Correctional Institute

SHIRLEY D. MINTER *(center left)*
Unit Manager, Federal Correctional Institute
PREVIOUS POSITIONS: Case Manager; Teacher; Activities Coordinator;
Correctional Officer

DAVID E. RIDDLE *(center right)*
Case Manager, Federal Correctional Institute
PREVIOUS POSITIONS: Correctional Officer; Community Probation Officer

OBIE CONDRY, JR. *(right)*
Correctional Counselor
PREVIOUS POSITIONS: Correctional Officer; Correctional Supervisor

F. MICHELLE TAYLOR
Graduate Assistant
PREVIOUS POSITIONS: Graduate
Assistant/Instructor; Guardian Ad
Litem; Instructor of Criminal Justice;
Advisor: Society of Criminal Justice

JACK C. STEELE
Securex, Inc.

JAMES T. "TIM" MOORE
Commissioner, Florida
Department of Law Enforcement
PREVIOUS POSITIONS: Criminal
Information Input Technician;
Criminal Justice Reporting
Systems Specialist; Standards
and Training Specialist;
Director, Division of Staff
Services; Deputy Director,
Division of Staff Services;
Deputy Commissioner

MELVIN L. TUCKER
Chief of Police,
Tallahassee, Florida
Previous Position:
FBI Agent

DEBRA RILEY
Police Officer, Crime Prevention Unit

MARK WHEELER and BRIX
K-9 Handler and Tactical Apprehension
and Control Team (T.A.C.) K-9
Previous Training: DEA Narcotics
School, K-9 Narcotics School, Basic
and Advanced Police K-9 School

JOSEPH W. HATCHETT
United States Circuit Judge—11th Circuit
PREVIOUS POSITIONS: Assistant United
States Attorney; United States Magistrate;
Justice, Supreme Court of Florida

CURT McKENZIE
Lieutenant, Leon County Jail

HOWARD SCHLEICH
Captain, Leon County
Jail

JOANN VAN METER
Lieutenant; Watch Commander of Police Patrol Division
PREVIOUS POSITIONS: Sergeant, Criminal Investigations of Sex Crimes and Child Abuse; Crime Prevention Officer; Homicide Investigator; Undercover Drug Operative

SUE CARTER COLLINS
Police Legal Advisor
PREVIOUS POSITIONS: Correctional Officer; Deputy Sheriff; Felony Investigator for Public Defender's Office; Assistant Public Defender; Assistant State Attorney

have incorporated exclusionary rules into their statutes; thus, evidence seized illegally in juvenile cases may not be admitted as evidence against those juveniles. The issue of unreasonable searches and seizures has been raised in the context of searches that are unique to juveniles: searches of their school lockers. In 1985, in *New Jersey v. T.L.O.*, the Supreme Court gave some insight into what they might do in a locker search incident.

T.L.O. and another girl were observed smoking cigarettes in the girls' rest room. The teacher who made this observation reported the violation of school rules and the girls to the assistant principal's office. The girls denied that they smoked, but when the assistant principal requested to see their purses, he saw a package of cigarettes clearly visible. He removed the package and found marijuana paraphernalia, $40.98 in single bills and change, and a letter from T.L.O. to a friend. The letter requested the friend to sell marijuana at the school. The police were then summoned.[21]

The Supreme Court held that the Fourth Amendment does apply to school searches. However, the interest of the school in preventing delinquency must be balanced against the student's right to privacy. The Court adopted a reasonableness test; the search is justified if a teacher has reasonable grounds to believe that a student has violated the law or the rules of the school. The Court thought the search was reasonable in *T.L.O.*

Whether other school searches are reasonable will have to be determined on the basis of the facts of each case. But it is clear that the Court does not require that, before teachers conduct a lawful search, they must have a warrant or they must have probable cause to believe that a law has been violated. Violation of school rules will constitute sufficient reason for a legal search.

There are many unanswered questions regarding school searches. About the only general statement that can be made is that those searches do not require all of the procedures required in adult cases. It also appears that the issue is not the age of the juvenile, but the status of being a student. Any search that would otherwise be unreasonable would not be so if the juvenile consented to the search. The consent by juveniles must be voluntary and knowledgeable, the same rules that apply to adults who consent to searches.

Detention   Most juveniles who are taken into custody are taken without a summons or a warrant. Police then face the problem of what to do with the persons in their custody. As Table 17.1 shows, official arrest data for 1987 indicate that police released 30.3 percent of the juvenile offenders they took into custody; 62 percent were referred to juvenile court jurisdiction.

Many states have a statutory requirement that, when juveniles are taken into custody, their parents must be notified immediately. Most are released to their parents; when that is not possible or not reasonable, most jurisdictions require that juveniles be placed in special **detention centers** provided for juveniles.

The first national study of juvenile detention for more than a decade found fundamental and substantial changes had occurred in the use of juvenile detention facilities. Despite the consensus of professionals that such facilities should be used primarily to detain only those juveniles who

TABLE 17.1

Police Disposition of Juvenile Offenders Taken
into Custody, 1987

Total All Agencies	1,172,585 (100%)
Handled within department and released	355,602 (30.3%)
Referred to juvenile court jurisdiction	726,634 (62.0%)
Referred to welfare agency	16,807 (1.4%)
Referred to other police agency	12,289 (1.0%)
Referred to criminal or adult court	61,253 (5.2%)

Source: Federal Bureau of Investigation, *Uniform Crime Reports, 1987* (Washington, D.C.: U.S. Government Printing Office, 1988), p. 240, footnotes omitted.

present a substantial threat to society's safety, the study found that juvenile detention facilities are being used as "short-term prisons for juveniles."

> These developments suggest that juvenile detention deserves much more public attention; we should not tolerate the perpetuation of detention centers as the "hidden closets" that conceal the failure of family, school, church, and other social institutions.[22]

As noted earlier in this chapter, the Supreme Court in *Schall v. Martin* upheld detaining juveniles for preventive detention. After noting that juveniles have a substantial interest in liberty, the Court nevertheless said, "But that interest must be qualified by the recognition that juveniles, unlike adults, are always in some form of custody." The Court reiterated its belief that courts have special powers over children as compared to adults. "[C]hildren, by definition, are not assumed to have the capacity to take care of themselves" and therefore, according to the Court, they need additional protection. Preventive detention of juveniles therefore may be appropriate to protect the juveniles themselves, not just to protect society, as in the case of preventive detention of adults, which the Court upheld in 1987.[23]

Juveniles in Jails   The power to detain juveniles, however, does not mean the power to detain them in jails rather than in special juvenile detention facilities. Yet, approximately 300,000 juveniles are detained in adult jail facilities each year. Nearly 25 percent of these have been accused of only status offenses, such as truancy and running away from home. Two-thirds of these juveniles will be released after their court hearings; but they will have suffered the harmful effects of being incarcerated in adult facilities before that decision. Some are raped; others commit suicide. "For every 100,000 juveniles placed in adult jails, 12 will commit suicide. This is eight times higher than the rate of suicide in secure juvenile detention centers.[24]

The Juvenile Justice and Delinquency Prevention Act, passed by Congress in 1974 and amended in 1977, 1980, and 1984, states that funds will

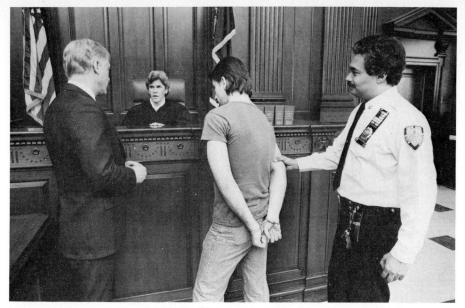

In some instances, police decide that it is necessary to take the juvenile into court handcuffed if the juvenile appears to be dangerous to himself or others. (Russ Kinne/Comstock)

be provided for juvenile justice and delinquency projects and programs to those states that comply with the mandates of the statute. Among other provisions is the phasing out of juvenile detention in adult jails. However, progress has been slow, with 1988 data indicating that 40 states are still not in compliance with the federal mandate.[25]

In 1987 a federal court in Iowa upheld the right of juveniles to bring legal action for the enforcement of the federal mandate. The case, *Hendrickson v. Griggs,* involves procedural issues beyond the scope of this chapter, but it is a step toward enforcing the federal mandate that requires, among other provisions, that juveniles be removed from adult jails.[26] Some states also have taken measures to prohibit jailing juveniles. In 1986, California, which had previously jailed large numbers of juveniles, enacted legislation prohibiting detaining juveniles in jails and lockups.[27]

On the other hand, one of the most progressive states in the criminal justice area, Minnesota, has not taken action to reduce the large number of juveniles detained in jails.

> Moreover, there is substantial opposition to banning the incarceration of juveniles in adult facilities by a large and well-organized segment of the professional juvenile justice community and by influential public interest organizations.[28]

Release on Bail Some states have granted juveniles the right to release on bail; others have denied that right; and still others have decided that it is not an issue because of the provision of special facilities for the detention of juveniles.

Despite efforts to keep juveniles out of jails, many are still held in jails pending processing of their cases. (Richard Hutchings/Photo Researchers)

Police Interrogation   Originally, it was assumed it would be therapeutic for children to confess what they had done; juveniles therefore had few procedural protections concerning police interrogation. Today the rule is that the confessions of juveniles may be used against them in court, provided those confessions are made voluntarily.

In 1971 when the Court decided *McKeiver*, it stated in a footnote that although it had not formally held that the *Miranda* case applies to juveniles, it was assuming the *Miranda* principles were fully applicable to the proceedings in *McKeiver*, despite the Court's holding in *McKeiver* that the juvenile is not entitled to all procedures of the criminal trial. Courts ruling on the issues generally have held that *Miranda* does apply to juvenile cases. The issues arise over whether juveniles may waive their *Miranda* rights. Some courts have refused to accept a juvenile waiver without parental guidance. Others have held that children cannot waive complicated legal rights, and thus it is permissible for police to question children in custody provided they do so in a fair manner.

Lineups, Showups, Fingerprints, and Pictures   Most statutes covering juvenile proceedings attempt to protect juveniles from some of the harshness of the criminal court and therefore prohibit publication of the pictures of suspects and the taking of fingerprints. The use of lineups and showups, however, has been left to the courts, which generally have held that the same standards applicable to adults must be applied in juvenile proceedings.[29]

Diversion   One method of decreasing the number of people who are incarcerated is to divert them from the criminal justice system to other facilities and programs.

Diversion literally means to turn aside or alter the nature of things. In the juvenile system diversion was originally thought to be a process that would divert juveniles from official juvenile or criminal proceedings. They would be referred out of those systems before a hearing. The diagram in Figure 17.4 points out that after investigation by a police officer, one of the alternatives is to refer and divert the juvenile to community resources.

Diversion in the juvenile field gained momentum after the 1967 President's Commission emphasized the need for this approach. In the 1970s, however, critics began to see the need for careful evaluation of diversion programs, noting that in many cases rather than diversion the result was net widening. Juveniles who would not have been processed in the system previously were now brought in under the disguise of diversion.[30]

After a thorough study of the literature evaluating diversion programs, Thomas G. Blomberg reached the conclusion that findings were "mixed and fragmented." Blomberg proposed a multigoal evaluation approach that would analyze the positive and negative results of juvenile diversion. Hesitant to abandon the concept of diversion, Blomberg emphasized:

> Certainly the net-widening results associated with diversion programs do not demonstrate failure of the diversion concept, but demonstrate instead failure in the implementation of diversion programs. As a result, diversion cannot as of yet be considered a failure or a success.[31]

Police officers may decide that questioning the juvenile on the scene is sufficient and not take him or her into custody. (Ed Lettau/ Photo Researchers)

Intake Screening   Figure 17.4 indicates the alternatives available at the intake screening stage of the juvenile justice process. Intake screening is supposed to screen out the juveniles who should be diverted; they may be released or referred to community agencies. Another alternative at intake is to release the juvenile to his or her parents pending the hearing. A third alternative is to detain (or continue detention should the juvenile already be in detention custody) the juvenile before the hearing.

A recent study of 620 youth referred to the juvenile court indicated that 23 percent were dropped at intake; 12 percent were handled informally, 15 percent were granted consent decrees, and 50 percent were referred for judicial court processing. The study also indicated that some of the cases dismissed involved serious offenses and noted that other research confirmed that it is not unusual for serious juvenile offense cases to be dismissed.[32]

Intake decisions are made by intake officers, who often are probation officers. Theoretically, they conduct an investigation before making the intake decision, but with heavy caseloads, this investigation may not be conducted thoroughly, if at all. Some states have placed statutory requirements on the intake officer regarding referrals out of the system or dismissals. For example, in some jurisdictions the intake officer may not dismiss a case without the written permission of the prosecutor. In others, the case may not be dismissed or diverted if the complaining witness insists that formal action proceed beyond this stage.

Preliminary Inquiry   If the child is detained with the intent that a petition will be filed to bring formal procedures, a hearing usually is held to determine whether there is reason to continue with the case. This is true whether the juvenile is being held as a dependent and neglected child or for alleged delinquency. The hearing must be held within a reasonable period after detention begins, but it does not involve all of the specific procedural safeguards.

Filing of the Petition   After the preliminary inquiry or hearing, the juvenile may be released from detention, or the case may be dismissed, in which case the child is dismissed. If there is no dismissal, the case may then proceed only with the filing of a **petition,** the formal document for filing against a juvenile in the juvenile system. This petition is in contrast to a grand jury indictment or a prosecutor's presentment in the adult criminal court.

The *Gault* case requires that juveniles and their parents must be given adequate notice of the charges and of the proceedings to follow. Most states require that the adjudicatory hearing be held within a specified period after the petition. If this does not occur, in some jurisdictions the case must be dismissed.

The Plea   Juveniles may admit or deny guilt; most admit that they committed the acts of which they are accused. This plea must be a knowing and voluntary one; and juveniles have the right to counsel if they are involved in proceedings that could lead to confinement in an institution.

After *Kent*, juvenile court statutes began to permit juveniles some discovery procedures. **Discovery** involves the right to find out what the opposing side is going to use in the case. This information is necessary for the juvenile and his or her attorney to know how best to proceed with the case, and it might significantly affect the juvenile's decision whether to admit or deny the allegations.

The Juvenile Court Hearing

The juvenile court hearing is for determining whether the juvenile is in need of supervision or whether the juvenile has committed an act over which the court has jurisdiction. If so, the Court must consider what to do with the juvenile.

Role of the Prosecutor   In the traditional juvenile court system, there was no place for a prosecutor. The proceedings were not adversarial; all parties were thought to be acting in the best interests of the child. Decisions whether to proceed would be made by intake officers.

In reality, however—whether the person is called an intake officer or a prosecutor—a person permitted to decide who will or will not be processed in the system has considerable power. Plea bargaining, a process used to determine most cases in the criminal court but thought to be inappropriate to juvenile proceedings, will take place. The question is not whether prosecutors will have power, but how much power they will have. Some jurisdictions restrict their power to dismiss the case after the petition is filed, but even then they have considerable discretion over determining in the first place whether to proceed with cases referred by the police or others.

Role of the Defense Attorney The defense attorney's primary function in a juvenile case is to make sure that the constitutional rights of the juvenile are protected during all of the proceedings. The attorney should be familiar with all the facts of the case and be prepared to present the defense at the hearing. The lack of formality in the hearing does not mean the defense is any less important in a juvenile than in a criminal court hearing.

The relationship between prosecutors and defense attorneys in the juvenile system is similar to the relationship they share in the criminal court system. They may serve as checks on the potential abuse of power, or they may cooperate to the point of violating the rights of juveniles. They also may serve diligently and competently, with the best interests of juveniles as their goals. But even those who take that perspective often find their goals thwarted by a system that has inadequate resources and insufficient personnel.

Role of the Probation Officer Another important person in the juvenile system is the probation officer, who will be actively involved in gathering information and evidence for the hearing and disposition of the case. Because the same officers will be involved in the supervision of juveniles placed on probation, the important question arises of whether probation officers can serve the dual function. Are they surveillance personnel or treatment personnel? What attitude might juveniles have toward people who are supposed to be counseling them when they realize those same persons were partly responsible for their being processed through the juvenile court?

Presentation of the Evidence and Adjudication The juvenile hearing may be much less formal than that of the criminal court, but the same general procedures take place. The prosecutor presents the evidence against the juvenile; the defense has an opportunity to cross-examine the witnesses, and some rules of evidence prevail. Hearsay evidence may be presented in a juvenile hearing, in contrast to an adult trial. Evidence is presented to the judge and not to a jury unless the jurisdiction provides for a trial by jury and the juvenile did not waive the right.

At the end of the presentation of evidence, there will be an adjudication of whether the juvenile did what he or she was accused of doing. Technically, the terms *guilty* and *not guilty* are not used in juvenile proceedings, although the obvious purpose is to determine whether the alleged acts actually were committed. To support a finding of responsibility, the evidence must be sufficient to convince the judge beyond a reasonable doubt.

Dispositions In traditional language, juveniles are not sentenced; dispositions are made. Dispositions tend to be indeterminate, although the court loses jurisdiction over the child when the child reaches the age of majority. Several types of dispositions are available. Figure 17.4 indicates that the court may take one of three routes. Nominal dispositions such as warnings and reprimands may be made. Conditional dispositions are similar to those in criminal courts: restitution, fine, community service, suspended disposition, or community supervision (probation). A final method of disposition is to place juveniles in secure or nonsecure facilities.

Particular attention should be given at this point to the use of restitution among juveniles, for it represents one of the most significant recent changes in disposition of juvenile cases. Anne L. Schneider's research on juvenile restitution notes that in 1977 fewer than 15 formal programs could be identified, compared to over 400 in 1985.[33] Schneider found some support for the assumption that juveniles required to pay restitution, compared to those sentenced in some other way, are less likely to be apprehended for further delinquent or criminal acts. But she emphasized that more research needs to be conducted on the relationship between recidivism and juvenile (and for that matter adult) restitution.[34]

What procedures must be followed at the disposition hearing? In *Gault*, the Supreme Court specifically stated that it was not answering the question of what due process rights apply to the pre- or postadjudicatory hearing stage of the juvenile process. The procedures required therefore are required by state statutes or by state court decision, and they vary from state to state. Since most juvenile cases do not involve a dispute over the facts, the disposition hearing becomes the most significant part of the process, and the right to counsel is important. Normally it is a separate hearing from that of adjudication, and it will be preceded by an investigative report, or social report, on which the disposition may be based.

The social report is crucial to the philosophy that juveniles are to be treated individually and that it is possible to rehabilitate them. The social study should include any information that might have a bearing on assessing the needs of the particular child. The types of evidence that may be admitted at the dispositional stage are much broader than those permitted at the adjudicatory hearing.

Rod Matthews, 15, listens in adult court as the jury delivers a guilty charge of second degree murder. Matthews was sentenced to life in prison for the beating death of his classmate. (UPI Bettmann Newsphotos)

Right to Appeal   In *Gault*, the Court refused to rule that there is a constitutional right to appeal from a juvenile court decision, but since *Gault* all jurisdictions have by statute made some provisions for appeal.

The Juvenile in the Criminal Court

Most states provide that in certain cases juveniles may be tried in criminal courts. This may be permitted because both courts have jurisdiction, the offenses are excluded from the jurisdiction of the juvenile court, or there is a waiver from the juvenile to the criminal court. This last procedure, also called *transfer* or **certification**, means just what the words say: the juvenile court waives jurisdiction, the case is transferred from the juvenile to the criminal court, or the court certifies that the juvenile should be tried as an adult. When certification occurs, the juvenile will go through the same procedures and have the same constitutional rights as adults tried in criminal courts. Waiver or certification does not occur often. In 1987, 3,058 juvenile cases in 23 states were disposed of by adult courts. California accounted for 73.6 percent of those cases.[35]

Certification is extremely important because it may result in far more severe consequences to the juvenile than if he or she had remained under the juvenile court's jurisdiction. The procedures that must be followed differ from state to state. In some states the prosecutor makes the decision; in others the decision is made by the juvenile court judge. Here are some general observations:

> Most jurisdictions require that the child be over a certain age and be charged with a particularly serious offense before jurisdiction may be waived.
>
> A number of other states permit waiver of jurisdiction over children above a certain age, without regard to the nature of the offense charged.
>
> Some other jurisdictions placed no limitations on waiver, permitting waiver without regard to the age of the child or the nature of the offense.
>
> Finally, a number of states permit waiver based on a combination of these factors.[36]

The procedural requirements for waiver were articulated by the Supreme Court in the *Kent* case. Although that case applied only to the statute in question in Washington, D.C., most courts have interpreted *Kent* as stating the minimum due process requirements for transfer of a juvenile from the juvenile court to the criminal court. The juvenile is entitled to a hearing on the question of transfer, and the right to counsel attaches to that hearing. Upon request, counsel must be given access to the social record that the court has compiled on the juvenile. If jurisdiction is waived, the juvenile must be given a statement of the reasons for the waiver.

Some statutes give jurisdiction to criminal courts over juveniles who commit specified serious crimes, such as murder, but permit the criminal court to transfer the case to juvenile court. New York is an example. Under the New York statute, children age 13 or older who are charged with second-degree murder and children 14 or older who are charged with any one of a number of serious crimes (including burglary, sodomy in the first degree, aggravated sexual abuse, manslaughter in the first degree, murder, rape, and robbery) are under the exclusive jurisdiction of the criminal court. But the criminal court may transfer the case to the juvenile court by a process known as *reverse certification*.[37]

SPECIAL SENTENCING OF VIOLENT YOUNG JUVENILES

Texas enacted legislation that provides a third type of system for handling young juveniles who commit serious crimes. The 1987 Texas statute is aimed at 13- and 14-year-olds who commit serious crimes. They are below the 15-year minimum age for transfer of cases to the criminal court, but the seriousness of their offenses, it is argued, warrants harsher treatment than is available through the juvenile court.

The Texas statute thus provides that a juvenile who has been adju-

Many violent crimes are committed by juveniles. Here, police officers apprehend a teenager who was accused of armed robbery and auto theft. He was also driving without a license, and a loaded, semiautomatic pistol was found in the car. (Alan Byrd/Tallahasse Democrat)

dicated delinquent for one of six serious, violent offenses (capital murder, murder, aggravated sexual assault, aggravated kidnapping, deadly assault on a law enforcement or corrections officer or a court participant, and attempted capital murder) may be sentenced to up to 30 years. The first year will be spent in those facilities designed for juveniles and operated by the Texas Youth Commission (TYC).

A juvenile who is not paroled by the TYC by the time he or she reaches the age of majority (18), may be transferred to the jurisdiction of the Texas Department of Corrections (TDC) to serve the remainder of the term. This system permits an alternative in those cases in which the prosecutor prefers not to ask for transfer of the case to the criminal court but thinks the crime warrants harsher punishment than would be available under traditional juvenile court approaches.[38]

THE JUVENILE IN CORRECTIONS

In 1987, 80,869 juveniles were under state care in residential or nonresidential facilities. Of the juveniles released from state care in 1987, the average stay had been 11 months, ranging from a high of 35 months in Massachusetts to a low of 4 months in Minnesota.[39] Characteristics of youth in custody in 1987 are reported in Spotlight 17.3, which contains information on the first Bureau of Justice Statistics (BJS) survey of youth confined in long-term institutions.

SPOTLIGHT 17.3
SURVEY OF YOUTH IN CUSTODY, 1987

Results from a nationally representative survey of juveniles and young adults in long-term, State-operated juvenile institutions indicate that nearly 40% were being held for a violent offense. More than 60% used drugs regularly, and almost 40% were under the influence of drugs at the time of their offense. Less than a third lived with both parents while they were growing up. More than half of all residents in these institutions reported that a family member had been incarcerated at some time in the past.

The 1987 survey was based on personal interviews with a nationally representative sample of 2,621 residents from among the more than 25,000 individuals confined in long-term, State-operated juvenile institutions. Interviews were carried out in 50 institutions in 26 States. Primarily as a result of the inclusion of California's Youth Authority facilities, more than a quarter of the sample was made up of young adults who are age 18 and older. For the purposes of this report, this older population will be referred to as young adults, while those less than the age of 18 will be referred to as juveniles. All residents regardless of age will be referred to as youth. . . .

Other findings from the survey include the following:

- An estimated 60.5% of the juveniles and young adults were between the ages of 15 and 17; 12.4% were age 14 or younger; and 27.2% were 18 years of age or older.
- Among all the juveniles and young adults held in long-term, State-operated juvenile institutions, 93.1% were male. An estimated 53.1% were white; 41.1% were black; and 5.7% were American Indians, Asians, Alaska Natives, or Pacific Islanders. An estimated 18.9% were of Hispanic origin.

- About 70% of the juveniles and young adults did not live with both parents while they were growing up. More than half (54%) reported having primarily lived in a single-parent family.
- Among the juveniles in these facilities, 39.3% were held for a violent offense, 45.6% for a property offense, 5.6% for a drug offense, and 7.2% for a public-order offense. Just over 2% were confined for a juvenile status offense, such as truancy, running away, or incorrigibility.
- Almost 43% of the juveniles had been arrested more than 5 times, with over 20% of them having been arrested more than 10 times in the past.
- Approximately 4 of 5 juveniles (82.2%) reported previously having been on probation, and 3 of 5 (58.5%) reported having been committed to a correctional institution at least once in the past.
- An estimated 97% of all juveniles and 98% of the young adults were found to have a current or prior violent offense or to have previously been on probation or sent to a correctional institution.
- This majority of the juveniles held for violent offenses reported that their victims were male (58.1%), white (61.6%), and under the age of 21 (54.2%). Over 40% of these victims were strangers to the offender, and approximately 12% were relatives.
- More than 80% of the residents reported the prior use of an illegal drug. Almost 40% of those who had previously used drugs began using drugs before the age of 12.
- Nearly half (47.6%) of the juveniles reported that they were under the influence of either drugs or alcohol at the time of their current offense.

Source: Allen J. Beck et al., Bureau of Justice Statistics (Washington, D.C.: U.S. Department of Justice, September 1988), p. 1, footnote omitted.

Historical Background of Closed Institutions

Placement of juveniles in closed institutions is a relatively new practice. In the 1700s and early 1800s, it was thought that the family, the church, and other social institutions should handle juvenile delinquents. Jail was the only form of incarceration and it was primarily used for detention pending trial. From 1790 to 1830, the traditional forms of social control began to break down as mobility and town sizes increased. Belief in sin as the cause of delinquency was replaced by a belief in community disorganization. Some method was needed whereby juveniles could be put back into an orderly life. It was decided that the institution, the house of refuge, the well-ordered asylum patterned after the family structure, was the answer.

The institutional model was used for juveniles, adult criminals, the aged, the mentally ill, orphans, unwed mothers, and vagrants. By institutionalizing these persons, their lives could once again become ordered as they were removed from the corruption of society. Life in the total institution was characterized by routine, head counts, bells to signal the beginning and the end of activities, and marching to all activities.[40]

By the 1850s many people were admitting that custody was all the institutions offered. Overcrowding, lack of adequate staff, and heterogeneous populations led to the realization that institutionalization was not accomplishing its purpose. The next concept for juveniles was the **training school**, often built around a cottage system. It was thought that cottage parents would create a homelike atmosphere. Hard work, especially farm work, was emphasized.

Types of Institutions for Juveniles

Despite the movement toward diversion of juveniles from closed institutions, today most juveniles who are under the care and custody of the state are confined in public institutions or in the traditional training school. Detention centers and shelters are used to confine juveniles who have been referred to the juvenile court and are awaiting disposition by that court. These facilities are used for detention of juveniles who cannot be detained in their own homes. A child who is to be placed in a correctional institution, may be held temporarily in a reception or diagnostic center, pending a decision concerning which institution would mean the best placement for the child. Our primary concern here is with the facilities in which the juveniles are eventually placed for their confinement, and those are of three basic types.

The training school, which houses most of the confined juveniles, generally is the largest of the facilities. It was the first type of widely accepted facility for the confinement of juveniles, and it is the most secure. Some jurisdictions also operate other types of facilities that are less secure, such as ranches, forestry camps, or farms. These generally are located in rural areas and permit greater contact with the community than the training school.

The least physically secure facilities are group homes. Unlike foster homes, which are community-based facilities in which one or more juveniles live with a family, many group homes are really small institutions. Most are operated by a staff not a family. The cost per juvenile is twice as high for staff-operated group homes as for family-type group homes or foster care. They have been highly criticized as a poor substitute for family-operated group homes because they remove the positive influence of the family atmosphere.[41]

In many juvenile institutions an attempt has been made to make the facility as homelike as possible. A campuslike environment or cottage setting is not uncommon, with a small number of juveniles housed in each building along with cottage or house parents. Despite these efforts, the architecture of many of the facilities for juveniles reflects the premise that all who are confined there must face the same type of security as those few who actually need the secure environment. Security, of course, is very important, but the facilities should not preclude rehabilitation opportunities.

Treatment and Juvenile Corrections

Special facilities for juveniles originally were established to isolate them from the harmful effects of society and from incarcerated adults. Later, with the development of the juvenile court, the philosophy of treatment rather than punishment of the juvenile became predominant. Various commissions during the past century, however, have pointed out the failure of juvenile corrections to provide adequate services and programs to enable the implementation of this treatment philosophy. Recently the courts have entered the picture. They have required some elements of due process in the adjudication of juveniles, changes in the disciplinary handling of institutionalized juveniles, and changes in the degree and kinds of services provided in those institutions.

The assignment of juveniles to special facilities for the purpose of treatment, after juveniles have been through proceedings that do not involve all elements of due process, raises the critical issue of whether juveniles have a right to treatment programs while they are confined, as the goal of rehabilitation had provided the justification for a lack of due process in juvenile proceedings. The Supreme Court has discredited the practice of using the philosophy of rehabilitation to deny juveniles their basic constitutional rights, and it has acknowledged that rehabilitation has failed. Yet, the Court has indicated its support for retention of at least part of the *parens patriae* philosophy in juvenile proceedings.

Scholars and many courts have taken the position that, under the doctrine of *parens patriae*, juveniles have given up some of their constitutional rights in order to be processed through a system that is based on treatment not punishment. Therefore, the state must provide that treatment or relinquish custody of the child. The right to treatment also is based on cases involving the rights of the mentally ill who are confined.

The Supreme Court has not decided a case on the constitutional right to treatment for juveniles, although the opinion of the Court in *O'Conner v. Donaldson*, a case involving confinement of the mentally ill, indicates that the Court might not hold that juveniles have a constitutional right to treatment.[42] Some lower courts have held that juveniles have a statutory or constitutional right to treatment, but most of those cases that have not been reversed were decided prior to *O'Conner*.[43]

Special treatment programs, such as for alcohol abuse, may be more effective with juveniles than incarceration in correctional facilities. (Michael D. Sullivan/TexaStock)

Some of the earlier decisions, decided before *O'Conner*, have been reversed on appeal. An example is the case of *Morales v. Turman*, a Texas case that has been in the federal courts since 1973, when the lower court found numerous violations of statutory and constitutional rights of the children confined in the Texas juvenile system. The lower court held that the children had a constitutional right to treatment, but that conclusion was questioned by the federal appellate court, and the case is generally interpreted as not recognizing a constitutional right to treatment.[44]

A 1983 federal court rejected the constitutional right to treatment argument.

> We therefore agree . . . that, although rehabilitative training is no doubt desirable and sound as a matter of policy and perhaps of state law, plaintiffs have no constitutional right to that rehabilitative training.

The Supreme Court refused to hear the case, thus permitting the decision of the federal appellate court to stand.[45]

The Juvenile in the Community: Probation and Parole

Juveniles, like adults, may be released from institutions and placed on parole, usually called **aftercare** with juveniles. On January 1, 1987, 26,879 juveniles were under aftercare supervision in 43 jurisdictions.[46]

Historically, juveniles, like adult offenders, have had no right to early release, but most juveniles do not remain in confinement for long periods of time. They usually are released to aftercare, but the juvenile who violates the terms of that release, may be returned to confinement. The rules that the Supreme Court has applied to adult parole and probation revocation generally have been applied to juveniles, although some lower courts or statutes have granted juveniles more due process and some have granted less.

The type of aftercare of juveniles is important. Aftercare should begin with prerelease programs while the juvenile still is in confinement. There are two kinds of prerelease programs in juvenile institutions. In the first type, juveniles may be given furloughs or weekend passes to visit their families, thus permitting a gradual reentry into society. In the second type, the inmates may be moved to special cottages within the institution, where they live for a period of time with other inmates who are almost ready to be released and where special programs are provided to prepare them for that release. The length of the aftercare period will depend on the needs of each child.

Effect of Institutionalization on Juveniles

The Advisory Commission advocated that where possible, juvenile delinquents should be diverted from institutionalization. The commission concluded:

The failure of major juvenile and youth institutions to reduce crime is incontestable. Recidivism rates, imprecise as they may be, are notoriously high. The younger the person when entering an institution, the longer he is institutionalized, and the farther he progresses into the criminal justice system, the greater his chance of failure.[47]

The advisory commission emphasized that these institutions are places of punishment, and they do not have a significant effect on deterrence. They temporarily remove juveniles from society. In that sense, society is protected, but the changes in the offender during that incarceration are negative not positive. The institutions are geographically isolated, which hinders delivery of services from outside the institution, decreases visits from family and friends, reduces opportunities for furloughs home, and limits the availability of staff. Many of these institutions have outlasted their functions. Their architecture has left the institutions inflexible in a time when flexibility is greatly needed. They were built to house too many people for maximum treatment success. The large numbers have resulted in an excessive emphasis on security and control. The advisory commission maintained that these institutions are dehumanizing and that they create an unhealthy need for dependence.

The traditional juvenile correctional institution must change. It no longer can continue to house failures; it must share a major responsibility for the reintegration of those juveniles into society, but as institutions change their goals, the public must bear its share of responsibility. It no longer can be assumed that the major responsibility for institutionalized juveniles lies with the officials at those institutions. The public must be involved in the planning, the goals, and the programs as well as in the efforts toward reintegration into the community. Most important, the public must give full acceptance to these institutional and community programs for juveniles. The advisory commission concluded its discussion of juvenile corrections by saying, "It is no surprise that institutions have not been successful in reducing crime. The mystery is that they have not contributed even more to increasing crime."[48]

It appears that most closed institutions for juveniles have not been successful and that the least effective are the large institutions.[49] Yet, children whose only offense is that they are emotionally disturbed or incorrigible are not only confined but often confined for longer periods of time than those who have committed more serious offenses.

Confronted by aggressive peers, intolerant staff, and the rigidity of organizational rules, they feel the time confined is a living hell. It is not surprising that many vent their anger toward society upon returning to the community.[50]

Deinstitutionalization

Dissatisfaction with closed institutions has led to several movements. One is diversion. Another is community corrections. A third movement, related to diversion and community corrections, is deinstitutionalization. This movement began with an emphasis on probation, foster homes, and community treatment centers for juveniles. The establishment of the California Youth Authority in the early 1960s and the closing of the institutions for juveniles in Massachusetts in 1970 and 1971 gave impetus to the movement.

What caused this movement toward deinstitutionalization for juveniles? Some say it began in the early 1960s when the government began granting money to localities to improve conditions in delinquency. Others say it began when social scientists began to assume the role of clinician and became involved in policy decision making at the local and federal levels. Still others point to the interest of lawyers in the 1960s and 1970s in reforming the juvenile court.

Andrew T. Scull takes the position that the movement was motivated primarily by a desire to save the costs of constructing new facilities and repairing existing ones.[51] Whatever the reasons, it is clear that this movement is unlike most others in the field. It involves a major change: abandoning the large institution and replacing it with a different concept of corrections. The era of the large institution has been summarized as follows:

> [T]he penal institution has been dissected like a cadaver in a morgue. No organ, no angle, no aspect has defied scrutiny and commentary. The net result of these analyses has been a literature which has hardened attitudes toward the institution as a snake pit; as a demonic invention conceived with the best of intentions but which, like so many other innovations grounded in the blind zeal of reformers, turn out to be as bad as or worse than the practices they replace. The pendulum has swung to the point that modern reformers—both law and professional—would demolish the institution stone by stone.[52]

That is precisely what Jerome G. Miller advocated in Massachusetts.

In 1969, Jerome Miller took charge of the Department of Youth Services in Massachusetts. At first he attempted to reform the system, but "after 15 months of bureaucratic blockades, open warfare with state legislators, and sabotage by entrenched employees, Miller abandoned reform and elected revolution."[53] Between 1969 and 1973, Miller closed the state juvenile institutions, placing juveniles in community-based facilities.

The Massachusetts experiment with deinstitutionalization has been evaluated by a team of social scientists from Harvard University. In the early stages of evaluation, they concluded guardedly that the experiment was a success. In 1977 the tentative conclusions were questioned. The recidivism rates of the youth had not increased or decreased; therefore, it might be concluded that deinstitutionalization, though no better, was no worse than institutionalization and certainly more humane. However, the evaluators reported a crisis in the reaction of the public, the courts, and the police.

Public concern in Massachusetts mainly was over the need for more secure facilities. A task force appointed to consider the issue concluded,

> We are left with a picture of the reformed agency showing clear signs of difficulty and crisis in the political structure that supports it and some suggestions of difficulty in its actual operations.

The evaluators were specifically looking at the results of the use of extreme tactics in effecting reform.[54] Empirical studies of the Massachusetts system in the 1980s are contradictory regarding the success or failure of deinstitutionalization.

Deinstitutionalization also may be the government's reponse to court pressures or orders to improve juvenile institutions. In late 1988, Maryland closed the Montrose School, a secure facility for juveniles. Threatened lawsuits over conditions; an environmental group threatening to sue because of the facility's sewer system, and two suicides, among other reasons, led to closing this facility. Youths were placed in alternative programs, an appropiate move because many of the confined juveniles were being incarcerated for status offenses.[55]

In evaluating deinstitutionalization, we must raise the issue of whether the negative effects of institutionalization at least to some extent, also will crop up in community treatment centers or other forms of handling juveniles. Maynard L. Erickson, in responding to the argument that large juvenile institutions should be abolished because they are schools for crime, points out that, in many cases, those large institutions are confining juveniles who previously have been in the smaller institutions. The latter therefore must take responsibility for at least part of the failure of the correctional system to rehabilitate juveniles. Furthermore, says Erickson, replacing the large institutions with smaller facilities "may not really change the amount of teaching and learning that takes place among offenders."[56] If juveniles who already have a strong orientation toward crime are confined together, they may continue to infect and teach each other.

JUVENILES AND CAPITAL PUNISHMENT

One final issue in criminal justice also applies to juveniles. The execution in January 1986 of James Terry Roach, then 25 but executed for a crime he committed when he was 16, raised the issue of whether capital punishment should be imposed on juveniles. In an earlier case, Monty Lee Eddings, who was 15 when he murdered the Oklahoma highway patrol officer who stopped him for a traffic violation, was successful in the appeal of his death sentence to the Supreme Court. Eddings's attorney argued that executing a person for a crime committed while a juvenile constitutes cruel and unusual punishment. The Supreme Court did not decide that issue but sent the case back for resentencing on the ground that the lower court did not consider mitigating circumstances in sentencing. The trial court then considered the mitigating circumstances and again sentenced Eddings to death. Before his case reached the Supreme Court a second time, the Court of Criminal Appeals of Oklahoma changed his sentence from death to life imprisonment.[57]

In 1985 the Court upheld the death sentence of a defendant who was 18 at the time he committed his particularly atrocious capital crime.[58] But on the last day of its 1987–1988 term, the Court announced its decision in *Thompson v. Oklahoma*, in which it reversed the capital sentence of William Wayne Thompson, who was 15 when he committed the crime for

In its 1988–89 term, the U.S. Supreme Court held that execution of offenders for crimes committed while they were 16 and 17 is not cruel and unusual punishment. James Terry Roach, pictured here, was executed in 1986 for a crime he committed while he was sixteen. (AP/Wide World Photos)

which he was given the death penalty. In *Thompson*, a majority of the Court agreed that execution of an individual who was 15 at the time he committed a capital crime is cruel and unusual punishment even though the crime was particularly heinous. The following excerpt from the Court's opinion details the relevant facts of this important case and gives a brief statement of the Court's reasons for its conclusion that execution of Thompson would constitute cruel and unusual punishment.

The Court also decided a procedural issue concerning the admission of evidence, but the relevant issue in this chapter is the holding on capital punishment. In deciding whether capital punishment of a person who was 15 when he committed the crime constitutes cruel and unusual punishment in violation of the Eighth Amendment, the Court used the standard established in *Trop v. Dulles*, decided in 1958. The standard is "the evolving standards of decency that mark the progress of a maturing society."[59]

But how does a judge decide whether that standard has been met? The Court looked at legislative enactments and jury decisions (only 5 of the 1,393 persons sentenced to death between 1982 and 1986 were less than 16 when they committed the crimes for which they were sentenced) and decided that the "evolving standards of decency" preclude executing one so young.[60]

Thompson v. Oklahoma

Only a brief statement of facts is necessary. In concert with three older persons, petitioner actively participated in the brutal murder of his former brother-in-law in the early morning hours of January 23, 1983. The evidence disclosed that the victim had been shot twice, and that his throat, chest, and abdomen had been cut. He also had multiple bruises and a broken leg. His body had been chained to a concrete block and thrown into a river where it remained for almost four weeks. Each of the four defendants was tried separately and each was sentenced to death. . . .

It is generally agreed "that punishment should be directly related to the personal culpability of the criminal defendant." There is also broad agreement on the proposition that adolescents as a class are less mature and responsible than adults. We stressed this difference in explaining the importance of treating the defendant's youth as a mitigating factor in capital cases:

> But youth is more than a chronological fact. It is a time and condition of life when a person may be most susceptible to influence and to psychological damage. Our history is replete with laws and judicial recognition that minors, especially in their earlier years, generally are less mature and responsible than adults. Particularly during the formative years of childhood and adolescence, minors often lack the experience, perspective, and judgment expected of adults. . . .

[The Court then quoted with approval the following passage from the 1978 Report of the Twentieth Century Fund Task Force on Sentencing Policy toward Young Offenders]:

> Adolescents, particularly in the early and middle teen years, are more vulnerable, more impulsive, and less self-disciplined than adults. Crimes committed by youths may be just as harmful to victims as those committed by older persons, but they deserve less punishment because adolescents may have less capacity to control their conduct and to think in long-range terms than adults. Moreover, youth crime as such is not exclusively the offender's fault.

Thus, the Court has already endorsed the proposition that less culpability should attach to a crime committed by a juvenile than to a comparable crime committed by an adult. The basis for this conclusion is too obvious to require extended explanation. Inexperience, less education, and less intelligence make the teenager less able to evelute the consequences of his or her conduct while at the same time he or she is much more apt to be motivated by mere emotion or peer pressure than is an adult. The reasons why juveniles are not trusted with the privileges and responsibilities of an adult also explain why their irresponsible conduct is not as morally reprehensible as that of an adult.

    [The Court then discussed the two principal social purposes served by the death penalty—retribution and deterrence—and concluded that neither is applicable to juveniles. Capital punishment] is, therefore, "nothing more than the purposeless and needless imposition of pain and suffering," and thus an unconstitutional punishment.

The Court's decision in *Thompson* bans capital punishment for youths who are under 16 when they commit a capital offense. It does not answer the question of whether capital punishment is cruel and unusual when imposed on youths between the ages of 16 and 18 at the time the capital murder is committed. The Court makes this very clear in its opinion, noting that it has been asked to declare capital punishment unconstitutional for all youths under 18.

> Our task today, however, is to decide the case before us; we do so by concluding that the Eighth and Fourteenth Amendments prohibit the execution of a person who was under 16 years of age at the time of his or her offense.

During the last week of its 1988–89 term, the Supreme Court decided the cases of two death row inmates who committed murder while they were juveniles. The Court held that capital punishment for these youths does not constitute cruel and unusual punishment. Excerpts from this controversial opinion, decided by a 5–4 vote, are reprinted below.[61]

Stanford v. *Kentucky*

The first case involves the shooting death of 20-year-old Baerbel Poore. . . . Petitioner Kevin Stanford committed the murder on January 7, 1981, when he was approximately 17 years and 4 months of age. Stanford and his accomplice repeatedly raped and sodomized Poore during and after their commission of a robbery at a gas station where she worked as an attendant. They then drove her to a secluded area near the station, where Stanford shot her point-blank in the face and then in the back of her head. The proceeds from the robbery were roughly 300 cartons of cigarettes, two gallons of fuel and a small amount of cash. . . .

The second case . . . involves the stabbing death of Nancy Allen, a 26-year-old mother of two who was working behind the sales counter of the convenience store she and David Allen owned and operated. . . . Petitioner Heath Wilkins committed the murder on July 27, 1985, when he was approximately 16 years and 6 months of age. The record reflects that Wilkins' plan was to rob the store and murder "whoever was behind the counter" because "a dead person can't talk." While Wilkins' accomplice Patrick Stevens, held Allen, Wilkins stabbed her, causing her to fall to the floor. When Stevens had trouble operating the cash register, Allen spoke up to assist him, leading Wilkins to stab her three more times in her chest. Two of these wounds penetrated the victim's heart. When Allen began to beg for her life, Wilkins stabbed her four more times in the neck, opening her carotid artery. After helping themselves to liquor, cigarettes, rolling papers, and approximately $450 in cash and checks, Wilkins and Stevens left Allen to die on the floor. . . .

[After rejecting several arguments, including the assertion that capital punishment does not deter any juveniles from committing murder, the Court proceeded to decide the case on the basis of the Eighth Amendment's prohibition of "cruel and unusual punishment."]

The punishment is either "cruel and unusual" (i.e., society has set its face against it) or it is not. The audience for these arguments, in other words, is not this Court but the citizenry of the United States. It is they, not we, who must be persuaded. For as we stated earlier, our job is to identify the "evolving standards of decency"; to determine, not what they should be, but what they are. We have no power under the Eighth Amendment to substitute our belief in the scientific evidence for the society's apparent skepticism. . . .

We discern neither a historical nor a modern societal consensus forbidding the imposition of capital punishment on any person who murders at 16 or 17 years of age. Accordingly, we conclude that such punishment does not offend the Eighth Amendment's prohibition against cruel and unusual punishment.

SUMMARY

Focusing the last chapter in a criminal justice text on juvenile justice is appropriate, for in an analysis of this system most of the issues in the field of criminal justice come into focus. The juvenile system held the highest hopes for success in rehabilitation, reformation, and reintegration; but the juvenile system also contained some of the greatest deprivations of constitutional rights. In the name of "the best interests of the child," the state has taken away liberty without due process of law. Under the guise of treatment and rehabilitation not punishment, the juvenile court system has swept into its clutches many

who otherwise would not have been formally processed by the court system.

There is a need to treat juveniles differently from adults; there is a need to segregate them from adults in confinement; there is a need to offer them opportunities for improvement so they could succeed in a competitive world. Those needs no longer can be met by violating the rights of children.

This chapter has looked at the treatment of juveniles historically, traced the development of the juvenile court, and looked at the procedural requirements for that court today. The chapter has reviewed the major Supreme Court and lower court decisions concerning the rights of juveniles.

Discussion indicated that although not all procedural requirements of the criminal courts have been applied to juveniles, many of the due process rights have been extended to this special court. It is no longer sufficient to say that juveniles are not arrested, they are apprehended. They are not found guilty, they are adjudicated. They are not sentenced, but dispositions are made of their cases. The change in wording does not compensate for a lack of due process. In many respects criminal and juvenile courts are similar today. On the other hand, states have some room to experiment in their juvenile systems. Trial by jury is not required but has been extended by statute to juvenile courts in some states.

This chapter has pointed out that the crime rates among juveniles are not rising at alarming rates, as some have feared. More important, the violent crimes by juveniles appear to be committed by a few, but those violent few commit a large percentage of the total crimes committed by juveniles. Concern with this violence and with recidivism has led some states to pass statutes giving the criminal courts jurisdiction over juveniles who commit serious crimes. In other states, the juvenile court, after a proper hearing, may waive jurisdiction over a juvenile who has committed a serious crime.

All reforms have problems, and one problem with the get-tough laws concerning juveniles has been the unwillingness of courts and juries to convict if they know there will be an automatic penalty that they consider too severe. Thus, the get-tough policy could result in less, not more, protection for the community. It is always important to evaluate changes carefully for that reason. Insufficient attention has been given to evaluating legislative changes in the juvenile system.

Juveniles also have received differential treatment in corrections, although it is not at all clear that those differences are always positive. Indefinite detention of juveniles under the guise that they are being treated when they are only being detained has been held to be inappropriate by courts. Unfortunately, disillusionment with treatment and rehabilitation in many jurisdictions has resulted in a decreased emphasis on treatment, even in the case of juveniles. At the other extreme has been the position that institutionalization is bad for juveniles and therefore should be abandoned, with juveniles being cared for in some type of community treatment facility.

STUDY QUESTIONS

1. How were juveniles treated historically?

2. What events led to the emergence of the juvenile court in this country?

3. What are the basic ways in which the juvenile court and the adult criminal court differ?

4. Briefly describe what the Supreme Court held in each of the following cases: *Kent, Gault, Winship, McKeiver, Breed,* and *Schall.*

5. What is meant by the *violent few*?

6. What is *diversion*? How does the concept apply to juveniles?

7. What is the relationship of the police to juveniles?

8. Describe the role of the prosecutor and of the defense attorney.

9. Why are some juveniles tried in adult criminal courts?

10. Why did separate institutions for juveniles develop? Are they successful? Should they be continued? What is meant by deinstitutionalization?

11. Should juveniles ever be sentenced to capital punishment? What are the issues? What is the current legal status of capital punishment of juveniles?

ENDNOTES

1. For a concise, recent, text on juvenile delinquency, see Arnold Binder, Gilbert Geis, and Dickson Bruce, *Juvenile Delinquency: Historical, Cultural, Legal Perspectives* (New York: Macmillan Publishing Co., 1988).

2. F. Nicholas, "History, Philosophy, and Proce-

dures of Juvenile Courts," *Journal of Family Law* 1 (Fall 1961): 158–59.

3. Orman Ketcham, "The Unfulfilled Promise of the American Juvenile Courts," in Margaret Keeney Rosenheim, ed., *Justice for the Child* (New York: Free Press, 1962), p. 24.

4. See Alexander W. Pisciotta, *"Parens Patriae,* Treatment and Reform: The Case of the Western House of Refuge, 1849–1907," *New England Journal of Criminal and Civil Confinement* 10 (Winter 1984): 65–86.

5. Commonwealth v. Fisher, 62 At. 198, 199, 200 (Pa. 1905).

6. Kent v. U.S., 383 U.S. 541, 556 (1966).

7. See Anthony Platt, *The Child Savers* (Chicago: University of Chicago Press, 1969).

8. John R. Sutton, "The Juvenile Court and Social Welfare: Dynamics of Pregressive Reform," *Law and Society Review* 19, no. 1 (1985): 142.

9. Federal Bureau of Investigation, *Crime in the United States: Uniform Crime Reports, 1987* (Washington, D.C.: U. S. Government Printing Office, 1987), p. 180.

10. Ibid., p. 170.

11. Donna Martin Hamparian et al., *The Young Criminal Years of the Violent Few* (Washington, D.C.: U.S. Government Printing Office, June 1985).

12. Smith *ex rel.* Daily Mail Publishing Co. v. Smith, 443 U.S. 97 (1979).

13. Kent v. U.S., 383 U.S. 541, 554–55, (1966), footnotes omitted.

14. *In re* Gault, 387 U.S. 1, 19–21, 26–28, (1967), footnotes omitted.

15. *In re* Winship, 397 U.S. 358 (1970), quoting *in re* Gault.

16. McKeiver v. Pennsylvania, 403 U.S. 528, 543 (1971).

17. McKeiver v. Pennsylvania, 403 U.S. 528, 547 (1971).

18. Breed v. Jones, 421 U.S. 519, 533 (1975), *remanded*, 519 F. 2d 1314 (9th Cir. 1975).

19. Schall v. Martin, 467 U.S. 253 (1984).

20. Samuel M. Davis, *Rights of Juveniles: The Juvenile Justice System* (New York: Clark Boardman Co., 1985), p. 3–4.

21. New Jersey v. T.L.O., 469 U.S. 325 (1985).

22. Ira M. Schwartz et al., "Juvenile Detention: The Hidden Closets Revisited," *Justice Quarterly* 4 (June 1987): 234. See also Barry Krisberg et al., "The Watershed of Juvenile Justice Reform," *Crime and Delinquency* 32, no. 1 (1986): 3–38.

23. Schall v. Martin, 467 U.S. 253, 265. The adult preventive detention case is U.S. v. Salerno, 481 U.S. 739 (1987), discussed in Chapter 10 of this text.

24. The American Correctional Association in cooperation with The National Coalition for Jail Reform, *Jails in America: An Overview of Issues,* (College Park, Md.: American Correctional Association, 1985), p. 27.

25. See Harry F. Swanger, "Hendrickson v. Griggs: A Review of the Legal and Policy Implications for Juvenile Justice Policymakers," *Crime and Delinquency* 34 (April 1988): 209–227.

26. Hendrickson v. Griggs, 672 F. Supp. 1126 (N.D. Iowa 1987). For a discussion, see ibid., and Mark Soter, "Litigation on Behalf of Children in Adult Jails," *Crime and Delinquency* 34 (April 1988): 190–208.

27. CAL. WELF. & INST. CODE, Statutes of 1986, Ch. 1271. For a discussion, see David Steinhart, "California Legislature Ends the Jailing of Children: The Story of a Policy Reversal," *Crime and Delinquency* 34 (April 1988): 150–68.

28. Ira M. Schwartz et al., "The Jailing of Juveniles in Minnesota: A Case Study," *Crime and Delinquency* 34 (April 1988): 149.

29. See Davis, *Rights of Juveniles*, pp. 3-64.1–3-69.

30. Thomas G. Blomberg, "Widening the Net: An Anomaly in the Evaluation of Diversion Programs," in Malcolm W. Klein and Katherine S. Tellmann, eds., *Handbook of Criminal Justice Evaluation* (Beverly Hills, Calif.: Sage Publications, 1980), pp. 571–93.

31. Ibid., p. 585. See also Blomberg, "Diversion's Disparate Results and Unresolved Questions: An Integrative Evaluation Perspective," *Journal of Research in Crime and Delinquency* 20 (January 1983): 24–38. For other evidence on the diversion debate, see Edwin M. Lemert, "Diversion in Juvenile Justice: What Hath Been Wrought?" *Journal of Research in Crime and Delinquency* 18 (January 1981): 34–46; and Scott H. Decker, "A Systematic Analysis of Diversion: Net Widening and Beyond," *Journal of Criminal Justice* 13, no. 3 (1985): 207–16.

32. Belinda R. McCarthy, "Case Attriuion in the Juvenile Court: An Application of the Crime Control Model," *Justice Quarterly* 4 (June 1987): 237–55.

33. Anne L. Schneider, "Restitution and Recidivism Rates of Juvenile Offenders: Results from Four Experimental Studies," *Criminology* 40 (August 1986): 533–52. See also Anne L. Schneider, ed., *Guide to Juvenile Restitution Programs* (Washington, D.C.: National Criminal Justice Reference Service and Government Printing Office, 1985).

34. Schneider, "Restitution and Recidivism Rates," *ibid.*

35. George Camp and Camille Camp, *The Corrections Yearbook* (South Salem, N.Y.: Criminal Justice Institute, 1988), p. 64.

36. Davis, *Rights of Juveniles*, pp. 4-3–4-5.

37. New York FAM. CT. ACT, Section 301.2(1)(b).

38. Act of June 17, 1987, Ch. 385, Tex. Sess. Law Serv. 3764 (Vernon) (effective 1 September 1987). For a detailed discussion of the legislative

history of this statute and the implications of the statute, see Robert O. Dawson, "The Third Justice System: The New Juvenile–Criminal System of Determinate Sentencing For the Youthful Violent Offender in Texas," *St. Mary's Law Journal* 19 (No. 4, 1988): 943–1016.

39. Camp and Camp, *Corrections Yearbook*, pp. 50, 51.

40. See David J. Rothman, *The Discovery of the Asylum* (Boston: Little, Brown and Co., 1971).

41. Joseph R. Rowan and Charles J. Kehoe, "Let's Deinstitutionalize Group Homes," *Juvenile and Family Court Journal* 36 (Spring 1985): 1–4.

42. O'Conner v. Donaldson, 422 U.S. 563 (1975), *remanded*, 519 F. 2d 59 (5th Cir. 1975).

43. See, for example, Nelson v. Heyne, 355 F. Supp. 451 (N.D. Ind. 1972), *aff'd*, 491 F. 2d 352 (7th Cir. 1974), *cert. denied* 417 U.S. 976 (1974).

44. This case has had a long history that cannot be detailed here, but the citations and decisions may be traced through Morales v. Turman, 569 F. Supp.332 (E.D. Tex., 1983) and 820 F. 2d 728 (5th Cir. 1987).

45. Santana v. Collazo, 714 F. 2d 1172, 1177 (1st Cir. 1983), *cert. denied*, 466 U.S. 974 (1984), *appeal after remand*, 793 F. 2d 41 (1st Cir. 1986). For a discussion of treatment for institutionalized juveniles, see Steven P. Lab and John T. Whitehead, "An Analysis of Juvenile Correctional Treatment," *Crime and Delinquency* 54 (January 1988): 60–83.

46. Camp and Camp, *Corrections Yearbook*, p. 52.

47. The National Advisory Commission on Criminal Justice Standards and Goals, *Corrections* (Washington, D.C.: U.S. Government Printing Office, 1973), p. 350.

48. Ibid., pp. 350–52.

49. See also Theodore M. Newcomb, "Characteristics of Youths in a Sample of Correctional Programs: Differences Associated with Programs and Time Spent in Them," *Journal of Research in Crime and Delinquency* 15 (January 1978): 3–24.

50. Clemens Bartollas, Stuart J. Miller, and Simon Dinitz, *Juvenile Victimization: The Institutional Paradox* (New York: John Wiley and Sons, 1976), p. 166.

51. Andrew T. Scull, *Decarceration: Community Treatment and the Deviant: A Radical View*, 2d ed. (New Brunswick, N.J.: Rutgers University Press, 1984).

52. Bartollas, Miller, and Dinitz, *Juvenile Victimization*, pp. 262–63.

53. *Time* (30 August 1976), p. 63.

54. Alden D. Miller, Lloyd E. Ohlin, and Robert B. Coates, "The Aftermath of Extreme Tactics in Juvenile Justice Reform: A Crisis Four Years Later," in David F. Greenberg, ed., *Corrections and Punishment*, Sage Criminal Justice System Annuals (Beverly Hills, Calif.: Sage Publications, 1977), p. 245.

55. "Closing of Training School in Maryland Cited as Model Reform," *Criminal Justice Newsletter* 19 (15 November 1988): 5. A 42-page report on the closing of the Montrose School is available from the Center for the Study of Youth Policy, the University of Michigan, 1015 East Huron Street, Ann Arbor, Michigan 48104.

56. Maynard L. Erickson, "Schools for Crime?" *Journal of Research in Crime and Delinquency* 15 (January 1978): 32–33.

57. Eddings v. Oklahoma, 455 U.S. 104, 115 (1982).

58. Baldwin v. Alabama, 472 U.S. 372 (1985).

59. Trop v. Dulles, 356 U.S. 6, 101 (1958) (plurality opinion).

60. Thompson v. Oklahoma, 479 U.S. 830 (1988), cases and citations omitted.

61. Stanford v. Kentucky, No. 87-5765 (June 26, 1989), footnotes and citations omitted.

Criminal Justice: Spotlight on the Present and the Future

The Preface to this text began by noting that many consider crime to be the major domestic problem in the United States. Clearly the subject was a critical factor in the 1988 presidential election, as Vice-President George Bush's campaign ads during the latter weeks of the campaign centered on the brutal crimes committed by Willie Horton while he was on a furlough release from a Massachusetts prison. The impact of the Willie Horton ads in defeating Massachusetts governor Michael Dukakis indicates more about emotional than factual reactions to crime. Furloughs are permitted in many states and the federal system; most are successful; and even if they were not, the U.S. president will probably have little impact on changes in that system.

The thrust of this text has been to look beyond the campaign ads and other public statements about crime and encourage the reader to think carefully about crime facts and their implications. It is imperative that the facts be analyzed carefully in light of social science research as well as philosophical and moral feelings about those facts. It also is important to consider the impact that any change in one area of the criminal justice system will have on other aspects of that system. Failure to do this accounts for some of the most serious problems faced by the criminal justice system today.

In assessing the present and future of the criminal justice system, this Epilogue is organized around the basic outline of the text: the criminal event, policing, the criminal court system, confinement and corrections, and the juvenile justice system.

THE CRIMINAL EVENT

Problems of Definition and Measurement

Perhaps the most difficult problem in studying the criminal justice system is defining and measuring the basis of that system: crimes. Legal definitions differ among the various states and the federal system, and court interpretations of those definitions also are inconsistent. There is no reason

Willie Horton, Jr., left, stabbed Clifford Barnes, right, and twice raped Barnes's fiancee while Horton was on a prison furlough. Barnes is shown with Donna Cuomo, whose brother was killed by Horton in 1974. The Horton case became an important issue in the 1988 presidential election. (AP/Wide World Photos)

to expect that this will change. Perhaps, that is as it should be, for permitting individual states to define crime and enact legislation about crime enables them to take account of the differences in behavior and in feelings about that behavior throughout the country. Such changes also permit the criminal justice system to grow and develop as we gain more insight into human behavior. For example, over the years attitudes in the medical profession toward whether alcoholism is a disease have changed. Unfortunately, as indicated in Chapter 1, the U.S. Supreme Court has not agreed. Perhaps in time that, too, will change.

Permitting differences in definitions of crime, however, makes it impossible for us to compile accurate crime data. And even if we had uniform definitions and interpretations of those definitions, accurate data still would be hampered by our inability to detect all criminal activity.

Despite these problems, some analysis can be made of the best crime data available. The latest figures available from the FBI, the 1987 *Uniform Crime Reports,* indicate only slight changes in rates of violent crimes between 1986 and 1987 and an increase of 3 percent for property crime rates. These data, however, indicate a significant rise when compared with 1983 and 1978, and statisticians emphasize that it is important to view crime data over several years.[1]

Victimization data also indicate that crime is rising. After a decline for several years, the 1987 data showed a 1.8 percent increase over 1986, although the data still indicated less crime than in 1981, the peak year since the Bureau of Justice Statistics began collecting victimization data.[2]

Fear of Crime

For some reasons, however, actual data may not be as important as *perceptions* of these data. Late 1988 studies in New York indicated that one-

Pieces of Pam Am Flight 103, left, and mourners, right, illustrate the incredible tragedy that occurred when the aircraft exploded in the sky, killing all on board and some on the ground. Terrorists are reportedly responsible for the tragedy. (Topham/The Image Works; AP/Wide World Photos)

third of transit riders in that city perceived subway crime to be four times as high as the actual data. This "exaggerated perception of crime . . . threatens to erode ridership and confidence in the system."[3]

Chapter 4's discussion of crime victims indicated that fear of crime is not necessarily correlated with probability of becoming a crime victim. Women and the elderly express greater fear of becoming crime victims than the data warrant; young men (black) are the most frequent victims of crime. Exaggerated fear of crime may also result from the 1988 bombing of Pan Am 103 in Scotland during its flight from London to New York.

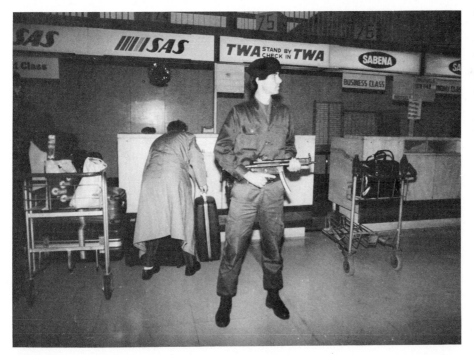

Greek antiterrorist police officer stands guard in Athens airport, representing increased airport security since the terrorist bombing of Pam Am Flight 103 that caused its crash over Scotland in late 1988. (AP/Wide World Photos)

That tragedy, which resulted in the deaths of all 259 passengers and crew members as well as some individuals on the ground, may not reflect a new trend in international terrorism. But it will probably cause some to alter their plans for international travel, and it already has resulted in increased security at international airports.

Understanding Criminal Behavior

Detecting and measuring criminal activity may be aided by increased understanding of the causes of such activity. In a survey text of this nature it is not possible to explore all of the ramifications of causation: one chapter was devoted to an overview of the subject. A more extensive exploration of the biological, psychological, genetic, chemical, and neurological as well as the traditional sociological and economic causes of crime is needed.

The importance of research on the causes of criminal behavior was emphasized in a provocative article, published in 1978, by the late criminologist Donald R. Cressey, who discussed his concern with the need for sociologists and criminologists to become more involved in developing and testing theories of human behavior. Referring to a 1967 prediction he made about the future content of criminology courses as combining legal and social science knowledge, Cressey expressed his concern that such has not occurred. Rather, he declared, "there seems to have been a smothering of social science knowledge as criminology has expanded."[4]

In his 1967 prediction, Cressey had hoped that criminologists would use their knowledge of social science not only to further their understanding of why criminals behave as they do but also to apply this knowledge to analyze why courts, police, prosecutors, judges, and legislators behave as they do. Instead, many criminologists have moved toward a policy orientation. Some have abandoned attempts to find cause-and-effect relationships in human behavior and have become antagonistic to such scientific efforts, as they spend an increasing amount of time attempting to "do something" about crime. The administration of the criminal law, rather than an understanding of crime and criminals, has become the focus. Cressey concluded:

> The typical modern criminologist is a technical assistant to politicians bent on repressing crime, rather than a scientist seeking valid propositions stated in a causal framework. If cause—and with it the search for generalizations—goes out the window, criminology will become even more of a hodgepodge than it is now. In the long run, the nation will be worse off as a result.[5]

Concern with the failures of criminology and criminal justice also was discussed by criminologist C. R. Jeffery. The Jeffery and Cressey articles appeared with others in a *Criminology* symposium issue, "Criminology: New Concerns and New Directions." Jeffery outlined the failure of psychiatry and psychology between 1920 and 1950, when these disciplines were the basis for the treatment model in penal institutions. This failure he compared with

> failure of the sociological model as found in the war against poverty program in the 1960s era. The notion that the opportunity structure could be altered through education and job training, thus altering poverty and delinquency, was also a total disaster. The failure of criminology as a science of the individual was matched by its failure as a science of the social offender.[6]

On the other hand, Jeffery noted, the government's "war on crime," which resulted in the 1967 appointment of the President's Crime Commission, passage of the Safe Streets Act, and development of the Law Enforcement Assistance Administration, has been a failure as well. Even the government recognized the failure of LEAA, described by former Attorney General Griffin Bell as a "paper-shuffling operation which had failed to come up with new and innovative means to combat the ever-growing crime problem."[7]

Jeffery warned that increasing the police force and developing new types of hardware for combating crime would not be effective. He concluded that the treatment model has been abandoned

> at a time when the behavioral sciences are about to make a major contribution to our knowledge of human behavior. It is ironic that in the 1970s, when we are returning to an eighteenth-century punishment model of crime control, twenty-first-century breakthroughs are occurring in our understanding of human behavior.[8]

Jeffery emphasized the need for a major research effort "to join biology, medicine, psychology, criminology, and criminal law into a new crime prevention model. We must approach the crime problem as a behavioral problem and not as a political problem."[9]

A similar position was taken by criminologist Simon Dinitz when he referred to

> the propensity for modern scholars to forego hard scholarly work in order to assume leadership roles in the intoxicating world of social and ideological movements. Such has too often occurred to the detriment of the scholars and the field. In only a few historical periods was it considered inappropriate for intellectual types to get involved in sociopolitical movements. In these periods scholarly productivity frequently blossomed, in stark contrast to the present when the media consume ideas like prisons consume people.[10]

Although not all criminologists agree with this position, it is clear that if criminologists wish to be taken seriously, they must find some ideas based on scientific findings. Cressey's warning should be heeded:

> Criminologists should not abandon science to become policy advisors in this repressive war on crime. Neither should they retreat into broad intellectualizing accompanied by political proselytizing. . . . They . . .

should sharpen their scientific research tools and put them to work on studies designed to secure comprehension of the conditions under which criminal laws are enacted, enforced, and broken. If they do so, and come up with some reasonable generalizations, politicians might listen to them, just as politicians listened to Bentham, Beccaria, Voltaire, and even Freud.[11]

Drugs and the Criminal Event

Although the relationship between drugs and crime is not an easy one to assess, numerous people arrested today are or have been involved with illegal drugs. The impact of the drug problem is enormous, and as Spotlight E.1 indicates, is one of the major problems in the entire criminal justice system.

Despite the drug problem, according to a recent U.S. Justice Department report, recent research indicates the following:

1. Very recent cocaine and heroin abusers constitute a majority of the arrestees and inmates in jails and prisons in New York City and some other jurisdictions.
2. Frequent users of heroin and cocaine in the general population exhibit a multiproblem life-style that may include a pattern of persistent criminal behavior.
3. Criminal justice agencies, with rare exceptions, do not seek or use information about the drug use of persons who are arrested or convicted of crimes.
4. To the extent that criminal sanctions are applied, their ability to interrupt the life-style of the vast majority of cocaine-heroin abusers is minimal.
5. Existing evidence does not show that criminal justice sanctions (fine, probation, or parole, or length of time served) reduce criminality or drug use more effectively than drug treatment among cocaine-heroin abusers.[12]

Increased drug arrests have put pressure on the entire criminal justice system. In early 1989, with 80 percent of all crimes traced to drugs, Connecticut prison officials announced that despite early prison releases to accommodate the incoming inmate populations, the state's prisons simply cannot keep pace. The correction commissioner described prisons as follows:

> It's a world where people have no place to keep their belongings, where sewage systems back up, where everything is fast-tracked to deal with numbers, not quality. We just can't absorb the growth.[13]

In Florida, where prison populations continue to soar, the state attorney is considering a plan to divert first-time drug offenders to drug-rehabilitation programs or place them on probation. "Officials say the volume of crack-cocaine cases is bogging down the court system, crowding

SPOTLIGHT E.1
WAR ON DRUGS OVERWHELMING LEGAL SYSTEM, BAR STUDY SAYS

The war on drugs is overwhelming a criminal justice system whose greatest problem is a lack of resources, not the legal protections afforded to criminal suspects, a two-year study by the American Bar Association has concluded.

"The entire system is starved: police, prosecution, criminal defense, courts and corrections," said the report, released Wednesday. "As currently funded, the criminal justice system cannot provide the quality of justice that the public legitimately expects and that the people working within the system wish to deliver."

Less than 3 percent of all government spending in the United States went to support civil and criminal justice activities in the fiscal year 1985, according to a Federal study released previously.

Resources Are Overwhelmed

The bar association's study concluded that those resources, which it said were already scant, were being overwhelmed by a vast and largely unsuccessful battle against illegal drugs. It said that while the courts were clogged, the drug problem "is growing worse, and law enforcement has been unable to control" it.

The study was conducted by a panel headed by Samuel Dash, a law professor at Georgetown University who is the former chief counsel to the Senate Watergate Committee.

The study said that while the Supreme Court's Miranda decision holding that the police are required to warn suspects of their rights before questioning had little detrimental effect on law enforcement, although it "has sparked heated controversy on a political level."

'Not Considered Troublesome'

"The restrictions it imposes on custodial interrogation of suspects are not considered troublesome by either police or prosecutors," the study's panelists reported.

Eighty-seven percent of the prosecutors surveyed said that no more than 5 percent of their cases were dismissed because of problems involving the requirements of the Miranda decision.

The rule under which evidence obtained illegally by the police is excluded from use in court has also caused few major problems, the study concluded. Some police officials, in fact, told the association's panel that the demands of the exclusionary rule had promoted professionalism in the nation's police departments.

Most prosecutors put the number of cases dismissed because of the exclusionary rule at 5 percent or less, while three-quarters of the judges and defense lawyers polled said suppression motions succeeded 10 percent or less of the time.

Data from Testimony

The study was based on testimony from the legal community and a national telephone survey of police officers; prosecutors, defense lawyers and judges.

"Police, prosecutors and judges told the committee that they have been unsuccessful in making a significant impact on the importation, sale and use of illegal drugs, despite devoting much of their resources to the arrest, prosecution and trial of drug offenders," the panel reported.

"These extraordinary efforts," it said, "have instead distorted and overwhelmed the criminal justice system, crowding dockets and jails, and diluting law enforcement and judicial efforts to deal with other major criminal cases."

The panel recommended that the association set up a special commission to study and re-evaluate national, state and local strategies in dealing with the drug problem and to educate the public and lawmakers as well as government policymakers.

Source: "War on Drugs Held Burdening Justice," *New York Times* (5 December 1988), p. 11. Copyright © 1988 by The New York Times Company. Reprinted by permission.

the jails and failing to cut down on the drug trade," and judges complain that they spend so much time with arraignments and pretrial proceedings in crack cases that they do not have time to try more serious felony cases.[14]

One effort to combat the drug problem has been to order drug testing in the work place. On March 21, 1989, the U.S. Supreme Court decided two cases involving whether such tests are constitutional. By a 7–2 vote, the Court upheld administrative regulations governing drug testing of railroad workers. By a 5–4 vote the Court upheld drug testing for certain customs workers.[15] Drug problems may be expected to continue to increase in the near future, and drug arrests and convictions will continue to clog the already tremendously overcrowded criminal justice system.

POLICING

Policing in the 1980s has raised numerous problems and attempted solutions. With financial cut-backs in many jurisdictions, police departments have been forced to fight drug and other crime problems without the expansion needed to cope effectively with those problems. Many departments have not been able to enforce the higher educational and training requirements recommended by earlier national commissions and adopted by their own departments.

Violence

Violence against police has increased, with the 72 officers killed in the line of duty during 1987 representing an increase of 6 deaths over 1986, but that increase followed a decline in 1986 when the number of officers killed in a year was lower than for any year since 1968.[16]

Highly publicized cases of violence against police committed by persons on release from prison or while on jail or prison furloughs again raises the system impact of criminal justice. Early release in one segment of the system may negatively affect other aspects of the system. This problem was illustrated by the 1988 slaying of two Miami, Florida, policemen, allegedly shot in the head by Charles Harry Street, who had been released from prison 10 days prior to the shooting. Street had served 8 years in prison for attempted murder.[17]

Policing and Defendants' Rights

The text discussed police concern with the *Miranda* decision that requires them to issue warnings to suspects about their constitutional rights. It also discussed some recent cases that have altered that rule as the Court adopted the inevitable discovery and the good faith doctrines.

Since the completion of those earlier discussions, the Court in *Arizona v. Youngblood* held that the police are not obligated to preserve all evidence that might potentially exonerate the defendant. In this case, the

Court specifically held that the officer's failure to preserve and perform scientific tests on semen samples found on a sodomy victim's clothing did not violate the defendant's constitutional rights. In such cases, ruled the Court majority, the defendant's constitutional rights are not violated unless he or she can prove that the police acted in *bad faith*.[18]

Such decisions by the Court lead many to argue that the Court is diminishing suspects' constitutional rights. The Court's division on the cases is critical. The older justices are frequently the dissenters in these cases, and speculation of retirement among one or more of them is frequently discussed. If President George Bush has the opportunity to appoint one or more members of the U.S. Supreme Court, we can expect a conservative appointment. And in all probability that would change the nature of some of these close votes.

Private Security

Another significant change occurring in policing is the growing trend toward private security. The director of the National Institute of Justice recently reported that "nearly as much money is now paid by governments to private security companies as is spent for public law enforcement by the federal and state governments combined."[19] Private citizens are spending money on private security more frequently because they do not feel that public security is adequate. Home and business burglar alarms and private security guards are obvious manifestations of this development. But in 1988, national attention was focused on a Miami, Florida, neighborhood when citizens began blocking off public roads into their cul-de-sacs or neighborhoods.

Attorneys have argued that these barricades and private security guards are constitutional; others disagree. But the homeowner's reaction to the need for private security was articulated by the homeowner association's president, as follows:

> What else could we do? . . . Women were being followed home from the grocery store and robbed in the driveway. The gentleman across the street was robbed at gunpoint on his way home from church. We came to realize the police can't protect us; they're overwhelmed.[20]

There are problems between public and private security; those were discussed earlier in the text. These problems must be resolved, for it is clear that local, state, and the federal government, faced with increasing crime problems and budget deficits, cannot provide the security needed in their respective jurisdictions.

THE CRIMINAL COURT SYSTEM

Problems raised by public and private security and by increasing or decreasing defendants' rights were frequently the focus of former chief justice Warren E. Burger's attacks on the criminal justice system. In his 1981 annual address to the American Bar Association, Burger asked,

> Is a society redeemed if it provides massive safeguards for accused persons but does not provide elementary protection for its decent, law abiding citizens?

Specifically, Burger called for stricter bail release laws and policies, speedier trials, speedier appellate review of convictions, and some limitations on appellate review.[21]

In his 1984 annual address to the bar, Chief Justice Burger noted that recent public opinion polls showed that the public's confidence in lawyers in the United States is declining sharply, though at the same time, the number of lawyers is increasing dramatically. The United States now has two-thirds of all the lawyers in the world, and one-third of those entered practice within the past 5 years. We might think that the increase in lawyers would create healthy competition, resulting in better service and more reasonable fees; yet, as pointed out by Derek Bok, the former dean of the Harvard Law School and now the president of that university, "The blunt, inexcusable fact is that this nation, which prides itself on efficiency and justice, has developed a legal system that is the most expensive in the world."[22]

Despite the cost of our legal system and the abundance of lawyers, we are faced with a backlog in the courts, resulting in long delays for many trials. During this delay, many defendants wait in jail, and with the move toward using bail for preventive detention, even more defendants will be jailed awaiting these trials. The movement toward bail for the preventive detention of defendants thought to be dangerous raises what perhaps is the most difficult problem of the criminal justice system—the conflict between the rights of defendants and the rights of the rest of us to be protected from crime. That conflict is seen in many of the issues we have discussed in this book, including the Court's recent diminishing of the extent of the exclusionary rule.

Increased Litigation on the Exclusionary Rule Exceptions

Changes in what police can and cannot do with regard to evidence during the search of a suspect or a victim may have unanticipated and negative repercussions even to those who welcome the Court's change. These potential effects illustrate the *system impact* of changes. The already crowded courtrooms may become more so with increased litigation over issues surrounding the exclusionary rule.

This litigation may focus on whether the evidence acquired in an alleged unconstitutional seizure would have been discovered anyway (the inevitable discovery exception) or was seized in good faith (the good faith rule). The more recent exception, requiring defendants to prove that police acted in bad faith in their failure to preserve evidence that might exonerate the defendant, may lead to increased litigation on that issue alone.

Other recent changes in the criminal court system also have implications for the future of that system, for victims, and for defendants. An Atlanta district judge ruled that AIDS-infected defendants must enter their guilty pleas and be sentenced by telephone rather than subject others to the spread of AIDS. This action, which has already raised considerable controversy, has been described by an American Civil Liberties Union member as "an outrage. . . . It is a degree of ignorance that I had thought we had put behind us."[23] The ACLU is appealing a 1988 Maryland case in which court personnel wore plastic gloves in dealing with a defendant who had AIDS. Such actions will force courts to decide between perceived danger (there is no evidence that permitting an AIDS victim to appear in court will endanger others) and defendants' constitutional rights.[24]

Evidence Changes

Changes in evidence requirements affect the criminal court system. Earlier discussions noted that some jurisdictions have relaxed their rules of evidence to permit hearsay testimony in cases of alleged sexual abuse of children. Refusal to do so in a recent Georgia case led to the acquittal of the alleged offender, who was accused of raping a 4-year-old. The child was too frightened to testify.[25] Permitting hearsay evidence, however, raises the issue of whether the defendant's constitutional right to confront his or her witnesses has been violated. Thus, when the evidence is permitted, more litigation may be expected on the issue of the defendant's rights.

Permitting the use of the results of a new forensic test, DNA, or genetic "fingerprinting," also is changing the criminal court system.

> Hailed as the single greatest forensic breakthrough since the advent of fingerprinting at the turn of the century, this procedure has been the key evidence in convictions that would not otherwise have been possible.[26]

Like many other innovations, the use of DNA has raised questions by judges and attorneys and is not yet universally accepted. Its use also raises questions about how far authorities may go in gathering and retaining evidence. For example, in Washington state's King County, which includes Seattle, plans were being made in early 1989 to take DNA samples from all convicted sex offenders. "The aim: a DNA library that will pinpoint the owners of genetic fingerprints left at the scenes of future crimes."[27]

New Defenses as Evidence

Permitting evidence of *post-traumatic stress syndrome* has also raised serious questions in the criminal courtroom. War veterans who suffered from combat; women who are beaten by their husbands; rape victims; and other violent crime victims have attempted to raise this defense. In some jurisdictions the defense has been permitted, but whether or not it is allowed, the introduction of this defense increases litigation on the issue of the defense alone. It can be expected that the issue of this and other "new" defenses will increase in the future.

Defense of Criminal Defendants

Arguments continue over the right of indigent defendants to *effective* assistance of counsel, with courts, including the Supreme Court, ruling that defendants have this right but not articulating clearly what the right includes. In June, 1989, the Supreme Court upheld capital punishment in the case of a mentally retarded defendant convicted in Texas and now awaiting execution for murder. As Spotlight E.2 indicates, Alan M. Dershowitz, a professor of law at Harvard and one of the country's most noted defense attorneys on death penalty issues, has raised the critical question of what constitutes effective assistance of counsel with respect to this case, *Penry v. Lynaugh*.[28]

Sentencing Issues

Sentencing has been the focus of significant changes in the criminal court system. As the text noted, the movement from a rehabilitation philosophy to one of retribution and just deserts has led to more definite sentences and in many cases, longer sentences by statute. These changes provide one of the best illustrations in the system of how changes in one area affect problems in other areas.

These sentencing changes in many instances were made without sufficient consideration of their long-term affects; nor have they achieved their primary goals. One of the alleged evils of the indeterminate sentencing structure, and thus a major reason for the movement toward more definite sentencing, was judicial sentencing disparity with few checks on that alleged disparity. But longer, more definite sentences have not in any way affected disparity that exists from one state to another or between the federal government and state systems.

Efforts to reduce or eliminate judicial sentencing disparity have not affected prosecutorial discretion or for that matter, the ability of the jury to acquit if they perceive that the mandatory sentence for conviction would be too severe. And there are few checks on prosecutorial discretion or on the power of the jury to acquit or convict.

Nor is there evidence that longer, more definite sentences have had the deterrent effect projected by their advocates. The deterrence issue is studied most frequently in the context of the death penalty and murder. Scholars disagree on the evidence and its meaning, but with increasing crime rates, it is becoming rather difficult to demonstrate a deterrent effect of the death penalty. A recent study of the death penalty and deterrence in Texas, "one of the top most active states in the use of the death penalty," led its authors to conclude that "there is no evidence of a deterrent effect of executions in the state of Texas."[29]

Another result of longer and more determinate sentences has been overcrowded jails and prisons, leading many jurisdictions to face court

SPOTLIGHT E.2
RETARDED MAN DESERVES BETTER LEGAL ASSISTANCE

The other day I went to the Supreme Court to observe the oral argument in one of the most important cases of the decade. The issue was whether it would be cruel and unusual punishment for the state of Texas to execute a mentally retarded man who had been convicted of a rape-murder. He was 32 years old, but the man had the intelligence of a 6-year-old, the emotional maturity of a 9-year-old, an IQ of 53, and a long history of abuse and institutionalization.

At stake was not just the life of John Paul Penry, whose case made headlines because his victim was the beautiful sister of football kicking star Mark Mosely. For as many as 300 other mentally retarded inmates on death row, the Penry decision may well mean the difference between institutionalization and death by electrocution or injection.

Watching a Supreme Court argument is usually a grand experience. I anticipated witnessing the high art of life-or-death advocacy—until the advocate for John Paul Penry strode up to the podium.

To say the least, his presentation was a disaster. The attorney spoke haltingly and his words were difficult to understand. He seemed not to understand some of the justices' questions. When he did, he frequently gave the wrong answers. He became so bogged down in technical detail that Justice Sandra Day O'Connor had to remind him, with only three minutes left in his argument time, that he had not addressed the main issue—whether it was constitutional to execute a mentally retarded prisoner.

How poorly the interests—the lives!—of retarded death row inmates were being represented! This well-intentioned, good-hearted lawyer was simply not up to the job of arguing a complex case in the Supreme Court.

As I watched him, I felt compassion for this lawyer who was so clearly out of his league. According to the *Forth Worth* (Texas) *Star-Telegram,* he had "retired comfortably from years of public service and joined a special legal assistance project that the Texas Department of Corrections had established to aid death row inmates with appeals."

Indeed, the fault did not lie with him—he was doing the best he could. Instead it lay squarely with the justice system, which had to rely on retired do-gooders to do the difficult work of trying to save lives. There simply weren't enough active and experienced lawyers willing to do the job.

Although it is a temptation to remain silent for the sake of a fellow lawyer, I cannot do so after what I observed in the Supreme Court. The lives of hundreds of mentally retarded inmates, unable to defend themselves or even to understand that they are not being well represented, lie in balance.

For too long, professionals, whether they be lawyers, doctors or airline pilots, have been unwilling to blow the whistle on their colleagues. Underqualified doctors have been permitted to perform delicate surgery because their peers were unwilling to say what they saw in the operating rooms. Lawyers have been equally malfeasant in failing to complain about colleagues who have accepted challenges beyond their capacities.

No intelligent criminal, facing even a year in prison, would have allowed a lawyer so obviously out of his depth to argue for his freedom before the justices. But John Paul Penry is mentally retarded. He can't tell the difference between a good lawyer and a poor one. He must depend on the judgment of others.

It would be a double travesty of justice for the Supreme Court, when it makes its decision in several months, to permit the execution of a mentally retarded "child" who could neither exercise good judgment in the commission of his crimes nor in the selection of his attorney.

Something must be done to assure the competence of the legal representation of death row inmates. When lawyers help the rich get richer through leveraged buyouts and other fancy financial footwork, those most in need of excellent legal representation—the mentally retarded, the poor, the homeless, the stateless—have to rely on well-motivated volunteers, retired lawyers and underpaid public defenders. There is something drastically wrong with this system.

If John Paul Penry is "put to sleep," as one of Penry's friends put it, it will not be because of his crimes alone—only 11 people were executed in America in all of 1988. It will be because he picked the wrong person to kill, he was born to the wrong parents, and the wrong lawyer represented him.

Source: Alan Dershowitz, "Retarded Man Deserves Better Legal Assistance," *St. Petersburg Times* (14 January 1989), p. 18A.

orders to reduce those populations. Additional facilities are costly and usually filled as soon as they are built. Many jurisdictions today have no alternative other than diversion from incarceration or early release of those already incarcerated.

CONFINEMENT AND CORRECTIONS

By far the greatest attention in the criminal justice system today is focused on the confinement of inmates. Earlier discussions have detailed the data indicating that most prisons and many jails are already overcrowded; that building new structures and expanding existing ones has not solved the problem; and that many prisons and jails are under federal court order to reduce their populations or to improve conditions within those institutions.

New York has begun to use barges to house jail inmates. The first barge, called the Bibby Venture, is a 386-bed facility located in the Hudson River.[30] Massachusetts correctional officials reported in mid-1988 that they had 12,260 prisoners in facilities built for 7,844. In one facility, inmates were sleeping on "hallway floors, desktops and former trade shops," and the facility was called a "sardine factory." Officials cited crowded conditions as a major cause of violence. "The smallest infraction is sensed as a major spark."[31] Prison overcrowding in Massachusetts was the main reason officials began using the furlough program so strongly criticized by the Republicans in the 1988 presidential campaign.

Despite the abolition of rehabilitation as a viable punishment philosophy in the late 1970s and the following decade, by the end of the 1980s, many jurisdictions were forced to seek alternatives to incarceration. Probation, home confinement with or without electronic surveillance, and early prison release were among those alternatives. These changes, however, have led some experts to conclude that rather than diverting individuals from incarceration, the programs are widening the net of state control over citizens, perhaps leading to a "minimum security society" in which "ever-increasing state intervention and control can be anticipated." Professor Thomas G. Blomberg continues his comments by emphasizing that research documents "that diversion practices are being applied largely to individuals and families previously not subject to contact with the criminal justice system."[32]

THE JUVENILE JUSTICE SYSTEM

The problems of juvenile crime have become even more dramatic with recent incidents involving young children actively pursuing a life of crime. In January, 1989, a 5-year-old New York City kindergarten student brought a loaded gun to school, gave it to his teacher, and told her that a man gave it to him on the way to school. In Tallahassee, Florida, an 11-year-old was apprehended for repeatedly burglarizing a home not far from the affluent neighborhood in which he lived with his parents. He spread women's panties around the home, hoping, he said, to convince police that an older person committed the crimes.

Such incidents, shocking though they may be, are not the main problem with juvenile crime, however. Although most juveniles may engage in some delinquent activities, most do not become chronic delinquents or criminals. But those who do become chronic offenders are responsible for most crimes committed by juveniles. The system is not handling these, as indicated by this comment from a federal study published in 1988:

> One of the major deficiencies of the juvenile justice system is the number of chronic serious juvenile offenders who slip through the cracks time and again. They continue their delinquent behavior, confident their often-violent actions probably will go unpunished. Unfortunately, they are often right.[33]

Concern with chronic juvenile offenders, particularly when they commit violent crimes, in some jurisdictions has led to special legislation provisions to remove such offenders from the juvenile court and treat them as adult criminals. It also has led to general criticism of the juvenile court system and a more punitive philosophy than was envisoned by the founders of the special court for children.

Of particular concern in the juvenile court system today is the issue of whether capital punishment is a proper sanction for those who commit murders while still juveniles. The Court has already ruled unconstitutional the capital punishment of youths who are under 16 when they commit capital crimes, but it also has approved the execution of those who were 16 and 17 when they did so.

CONCLUSION

In a 1985 publication, I concluded that the

> greatest danger we face now is to conclude, without further evidence, that the decreasing crime rate is *caused* by the recent return to determinate and longer sentences, with the accompanying

just deserts punishment philosophy. I predicted that "such a conclusion would lead to an even larger reduction in prison educational, vocational, and treatment programs."[34]

The Reagan administration did indeed take "credit" for the decrease in crime during its earlier years but made little mention of the increases toward the end of his administration. Prisons cut back on rehabilitative programs; use of alternatives to prison, including early release through parole, were cut. But the increasing number of inmates forced officials to look again at their criminal justice systems.

Our basic mistake is to assume that quick fixes will work. Most of the changes that we have made

in the criminal justice system and corrections may be viewed as short-term efforts to solve the problem of crime. One authority has termed our recent efforts *barbed wire justice*, concluding,

> Prisons do prevent crime: imprisonment keeps prisoners from committing additional crimes, and capital punishment assures us that they won't commit another crime. It is not clear, however, whether this strategy really stops crimes or whether it merely postpones them, at great public expense until the "overcorrected" and embittered inmate is finally released.[35]

That comment, made by a clinical psychologist in a correctional institution, emphasizes our real problem, which can be solved, if at all, only with the assistance of social scientists, for they are the only ones in a position to tell us what *causes* crime.

Americans need to face the issue of crime in terms of long-range solutions. We may not have all of the answers, but we will never have any of them if we continue to hide behind a punitive policy of longer sentences without carefully studying and assessing what happens to those on whom those sentences are imposed.

The next decade will be a critical one in this country, and attorneys and social scientists must confront the complicated problems of the criminal justice system. Citizens must realize that the answers are not simple; indeed, they are complex and costly and require the understanding and cooperation of us all.

ENDNOTES

1. *Crime in the United States: Uniform Crime Reports, 1987* (Washington, D.C.: U.S. Government Printing Office, 1988), p. 41.
2. Bureau of Justice Statistics, *Criminal Victimization 1987* (Washington, D.C.: U.S. Department of Justice, October 1988), p. 1.
3. "Battling Subway Crime, Both Real and Perceived," *New York Times* (2 October 1988), p. 20.
4. Donald R. Cressey, "Criminological Theory, Social Science, and the Repression of Crime," *Criminology* 16 (August 1978): 173.
5. Ibid., p. 177.
6. C. R. Jeffery, "Criminology as an Interdisciplinary Behavioral Science," *Criminology* 16 (August 1978): 153–154.
7. Quoted in ibid., p. 154.
8. Ibid., p. 156.
9. Ibid., p. 166.
10. Simon Dinitz, "Nothing Fails like a Little Success," *Criminology* 16 (August 1978): 230–31.
11. Cressey, "Criminological Theory," pp. 188–89.
12. Harry K. Wexler et al., *A Criminal Justice System Strategy for Treating Cocaine-Heroine Abusing Offenders in Custody* (Washington, D.C.: National Institute of Justice, U.S. Department of Justice, June, 1988), pp. 3, 4, 5.
13. Craig Wolff, "Swamped by Drug-Related Arrests, Connecticut Releases Inmates Early," *New York Times* (2 January 1989), p. 10.
14. "Drug Cases Overloading Court System," *Tallahassee Democrat* (7 August 1988), p. 30.
15. The cases heard by the Court are Skinner v. Railway Labor Executives' Association, 109 S. Ct. 1402 (1989) and National Treasury Employees Union v. Von Raab, 109 S. Ct. 1384 (1989).
16. *Uniform Crime Reports, 1987*, p. 228.
17. "Two Miami Policemen Slain in Struggle," *New York Times* (29 November 1988), p. 4.
18. Arizona v. Youngblood, 109 S. Ct. 333 (1988).
19. Marcia Chaiken and Jan Chaiken, *Public Policing—Privately Provided* (Washington, D.C.: National Institute of Justice, U.S. Department of Justice, June 1987), Foreword, p. iii.
20. Jeffrey Schmalz, "Fearful and Angry Floridians Erect Street Barriers to Crime," *New York Times* (6 December 1988), p. 1.

21. Warren E. Burger, "Annual Report to the American Bar Association by the Chief Justice of the United States," *American Bar Association Journal* 67 (March 1981): 293.
22. Chief Justice Warren E. Burger, "The State of Justice," *American Bar Association Journal* 70 (April 1984): 63, quoting Bok.
23. "Judges Make AIDS Victims Enter Pleas by Phone," *St. Petersburg Times* (15 December 1988), p. 6A.
24. Ibid.
25. "Man Accused of Raping Girl Is Acquitted," *Atlanta Constitution* (8 December 1988), p. 1.
26. "Convicted by Their Genes," *Time* (31 October 1988), p. 74.
27. Ibid.
28. Penry v. Lynaugh, No. 87-6177 (June 26, 1989).
29. Scott H. Decker and Carol W. Kohfeld, "Capital Punishment and Executions in the Lone Star State: A Deterrence Study," *Criminal Research Bulletin* 3 (Huntsville, Tex.: Sam Houston State University Criminal Justice Center, 1988), pp. 1, 6.
30. "Prison Barge to Be Moored at Greenwich Village Pier," *New York Times* (29 October 1988), p. 11.
31. "Crowded Prisons Pose Crisis in Massachusetts," *New York Times* (20 July 1988), p. 11.
32. Thomas G. Blomberg, "Criminal Justice Reform and Social Control: Are We Becoming a Minimum Security Society?" in John Lowman et al., *Transcarceration: Essays in the Sociology of Social Control* (Brookfield, Vt.: Gower Publishing Co., 1987). See also Andrew Scull, *Decarceration: Community Treatment and the Deviant: A Radical View*, 2d ed. (New Brunswick, N.J.: Rutgers University Press, 1984).
33. American Institute for Research, *Evaluation of the Habitual Serious and Violent Juvenile Offender Program: Executive Summary* (Washington, D.C.: U.S. Department of Justice, January 1988), p. 2.
34. Sue Titus Reid, *Crime and Criminology*, 4th ed. (New York: Holt, Rinehart and Winston, 1985), p. 617.
35. Aris T. Papas, "Barbed Wire Justice," *Corrections Today* 46 (June 1984): 56.

Appendix A

SELECTED AMENDMENTS
OF THE UNITED STATES CONSTITUTION

Amendment I (1791)

Congress shall make no law respecting an establishment of religion, or prohibiting the free exercise thereof; or abridging the freedom of speech, or of the press; or the right of the people peaceably to assemble, and to petition the Government for a redress of grievances.

Amendment IV (1791)

The right of the people to be secure in their persons, houses, papers, and effects, against unreasonable searches and seizures, shall not be violated, and no Warrants shall issue, but upon probable cause, supported by Oath or affirmation, and particularly describing the place to be searched, and the persons or things to be seized.

Amendment V (1791)

No person shall be held to answer for a capital, or otherwise infamous crime, unless on a presentment or indictment of a Grand Jury, except in cases arising in the land or naval forces, or in the Militia, when in actual service in time of War or public danger; nor shall any person be subject for the same offence to be twice put in jeopardy of life or limb; nor shall be compelled in any criminal case to be a witness against himself, nor be deprived of life, liberty, or property, without due process of law; nor shall private property be taken for public use, without just compensation.

Amendment VI (1791)

In all criminal prosecutions, the accused shall enjoy the right to a speedy and public trial, by an impartial jury of the State and district wherein the crime shall have been committed, which district shall have been previously ascertained by law, and to be informed of the nature and cause of the accusation; to be confronted with the witnesses against him; to have compulsory process for obtaining witnesses in his favor, and to have the Assistance of Counsel for his defence.

Amendment VIII (1791)

Excessive bail shall not be required, nor excessive fines imposed, nor cruel and unusual punishments inflicted.

Amendment XIV (1868)

Section 1.   All persons born or naturalized in the United States, and subject to the jurisdiction thereof, are citizens of the United States and of the State wherein they reside. No state shall make or enforce any law which shall abridge the privileges or immunities of citizens of the United States; nor shall any State deprive any person of life, liberty, or property, without due process of law; nor deny to any person within its jurisdiction the equal protection of the laws.

Section 5.   The Congress shall have power to enforce, by appropriate legislation, the provisions of this article.

Appendix B

HOW TO READ A COURT CITATION

Pugh v. Locke, 406 F. Supp. 38 (M.D. Ala. 1976), *aff'd sub nom,* Newman v. State of Alabama, 559 F. 2d 238 (5th Cir. 1977), *cert. denied* 428 U.S. (1978).

Original Citation

[Pugh v. Locke][1] [406][2] [F. Supp.][3] [318][4] [M.D.Ala.][5] [1976][6].

    1. Name of case
    2. Volume number of reporter where case is found
    3. Name of reporter; *see* Abbreviations for Commonly Used Reporters
    4. Page in the reporter the decision begins
    5. Court deciding the case
    6. Year decided

Additional Case History

[*aff'd sub nom*][7] [Newman v. State of Alabama][8] [559][9] [F. 2d][10] [238][11] [(5th Cir. 1977)][12] [*cert. denied*][13] [438][14] [U.S.][15] [915][16] [1978][17]

    7. Affirmed under a different name
    8. The name under which the case was affirmed
    9. Volume number
  10. Abbreviated name of reporter
  11. Page number
  12. The court deciding the case and the date decision was given
  13. Additional history—appeal to U.S. Supreme Court denied
  14. Volume number of denial citation
  15. Abbreviated name of reporter
  .16. Page number
  17. Year denied

Abbreviations for Commonly Used Reporters for Court Cases

Decisions of the United States Supreme Court

S. Ct.: Supreme Court Reporter
U.S.: United States Reports

Decisions from Other Courts: A Selected List

At., At. 2d: Atlantic Reporter, Atlantic Reporter Second Series
Cal. Rptr: California Reporter
F. 2d: Federal Reporter Second Series
F. Supp: Federal Supplement
N.Y. S. 2d: New York Supplement Second
N.W., N.W. 2d: North Western Reporter, North Western Reporter Second Series
N.E., N.E. 2d: North Eastern Reporter, North Eastern Reporter Second Series
P., P. 2d: Pacific Reporter, Pacific Reporter Second Series
S.E., S.E. 2d: South Eastern Reporter, South Eastern Reporter Second Series

Definitions

Aff'd.   Affirmed; the appellate court agrees with the decision of the lower court.

Aff'd sub nom.   Affirmed under a different name; the case at the appellate level is sometimes given a different name.

Aff'd per curium.   Affirmed by the courts. The opinion is written by "the court" instead of by one of the judges; a decision affirmed but no written opinion is issued.

Cert. denied.   Certiorari denied; the Supreme Court, either the state supreme court or the U.S. Supreme Court, refuses to hear and decide the case.

Concurring opinion.   An opinion agreeing with the court's decision, but offering different reasons.

Dissenting opinion.   An opinion disagreeing with the reasoning and result of the majority opinion.

Reh'g. denied.   Rehearing denied, the court's refusal to retry a case.

Remanded.   The appellate court sending a case back to the lower court for further action.

Rev'd.   Reversed, overthrown, set aside, made void; the appellate court reverses the decision of the lower court.

Rev'd and remanded.   Reversed and remanded; the appellate court reverses the decision and sends the case back for further action.

Vacated.   Abandoned, set aside, made void; the appellate court sets aside the decision of the lower court.

Glossary

Acquittal. Legal verification of the innocence of a person in a criminal trial.

Adjudication. The process of decision making by a court. Normally used to refer to juvenile proceedings.

Administrative law. Rules and regulations made by agencies to which power has been delegated by the legislature. Administrative agencies also investigate and decide cases concerning potential violations of these rules.

Adversary system. The American system for settling disputes in court. A defense attorney and a prosecuting attorney each attempt to convince a judge or a jury of his or her version of the case.

Aftercare. Providing continued supervision of juveniles after they are released from a correctional facility; similar to the term *parole* in regard to adults.

Anomie. Normlessness or lawlessness; refers to the lack of cohesion in a society, resulting in a situation that is more conducive to deviant behavior.

Appeal. A stage in a judicial proceeding in which a higher court is asked to review the case decided by a lower court.

Appellant. The loser in a court case who seeks a review of that case in a higher court.

Appellate jurisdiction. *See* **Jurisdiction.**

Appellee. The winning party in a lower court who speaks on appeal against reversing the lower court's decision.

Arraignment. A hearing before a judge during which the defendant is identified, hears the formal reading of the charges, is read his or her legal rights, and enters a plea of guilty or not guilty to the charges.

Arrest. The act of taking a person into custody in order to make a criminal charge against that person.

Arson. The malicious burning of the structures of another, or of one's own, with the intent to defraud.

Assault. Technically, a threat to commit a battery, but often used to refer to a battery. Aggravated assault involves a battery inflicted by use of a deadly weapon such as a knife or gun. *See also* **Battery.**

Assigned counsel. An attorney appointed and paid by the court to represent a defendant who does not have funds to hire a private attorney.

Bail. Money or property posted by the defendant after arrest and before trial to guarantee that he or she will appear for trial, sentencing, or imprisonment. If the defendant does not appear, the money or property is forfeited to the state.

Battered woman's syndrome. Violent reactions leading to murder of women who have been battered by their husbands; this syndrome has been used successfully in some cases in which women have been tried for the murder of their husbands.

Battery. An unlawful beating or other wrongful, offensive roughing of another person without the consent of that person. *See also* **Assault.**

Beyond a reasonable doubt. The evidence required for conviction in a criminal case; means a lack of uncertainty; the facts presented to the judge or jury are sufficient to lead a reasonable person to conclude without question that the defendant committed the act for which he or she is charged. In contrast to the standard required in a civil case: a preponderance of the evidence, meaning that the facts indicate that more probably than not, the facts are as the plaintiff has argued.

Bond. A written document indicating that the defendant or his or her sureties will assure the presence of that defendant at a criminal proceeding, and if not, will forfeit the security posted for the bond.

Booking. The official recording of the name, photograph, and fingerprints of a suspect, along with the offense charged and the name of the officer who made the arrest.

Bow Street Runners. Mid-eighteenth-century London system that gave the police powers of investigation and arrest to constables who were given some training and paid a portion of the fines in successfully prosecuted cases.

Building tenders. Inmates in supervisory positions used to assist prison officials with maintenance of the institution and control of other inmates.

Burglary. Illegally or forcibly entering any enclosed structure in order to commit a crime, usually theft.

Capital punishment. Punishment by death. In the United States, only first-degree murder under certain circumstances qualifies.

Case law. Legally binding court interpretations of written laws or rules made by courts in the absence of both written laws and past court decisions. *See* **Common law.**

Causation. The idea that in order to hold people accountable for their actions, a cause-and-effect relationship must be established between those actions and a harmful consequence.

Certification. Process used to remove juveniles from the jurisdiction of the juvenile court to that of the criminal court; also called *transfer* or *waiver.*

Charge. The formal assertion that a person is guilty of a particular offense. Instructions a judge gives a jury on matters of law and other possible verdicts.

Charge bargaining. A negotiation process between the prosecutor and defense attorney for the dismissal of one or more charges against the defendant in return for the defendant's plea of guilty to the remaining charges.

Child abuse. Actions by any adult who purposefully, not from neglect, inflicts physical or sexual harm on children. Child abuse may also include excessive psychological mistreatment.

Circumstantial evidence. Evidence that may be inferred from a fact or a series of facts. *See also* **Direct evidence.**

Civil death. The practice of declaring convicted persons civilly dead by eliminating their civil rights such as voting, contracting, and the right to sue or be sued.

Civil law. Distinguished from criminal law as that law pertaining to private or civil rights.

Civil rights. Sometimes called *civil liberties;* refers to all the natural rights guaranteed by the Constitution such as free speech and the right to religious beliefs and practices; also refers to the body of law concerning natural rights.

Classical school. School of thought that believed human behavior is rational, based on a pleasure-pain principle, and people will not commit crimes if the pain of punishment is greater than the pleasure of the crime.

Classification. The assignment of new prisoners to the housing, security status, and treatment program that best fits their needs.

Commissary. Refers both to the prison store and to the incidental items sold to inmates. May also be an inmate's account, which is debited when an item is purchased.

Common law. Broadly defined, the legal theory and law that originated in England and is also used in the United States. More specifically, common law consists of the guidelines, customs, traditions, and judicial decisions that courts use in decision making. It is contrasted to the constitution and written law.

Community-based corrections. Punishment that emphasizes assimilation into the community. Instead of imprisonment, the offender may be put on probation or placed in programs such as work release, foster homes, halfway houses, parole, and furlough.

Community service. Punishment assigning the offender to community service or work projects. Sometimes, it is combined with restitution or probation.

Complaint. The formal assertion that a violation of the law or a crime has been committed.

Concurrent jurisdiction. *See* **Jurisdiction.**

Concurrent sentences. *See* **Consecutive sentences.**

Concurring opinion. A judge's written opinion agreeing with the result in a case, but disagreeing with the reasoning of the majority opinion.

Conflict approach. In contrast to the consensus approach, views laws as in conflict, disharmony, clash. Proponents do not agree on the nature or the source of the conflict.

Conjugal visiting. Providing prisoners with opportunities for sexual and other social contacts with their spouses in an unsupervised, private setting.

Consecutive sentences. Terms of imprisonment for more than one offense that must be served one following the other. If a defendant receives a 3-year term for robbery and a 5-year term for assault, the consecutive sentence adds to a total of 8 years; in the same case, a concurrent sentence would add to a total of only 5 years.

Consensus approach. In contrast to the conflict approach, views laws as representing the consensus or agreement of society. Laws represent the values and norms of society, not of special interest groups.

Constable. An officer of a municipal corporation who has duties similar to those of a sheriff, such as preserving the public peace, executing papers from the court, and maintaining the custody of juries.

Constitutional causes of crime. An explanation that the physical characteristics of a person's body influence criminal behavior.

Contempt of court. An act done to embarrass, humiliate, or undermine the power of the court; may be civil or criminal; often is declared by a judge whose order has been violated.

Continuance. An adjournment of a trial or other proceeding until a later date.

Contraband. Any item—such as weapons, drugs, or alcohol—for which possession in prison is either illegal or violates prison rules; outside prison, may refer to any item that it is unlawful to possess.

Conviction. The court's judgement that the defendant is guilty of the criminal charge.

Corporal punishment. Physical punishment such as beatings or whippings.

Correctional officers. Corrections employees with supervisory power over suspects or convicted offenders in custody.

Crime. An illegal act of omission or commission that is punishable by law.

Crime Classification System (CCS). A system for collecting data on the severity of crimes, and on the effect those crimes have on victims.

Crime control model. A model of crime that places great emphasis on controlling crime; this goal is considered to be more important than the due process rights of defendants, which may be sacrificed for rigorous crime control.

Crime rate. The crimes per 100,000 population.

Crimes known to the police. All serious criminal offenses that have been reported to the police, for which the police have sufficient evidence to believe the crimes were committed.

Criminal. A person found guilty of an act that violates the criminal law.

Criminal justice system. The entire system of criminal prevention, detection, apprehension, trial, and punishment.

Criminal law. The statutes defining acts so offensive that they threaten the well-being of the entire state, and requiring that the accused be prosecuted by the government.

Criminologists. People who systematically study crime, criminal behavior, the reaction of society to crime and criminals, and the evolution of law.

Cross-examination. The questioning of a witness by adversary counsel after one attorney concludes the direct examination.

Cruel and unusual punishment. The punishment prohibited by the Eighth Amendment to the U.S. Constitution as interpreted by the courts. Some examples are torture, prison conditions that "shock the conscience," excessively long sentences, and the death penalty for rape without homicide.

Curtilage. Enclosed ground and buildings immediately around a dwelling.

Custody. Legal control over a person or property; physical responsibility for a person or thing.

Date rape. Sexual intercourse without the consent of the victim, perpetrated by a person the victim has voluntarily selected for a social occasion. The victim may have voluntarily engaged in some form of intimate interaction but did not agree to sexual intercourse.

Deadly force. Force likely to cause serious bodily injury or death.

Defendant. The person charged with a crime and against whom a criminal proceeding has begun or is pending.

Defense. A response by the defendant in a criminal or civil case. It may consist only of a denial of the factual allegations of the prosecution (in a criminal case) or of the plaintiff (in a civil case). If the defense offers new factual allegations in an effort to negate the charges, there is an affirmative defense.

Defense attorney or counsel. The counsel for the defendant in a criminal proceeding, whose main function is to protect the legal rights of the accused.

Deinstitutionalization. The substitution of community-based programs for confinement in prison.

Demonstrative evidence. Real evidence; the kinds of evidence that are apparent to the senses, in contrast to evidence presented by the testimony of other people.

Depositions. Oral testimony taken from the opposing party or a witness for the opposing party. Depositions are taken out of court but under oath. They are recorded verbatim, usually by a court reporter. Counsel for both sides are present. Depositions are used when the deposed may not be able to appear in court.

Deprivation model. A model of prisonization based on the idea that the prisoner's subculture stems from the way inmates adapt to the severe psychological and physical losses imposed by imprisonment.

Detention. *See* **Pretrial detention.**

Detention center. A facility for the temporary confinement of juveniles in custody who are awaiting court disposition.

Determinate sentence. The legislature determines the length of a sentence for a specific crime; the parole board, correctional institution, or judge cannot make changes in the sentence length. The judge, however, may have the power to suspend the sentence or to impose probation rather than a term of years.

Deterrence. Punishment philosophy based on the assumption that the acts of potential offenders can be prevented. *Individual deterrence* refers to the prevention of additional criminal acts on the part of the specific individual being punished; *general deterrence* refers to the presumed effect that punishing one offender will have on other potential offenders.

Dicta. Written portions of a judge's opinion that are not part of the actual ruling of the court and which, therefore, are not legally binding precedents for future court decisions.

Differential association. A sociological learning theory developed by Edwin Sutherland and postulating that criminal behavior is learned just like any other forms of behavior; the learning occurs in small groups and is characterized by learning to define illegal behavior as acceptable.

Differential opportunity. An approach to explaining delinquent and criminal behavior that emphasizes the access people do or do not have to both legal and illegal ways of meeting goals.

Directed verdict. Upon a finding of insufficient evidence to convict a defendant, the judge may direct the jury to return a verdict of not guilty. The judge may not direct a verdict of guilty.

Direct evidence. Evidence offered by an eyewitness who testifies to what he or she saw, heard, tasted, smelled, or touched.

Direct examination. Examination conducted by the attorney who called the witness; after that witness is cross-examined by opposing counsel, the counsel may redirect questions to the witness.

Discovery. A legal motion requesting the disclosure of information held by the opposing counsel. In criminal law the defense counsel files a discovery motion to obtain information from the police and the prosecutor.

Discretion. The authority in the criminal justice system to make decisions based on one's own judgment rather than on legal rules. The result can be not only inconsistent handling of offenders but also actions tailored to individual circumstances.

Disposition. The final decision of a court in a criminal proceeding to accept a plea of guilty, find the defendant guilty or not guilty, or to terminate the proceedings against the defendant.

Diversion. The offender is removed from the criminal proceeding to accept a plea of guilty, find the defendant guilty, or to terminate the proceedings against the defendant.

Domestic violence. Causing serious physical harm or threatening such harm to a member of the family or household, including spouses, ex-spouses, parents, children, persons otherwise related by blood, persons living in the household, or persons who formerly lived there.

Double celling. Two or more inmates are housed together in a jail or prison cell; also called *double bunking*.

Due process. Constitutional principle that a person should not be deprived of life, liberty, or property without reasonable and lawful procedures that must be made available in any criminal action, including postconviction procedures such as prison disciplinary hearings or parole revocations.

Due process model. In contrast to the crime control model, the due process model of crime control emphasizes the rights of defendants: crime control may be less efficient, but the individual constitutional rights of defendants take priority in this approach. For example, a confession that is obtained in violation of the defendant's rights must be excluded at the trial.

Ecology. The study of the distribution of people and their activities in time and space; used in the study of criminal and other kinds of deviant behavior in relationship to characteristics of the environment in which the behavior occurs.

Entrapment. A defense asserting that a crime has been instigated by a government agent who offers inducements to commit a crime or makes false representations.

Equal protection. All persons under like circumstances must receive the same treatment in the criminal justice system; they may not be discriminated against because of race, sex, minority status, or religion.

Exclusionary rule. Excludes from a criminal trial evidence that is secured as the result of illegal action by law enforcement officers.

Exclusive jurisdiction. *See* **Jurisdiction.**

Felony. A serious offense such as murder, armed robbery, or rape. Punishment ranges from 1 year imprisonment in a state or federal institution to execution.

Felony murder. An unlawful killing of a person that occurs while attempting to commit or while committing another felony, such as robbery, rape, or arson.

Fine. The convicted offender is punished by paying a sum of money to a court in addition to or instead of other punishment.

Fleeing felon rule. Common-law rule that permitted police to shoot at any fleeing felon; the rule has been greatly modified to require circumstances involving (1) the threat of serious injury or death of the officer or others, (2) the prevention of an escape if the suspect threatens the officer with a gun, or (3) the officer's having probable cause to believe the suspect has committed or threatened to commit serious bodily harm. If possible, a warning should be given.

Folkways. Norms of behavior stemming from the habits, behavior, or customs of a certain group or society.

Frankpledge. In old English law, a system whereby the members of a tithing had corporate responsibility for the behavior of all members over fourteen years old.

Free Venture Program. Program begun by federal government to encourage the development in state prisons of meaningful job opportunities for inmates. The program uses business principles and practices in an attempt to make prison industries profitable.

Frisk. Patting down or running one's hands quickly over a person's body to determine whether the suspect has a weapon; this is in contrast to search, which is a more careful and thorough examination.

Furlough. An authorized, temporary leave from a correctional facility in order to attend a funeral, visit the family, or attempt to secure employment.

General deterrence. *See* **Deterrence.**

Good faith exception. Provision that illegally obtained evidence will not be excluded from a subsequent trial if it can be shown that the police secured the evidence in good faith, meaning that they reasonably believed that they were acting in accordance with the law.

Good-time credits. Days subtracted from an inmate's prison term, awarded for satisfactory behavior during incarceration.

Grand jury. A group of citizens, convened by legal authority, that evaluates evidence to ascertain whether a crime has been committed and whether there is sufficient evidence against the accused to justify prosecution. If so, the grand jury returns an indictment.

Granny bashing. Bodily abuse of aged parents.

Guards. The traditional term for corrections employees who supervise suspects or convicted offenders in custody.

Habeas corpus. A written court order requiring that the accused be brought to court to determine the legality of custody and confinement.

Hands-off doctrine. A policy used by courts to justify nonintervention in the daily administration of correctional facilities.

Harmless errors. Minor or trivial errors not deemed sufficient to harm the rights of the parties who assert the errors. Cases are not reversed on the basis of harmless errors.

Hearsay evidence. Secondhand evidence of which the witness does not have personal knowledge, but merely repeats something the witness says he or she heard someone else say.

Hedonism. The concept that people avoid pain and choose pleasure.

House arrest. A form of probation in which the offender is permitted to live at home but is restricted in his or her movements to and from the home. Curfew will probably be imposed and the offender will be subject to unannounced visits from a probation officer. In some cases, electronic devices will be used to monitor the activities of the probationer.

Humanitarianism. In penal philosophy, the doctrine advocating the removal of harsh, severe, and painful conditions in penal institutions.

Hundred. In English law, a combination of ten tithings as part of the system of frankpledge. *See* **Tithings** *and* **Frankpledge.**

Implicit bargaining. The informal practice of giving lesser sentences to those defendants who plead guilty compared with those who do not.

Importation model. A theory of prisonization based on the idea that the inmate subculture arises not only from internal prison experiences, but also from the external patterns of behavior the inmates bring to prison.

Incapacitation. A punishment theory usually implemented by imprisoning an offender to prevent the commission of any other crimes by that person.

Incarceration. Imprisonment in a jail, prison, or other type of penal institution.

Incest. Sexual relations between close relatives other than husband and wife. Relations between father and daughter are the most common.

Indeterminate sentence. Sentence of a person to prison without imposition of a definite term of years. Parole boards or professionals at the penal institution determine when the inmate will be released.

Index offenses or crimes. The FBI's *Uniform Crime Reports* of the occurrences of the eight crimes considered most serious: murder and nonnegligent manslaughter, forcible rape, robbery, aggravated assault, burglary, larceny–theft, motor vehicle theft, and arson.

Indictment. The written accusation of a grand jury, formally stating that probable cause exists to believe that the suspect committed a felony. An indictment arises from evidence presented by the prosecutor to the grand jury, in contrast to a presentment issued without the prosecutor's participation.

Indigent defendants. Those defendants who meet financial eligibility requirements to qualify for an attorney paid by the state.

Individual deterrence. *See* **Deterrence.**

Inevitable discovery rule. Provides that evidence illegally secured by police will not be excluded from the subsequent trial of the suspect, provided it can be shown that the evidence would have been discovered anyway under legal means.

Informant. A person who gives information to law enforcement officials about a crime or planned criminal activity.

Information. A formally written document used to charge a person with a specific offense. Prosecutors issue informations, in contrast to grand juries, which issue indictments.

Initial appearance. The first appearance of the accused before a magistrate; if the accused is detained in jail immediately after arrest, he or she must be taken quickly to a magistrate for the initial appearance. At that point the magistrate will decide whether there is probable cause to detain the suspect and, if so, tell the suspect of the charges and of his or her constitutional rights, including the right to an attorney.

Inmate. A person whose freedom has been replaced by confinement in a prison, asylum, or similar institution.

Inquisitory system. A system in which the defendant must prove his or her innocence, in contrast to the adversary system, which has a presumption of innocence requiring the state to prove the defendant's guilt.

Intake decisions. (1) In prosecution, the first review of a case by an official in the prosecutor's office. Weak cases often are weeded out at this stage. (2) In juvenile court, the reception of a juvenile against whom complaints have been made. Decision to dismiss or proceed with the case will be made at this stage.

Intensive probation supervision (IPS). With small caseloads, probation officers provide more careful supervision than with larger caseloads; probationers are carefully supervised.

INTERPOL. A world police organization that was established for the purpose of cooperation among nations involved in common policing problems.

Interrogatories. A set of questions given to a party thought to have pertinent information that may be used at trial. The party completing the interrogatories must sign an oath that the statements are correct.

Jail. A local, regional, or federal facility used to confine persons awaiting trial as well as those serving short sentences.

Judge. An elected or appointed officer of the court who presides over a court of law; the final and neutral arbiter of law who is responsible for all court activities.

Judicial review. The authority of a court to check the power of the executive and legislative branches of government by deciding whether their acts defy rights established by the state and federal constitutions.

Jury. In a criminal case, a group of people who have been sworn in at court to listen to a trial and decide whether the defendant is guilty or not guilty. Juries in some jurisdictions can determine or recommend sentence.

Jurisdiction. The lawful exercise of authority; the area within which authority may be exercised, such as the geographical area within which a particular police force has authority. Courts may have *original* jurisdiction to hear the case; if more than one court has authority to hear the case, jurisdiction is *concurrent. Appellate* jurisdiction refers to the power of a court to hear the case on appeal. *Exclusive* jurisdiction means that only one court may hear the case.

Just deserts. The belief that whosoever commits a crime should suffer for it; also the amount or type of punishment a particular offender deserves to receive.

Juvenile. A young person under age for certain privileges such as voting or drinking alcoholic beverages. If accused of a criminal or juvenile offense, a juvenile usually is not tried by a criminal court but is processed in the juvenile court.

Juvenile court. The court having jurisdiction over juveniles accused of delinquent acts or offenses, or in need of supervision because they are being neglected or mistreated by their parents or guardians.

Juvenile delinquent. A person under legal age (the maximum age varies among the states from 16 to 21, but 18 is the most common) whom a juvenile court has determined to be incorrigible, in need of supervision, or in violation of a criminal statute.

Labeling perspective. An approach to the explanation of criminal behavior that emphasizes how and why an act is considered criminal rather than looking at why the individual committed the act.

Larceny–theft. The unlawful removal of someone else's property with the intention of keeping it permanently. Historically, small thefts were categorized as *petit larceny* and large thefts as *grand larceny.* The latter was punished by the death penalty, a punishment no longer permitted in the United States for larceny. Modern theft laws rarely distinguish between the two types of larceny.

Law Enforcement Assistance Administration (LEAA). Agency established by Congress in 1965; provided funding for development of police departments, police techniques, police education, and police training. It was abolished in 1982. Money for education was provided through the Law Enforcement Education Program (LEEP).

Law Enforcement Education Program (LEEP). *See* **Law Enforcement Assistance Administration.**

Lineup. A procedure in which a group of people are placed together in a line to allow the victim or an eyewitness to point out the suspected criminal.

Magistrate. A judge from the lower courts of the state or federal court system. Magistrates usually preside over arraignments, preliminary hearings, bail hearings, and minor offenses.

Mala in se. Actions that are intrinsically immoral, such as murder, forcible rape, and robbery.

Mala prohibita. Actions that are wrong because legislation prohibits them, although there may not be general agreement that they are wrong in themselves.

Mandatory sentence. Sentences with lengths imposed by the legislature when no discretion is given the judge concerning the sentence. If the defendant is convicted, the specified sentence must be imposed. This is in contrast to determinate sentencing, in which the judge may have discretion to impose probation or suspend the specified sentence.

Manslaughter. The unlawful killing of a human being by a person who lacks malice in the act. Manslaughter may be *involuntary* (or negligent), the result of recklessness while committing an unlawful act such as driving while intoxicated; or *voluntary,* an intentional killing committed in the heat of passion.

Marshals. Sworn law enforcement officers who perform civil duties of the courts, such as the delivery of papers to begin civil proceedings. In some jurisdictions marshals may also serve papers for the arrest of criminal suspects, and escort prisoners from jail to court or into the community when they are permitted to leave the jail or prison temporarily.

Mens rea. The guilty or criminal intent of the accused at the time the criminal act is committed.

***Miranda* warning.** The rule stemming from *Miranda v. Arizona,* which stipulates that anyone in custody must be warned of certain rights before any questioning can take place. These rights include the right to remain silent and the right to counsel, which will be appointed if the suspect cannot afford to hire private counsel. If the warning is not given, or is given and then violated, any information obtained from the suspect may be inadmissible as evidence at trial.

Misdemeanor. A less serious offense, punishable by a fine, probation, or a short jail term; in contrast to a felony, a more serious crime.

Mistrial. A trial that cannot stand; is invalid; judges may call a mistrial for such reasons as an error on the part of counsel, the death of a juror or counsel, or the inability of the jury to reach a verdict.

Model Penal Code. A systemized statement of criminal law by the American Law Institute. This code is frequently used as the model for writing new criminal laws.

Molly Maguires. A powerful secret police organization in the 1870s in Pennsylvania. These terrorists seriously threatened the Pennsylvania economy.

Moot. The term used to describe a controversy that has ended or evolved to the stage where a court decision on that particular case is no longer relevant or necessary; this is a limitation on the power of courts to decide a case.

Mores. The manners and ways of a social group that have become acceptable behavior and are essential to its welfare and survival, but have not become a part of the group's criminal law.

Motion. A document submitted to the court asking for an order or a rule.

Motor vehicle theft. Stealing an automobile, in contrast to stealing an automobile part, or larceny–theft from an automobile.

Murder. The unlawful killing of another person with either express or implied aforethought. May be defined by degrees in view of the circumstances.

National Crime Survey (NCS). Crime data collected by the Bureau of Justice Statistics (BJS) and based on surveys of people to determine who has been victimized by crime.

National Incident-Based Reporting System (NIBRS). A new reporting system utilized by the FBI in collecting crime data. In this system a crime is viewed along with all its components, including type of victim, type of weapon used, location of the crime, alcohol/drug influence, type of criminal activity, relationship of victim to offender, residence of victims and arrestees, and a description of property and its value. This system includes 22 crimes, rather than the 8 that constitute the FBI's Part I offenses of serious crimes.

National Youth Survey (NYS). Program for gathering data on crime by interviewing adolescents over a five-year period. The program has been structured to overcome many of the criticisms of other self-report studies.

Neoclassical School. School of thought maintaining that the accused should be exempted from conviction if circumstances prevented the exercise of free will.

Nolo contendere. Literally means "I will not contest it." In a criminal case this plea has the legal effect of a guilty plea, but the plea cannot be used against the defendant in a civil action brought on the same act. It might be used in a case involving a felony charge of driving while intoxicated. A guilty plea could be used as evidence of liability in a civil action of wrongful death filed by the family of the victim who died in the accident. This plea would require that the plaintiff in the civil action prove liability.

Norms. The rules or standards of behavior shared by members of a social group which define appropriate behavior. *See* **Mores.**

Offender. A person who has committed a criminal offense.

Offense. A violation of the criminal law.

Original jurisdiction. *See* **Jurisdiction.**

Paralegal. A person who is not a licensed attorney but who has some training in legal skills and works under the supervision of a licensed attorney. Paralegals may conduct interviews, investigations, legal research, and perform many functions in court, such as filing motions. Many schools now have paralegal programs for training for this relatively new profession.

Pardon. An act exempting a convicted offender from punishment. The pardon may be complete or partial, exempting only part of the punishment.

Parens patriae. Parent of the country; doctrine from English common law that was the basis for allowing the state to take over guardianship of the child; in this country, the basis of the juvenile court. The doctrine presumes that the state will act in the best interests of the child.

Parole. The status of an offender who is released before the completion of the sentence but who must be supervised in the community by a parole officer.

Parole board. A panel at the state or federal level that decides whether an inmate will be released from an institution before the expiration of the sentence.

Parole officer. Government employee who supervises and counsels inmates paroled in the community.

Parole revocation. The process of returning a released offender to an institution for violating technical conditions of parole, or for violating the criminal law.

Penitentiary. Historically, an institution intended to isolate convicted offenders from one another, giving them time to reflect on their bad acts and become penitent. Later, synonymous with prison.

Peremptory challenge. A challenge that may be used by the prosecution or the defense to excuse a potential juror from the jury panel. No reason need be given. Each attorney gets a specified number of these challenges.

Petition. The formal document for filing an action in juvenile court, in contrast to a grand jury indictment or prosecutor's presentment in the criminal court.

Petit jury. Literally means small, minor, or inconsiderate; used to distinguish a trial jury from a grand jury.

Plaintiff. In a civil suit, the person who brings the complaint against the defendant; the person harmed by the defendant.

Plea bargaining. The process of negotiation between the defense and the prosecution before the trial of a defendant. The process may involve reducing or dropping of some charges, or a recommendation for leniency in exchange for a plea of guilty on another charge or charges.

Police. A local government official authorized to enforce the law and to maintain order, using physical force if necessary.

Positivists. Theorists who believed that punishments for a particular crime should not be predetermined but should be tailor-made for the individual criminal. This position was based on the assumption that behavior can be studied, understood, and changed.

Posse. Rural police system in which the sheriff may call into action any number of citizens over a certain age if they are needed to assist in law enforcement.

Prejudicial errors. Errors that substantially affect the rights of parties and therefore may result in the reversal of a case.

Preliminary hearing. An appearance before a lower-court judge to determine whether there is sufficient evidence to submit to the grand jury or to the trial court. Preliminary hearings also may include the bail decision.

Presentence investigation (PSI). Investigation of the background and characteristics of the defendant; may include information that would not be admissible at the trial; presented to the judge to be used in determining sentence.

Presentment. A document issued by a grand jury stating that probable cause exists to believe that the suspect committed the crime. Presentments are issued without the participation of the prosecutor. *See also* **Indictments.**

Presumption of innocence. A cornerstone of the adversary system; says a defendant is innocent unless and until the prosecution proves guilt beyond a reasonable doubt.

Presumptive sentence. The normal sentence is specified by statute for each offense; judges are permitted to deviate from that sentence but usually may do so only under specified circumstances or must give reasons for the deviation.

Pretrial detention. Detention of a defendant in jail between arrest and trial, either because the judge has refused bail or the defendant cannot meet the requirements of bail. Generally the purpose is to assure the presence of the accused at trial. May also refer to *preventive detention* of defendants thought to present a danger to themselves, to others, or both if released pending trial.

Preventive detention. *See* **Pretrial detention.**

Prison. Federal or state penal facility for detaining adults sentenced to a year or longer after conviction of a crime.

Prisonization. The adaptation of an inmate to the subculture of prison life.

Private security forces. Persons employed by private agencies instead of governmental ones to provide security from criminal activity.

Proactive. The police take the initiative in finding criminals rather than depending on the reports of citizens.

Probable cause. In search warrant cases, a set of facts and circumstances that lead to the reasonable belief that the items sought are located in a particular place. In arrest cases, the facts and circumstances lead to the reasonable belief that the suspect has actually committed a crime.

Probation. A type of sentence that places the convicted offender under the supervision of a probation officer within the community instead of imprisonment. The term also refers to the part of the criminal justice system that is in charge of all aspects of probation.

Probation officer. Government official responsible for supervising persons on probation, and for writing the presentence reports on offenders.

Probation revocation. The process of declaring that a sentenced offender violated the terms of probation. If probation involved a suspended prison or jail sentence, the revocation may mean that the original sentence will be invoked and the individual will be sent to prison or jail.

Property crimes. Crimes aimed at the property of another person rather than at the person. In the FBI's serious offense category, property crimes include arson, larceny–theft, vehicular theft, and burglary.

Pro se. "On behalf of self;" acting as one's own attorney.

Prosecution. The process that occurs when the state (or federal government) begins the formal process in a criminal case. The action is taken by a prosecuting attorney, a government official whose duty is to initiate and maintain criminal proceedings on behalf of the government against persons accused of committing crimes.

Prosecutor or prosecuting attorney. A government official responsible for representing the state in criminal proceedings against an offender.

Public defender. An attorney retained and paid by the government to represent indigent defendants in criminal proceedings.

Rape. Historically, unlawful sexual intercourse with a woman; called *forcible rape* if obtained against the will of the woman by the use of threats of force; called *statutory rape* if the sexual intercourse is consensual between a man and a girl who is under the age of consent. More recently some rape statutes have been rewritten to include male victims, as well as penetration of any bodily opening by any instrument, including but not limited to the male sexual organ.

Rape trauma syndrome. Predictable reactions of rape victims, including an initial acute reaction in which the victim's life is seriously disrupted, followed by a long-term phase in which the victim's symptoms decrease and a period of readjustment and reconstruction follows.

Reactive. The police depend on the reports of citizens to find criminals, rather than working independently; an important process since police are not in a position to observe most criminal behavior.

Recidivist. Repeated committer of crimes, released inmates relapsing into previous behavior or ways.

Recusal. To remove oneself from a proceeding; judges who have a conflict of interest in a case should recuse themselves.

Reformatory. Early correctional facility that was less physically secure, and that emphasized the changing or reformation of the offender; usually used to refer to institutions.

Rehabilitation. Philosophy of punishment based on a belief that the offender can and will change to a law-abiding citizen through treatment programs and facilities. Rehabilitation may be most likely to occur in community-based programs rather than during incarceration in penal institutions. The "rehabilitative ideal" was embodied in probation, parole, the indeterminate sentence, and the juvenile court.

Reintegration. Punishment philosophy emphasizing the return of the offender to the community so that employment, family ties, and education can be restored.

Release on Recognizance (ROR). The practice of releasing without bail bond an offender before trial because circumstances suggest the unlikelihood of flight to avoid prosecution.

Restitution. Punishment that requires the offender to repay the victim with services or money. This punishment may be instead of or in addition to other punishment or fines. It can also be a requirement of parole.

Retribution. *See* **Just deserts.**

Right to counsel. The right to be represented by an attorney at crucial stages in the criminal system; indigent defendants have the right to counsel provided by the state.

Robbery. The use of force or fear to take personal property belonging to another against that person's will.

Sanction. A penalty or punishment that is imposed upon a person in order to enforce the law.

Search and seizure. Examining a person or a person's property and taking items that may be evidence of criminal activity; usually, to be lawful, must be accompanied by a search warrant; unreasonable searches and seizures are prohibited.

Search Warrant *See* **Warrant.**

Self-report data (SRD). The process of collecting data on crime by asking people, usually by use of anonymous questionnaires, about their criminal activity.

Sentence. The punishment for a convicted offender, decided upon by a judge or jury.

Sentence bargaining. A negotiation process between the prosecutor and defense attorney for the prosecutor's recommendation of a reduced sentence in exchange for the defendant's plea of guilty.

Sentence disparity. Inequalities and differences that result when people found guilty of the same crime receive sentences varying in length and type, without reasonable justification for those differences.

Sexual abuse. Any physical or psychological mistreatment pertaining to a person's sex or sex organs. The term includes child pornography, sexual harassment of adult women, and sexual molestation of children, as well as sexual abuse of adults.

Sheriff. The chief law enforcement officer in a county, usually chosen by popular election.

Silent system. In penitentiaries, historically the practice of not allowing offenders to speak with one another.

Social control. Informal and formal methods of getting members of society to conform to the norms. The most formal method is law; informal methods are customs, folkways, and mores.

Socialization. The basic lifelong social process by which an individual is integrated into a social group by learning its culture, values, and social roles.

Social system. The interrelationship of social positions, norms, values, structures, and agencies within a society; a group of interacting individuals who are considered a social unit because of common norms, values, and objectives that bind them together.

Specific deterrence. *See* **Deterrence.**

Standing. In the legal system, the doctrine mandating that courts cannot recognize a party to a suit unless that person has a personal stake or direct interest in the outcome of the suit.

Stare decisis. "Let the decision stand." The doctrine that courts will abide by or adhere to the rulings of previous court decisions when deciding cases with substantially the same facts.

Status offenses. A class of crime that does not consist of proscribed action or inaction, but of the personal condition or characteristic of the accused, for example, being a vagrant. In juvenile law, may refer to a variety of acts that would not be considered criminal if committed by an adult; for example, being insubordinate, truant, or a runaway.

Statutory law. Law that the legislature has originated and passed by a written enactment.

Statutory rape. *See* **Rape.**

Subculture. A group of significant size whose behavior differs markedly from the behavior of the dominant groups of society.

Subpoena. A command issued by the court, ordering a person to appear in court at a specified time and place for the purpose of giving testimony on a specified issue. Persons may also be ordered to bring documents pertinent to the case; that order is called a subpoena *duces tecum.*

Sub-rosa economic system. Informal economic system among inmates in which contraband dealings and gambling exist under a strict set of inmate-created rules.

Summons. A formal document issued by a court to notify a person that his or her presence is required for a particular reason in a particular court at a specified day and time.

Team policing. The use of more than one officer, each with different types of training, to work together within a particular area.

Theft. *See* **Larceny–theft.**

Tithings. In English history, a system of ten families who had responsibility for the behavior of members over the age of fourteen. Tithings were also important in protecting the group from outsiders.

Tort. A noncriminal (civil) wrong or injury arising from a breach of legal duty for which one may be sued in civil court for damages to person or property, or for wrongfully causing a death. Some actions may constitute both torts and crimes.

Training school. A secure correctional facility to which juveniles are confined on court order.

Transportation. Historically, the practice of punishing criminals by exiling them to another country, usually far away.

Trial. In criminal law, court proceedings during which a judge, a jury, or both listen to the evidence as presented by the defense and the prosecution and determine whether the defendant is guilty beyond a reasonable doubt.

True bill. The prosecutor's indictment, returned with the approval of the grand jury. After hearing the prosecutor's evidence, the grand jury determines that the indictment is accurate; that is, it is a true bill.

Uniform Crime Reports (UCR). Official data on crime, collected and published by the Federal Bureau of Investigation (FBI) and based on "crimes known to the police"—crimes reported to or observed by the police, and that the police have reason to believe were actually committed.

Venue. Location of the trial; change of venue refers to the removal of the trial from the location where it would normally be tried to another location, either to avoid public pressure or to obtain an impartial jury.

Victim compensation programs. Plans for assisting crime victims in making social, emotional, and economic adjustments.

Victimology. The discipline that studies the nature and causes of victimization as well as programs for aiding victims and preventing victimization.

Victim precipitation. Bringing about a criminal act by the actions of the victim.

Violent crimes. Those crimes defined by the FBI's *Uniform Crime Reports* as serious crimes against the person. They include rape (forcible), robbery, murder and non-negligent manslaughter, and aggravated assault.

Voir dire. To speak the truth; the process of questioning prospective jurors to determine their qualifications and desirability for serving on a jury.

Waiver. The giving up or relinquishing of one's rights, such as the right to counsel or to a jury trial. Waivers must be knowing and intelligent; that is, the defendant must understand what is being relinquished. Some rights may not be waived.

Warden. Historical term for the chief administrative officer in a correctional facility.

Warrant. A court-issued writ authorizing an officer to arrest a suspect or to search a person or place.

Watch system. A system charged with the duties of overseeing, patrolling, or guarding an area or a person. Watchmen were prominent in the early watch system of policing.

White-collar crime. The illegal actions of corporations or individuals, committed while pursuing their legitimate occupations; for example, consumer fraud, bribery, and embezzlement.

Workhouse. English institution used for the purpose of confining offenders who were forced to work at unpleasant tasks; offenders were also physically punished. The concept is used in some places today to refer to institutions that emphasize reformation or rehabilitation through work.

Work release. Release of an inmate to attend school or work outside the institution, but requiring that person to return to the institution at specified times.

Writ. *See* **Writ of certiorari.**

Writ of certiorari. *Certiorari* literally means "to be informed of"; a *writ* is an order from a court giving authority for an act to be done or ordering that it be done; a writ of certiorari is used by courts that have discretion to determine which cases they will hear. It is most commonly used now by the U.S. Supreme Court when cases are appealed to that court from lower courts.

Case Index

Name Index

Thomas, Charles W., 522–523
Thrasher, Frederic M., 83, 98n
Trebach, Arnold S., 28–29, 31n

van den Haag, Ernest, 435,
   465n–466n
Vollmer, August, 163–164, 167

von Hirsch, Andrew, 435, 465n,
   626n

Whitaker, Gordon P., 225, 259n
Wilson, James Q., 58n, 73–74, 97n,
   182–185, 210, 217n–218n, 225, 239,
   259n–260n

Wilson, O. W., 163–164, 177n, 211, 218n
Wolfgang, Marvin E., 94, 98n–99n,
   133n, 346n, 538n

Yllo, Kersti, 122, 134n

Zeisel, Hans, 427n, 466n

General Index

decisions of, 268
efficiency of, 280–281
First Amendment, 128
history and purpose, 276–277
operation, 278–281
plea bargaining, approval of, 378–379
power, 269–270
rulings on right to appointed counsel, 327–332

Team policing, 174
Texas Ranger, 151–153
Theft, 319
Tithings, 141
Torts, 17–18, 257
Training school, 658–659
Transportation as punishment, 473, 478
Trial
closing statements, 417–418
defendant's rights, 10–12, 392–407
defenses, 23, 69, 283, 416
delay of, 293–297
evidence, See Evidence
jury, 408–410
media during, 398
mistrial, 412, 422
opening statements, 410–411
process, 407, 424
witnesses, 413–414
True bill, 359

Uniform Crime Reports, 35–42
compared to NCS, 36t, 45
limitations, 39–42
statistics, 48–57

Venue, 365
Verdict, 420–422

Victimization, surveys of, 43, 672. See also NCS; Self-report data
Victimology, 103
Victim-precipitation, 124
Victims
Blacks, 105, 109, 247–248
cases most likely to be prosecuted, 319
characteristics, 104–107
children, 113–118, 126–127, 320–321
compensation, 129–130
crime reporting, 37, 39–40
economic loss, 109–110
elderly, 105, 111, 113
homicide, 75, 94, 319
income, 104
juvenile, 113–118
National Organization for Victim Assistance, 103
plea bargaining, 380–381
of police misconduct, 245–248
precipitated crime, 124
prisoners, 529–530
race, 118–122
rape, 39, 108–109, 118–122, 124, 353
relationship with criminal justice system, 122–130
relationship with criminals, 108, 319
severity of, 47
sex distribution, 105
statistics, 104–105, 109, 115–116, 118–122
study of, 103–109
suffering of, 123
as witness at trial, 413–414
women, 105, 118–122, 319
Violence

home, 112–113, 120–122, 124, 126, 228
police and, 242–248, 677
in prisons, 508, 526, 529–532, 575–580
See also Violent crimes
Violent crimes, 75–76
clearance of, 37–38
definition, 50
deterrence, 67
reporting of, 39
risk of, 105, 108–109, 113
statistics, 38–39, 53–56, 90, 108–109, 672

Warden, 476, 506–509
Warrants, 194–204
Watch system, 141–144
White collar crimes, 42, 314
Wiretapping, 354–351
Women
battered woman's syndrome, 283
criminals, 89–91
correctional officers (guards), 511, 513–516
death row, 449
defendant, 11
fear of crime, 111
jail inmates, 493–494
judges, 288–289
police, 232–238
prisoners, 485–486, 532–535, 569–571
prisons for, 485
sentencing, 455
sheriffs, 149
victims, 105, 111, 118–122, 319
Workhouse, 475, 492
Work release, 593–595

XYY chromosomal abnormality, 414